Multicultural Education

Multicultural Education

Issues and Perspectives

UPDATED FOURTH EDITION

NEW FEATURE ON AMERICAN MUSLIMS

Edited by

JAMES A. BANKS

University of Washington, Seattle

CHERRY A. McGEE BANKS

University of Washington, Bothell

JOHN WILEY & SONS, INC.

Photo Credits Part 1 Top: James Schepf/ Liaison Agency, Inc. Center: Hunter Freeman/ Liaison Agency, Inc. Bottom: Ian Shaw/ Tony Stone Images/ New York, Inc. **Part 2** Top: Steve Liss/ Liaison Agency, Inc. Center: Jonathon Selig/ Tony Stone Images/ New York, Inc. Bottom: Mary Kate Denny/ Tony Stone Images/ New York, Inc. **Part 3** Top: Steve Dunwell/ The Image Bank. Center: Peter Cade/ Tony Stone Images/ New York, Inc. Bottom: Charles Gupton/ The Stock Market. **Part 4** Top: Gabe Palmer/ The Stock Market. Center: Ellen B. Senisi/ The Image Works. Bottom: Anthony Suau/ Liaison Agency, Inc. **Part 5** Top: Don Smetzer/ Tony Stone Images/ New York, Inc. Center: Stephen Derr/ The Image Bank. Bottom: Paul Merideth/ Tony Stone Images/ New York, Inc. **Part 6** Top: Amwell/ Tony Stone Images/ New York, Inc. Center: ©Syracuse Newspapers/ John Berry/ The Image Works. Bottom: Zigy Kaluzny/ Tony Stone Images/ New York, Inc.

Acquisitions Editor	Brad Hanson
Marketing Manager	Kevin Molloy
Production Services Manager	Jeanine Furino
Production Editor	Sandra Russell
Cover Designer	Kevin Murphy
Photo Editor	Lisa Gee
Production Management Services	Grace Sheldrick/Wordsworth Associates

This book was typeset in 10/12 Times Roman by Techbooks and printed and bound by Malloy Lithographing, Inc. The cover was printed by Lehigh Press, Inc.

The paper in this book was manufactured by a mill whose forest management programs include sustained yield harvesting of its timberlands. Sustained yield harvesting principles ensure that the number of trees cut each year does not exceed the amount of new growth.

This book is printed on acid-free paper.

ISBN 0-471-22813-3

Printed in the United States of America

10 9 8 7 6 5 4 3 2 1

Preface

Issues, problems, and opportunities related to diversity are paramount in the twenty-first century. As the population within the United States and the world increases, political upheaval, world migration, and transnational economic linkages are bringing peoples throughout the world into increased contact, cultural interaction, and conflict. When the new century began, the world population had reached 6 billion; the United States population was 274.6 million. Race, ethnic, language, and class diversity was deepening in the United States. Non-Hispanic Whites made up 69.1 percent of the U.S. population in 2000. However, the U.S. Census projects that the Non-Hispanic White percentage of the nation's population will decrease in the coming years and that racial, ethnic, cultural, and language diversity will deepen in the United States.

Diversity in the United States will become increasingly reflected in the nation's schools, colleges, and universities. The 1990 Census indicated that 14 percent of school-age youths in the United States spoke a first language other than English at home. Consequently, large numbers of students in the nation's schools are English language learners.

Thirty-five percent of students enrolled in grades 1 to 12 in public schools in 1995 were students of color. It is projected that students of color will make up about 48 percent of the nation's school-age youth by the year 2020.

Many of the nation's students are poor. About 36.6 million people in the United States were living in poverty in 1999, including 1 in 5 students. The gap between the rich and the poor is also widening. In 1997, the top 1 percent of households owned 40 percent of the national wealth.

These demographic, social, and economic trends have important implications for education in the twenty-first century. As the nation's students become increasingly diverse, most of the nation's teachers remain White, middle-class, and female. Approximately 87 percent of the nation's teachers are White, and 72 percent are female.

An important aim of teacher education in the first decades of the new century is to help teachers acquire the knowledge, values, and behaviors needed to work effectively with students from diverse groups. Teachers also need to acquire the knowledge and skills necessary to help students from mainstream groups to develop cross-cultural knowledge, values, and competencies.

Multicultural Education: Issues and Perspectives, Fourth Edition, is designed to help present and future educators acquire the concepts, paradigms, and explanations needed to become effective practitioners in culturally, racially, and language-diverse classrooms and schools. This Fourth Edition has been revised to reflect current and emerging research, concepts, and debates about the education of students from both genders and from different cultural, racial, ethnic, and language groups. Exceptionality is a part of our concept of diversity because there are exceptional students in each group discussed in this book.

Chapter 4 is new to this edition. The modified titles of Chapters 6, 11, 16, and 17 reflect their substantial revisions. The new co-authors of Chapters 14 and 15 bring important knowledge and perspectives to these chapters. Each chapter in *Multicultural Education*, Fourth Edition, contains new census data, statistics, interpretations, and developments. The Multicultural Resources in the Appendix have been substantially revised and updated. Few of the books listed in the previous edition are in this Fourth Edition. The Glossary has been revised to incorporate new census data and interpretations.

This book consists of six parts. The chapters in Part I discuss how race, gender, class, and exceptionality interact to influence student behavior. Social class and religion and their effects on education are discussed in Part II. Part III describes how educational opportunity differs for female and male students and how schools can foster gender equity. The issues, problems, and opportunities for educating students of color and students with language differences are discussed in Part IV. Chapter 11, on the colorblind perspective, highlights the importance of race when teaching about differences. Part V focuses on exceptionality, describing the issues involved in creating equal educational opportunity for students who have disabilities and for those who are gifted. The final part of *Multicultural Education*, Fourth Edition, Part VI, discusses multicultural education as a process of school reform and ways to increase student academic achievement. The Appendix consists of a list of books for further reading. The Glossary defines many of the key concepts and terms throughout the book.

This updated Fourth Edition contains a new feature on American Muslims. It is a condensed version of a chapter in *A New Religious America: How A "Christian Country" has Become the World's Most Religiously Diverse Nation* by Diana L. Eck, professor of comparative religion at Harvard University.

ACKNOWLEDGMENTS

We are grateful to the authors who revised their chapters for this Fourth Edition of *Multicultural Education*, to Jean Anyon for writing and revising a new chapter for this edition, to Jill Bevan-Brown for enriching Chapter 14 with examples from Maori culture and education in New Zealand, and to Janet Ward Schofield for the important revisions she made in Chapter 11, which is reprinted from another publication. We also thank Elizabeth E. Cohen of Stanford University and Michael Knapp of the University of Washington for their helpful comments on a draft of Chapter 4 that enabled Jean Anyon to strengthen it. We are grateful to William Heward, Michael Knapp, Luanna Meyer, Sonia Nieto, Carlos J. Ovando, David Sadker, Betty Schmitz, and James K. Uphoff for recommending sources for the Multicultural Resources part of the Appendix.

We thank Yukari Takimoto, a research assistant in the Center for Multicultural Education at the University of Washington, for her work on the citations and references.

Grace Sheldrick, Wordsworth Associates, has provided the editorial and production service for our books for more than a decade. We are grateful to her for her professionalism and wisdom. Our daughters, Angela and Patricia, continue to be a source of encouragement and inspiration for our work.

J. A. B.
C. A. M. B.

Brief Contents

Contents

Multicultural Education

Multicultural teaching and school reform reflect the academic, social, and cultural needs of students from diverse groups.

PART I

Issues and Concepts

The three chapters in the first part of this book define the major concepts and issues in multicultural education, describe the diverse meanings of culture, and describe the ways in which such variables as race, class, gender, and exceptionality influence student behavior. Various aspects and definitions of culture are discussed. Culture is conceptualized as a dynamic and complex process of construction; its invisible and implicit characteristics are emphasized. The problems that result when culture is essentialized are described.

Multicultural education is an idea, an educational reform movement, and a process whose major goal is to change the structure of educational institutions so that male and female students, exceptional students, and students who are members of diverse racial, ethnic, language, and cultural groups will have an equal chance to achieve academically in school. It is necessary to conceptualize the school as a social system in order to implement multicultural education successfully. Each major variable in the school, such as its culture, its power relationships, the curriculum and materials, and the attitudes and beliefs of the staff, must be changed in ways that will allow the school to promote educational equality for students from diverse groups.

To transform the schools, educators must be knowledgeable about the influence of particular groups on student behavior. The chapters in this part of the book describe the nature of culture and groups in the United States as well as the ways in which they interact to influence student behavior.

CHAPTER I

Multicultural Education: Characteristics and Goals

James A. Banks

THE NATURE OF MULTICULTURAL EDUCATION

Multicultural education is at least three things: an idea or concept, an educational reform movement, and a process. Multicultural education incorporates the idea that all students—regardless of their gender and social class and their ethnic, racial, or cultural characteristics—should have an equal opportunity to learn in school. Another important idea in multicultural education is that some students, because of these characteristics, have a better chance to learn in schools as they are currently structured than do students who belong to other groups or who have different cultural characteristics.

Some institutional characteristics of schools systematically deny some groups of students equal educational opportunities. For example, in the early grades, girls and boys achieve equally in mathematics and science. However, the achievement test scores of girls fall considerably behind those of boys as children progress through the grades (American Association of University Women Educational Foundation, 1998; Sadker & Sadker, 1994). Girls are less likely than boys to participate in class discussions and to be encouraged by teachers to participate. Girls are more likely than boys to be silent in the classroom. However, not all school practices favor males. As Sadker and Sadker point out in Chapter 6, boys are more likely to be disciplined than are girls, even when their behavior does not differ from that of girls. They are also more likely than girls to be classified as learning disabled. Males of color, especially African American males, experience a highly disproportionate rate of disciplinary actions and suspensions in school. Some writers have described the situation of African American males as a "crisis" and have called them "endangered" in U.S. society (Gibbs, 1988).

In the early grades, the academic achievement of students of color such as African Americans, Latinos, and American Indians is close to parity with the achievement of White mainstream students. However, the longer these students of color remain in school, the more their achievement lags behind that of White mainstream students. Social-class status is also strongly related to academic achievement. Anyon, in Chapter 4, describes how the educational opportunities are much greater for students attending affluent suburban schools than for those who attend inner-city schools. She develops these ideas further in her book (Anyon, 1997). Exceptional students, whether they are physically or mentally disabled or gifted and talented, often find that they do not experience equal educational opportunities in the schools. The chapters in Part V of this book describe the problems that such exceptional students experience in schools and suggest ways that teachers and other educators can increase their chances for educational success.

Multicultural education is also a reform movement that is trying to change the schools and other educational institutions so that students from all social class, gender, racial, language, and cultural groups will have an equal opportunity to learn. Multicultural education involves changes in the total school or educational environment; it is not limited to curricular changes. The variables in the school environment that multicultural education tries to transform are discussed later in this chapter and illustrated in Figure 1.5. Multicultural education is also a process whose goals will never be fully realized.

Educational equality, like liberty and justice, are ideals toward which human beings work but never fully attain. Racism, sexism, and discrimination against people with disabilities will exist to some extent no matter how hard we work to eliminate these problems. When prejudice and discrimination are reduced toward one group, they are usually directed toward another group or they take new forms. Whenever groups are identified and labeled, *categorization* occurs. When categorization occurs, members of in-groups favor in-group members and discriminate against out-groups. This process can occur without groups having a history of conflict, animosity, or competition, and without them having physical differences or any other kind of important difference. Social psychologists call this process *social identity theory* or the *minimal group paradigm* (Rothbart & John, 1993; Smith & Mackie, 1995). Because the goals of multicultural education can never be fully attained, we should work continually to increase educational equality for all students.

Multicultural education must be viewed as an ongoing process, and not as something that we "do" and thereby solve the problems that are the targets of multicultural educational reform. When I asked one school administrator what efforts were being taken to implement multicultural education in his school district, he told me that the district had "done" multicultural education last year and that it was now initiating other reforms, such as improving the students' reading scores. This administrator not only misunderstood the nature and scope of multicultural education, but he also did not understand that it could help raise the students' reading scores. A major goal of multicultural education is to improve academic achievement (Banks & Banks, 1995).

MULTICULTURAL EDUCATION: AN INTERNATIONAL REFORM MOVEMENT

Since World War II, many immigrants and groups have settled in the United Kingdom and in nations on the European continent, including France, the Netherlands, Germany, Sweden, and Switzerland (Figueroa, 1995; Hoff, 1995). Some of these immigrants, such as the Asians and West Indians in England and the North Africans and Indochinese in France, have come from former colonies. Many Southern and Eastern European immigrants have settled in Western and Northern European nations in search of upward social mobility and other opportunities. Groups such as Italians, Greeks, and Turks have migrated to Northern and Western European nations in large numbers. Ethnic and immigrant populations have also increased significantly in Australia and Canada since World War II (Allan & Hill, 1995; Moodley, 1995).

Most of the immigrant and ethnic groups in Europe, Australia, and Canada face problems similar to those experienced by ethnic groups in the United States. Groups such as the Jamaicans in England, the Algerians in France, and the Aborigines in Australia experience achievement problems in the schools and prejudice and discrimination in both the schools and society at large. The problems that Greeks and Italians experience in Australia indicate that race is not always a factor when ethnic conflict and tension develop.

The United Kingdom, various nations on the European continent, and Australia and Canada have implemented a variety of programs to increase the achievement of ethnic and immigrant students and to help students and teachers develop more positive attitudes toward racial, cultural, ethnic, and language diversity (Banks & Lynch, 1986; Figueroa, 1995).

THE HISTORICAL DEVELOPMENT OF MULTICULTURAL EDUCATION

Multicultural education grew out of the ferment of the civil rights movement of the 1960s. During this decade, African Americans embarked on a quest for their rights that was unprecedented in the United States. A major goal of the civil rights movement of the 1960s was to eliminate discrimination in public accommodations, housing, employment, and education. The consequences of the civil rights movement had a significant influence on educational institutions as ethnic groups—first African Americans and then other groups—demanded that the schools and other educational institutions reform their curricula so that they would reflect their experiences, histories, cultures, and perspectives. Ethnic groups also demanded that the schools hire more Black and Brown teachers and administrators so that their children would have more successful role models. Ethnic groups pushed for community control of schools in their neighborhoods and for the revision of textbooks to make them reflect the diversity of peoples in the United States.

The first responses of schools and educators to the ethnic movements of the 1960s were hurried. Courses and programs were developed without the thought and careful planning needed to make them educationally sound or to institutionalize them within the educational system. Holidays and other special days, ethnic celebrations, and courses that focused on one ethnic group were the dominant characteristics of school reforms related to ethnic and cultural diversity during the 1960s and early 1970s. Grant and Sleeter, in Chapter 3, call this approach "single group studies." The ethnic studies courses developed and implemented during this period were usually electives and were taken primarily by students who were members of the group that was the subject of the course.

The visible success of the civil rights movement, plus growing rage and a liberal national atmosphere, stimulated other marginalized groups to take actions to eliminate discrimination against them and to demand that the educational system respond to their needs, aspirations, cultures, and histories. The women's rights movement emerged as one of the most significant social reform movements of the late twentieth century (Schmitz, Butler, Rosenfelt, & Guy-Sheftal, 1995). During the 1960s and 1970s, discrimination against women in employment, income, and education was widespread and often blatant. The women's rights movement articulated and publicized how discrimination and institutionalized sexism limited the opportunities of women and adversely affected the nation. The leaders of this movement, such as Betty Friedan and Gloria Steinem, demanded that political, social, economic, and educational institutions act to eliminate sex discrimination and to provide opportunities for women to actualize their talents and realize their ambitions (Steinem, 1995). Major goals of the women's rights movement included equal pay for equal work, the elimination of laws that discriminated against women and made them second-class citizens, the hiring of more women in leadership positions, and greater participation of men in household work and child rearing.

When *feminists* (people who work for the political, social, and economic equality of the sexes) looked at educational institutions, they noted problems similar to those identified by ethnic groups of color. Textbooks and curricula were dominated by men; women were largely invisible. Feminists pointed out that history textbooks were dominated by political and military history—areas in which men had been the main participants (Trecker, 1973). Social and family history and the history of labor and of ordinary people were largely ignored. Feminists pushed for the revision of textbooks to include more history about the important roles of women in the development of the nation and the world. They also demanded that more women be hired for administrative positions in the schools. Although most teachers in the elementary schools were women, most administrators were men.

Other marginalized groups, stimulated by the social ferment and the quest for human rights during the 1970s, articulated their grievances and demanded that institutions be reformed so they would face less discrimination and acquire more human rights. People with disabilities, senior citizens, and gay rights advocates were among the groups that organized politically during this period and made significant inroads in changing institutions and laws. Advocates for citizens with disabilities attained significant legal victories during the 1970s. The Education for All Handicapped Children Act of 1975 (P.L. 94–142), which required that students with disabilities be educated in the least restricted environment and institutionalized the word *mainstreaming* in education, was perhaps the most significant legal victory of the movement for the rights of students with disabilities in education (see Chapters 13 and 14).

HOW MULTICULTURAL EDUCATION DEVELOPED

Multicultural education emerged from the diverse courses, programs, and practices that educational institutions devised to respond to the demands, needs, and aspirations of the various groups. Consequently, as Grant and Sleeter point out in Chapter 3, multicultural education is not in actual practice one identifiable course or educational program. Rather, practicing educators use the term *multicultural education* to describe a wide variety of programs and practices related to educational equity, women, ethnic groups, language minorities, low-income groups, and people with disabilities. In one school district, multicultural education may mean a curriculum that incorporates the experiences of ethnic groups of color; in another, a program may include the experiences of both ethnic groups and women. In a third school district, this term may be used the way it is by me and by other authors, such as Grant and Sleeter (1986a) and

Nieto (1999); that is, to mean a total school reform effort designed to increase educational equity for a range of cultural, ethnic, and economic groups. This broader and more comprehensive notion of multicultural education is discussed in the last part of this chapter. It differs from the limited concept of multicultural education, in which it is viewed as curriculum reform.

MULTICULTURAL EDUCATION AND TENSION AMONG DIVERSE GROUPS

The challenge to multicultural educators, in both theory and practice, is how to increase equity for a particular marginalized group without further limiting the opportunities of another such group. Even though the various groups that are targeted for empowerment and equity in multicultural education share many needs and goals, sometimes they perceive their needs as divergent, conflicting, and inconsistent, as some feminist and ethnic group advocates have in the past (Albrecht & Brewer, 1990). Butler describes this phenomenon in Chapter 8. A major cause of the tension among various marginalized groups may be institutionalized practices within society that promote tension, conflict, and divisiveness among them. If this is the case, as some radical scholars suggest (Barton & Walker, 1983), perhaps an important goal of multicultural education should be to help students who are members of particular marginalized groups better understand how their fates are tied to those of other powerless groups and the significant benefits that can result from multicultural political coalitions. These coalitions could be cogent vehicles for social change and reform. Jesse Jackson's attempt to form what he called a Rainbow Coalition at the national level in the 1980s had as a major goal the formulation of an effective political coalition made up of people from both gender groups and from different racial, ethnic, cultural, and social-class groups.

THE NATURE OF CULTURE IN THE UNITED STATES

The United States, like other Western nation-states such as the United Kingdom, Australia, and Canada, is a multicultural society. The United States consists of a shared core culture as well as many subcultures. In this book, we call the larger shared core culture the *macroculture;* the smaller cultures, which are a part of the core culture, are called *microcultures.* It is important to distinguish the macroculture from the various microcultures because the values, norms, and characteristics of the mainstream (macroculture) are frequently mediated by, as well as interpreted and expressed differently within, various microcultures. These differences often lead to cultural misunderstandings, conflicts, and institutionalized discrimination.

Students who are members of certain cultural, religious, and ethnic groups are sometimes socialized to act and think in certain ways at home but differently at school. One example of this behavior is children who are taught the creation story in the book of Genesis at home but who are expected to accept in school the evolutionary explanation of the development and emergence of human beings. A challenge that multicultural education faces is how to help students from diverse groups mediate between their home and community cultures and the school culture. Students should acquire the knowledge, attitudes, and skills needed to function effectively in each cultural setting. They should also be competent to function within and across other microcultures in their society, within the national macroculture, and within the world community.

The Meaning of Culture

Bullivant (1993) defines culture as a group's program for survival in and adaptation to its environment. The cultural program consists of knowledge, concepts, and values shared by group members through systems of communication. Culture also consists of the shared beliefs, symbols, and interpretations within a human group. Most social scientists today view culture as consisting primarily of the symbolic, ideational, and intangible aspects of human societies. The essence of a culture is not its artifacts, tools, or other tangible cultural elements but how the members of the group interpret, use, and perceive them. It is the values, symbols, interpretations, and perspectives that distinguish one people from another in modernized societies; it is not material objects and other tangible aspects of human societies (Kuper, 1999). People within a culture usually interpret the meanings of symbols, artifacts, and behaviors in the same or in similar ways.

Identifying and Describing the U.S. Core Culture

The United States, like other nation-states, has a shared set of values, ideations, and symbols that constitute the core or overarching culture. This culture is shared to some extent by all the diverse cultural and ethnic groups that make up the nation-state. It is difficult to identify and describe the overarching culture in the United States because it is such a diverse and complex nation. It is easier to identify the core culture within an isolated premodern society, such as the Maoris before the Europeans came to New Zealand, than within highly pluralistic, modernized societies such as the United States, Canada, and Australia (Lisitzky, 1956).

When trying to identify the distinguishing characteristics of U.S. culture, one should realize that the political institutions within the United States, which reflect some of the nation's core values, were heavily influenced by the British. U.S. political ideals and institutions were also influenced by Native American political institutions and practices, especially those related to making group decisions, such as in the League of the Iroquois (Weatherford, 1988).

Equality

A key component in the U.S. core culture is the idea, expressed in the Declaration of Independence in 1776, that "all men are created equal, that they are endowed by their Creator with certain unalienable rights, that among these are life, liberty, and the pursuit of happiness" (Declaration of Independence, 1968, pp. 447–449). When this idea was expressed by the nation's founding fathers in 1776, it was considered radical. A common belief in the eighteenth century was that human beings were not born with equal rights; that some people had few rights and others, such as kings, had divine rights given by God. When considering the idea that "all men are created equal" is a key component of U.S. culture, one should remember to distinguish between a nation's ideals and its actual practices, as well as between the meaning of the idea when it was expressed in 1776 and its meaning today. When the nation's founding fathers expressed this idea in 1776, their conception of men was limited to White males who owned property (Foner, 1998). White men without property, White women, and all African Americans and Indians were not included in their notion of people who were equal or who had "certain unalienable rights."

Although the idea of equality expressed by the founding fathers in 1776 had a very limited meaning at that time, it has proven to be a powerful and important idea in the quest for human rights in the United States. Throughout the nation's history since 1776, marginalized and excluded groups such as women, African Americans, Native Americans, and other cultural and ethnic groups have used this cogent idea to justify and defend the extension of human rights to them and to end institutional discrimination, such as sexism, racism, and discrimination against people with disabilities. As a result, human rights have gradually been extended to various groups throughout U.S. history. The extension of these rights has been neither constant nor linear. Rather, periods of extension of rights have often been followed by periods of retrenchment and conservatism. Schlesinger (1986) calls these patterns "cycles of American history." The United States is still a long way from realizing the ideals expressed in the Declaration of Independence in 1776. However, these ideals remain an important part of U.S. culture and are still used by marginalized groups to justify their struggles for human rights and equality.

Individualism and Individual Opportunity

Two other important ideas in the common overarching U.S. culture are individualism and individual social mobility (Stewart & Bennett, 1991). Individualism as an ideal is extreme in the U.S. core culture. Individual success is more important than commitment to family, community, and nation-state. An individual is expected to experience success by his or her sole efforts. Many people in the United States believe that a person can go from rags to riches within a generation and that every American-born boy can, but not necessarily will, become president.

Individuals are expected to experience success by hard work and to pull themselves up by their bootstraps. This idea was epitomized by fictional characters such as Ragged Dick, one of the heroes created by the popular writer Horatio Alger. Ragged Dick attained success by valiantly overcoming poverty and adversity. A related belief is that if you do not succeed, it is because of your own shortcomings, such as being lazy or unambitious; failure is consequently your own fault. These beliefs are taught in the schools with success stories and myths about such U.S. heroes as George Washington, Thomas Jefferson, and Abraham Lincoln. The beliefs about individualism in U.S. culture are related to the Protestant work ethic. This is the belief that hard work by the individual is morally good and that laziness is sinful. This belief is a legacy of the British Puritan settlers in colonial New England. It has had a powerful and significant influence on U.S. culture.

Groups and Individual Opportunity

The belief in individual opportunity has proven tenacious in U.S. society. It remains strong in American culture despite the fact that individuals' chances for upward social, economic, and educational mobility in the United States are highly related to the social-class, ethnic, gender, and other ascribed groups to which they belong (Knapp & Woolverton, 1995). Social scientists have amply documented the extent of social-class stratification in the United States and the ways in which people's chances in life are affected by the groups to which they belong (Rose, 1992; Willis, 1977). Jencks and his associates (1972) have thoroughly documented the extent to which educational opportunity and life chances are related to social class. The chapters in this book on social class, gender, and ethnicity belie the notion that individual opportunity is a dominant characteristic of U.S. society. Yet the belief in individual opportunity remains strong in the United States.

Individualism and Groupism

Although the groups to which people belong have a cogent influence on their life chances in the United States, Americans—particularly those in the mainstream—are highly individualistic in their value orientations and behaviors. The nuclear family reinforces individualism in U.S. culture. One result of the strong individualism is that married children usually expect their older parents to live independently or in homes for senior citizens rather than with them.

The strong individualism in U.S. culture contrasts sharply with the groupism and group commitment found in Asian nations, such as China and Japan (Butterfield, 1982; Reischauer, 1981). Individualism is viewed rather negatively in these societies. One is expected to be committed first to the family and group and then to oneself. Some U.S. social scientists, such as Lasch (1978) and Bellah and associates (1985), lament the extent of individualism in U.S. society. They believe it is harmful to the common national culture. Some observers believe that groupism is too strong in China and Japan and that individualism should be more valued in those nations. Perhaps modernized, pluralistic nation-states can best benefit from a balance between individualism and groupism, with neither characteristic dominating.

Expansionism and Manifest Destiny

Other overarching U.S. values that social scientists have identified include the desire to conquer or exploit the natural environment, materialism and consumption, and the belief in the nation's inherent superiority. These beliefs justified Manifest Destiny and U.S. expansion to the West and into other nations and the annexation of one-third of Mexico's territory in 1848. These observations, which reveal the less positive side of U.S. national values, have been developed by social scientists interested in understanding the complex nature of U.S. society (Appleby, Hunt, & Jacob, 1994; Greenbaum, 1974).

Greenbaum (1974) believes that distance is also a key value in U.S. society. He uses this word to describe the formal nature of bureaucratic institutions, as well as unfriendliness and detachment in social relationships. Greenbaum argues that the Anglo-Saxon Protestants, the dominant cultural group in U.S. society, have often used distance in their relationships with other ethnic and cultural groups to keep them confined to their social-class status and group.

In his discussion of the nature of values in U.S. society, Myrdal (1962) contends that a major ethical inconsistency exists in U.S. society. He calls this inconsistency "the American dilemma." He states that American Creed values, such as equality and human dignity, exist in U.S. society as ideals. However, they exist alongside the institutionalized discriminatory treatment of African Americans and other ethnic and cultural groups in U.S. society. This variance creates a dilemma in the American mind because Americans try to reconcile their democratic ideals with their treatment of marginalized groups. Myrdal states that this dilemma has been an important factor that has enabled ethnic groups to fight discrimination effectively. In their efforts to resolve their dilemma when the inconsistencies between their ideals and actions are pointed out to them by human-rights advocates, Americans, according to Myrdal, often support the elimination of practices that are inconsistent with their democratic ideals or the American Creed. Some writers have refuted Myrdal's hypothesis and contend that most individuals in the United States do not experience such a dilemma (Ellison, 1995).

Microcultures in the United States

A nation as culturally diverse as the United States consists of a common overarching culture, as well as of a series of microcultures (see Figure 1.1). These microcultures share most of the core values of the nation-state, but these values are often mediated by the various microcultures and are interpreted differently within them. Microcultures sometimes have values that are somewhat alien to the national core culture. Also, some of the core national values and behaviors may seem somewhat alien in certain microcultures or may take on different forms.

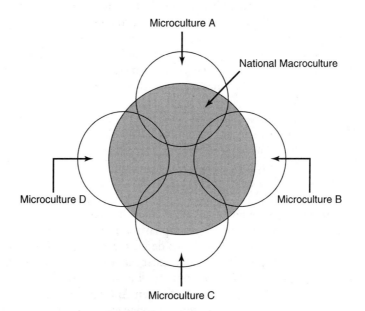

Figure 1.1 Microcultures and the National Macroculture

The shaded area represents the national macroculture. A, B, C, and D represent microcultures that consist of unique institutions, values, and cultural elements that are nonuniversalized and are shared primarily by members of specific cultural groups. A major goal of the school should be to help students acquire the knowledge, skills, and attitudes needed to function effectively within the national macroculture, their own microcultures, and within and across other microcultures.

Source: James A. Banks. *Multiethnic Education: Theory and Practice*, 2nd ed., p. 75. Boston: Allyn and Bacon, 1988. Used with permission of the publisher.

The strong belief in individuality and individualism that exists within the national macroculture is often much less endorsed by some ethnic communities and is somewhat alien within them. African Americans and Latinos who have not experienced high levels of cultural assimilation into the mainstream culture are much more group oriented than are mainstream Americans. Schools in the United States are highly individualistic in their learning and teaching styles, evaluation procedures, and norms. Many students, particularly African Americans, Latinos, and Native Americans, are group-oriented (Irvine & York, 1995; Shade, Kelly, & Oberg, 1997). These students experience problems in the highly individualistic learning environment of the school. Teachers can enhance the learning opportunities of these students, who are also called field dependent or field sensitive, by using cooperative teaching strategies that have been developed and field-tested by researchers such as Slavin (1995) and Cohen (1994).

Some emerging theories indicate that female students may have preferred ways of knowing, thinking, and learning that differ to some extent from those most often preferred by males (Goldberger, Tarule, Clinchy, & Belenky, 1996; Halpern, 1986; Taylor, Gilligan, & Sullivan, 1995). Maher (1987) describes the dominant inquiry model used in social science as male constructed and dominated. She contends that it strives for objectivity: "Personal feelings, biases, and prejudices are considered inevitable limitations" (p. 186). Feminist pedagogy is based on different assumptions about the nature of knowledge and results in a different teaching method. According to Maher and Tetreault (1994), feminist pedagogy enhances the learning of females and deepens the insight of males. In Chapter 7, Tetreault describes feminist pedagogy techniques she uses to motivate students and to enhance their understandings.

After completing a major research study on women's ways of knowing, Belenky and her colleagues (1986) concluded that conceptions of knowledge and truth in the core culture and in educational institutions "have been shaped throughout history by the male-dominated majority culture. Drawing on their own perspectives and visions, men have constructed the prevailing theories, written history, and set values that have become the guiding principles for men and women alike" (p. 5).

These researchers also found an inconsistency between the kind of knowledge most appealing to women and the kind that was emphasized in most educational institutions. Most of the women interviewed in their study considered personalized knowledge and knowledge that resulted from first-hand observation most appealing. However, most educational institutions emphasize abstract, "out-of-context" knowledge (Belenky et al., 1986, p. 200). Ramírez and Castañeda (1974) found that Mexican American students who were socialized within traditional cultures also considered personalized and humanized knowledge more appealing than abstract knowledge. They also responded positively to knowledge that was presented in a humanized or story format.

Research by Gilligan (1982) provides some clues that help us better understand the findings by Belenky and her colleagues about the kind of knowledge women find most appealing. Gilligan describes caring, interconnection, and sensitivity to the needs of other people as dominant values among women and the female microculture in the United States. By contrast, she found that the values of men were more characterized by separation and individualism.

A major goal of multicultural education is to change teaching and learning approaches so that students of both genders and from diverse cultural, ethnic, and language groups will have equal opportunities to learn in educational institutions. This goal suggests that major changes ought to be made in the ways that educational programs are conceptualized, organized, and taught. Educational approaches need to be transformed.

In her research on identifying and labeling students with mental retardation, Mercer (1973) found that a disproportionate number of African American and Mexican American students were labeled mentally retarded because the testing procedures used in intelligence tests "reflect the abilities and skills valued by the American core culture," (p. 32) which Mercer describes as predominantly White, Anglo-Saxon, and middle and upper class. She also points out that measures of general intelligence consist primarily of items related to verbal skills and knowledge. Most African American and Latino students are socialized within microcultures that differ in significant ways from the U.S. core culture. These students often have not had an equal opportunity to learn the knowledge and skills that are measured in mental ability tests. Consequently, a disproportionate percentage of African American and Latino students are labeled mentally retarded and are placed in classes for slow learners. Mental retardation, as Mercer points out, is a socially determined status. When students are placed in classes for the mentally retarded, the self-fulfilling prophecy develops. Students begin to act and think as though they *are* mentally retarded (Banks, 2000).

Groups and Group Identification

Thus far, this chapter has discussed the various microcultures that make up U.S. society. Individuals learn the values, symbols, and other components of their culture from their social group. The group is the social system that carries a culture. People belong to and live in social groups (Bullivant, 1993). A group is a collectivity of persons who share an identity, a feeling of unity. A group is also a social system that has a social structure of interrelated roles (Theodorson & Theodorson, 1969). The group's program for survival, values, ideations, and shared symbols constitutes its culture (Kuper, 1999).

The study of groups is the major focus in sociology. Sociologists believe that the group has a strong influence on the behavior of individuals, that behavior is shaped by group norms, and that the group equips individuals with the behavior patterns they need in order to adapt to their physical, social, and metaphysical environments. Sociologists also assume that groups have independent characteristics; they are more than aggregates of individuals. Groups possess a continuity that transcends the lives of individuals.

Sociologists also assume that knowledge about groups to which an individual belongs provides important clues to and explanations for the individual's behavior. Goodman and Marx (1982) write, "Such factors as shared religion, nationality, age, sex, marital status, and education have proved to be important determinants of what people believe, feel, and do" (p. 7). Although membership in a gender, racial, ethnic, social-class, or religious group can provide us with important clues about individuals' behavior, it cannot enable us to predict behavior. Knowing one's group affiliation can enable us to state that a certain type of behavior is probable. Membership in a particular group does not determine behavior but makes certain types of behavior more probable.

There are several important reasons that knowledge of group characteristics and modalities can enable us to predict the probability of an individual's behavior but not the precise behavior.

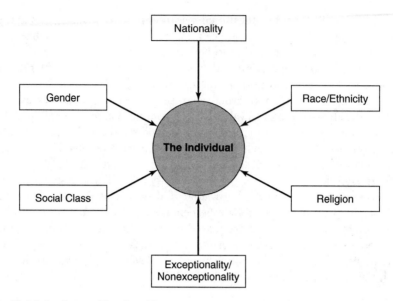

Figure 1.2 Multiple Group Memberships

An individual belongs to several different groups at the same time. This figure shows the major groups discussed in this book.

This is, in part, because each individual belongs to several groups at the same time (see Figure 1.2). An individual may be White, Catholic, female, and middle class, all at the same time. She might have a strong identification with one of these groups and a very weak or almost nonexistent identification with another. A person can be a member of a particular group, such as the Catholic church, and have a weak identification with the group and a weak commitment to the tenets of the Catholic faith. Religious identification might be another individual's strongest group identification. Identification with and attachments to different groups may also conflict. A woman who has a strong Catholic identification but is also a feminist might find it difficult to reconcile her beliefs about equality for women with some positions of the Catholic church, such as its prohibiting women from becoming ordained priests.

The more we know about a student's level of identification with a particular group and the extent to which socialization has taken place within that group, the more accurately we can predict, explain, and understand the student's behavior in the classroom. A knowledge of the importance of a group to a student at a particular time of life and within a particular social context will also help us understand the student's behavior. Ethnic identity may become more important to a person who becomes a part of an ethnic minority when he or she previously belonged to the majority. Many Whites who have moved from the U.S. mainland to Hawaii have commented on how their sense of ethnic identity increased and they began to feel marginalized. Group identity may also increase when the group feels threatened, when a social movement arises to promote its rights, or when the group attempts to revitalize its culture.

The Teaching Implications of Group Identification

What are the implications of group membership and group identity for teaching? As you read the chapters in this book that describe the characteristics of the two gender groups and of social-class, racial, ethnic, religious, language, and exceptional groups, bear in mind that individuals within these groups manifest these behaviors to various degrees. Also remember that individual students are members of several of these groups at the same time. Above, the core U.S. culture is described as having highly individualistic values and beliefs. However, research by Gilligan (1982) indicates that the values of women, as compared with those of men, are more often characterized by caring, interconnection, and sensitivity to the needs of others. This observation indicates how core values within the macroculture are often mediated by microcultures within various gender, ethnic, and cultural groups.

As stated above, researchers have found that some students of color, such as African Americans and Mexican Americans, often have field-sensitive learning styles and therefore prefer more personalized learning approaches (Ramírez & Castañeda, 1974). Think about what this means. This research describes a group characteristic of these students and not the behavior of a particular African American or Mexican American student. It suggests that there is a higher probability that these students will have field-sensitive learning styles than will middle-class Anglo-American students. However, students within all ethnic, racial, and so-cial-class groups have different learning styles (Irvine & York, 1995). Those groups influence students' behavior, such as their learning style, interactively, because they are members of several groups at the same time. Knowledge of the characteristics of groups to which students belong, about the importance of each of these groups to them, and of the extent to which individuals have been socialized within each group will give the teacher important clues to students' behavior.

The Interaction of Race, Class, and Gender

When using our knowledge of groups to understand student behavior, we should also consider the ways that such variables as class, race, and gender interact and intersect to influence student behavior. Middle-class and more highly assimilated Mexican American students tend to be more field independent than do lower-class and less assimilated Mexican American students. African American students tend to be more field-dependent (group oriented) than are White students; females tend to be more field-dependent than are male students. Therefore, it can be hypothesized that African American females would be the most field-dependent when compared to African American and White males and White females. This finding was made by Perney (1976).

Unfortunately, the researcher did not include a social-class measure in the study. After a comprehensive review of research on the ways that race, class, and gender influence student behavior in education, Grant and Sleeter (1986b) concluded that we must look at the ways these variables interact in order to fully understand student behavior.

Figure 1.3 illustrates how the major groups discussed in this book—gender, race or ethnicity, social class, religion, and exceptionality—influence student behavior, both singly and interactively. The figure also shows that other variables, such as geographic region and age, also influence an individual's behavior. The ways these variables influence selected student behaviors are described in Table 1.1.

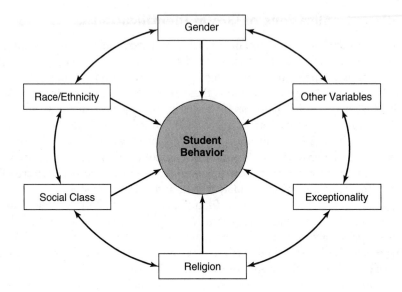

Figure 1.3 The Intersection of Variables

The major variables of gender, race or ethnicity, social class, religion, and exceptionality influence student behavior, both singly and interactively. Other variables, such as region and age, also influence student behavior.

Table 1.1 Singular and Combined Effects of Variables

Student Behavior	Gender Effects	Race/ Ethnicity Effects	Social- Class Effects	Religious Effects	Combined Effects
Learning Styles (Field Independent/Field Dependent)	X[a]	X			X
Internality/Externality			X		
Fear of Success	X	X			?
Self-Esteem	X	X			?
Individual vs. Group Orientation	X	X	X		?

[a]An X Indicates that the variable influences the student behavior that is described in the far-left column. An X in the far-right column means that research indicates that two or more variables combine to influence the described behavior. A question mark indicates that the research is unclear about the combined effects of the variables.

THE SOCIAL CONSTRUCTION OF CATEGORIES

The major variables and categories discussed in this book, such as gender, race, ethnicity, class, and exceptionality, are social categories (Berger & Luckman, 1967; Mannheim, 1936). The criteria for whether an individual belongs to one of these categories are determined by human beings and consequently are socially constructed. Religion is also a social category. Religious institutions, symbols, and artifacts are created by human beings to satisfy their metaphysical needs.

These categories are usually related to the physical characteristics of individuals. In some cases, as when they are individuals with severe or obvious physical disabilities, the relationship between the labels given to individuals and their physical characteristics is direct and would be made in almost any culture or social system. The relationship between categories that are used to classify individuals and their physical characteristics, however, is usually indirect and complex. Even though one's sex is determined primarily by physical characteristics (such as genitalia, chromosome patterns, etc.,), gender is a social construction created and shaped by the society in which individuals and groups function.

Gender

Gender consists of the socially and psychologically appropriate behavior for males and females sanctioned by and expected within a society. Gender-role expectations vary across cultures and at different times in a society and within microcultures in the same society. Traditionally, normative behavior for males and females has varied among mainstream Americans, African Americans, Native Americans, and Hispanic Americans. Gender-role expectations also vary somewhat across social classes within the same society. In the White mainstream society in the 1940s and 1950s, upper-middle-class women often received negative sanctions when they worked outside the home, whereas women in working-class families were frequently expected to become wage earners.

Race

Race is a socially determined category that is related to physical characteristics in a complex way (Jacobson, 1998). Two individuals with nearly identical physical characteristics, or phenotypes, can be classified as members of different races in two different societies (Nash, 1999). In the United States, where racial categories are well defined and highly inflexible, an individual with any acknowledged or publicly known African ancestry is considered Black (Davis, 1991). One who looks completely Caucasian but who acknowledges some African ancestry is classified as Black. Such an individual would be considered White in Puerto Rico. In Puerto Rico, hair texture, social status, and degree of eminence in the community are often as important as—if not more important than—physical characteristics in determining an individual's racial group or category. There is a saying in Puerto Rico that "money lightens," which means that upward social mobility considerably enhances an individual's opportunity to be classified as White. There is a strong relationship between race and social class in Puerto Rico and in most other Caribbean and Latin American nations.

Our discussion of race as a social category indicates that the criteria for determining the characteristics of a particular race vary across cultures, that an individual considered Black in one society may be considered White in another, and that racial categories reflect the social, economic, and political characteristics of a society.

Social Class

Social scientists find it difficult to agree on criteria for determining social class. The problem is complicated by the fact that societies are constantly in the throes of change. During the 1950s, social scientists often attributed characteristics to the lower class that are found in the middle class today, such as single-parent and female-headed households, high divorce rates, and substance abuse. Today, these characteristics are no longer rare among the middle class, even though their frequency is still higher among lower-class families. Variables such as income, education, occupation, life-style, and values are among the most frequently used indices to determine social-class status in the United States (Warner, with Meeker & Eells, 1960). However, there is considerable disagreement among social scientists about which variables are the most important in determining the social-class status of an individual or family.

Social-class criteria also vary somewhat among various ethnic and racial groups in the United States. Teachers, preachers, and other service professionals were upper class in many rural African American communities in the South in the 1950s and 1960s but were considered middle class by mainstream White society. The systems of social stratification that exist in the mainstream society and in various microcultures are not necessarily identical.

Exceptionality

Exceptionality is also a social category. Whether a person is considered disabled or gifted is determined by criteria developed by society. As Shaver and Curtis (1981) point out, disabilities are not necessarily handicaps, and the two should be distinguished. They write, "A disability or combination of disabilities becomes a handicap only when the condition limits or impedes the person's ability to function normally" (p. 1). A person with a particular disability, such as having one arm, might have a successful college career, experience no barriers to his achievements in college, and graduate with honors. However, he may find that when he tries to enter the job market, his opportunities are severely limited because potential employers view him as unable to perform well in some situations in which, in fact, he could perform effectively (Shaver & Curtis, 1981). This individual has a disability but was viewed as handicapped in one situation—the job market—but not in another—his university.

Mercer (1973) has extensively studied the social process by which individuals become labeled as persons with mental retardation. She points out that even though their physical characteristics may increase their chance of being labeled persons with mental retardation, the two are not perfectly correlated. Two people with the same biological characteristics may be considered persons with mental retardation in one social system and not in another social system. An individual may be considered a person with mental retardation at school but not at home. She writes, "Mental retardation is not a characteristic of the individual, nor a meaning inherent in behavior, but a socially determined status, which [people] may occupy in some social systems and not in others" (p. 31). She states that people can change their role by changing their social group.

The highly disproportionate number of African Americans, Latinos, and particularly males classified as learning disabled by the school indicates the extent to which exceptionality is a social category. Mercer (1973) found that the school labeled more people mentally retarded than did any other institution. Many African American and Latino students who are labeled mentally retarded function normally and are considered normal in their homes and communities. Boys are more often classified as mentally retarded than are girls. The school, as Mercer and other researchers have pointed out, uses criteria to determine the mental ability of students of color that conflict with their home and community cultures. Some students in all ethnic and cultural groups are mentally retarded and deserve special instruction, programs, and services, as the authors in Part Five of this book suggest. However, the percentage of students of color in these programs is too high. The percentage of students in each ethnic group labeled mentally retarded should be about the same as the total percentage of that group in school.

Giftedness is also a social category (Sapon-Shevin, 1994). Important results of the socially constructed nature of giftedness are the considerable disagreement among experts about how the concept should be defined and the often inconsistent views about how to identify gifted students (Ford, 1996). The highly disproportionate percentage of middle- and upper-middle-class mainstream students categorized as gifted compared to lower-class students and students of color such as African Americans, Latinos, and Native Americans is also evidence of the social origin of the category. Many students who are classified as gifted do have special talents and abilities, and they do need special instruction.

In Chapter 15, Subotnik and LeBlanc describe the characteristics of these students and ways in which their needs can be met. However, some students who are classified as gifted by school districts merely have parents with the knowledge, political skills, and power to force the school to classify their children as gifted, which will provide them with special instruction and educational enrichment (Sapon-Shevin, 1994). In some racially mixed school districts, the gifted programs are made up primarily of middle-class and upper-middle-class mainstream students.

Schools should try to satisfy the needs of students with special gifts and talents; however, they should also make sure that students from all social-class, cultural, language, and ethnic groups have an equal opportunity to participate in programs for academically and creatively talented students. If schools or districts do not have a population in their gifted programs that represents their various cultural, racial, language, and ethnic groups, steps should be taken to examine the criteria used to identify gifted students and to develop procedures to correct the disproportion. Both excellence and equality should be major goals of education in a pluralistic society.

THE DIMENSIONS OF MULTICULTURAL EDUCATION

When many teachers think of multicultural education, they think only or primarily of content related to ethnic, racial, and cultural groups. Conceptualizing multicultural education exclusively as content related to various ethnic and cultural groups is problematic for several reasons. Teachers who cannot easily see how their content is related to cultural and normative issues will easily dismiss multicultural education with the argument that it is not relevant to their disciplines. This is done frequently by secondary math and science teachers.

The irrelevant-of-content argument can become a legitimized form of resistance to multicultural education when it is conceptualized primarily or exclusively as content. Math and science teachers often state, "Multicultural education is fine for social studies and literature teachers, but it has nothing to do with me. Math and science are the same, regardless of the culture or the kids." Multicultural education needs to be more broadly defined and understood so that teachers from a wide range of disciplines can respond to it in appropriate ways and resistance to it can be minimized.

Multicultural education is a broad concept with several different and important dimensions (Banks, 1995a). Practicing educators can use the dimensions as a guide to school reform when trying to implement multicultural education. The dimensions are (1) content integration, (2) the knowledge construction process, (3) prejudice reduction, (4) an equity pedagogy, and (5) an empowering school culture and social structure. Each dimension is defined and illustrated below.

Content Integration

Content integration deals with the extent to which teachers use examples and content from a variety of cultures and groups to illustrate key concepts, principles, generalizations, and theories in their subject area or discipline. The infusion of ethnic and cultural content into the subject area should be logical and not contrived.

More opportunities exist for the integration of ethnic and cultural content in some subject areas than in others. In the social studies, the language arts, and music, frequent and ample opportunities exist for teachers to use ethnic and cultural content to illustrate concepts, themes, and principles. There are also opportunities to integrate multicultural content into math and science. However, the opportunities are not as ample as they are in social studies, the language arts, and music.

The Knowledge Construction Process

The knowledge construction process relates to the extent to which teachers help students to understand, investigate, and determine how the implicit cultural assumptions, frames of references, perspectives, and biases within a discipline influence the ways in which knowledge is constructed within it (Banks, 1996).

Students can analyze the knowledge construction process in science by studying how racism has been perpetuated in science by genetic theories of intelligence, Darwinism, and eugenics. In his important book *The Mismeasure of Man*, Gould (1996) describes how scientific racism developed and was influential in the nineteenth and twentieth centuries. Scientific racism has had and continues to have a significant influence on the interpretations of mental ability tests in the United States.

The publication of *The Bell Curve* (Herrnstein & Murray, 1994), its widespread and enthusiastic public reception, and the social context out of which it emerged provide an excellent case study for discussion and analysis by students who are studying knowledge construction (Kincheloe, Steinberg, & Gresson, 1996). Herrnstein and Murray contend that low-income groups and African Americans have less cognitive abilities than do other groups and that these differences are inherited. Students can examine the arguments made by the authors, their major assumptions, and how their conclusions relate to the social and political context.

Gould (1994) contends that Herrnstein and Murray's arguments reflect the social context of the times, "a historical moment of unprecedented ungenerosity, when a mood for slashing social programs can be powerfully abetted by an argument that beneficiaries cannot be helped, owing to inborn cognitive limits expressed as low I.Q. scores" (p. 139). Students should also study counterarguments to *The Bell Curve* made by respected scientists. Two good sources are *The Bell Curve Debate: History, Documents, Opinions*, edited by Jacoby and Glauberman (1995); and *Measured Lies: The Bell Curve Examined*, edited by Kincheloe, Steinberg, and Gresson (1996).

Students can examine the knowledge construction process in the social studies when they study such units and topics as the European discovery of America and the westward movement. The teacher can ask the students the latent meanings of concepts such as the European discovery of America and the New World. The students can discuss what these concepts imply or suggest about the Native American cultures that had existed in the Americas for about 40,000 years before the Europeans arrived. When studying the westward movement, the teacher can ask the students, "Whose point of view or perspective does this concept reflect, that of the European Americans or the Lakota Sioux?" "Who was moving west?" "How might a Lakota Sioux historian describe this period in U.S. history?" "What are other ways of thinking about and describing the westward movement?"

Prejudice Reduction

Prejudice reduction describes lessons and activities teachers use to help students develop positive attitudes toward different racial, ethnic, and cultural groups. Research indicates that children come to school with many negative attitudes toward and misconceptions about different racial and ethnic groups (Banks, 2000; Stephan, 1999). Research also indicates that lessons, units, and teaching materials that include content about different racial and ethnic groups can help students to develop more positive intergroup attitudes if certain conditions exist in the teaching situation (Banks, 1995b). These conditions include positive images of the ethnic groups in the materials and the use of multiethnic materials in a consistent and sequential way.

Allport's (1954) *contact hypothesis* provides several useful guidelines for helping students to develop more positive interracial attitudes and actions in contact situations. He states that contact between groups will improve intergroup relations when the contact is characterized by these four conditions: (1) equal status; (2) cooperation rather than competition; (3) sanction by authorities such as teachers and administrators; and (4) interpersonal interactions in which students become acquainted as individuals.

An Equity Pedagogy

Teachers in each discipline can analyze their teaching procedures and styles to determine the extent to which they reflect multicultural issues and concerns. An equity pedagogy exists when teachers modify their teaching in ways that will facilitate the academic achievement of students from diverse racial, cultural, gender, and social-class groups (Banks, C. A. M., & Banks, J. A., 1995). This includes using a variety of teaching styles and approaches that are consistent with the wide range of learning styles within various cultural and ethnic groups, being demanding but highly personalized when working with groups such as Native American and Alaskan students, and using cooperative learning techniques in math and science instruction in order to enhance the academic achievement of students of color (Davidson, 1990).

Several chapters in this book discuss ways in which teachers can modify their instruction in order to increase the academic achievement of students from different cultural groups and from both gender groups, including the chapters that constitute Parts III and IV.

An Empowering School Culture

Another important dimension of multicultural education is a school culture and organization that promotes gender, racial, and social-class equity. The culture and organization of the school must be examined by all members of the school staff. They all must also participate in restructuring it. Grouping and labeling practices, sports participation, disproportionality in achievement, disproportionality in enrollment in gifted and special education programs, and the interaction of the staff and the students across ethnic and racial lines are important variables that need to be examined in order to create a school culture that empowers students from diverse racial and ethnic groups and from both gender groups.

Figure 1.4 summarizes the dimensions of multicultural education described above. The next section of this chapter identifies the major variables of the school that must be changed in order to institutionalize a school culture that empowers students from diverse cultural, racial, ethnic, and social-class groups.

The School as a Social System

To implement multicultural education successfully, we must think of the school as a social system in which all of its major variables are closely interrelated. Thinking of the school as a social system suggests that we must formulate and initiate a change strategy that reforms the total school environment to implement multicultural education. The major school variables that must be reformed are presented in Figure 1.5.

Reforming any one of the variables in Figure 1.5, such as the formalized curriculum or curricular materials, is necessary but not sufficient. Multicultural and sensitive teaching materials are ineffective in the hands of teachers who have negative attitudes toward different racial, ethnic, and cultural groups. Such teachers are rarely likely to use multicultural materials or are likely to use them detrimentally. Thus, helping teachers and other members of the school staff to gain knowledge about diverse groups and democratic attitudes and values is essential when implementing multicultural programs.

To implement multicultural education in a school, we must reform its power relationships, the verbal interaction between teachers and students, the culture of the school, the curriculum, extracurricular activities, attitudes toward minority languages (Beykont, 2000), the testing program, and grouping practices. The institutional norms, social structures, cause-belief statements, values, and goals of the school must be transformed and reconstructed.

Major attention should be focused on the school's hidden curriculum and its implicit norms and values. A school has both a manifest and a hidden curriculum. The manifest curriculum consists of such factors as guides, textbooks, bulletin boards, and lesson plans. These aspects of the school environment are important and must be reformed to create a school culture that promotes positive attitudes toward diverse cultural groups and helps students from these groups

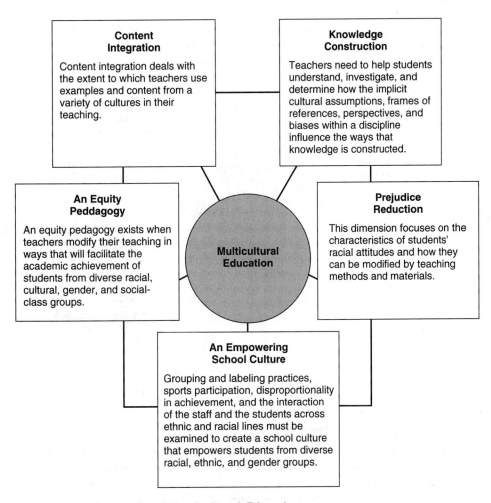

Content Integration

Content integration deals with the extent to which teachers use examples and content from a variety of cultures in their teaching.

Knowledge Construction

Teachers need to help students understand, investigate, and determine how the implicit cultural assumptions, frames of references, perspectives, and biases within a discipline influence the ways that knowledge is constructed.

An Equity Peddagogy

An equity pedagogy exists when teachers modify their teaching in ways that will facilitate the academic achievement of students from diverse racial, cultural, gender, and social-class groups.

Multicultural Education

Prejudice Reduction

This dimension focuses on the characteristics of students' racial attitudes and how they can be modified by teaching methods and materials.

An Empowering School Culture

Grouping and labeling practices, sports participation, disproportionality in achievement, and the interaction of the staff and the students across ethnic and racial lines must be examined to create a school culture that empowers students from diverse racial, ethnic, and gender groups.

Figure 1.4   The Dimensions of Multicultural Education

experience academic success. However, the school's hidden or latent curriculum is often more cogent than is its manifest or overt curriculum. The latent curriculum has been defined as the one that no teacher explicitly teaches but that all students learn. It is that powerful part of the school culture that communicates to students the school's attitudes toward a range of issues and problems, including how the school views them as human beings and its attitudes toward males, females, exceptional students, and students from various religious, cultural, racial, and ethnic groups. Jackson (1992) calls the latent curriculum the "untaught lessons."

When formulating plans for multicultural education, educators should conceptualize the school as a microculture that has norms, values, statuses, and goals like other social systems. The school has a dominant culture and a variety of microcultures. Almost all classrooms in the United States are multicultural because White students, as well as Black and Brown students, are socialized within diverse cultures. Teachers also come from many different groups. Many

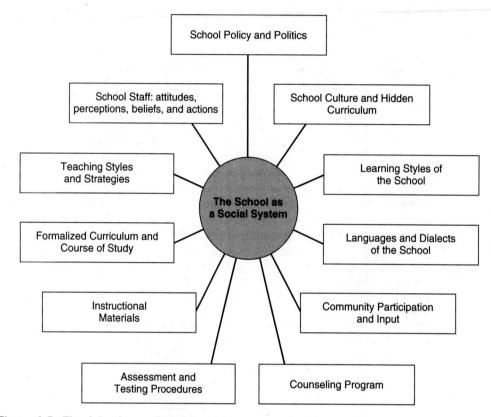

Figure 1.5 The School as a Social System

The total school environment is a system consisting of a number of major identifiable variables and factors, such as a school culture, school policy and politics, and the formalized curriculum and course of study. Any of these factors may be the focus of initial school reform, but changes must take place in each of them to create and sustain an effective multicultural school environment.

Source: Adapted with permission from James A. Banks (Ed.), *Education in the 80s: Multiethnic Education* (Washington, DC: National Education Association, 1981), Figure 2, p. 22.

teachers were socialized in cultures other than the Anglo mainstream, although these may be forgotten and repressed. Teachers can get in touch with their own cultures and use the perspectives and insights they acquired as vehicles for helping them relate to and understand the cultures of their students.

The school should be a cultural environment in which acculturation takes place; teachers and students should assimilate some of the views, perspectives, and ethos of each other as they interact. Teachers and students will be enriched by this process, and the academic achievement of students from diverse groups will be enhanced because their perspectives will be legitimized in the school. Both teachers and students will be enriched by this process of cultural sharing and interaction.

SUMMARY

Multicultural education is an idea stating that all students, regardless of the groups to which they belong, such as those related to gender, ethnicity, race, culture, language, social class, religion, or exceptionality, should experience educational equality in the schools. Some students, because of their particular characteristics, have a better chance to succeed in school as it is currently structured than have students from other groups. Multicultural education is also a reform movement designed to bring about a transformation of the school so that students from both genders and from diverse cultural, language, and ethnic groups will have an equal chance to experience school success. Multicultural education views the school as a social system that consists of highly interrelated parts and variables. Therefore, in order to transform the school to bring about educational equality, all the major components of the school must be substantially changed. A focus on any one variable in the school, such as the formalized curriculum, will not implement multicultural education.

Multicultural education is a continuing process because the idealized goals it tries to actualize—such as educational equality and the eradication of all forms of discrimination— can never be fully achieved in a human society. Multicultural education, which was born during the social protest of the 1960s and 1970s, is an international movement that exists in various nations on the European continent and in Australia, the United Kingdom, and Canada. A major goal of multicultural education is to help students to develop the knowledge, attitudes, and skills needed to function within their own microcultures, the U.S. macroculture, other microcultures, and within the global community.

Questions and Activities

1. What are the three components or elements of multicultural education?
2. How does Banks define multicultural education?
3. Find other definitions of multicultural education in several books listed under the category "Issues and Concepts" in the Appendix. How are the definitions of multicultural education in these books alike and different from the one presented in this chapter?
4. In what ways did the civil rights and women's rights movements of the 1960s and 1970s influence the development of multicultural education?
5. Ask several teachers and other practicing educators to give you their views and definitions of multicultural education. What generalizations can you make about their responses?
6. Visit a local school and, by observing several classes as well as by interviewing several teachers and the principal, describe what curricular and other practices related to multicultural education have been implemented in the school. Share your report with your classmates or workshop colleagues.
7. What major tensions exist among groups such as various racial and ethnic groups and between feminists and ethnic minorities? Can multicultural education help reduce such tensions? If so, how?

8. What is a macroculture? A microculture?

9. How is culture defined? What are the most important components of culture in a modernized society?

10. List and define several core or overarching values and characteristics that make up the macroculture in the United States. To what extent are these values and characteristics consistent with practices in U.S. society? To what extent are they ideals that are inconsistent with realities in U.S. society?

11. What problems result when ideals in U.S. society are taught to students as if they were realities? Give examples of this.

12. How is individualism viewed differently in the United States and in nations such as China and Japan? Why? What are the behavioral consequences of these varying notions of individualism?

13. What is the American dilemma defined by Myrdal? To what extent is this concept an accurate description of values in U.S. society? Explain.

14. How do the preferred ways of learning and knowing among women and students of color often influence their experiences in the schools as they are currently structured? In what ways can school reform help make the school environment more consistent with the learning and cognitive styles of women and students of color?

15. In what ways does the process of identifying and labeling students with mental retardation discriminate against groups such as African Americans and Latinos?

16. In what ways can the characteristics of a group help us understand an individual's behavior? In what ways are group characteristics limited in explaining an individual's behavior?

17. How do such variables as race, class, and gender interact to influence the behavior of students? Give examples to support your response.

18. What is meant by the "social construction of categories"? In what ways are concepts such as gender, race, social class, and exceptionality social categories?

19. List and define the five dimensions of multicultural education. How can these dimensions be used to facilitate school reform?

References

Albrecht, L. and Brewer, R. M. (Eds.). (1990). *Bridges of Power: Women's Multicultural Alliances*. Philadelphia: New Society Publishers.

Allan, R. and Hill, B. (1995). Multicultural Education in Australia: Historical Development and Current Status. In J. A. Banks and C. A. M. Banks (Eds.), *Handbook of Research on Multicultural Education* (pp. 763–777). New York: Macmillan.

Allport, G. W. (1954). *The Nature of Prejudice*. Reading, MA: Addison-Wesley.

American Association of University Women Educational Foundation. (1998). *Gender Gaps: Where Schools Still Fail Our Children*. Washington, DC: Author.

Anyon, J. (1997). *Ghetto Schooling: A Political Economy of Urban Educational Reform.* New York: Teachers College Press.

Appleby, J., Hunt, L., and Jacob, M. (1994). *Telling the Truth about History.* New York: Norton.

Banks, C. A. M. and Banks, J. A. (1995). Equity Pedagogy: An Essential Component of Multicultural Education. *Theory into Practice, 34*(3), 152–158.

Banks, J. A. (1995a). Multicultural Education: Historical Development, Dimensions, and Practice. In J. A. Banks and C. A. M. Banks (Eds.), *Handbook of Research on Multicultural Education* (pp. 3–24). New York: Macmillan.

Banks, J. A. (1995b). Multicultural Education: Its Effects on Students' Racial and Gender Role Attitudes. In J. A. Banks and C. A. M. Banks (Eds.), *Handbook of Research on Multicultural Education* (pp. 617–627). New York: Macmillan.

Banks, J. A. (Ed.) (1996). *Multicultural Education, Transformative Knowledge, and Action.* New York: Teachers College Press.

Banks, J. A. (2000). The Social Construction of Difference and the Quest for Educational Equality. In R. Brandt (Ed.), *Education in a New Era* (pp. 21–45). Arlington, VA: Association for Supervision and Curriculum Development.

Banks, J. A. (2001). *Cultural Diversity and Education: Foundations, Curriculum, and Teaching* (4th ed.). Boston: Allyn and Bacon.

Banks, J. A. and Banks, C. A. M. (Eds.). (1995). *Handbook of Research on Multicultural Education.* New York: Macmillan.

Banks, J. A. and Lynch, J. (Eds.). (1986). *Multicultural Education in Western Societies.* London: Cassell.

Barton, L. and Walker, S. (Eds.). (1983). *Race, Class and Education.* London: Croom Helm.

Belenky, M.F., Clinchy, B. M., Goldberger, N. R., and Tarule, J. M. (1986). *Women's Ways of Knowing: The Development of Self, Voice and Mind.* New York: Basic Books.

Bellah, R. N., Madsen, R., Sullivan, W. M., Swidler, A., and Tipton, S. M. (1985). *Habits of the Heart: Individualism and Commitment in American Life.* New York: Harper and Row.

Berger, P. L. and Luckman, T. (1967). *The Social Construction of Reality: A Treatise in the Sociology of Knowledge.* New York: Doubleday and Co.

Beykont, Z. F. (Ed.). (2000). *Lifting Every Voice: Pedagogy and Politics of Bilingualism.* Cambridge, MA: Harvard Education Publishing Group.

Bullivant, B. (1993). Culture: Its Nature and Meaning for Educators. In J. A. Banks and C. A. M. Banks (Eds.), *Multicultural Education: Issues and Perspectives* (2nd ed.) (pp. 29–47). Boston: Allyn and Bacon.

Butterfield, F. (1982). *China: Alive in the Bitter Sea.* New York: Bantam Books.

Cohen, E. G. (1994). *Designing Groupwork: Strategies for Heterogeneous Classrooms* (2nd ed.). New York: Teachers College Press.

Davidson, N. (Ed.). (1990). *Cooperative Learning in Mathematics: A Handbook for Teachers.* Menlo Park, CA: Addison-Wesley.

Davis, F. J. (1991). *Who Is Black? One Nation's Definition.* University Park: The Pennsylvania State University.

Declaration of Independence. (1968). In *The Annals of America,* Vol. 2 (pp. 447–449). Chicago: Encyclopaedia Britannica.

Ellison, R. (1995). An American Dilemma: A Review. In J. F. Callahan (Ed.), *The Collected Essays of Ralph Ellison* (pp. 328–340). New York: The Modern Library.

Figueroa, P. (1995). Multicultural Education in the United Kingdom: Historical Development and Current Status. In J. A. Banks and C. A. M. Banks (Eds.), *Handbook of Research on Multicultural Education* (pp. 778–800). New York: Macmillan.

Foner, E. (1998). *The Story of American Freedom*. New York: Norton.

Ford, D. Y. (1996). *Reversing Underachievement among Gifted Black Students*. New York: Teachers College Press.

Gibbs, J. T. (Ed.). (1988). *Young, Black, and Male in America: An Endangered Species*. Dover, MA: Auburn House Publishing.

Gilligan, C. (1982). *In a Different Voice: Psychological Theory and Women's Development*. Cambridge, MA: Harvard University Press.

Goldberger, N., Tarule, J., Clinchy, B., and Belenky, M. (Eds.). (1996). *Knowledge, Difference and Power*. New York: Basic Books.

Goodman, N. and Marx, G. T. (1982). *Society Today* (4th ed.). New York: Random House.

Gould, S. J. (1994). Curveball. *The New Yorker, 70*(38), 139–149.

Gould, S. J. (1996). *The Mismeasure of Man* (revised & expanded ed.). New York: Norton.

Grant, C. A. and Sleeter, C. E. (1986a). *After the School Bell Rings*. Philadelphia: The Falmer Press.

Grant, C. A. and Sleeter, C. E. (1986b). Race, Class, and Gender in Education Research: An Argument for Integrative Analysis. *Review of Educational Research, 56*, 195–211.

Greenbaum, W. (1974). America in Search of a New Ideal: An Essay on the Rise of Pluralism. *Harvard Educational Review, 44*, 411–440.

Halpern, D. F. (1986). *Sex Differences in Cognitive Abilities*. Hillsdale, NJ: Lawrence Erlbaum Associates, Inc.

Herrnstein, R. J. and Murray, C. (1994). *The Bell Curve: Intelligence and Class Structure in American Life*. New York: The Free Press.

Hoff, G. (1995). Multicultural Education in Germany: Historical Developments and Current Status. In J. A. Banks and C. A. M. Banks (Eds.), *Handbook of Research on Multicultural Education* (pp. 821–838). New York: Macmillan.

Irvine, J. J. and York, E. D. (1995). Learning Styles and Culturally Diverse Students: A Literature Review. In J. A. Banks and C. A. M. Banks (Eds.), *Handbook of Research on Multicultural Education* (pp. 484–497). New York: Macmillan.

Jackson, P. W. (1992). *Untaught Lessons*. New York: Teachers College Press.

Jacobson, M. F. (1998). *Whiteness of a Different Color: European Immigrants and the Alchemy of Race*. Cambridge, MA: Harvard University Press.

Jacoby, R. and Glauberman, N. (Eds.). (1995). *The Bell Curve Debate: History, Documents, Opinions*. New York: Times Books/Random House.

Jencks, C., Smith, M., Acland, H., Bane, M. J., Cohen, D., Gintis, H., Heyns, B., and Michelson, S. (1972). *Inequality: A Reassessment of the Effect of Family and Schooling in America*. New York: Basic Books.

Kincheloe, J. L., Steinberg, S. R., and Gresson, A. D. III (Eds.). (1996). *Measured Lies: The Bell Curve Examined*. New York: St. Martin's.

Knapp, M. S. and Woolverton, S. (1995). Social Class and Schooling. In J. A. Banks and C. A. M. Banks (Eds.), *Handbook of Research on Multicultural Education* (pp. 548–569). New York: Macmillan.

Kuper, A. (1999). *Culture: The Anthropologists' Account.* Cambridge, MA: Harvard University Press.

Lasch, C. (1978). *The Culture of Narcissism.* New York: Norton.

Lisitzky, G. (1956). *Four Ways of Being Human: An Introduction to Anthropology.* New York: Viking Press.

Maher, F. A. (1987). Inquiry Teaching and Feminist Pedagogy. *Social Education, 51*(3), 186–192.

Maher, F. A. and Tetreault, M. K. (1994). *The Feminist Classroom.* New York: Basic Books.

Mannheim, K. (1936). *Ideology and Utopia: An Introduction to the Sociology of Knowledge.* New York: Harcourt Brace.

Mercer, J. R. (1973). *Labeling the Mentally Retarded: Clinical and Social System Perspectives on Mental Retardation.* Berkeley: University of California Press.

Moodley, K. A. (1995). Multicultural Education in Canada: Historical Development and Current Status. In J. A. Banks and C. A. M. Banks (Eds.), *Handbook of Research on Multicultural Education* (pp. 801–820). New York: Macmillan.

Myrdal, G. with the assistance of Sterner, R. and Rose, A. (1962). *An American Dilemma: The Negro Problem and Modern Democracy* (anniv. ed.). New York: Harper and Row.

Nash, G. B. (1999). *Forbidden Love: The Secret History of Mixed-Race America.* New York: Henry Holt.

Nieto, S. (1999). *The Light in Their Eyes: Creating Multicultural Learning Communities.* New York: Teachers College Press.

Perney, V. H. (1976). Effects of Race and Sex on Field Dependence–Independence in Children. *Perceptual and Motor Skills, 42,* 975–980.

Ramírez, M. and Castañeda, A. (1974). *Cultural Democracy, Bicognitive Development and Education.* New York: Academic Press.

Reischauer, E. O. (1981). *The Japanese.* Cambridge, MA: Harvard University Press.

Rose, S. J. (1992). *Social Stratification in the United States.* New York: The New Press.

Rothbart, M. and John, O. P. (1993). Intergroup Relations and Stereotype Change: A Social-Cognitive Analysis and Some Longitudinal Findings. In P. M. Sniderman, P. E. Telock, and E. G. Carmines (Eds.), *Prejudice, Politics, and the American Dilemma* (pp. 32–59). Stanford: Stanford University Press.

Sadker, M. P. and Sadker, D. M. (1994). *Failing at Fairness: How America's Schools Cheat Girls.* New York: Charles Scribner's Sons.

Sapon-Shevin, M. (1994). *Playing Favorites: Gifted Education and the Disruption of Community.* Albany: State University of New York Press.

Schlesinger, A. M., Jr. (1986). *The Cycles of American History.* Boston: Houghton Mifflin.

Schmitz, B., Butler, J., Rosenfelt, D., and Guy-Sheftal, B. (1995). Women's Studies and Curriculum Transformation. In J. A. Banks and C. A. M. Banks (Eds.), *Handbook of Research on Multicultural Education* (pp. 708–728). New York: Macmillan.

Shade, B. J., Kelly, C., and Oberg, M. (1997). *Creating Culturally Responsive Classrooms.* Washington, DC: American Psychological Association.

Shaver, J. P. and Curtis, C. K. (1981). *Handicapism and Equal Opportunity: Teaching about the Disabled in Social Studies.* Reston, VA: The Foundation for Exceptional Children.

Slavin, R. E. (1995). Cooperative Learning and Intergroup Relations. In J. A. Banks and C. A. M. Banks (Eds.), *Handbook of Research on Multicultural Education* (pp. 628–634). New York: Macmillan.

Smith, E. R. and Mackie, D. M. (1995). *Social Psychology.* New York: Worth Publishers, Inc.

Steinem, G. (1995). *Outrageous Acts and Everyday Rebellions.* New York: Holt.

Stephan, W. G. (1999). *Reducing Prejudice and Stereotyping in Schools.* New York: Teachers College Press.

Stewart, E. C. and Bennett, M. J. (1991). *American Cultural Patterns: A Cross-Cultural Perspective.* Yarmouth, ME: Intercultural Press.

Taylor, J. M., Gilligan, C., and Sullivan, A. M. (1995). *Between Voice and Silence: Women and Girls, Race and Relationships.* Cambridge, MA: Harvard University Press.

Theodorson, G. A. and Theodorson, A. G. (1969). *A Modern Dictionary of Sociology.* New York: Barnes and Noble.

Trecker, J. L. (1973). Teaching the Role of Women in American History. In J. A. Banks (Ed.), *Teaching Ethnic Studies: Concepts and Strategies* (pp. 279–297). Washington, DC: National Council for the Social Studies. (NCSS 43rd Yearbook)

Warner, W. L. with Meeker, M. and Eells, K. (1960). *Social Class in America* (reissued ed.). New York: Harper Torchbooks.

Weatherford, J. (1988). *Indian Givers: How the Indians of the Americas Transformed the World.* New York: Fawcett Columbine.

Willis, P. (1977). *Learning to Labor.* New York: Columbia University Press.

CHAPTER 2

Culture in Society and in Educational Practices

Frederick Erickson

A group of first graders and their teacher are in the midst of a reading lesson in a classroom in Berkeley, California. The children read aloud in chorus from their reading book:

1 T: All right, class, read that and remember your endings.

2 CC: What did Little Duck see? (final t of "what" deleted)

3 T: What. (emphasizing final t)

4 CC: What (final t deleted as in turn 2)

5 T: I still don't hear this sad little "t."

6 CC: What did—what did—what—(final t's deleted)

7 T: What.

8 T&CC: What did Little Duck see? (final t spoken)

9 T: OK, very good

(From Piestrup, 1973, pp. 96–97)

What is cultural in this picture? How are those aspects of culture, and other aspects as well, related to issues of multicultural education? This chapter tries to answer these questions by considering various ways in which culture has been thought of and how those varying definitions of culture have relevance for education in general and for multicultural education in particular. The chapter first surveys a number of issues broadly in an overview. Later in the chapter, as the issues are revisited more closely, pertinent citations are included.

CULTURE: AN OVERVIEW

In a sense, everything in education relates to culture—to its acquisition, its transmission, and its invention. Culture is in us and all around us, just as is the air we breathe. It is personal, familial, communal, institutional, societal, and global in its scope and distribution.

Yet culture as a notion is often difficult to grasp. As we learn and use culture in daily life, it becomes habitual. Our habits become for the most part invisible to us. Thus, culture shifts in and outside our reflective awareness. We do not think much about the structure and characteristics of culture as we use it, just as we do not think reflectively about any familiar tool in the midst of its use. If we hammer things a lot, we do not think about the precise weight or chemical composition of the steel of the hammer, especially as we are actually hammering; and when we speak to someone we know well we are unlikely to think reflectively about the sound system, grammar, vocabulary, and rhetorical conventions of our language, especially as we are doing things in the midst of our speaking.

Just as hammers and languages are tools by which we get things done, so is culture; indeed, culture can be thought of as the primary human toolkit. Culture is a product of human creativity in action; once we have it, culture enables us to extend our activity still further. In the sense that culture is entirely the product of human activity, an artifact, it is not like the air we breathe. By analogy to computers, which are information tools, culture can be considered as the software—the coding systems for doing meaning and executing sequences of work—by which our human physiological and cognitive hardware is able to operate so that we can make sense and take action with others in daily life. Culture structures the "default" conditions of the everyday practices of being human.

Another way to think of culture is as a sedimentation of the historical experience of persons and of social groupings of various kinds, such as nuclear family and kin, gender, ethnicity, race, and social class, all with differing access to power in society. We have become increasingly aware that the invention and sharing of culture (in other words, its production and reproduction) happen through processes that are profoundly political in nature, having to do with access to and distribution of social power. In these processes of cultural production and reproduction, the intimate politics of immediate social relations face-to-face are combined with a more public politics in the social forces and processes of economy and society writ large. How does the sedimentation of historical experience as culture take place? What are the micro- and macropolitical circumstances in which culture is learned and invented? How does culture get distributed, similarly and differently within and across human groups and within and between human generations?

These are questions not only for social scientists or for social philosophers to address; they also are questions that raise issues that are essential for educators to consider. Culture, as it is more and less visible and invisible to its users, is profoundly involved in the processes and contents of education. Culture shapes and is shaped by the learning and teaching that happen during the practical conduct of daily life within all the educational settings we encounter as learning environments throughout the human life span, in families, in school classrooms, in community settings, and in the workplace. There is some evidence that we begin to learn culture in the womb, and we continue to learn new culture until we die. Yet people learn differing sets and subsets of culture, and they can unlearn culture—shedding it as well as adopting it. At the individual and at the group level, some aspects of culture undergo change and other aspects stay the same, within a single human life and across generations.

Educators address these issues every time they teach and every time they design curriculum. They may be addressed by educators explicitly and within conscious awareness, or they may be addressed implicitly and outside conscious awareness. But at every moment in the conduct of educational practice, cultural issues and choices are at stake. This chapter makes some of those issues and choices more explicit.

Two final orienting assumptions are implicit in the previous discussion. First, everybody is cultural, and although there is no evidence base on which to decide that any particular cultural ways are intrinsically more valuable than others—more inherently superior or inferior—it is a plain political fact that not all cultural practices are equal in power and prestige in the United States or in any other country. Every person and social group possesses and uses culture as a tool for the conduct of human activity. This means that culture is not the possession or characteristic of an exotic other, but of all of us, the dominant and the dominated alike. In other words, and to put it more bluntly, within U.S. society White people are just as cultural as are people of color (indeed the terms *White* and *people of color* represent cultural categories that are socially constructed). Moreover, White Anglo-Saxon Protestants (WASPs) are just as cultural as are Jews or Catholics; men are just as cultural as women; adults are just as cultural as teenagers; Northerners are just as cultural as Southerners; English speakers are just as cultural as the speakers of other languages; and native-born Americans are just as cultural as immigrants or citizens who reside in other countries. This is to say, Americans of African or European or Asian descent are just as cultural as people who live in Africa, Europe, or Asia. To reiterate, everybody in the world is cultural, even though not all culture is equal in power and prestige.

The second orienting assumption is that everybody is multicultural. Every person and every human group possesses both culture and cultural diversity. For example, Americans of Mexican descent are not culturally identical to Puerto Ricans who live on the mainland, but not all Mexican Americans or Puerto Ricans (or White Episcopalians, for that matter) are culturally identical even if they live in the same neighborhood and attend the same school or church. Members of the same family also are culturally diverse. In fact, we often encounter cultural difference as individual difference, as well as encountering culture in its more institutionalized manifestations, such as school literacy, the legal system, or the broadcast media. An important way we meet culture is in the particular people with whom we interact daily.

It is not possible for individuals to grow up in a complex modern society without acquiring differing subsets of culture—differing software packages that are tools that can be used in differing kinds of human activity; tools that in part enable and frame the activities in which they are used. From the nuclear family, through early and later schooling, through peer networks, and through life at work, we encounter, learn, and to some extent help create differing microcultures and subcultures. Just as everyone learns differing variants and styles of the various languages we speak so that everybody is multilingual (even those of us who only speak English), so everybody is multicultural. No matter how culturally isolated a person's life may appear, in large-scale modern societies (and even in small-scale traditional societies) each member carries a considerable amount of that society's cultural diversity inside. This insight is in an article by Goodenough (1976)—"Multiculturalism as the Normal Human Experience."

If it is true that every person and human group is both cultural and multicultural, then a multicultural perspective on the aims and conduct of education is of primary importance. That assumption guides this chapter. First it considers a variety of definitions of culture. Then it discusses issues of how culture is organized and distributed in society that have special relevance for education. The discussion comments on teaching and learning in multicultural classrooms, in the light of the conceptions of culture previously discussed. The chapter concludes with a discussion of the diversity of culture not only within society but also within the person and the implications of that diversity for multicultural education.

ALTERNATIVE DEFINITIONS AND CONCEPTIONS OF CULTURE

Attempts at formal definitions of culture have not been fruitful; even the experts have not been able to agree on what culture *really* is. Yet some ways of thinking about culture seem increasingly to be inadequate and misleading and others are more useful. Presented here is a range of definitions, emphasizing the differing conceptions of culture that underly the various definitions.

Culture as Cultivation

All conceptions of culture imply a distinction between the cultural and the natural. Cultivation transforms the natural, in a social sense, just as agriculture transforms nature in a biological and chemical sense. Cultivating the soil makes for fewer weeds than in nature (indeed, the distinction between what is considered weed and what is considered plant is a cultural one). Cultivation requires effort and method—it evokes images of straight furrows, of working, and of planning for the future harvest.

The agricultural metaphor for culture bears a family resemblance to an artistic one. In the fine arts, cultivation also involves disciplining the natural—the fingers learn to find keys on the piano; the painter's eye and hand and the ballerina's feet are schooled by artistic convention. Thus, in ordinary use, culture has come to mean high culture—what we find in the museum, the symphony hall, the theater, the library. In those institutions we find cultural products whose value is defined by elite tastes, which are defined and framed reflexively by those cultural products.

In contrast to prestigious high culture there is also low culture—popular culture—which is another sense in which the term *culture* is used. Some artifacts of U.S. popular culture, such as blue jeans and popular music, have been adopted throughout the world. In the realm of popular culture, fashions change across time and across various social groups and social sectors, just as they do in the realm of high culture. We have diverse artifacts and practices of popular culture with differential appeal, such as classic rock 'n roll, rap, country, and Cajun music. We have Western cowboy boots, motorcycle boots, hiking boots, upland game hunting boots, and Nike basketball sneakers, each with a different resonance among subgroups within U.S. society, and each potentially able to serve as badges of personal and group identity.

In the social sciences, the term *culture* refers to phenomena that are less mystifying than those of so-called high culture and less sensational than those of popular culture. In the social scientific sense, culture is seen as something everyone has and makes use of routinely, regardless of social position. It refers to the patterns for sense-making that are part of the organization of the conduct of everyday life.

This egalitarian notion of culture arose among Western Europeans in the Enlightenment (Vico, 1744/1968), and it developed further in the early Romantic period, foreshadowed by Rousseau and continued by the brothers Grimm and by von Humboldt. The Grimms collected folktales from German peasants whose language and folk knowledge had been made fun of by aristocrats in earlier times. This shift toward greater respect for the lifeways of ordinary people happened between the mideighteenth and the early nineteenth centuries.

Culture as Tradition

By the early nineteenth century, culture was beginning to be seen as tradition—that which is handed down across generations. Within anthropology during the nineteenth century, culture was seen as a sum total of social inheritance. In 1871, anthropologist Sir Edward Burnett Tylor presented this broad definition: "Culture or Civilization . . . is that complex whole which includes knowledge, belief, art, morals, law, custom, and any other capabilities and habits acquired by man as a member of society" (Tylor, 1871/1970, p. 1).

As genetic theory was developing, culture came to be seen as a kind of gene pool existing at the level of social symbolism and meaning rather than biology. By 1917, a U.S. anthropologist called culture the "superorganic," meaning that it had an ideational rather than material existence (Kroeber, 1917). Following Tylor and others, Kroeber assumed that culture was a whole system consisting of interrelated parts, not literally a living organism but metaphorically similar to one.

Yet the notion of culture remained fuzzy among social scientists. Near the end of his career, Kroeber collaborated with Kluckhohn in a review of the uses of the term *culture*. Their review of anthropology and sociology publications turned up hundreds of citations and differing shadings of meaning for the word (Kroeber & Kluckhohn, 1952). Since then, no scholar has tried to claim a single, authoritative meaning of the term.

Culture as Information Bits

Currently, one conception of culture considers it by analogy to information bits in a computer as well as to genetic information in a breeding population. According to this view, culture can be thought of as consisting of many small chunks of knowledge that are stored as a large pool of information within a bounded social group (see Goodenough, 1981). No single member of the group has learned all knowledge that is possessed within the group as a whole. The amounts and kinds of information known are seen as varying widely across individuals and subgroups within the total population.

This variation can be understood by analogy to language. What we call a *language* has a sound system (pronunciation), a syntax (grammar), and a lexicon (vocabulary). Those who understand the literal meaning of a sound system, a syntax, and a lexicon are termed members of the same *language community*. Subsets of the language are called dialects—they are spoken by members of subgroups within the overall language community. Dialects may vary in some aspects of pronunciation of vowels or consonants, or in some aspects of grammar, or in vocabulary, but any dialect is still intelligible overall to speakers of other dialects within the language. Each person within a language community speaks a unique form of that language, called an *idiolect* (i.e., no one individual actually speaks "English"; all individuals pronounce the language sounds in slightly differing ways and use grammar and vocabulary in individually distinct ways, in a kind of personal dialect). By this analogy, an overall general culture = language, while dialect = subculture, and idiolect = microculture, which can be thought of as a personal or immediately local variation on a subculture or general culture.

Culture as Symbol System

Another conception considers culture as a more limited set of large chunks of knowledge—conceptual structures that frame or constitute what is taken as "reality" by members of a social group (Geertz, 1973). These central organizing constructs—core symbols—are seen as being shared widely throughout the group. The routine ways of acting and making sense that are used by members of the group tend to repeat the major framing patterns again and again, just as within a musical composition many variations can be written on a few underlying thematic elements. This conception of culture emphasizes relatively tight organization of patterns, coherence in the overall meaning system, and identical (or at least closely shared) understanding of symbols and shared sentiments regarding those symbols among the members of the social group.

Culture as Social Process

A third conception treats social structure and culture as intertwined (Bourdieu, 1977; Bourdieu & Passeron, 1977; Williams, 1983). Some work within this stream of approaches emphasizes the diversity of cultural knowledge within a given social unit (Barth, 1969; 1989). Cultural difference is seen as tracing lines of status, power, and political interest within and across the subgroups and institutions found in the total social unit. This variation in cultural difference within a social unit can be seen as analogous to the ways in which differences in air pressure or temperature are displayed on a weather map. There is variation in temperature in the earth's atmosphere, and it is nonrandomly distributed. There is variation in culture within a human society or social unit, and it, too, is nonrandomly distributed, closely related to the differential allocation of power and prestige within the society.

One school of thought within this third mode sees culture not so much as a cognitive template for the routine conduct of everyday life, but as residing in the conduct of everyday life itself (Bourdieu, 1977; Ortner, 1984). This conduct is seen as practice, as routine activity that is habitual and goal-directed (Connell, 1982). Practices are daily and customary, but they also tend toward a projected outcome, although the aims in such "projects" may not be entirely conscious ones. Thus, the person engaged in the practical conduct of everyday life can be seen as not simply following cultural "rules" (as in the first conception of culture) or as responding to cultural symbols always in the same ways (as is implied in the second conception of culture), but as being strategic—an active agent who uses culture as tools adaptively, employing novel means when necessary to achieve desired ends.

The first and second conceptions of culture can be criticized as presuming that human actors are the passive recipients of shaping by their social circumstances and that once having acquired culture passively (through learning) they are on "automatic pilot," capable only of following general cultural rules or scripts and incapable of acting adaptively in unique local circumstances. These views consider the cultural actor as a robot or as a "social dope" (Garfinkel & Sacks, 1970); they leave no room for human agency. Practice theory, on the other hand, takes realistic account of how habitual and conservative our daily conduct is, but it leaves room for the assumption that individuals can make sense adaptively within their practices, rather than simply following cultural rules.

The school of thought that sees culture as inherently related to issues of social structure and power also tends to see culture as arising through social conflict, with the possibility of differing interest groups becoming progressively more culturally different across time even though the groups may be in continual contact. From this perspective the emphasis is not on culture as a general integrated system but on the content of cultural knowledge and practice within the specific life situations of the persons and groups by whom such knowledge is held and such practices are undertaken. Two key questions in this perspective are: "Given certain kinds of daily experience, what kinds of sense do people make of it?" and, "How does this sense-making influence their customary actions?" This position assumes that new culture—whether conceived as small information bits or as larger structures of concept and activity—is being transformed continually within the contradictions experienced in daily life. These new cultural forms are accepted, learned, and remembered, or rejected, ignored, and forgotten, depending on where one sits in the social order, and depending on the particular circumstances in the situation in which the new culture is invented.

Overall, the third conception of culture emphasizes three related points: (1) the systematic variation of culture in relation to the allocation of power in society; (2) social conflict as a fundamental process by which cultural variation is organized, through which traditional culture is being simultaneously forced on people and contested, and through which new culture is continually being invented; and (3) human agency in the use of cultural tools, both tools inherited through tradition and tools invented through their use in practice within changing circumstances (Giddens, 1984).

Culture as Motive and Emotion

Another contemporary approach considers both the cognitive and the emotional/motivational force of culture (Lutz, 1990). We learn customs, but why do we become emotionally attached to them? How do we come to desire and work for ends and to use means for reaching those ends that are culturally enjoined? We do not act on culturally defined goals simply because we are forced to do so, although in situations of unequal power subordinates may fake it— they may feign more allegiance to cultural norms such as politeness or diligence than they in fact are feeling. Still, culturally defined love objects are genuinely yearned for, culturally defined careers do become the objects of genuine aspiration and striving, and customs that are culturally defined as repulsive, such as eating sea slugs, evoke strong emotional reactions of disgust in some social groups, even though those same food practices are seen as normal or even highly desirable in other social groups.

Contemporary neuroscience shows that when we engage in routine activities not only are the neural networks activated that involve prior cognitive learning (i.e., neural connections to the cerebral cortex), but also that neural connections to our emotional states at the time of initial learning are also activated (i.e., neural connections to the limbic system). Thus, our repetition of certain customary activities evokes and reinforces emotional feelings as well as thoughts and skills (D'Andrade & Strauss, 1992). Through continued participation in daily life we thus acquire cultural models for its conduct that involve feeling in our knowing. In an important sense that went unrecognized in earlier cognitive psychology, all of our cognitions are "hot cognitions" and learning is a profoundly emotional activity as well as a cognitive one.

Now, more than forty years since Kroeber and Kluckhohn's review of social scientists' use of the term *culture*, formal definitions, while overlapping, still do not agree exactly (Kuper, 1999). Yet culture is generally seen as a product of human activity that is used as a tool. It is seen as being learned and transmitted from our elders and also as invented within current situations. How much and in what ways culture is shared within and between identifiable human groups are issues on which there is much debate currently. Power and politics seem to be involved in the processes by which culture is learned, shared, and changed. Culture, in other words, takes shape in the weight of human history. Some aspects of culture are explicit, and others are implicit, learned, and shared outside conscious awareness. Our moods and desires as well as our thoughts are culturally constructed.

Culture can be thought of as a construction—it constructs us and we construct it. That is, all thoughts, feelings, and human activity are not simply natural, but are the result of historical and personal experiences that become sedimented as culture in habit. Culture varies, somehow, from one person or group to another. Since our subjective world—what we see, know, and want—is culturally constructed, and since culture varies, persons really do not inhabit the same subjective worlds even though they may seem to do so. Even though some of us show up in what seems to be the same event, how we experience it is never quite the same across the various individuals who have joined together in interaction. Thus, no single or determinative human world is a fixed point of reference. Individually and collectively, we make cultural worlds and they are multiple. This point has profound implications for educators, as is discussed in the following sections.

As human beings not only do we live in webs of meaning, caring, and desire that we ourselves create and that create us, but those webs also hang in social gravity (Geertz, 1973, p. 5). Within the webs all our activity is vested in the weight of history; that is, in a social world of inequality all movement is up or down. Earlier conceptions of culture described it and human actions guided or framed by it as existing in a universe without gravity. Movement was thus unconstrained; it had no effort, no force. There was no domination or subordination, no resistance or compliance in such a cultural world. In more recent conceptions of culture, we are coming to see that living in a gravity-ridden social and cultural universe we always have weight. We are culturally constructed and constructing beings, and in that construction we are never standing still.

CULTURAL ISSUES IN EDUCATION AND SOCIETY

The previous discussion provides a framework for the four main issues that have special relevance for educators: (1) the notion of culture as invisible as well as visible; (2) the politics of cultural difference in school and society; (3) the inherent diversity of cultures and subcultures within human social groups; and (4) the diversity of cultures within the individual—a perspective on the self as multiculturally constructed.

Invisible Culture

The distinction between visible and invisible culture has also been called explicit/implicit or overt/covert (Hall, 1959; 1976; Philips, 1983). Much of culture is not only held outside conscious awareness but is also learned and taught outside awareness—hence, neither the cultural insiders nor the newcomers are aware that certain aspects of their culture exist. In multicultural education and in discussions of cultural diversity more generally the focus has been on visible, explicit aspects of culture, such as language, dress, food habits, religion, and aesthetic conventions. While important, these visible aspects of culture, which are taught deliberately and learned (at least to some extent) consciously, are only the tip of the iceberg of culture.

Implicit and invisible aspects of culture are also important. How long in clock time one can be late before being impolite, how one conceives or experiences emotional or physical pain, how one displays such pain behaviorally, what topics should be avoided at the beginning of a conversation, how one shows interest or attention through listening behavior, how loud is too loud or not loud enough in speaking, how one shows that one would like the speaker to move on to the next point—these are all aspects of culture that we learn and use without realizing it. When we meet other people whose invisible cultural assumptions and patterns for action differ from those we have learned and expect implicitly, we usually do not recognize what they are doing as cultural in origin. Rather, we see them as rude or uncooperative. We may apply clinical labels to the other people—passive aggressive, low self-esteem.

Differences in invisible culture can be troublesome in circumstances of intergroup conflict. The difficulty lies in our inability to recognize others' differences in ways of acting as cultural rather than personal. We tend to naturalize other people's behavior and blame them—attributing intentions, judging competence—without realizing that we are experiencing culture rather than nature.

Modern society exacerbates the difficulties that can result from differences in invisible culture. Formal organizations and institutions, such as hospitals, workplaces, the legal system, and schools, become collection sites for invisible cultural difference. If the differences were more visible, we might see less misattribution, in the absence of intergroup conflict. For example, if we were to meet a woman in a hospital emergency room who was wearing exotic dress, speaking a language other than English, and carrying food that looked and smelled strange, we would not assume that we understood her thoughts and feelings or that she necessarily understood ours. Yet when such a person is dressed similarly to us, speaks English, and does not differ from us in other obvious ways, we may fail to recognize the invisible cultural orientations that differ between us, and a cycle of mutual misattribution can start.

Anthropologists with linguistic and cognitive orientations have identified aspects of invisible culture (Gumperz, 1982; Hymes, 1974). They make a helpful distinction between language community and speech community or network. People in the same language community share knowledge of the sound system, grammar, and vocabulary of a language. But within the same language community there are diverse speech communities or networks—sets of persons who share assumptions about the purposes of speaking, modes of politeness, topics of interest, ways of responding to others. Those cultural assumptions concerning ways of speaking differ considerably, even though at a general level all are uttering the same language. That is, language community differences are visible, but speech community differences are often invisible.

Yet cultural difference, visible and invisible, does not always lead to trouble between people. These differences become more troublesome in some circumstances than in others. That leads to a consideration of the circumstances of intercultural contact.

The Politics of Cultural Difference: Boundaries and Borders

The introductory discussion states that cultural difference demarcates lines of political difference, and often of domination. By analogy to a weather map, boundaries of cultural difference can be seen as isobars of power, rank, and prestige in society. One can trace boundaries of networks of members who share cultural knowledge of various sorts, of language, social ideology and values, religious beliefs, technical knowledge, preferences in aesthetic tastes—in recreation and sport, in personal dress and popular music tastes, and in cultivated tastes in the fine arts, cuisine, and literature. Because these preferences have differing prestige value, they have been called cultural capital (Bourdieu, 1977; Bourdieu & Passeron, 1977). Such preferences also become symbols, or badges of group identity—markers of ethnicity, religion, gender, or social class.

The presence of cultural difference in society does not necessarily lead to conflict, however, nor need it lead to difficulty in education. The presence of conflict depends on whether cultural difference is being treated as a *boundary* or as a *border* (Barth, 1969; Giroux, 1991; McDermott & Gospodinoff, 1979/1981). *A cultural boundary refers to the presence of some kind of cultural difference.* As noted earlier, cultural boundaries are characteristic of all human societies, traditional as well as modern. *A border is a social construct that is political in origin.* Across a border power is exercised, as in the political border between two nations.

When a cultural boundary is treated as a cultural border, differences in rights and obligations are powerfully attached to the presence or absence of certain kinds of cultural knowledge. Consider, for example, the political/cultural border between the United States and Mexico. On either side of the border are people who speak English and people who speak Spanish; that is, the boundaries of language community cross over the lines demarcating national citizenship. Yet on either side of the border, fluency in Spanish—which is an aspect of cultural knowledge— is differentially rewarded or punished. On the Mexican side of the border, fluency in Spanish is an advantage legally, educationally, and in the conduct of much daily life, while on the United States side, the same cultural knowledge is disadvantaged; indeed in parts of South Texas, speaking Spanish is still stigmatized.

When one arrives at a cultural border, one's cultural knowledge may be held up for scrutiny— stopped and frisked. An ancient example comes from the Book of Judges. At approximately 800 B.C., the Hebrews were not yet fully unified politically under a monarch and they had not yet completely occupied the territory of Canaan. They were a loose federation of kinship groups or clans that periodically came together in an unstable and tense alliance against common enemies. A dispute broke out between soldiers of two of the clans, the men of Ephraim and the men of Gilead. After defeat in a battle with the Ammonites, the common enemy, the men of Ephraim were trying to escape across fords in the Jordan River. The fords were guarded on the Hebrew-occupied side of the river by Gileadites. The men of Gilead checked the clan identity of the re-treating soldiers by testing their cultural knowledge: "When any of the fugitives of Ephraim said, 'Let me go over,' the men of Gilead said to him, 'Are you an Ephraimite?' When he said, 'No,' they said to him, 'Then say Shibboleth.' He said 'Sibboleth,' for he could not pronounce it correctly. Then they seized him and slew him at the fords of the Jordan" (Judges 12: 5b-6a, RSV). The two clans of Hebrews differed in their pronunciation of the initial sibilant in the word *Shibboleth*. The Gileadites used the /sh/ phoneme for that consonant, while the Ephraimites used the /s/ phoneme. The Gileadite soldiers were aware of this cultural difference and made use of it to construct a sociolinguistic test at a geographic and political border, which, because of the test imposed, became a cultural border as well.

In modern societies the same thing can happen when one enters the emergency room of a hospital and speaks to an admitting clerk, or when one speaks to the maitre d' at a restaurant. It also can happen in school classrooms. Yet cultural boundaries (the objective presence of cultural difference) need not necessarily be treated as cultural borders. This is a matter of socially constructed framing.

The framing of cultural difference as boundary or as border can change over time. Sometimes that change is very rapid, as in the following example (Fanon, 1963). In Algeria shortly before France gave up colonial rule, the pronunciation of the announcers on the state radio was made a cultural border issue by the independence movement. Complaints were voiced that Radio Algiers was not employing native Algerians. This practice was seen as another symbol of colonial oppression by France. Radio Algiers sent out a statement that its announcers were in fact Algerians. The independence movement then asked why the radio announcers spoke cosmopolitan French rather than the Algerian dialect. The complaints about the announcers became increasingly strident in the independence-oriented press, right up to Independence Day. After that day the announcers on Radio Algiers continued to speak cosmopolitan French but public complaint ended instantly. The reason for the complaint was gone, and so a small feature of cultural difference, which had been framed for a time as a cultural border, was reframed as a cultural boundary.

These two examples suggest that cultural difference, rather than being considered a cause of conflict in society (and in education), is more appropriately seen as a resource for conflict. If people have a reason to look for trouble, cultural difference—especially one that becomes a badge of social identity—can be used to start a fight. But the causes of the fight go beyond the cultural difference itself.

Cultural Differentiation as a Political Process

What happens over time when certain aspects of cultural difference get treated as border issues? Examples from language suggest that the differences become more extreme on either side. This suggests that political conflict, explicit and implicit, is a major engine of culture change. Such conflict generates cultural resistance. Labov (1963) found that on Martha's Vineyard, a small island off the coast of Massachusetts, certain sound features in the islanders' dialect became increasingly divergent from the more standard English spoken by summer tourists as the number of tourists staying on the island in the summer increased over time, although the islanders were not aware that this was happening. First-hand contacts with a standard model of American English had been increasing for the islanders, but across a generation their speech was becoming more different from that of the mainlanders.

A similar process of divergence was reported as taking place across the time span of half-hour interviews in experimental situations (Giles & Powesland, 1975). Speakers of differing British regional dialects were paired for two-person discussions. In some discussions, mild discomfort and conflict was experimentally introduced, while in other discussions conflict was not introduced. In the discussions with conflict and discomfort, by the end of a half-hour each person was speaking a broader form of his or her regional dialect than before the discussion began. In other words, if a Yorkshireman were talking to a person from Dorsetshire, he would become more distinctly Yorkshire in his pronunciation and the Dorset man would become more Dorsetshire in his pronunciation as the conversation between the two progressed. Conversely, when conflict was not introduced and the two parties spoke comfortably, pronunciation features that differed between their two dialects became less distinct—they were converging in speech style rather than diverging.

This example suggests that cultural divergence is a result rather than a cause of social conflict. Bateson et al. (1972) called the tendency of subsystems to evolve in increasingly differentiated ways complementary *schismogenesis*, which seems to be the process by which cultural resistance over time results in culture change. It should be emphasized, however, that such change can occur entirely outside the conscious awareness of those involved in it as well as in situations of more explicit, conscious awareness in which people are deliberate regarding the change they are struggling to produce.

The classic view of culture in social science was as a total system, with integrated parts, the operation of which tended toward maintaining a steady state. As we have seen, culture now seems to be more labile than that—variable in the moment. This raises the question of how we conceive of culture change—as loss, as gain, as a mixture of both, or less evaluatively as change. We must also consider how culture is shared within human groups. We usually think of ethnic and racial groups (and perhaps of gender categories as well) as necessarily identifying cultural boundaries. Such groups, we may assume, are defined by shared culture among their members. Barth (1969) contends, however, that culture sharing is not the crucial defining attribute of ethnic group membership. Rather, the ethnic or racial group is more appropriately considered as an economic and political interest group. Features of culture may be considered as identity badges, indicating group membership. But culture sharing is not essential for this, according to Barth. There may be much cultural diversity within the same named social category. He used as an example the Pathans, who live as a numerical minority on one side of the border between Pakistan and Afghanistan and as a majority on the other side. Some Pathans are herders—more so on the Afghan side of the border. Other Pathans are farmers—more on the Pakistani side. Yet both herders and farmers will identify as Pathan and are so regarded by ethnic others on either side of the border.

Culture Change as Culture Loss—or Not

When we think of ethnic/racial groups and cultural groups as having the same boundaries— the traditional view—we sometimes think of culture change as culture loss. Members of an ethnic group can blame themselves for losing a language, a religion, a household practice. Native Americans, for example, have mourned the passing of old culture and have gone beyond mourning to self-blame, considering themselves less Indian than their forebears. Yet if a Koyukon Athabaskan now uses a snowmobile rather than a dog team and sled, does that mean he or she is any less Koyukon than before? Not necessarily, if we follow Barth's analysis. What is essential for the maintenance of ethnic groups and ethnic identity are not the specifics of culture traits practiced by the members; rather, being ethnic counts economically and politically in the larger society. Even the specific ways in which it counts to be ethnic can change; yet if there continue to be economic and political consequences of being identified as ethnic, especially if that is to the advantage of the members, then the ethnic group continues.

The classic view makes culture the defining attribute of ethnic identity. It becomes easy then to see culture change as culture loss. This can be thought of as the leaky bucket perspective on culture change: as if culture were held in a human group as water is contained in a bucket. Change then becomes the holes in the bucket. As one carries such a bucket over time and space, the water gradually drains out. Alternatively, we can conceive of the bucket of culture as always full. Air may replace the water, but the bucket is never empty. The contemporary

Koyukon society, with its snowmobile practices, can be considered just as full culturally as the Koyukon society in the days of sled and dog team. What is in the bucket is different now, but the bucket is still not empty. During the summer people in an Odawa community in Northern Ontario wear tee shirts as they fish from aluminum boats powered by outboard motors. They no longer wear buckskin and use birchbark canoes. Yet they continue to fish, and they do so with differing fishing rights from those of White Canadians. Moreover, they still consider themselves Odawa, as distinct from White Canadians in neighboring villages who also fish from aluminum boats while wearing tee shirts.

Culture and Collective Identity Formation

To call something cultural has in itself political implications. Because so many aspects of culture are transparent to its users in their use, ordinarily we do not think about or notice them. Yet in complex and diverse modern societies, as ethnic, racial, religious and gender identifications become self-aware among identification group members, they begin to notice their customary practices and to identify them as cultural. As with ethnic identification, cultural identification is always relational and comparative—with reference to an other. In the early nineteenth century, for example, German *Kultur* began to be invoked by German intellectuals in contrast and opposition to the French and Italians, whose tastes in literature and music, architecture, and clothing had previously set the standard of what was desirable in upper-class polite society. Without the presence of French and Italian models to compete with, Germans may not have become so aware of their own Germanness. This awareness progressed beyond rediscovery to invention, with German intellectuals such as Wagner helping to create a Germanic heritage with the support of the ruling interests in German society. With this rise in in-group awareness and solidarity came a heightened awareness of boundaries with non-Teutonic others. To the extent that this perception of out-groups was invidious, the boundaries became borders.

We see a similar phenomenon today with the rise of religious nationalism and of ethnic and racial nationalism. With in-group identification there is always the possibility for treating boundaries as borders. Especially when heightening of cultural awareness and identification is used as a political strategy for changing power relations in society, or for legitimating territorial or colonial expansion, in-group solidarity and identification can become demonic. As Said notes (1978) in commenting on the colonial relationship between Europe and a perceived Orient that was a cultural creation of Europeans themselves, when more powerful nations or interest groups identify some Other as exotic and different there can be a tendency for the more powerful to project their own flaws, contradictions, and hostilities on the constructed Other. Such projections are reciprocated by those who have been "Othered" in a process of mutual border framing. Through this process of projective "Othering," negative cultural stereotypes result, making the fostering of intercultural and multicultural awareness a tricky business indeed.

Ethnic identification need not necessarily lead to Othering in the negative sense, however—the comparisons with those who differ from "Us" need not be invidious. Cultural differences can be framed as boundaries rather than as borders even though such framing takes effort to maintain. It should be noted, however, that an increase in the deliberateness and intensity of cultural awareness necessarily involves a comparative awareness. The construction of in-group identity is a relational process through which a definition of Other as well as of Self, of Them as well as of Us—and in the case of subordinated groups a specific identification of aspects of oppression—becomes more focal in conscious awareness.

TEACHING AND LEARNING MULTICULTURALLY

Emphasizing Invisible as Well as Visible Culture

Schools can support or hinder the development of healthy identity and of intergroup awareness. The discussion now turns to teaching and learning in classrooms (see Mehan et al., 1995). This chapter emphasizes the importance of culture and criticizes our tendencies to essentialize it. When we essentialize culture, assuming that all persons in a given social category are culturally similar and focusing on the unitary cultures of various Others without reflecting on our own cultures and their diversity, we open a Pandora's box of opportunity for negative attribution. Sometimes social scientific notions of culture, especially of culture as a unified system and of group membership as culturally defined, have provided a justification for intergroup stereotypes. When these stereotypes come with social scientific warrant, we call them neostereotypes.

Teaching about the cultural practices of other people without stereotyping or misinterpreting them and teaching about one's own cultural practices without invidiously characterizing the practices of other people should be the aims of multicultural education. In situations of intergroup conflict these aims can be ideals that are difficult to attain. Educators should face such difficulty realistically.

One problem in multicultural curriculum and pedagogy is the overemphasis on visible (explicit) culture at the expense of the invisible and implicit. Focusing mainly on explicit culture can be misleading. Even when we do this respectfully of the lifeways of others, focus on visible culture easily slides into too comfortable a stance for considering other people—a stance of cultural romance or cultural tourism.

Particular traits of visible culture, often treated in isolation, have become the basis for much of what we teach about cultural diversity in schools. Some educators speak critically of "piñata curriculum," "snowshoe curriculum," and "holidays and heroes" in characterizing this approach.

By treating cultural practices as sets of static facts, we trivialize them in superficiality and we make it seem as if culture were necessarily unchanging. What if Mexican Americans were to have a party and not break a piñata? Would they be any less Mexican? In Alaskan Athabascan villages, snowmobiles rather than sled dogs and snowshoes are the preferred mode of winter transportation. Are the villagers any less Indian? They are, only if we adopt an essentialist view of culture, with its accompanying "leaky bucket" image of culture change.

A way to teach about explicit culture without overgeneralizing about the lifeways of other people is to emphasize the variability of culture within social groups and the continual presence of cultural change as well as cultural continuity across time. Unfortunately, published multicultural materials that have an essentialist emphasis may not lend themselves well to this method. Yet in every classroom there is a resource for the study of within-group cultural diversity as well as between-group diversity. That resource is the everyday experience and cultural practices of the students and teachers themselves. (This is most easily done in a self-contained classroom, and so this discussion may seem most relevant for elementary school teaching, but many of the issues and approaches mentioned can be undertaken by high school and college teachers as well.)

Critical Autobiography as Curriculum and as Action Research

Critically reflective autobiography by students and oral history of their families—a form of community action research—can become important parts of a multicultural curriculum. Even in a classroom with a student population highly segregated by race or by social class, reflective investigation of their own lives and of family and local community histories by students will reveal diversity as well as similarity (hooks, 1993; Skilton Sylvester, 1994; Torres-Guzmán, 1992; Wiggington, 1986; Witherell & Noddings, 1991). Not all the Italian Americans in a classroom have had the same family experience of immigration. Not all the African American students whose forebears moved from the rural South to a large city have had the same experience of urbanization. As a result of differing life experiences there are differences in cultural funds of knowledge between families who on the surface appear to be demographically similar— differences in family microcultures (see Moll, 1990).

Some of these differences across families also reveal similarity—as in variations on a common theme of life experience, such as that of the experience of racism by African Americans. But not all the experiences, even of racism within a given racial group, are identical. Thus, diversity and similarity always accompany one another in the real stories of people in human groups. Those stories have involved struggles to change, to resist. Contemporary community issues, as students address them through local community study, also provide opportunities for students to take action to improve the circumstances of their lives and, in the process, come to see themselves and their families not simply as passive recipients of social and cultural influences, but as active agents who are making sense and making their lives.

Direct connections between the daily lives of students outside the classroom and the content of instruction in history, social studies, and literature can make the stated curriculum come alive. These connections also afford the teacher an opportunity to learn the cultural backgrounds and cultural diversity that he or she confronts with each set of students. As stated earlier, formal organizations in modern societies become collection sites for cultural diversity. This is true for every school classroom. Each new set of students represents a unique sampling from the universe of local cultural diversity present in the school area. Simply knowing that one has three Haitian students and four Cambodian students—or seventeen girls and eleven boys—in a certain classroom, for example, does not tell that teacher anything (necessarily) about the specific cultural backgrounds of those students and their families and their assumptions about ethnicity, race, or gender, given the cultural diversity that is possible within any social category. The teacher's tasks are to know not only about Haitians or Cambodians in general, or about girls and boys in general, but also about these students in particular. By making particular student culture and family history a deliberate object of study by all the students in the classroom, the teacher can learn much about what he or she needs to know in order to teach the particular students in ways that are sensitive and powerfully engaging, intellectually and emotionally.

As our standards for what students need to learn change from the lower-order mastery of facts and simple skills to higher-order reasoning and the construction of knowledge that is personally distinctive and meaningful (in other words, as we move from an essentialist understanding of curriculum, teaching, and learning to a more constructivist one), our conceptions of culture in muliticultural education also need to become more constructivist and less essentialist. Teaching about culture as socially constructed and continually changing is thus consistent with contemporary definitions of good pedagogy as well as being consistent with recent developments in culture theory and social theory.

Reframing Borders as Boundaries in the Classroom

This approach frames the cultural diversity to be found in the classroom group in terms of cultural boundaries rather than cultural borders. Even when cultural difference and group identity are highly politicized in the wider society, by approaching the culture of students forthrightly in the classroom they can be depoliticized to a remarkable extent (or perhaps we might think of it as being repoliticized in a positive rather than negative frame).

A problem comes with teaching second-culture skills and knowledge as morality rather than as pragmatic skills for survival and success. Delpit (1995) observes that for students of color in the United States the school's "second-culture" often appears alien and dominating. Culturally mainstream ways of speaking and writing represent a "language and culture of power" that minority students need to master for success in the wider society. But this culture of power can be taught unsuccessfully in two ways. In the first, the teacher attempts to teach the second-culture skills in a moralizing way—the right way to act and to be. This approach is likely to stimulate student resistance and thus is a teaching strategy that risks student refusal to learn. (Consider the word *ain't*. Teachers for generations have been teaching working-class students not to say *ain't* as a moral lesson. Yet inside and outside the classroom the students still say *ain't*.)

Another unsuccessful way to teach a second-culture skill is implicitly, according to Delpit. She observes that among well-meaning middle-class White teachers, some aspects of the language of power are part of the teacher's own invisible culture. Taking it for granted herself, she does not teach it explicitly to working-class African American students.

Delpit (1995) recommends an alternative approach—to teach second-culture skills explicitly and carefully but without moralizing. The school's language and culture of power can be presented as a situational dialect, to be used pragmatically for special situations, such as job interviews, formal writing, and college admissions interviews. When combined with reflective self-study of the student's own language use in the family, among peers, and in the neighborhood—study by which the student explores his or her own repertoire of differing speech styles used in differing situations—explicit teaching and learning of the language of power can be framed not as a matter of cultural borders but of cultural boundaries. This approach takes a critical and strategic view of multiculturalism, for survival reasons.

Multicultural Pedagogy as Emancipatory

Other multicultural educators recommend a critical approach to cultures of domination and to the phenomenon of domination. Ladson-Billings (1994) describes African American and White teachers who are effective with African American students. They taught in a variety of styles, but one common approach was to deal directly and explicitly with issues of injustice and oppression and the privileging of mainstream knowledge and perspectives as they came up in the curriculum and in the reported daily experiences of their students. Trueba (1994), Nieto (1999), McCarthy (1993), Perry and Fraser (1993), Sleeter and Grant (1993), Apple (1996), and Giroux (1991) all recommend a similar approach, sometimes called critical pedagogy, counter-hegemonic pedagogy, or emancipatory pedagogy.

Cultural hegemony refers to the established view of things—a commonsense view of what is and why things happen that serves the interests of those people already privileged in a society. When the school presents a comfortable established view of the nature of U.S. society and of the goodness and inherent rightness of school knowledge and school literacy, that is hegemonic. Students whose lives are not affirmed by the establishment seem intuitively not to accept hegemonic content and methods of instruction. They often resist, consciously or unconsciously, covertly as well as overtly.

Multicultural education has an opportunity and a challenge to be counter-hegemonic. When such issues as racism, class privilege, and sexism are left silent in the classroom, the implicit message for students of color appears to be that the teacher and the school do not acknowledge that experiences of oppression exist. If only the standard language, the standard American history, and the voices and lives of White men appear in the curriculum, then the further implicit message (by what is left in and what is left out of the knowledge presented as legitimate by the school) seems to be that the real United States and real school are only about the cultural mainstream and its establishment ideology. This approach especially marginalizes the students of color who come to school already marginalized by life experience and by the historical experience of oppression in their ethnic or racial communities. Such a hegemonic approach also marginalizes female students (Sadker & Sadker, 1994). Marginalization is alienating, and one response to alienation is resistance—the very thing that makes teaching and learning more difficult for students and their teachers.

Ironically, for teachers to name and acknowledge tough social issues, rather than turning students against school and the teacher, makes it more possible for students who have experienced oppression to affiliate with the teacher and with school learning. By taking the moralizing that characterizes culturally hegemonic teaching out of the picture, reframing second-culture acquisition as strategically instrumental rather than inherently right, a teacher facilitates second-culture learning by students from nonmainstream backgrounds. Through such teaching, cultural borders are reframed as boundaries, and the politics of the dominant culture and cultures are, to some extent at least, depoliticized in the classroom. The cycles of resistance and schismogenesis that are stimulated by hegemonic curriculum and teaching do not get set off.

The role of resistance to cultures of domination in student disaffiliation from school learning is a fundamental issue in public education in the United States, Canada, Australia, and also in Britain and the rest of Europe (Apple, 1996; Giroux, 1983; Willis, 1977). Ogbu (1987/1992) has argued that for students of "caste-like" minority background in the United States (from groups with historic experiences of stigma and limitation of economic opportunity, such as African Americans, Mexican Americans, Puerto Ricans, and Native Americans), resistance to school is almost inevitable because of the effects of group history. Fordham (1996) has shown that African American high school students in Washington, DC, defined achieving in school as "acting White." Other scholars, (Erickson, 1987/92; Foley, 1991; Trueba, 1994) have acknowledged Ogbu's insight while observing that student resistance can come not only as a result of group history of oppression, but also of oppressive and alienating circumstances of teaching and learning within the school itself. Another difficulty with Ogbu's position is that it leaves no room for the possibility of school change.

A major theme here is that when business is done as usual in school, student resistance results from that, as well as from influences from the wider society on students. In the short run, we cannot change the wider society. But we can make school learning environments less alienating. Multicultural education, especially critical or antiracist multicultural education, is a way to change the business-as-usual of schools. When that happens, as Ladson-Billings (1994) and others have shown, minority students of the backgrounds categorized as "caste-like" rise to the occasion. When treated with dignity and taught skillfully, such students affiliate with the school and achieve. Moll & Greenberg (1990; see also Moll, 1998) shows that minority students' families in their cultural practices maintain *funds of knowledge* that can be made use of in curriculum as teachers learn what those practices are, and the kinds of knowledge and skill they entail. Gutierrez, in a series of compelling studies of classroom teaching (Gutierrez, Baquedano-López, Alvarez, & Chiu 1999; Gutierrez, Baquedano-López, & Tejeda 1999; Gutierrez, Rymes, & Larson 1995), shows that learning is enhanced (as is student morale—the will to learn) when teachers in classroom discourse make use of language and speech styles from students' homes and from popular culture. This bridging pedagogy between official school knowledge and unofficial knowledge creates an intermediate "third space"—a hybrid discourse that allows students to use the voices they bring to the classroom as they begin to affiliate with school voices and discourses and to appropriate them as their own. In such classrooms the price of school success is not that one give up one's own self and voice to adopt a new and alien one. Rather, the student adds new voices and discourses to those the student already has, and the teacher through her own language use respects both the voices that are familiar to the student and those that are new.

Group history of oppression no doubt makes students and parents wary of school and its claims that the standard ways of teaching are good for you. That is, trust of a school's good intentions, especially by students and parents of color, is not automatic. But relationships of mutual trust and respect can be established between teachers and students in the classroom. Sensitive multicultural pedagogy is one foundation for such trust.

Conventional Teaching as Cultural Border Wars

Conversely, for teachers to treat the dominant culture in the curriculum as a matter of cultural borders rather than of boundaries can make the classroom an unsafe place for students. It makes the classroom learning environment untrustable and can invite student resistance. A vivid example of such culture conflict is seen in the first-grade reading lesson cited at the beginning of this chapter:

   1 T: All right, class, read that and remember your endings.
   2 CC: What did Little Duck see? (final t of "what" deleted)
   3 T: What. (emphasizing final t)
   4 CC: What (final t deleted as in turn 2)
   5 T: I still don't hear this sad little "t."
   6 CC: What did—what did—what—(final t's deleted)

7 T: What.

8 T&CC: What did Little Duck see? (final t spoken)

9 T: OK, very good

The example comes from first-grade classrooms in Berkeley, California, attended by both predominantly working-class African American children and predominantly middle-class White children (Piestrup, 1973, pp. 96–97). In some classrooms the teachers were African American, and in others the teachers were White.

Piestrup (1973) found the phenomenon of language style divergence that increases over time in situations of conflict, also reported by Labov (1963) and Giles and Powesland (1975). At the beginning of the school year many of the African American children spoke Black dialect (sometimes termed Black Nonstandard Vernacular). In the classrooms in which the teachers—whether African American or White—negatively sanctioned the children's use of Black dialect, by the end of the year those children spoke a broader form of the dialect in the classroom than they had done at the beginning of the year. The converse was also true in Piestrup's findings. Regardless of whether the teacher was African American or White, if the teacher did not publicly rebuke children for speaking Black dialect, by the end of the year those children's classroom speech more closely approached standard English.

The transcribed example shows one scene of rebuke for language style that Piestrup found in a number of the classrooms. Here, the teacher was correcting African American children's nonstandard pronunciation. An alternative focus of instruction could have been comprehension—understanding what was in the story. The teacher chose to focus on final consonant deletion (the final /t/ in the word *what*). In so doing the teacher was making that cultural feature of language style a cultural border issue—just as the Ephraimites treated the pronunciation of the final sound in the word *Shibboleth* so long ago. But the children's not articulating the final /t/ in *what* could have been treated as a cultural boundary issue.

Framed in that way, the speech-style difference (which probably did not interfere with the teachers' ability to hear the child's speech as intelligible in terms of literal, referential meaning) need not have gotten in the way of the discussion. Rather, the teacher, the child, and the other children in the group could have gone on to consider what Little Duck saw. There is now considerable evidence that pronouncing words in a nonstandard way does not interfere with children's ability either to decode written standard English (that is, to read letter combinations as identifiable words) or to understand the sense of a written passage at the level of a sentence or paragraph.

Why did the teacher insist on the final /t/? One explanation could be class bias or some other source of ethnocentrism, since final consonant deletion is not correct in terms of the dominant cultural style of official school literacy. Another, related explanation is possible. Deletion of a final /t/ also violates a key cultural assumption in one of professional subculture of educators—the assumption from behaviorist learning theory that mastery of subskills (such as pronouncing the final consonant) must necessarily precede mastery of more complex skills (such as comprehension at the word or sentence level). This ladder-of-skills cultural belief of educators is increasingly being challenged by advocates of whole language approaches to literacy as well as by sociolinguists and cognitive psychologists who study processes of learning to read.

Both sets of beliefs can be seen as hegemonic, reinforcing one another's common-sense validity. The general cultural value of correctness of standard English seems to be confirmed by the professional cultural belief in a ladder-of-skills approach to pedagogy. Of course, the teacher should correct mistakes, the reasoning goes; that's the teacher's job. Thus, we see how what may have begun as an ethnic and social-class marker in speech style (standard English) gets used as a sociolinguistic test at a cultural border in what seems to be a professionally responsible pedagogy. The justification of that pedagogy results in ways of teaching that are culturally biased and needlessly alienating for students who come to school speaking a dialect other than the culturally dominant one.

Between teachers and students, the discomfort of such interchanges as shown in the example, repeating day after day across the school year, according to Piestrup, led to dialect divergence on the part of the students. Considering that these were first graders, not adolescents, we can see the dialect divergence as a nondeliberate form of student resistance on the part of the students, outside their conscious awareness. These regressive social relationships between teachers and students, which become more negative, can happen for many reasons, not only because of cultural difference; when cultural difference is treated as a border issue in the classroom, it becomes a rich resource for ongoing conflictual relationships between teachers and students (McDermott & Gospodinoff, 1979/81).

In the previous example, the cultural assumptions behind the standard pedagogy are so much a part of professional common sense that we might consider them an aspect of invisible culture. The teacher might say, "I wasn't doing anything cultural; I was just teaching the children to read correctly." The children's lack of cooperation might not be seen as cultural resistance. Rather, the cultural issue might be clinicalized. The uncooperative children might be seen as passive-aggressive or as suffering from low self-esteem. If they shifted in their seats a lot they might be considered hyperactive.

Aspects of invisible culture often get used as diagnostic indicators with clinical significance, especially in the early grades. For example, if a child comes from a home in which adults do not routinely ask them teacherlike known-information questions (questions to which the adults already know the answer), such questions by a teacher can seem confusing or intimidating initially (Heath, 1983). "What color is this?" the kindergarten teacher says on the first day of school, holding up a red piece of construction paper in front of an African American child whose mother is on welfare. "Aonh-oh" (I don't know) the child replies, thinking there must be some trick, because anybody can see that the paper is red. "Lacking in reading readiness," the teacher thinks to herself, writes this in the child's permanent record, and assigns the child to the bottom reading group.

Once again we find ourselves with the Ephraimites on the banks of the Jordan River, witnessing the consequences of a cultural border test. Yet because we do not recognize knowing about teacherlike questions as a distinct cultural skill, we may not see the teacher's informal readiness test as cultural, or as culturally biased. Such framing of cultural difference as a border can be done inadvertently by teachers who are members of the cultural minority student's own ethnic group and speech community as well as by teachers who are of majority background. Recall that Piestrup (1973) found the African American students' speech style diverging from the standard style in classrooms where such speech style was rebuked, regardless of whether the teacher was White or African American. What mattered was not the race of the teacher but the teacher's cultural practices in pedagogy—responsive or unresponsive?

The cultural responsiveness or relevance of a classroom learning environment can differ in contradictory ways between the visible and the invisible aspects of culture. For example, in the same multiracial kindergarten or first-grade classroom in which a teacher uses informal tests of reading readiness that treat invisible cultural knowledge and skill as a cultural border (such as recognition of teacher questions and how to answer them) the teacher may have put a picture of Frederick Douglass on the wall, read a book about his life, presented information on West Africa in a positive light, and taught basic vocabulary in Yoruba or Swahili. Yet hanging a picture of Douglass, the African American abolitionist, on the wall next to a picture of George Washington, the White slave holder, or introducing students to an African language does not make that classroom fully multicultural, if invisible aspects of the communicative cultural practices of African American students are still being treated in invidious ways.

Such contradictions between formal and informal culture must be confusing and alienating for students, even though that alienation may be experienced by them outside conscious awareness. This is why attention to issues of invisible informal culture as well as those of visible formal culture seems so important for the success of attempts at multicultural education. And in all this work we must investigate critically our notions of failure and success itself, for "school failure" and "school success" are themselves cultural constructions, generally within society and locally within each classroom (see Varenne & McDermott, 1998).

CONCLUSION: ON DIVERSITY OF TONGUES AND THEIR EDUCATIONAL POTENTIAL

The Russian literary critic Bakhtin (1981) provides us with a final way to consider culture in its continuity and in its diversity, as transmitted across generations and as invented in the present moment. He studied the novel as it emerged in the sixteenth and eighteenth centuries in Spain and France and in England respectively and as it developed in England, France, and Russia in the nineteenth centuries. Bakhtin noted that the classic novelists depicted a variety of ways of speaking across their various characters who differed in social class, gender, and region. That diversity he called *heteroglossia*, from the Greek meaning "differing tongues." He believed that a fine novel encapsulated key aspects of the total diversity in speech styles found in the society at the historical moment in which that novel was written. To produce such a text convincingly the author must have incorporated the diversity of tongues present in the society.

Bakhtin (1981) also observed a personal heteroglossia within the characters of the novel akin to that in its author. For example, in Cervantes' *Don Quixote* Bakhtin noticed that usually the good Don, of bourgeois background, spoke in an imitation of the literary romance. Thus, his speech style sounded like the Spanish of the nobility. Sancho Panza, the peasant, usually spoke in the speech style of the lower classes. Yet once in a while, when engaged with the Don, or when reflecting to himself on what he had been experiencing, Sancho's speech drifted slightly toward the more prestigious style of Spanish. This tendency, apparent from the beginning of the modern novel, was more pronounced in nineteenth-century French and Russian novels. Russian serfs, for example, were depicted as speaking in a variety of speech styles—what Bakhtin called "social languages"—some more elevated and agentive, some more subordinated and passive. World view, personal status, and agency seemed to shift, as did the character's language style.

Bakhtin's insights suggest ways of understanding how cultural diversity is organized and distributed within a society and within persons. There is heteroglossia within a society. Members of distinct social categories and social networks speak more often than not in differing ways (reminiscent of the "speech community" notion discussed earlier). Men do tend to speak differently from women, African Americans from Whites, working-class people from upper-middle-class people, gay from straight, fundamentalist Christians from Unitarians, physicians from lawyers (and physicians from nurses). These ways of speaking are relatively continuously distributed within the various social groupings; they become badges of identity of such groupings; and for the most major social categories such as class, gender, race and ethnicity, and religion these social languages tend to persist across generations. In other words, social divisions and cultural and linguistic diversity appear to be consistently reproduced in society across time.

Moreover, the differing ways of speaking carry with them differing points of view that are the result of differing life experiences of the speakers and, as the feminist slogan puts it, "the personal is political." Thus, the historical experience of a group and its particular political interests in assuming that things are really one way rather than some other—its ideology—come with the social language of the group, as uttered by a particular member of that group. Ways of speaking, then, are discourses—whole sets of assumptions about the world and roles for being in the world that are entailed in certain ways of creating oral and written texts (Foucault, 1979; Gee, 1990). Much more is involved than language style alone. To the extent that various group interests and their discourses are involved with the distribution of power in society, there can be conflict and contradiction between ways of speaking and thinking as well as between social groupings. A discourse is in a sense a social institution or a subculture.

Yet the consistency of cultural reproduction is not unitary or absolute. There is also heteroglossia within persons. Each person's life experiences differs somewhat from those of other people, and every person lives in a variety of social situations each day. Differing social situations provide differing ecologies of relationship with other people. They evoke differing aspects of the individual's overall repertoire of ways of speaking. One speaks differently to one's mother than to one's siblings, to one's teacher than to one's mother. Sometimes in complex relationships, such as that between an employer or supervisor who is also a friend or between spouses who are simultaneously lovers, parents, and administrators of household resources, a variety of interrelated voices are evoked from moment to moment in what appears to be the same social situation. The utterances of persons in dialogue lean on one another in mutual influence, Bakhtin claimed. Thus, the phenomenon of ways of speaking (and of discourses) is inherently labile as well as stable. Culture at the group level varies in part because individuals differ among one another and within themselves as they find themselves in differing social circumstances. In other words, there is an inherent hybridity in cultural practices (see Arteaga, 1994; Gutierrez, Baquedano-López, & Tejeda, 1999; and Valle & Torres, 1995)—a blending of sources and voices in which new combinations and recombinations of old elements with new ones are continually being made.

As diverse persons show up in the scenes of daily life they bring their heteroglossia with them. There can be affiliation as well as conflict across those cultural differences. And discourses can be contested; they can be interrupted or interrogated. When that happens the assumptions of the discourse become visible and available for criticism. If a person or a group were to change discourses in a conflict that would be to take a different stance in the world. One may feel as if that is not permitted or as if that is one's right.

Since the discourses vary within persons as well as between groups, whatever conflict or affiliation there may be between the discourses in society is experienced within the personality. This means that the diversity of tongues and of voices within the person has profound emotional content and profound significance for personal identity and wholeness.

Schools are collection sites for diversity of voice and identity. Schools ask of students that they try on new discourses, new ways of speaking and thinking, new ways of being a self, and to appropriate them as their own. At their best, schools ask this of teachers as well, in order that they may come into closer awareness of and engagement with the voices of their students and also develop intellectually within their careers, appropriating within themselves more of the various discourses and literacies of their society. That is personally risky business, both for students and teachers. When discourses, or cultures, are in conflict in society then conflict can be experienced within the self over which discourses are being tried on.

Students and teachers come to school already having appropriated multiple voices and cultures. One task of education can be reflection on the voices one already has. Multicultural education, especially that which considers invisible as well as visible culture, can assist in that process of personal and group reflection. Teachers and students, by looking within themselves, can come to see that everybody is cultural and multicultural, including themselves. By listening to the discourses around them and also within them and by testing how those discourses feel— more like self, more like other, owned or alienated—students and their teachers can valorize many discourses, treating them as inherently of equivalent worth, even though not all the discourses and cultures are treated as equal in power and prestige in the world outside the classroom. If school is a secure place to try on new cultures and voices, if cultural diversity is treated as boundaries rather than as borders, then students and their teachers can establish safe "third" spaces in which to explore growing relationships with new cultures and old ones. This "third-space" pedagogy (Gutierrez, Baquedano-López, Alvarez, & Chiu, 1999) makes legitimate within the walls of the classroom the cultural hybridity that students and teachers bring to it.

Ultimately, for persons in complex multicultural societies, growth into maturity involves coming to terms with the diversity of voices and cultures within. This is especially the case when the cultures and voices have been in conflict in the wider society and when the person is a member of a dominated group. Then, coming to terms with one's own diversity means making some kind of just peace with the voices within. For example, in every man there are the voices of women, and in every woman there are the voices of men. Are these voices alien and in conflict within the person, or have they been appropriated within the self? Can a woman come to terms with the male voices within without acquiescing to male hegemony and adopting an alienated self? In every White person in the United States, because of our historical experience, there are not only White voices but also Black ones. What do those voices sound more like—Amos and Andy or Frederick Douglass? Aunt Jemima or Alice Walker? How have those voices been appropriated within the person, and what role has the school played in facilitating that process? In every African American in the United States there are not only Black voices but also White ones. How can the African American come to terms with the White voices within, forgiving and making peace with them, coming to own them while at the same time affirming and owning the Black voices, holding a continuing sense of the injustice of continuing racism? Doing all of that is necessary to mature into full adulthood as an African American (Cross, 1991; Helms, 1990).

To come to terms with the diversity of voices within is an educative task for society, for the individual, and for the school. It is what growing up means in a multicultural society and in a multicultural world. When the voices of the school curriculum and of its teaching and learning are fully multicultural, then the appropriation of multiple voices—in dignity and without coercion, keeping a critical stance without despair—becomes possible for all students. This is a noble aim for multicultural education. How difficult it is to achieve, yet how necessary. This becomes more apparent to educators as we become able to think more deeply about culture, its nuances, and its diversity in school and in society.

AFTERWORD

> What we are talking about is creating a new tradition, telling "new stories" that are fundamentally different by virtue of the role that the lives of the historically oppressed have assumed in their construction. This is a matter of redefining American culture, not once and for all, but in the negotiated meanings that are always emerging out of a curricular process. It is in the day-to-day interactions of teachers and students, dealing with a transformed curriculum and attempting to create a transformed, democratic classroom, that the new common culture will be created and continually recreated. (Perry & Fraser, 1993, pp. 19–20)

Questions and Activities

1. The author describes six conceptions of culture: (1) culture as cultivation; (2) culture as tradition; (3) culture as information bits; (4) culture as a symbol system; (5) culture as social process; and (6) culture as motive and emotion. Form groups in your class or workshop that consist of five people each to explore the diverse meanings of culture. Ask one student or workshop participant in each group to become an expert on one conception of culture given by the author. Discuss how the different conceptions of culture are both alike and different. Explain each definition by giving examples.

2. What does the author mean by "implicit and invisible aspects of culture"? In what ways are these aspects of culture important? Give some examples of invisible aspects of culture. What are some nonexamples of the concept?

3. In what ways might differences in invisible culture cause conflict? Give specific examples.

4. According to the author, what problems result when teachers focus on visible (explicit) culture at the expense of invisible and implicit culture? What kinds of educational practices result when teachers focus on visible and tangible aspects of culture?

5. How does the author distinguish between a cultural boundary and a cultural border? Why is this distinction important? Is a cultural boundary always a cultural border? Explain.

6. According to the author, does cultural change necessarily mean cultural loss? Explain why or why not.

7. The author states that we sometime "essentialize" culture. What does he mean? What problems result, in his view, when culture is essentialized?

8. The author states that "our conceptions of culture in multicultural education need to become more constructivist and less essentialist." Explain what he means by this statement and its implications for educational practice.

9. The author states that "Multicultural education has an opportunity and a challenge to be counter-hegemonic." Explain the meaning of this statement and give examples of how this might be done by classroom teachers.

References

Apple, M. W. (1996). *Cultural Politics and Education*. Buckingham: Open University Press.

Arteaga, A. (1994). *An Other Tongue: Nation and Ethnicity in the Linguistic Borderlands*. Durham, NC: Duke University Press.

Bakhtin, M. M. (1981). *The Dialogic Imagination*. M. Holquist (Ed.). Trans. by C. Emerson and M. Holquist. Austin: University of Texas Press.

Barth, F. (1969). *Ethnic Groups and Boundaries: The Social Organization of Culture Difference*. Boston: Little, Brown.

Barth, F. (1989). The Analysis of Culture in Complex Societies. *Ethnos 54*, 120–142.

Bateson, G., Jackson, D., Haley, J., and Weakland, J. (1972). Toward a Theory of Schizophrenia. In G. Bateson (Ed.), *Steps Toward an Ecology of Mind* (pp. 201–227). New York: Ballantine Books.

Bourdieu, P. (1977). *Outline of a Theory of Practice*. Cambridge Studies in Social Anthropology 16. New York: Cambridge University Press.

Bourdieu, P. and Passeron, J. C. (1977). *Reproduction: In Education, Society and Culture*. Beverly Hills, CA: Sage Books.

Connell, R. (1982). *Making the Difference: Schools, Families, and Social Division*. Sydney: Allen and Unwin.

Cross, W. E. (1991). *Shades of Black: Diversity in African American Identity*. Philadelphia: Temple University Press.

D'Andrade, R. G. and Strauss, C. (Eds.). (1992). *Human Motives and Cultural Models*. New York: Cambridge University Press.

Delpit, L. (1995). *Other People's Children: Cultural Conflict in the Classroom*. New York: New Press.

Erickson, F. (1987/1992). Transformation and School Success: The Politics and Culture of Educational Achievement. Anthropology and Education *Quarterly, 18*(4), 335–356.

Fanon, F. (1963). *The Wretched of the Earth*. Trans. by C. Farrington. New York: Grove Press.

Foley, D. E. (1991). Reconsidering Anthropological Explanations of Ethnic School Failure. *Anthropology and Education Quarterly, 22*(1), 60–86.

Fordham, S. (1996). *Blacked Out: Dilemmas of Race, Identity, and Success at Capital High.* Chicago: The University of Chicago Press.

Foucault, M. (1979). *Discipline and Punish: The Birth of the Prison.* New York: Random House/Vintage Books.

Garfinkel, H. and Sacks, H. (1970). The Formal Properties of Practical Actions. In J. C. McKinney and E. A. Tiryakian (Eds.), *Theoretical Sociology* (pp. 331–336). New York: Appleton-Century-Crofts.

Gee, J. (1990). *Social Linguistics and Literacies: Ideology in Discourses.* Philadelphia: The Falmer Press.

Geertz, C. (1973). *The Interpretation of Cultures.* New York: Basic Books.

Giddens, A. (1984). *The Constitution of Society: Outline of the Theory of Structuration.* Berkeley: University of California Press.

Giles, H. and Powesland, P. F. (1975). *Speech Style and Social Evaluation.* London: Academic Press.

Giroux, H. A. (1983). Theories of Reproduction and Resistance: A Critical Analysis. *Harvard Educational Review, 53,* 257–293.

Giroux, H. (1991). *Border Crossings: Cultural Workers and the Politics of Education.* New York: Routledge.

Goodenough, W. (1976). Multiculturalism as the Normal Human Experience. *Anthropology and Education Quarterly,* 7(4), 4–7.

Goodenough, W. (1981). *Culture, Language and Society.* Menlo Park, CA: Benjamin/Cummins Publishing.

Gumperz, J. J. (1982). *Discourse Strategies.* New York: Cambridge University Press.

Gutierrez, K., Baquedano-López, P., Alvarez, H., and Chiu, M. (1999). Building a Culture of Collaboration through Hybrid Language Practices. *Theory into Practice* 38(2), 87–93.

Gutierrez, K., Baquedano-López, P., and Tejeda, C. (1999). Rethinking Diversity: Hybridity and Hybrid Language Practices in the Third Space. *Mind, Culture, and Activity* 6(4) 286–303.

Gutierrez, K., Rymes, B., and Larson, J. (1995). Script, Counterscript, and Underlife in the Classroom: James Brown versus Brown vs. Board of Education. *Harvard Educational Review* 65(3), 445–471.

Hall, E. T. (1959). *The Silent Language.* New York: Doubleday.

Hall, E. T. (1976). *Beyond Culture.* New York: Doubleday.

Heath, S. B. (1983). *Ways with Words: Language, Life, and Work in Communities and Classrooms.* New York: Cambridge University Press.

Helms, J. (1990). *Black and White Racial Identity.* New York: Greenwood Press.

hooks, b. (1993). Transformative Pedagogy and Multiculturalism. In T. Perry and J. W. Fraser (Eds.), *Freedom's Plow: Teaching in the Multicultural Classroom* (pp. 91–98). New York: Routledge.

Hymes, D. H. (1974). *Foundations in Sociolinguistics: An Ethnographic Approach.* Philadelphia: University of Pennsylvania Press.

Kroeber, A. L. (1917). The Superorganic. *American Anthropologist, 19,* 163–213.

Kroeber, A. L. and Kluckhohn, C. (1952). *Culture: A Critical Review of Concepts and Definitions,* Vol. 47(1). Cambridge, MA: Peabody Museum of American Archaeology and Ethnology, Harvard University.

Kuper, A. (1999). *Culture: The Anthropologists' Account.* Cambridge, MA: Harvard University Press.

Labov, W. (1963). The Social Motivation of a Sound Change. *Word, 19,* 273–309.

Ladson-Billings, G. (1994). *The Dreamkeepers: Successful Teachers of African-American Children*. San Francisco: Jossey-Bass Publishers.

Lutz, C. A. (1990). *Language and the Politics of Emotion*. New York: Cambridge University Press.

McCarthy, C. (1993). After the Canon: Knowledge and Ideological Representation in the Multicultural Discourse on Curriculum Reform. In C. McCarthy and W. Crichlow (Eds.), *Race, Identity, and Representation in Education* (pp. 289–305). New York: Routledge.

McDermott, R. P. and Gospodinoff, K. (1979/1981). Social Contexts for Ethnic Borders and School Failure. In A. Wolfgang (Ed.), *Nonverbal Behavior: Applications and Cultural Implications* (pp. 175–195). New York: Academic Press.

Mehan, H., Wills, J. S., Okamoto, D., and Lintz, A. (1995). Ethnographic Studies of Multicultural Education in Classrooms and Schools. In J. A. Banks and C. A. M. Banks (Eds.), *Handbook of Research on Multicultural Education* (pp. 129–144). New York: Macmillan.

Moll, L. C. (Ed.). (1990). *Vygotsky and Education: Instructional Implications and Applications of Sociohistorical Psychology*. New York: Cambridge University Press.

Moll, L. (1998) *Funds of Knowledge for Teaching: A New Approach to Culture in Education*. Keynote address delivered to the Illinois State Board of Education, 21st Annual Statewide Conference for Teachers of Linguistically and Culturally Diverse Students. Springfield, IL, February.

Moll, L. and Greenberg, J. (1990). Creating Zones of Possibilities: Combining Social Contexts for Instruction. In L. C. Moll (Ed.), *Vygotsky and Education* (pp. 319–348). New York: Cambridge University Press.

Nieto, S. (Ed.). (1999). *The Light in Their Eyes: Creating Multicultural Learning Communities*. New York: Teachers College Press.

Ogbu, J. U. (1987/1992). Variability in Minority School Performance: A Problem in Search of an Explanation. *Anthropology and Education Quarterly, 18*(4), 312–334.

Ortner, S. B. (1984). Theory in Anthropology since the Sixties. *Comparative Studies in Society and History, 26*(1), 126–166.

Perry, T. and Fraser, J. W. (Eds.). (1993). *Freedom's Plow: Teaching in the Multicultural Classroom*. New York: Routledge.

Philips, S. U. (1983). *The Invisible Culture: Communication in School and Community on the Warm Springs Indian Reservation*. New York: Longman.

Piestrup, A. M. (1973). *Black Dialect Interferences and Accommodations of Reading Instruction in First Grade*. Washington, DC: National Institute of Mental Health. (ERIC Document Reproduction Service No. ED 119113)

Sadker, M. and Sadker, D. (1994). *Failing at Fairness: How America's Schools Cheat Girls*. New York: Scribner's.

Said, E. W. (1978). *Orientalism*. New York: Pantheon Books.

Skilton Sylvester, P. (1994). Elementary School Curricula and Urban Transformation. *Harvard Educational Review 64*, 309–331.

Sleeter, C. E. and Grant, C. A. (1993). *Making Choices for Multicultural Education*. New York: Merrill/Macmillan.

Torres-Guzmán, M. (1992). Stories of Hope in the Midst of Despair: Culturally Responsive Education for Latino Students in an Alternative High School in New York City. In M. Saravia-Shore and S. F. Arvizu (Eds.), *Cross-Cultural Literacy: Ethnographies of Communication in Multiethnic Classrooms* (pp. 477–490). New York: Garland Publishing, Inc.

Trueba, H. T. (1994). Reflections on Alternative Visions of Schooling. In *Anthropology and Education Quarterly*. Theme Issue: Alternative Visions of Schooling: Success Stories in Minority Settings. G. Ernst, E. Statzner, and H. Trueba (Eds.), *25*(3), 376–393.

Tylor, E. B. (1871/1970). *Primitive Culture: Researches into the Development of Mythology, Philosophy, Religion, Language, Art, and Custom.* London: Murray.

Valle, V. and Torres, R. (1995). The Idea of Mestizaje and the 'Race' Problematic: Racialized Media Discourse in a Post-Fordist Landscape. In A. Darder (Ed.), *Culture and Difference: Critical Perspectives on the Bicultural Experience in the United States* (pp. 139–153). Westport, CT: Bergin and Garvey.

Varenne, H. and McDermott, R. (1998). *Successful Failure: The School America Builds.* Boulder, CO: Westview Press.

Vico, G. (1744/1968). *The New Science of Giambattista Vico* (rev. ed.). Trans of the 3rd ed. (1744) by T. G. Bergin and M. H. Frisch. Ithaca, NY: Cornell University Press.

Wiggington, S. (1986). *Sometimes a Shining Moment: The Foxfire Experience.* Garden City, NY: Anchor Books.

Williams, R. (1983). *Culture and Society.* New York: Columbia University Press.

Willis, P. E. (1977). *Learning to Labor: How Working Class Kids Get Working Class Jobs.* New York: Columbia University Press.

Witherell, C. and Noddings, N. (1991). *Stories Lives Tell: Narrative and Dialogue in Education.* New York: Teachers College Press

CHAPTER 3

Race, Class, Gender, and Disability in the Classroom

Carl A. Grant and
Christine E. Sleeter

Schools have always been a focal point of debate. What should be taught? How should students be organized for instruction? How should teachers be prepared? What constitute acceptable standards? As we enter the twenty-first century, several developments and tensions in society have fueled renewed debate about schooling.

First, as transnational corporations have exported jobs to Third World nations in order to cut wages, many middle-class and working-class people in the United States experienced an erosion of their life-styles, and the poverty level rose, especially among women and children. Compared to the postwar economic boom, the 1980s and early 1990s were decades in which people in the United States had to learn to settle for less: fewer jobs were available, prices rose, real income of a large proportion of the population fell, and White middle-class families experienced some of the hard times poor families had always lived with (Newman, 1993; Rivlin, 1992; Shor, 1986). Between 1983 and 1995, the average household net worth of the 1 percent wealthiest families grew by 17 percent, while the average net worth of the bottom 95 percent fell; the poorest 40 percent of U.S. households dropped by 79 percent (Collins, Leondar-Wright, & Sklar, 1999). Although the late 1990s saw an economic boom for those at the upper end of the economic spectrum, many people had grown skeptical of their ability to achieve the American dream. Katherine Newman (1993) listened to people describing their concerns and fears:

> I'll never have what my parents had. I can't even dream of that.
> I'm living a lifestyle that's way lower than it was when I was
> growing up and it's depressing . . . . Even if you are a hard worker
> and you never skipped a beat, you followed all the rules, did
> everything they told you you were supposed to do, it's still
> horrendous. (p. 3)

Furthermore, domestic social problems such as drug use and teen pregnancy seemed to be concentrated in a growing underclass dependent on welfare. Middle-class people in the United

States, increasingly concerned about their ability to maintain their own standard of living, have become less tolerant of those who are poor. As schooling has become increasingly a prerequisite for employment, its payoff has seemed less certain, and competition for the good jobs has seemed keener.

Second, the United States has experienced tremendous growth in ethnic and racial diversity, especially through immigration, and public debate about what that diversity should mean has become prolific. By 1999, the population was 72 percent non-Hispanic White, 12 percent African American, 11 percent Latino, 4 percent Asian and Pacific Islander, and 1 percent Native American (U.S. Bureau of the Census, 1999). Whites were no longer the majority in many cities, and in California no racial or ethnic group held a majority in the public schools. About half of the nation's immigrants during the 1990s were from Central and South America and the Caribbean, the largest number coming from Mexico (Foreign-Born Population, 1998). Of the U.S. population, 86 percent spoke English only at home, while 14 percent spoke a language other than English.

Popular discussions commonly centered on trying to identify what we have in common in order to promote national unity. While some people argued that new commonalities could be forged from diverse cultural input, others insisted that all immigrants must be turned into "Americans" who embrace traditional definitions of U.S. culture. Discussions of immigration often publicized Asians as the model minority, attributing their presumed success to their embracing of traditional U.S. culture and values. Educators agreed that schools would need to respond to growing racial and ethnic diversity, but disagreed about whether schools should promote cultural assimilation or pluralism.

Third, racial minority groups experienced tension between achieving steady gains in education, as reflected in years of schooling obtained, SAT scores, and other standardized test scores; and simultaneous lack of economic progress and even erosion of gains in life-style, economic status, and rights. For example, between 1970 and 1987 the White–African American education gap closed from 2.3 years to 3 months (U.S. Bureau of the Census, 1989, p. 69) and has since remained at 3 to 4 months (National Center for Education Statistics, 1999). At the same time, however, poverty and unemployment hit communities of color harder than White communities (U.S. Bureau of the Census, 1992), and communities of color experienced assaults on legal protections, such as passage of Propositions 187 (aimed at reducing immigration), 209 (aimed at ending affirmative action), and 227 (aimed at ending bilingual education) in California. These occurrences led to growing frustration. For example, Terkel (1988) reported the following comment:

> I think Reagan made it very accepted to be a white bigot. It's the most fashionable thing. Now they say: America is white. America isn't single women on welfare. Why should us taxpayers support these people who ride on our backs and bring this country down? I'm afraid of what's gonna happen to blacks in this country. There are a fortunate few who will get over. But for the many, no way . . . . The dividing line is becoming clear and the bitterness is growing. You can't help but wonder why. (pp. 67–68)

Even Asian Americans, held up as the model group who had made it, were not nearly as successful uniformly as the media suggested. It is revealing that some of the most outspoken critics of this stereotype have been Japanese Americans, the group often touted as most successful (Jiobu, 1988; Omatsu, 1994; Suzuki, 1989; Takaki, 1989). But many people in the United States, seeing White women and people of color in professional and administrative positions, believed racism and sexism were no longer problems. Ironically, despite gains in years of schooling and test scores, following the reform reports of the early 1980s, racial and ethnic minority children were often described as "at risk of failure" rather than as "promising achievers" (Swadener, 1990).

People in the United States with disabilities also experienced both gains and losses. Although special education had expanded services to students with disabilities in schools, they, too, were disproportionately hit by economic losses and threatened by the raising of standards in schools. A triumph was passage of the Americans with Disabilities Act, designed to protect people with disabilities from discrimination, but some observers adopted a wait-and-see attitude because of many loopholes in the act (The Americans with Disabilities Act: Where We Are Now?, 1991).

Fourth, universities became actively engaged in promoting diversity. Since the 1960s, there have been growing bodies of scholarship by scholars of color, women, and critical theorists who created new ethnic studies and women's studies courses, programs, and curricular requirements (Banks & Banks, 1995). You may have taken such a course yourself. The amount of research and curriculum that was multicultural mushroomed, advancing perspectives that differed in some cases sharply from those of most political and economic leaders. At the same time, ethnic studies programs on several campuses found themselves under renewed attack in the wake of passage of conservative state laws such as Proposition 209 in California (Martinez, 1999).

Fifth, the work of schools has been driven by a rapidly growing standards and testing movement. This movement began with the 1983 *Nation at Risk Report*'s warning that U.S. preeminence on the world stage was being eroded by the mediocre performance of its educational institutions. A call to raise student achievement levels led to the 1989 Educational Summit in Charlottesville, where President George Bush and the nation's governors unveiled Goals 2000, declaring that every child in the United States would meet rigorous standards of academic achievement by the year 2000. After a brief attempt to develop national standards in the early 1990s, the task of standard writing quickly devolved to the states. At the state level, task forces across the nation wrote or elaborated on state standards for student and teacher performance, and systems of testing were put into place. Currently, every state but Iowa has state curriculum standards, and most have mandatory standardized assessment programs. As a vice principal recently remarked to one of us, "Everything in our school is being driven by tests." Many advocates of multicultural education quickly found attention to diversity and equity being replaced by attention to standards and student test scores.

All of this may seem removed from you and your classroom. But students whose parents have been experiencing the tensions discussed here are in your classroom, and local community and business leaders as well as spokespeople for oppressed groups are probably recommending what they believe schools should do to address these issues. And probably you have come across reports of tensions surrounding these issues in the media. For example, as the states of California and New York have wrestled with what a multicultural curriculum should look like, and as universities have begun requiring multicultural coursework, critics have charged minority groups with attempting to tear the United States apart (Schlesinger, 1992).

Yet, advocates of multicultural education argue that most curricula are no more than cosmetically multicultural (Sleeter & Grant, 1991), and that weak treatments of historic injustices mask very real concerns.

A major thread running through the debates about schooling is the relative importance of preparing students for jobs versus preparing them as citizens. Schools have always done both, but recently much of the talk about what schools should do has emphasized job preparation and maintained silence about citizenship. What kind of a nation do we want for ourselves and our children, given the challenges and problems we have been facing? How should limited resources be distributed, given our diversity and virtually everyone's desire for a good life? How should we address the fact that there are not enough good jobs to go around? And who gets to decide the most effective ways of educating children from diverse backgrounds?

Most students we teach usually give one of three reasons for wanting to become teachers: (1) they love kids, (2) they want to help students, (3) they want to make school more exciting than when they were students. If one of these is the reason you chose to enter the teaching profession, then we hope you will see the demographic and social trends described above as being challenging and will realize that your love and help are needed, not just for some students, but for all students.

This chapter discusses the importance of race, class, gender, language, and disability in classroom life and provides alternative approaches to dealing with these issues in the classroom.

RACE, CLASS, GENDER, LANGUAGE, DISABILITY, AND CLASSROOM LIFE

Ask yourself what you know about race, class, gender, language, and disability as they apply to classroom life. Could you write one or two good paragraphs about what these words mean? How similar or different would your meanings be from those of your classmates? How much do these ascribed characteristics influence the way you think about teaching? If you and your classmates organize into small discussion groups (try it) and listen closely to each other, you will probably notice some distinct differences in the ways you see the importance of these factors. The point of such an exercise is not to show that you have different ideas and interpretations, but to challenge you to think clearly about what your ideas and interpretations mean for working with your students: How will you bring excellence and equity to your teaching?

Race, social class, and gender are used to construct categories of people in society. On your college application form, you were probably asked to indicate your race, gender, disability, and parents' place of employment. Most institutions want to know such information. It provides the institution with the ability to analyze and report data related to any or all of your ascribed characteristics. Social scientists studying school practices often report results according to race, class, home language, or gender. As a teacher, it is essential for you to understand how the dynamics of race, class, language, gender, and disability can influence your knowledge and understanding of your students. It is also important for you to consider these dynamics collectively and not separately. Each of your students is a member of multiple status groups, and these simultaneous memberships, in interaction with dynamics in the broader society, influence the students' perceptions and actions.

For example, a child in the classroom is not just Asian American but also male, middle class, native-English speaking, and not disabled. Thus, he is a member of an oppressed racial group, but also of a gender group and a social class that historically have oppressed others. Therefore, his view of reality and his actions based on that view will differ from those of a middle-class Asian American girl whose first language is Korean, or a lower-class Asian American boy whose first language is Hmong and who has spina bifida. A teacher's failure to consider the integration of race, social class, and gender could lead at times to an oversimplified or inaccurate understanding of what occurs in schools, and therefore to an inappropriate or simplistic prescription for educational equity and excellence. You may have noticed, for example, teachers assuming (often mistakenly) that middle- and lower-class Mexican American students identify strongly with each other and that they view issues in much the same way, or that African American male students have the same goals and views as African American female students.

We often begin working with teacher education students by having them take a self-inventory of the sociocultural groups they have been exposed to in their own schooling, religious, or work situations. The more honest you are in thinking about your familiarity with the backgrounds of different children, the more readily you can begin to learn about people to whom you have had little exposure. It will be a much greater limitation on your ability to teach well if you assume you know more about different students than you actually know, than if you recognize whose lives are unfamiliar to you, so that you can learn.

APPROACHES TO MULTICULTURAL EDUCATION

Educators often work with students of color, students from low-income backgrounds, and White female students according to one of five approaches to multicultural education. As we briefly explain these approaches, ask yourself which approach you are most comfortable using in your teaching. Before we begin this discussion, you should understand two important points. First, space does not allow for a complete discussion of each approach; for a thorough discussion, please refer to *Making Choices for Multicultural Education: Five Approaches to Race, Class and Gender* (Sleeter & Grant, 1999). Second, if you discover that you are a true eclectic or that none of the approaches satisfies your teaching style, that is fine, as long as you are not straddling the fence. Indecision, dissatisfaction, and frustration in teaching style and technique may confuse your students. Also, to be the dynamic teacher you want to be, you need a teaching philosophy that is well thought out and makes learning exciting for your students. Good teaching requires that you have a comprehensive understanding of what you are doing in the classroom, why, and how you are doing it.

Teaching the Exceptional and Culturally Different

If you believe that a teacher's chief responsibility is to prepare all students to fit into and achieve within the existing school and society, this approach may be particularly appealing to you. It may be especially appealing if students of color, special-education students, White female students, language-minority students, or low-income students are behind in the main subject areas of the traditional curriculum. The goals of this approach are to equip students with the cognitive skills, concepts, information, language, and values traditionally required by U.S. society, and eventually to enable them to hold a job and function within society's institutions and culture. Teachers using this approach often begin by determining the achievement levels of students, comparing their achievement to grade-level norms, and then working diligently to help those who are behind to catch up.

A good deal of research documents learning strengths of students of different sociocultural groups, suggesting that if a teacher learns to identify and build on their strengths, students will learn much more effectively than if a teacher assumes the child cannot learn very well. For example, Shade (1989) synthesized research on the learning style of African Americans and concluded that, "from all indications their knowledge is gained most effectively through kinetic and tactile senses, through the keen observation of the human scene, and through verbal description. This difference in perception manifests itself, not only in worldview but also in modality preference, cue selection, and pictorial perception" (p. 110). Teachers who understand this will read the classroom behavior of such children accurately and will adjust their instructional processes accordingly without lowering their expectations for learning.

As another example, gender differences in math achievement may be due partly to instructional styles that favor males. Fennema and Peterson (1987) suggest that girls learn math better when taught through cooperative rather than competitive procedures. More recently, Pearson (1992) discovered that, at the college level, the majority of the female students studied preferred a more collaborative and intimate learning environment. Based on a review of research on bilingual education, Snow (1994) concludes that developing a strong foundation in children's primary language provides a sturdy base for literacy development and cognitive growth. Programs that treat languages other than English as a problem to remediate rather than as a resource to develop cut language minority children off from language skills with which they enter school.

Starting where the students are and using instructional techniques and content familiar to them are important. For example, one teacher who used this approach helped two African American students who had moved from a large urban area to a much smaller college town to catch up on their writing skills by having them write letters to the friends they left in the city. A second teacher grouped the girls in her ninth-grade class who were having problems in algebra, allowing them to work together, support one another, and not be intimidated by the boys in the class who had received the kind of socialization that produces good math students. A third teacher provided two students with learning disabilities with materials written at their reading level that covered concepts comparable to those the rest of the class was reading. A fourth teacher placed two Latino students with limited English-speaking abilities into a transitional bilingual program. A teacher may believe that only one or two students in the classroom need this approach, or that all of them do, especially if the school is located in an inner-city community or barrio.

In sum, the heart of this approach is building bridges for students to help them acquire the cognitive skills and knowledge expected of the so-called average White middle-class student. This approach accepts that there is a body of knowledge all students should learn, but that teachers should teach that knowledge in whatever way works so students understand and learn it.

Human Relations Approach

If you believe that a major purpose of the school is to help students learn to live together harmoniously in a world that is becoming smaller and smaller, and if you believe that greater social equality will result if students learn to respect one another regardless of race, class, gender, or disability, then this approach may be of special interest to you. Its goal is to promote a feeling of unity, tolerance, and acceptance among people: "I am okay and you are okay."

The human relations approach teaches positive feelings among all students, promotes group identity and pride for students of color, reduces stereotypes, and works to eliminate prejudice and biases. For example, a teacher of a fourth-grade multiracial, mainstreamed classroom spends considerable time during the first two weeks of each semester, and some time thereafter, doing activities to promote good human relations in the class. Early in the semester he uses a sociogram to learn student friendship patterns and to make certain that every child has a buddy. He also uses this activity to discover how negative or positive the boy-girl relationships are. He uses sentence-completion activities to discover how students are feeling about themselves and their family members. Based on these data, he integrates into his curriculum concepts of social acceptance and humanness for all people, the reduction and elimination of stereotypes, and information to help students feel good about themselves and their people. Also he regularly brings to his classroom speakers who represent the diversity in society to show all students that they too can be successful.

The curriculum for the human relations approach addresses individual differences and similarities. It includes contributions of the groups of which the students are members and provides accurate information about various ethnic, racial, disability, gender, or social-class groups about whom the students hold stereotypes. Instructional procedures include a good deal of cooperative learning, role playing, and vicarious or real experiences to help the students develop appreciation of others. Advocates of this approach suggest that it should be comprehensive, integrated into several subject areas, and schoolwide. For example, a school attempting to promote gender equality is working at cross-purposes if lessons in language arts teach students to recognize sex stereotypes, while in the science class girls are not expected to perform as well as boys and thus are not pushed to do so. These contradictory attitudes simply reaffirm sex stereotypes.

While the teaching-the-exceptional-and-culturally-different approach emphasizes helping students acquire cognitive skills and knowledge in the traditional curriculum, the human relations approach focuses on attitudes and feelings students have about themselves and each other.

Single-Group Studies Approach

We use the phrase *single-group studies* to refer to the study of a particular group of people, for example, Asian American studies or Native American studies. The single-group studies approach seeks to raise the social status of the target group by helping young people examine how the group has been oppressed historically and what its capabilities and achievements have been. Unlike the two previous approaches, this one (as well as the next two) views school knowledge as political rather than neutral and presents alternatives to the existing Eurocentric, male-dominant curriculum. It focuses on one specific group at a time so the history, perspectives, and worldview of that group can be developed coherently, rather than piecemeal. It also examines the current social status of the group and actions taken historically as well as contemporarily to further the interests of the group. Its advocates hope that students will develop more respect for the group and also the knowledge and commitment to work to improve the group's status in society.

Single-group studies are oriented toward political action and liberation. For example, in his discussion of the development of Asian American studies, Omatsu (1994) explains that

> the redefinition [of the Asian American experience] began with an
> analysis of power and domination in American society. It provided a
> way for understanding the historical forces surrounding us. And
> most importantly, it presented a strategy and challenge for changing
> our future. (p. 33)

Women's studies, according to Westkott (1983), is intended "to change the sexist world." Women's studies corrects history that has been written almost solely by White men about White men. It teaches students about the oppression women face and provides female students with accurate knowledge, purpose, and understanding of themselves. For students of color, ethnic studies provides the intellectual offensive for the social and political struggle for liberation and cultural integrity (Cortada, 1974). The student works to develop what Freire (1973) calls a "critical consciousness."

Since the late 1960s and early 1970s, scholars have generated an enormous amount of research about various oppressed groups and have begun to map out new conceptual frameworks within various disciplines. For example, Afrocentric scholars redefined the starting point of African American history from slavery to ancient Africa, and in the process rewrote story lines for African American history. Beginning history with a group other than European males enables one to view historic events very differently. A group's story may begin in Asia and move east, or South or Central America and move north, or Europe and move west, or right here on the North American continent thousands of years ago. Further, the story is different if one views the group as having started from a position of strength (for example, African civilizations [Gates, 1999]), then having been subjugated and now attempting to rebuild that strength, rather than starting in a position of weakness (such as slavery) and now attempting to rise.

A single-group studies curriculum includes units or courses about the history and culture of a group (for example, African American history, Chicano literature, disability studies). It teaches how the group has been victimized and has struggled to gain respect, as well as about current social issues facing the group. It is essential that such curricula be based on scholarship by people who have studied the group in depth, rather than on your own ideas about what you think might be important.

Beginning in the late 1980s, Afrocentric curricula and schools received considerable publicity and discussion. As reported in *Education Week*,

> School districts in Atlanta, Indianapolis, Milwaukee, Pittsburgh,
> Washington, and other cities are in various stages of adopting
> Afrocentric programs inspired, in part, by a curriculum pioneered in
> the predominantly white Portland, Ore. school system. (Viadero,
> 1990, p. 1)

Afrocentric schools represent a serious attempt to implement the single-group studies approach because of the failure of schools to successfully educate African American children. Afrocentric public schools have received considerable publicity during the 1990s. However, Ratteray (1990) points out that more than 400 independent African American schools exist, a few being more than 100 years old. The main rationale for such schools is that "Current practice, even in desegregated settings, effectively excludes African American males [and females, to a lesser degree] from the mainstream culture" (Leake & Leake, 1992, p. 25). Pollard and Ajirotutu (1999) reported a five-year study of one Afrocentric middle school in Milwaukee. The greatest problem they found was high staff turn-over, making consistent implementation of school reform difficult. Over the five years, student attendance improved, and suspensions and truancy dropped. Academic achievement gains were mixed. Their major recommendation was that such schools need a stable staff, with a consistent program of staff development, led by an administrative team with a clear vision.

Developments such as this have sparked much controversy. While many African American educators maintain that they are an antidote to the "colonial Western approach to history and academic work" and that they develop strong self-concepts in African American students, opponents maintain that such curricula are too politicized and stretch truth (Leo, 1990). From our perspective, all curricula and school programs are political and try to teach someone's version of the truth; at least Afrocentric curricula are more direct about this than are traditional Eurocentric, male-dominant curricula.

Although single-group studies focus mainly on the curriculum, they also give some attention to instructional processes that benefit the target group. Women's studies programs, for example, have developed what is known as "feminist pedagogy" (see Chapter 7). This is a teaching approach that attempts to empower students. The main idea is that in the traditional classroom, women are socialized to accept other people's ideas. By reading text materials that were written mainly by men, providing a male interpretation of the world, women learn not to interpret the world for themselves. In the feminist classroom, women learn to trust and develop their own insights. The feminist teacher may assign material to read and may encourage students to generate discussion and reflections about the material. The discussion and personal reflection are important parts of the process, during which "control shifts from me, the teacher, the arbiter of knowing, to the interactions of students and myself with the subject matter" (Tetreault, 1989, p. 137).

In summary, the single-group studies approach is aimed toward social change. It challenges the knowledge normally taught in schools, arguing that knowledge reinforces control by White wealthy men over everyone else. It offers an in-depth study of oppressed groups for the purpose of empowering group members, developing in them a sense of pride and group consciousness, and helping members of dominant groups understand where others are coming from.

Multicultural Education Approach

Multicultural education has become the most popular term used by educators to describe education for pluralism. We apply this term to a particular approach that most multicultural education theorists prefer. As you will notice, this approach synthesizes many ideas from the previous three approaches.

The societal goals of this approach are to reduce prejudice and discrimination against oppressed groups, to work toward equal opportunity and social justice for all groups, and to effect an equitable distribution of power among members of the different cultural groups. The multicultural education approach attempts to reform the total schooling process for all children, regardless of whether the school is an all-White suburban school or a multiracial urban school. Schools that are reformed around principles of pluralism and equality would then contribute to broader social reform.

Various practices and processes in the school are reconstructed so the school models equality and pluralism. For example, the curriculum is organized around concepts basic to each discipline, but content elaborating on those concepts is drawn from the experiences and perspectives of several different U.S. groups. If you are teaching literature, you select literature written by members of different groups. This not only teaches students that groups other than Whites have produced literature; it also enriches the concept of literature because it enables students to experience different literature forms that are common to all writing. For example, the universal struggle for self-discovery and cultural connection within a White-dominant society can be examined by reading about a Puerto Rican girl in *Felita* (Mohr, 1990), a Chinese girl in *Dragonwings* (Yep, 1975), an African American boy in *Scorpions* (Myers, 1990), and a European American girl in *The Great Gilly Hopkins* (Paterson, 1987).

It is also important that the contributions and perspectives you select depict each group as the group would depict itself and show the group as active and dynamic. This requires that you learn about various groups and become aware of what is important and meaningful to them. For example, teachers wishing to teach about famous Native Americans should ask members of different Native American tribes whom they would like to see celebrated, instead of holding up to their students Pocahontas, Kateri Tekakwitha, or Sacajawea. These Native Americans are often thought among their people to have served White interests more than Native American interests. Additionally, African Americans are becoming increasingly concerned because the African American athlete or entertainer is often held up as the hero and heroine for the group, instead of African Americans who have done well in other areas of life, such as science or literature.

In this approach, instruction starts by assuming that students are capable of learning complex material and performing at a high level of skill. Each student has a personal, unique learning style that teachers discover and build on when teaching. The teacher draws on and uses the conceptual schemes (ways of thinking, knowledge about the world) that students bring to school. Cooperative learning is fostered, and both boys and girls are treated equally, in a nonsexist manner. A staff as diverse as possible is hired and assigned responsibilities nonstereotypically. More than one language is taught; all students become at least bilingual. The multicultural education approach, more than the previous three, advocates total school reform to make the school reflect diversity. It also advocates giving equal attention to a variety of cultural groups regardless of whether specific groups are represented in the school's student population.

Education That Is Multicultural and Social Reconstructionist

Reflect back on the various forms of social inequality mentioned at the opening of this chapter. Education that is multicultural and social reconstructionist deals more directly than the other approaches have with oppression and social structural inequality based on race, social class, gender, and disability. Its purpose is to prepare future citizens to reconstruct society so that it better serves the interests of all groups of people, especially those who are of color, poor, female, and/or with disabilities. The phrase *education that is multicultural*, Grant (1978) explains, means that the entire education program is redesigned to reflect the concerns of diverse (race, class, gender, and disability) groups. Its orientation and focus are on the whole education process. Social reconstructionism seeks to reconstruct society toward greater equity in race, class, gender, and disability. This approach also questions ethics and power relations embedded in the new global economy. It draws on the penetrating vision of George Bernard Shaw (1980), who exclaimed, "You see things, and you say, 'Why?' But I dream things that never were, and I say, 'Why not?'" (p. 681).

As noted above, this approach extends the multicultural education approach, in that the curriculum and instruction of these two approaches are very similar. However, there are four practices unique to education that is multicultural and social reconstructionist.

First, democracy is actively practiced in the schools. Having students read the U.S. Constitution and hear lectures on the three branches of government is a passive way to learn about democracy. For students to understand democracy they must live it. They must practice politics, debate, social action, and the use of power. In the classroom this means that students will be given the opportunity to direct a good deal of their learning and to learn how to be responsible for that direction. This does not mean that teachers abdicate the running of their classroom to the students, but rather that they guide and direct students so they learn how to learn and develop skills for wise decision-making. Shor (1980) described this as helping students become subjects rather than objects in the classroom, and Freire (1985) said it will produce individuals "who organize themselves reflectively for action rather than men [and women] who are organized for passivity" (p. 82).

Second, students learn how to analyze institutional inequality within their own life circumstances. Freire (1973) distinguished between three kinds of consciousness: critical consciousness, magical consciousness, and naive consciousness:

> Critical consciousness represents things and facts as they exist empirically, in their causal and circumstantial correlations, naive consciousness considers itself superior to facts, in control of facts, and thus free to understand them as it pleases. Magic consciousness, in contrast, simply apprehends facts and attributes them to a superior power by which it is controlled and to which it must therefore submit. (p. 44)

To put it another way, a person with critical consciousness wants to know how the world actually works and is willing to analyze the world carefully, for himself or herself. A person with naive or magic consciousness does not do that. If one sees the world through magic, one assumes that one cannot understand or affect the world; things just happen. If one sees the world naively, one assumes cause-effect relationships that one wants to assume or that one has been told exist, without investigating them or thinking critically, for oneself.

In a stratified society, Freire (1973) argued that most ordinary people see the world naively or magically, as the elite would wish them to see it. Either they believe that they have no power to change the way the world works for them, or they believe that their problems have no relationship to their position in the power hierarchy. For example, students are taught that education is the doorway to success and that if they obey the teacher and do their work they will succeed. However, studies indicate that many students of color who comply with school rules and teachers' requests still do not receive the career guidance and school work necessary for becoming successful (Grant & Sleeter, 1986). Furthermore, education pays off better for White males than for all others. For example in 1994, the average full-time working White male with four years of high school earned $26,125, whereas the average Black and Latino full-time working male with the same amount of education earned $18,525 and $19,667 respectively. For full-time working women, these figures were $15,078 (White women), $14,333 (Black women), and $14,313 (Latino women) (U.S. Bureau of the Census, 1999). This approach teaches students to question what they hear about how society works from other sources and to analyze the experiences of people like themselves in order to understand more fully what the problems actually are so they can prepare themselves to change unfair social processes.

Third, students learn to use social action skills. Bennett (1990) describes social action skills as "the knowledge, attitudes and skills that are necessary for active citizen participation" (p. 307). In this approach the school is seen as a laboratory or training ground for preparing students to be more socially active. Banks (1994) says that oppressed ethnic groups

> must also develop a sense of political efficacy, and be given practice in social action strategies which teaches them how to get power without violence and further exclusion . . . . A curriculum designed to help liberate marginalized ethnic groups should emphasize opportunities for social action, in which students have experience obtaining and exercising power. (p. 216)

For example, some stories that elementary school children read could deal with issues involving discrimination and oppression and could suggest ways to deal with such problems. Students of all ages can be taught to identify sexist advertising of products sold in their community and how to take action to encourage advertisers to stop these types of practices. Advocates of this approach do not expect children to reconstruct the world, but they do expect the schools to teach students how to do their part in helping the nation achieve excellence and equity in all areas of life.

Fourth is building bridges across various oppressed groups (e.g., people who are poor, people of color, and White women) so they can work together to advance their common interests. This is important because it can energize and strengthen struggles against oppression. However, getting groups to work together is difficult because members often believe that they would have to place some of their goals second to those of other groups. Further, racial groups find themselves divided along gender and class lines to the extent that middle-class males of all colors fail to take seriously the concerns of women and of lower-class members of their own groups. Childs (1994) describes "transcommunal" organizations, such as the African American/Korean alliance in Los Angeles, which bring different groups together to identify and work on common concerns. Albrecht and Brewer's book (1990), *Bridges of Power: Women's Multicultural Alliances*, addresses concerns and issues women face in attempting to coalesce across racial and social-class lines.

You now have an idea of the approaches used to teach multicultural education. Which one best suits your teaching philosophy and style? An equally important question is, Which approach will best help to bring excellence and equity to education? This chapter next provides an example of how one teacher brings both excellence and equity to her classroom.

MS. JULIE WILSON AND HER APPROACH TO TEACHING

The following example describes a few days in the teaching life of Ms. Julie Wilson, a first-year teacher in a medium-large city. Which approach to multicultural education do you think Ms. Wilson is using? With which of her teaching actions do you agree or disagree? What would you do if assigned to her class?

May 23

Julie Wilson was happy, but also sad that she had just completed her last exam at State U. As she walked back to her apartment, she wondered where she would be at this time next year. She had applied for ten teaching positions and had been interviewed three times. As Julie entered her apartment building, she stopped to check the mail. A large, fat, white envelope addressed to her was stuffed into the small mailbox. She hurriedly tore it open and quickly read the first sentence. "We are pleased to offer you a teaching position . . . ." Julie leaped up the stairs three at a time. She burst into the apartment, waving the letter at her two roommates. "I've got a job! I got the job at Hoover Elementary. My first teaching job, a fifth-grade class!"

Hoover Elementary had been a part of a desegregation plan that brought together students from several different neighborhoods in the city. Hoover was situated in an urban-renewal area to which city officials were giving a lot of time and attention and on which they were spending a considerable amount of money. The city officials wanted to bring the Whites back into the city from suburbs and to encourage the middle-class people of color to remain in the city. They also wanted to improve the life chances for the poor. Julie had been hired because the principal was looking for teachers who had some record of success in working with diverse students. Julie had a 3.5 grade point average and had worked with a diverse student population in her practicum and student teaching experience. She had strong letters of recommendation from her cooperating teacher and university supervisor. Julie also had spent her last two summers working as a counselor in a camp that enrolled a wide diversity of students.

August 25

Julie was very pleased with the way her classroom looked. She had spent the last three days getting it ready for the first day of school. Plants, posters, goldfish, and an old rocking chair added to the warmth of an attractive classroom. There was also a big sign across the room saying "Welcome Fifth Graders." Tomorrow was the big day.

August 26

Twenty-eight students entered Julie's classroom: fifteen girls and thirteen boys. There were ten White students, three Hmong students, six Latino students, and nine African American students. Three of the students were learning disabled, and one was in a wheelchair. Eleven of the students were from middle-class homes, nine were from working-class homes, and the remaining eight were from very poor homes. Julie greeted each student with a big smile and a friendly hello as they entered the room. She asked their names and told them hers. She then asked them to take the seat with their name on the desk.

After the school bell rang, Julie introduced herself to the whole class. She told them that she had spent most of her summer in England, and that while she was there she had often thought about this day—her first day as a teacher. She talked briefly about some of the places she had visited in England as she pointed to the places on a map. She concluded her introduction by telling them a few things about her family. Her mother and father owned a dairy farm in Wisconsin, and she had one older brother, Wayne, and two younger sisters, Mary and Patricia. Julie asked if there were any students new to the school. Lester, an African American male, raised his hand, along with a female Hmong student, Mai-ka, and two Latino students, Maria and Jesus. Julie asked Mai-ka if she would like to tell the class her complete name, how she had spent her summer, and one favorite thing she liked to do. Then she asked the same of the other three. After Mai-ka and Michael finished introducing themselves, Julie invited the other students to do the same. Julie then asked Lourdes to tell Mai-ka, Maria, Jesus, and Michael about Hoover Elementary.

Once the opening greetings were completed, Julie began a discussion about the importance of the fifth grade and how special this grade was. She explained that this is a grade and class where a lot of learning would take place, along with a lot of fun. As Julie spoke, the students were listening intently. Julie radiated warmth and authority. Some of the students glanced at each other unsmilingly as she spoke of the hard work; however, when she mentioned "a lot of fun," the entire class perked up and looked at each other with big grins on their faces.

Julie had begun working on her educational philosophy in the Introduction to Education course at State U. Although she was continually modifying the way she thought about teaching, her basic philosophical beliefs had remained much the same. One of her major beliefs was that the students should actively participate in planning and shaping their own educational experiences. This, she believed, was as important for fifth graders as twelfth graders.

Julie asked the class if they were ready to take care of their classroom governance— deciding on rules, helpers, a discipline code, and time for classroom meetings. The class responded enthusiastically. The first thing the students wanted to do was to decide on the class rules. Several began to volunteer rules:

> "No stealing."
>
> "No rock throwing on the playground."
>
> "No sharpening pencils after the bell rings."
>
> "No fighting."

As the students offered suggestions, Julie wrote them on the chalkboard. After giving about sixteen suggestions, the class concluded. Julie commented, "All the rules seem very important"; she then asked the class what they should do with the rules. One student, Richard, suggested that they be written on poster board and placed in the upper corner of the room for all to see. Other class members said, "Yes, this is what we did last year in fourth grade." William, however, said, "Yes, we did do this, but we rarely followed the rules after the first day we made them." Julie assured the class this would not be the case this year, and that they would have a weekly classroom meeting, run by an elected official of the class. She then asked if they thought it would be helpful if they wrote their rules using positive statements, instead of "no" or negative statements. The class said yes and began to change statements such as "no stealing" to "always ask before borrowing," and "no rock throwing" to "rock throwing can severely hurt a friend." Once the rules were completed, the class elected their officers.

After the classroom governance was taken care of, Julie asked the students if they would like her to read them a story. An enthusiastic yes followed her question. Julie glanced at the clock as she picked up *To Break the Silence* (Barrett, 1986) from the desk. The book is a varied collection of short stories, especially for young readers, written by authors of different racial backgrounds. It was 11:35. She could hardly believe the morning had gone by so quickly. She read for twenty minutes. All the students seemed to be enjoying the story, except Lester and Ben, two African American male students. Lester and Ben were drawing pictures, communicating nonverbally between themselves, and ignoring the rest of the class members. Julie decided that because they were quiet and not creating a disturbance she would leave them alone.

After lunch, Julie had the class do two activities designed to help her learn about each student both socially and academically. She had the students do a self-concept activity, in which they did sentence completions that asked them to express how they felt about themselves. Then she had them play math and reading games to assess informally their math and reading skills. These activities took the entire afternoon, and Julie was as pleased as the students when the school day came to an end.

When Julie arrived at her apartment, she felt exhausted. She had a quick dinner and shower and then crawled into bed. She set the alarm for 7 P.M., and fell quickly asleep.

By 10:30 that night she had examined the students' self-concept activity and compared the information she had collected from the informal math and reading assessment with the official information from the students' cumulative record cards. She thought about each student's achievement record, social background, race, gender, and exceptionality. She said aloud, "I need to make plans soon to meet every parent. I need to find out about the students' lives at home, the parents' expectations, and if I can get some of them to volunteer."

Julie turned off her desk lamp at 11:45 to retire for the evening. She read a few pages from Richard Wright's *Native Son* and then turned out the light. Tonight she was going to sleep with less tension and nervousness than she had the night before. She felt good about the way things had gone today and was looking forward to tomorrow. As Julie slept, she dreamed of her class. Their faces and most of their names and backgrounds floated through her mind.

Eight of the ten White students were from Briar Creek, a middle-class single-unit housing community; these students were performing at grade level or above in all scholastic areas, and each of them was at least a year ahead in some core area subject. Charles, who had used a wheelchair since being in an automobile accident three years ago, was three years ahead in both reading and math. However, Elaine and Bob had chosen a mixture of positive and negative adjectives when doing the self-concept activity, and this concerned Julie. She would keep her eye on them to try to determine the cause of their problems.

Estelle and Todd, the other two White students, were between six months and a year behind in most academic areas. Estelle had been diagnosed as learning disabled, but the information in her personal cumulative file folder seemed ambiguous about the cause of her problem. Julie wondered if Estelle was classified as L.D. based on uncertain reasons. She recalled an article that discussed the learning-disability label as being a social construction rather than a medical condition.

All three of the Hmong students were at grade level or very close in their subjects. However, two of them, Mai-ka and Chee, were having some difficulty speaking English. The Thao family owned a restaurant in the neighborhood. The rumor mill reported that they were doing very well financially, so well that they had recently opened a restaurant in the downtown area of the city. All of the six Latino students were Mexican American, born in the United States. Maria, José, and Lourdes were bilingual, and the other three were monolingual, with English being their primary language. Maria, José, and Lourdes were from working-class homes, and Richard, Jesus, and Carmen were from very poor homes. Lourdes, Carmen, and Richard's achievement scores were at least two years ahead of their grade level. José was working at grade level, and Maria and Jesus were one to two years behind.

Five of the African American students—Lester, Ben, Gloria, Sharon, and Susan—were all performing two years behind grade level in all core area subjects. All five lived in the Wendell Phillips low-rent projects. Two African American students—Shelly and Ernestine—lived in Briar Creek and were performing above grade level in all academic areas. Dolores and Gerard lived in Chatham, a working-class predominantly African American neighborhood; both were performing above grade level in all subjects, except Gerard, who was behind in math. Gerard also had chosen several negative words when doing the self-concept activity.

All students in Julie's class were obedient and came from families that encouraged getting a good education.

May 25, 7:30 A.M.

Julie liked arriving early at school. The engineer, Mike, usually had a pot of coffee perking when she arrived. This was her time to get everything ready for the day. She had been teaching for almost one school year and was proud and pleased with how everything was going. The school principal, Mr. Griffin, had been in her class three times for formal visits and had told others, "Julie is an excellent teacher." He usually offered her one or two minor suggestions, such as "Don't call the roll every day; learn to take your attendance silently," and "The museum has an excellent exhibit on food and the human body your class may enjoy."

Julie had also been surprised by several things. She was surprised at how quickly most of the teachers left school at the end of the day. Out of a staff of twenty classroom teachers, only about five or six came early or stayed late. Even more surprising to her was how she and the other teachers who either came early or stayed late were chided about this behavior. She was surprised at the large number of worksheets and ditto sheets used and at how closely many teachers followed the outline in the books regardless of the needs of students. Also, she noticed, there was a common belief among the staff that her instructional style would not work.

Julie had made several changes in the curriculum. She had adopted a tradebook approach to reading and integrated that with her language arts. She made available to the students a wide assortment of books that featured different races, exceptionalities, and socioeconomic classes. In some stories, both males and females were featured doing traditional as well as nontraditional activities. Stories were set in urban and rural settings, and some featured children with disabilities. It had taken Julie several months to acquire such a diverse collection of books for her students, and she had even spent some of her own money for the books, but the excitement the students had shown about the materials made the expense worthwhile.

She also had several computers in her class. A computer lab was down the hall, but Julie wanted her students to use the computer on a regular basis. When she discovered that Richard's father owned a computer store, she convinced him to lend the class two iMacs, and she convinced Mr. Griffin to purchase six more at cost. Several of the students from Briar Creek had computers at home. Charles and Elaine, Julie discovered, were wizards at the computer. Julie encouraged them to help the other students (and herself—since she had taken only one computer course at State U). The two students enjoyed this assignment and often had a small group of students remain after school to receive their help. Julie was pleased at how well Charles and Elaine handled this responsibility. Lester and Ben were Charles's favorite students, they liked the computer, but Julie believed they liked Charles and his electric wheelchair even more. Julie had heard them say on several occasions that Charles was "cool." Lester's and Ben's work was showing a steady improvement, and Charles enjoyed having two good friends. This friendship, Julie believed, had excellent mutual benefits for all concerned, including herself.

Julie's mathematics pedagogy was built on two principles. First, she built on the thinking and life experiences of the students. Second, she sought to provide students with insights into the role of mathematics within the various contexts of society. These two principles of mathematics pedagogy guided her daily teaching. Julie often took her class to the supermarket, to the bank, and to engineering firms. She made certain that she selected firms that employed men and women of color and White women in positions of leadership. She often requested that a representative from these groups spend a few minutes with the students, explaining their roles and duties. On one occasion, Julie's students questioned a federal government official about the purpose and intent of the U.S. Census. One biracial student asked, "How are racial categories constructed?"

Julie took the students on field trips to supermarkets in different areas of town so the students could compare prices and quality of products (e.g., fruit, meat, and vegetables) between the suburban area and the inner-city area. On two occasions this led to a letter-writing campaign to the owner of the food chain to explain their findings. The students also wondered why the cost of gas was cheaper in the suburban areas than in the inner-city area. This became a math, social studies, and language arts lesson. Letters were written and interviews conducted to ascertain the cost of delivering the gas to the inner city as compared to the suburban area of the city, and to ascertain the rental fee for service station property in the inner city in comparison to the suburban areas. Math skills were used to determine if there needed to be a difference in gas prices between the areas after rental fees and delivery charges were taken into consideration.

Julie used advertisements and editorials from newspapers and magazines to help students see the real-life use of such concepts as sexism, justice, and equity. Julie supplemented her social studies curriculum on a regular basis. She found the text biased in several areas. She would integrate into the assigned curriculum information from the history and culture of different racial and ethnic groups. For example, when teaching about the settling of the local community years ago, she invited a Native American female historian and a White historian to give views on how the settling took place and on problems and issues associated with it. She invited an African American historian and a Latino historian to discuss what was presently happening in the area. She had her students identify toys that had been made in Third World countries, and she explored with them child labor and low-wage work that many transnational corporations had put into place in order to maximize corporate profits.

Students were usually encouraged to undertake different projects in an effort to provide a comprehensive perspective on the social studies unit under study. Choices were up to the student, but Julie maintained high expectations and insisted that excellence in every phase of the work was always necessary for each student. She made certain that during the semester each student was a project leader. She also made certain that boys and girls worked together. For example, Julie knew that Ben, Lester, and Charles usually stayed close together and did not have a girl as a member of their project team. She also knew that Carmen was assertive and had useful knowledge about the project on which they were working. She put Carmen on the project team.

Julie did have two problems with her class that she could not figure out. Shelly and Ernestine did not get along well with any of the African American students, especially Ben and Lester. George and Hank, two White boys from Briar Creek, had considerable difficulty getting along with José and went out of their way to be mean to Lourdes and Maria. Julie was puzzled by George's and Hank's behavior; she did not think it was racially motivated because both of the boys got along pretty well with Shelly. She labored over this problem and discussed it with the school counselor. She wondered if she didn't have a problem related to a combination of race, class, and gender in George's and Hank's relationship with José, Lourdes, and Maria. She also concluded that she might have a social-class problem among the African American students.

Julie decided to discuss her concerns with the students individually. After some discussion, she discovered that Shelly's and Ernestine's problem with Ben and Lester was related to so-cial class and color. Both Shelly and Ernestine had very fair skin color. They had grown up in a predominantly White middle-class community and had spent very little time around other African American students. Ben and Lester were dark-skinned male students who lived in a very poor neighborhood. Julie felt that if her assumptions were true, she would need help with this problem. She was successful in getting an African American child psychiatrist to talk to her class. She did this in relationship to an art unit that examined "color, attitude, and feelings." His discussion enabled Julie to continue her discussion with Shelly and Ernestine and get them to examine their prejudice.

George and Hank admitted to Julie, after several discussions, that they did not care too much for any girls. But Hispanic girls who wore funny clothes and ate non-American foods were a big bore. It took Julie several months of talking with George and Hank, using different reading materials and having them all work on a group project under her direction, to get George and Hank to reduce some of their prejudices. At the end of the semester, Julie still believed this problem had not been completely resolved. Thus, she shared it with the sixth-grade teacher.

At the end of the school year, Julie felt very good about her first year. She knew she had grown as a teacher. She believed her professors at State U, her cooperating teacher, and her university supervisor would give her very high marks. They had encouraged her to become a reflective teacher—committed, responsible, and wholehearted in her teaching effort. Julie believed she was well on her way to becoming a reflective teacher, and she looked forward to her second year with enthusiasm.

She also realized that her sensitivity to things she did not know had grown, and she planned to engage in some learning over the summer. As she had become aware of resentments that students from low-income families felt toward students from upper-income families, she began to wonder what the city was doing to address poverty. She heard that the NAACP (National Association for the Advancement of Colored People), some Latino community leaders, and heads of homeless shelters were trying to work with the city council, and she wanted to find out more about how these groups viewed poverty in the city. She decided to join the NAACP so she could become more familiar with its activities. She also wanted to spend time with some Latino families, because before her teaching experience she had never talked directly with Latino adults; her principal suggested she should meet Luis Reyes, who directed a local community center and could help her do this. In addition, Julie felt somewhat overwhelmed by the amount of background information she had never learned about different groups in the United States and decided to start reading; because she enjoyed novels, she would start with some by Toni Morrison, Louise Erdrich, James Baldwin, and Maxine Hong Kingston. She would also read the novel by Sylvia Plath, *The Bell Jar*.

From what you know of Julie, what is her approach to multicultural education? Would you be comfortable doing as Julie did? Discuss Julie's teaching with your classmates. How would you change it?

CONCLUSION

In Julie's classroom, as in yours, race, class, gender, and disability are ascribed characteristics students bring to school that cannot be ignored. To teach with excellence, Julie had to affirm her students' diversity. Why do we say this?

For one thing, Julie needed to pay attention to her students' identities in order to help them achieve. She needed to acknowledge the importance of African American males to American life to hold the interest of Lester and Ben; she needed to acknowledge Mai-ka's and Chee's prior learning to help them learn English and school material; she needed to become familiar with her students' learning styles so her teaching would be most effective.

For another thing, Julie needed to pay attention to her students' personal and social needs to help them perceive school as a positive experience. Some of her students disliked other students because of prejudices and stereotypes. Some of her students did not know how to relate to people in wheelchairs or to people who looked or talked differently. Some of her students felt negative about their own abilities. These attitudes interfere not only with achievement, but also with one's quality of life, both as students today and later as adults in a pluralistic society.

Julie realized over the year the extent to which schools are connected with their social context. She remembered having to take a course called School and Society and had not understood why it was required. She remembered reading about societal pressures on schools; during the year, she had come to see how societal pressures translated into funding, programs, and local debates that directly affected resources and guidelines in her classroom. Further, she realized the extent to which students are connected with their own cultural context. The African American students, for example, emphasized their African American identity and did not want to be regarded as White; teachers who tried to be color blind regarded this as a problem, but teachers who found the community's diversity to be interesting saw it as a strength. On the other hand, immigrant students tried hard to fit in; Julie would not have understood why without considering why their families had immigrated and the pressures the children experienced.

Julie also knew that the future of the United States depends on its diverse children. Her students will all be U.S. adults one day, regardless of the quality of their education. But what kind of adults will they become? Julie wanted them all to be skilled in a variety of areas, to be clear and critical thinkers, and to have a sense of social justice and caring for others. Julie had some personal selfish motives for this: She knew her own well-being in old age would depend directly on the ability of today's children to care for older people when they become adults. She also knew her students of today would be shaping the society in which her own children would one day grow up. She wanted to make sure they were as well prepared as possible to be productive citizens who had a vision of a better society. She drew from all of the approaches, at one time or another, to address specific problems and needs she saw in the classroom. But the approach she emphasized, and the one that guided her planning, was education that is multicultural and social reconstructionist.

How will you approach excellence and equity in your own classroom? We can guarantee that all your students will have their identities shaped partly by their race, social class, and gender; all of them will notice and respond in one way or another to people who differ from themselves; and all of them will grow up in a society that is still in many ways racist, sexist, and classist. You are the only one who can guarantee what you will do about that.

Questions and Activities

1. Why is it important for teachers to strive to attain both excellence and equity for their students? What can you do to try to achieve both goals in your teaching?

2. What does each of these terms mean to you in relationship to classroom life: *race*, *language*, *class*, *gender*, and *disability*? How are your notions of these concepts similar to and different from those of your classmates?

3. Give an example of how such variables as race, language, class, and gender interact to influence the behavior of a particular student.

4. Name the five approaches to multicultural education identified by Grant and Sleeter. What are the assumptions and instructional goals of each approach?

5. In what significant ways does the "education that is multicultural and social reconstructionist" approach differ from the other four approaches? What problems might a teacher experience when trying to implement this approach in the classroom? How might these problems be reduced or solved?

6. Visit a school in your community and interview several teachers and the principal about activities and programs the school has implemented in multicultural education. Using the typology of multicultural education described by the authors, determine what approach or combination of approaches to multicultural education are being used

within the school. Share your findings with your classmates or fellow workshop participants.

7. Which approach to multicultural education is Ms. Wilson using? Which aspects of her teaching do you especially like? Which aspects would you change?

8. Which approach to multicultural education described by the authors would you be the most comfortable using? Why?

References

Albrecht, L. and Brewer, R. (1990). *Bridges of Power: Women's Multicultural Alliances*. Philadelphia: New Society Publishers.

Banks, J. A. (1994). *Multiethnic Education: Theory and Practice* (3rd ed.). Boston: Allyn and Bacon.

Banks, J. A. and Banks, C. A.M., (Eds.) (1995). *Handbook of Research on Multicultural Education*. New York: Macmillan.

Barrett, P. A. (Ed.). (1986). *To Break the Silence*. New York: Dell Publishing Company.

Bennett, C. E. (1990). *Comprehensive Multicultural Education* (2nd ed.). Boston: Allyn and Bacon.

Childs, J. B. (1994). The Value of Transcommunal Identity Politics. *Z Magazine* 7(7/8), 48–51.

Collins, C., Leondar-Wright, B., and Sklar, H. (1999). *Shifting Fortunes: The Perils of the Growing American Wealth Gap*. Boston: United for a Fair Economy.

Cortada, R. E. (1974). *Black Studies: An Urban and Comparative Curriculum*. Greenwich, CT: Xerox Publishing Group.

Fennema, E. and Peterson, P. L. (1987). Effective Teaching for Girls and Boys: The Same or Different? In D. C. Berliner and B. V. Rosenshine (Eds.), *Talks to Teachers* (pp. 111–125). New York: Random House.

Foreign-Born Population Tops 25 Million. (1998). *The Monterey County Herald*, April 9, A7.

Gates, H.L., Jr. (1999). *Wonders of the African World*. New York: Knopf.

Freire, P. (1973). *Education for Critical Consciousness*. New York: The Seaburg Press.

Freire, P. (1985). *The Politics of Education: Culture, Power, and Liberation*. Trans. by D. Macedo. Boston: Bergin and Garvey.

Grant, C. A. (1978). Education That Is Multicultural—Isn't That What We Mean? *Journal of Teacher Education, 29*, 45–49.

Grant, C. A. and Sleeter, C. E. (1986). *After the School Bell Rings*. Philadelphia: Falmer Press.

Jiobu, R. (1988). *Ethnicity and Assimilation*. Albany, NY: SUNY Press.

Leake, D. O. and Leake, B. L. (1992). Islands of Hope: Milwaukee's African American Immersion Schools. *The Journal of Negro Education 61*(1), 24–29.

Leo, J. (1990, Nov. 12). A Fringe History of the World. *U.S. News and World Report*, 25–26.

Martinez, E. (1999). The Cleansing of Ethnic Studies. *Z Magazine 12*(6), 31–37.

Mohr, N. (1990). *Felita*. New York: Bantam.

Myers, W. D. (1990). *Scorpions*. New York: Harper Trophy.

National Center for Education Statistics. (1999). [On-line]. Available: http://nces.ed.gov

Newman, K. S. (1993). *Declining Fortunes: The Withering of the American Dream*. New York: Basic Books.

Omatsu, G. (1994). The "Four Prisons" and the Movements of Liberation: Asian American Activism from the 1960s to the 1990s. In K. Aguilar-San Juan (Ed.), *The State of Asian America* (pp. 19–70). Boston: South End Press.

Paterson, K. (1987). *The Great Gilly Hopkins*. New York: Harper Trophy.

Pearson, C. S. (1992). Women as Learners: Diversity and Educational Quality. *Journal of Developmental Education, 16*(2), 2–4, 6, 8, 10, 38–39.

Pollard, D. S. and Ajirotutu, C. S. (1999). *Five Year Report: Malcolm X Academy*. Milwaukee, WI: African American Immersion Schools Evaluation Project.

Ratteray, J. D. (1990). African-American Achievement: A Research Agenda Emphasizing Independent Schools. In K. Lomotey (Ed.), *Going to School: The African-American Experience* (pp. 197–208). Albany, NY: SUNY Press.

Rivlin, A. M. (1992). *Reviving the American Dream: The Economy, the States, and the Federal Government*. Washington, DC: The Brookings Institution.

Schlesinger, A. M. (1992). *The Disuniting of America*. New York: Norton.

Shade, B. J. (1989). Afro-American Cognitive Patterns: A Review of the Research. In B. J. Shade (Ed.), *Culture, Style and the Educative Process* (pp. 94–115). Springfield, IL: Charles C Thomas Publisher.

Shaw, G. B. (1980). Back to Methuselah. In J. Bartlett (Ed.), *Familiar Quotations*. Boston: Little, Brown.

Shor, I. (1980). *Critical Teaching and Everyday Life*. Boston: South End Press.

Shor, I. (1986). *Culture Wars*. Boston: Routledge and Kegan Paul.

Sleeter, C. E. and Grant, C. A. (1991). Textbooks and Race, Class, Gender, and Disability. In M. W. Apple and L. K. Christian-Smith (Eds.), *Politics of the Textbook* (pp. 78–110). New York: Routledge, Chapman and Hall.

Sleeter, C. E. and Grant, C. A. (1999). *Making Choices for Multicultural Education: Five Approaches to Race, Class and Gender* (3rd ed.). New York: Wiley.

Snow, M. A. (1994). Primary Language Instruction: A Bridge to Literacy. In C. F. Leyba (Ed.), *Schooling and Language Minority Students: A Theoretical Framework* (2nd ed.), (pp. 133–164). Los Angeles: Evaluation, Dissemination and Assessment Center at California State University, Los Angeles.

Suzuki, B. (1989). Asian Americans as the 'Model Minority.' *Change* (Nov./Dec.), 13–19.

Swadener, E. B. (1990). Children and Families 'At Risk.' *Educational Foundations* (Fall), 17–39.

Takaki, R. (1989). *The Fourth Iron Cage: Race and Political Economy in the 1990's*. Paper presented at the Green Bay Colloquium on Ethnicity and Public Policy, Green Bay, WI.

Terkel, S. (1988). *The Great Divide: Second Thoughts on the American Dream*. New York: Pantheon Books.

Tetreault, M. K. T. (1989). Integrating Content about Women and Gender into the Curriculum. In J. A. Banks and C. A. M. Banks (Eds.), *Multicultural Education: Issues and Perspectives*, (pp. 124–144). Boston: Allyn and Bacon.

The Americans with Disabilities Act: Where Are We Now? (1991). *The Disability Rag 12*(1), 11–19.

U.S. Bureau of the Census. (1989). *Statistical Abstracts of the United States 1989*. Washington, DC: U.S. Government Printing Office.

U.S. Bureau of the Census. (1992). *Statistical Abstracts of the United States, 1992.* Washington, DC: U.S. Government Printing Office.

U.S. Bureau of the Census (1999). [On-line]. Available: http://www.census.gov

Viadero, D. (1990, November 28). Battle over Multicultural Education Rises in Intensity. *Education Week, 10,* 11.

Westkott, M. (1983). Women's Studies as a Strategy for Change: Between Criticism and Vision. In G. Bowles and R. D. Klein (Eds.), *Theories of Women's Studies* (pp. 210–218). London: Routledge and Kegan Paul.

Yep, L. (1975). *Dragonwings.* New York: Harper and Row.

Students from diverse religious and social-class groups experience equal status in classrooms and schools that have successfully implemented multicultural education.

Social Class
and Religion

The two chapters in Part II discuss the effects of two powerful variables on student behavior, beliefs, and achievement: social class and religion. Social class is a powerful variable in U.S. society despite entrenched beliefs about individual opportunity in the United States. As Anyon points out in Chapter 4, students who attend affluent suburban schools have more resources, better teachers, and better educational opportunities than do students who attend low-income, inner-city schools. Students from the lower, middle, and upper classes usually attend different kinds of schools and have teachers who have different beliefs and expectations about their academic achievement. The structure of educational institutions also favors middle- and upper-class students. Structures such as tracking, IQ tests, and programs for gifted and mentally retarded students are highly biased in favor of middle- and upper-class students.

Students who are socialized within religious families and communities often have beliefs and behaviors that conflict with those of the school. Religious fundamentalists often challenge the scientific theories taught by schools about the origin of human beings. They also attack textbooks and fictional books assigned by teachers that they believe violate or contradict their doctrines. Conflicts about the right to pray in the school sometimes divide communities.

The school should help students mediate between their home culture and the school culture. Uphoff, in Chapter 5, describes some promising ways in which this can be done.

CHAPTER 4

Inner Cities, Affluent Suburbs, and Unequal Educational Opportunity

Jean Anyon

Polls show that most White people in the United States believe that schools provide equal educational opportunity (Orfield & Yun, 1999). This chapter demonstrates that contrary to this belief, educational opportunity in the United States is not always equitable, with the contrast between inner-city and affluent suburban schools being the most glaring example of inequality. This chapter examines the differences between schooling in these two kinds of locales. Almost 80 percent of the country's low-income African American and Latino students live in the nation's fifty-one largest urban districts (National Center for Educational Statistics, 1996; 1998; Orfield & Yun, 1999). Although some African American and Latino families live in suburban localities, serious segregation exists within these communities, and low-income minorities in suburbs are likely either to attend schools in which children of color predominate, or to be placed in lower tracks of integrated schools (Freedman, 1999; Orfield & Easton, 1996; Orfield & Yun, 1999). However, America's large city school systems in the United States remain overwhelmingly (77 percent) non-White and poor (Anyon, 1997; Council of the Great City Schools, 1994), and affluent suburbs are almost entirely Caucasian (Baxandall & Ewen, 2000; Orfield & Yun, 1999). The separation of large numbers of upper-middle-class and wealthy Whites in affluent suburbs, and the majority of low-income African Americans and Latinos in inner cities, is unfortunately typical of U.S. metropolitan areas (Massey & Denton, 1993; Orfield & Yun, 1999). Because of this widespread segregation by income and race, comparisons of educational opportunity in inner cities and high-income suburbs can shed light not only on social class differences in schooling, but on inequalities in resources typically offered to significant percentages of low-income Blacks and Latinos and affluent Whites.

Although the focus of this chapter is the extensive inequalities of inner-city and affluent suburban education, it is important to note that, as Braddock (1990), Lucas (1999), and Oakes (1985) have pointed out, minority students in segregated suburban schools—as well as students of all colors in the lower track of almost any school—are likely to experience many of the inequalities documented here for inner-city schools. This chapter argues that unequal opportunity to learn may produce differential academic achievement by low-income urban and affluent suburban students, and that one consequence of this unequal achievement is inequality in future chances to obtain decent employment. The chapter also argues that chief among the underlying causes of unequal educational opportunity itself are the political and economic inequalities between central cities and more affluent suburbs. When students in inner-city schools are not prepared to compete economically with those from the affluent suburbs, the underlying causes of the differences in education are ultimately reinforced.

This chapter first discusses typical low-income urban and affluent suburban school conditions and resources, climate and culture, curriculum and instruction, and opportunities for teachers to improve their skills. Interspersed throughout are brief explanations of political and economic contributions to the creation of these educational differences. The final part of the chapter describes ideas that *all* teachers can use to counter unequal educational opportunity in their classrooms, schools, and communities.

DIFFERENCES BETWEEN AFFLUENT SUBURBAN AND INNER-CITY SCHOOLING

It is important to keep in mind, as the discussion unfolds, that the documentation of disadvantages in low-income urban schools, and of advantages in affluent suburban ones, is presented as describing typical but not universal circumstances. There are always exceptions to generalizations, no matter how widely a generalization may apply. Clearly, even wealthy districts may face problems of educational leadership, resources, student alienation, and discipline (Anyon, manuscript in progress). Every urban district has some outstanding teachers and educational programs, just as not all affluent suburban schools or teachers are of top quality. Moreover, it is important to point out that not all poor students are minority: Although a higher percentage of African Americans and Latinos live in poverty than do Whites, "less than half the poor [48 percent] are African American or Latino" (Blank, 1997, p. 15). Forty-eight percent of poor people nationally are White, and the remaining 4 percent are Native Americans, Asians, and other people of color (Blank, 1997).

Conditions and Resources

Suburban districts spend up to ten times as much on public education as do urban districts (Educational Testing Service, 1991; U.S. General Accounting Office, 1997). Despite the increases in state funds spent on city education systems in the last twenty years, almost 80 percent of large urban districts are funded at a lower rate than that of suburbs (U.S. General Accounting Office, 1997). Moreover, because urban districts typically spend up to one-quarter of their educational budgets to address the social and psychological needs of students living in high-risk poverty situations, a smaller percentage of urban educational funds is available for regular classroom programs (Firestone, Goertz, & Natriello, 1997). Because education in the United States has been paid for primarily by local property taxes, property-rich suburbs have had more money for this function than have the cities, which since the Great Depression of the 1930s have had less wealth to tax (Anyon, 1997). Federal tax incentives (as well as direct subsidies to developers and home buyers) financed family and business movement to the suburbs over the last fifty years and have contributed to the paucity of economic wealth in urban neighborhoods. In cities that have developed prosperous downtowns, like New York, Detroit, Los Angeles, Baltimore, and Boston, considerable wealth is concentrated in the central business and more affluent residential sections and has yet to be proportioned in a manner that would compensate for the poverty of low-income neighborhoods (Anyon, 1997).

In 1997, central cities held only 29 percent of the national population and comprised less than 12 percent of the national electorate (Anyon, 1997). After having been dominated for almost two centuries by rural elites, congressional as well as state legislatures are now numerically dominated by representatives of suburban taxpayers (Anyon, 1997; Edsall & Edsall, 1991; Judd & Swanstrom, 1994). Despite recent infusions of funds by most legislatures into urban school systems, money adequate to compensate for the long-term deterioration of school buildings, and past and current poverty of the schools and their students, has not been provided (Education Week, 1998; Kozol, 1991).

Consequences of long-term, inadequate school funding include decayed buildings not adequately maintained or capable of being wired for modern technology, too few computers, and insufficient instruction for teachers in how to use this technology (Educational Testing Service, 1997). In addition, inadequate funding often leads to the unavailability of sufficient curriculum materials and advanced course offerings; unequipped science labs; large classes in primary grades without teaching assistants; insufficient numbers of professionals to provide counseling, speech, and other services; and a minimum of athletics, art, or music classes (Annenberg Challenge, 1999; Johnson, 1999; U.S. Department of Education, 1993). Moreover, many urban districts do not have the resources to hire enough vice principals and office secretaries to allow principals the time to be effective instructional leaders (Anyon, 1980; 1997).

Affluent suburbs, on the other hand, typically have had the tax proceeds to provide and maintain attractive buildings, a full array of honors and other enrichment courses and clubs, well-supplied classrooms, and funds to prepare teachers to use new materials, and sufficient numbers of trained support staff such as psychiatrists, speech, and other supplementary classroom personnel. Most wealthy communities have the funds to hire support for school administrators, who are therefore able to pay more attention to the improvement of instruction and student performance. In cases where the community feels property taxes need to be augmented, residents have the educational skills and social clout necessary to raise additional moneys through grant proposals and other fund-raising activities. These funds are used to purchase playground equipment, athletics equipment and other expenses of team sport competitions, the services of librarians and books for school libraries, and other resources (Anyon, 1981; 1997; Firestone, Goertz, & Natriello, 1997; Johnson, 1999; Kohn, 1998; U.S. Department of Education, 1993).

Curriculum and Instruction

What counts as knowledge in many classroom lessons and curriculum materials in inner-city schools are the mechanics of phonics, writing, spelling, and math. Such information, called "basic skills," is typically presented to students in workbooks and on dittos (Anyon, 1980; 1997; Education Trust, 1996; Haberman, 1996; Oakes, 1985). While the mechanics of communication and mathematics are certainly important, they often dominate the inner-city curriculum to the exclusion of other, more conceptual, analytical, and critical understandings, analyses, and content areas (Anyon, 1994; 1995; Haberman, 1996). Studies of big-city school systems document the superficiality of social studies and science content offered to inner-city high school students and the lack of honors courses in which students can participate (Annenberg Challenge, 1999; Anyon, 1997; Christman & Macpherson, 1996; Consortium on Chicago School Research, 1996a) . The Education Trust (1996) points out that "nearly one in four central-city schools . . . had vacancies that they could not fill with a qualified teacher. In response, principals use substitutes, hire less-qualified teachers, or cancel courses. Consequently, central-city high school students have only about a 50 percent chance of having a qualified math or science teacher" (p. 7).

In affluent suburban schools, on the other hand, one most often finds a wide range of courses and topics of study, richly illustrated texts and trade books, and student research resources of many kinds. What counts as knowledge in these settings will include the mechanics of language and math but is more likely also to involve high-status systems of understanding found in the social and natural sciences and the humanities (Anyon, 1980, p. 81; Education Trust, 1996; Haberman, 1996). The fuller curriculum offered in affluent schools can provide motivation and intellectual challenge and can offer opportunities for students to excel academically that are not present in a curriculum that concentrates on basic skills.

For example, social studies teachers in an affluent suburban district I studied used an elementary textbook series entitled *Concepts and Inquiry,* written by staff at The Educational Research Council Social Science Program. This series discusses at length such topics as social class, the power of dominant ideas, and competing world views. Using a text from this series (Bostick, Davis, Gramm, Steinback, & Zweig, 1977), the district's objectives for fourth- and fifth-grade social studies included the following: "To understand the roles of savings, capital, trade, education, skilled labor, skilled managers, and cultural factors (religious beliefs, attitudes toward change) in the process of economic development"; "to distinguish a mixed economy from a totalitarian system"; "to understand the power of controlling ideas"; and "to understand that the controlling ideas of Western culture came largely from two preceding cultures: the Judaic and Greco-Roman" (p. 19).

Fifth-grade teachers in that affluent school discuss their curriculum:

> "It's not just academics; [the students] need to learn to think. They will have important jobs, and they need to be able to think things through."

> Referring to her science curriculum, one teacher said, "I try to get them to create an environment where they can solve problems—they manipulate variables and solve a problem."

> "Our students need the basics—to think through problems and to write well."

> "Our students will go to the best schools, and we have to prepare them."
> (Adapted from Anyon,1981; see also Anyon, manuscript in progress)

Observers such as Haberman (1996), Education Trust (1996), and Anyon (1994; 1995) have reported that teaching strategies in low-income urban classrooms tend to present students material that is comprised of unconnected social studies facts to be copied from the board or a book, lists of vocabulary words not in context to be looked up in a dictionary and put in sentences, arithmetic facts to memorize, and steps to follow to solve arithmetic problems. Students may be asked to recall, with very little discussion of issues or causes, bits of information not strung together by conceptual understanding or historical background. Haberman (1996) calls this approach to teaching "the pedagogy of poverty." One observer called central city social studies teaching "the 'trivial pursuit' approach to knowledge" (Guadelli, 1999, personal communication).

Editors of The Education Trust (1996) report observing inner-city high school students being required to color in the different parts of speech over and over, on a ditto. Perhaps the saddest lessons I have ever observed were members of an 8th-grade inner-city science class taking turns reading aloud from the safety manual of science equipment for equipment the school did not own, and a unit on Great Literature in which an 11th-grade class spent several months reading *about* great literature without ever reading the literature itself (see also New Jersey State Department of Education, 1994).

Teaching strategies in affluent suburban classrooms may, of course, be boring and rote, with the mechanics of language and math an important priority. However, observers have noted that classroom activities also typically include interactive discussion, field trips, independent student projects, and research (Anyon, 1980; 1981; manuscript in progress; Lester & Onore, 1990). Teachers in affluent suburban areas are more likely to be certified in the subject they are teaching and to have a fuller background of education courses (Annenberg Challenge, 1999). As Linda Darling-Hammond (1996) has pointed out, a teacher-preparation background typically produces teachers who are less authoritarian and more student-centered and who value student inquiry more highly than do teachers without this background.

The vast majority of school districts attempt to bring long-time teachers up to date and to improve the skills of all instructional personnel. As in other areas of education, sufficient funds are important. The lack of money in urban districts has meant that methods of upgrading the skills of urban teachers have typically involved half- or whole-day workshops with little or no follow up in teachers' classrooms, little if any paid time to visit master teachers in other schools or at conferences (to learn more about the new skill), a minimum of new materials with which to use the skill, and little peer pressure or administrative incentive to master the skill (Anyon, 1997; Philadelphia Children Achieving Challenge, 1996). A bright note in national school reform efforts of the 1990s was the introduction of funds to extend efforts to upgrade the skills of urban teachers. These efforts involve activities and resources long available in most affluent suburban districts (see, for example, Philadelphia Children Achieving Challenge, 1996).

Affluent suburbs most often have the funds to carry out a full range of activities to implement new teaching methodologies (such as in-class modeling, attendance at conferences, observations of teachers practiced in using the skill, and newly acquired resources to use). Moreover, the expectations and clout of the parent population usually ensure that districts use sanctions to motivate teachers to increase their pedagogical skills (Anyon, 1994; Kohn, 1998; Lester & Onore, 1990).

School Climate

Teachers are likely to face a difficult situation in inner-city schools. In addition to funding and curricular disadvantages described above, they typically confront students whose poverty and lack of family resources make their young lives highly stressful (Firestone, Goertz, & Natriello, 1997; Kotlowitz, 1991). Many central-city families do not have the financial resources to provide their children with sufficient food, clean clothes every day, warm coats, medical or dental care, toys, books or other belongings, or a quiet spot at home in which to do homework (Quint, 1995). Many students as young as seven or eight are responsible for feeding and caring for younger siblings while parents work at multiple jobs. Many elementary students care for ill relatives and are expected to find ways to bring food and income into the home. Due to a lack of adequate medical care, some suffer untreated long-term illness and physical, emotional, or other disabilities. Estimates by school personnel I have worked with are that up to 20 percent of students in inner-city schools are homeless or "hidden homeless" (bunking with relatives or friends) (Anyon, 1995).

These desperate circumstances make many students anxious and angry, and, as a result, perhaps aggressive, withdrawn, or confrontational. Such students can be difficult to teach. Moreover, many inner-city students express hopelessness about the future—as implied by this statement of a ten-year-old girl: "There ain't no jobs out there; that's why kids drop out" (Anyon, 1995). Both teachers and students are aware of the lack of decent prospects for urban non-college-bound youth. This knowledge can pervade the atmosphere of high poverty schools, producing what has been called a culture of resignation and despair (Anyon, 1997; Consortium on Chicago School Research, 1996a; 1996b).

Some teachers respond to the difficult situation by going out of their way to attempt to support and nurture their charges. Other teachers react to the overwhelming situation of their students, and to the lack of support their school districts provide them, with anger and frustration—transmitting these feelings to their classes in the form of unsympathetic attitudes, callous treatment, and unchallenging busy work (Anyon, 1997; Consortium on Chicago School Research, 1996a; 1996b; Philadelphia Children Achieving Challenge, 1996). Some inner-city teachers explain:

> "You can't teach here . . . everyday it's something. . . .
> Mornings the kids come in there's been a shooting or something,
> and that's all they can think about. It doesn't matter what
> techniques you use, it doesn't make any difference."
> "The [students] have so many problems . . . and nobody cares.
> The parents don't care, the kids don't care, and nobody does their
> job. Teachers 'get over' and take off whenever they feel like it."
> "We think, 'they're only going to sweep floors'—why teach
> them science?"
> "These students don't *deserve* [field trips]. They don't know
> how to act."
> "When you realize who they [the students are] you laugh, and
> you can't take it [teaching] seriously." (Anyon, 1997, p. 152)

Student responses to unsympathetic teachers may be hostile and uncooperative. Too many urban schools thus become chaotic, angry places, where students roam the halls and teachers scream at them to get in class, sit down, and be quiet.

The economic and political resources available to the majority of affluent families and schools typically produce classroom and school climates that are more conducive to teaching and learning. Of course, not all affluent students are angels, and some are troubled and difficult to deal with (think, for example, of the 1999 student killings at Columbine High School in Colorado); and certainly there are teachers whose classes are uncooperative and not well managed. But affluent families and schools can afford sufficient numbers of professionals—psychologists, medical personnel, tutors, and other specialists—as well as classroom assistants to help both students and teachers. Moreover, the past experiences of families and school personnel in affluent communities normally provide hope—a positive view of the future: the expectation that on a child's high school graduation, and with hard work, then college, perhaps graduate school, a decent job will result. Such anticipation of future rewards to educational effort can motivate students and teachers to work hard for high achievement.

Contrasts between poverty and affluent schools are apparent in the following passage, in which I describe my reactions to an affluent school after having spent several months observing and working with teachers in Marcy Elementary (a pseudonym), a K–8 inner-city school:

> After being in Marcy yesterday where chaos filled the halls, classrooms were devoid of children's drawings or stories, many ceilings were cracked with plaster falling, and teachers tried angrily and in vain to get the students to go back in their classrooms, I went into my daughter's third grade class today. She attends a "model" public school in an affluent neighborhood. Three-quarters of the parents are White professionals; most of the children of color who attend are from middle and upper-middle class families. It is widely known as a "very good school," and is occasionally written up in the *New York Times.*
>
> The contrast with the inner-city school was overwhelming. The kids were sitting, doing various activities, all over the room, on the floor, at tables—one boy was curled on top of a low book shelf, reading a book. The children were reading; writing; making Father's Day presents from brightly colored materials; and were working with manipulables of several kinds. Materials, books, and supplies were everywhere, and in abundance. The children's work was on display on the walls, hanging from the ceiling, and in the hall. Their murals and paper-maché projects decorated the back of the room. The T-shirts which they had tie-died and silk-screened for their "Olympics Field Day" were hanging from rope strung across the room, drying. The children were working easily, absorbed, in little clusters. Chatter filled the air, and smiles; and—most importantly—they seemed involved and interested in what they were doing. They seemed happy to be there.
>
> It seemed unbelievable to me how wonderful it was. It made me realize how far I had gone, over the last few months, toward accepting the starkness of Marcy's bare and vacant rooms, the angry, wounded-looking children, and the resentful, hostile teachers—as acceptable. (adapted from Anyon, 1997, p. 36)

CONSEQUENCES OF THESE DIFFERENCES

I argue that unequal opportunities to learn can result in unequal educational achievement, as affluent suburban students are provided the wherewithal to achieve—and to learn high-status knowledge, what some people call "social capital"—while inner-city youngsters are typically denied those opportunities (see also Duke, 1998). The differences in educational achievement, in turn, may reinforce economic inequalities, because the majority of inner-city youth are not prepared for and/or can not afford to go to college and have not been equipped by their schools with the academic skills demanded by the vast majority of decent jobs; they have been prepared only for low-skill jobs, almost all of which pay wages at or near the poverty threshold (Dembo & Morehouse, 1997; Mishel et al., 1999). Affluent youngsters, on the other hand, have been prepared by their schools for college, perhaps for professional study, and thus for the likelihood of managerial or professional positions. The economic inequality in the occupations, salaries, and ultimate places of residence of the urban poor and affluent suburbanites goes a long way toward reinforcing the political and economic differences that gave rise to the educational inequalities in the first place.

WHAT TEACHERS CAN DO

Where in this circle of unequal opportunity can teachers intervene? What kinds of difference can teachers make to interrupt the cycle of educational and social poverty and affluence? This final section describes tasks and resources that would be useful for all teachers and that would contribute to attitudes and practices promoting a more equitable distribution of possibilities for U.S. youth.

Teachers can develop in students of all classes and races a critical understanding of how U.S. society works, how economic and political systems have contributed to the privilege of some and the disadvantage of others, and how students in all locales can work to change the inequities. Teachers can foster such understandings by bringing into the curriculum the history of ordinary people—racial, ethnic, and labor history, for example—and by discussing ways in which their interests and those of powerful corporate and government groups often conflict (e.g., regarding pay at work, the right to organize labor unions, and the concentration of corporations that keeps consumer prices high, for example). Large corporate wealth and donations that influence government officials and policy; and attempts by corporations to influence political and other social choices of ordinary people through television shows and commercials, newspapers, textbooks and other school investments, and by Hollywood movies all need to be discussed (Chomsky, 1998; Domhoff, 1998; Herman & Chomsky, 1988; Zinn, 1999).

Teachers can introduce students to the methods that citizens have used to fight for their own rights and the rights of those who have been denied them. Lesson plans and units can be prepared that present these ideas to students in constructive ways. Elementary teachers and instructors in all secondary subjects can find ways to use the resources cited below to incorporate such information into their lessons.

Resources that will be useful include such progressive magazines as *Dollars and Sense,* *Teaching Tolerance,* and *Rethinking Schools.* Organizations such as the Anti-Defamation League of B'nai B'rith, Educators for Social Responsibility, National Labor Committee, Teaching for Change, Syracuse Cultural Workers, City Lore, and Teachers and Writers Collaborative have prepared excellent teaching materials. All have excellent web sites. Two particularly useful web sites with important links to teacher resources are www.teachingforchange.org (maintained by The Network of Educators on the Americas) and The Urban Education Web (www.eric-web.tc.columbia.edu, (maintained by Teachers College, Columbia University). Highly significant as models are histories of social movements like the civil rights movement of the 1950s and 1960s, the anti-Vietnam War movement, the women's movement, labor and Latino organizations, and ethnic struggles by Italian, Jewish, and Irish Americans, among others. The list of books in Table 4.1 can be helpful for locating background information and/or pedagogical resources to teach for a more just society.

Teachers in central cities need much support: better work environments, more and better teaching materials, and professional assistance of all kinds. Without these, it is extremely difficult to maintain excellence in one's day-in-and-day-out teaching. The committed, outstanding teachers I have observed in urban schools share at least two characteristics. First, they believe that their students have the capacity to learn what other students learn and can ultimately make positive contributions to society. Second, these teachers (as do most good teachers everywhere) typically acquire information about their students' cultures, histories, languages, and ways of achieving dignity—remembering that many of their students have struggled to survive in a hostile economic and social environment. These professionals demonstrate that they care about their students by not giving up on them and by working hard to teach them well.

Just as important, however, city teachers need to resist the pressures that lead to rote, ditto-driven modes of classroom instruction; they can seek out other professionals who attempt to teach for meaning and critical understanding in urban classrooms and do likewise (various teacher networks and organizations, like The National Writing Project, Urban Education at Teachers College, Columbia University, and others listed in this chapter are available on the Internet). Teachers in all kinds of locales can take initiatives to develop these sensitivities and locate resources to learn enough about groups of people who differ from themselves and, in affluent schools, who differ from their students, to develop respect for those who may be poorer, a different color, or speak a different language.

Teachers do not usually have the time or inclination to become involved in the community in which they teach. Nevertheless, teachers can and should reach out to community/ neighborhood groups; they can and should find out about such neighborhood assets as economic development groups, other nongovernmental organizations, political action citizen groups, parent coalitions, representatives of local hospitals and business corporations, fraternal orders, religious congregations, and social agencies.

Large numbers of active, involved groups exist in most urban and suburban communities. Teachers can invite members of these groups to classroom and school activities, with the intention of involving the organizations in efforts to (in the inner city) improve the schools and assist the families, and (in all neighborhoods) to offer suggestions for reaching out to disadvantaged groups. Lessons and units can be designed that introduce and involve students in interaction with residents of nursing homes, homeless shelters, economic development

Table 4.1 Teaching for Justice: Helpful Books

Anyon, J. (1997). *Ghetto Schooling: A Political Economy of Urban Educational Reform.* New York: Teachers College Press.

Ayres, B. (Ed.). (1996). *City Kids, City Teachers: Reports from the Front Row.* New York: New Press.

Ayres, B. and Greene, M. (Eds.). (1998). *Teaching for Social Justice: A Democracy and Education Reader.* New York: New Press.

Banks, J. A. (1997). *Teaching Strategies for Ethnic Studies* (6th ed.). Boston: Allyn and Bacon.

Bigelow, B. (1996). *Rethinking Our Classrooms: Teaching for Equity and Justice.* Milwaukee, WI: Rethinking Schools.

Collins, M. (1992). *"Ordinary" Children, Extraordinary Teachers.* Charlottesville, VA: Hampton Roads Publishing Co.

Debs, E. and Constantine, R. (1995). *Gentle Rebel: Letters of Eugene V. Debs.* Champagne: University of Illinois.

Delpit, L. (1996). *Other People's Children: Cultural Conflict in the Classroom.* New York: New Press.

Eldridge, D. (1997). *Teacher Talk: Multicultural Lesson Plans for the Elementary Classroom.* Needham Heights, MA: Allyn and Bacon.

Finn, P. (1999). *Literacy with an Attitude: Educating Working-Class Children in Their Own Self-Interest.* Albany, NY: SUNY Press.

Georgakas, D., and Surkin, M. (1998). *Detroit, I Do Mind Dying: A Study in Urban Revolution.* Cambridge, MA: South End Press.

King, J. (Ed.). (1997). *Preparing Teachers for Cultural Diversity.* New York: Teachers College Press.

King, M. L., Jr., and Foner, P. (1995 reprint). *The Black Panthers Speak.* New York: DaCapo Press.

King, M. L., Jr., and King, C. S. (1992). *I Have a Dream: Writings and Speeches That Changed the World.* San Francisco: Harper.

Knapp, M. (1995). *Teaching for Meaning in High-Poverty Classrooms.* New York: Teachers College Press.

Kohl, H. (1990 reissue). *36 Children.* New York: New American Library.

Kohl, H. (1996). *I Won't Learn From You and Other Thoughts on Creative Maladjustment.* New York: New Press.

Kraft, B. (1995). *Mother Jones: One Woman's Fight for Labor.* Boston: Clarion Books.

Ladson-Billings, G. (1997). *The Dreamkeepers: Successful Teachers of African-American Children.* San Francisco, CA: Jossey-Bass.

Table 4.1   Continued

Levin, M. (1998). *Teach Me! Kids Will Learn When Oppression Is the Lesson*. New York: Monthly Review Press.

Meier, D. (1997). *Learning in Small Moments: Life in an Urban Classroom*. New York: Teachers College Press.

Meier, D. (1995). *The Power of Their Ideas: Lessons for America from a Small School in Harlem*. Boston, MA: Beacon Press.

Parks, R. and Haskins, J. (1992). *Rosa Parks: My Story*. New York: Dial.

Perry, T. and Delpit, L. (Eds.). (1998). *The Real Ebonics Debate: Power, Language, and the Education of African-American Children*. Boston: Beacon.

Rathbone, C. (1998). *On the Outside Looking In: One Year in an Inner-City School*. New York: Atlantic Monthly Press.

Rose, M. (1993). *Possible Lives: The Promise of Public Education in America*. New York: Penguin Books.

Schneidewind, N. (1984). *Open Minds to Equality: A Sourcebook of Learning Activities to Promote Race, Sex, Class, and Age Equity*. Englewood Cliffs, NJ: Prentice-Hall.

Sleeter, C. (1996). *Multicultural Education as Social Activism*. Albany, NY: SUNY Press.

Weiner, L. (1999). *Urban Teaching: The Essentials*. New York: Teachers College Press.

Williams, B. (1996). *Closing the Achievement Gap: A Vision for Changing Beliefs and Practices*. Alexandria, VA: Association for Supervision and Curriculum Development.

Wilson, W. J. (1997). *When Work Disappears: The World of the New Urban Poor*. New York: Vintage Books.

Zinn, H. (1999). *A People's History of the United States* (20th anniversary ed.). New York: Harper Collins.

groups, businesses and religious organizations, daycare centers, soup kitchens, and political action groups concerned with voting, housing, job creation and training, urban renewal, and the building of low-income homes in affluent areas.

The publications listed in Table 4.2 can assist teachers who would like to involve the community and community organizations in school programs.

In urban areas, a number of community development groups work with educators and residents to link education reform and community development. Given the power of poverty and political isolation to make school reform in cities significantly more difficult than it would otherwise be, the results of these groups are impressive. They are a good source of advice and information for all teachers. Table 4.3 includes the national headquarters of each organization.

Table 4.2 Involving the Community in School Programs: Resources

Annenberg Institute of School Reform. (1998). *Reasons for Hope, Voices for Change: A Report of the Annenberg Institute on Public Engagement for Public Education.* Providence, RI: Author.

Cahill, M. (1998). *Schools and Community Partnerships: Reforming Schools, Revitalizing Communities.* Chicago: Cross City Campaign for Urban School Reform.

Cross City Campaign for Urban School Reform. (1996). *Building Bridges: Eight Case Studies of Schools and Communities Working Together.* Chicago: Author.

Cross City Campaign for Urban School Reform. (1998). *Community Organizing for School Reformers.* Chicago: Author.

Kretzmann, J. (1992). *Community Based Development and Local Schools: A Promising Partnership.* Evanston, IL: Center for Urban Affairs and Policy Research, Northwestern University.

Rivera, F. and Erlich, J. (1998). *Community Organizing in a Diverse Society* (3rd ed.). Boston: Allyn and Bacon.

Shirley, D. (1997). *Community Organizing for Urban School Reform.* Austin: University of Texas Press.

Teachers can call on representatives of these groups to make presentations to school staff, students, parents, and community organizations. Lesson plans and units can be written to involve classes with these groups. Successful programs that combine school and neighborhood coalitions have resulted from such contact (Anyon 1997; Finn 1999). Students in these collaborations can learn an important lesson: They can have a positive impact on their environment, on their lives, and on the lives of others.

TO MAKE A DIFFERENCE

In closing, I want to briefly address this question: "Why would a teacher seek employment in an inner-city school?" Committed, high-quality teaching in any community—urban, suburban, or rural—is fundamental to the readiness of each student to compete in the labor market and to participate fully in political and community life. A teacher in the central city can make a difference every time she or he connects with, supports, and nurtures a single student.

However, high-quality teaching is important for the society as a whole, as well: True democracy depends on an educated citizenry. Education that is seriously unequal throughout a social system not only threatens democratic political institutions, but it also legitimates and supports economic practices that create poverty (by, for example, allowing people in the United States to blame the victims—the inner city students). Depending on how one counts, between 30 and 55 million people have been living in poverty in the United States in recent years

Table 4.3 Community Development Groups

Association of Community Organizations for Reform Now (ACORN)
117 West Harrison Street, Room 200
Chicago, IL 60605

Center for Neighborhood Technology (publishes the monthly *Neighborhood Works*, which chronicles attempts nationwide to strengthen urban neighborhoods through community organizing)
2125 W. North Ave.
Chicago, IL 60647

Cross City Campaign for Urban School Reform
407 Dearborn Street, Suite 1725
Chicago, IL 60605

Highlander Center
1959 Highlander Way
New Market, TN 37820

Industrial Areas Foundation (IAF)
Texas Interfaith Education Fund
1106 Clayton Lane, Suite 120W
Austin, TX 78723

National Coalition of Education Activists
P.O. Box 679
Rhinebeck, NY 12572

National Council of La Raza
11 19th Street, NW
Washington, DC 20036

Network of Educators on the Americas
P.O. Box 73038
Washington, DC 20050

(Dembo & Morehouse, 1997; Schwarz & Volgy, 1993; U.S. Bureau of the Census, 1995). This, to my mind, presents a serious challenge to us all.

Throughout the history of the United States, citizens concerned with social justice have found ways to express their ideas and to work for change in laws and practices that would promote equality. As this chapter points out, workers have organized for rights on the job, for better pay, for employer-provided health care; and people of color have challenged discrimination in transportation, voting, housing, education, and job opportunities through legal means, nonviolent demonstrations, and—when needed—more aggressive measures. This work is not finished; millions of people are still denied full opportunity; the struggle continues. Although all teachers can contribute to movements for social justice, urban teachers are in an important location in regard to this effort.

Teaching well in U.S. inner cities is vital to social change, in part because of the concentration of poor people there. As we know, 80 percent of poor people of color live in central cities; but what is not so often discussed is that in some metropolitan areas most of the low-income students are White (e.g., Buffalo, NY) and, in fact, almost half of the poor White people in this country live in our central cities. Because so many of the poor live in close proximity in urban areas, their combined efforts—if channeled into constructive protest and organized into social movements—could lead to significant change.

Obtaining social justice on a large scale requires not only demonstrations and rallies, but also speaking in public, participating in and organizing community meetings, writing proposals and petitions, and working in many capacities with officials at city hall, in state and federal legislatures, in offices, and in nongovernmental organizations, including corporations and banks. Education is essential to these activities. Urban teachers can play a major role in social change by being committed to their students' potential and by teaching them well. The challenge to make a difference in urban schools is great, as is the opportunity.

Acknowledgement

I would like to thank Elizabeth G. Cohen and Michael S. Knapp, and especially James A. Banks, for very helpful suggestions on previous drafts of this chapter.

Questions and Activities

1. According to the author, why do affluent suburban schools have much more money than do schools in inner-city communities? How does the social-class status of the community in which students are socialized affect their life chances and educational opportunities?

2. What are some of the *challenges* and *opportunities* of teaching in inner-city schools? What are some of the *challenges* and *opportunities* of teaching in affluent suburban schools? In which kind of school do you think teachers can make the most difference? Why? In which kind of school would you prefer to teach? Why?

3. A number of teachers, scholars, and researchers have written powerful accounts of effective ways to teach low-income students of color. Working individually or with a group of classmates or workshop colleagues, read one account of such work with these students in one of the books listed below. Share the information with your class or workshop in an interesting presentation, such as a simulated television talk show, a role play, or using reader's theater:

    Collins, M. and Tamarkin, C. (1982). *Marva Collins' Way*. Boston: Houghton Mifflin.

    Darling-Hammond, L. (1997). *The Right to Learn: A Blueprint for Creating Schools That Work*. San Francisco: Jossey-Bass.

    Delpit, L. (1995). *Other People's Children: Cultural Conflict in the Classroom*. New York: The New Press.

    Lightfoot, S. L. (1983). *The Good High School: Portraits of Character and Culture*. New York: Basic Books. (Chapters 1 and 2)

Meier, D. (1995). *The Power of Their Ideas: Lessons for America*. Boston: Beacon Press.

Quint, S. (1994). *Schooling Homeless Children: A Model for America's Public Schools*. New York: Teachers College Press.

4. Spend several days observing in a low-income school in an inner city or in a rural community. Also, make observations in an affluent public or private school. If possible, interview several of the teachers in each school. Write a paper based on your observations. How are your observations similar to those made by the author of this chapter? How are they different? How are your observations similar to and different from those made by your classmates? Why?

References

Annenberg Challenge. (1999). Who's Teaching What, and to Whom? *Challenge Journal, 3*(2), 3.

Annenberg Institute for School Reform. (1998). *Reasons for Hope, Voices for Change: A Report of the Annenberg Institute on Public Engagement for Public Education*. Providence, RI: Author.

Anyon, J. (1980). Social Class and the Hidden Curriculum of Work. *Journal of Education, 162*(1), 67–92.

Anyon, J. (1981). Social Class and School Knowledge. *Curriculum Inquiry, 11*(1), 3–42.

Anyon, J. (1994). Teacher Development and Reform in an Inner City School. *Teachers College Record, 96*(1), 14–31.

Anyon, J. (1995) Inner City School Reform: Toward Useful Theory. *Urban Education, 30*(1), 1–11.

Anyon, J. (1997). *Ghetto Schooling: A Political Economy of Urban Educational Reform*. New York: Teachers College Press.

Anyon, J. (manuscript in progress). *A Political Economy of Opportunity in an Affluent Suburban School District: Only Some Students Get the Best*.

Ayres, B. (Ed.). (1996). *City Kids, City Teachers: Reports from the Front Row*. New York: New Press.

Ayres, B. and Greene, M. (Eds.). (1998). *Teaching for Social Justice: A Democracy and Education Reader*. New York: The New Press.

Baxandall, R. and Ewen, E. (2000). *Picture Windows: How the Suburbs Happened*. New York: Basic Books.

Bigelow, B. (1996). *Rethinking Our Classrooms: Teaching for Equity and Justice*. Milwaukee, WI: Rethinking Schools Ltd.

Blank, R. (1997). *It Takes a Nation: A New Agenda for Fighting Poverty*. Princeton, NJ: Princeton University Press.

Bostick, N., Davis, S., Gramm, W., Steinback, R., and Zweig, M. (1977). *Choices and Decisions: Economics and Society*. Boston, MA: Allyn and Bacon.

Braddock, J. (1990). *Tracking: Implications for Student Race-Ethnic Subgroups*. Baltimore: Johns Hopkins University Press.

Brecher, J. (1990). *Building Bridges: The Emerging Grassroots Coalition of Labor and the Community*. New York: Monthly Review Press.

Cahill, M. (1998). *Schools and Community Partnerships: Reforming Schools, Revitalizing Communities*. Chicago: Cross City Campaign for Urban School Reform.

Carson, C. and Foner, P. (1995 reprint). *The Black Panthers Speak*. New York: DaCapo Press.

Chomsky, N. (1998). *Propaganda and Control of the Public Mind*. Cambridge, MA: Ak Press Distribution.

Christman, J. and Macpherson, P. (1996). *The Five School Study: Restructuring Philadelphia's Comprehensive High Schools*. Philadelphia: Research for Action.

Collins, M. (1992). *"Ordinary" Children, Extraordinary Teachers*. Charlottesville, VA: Hampton Roads Publishing Co.

Consortium on Chicago School Research. (1996a). *A View from the Elementary Schools: The State of Reform in Chicago*. Chicago: Author.

Consortium on Chicago School Research. (1996b). *Charting Reform in Chicago: The Students Speak*. Chicago: Author.

Council of the Great City Schools. (1994). *National Urban Education Goals: 1992–1993 Indicators Report*. Washington, DC: Author.

Cross City Campaign for Urban School Reform. (1996). *Building Bridges: Eight Case Studies of Schools and Communities Working Together*. Chicago, IL: Author.

Cross City Campaign for Urban School Reform. (1998). *Community Organizing for School Reformers*. Chicago: Author.

Darling-Hammond, L. (1996). The Right to Learn and the Advancement of Teaching: Research, Policy, and Practice for Democratic Education. *Educational Researcher, 25(6)*, 5–17.

Debs, E. and Constantine, R. (1995). *Gentle Rebel: Letters of Eugene V. Debs*. Champagne: University of Illinois Press.

Delpit, L. (1995). *Other People's Children: Cultural Conflict in the Classroom*. New York: New Press.

Dembo, D. and Morehouse, W. (1997). *The Underbelly of the U.S. Economy: Joblessness and the Pauperization of Work in America*. New York: Council on International and Public Affairs and Apex Press.

Domhoff, G. (1998). *Who Rules America? Power and Politics in the Year 2000* (3rd ed.). Mountain View, CA: Mayfield Publishing Co.

Duke, N. (1998). For the Rich It's Richer: Print Experiences and Environments Offered to Children in Very Low- and Very High-SES First Grade Classrooms. Unpublished manuscript. East Lansing: Michigan State University.

Edsall, T. and Edsall, M. D. (1991). *Chain Reaction: The Impact of Race, Rights, and Taxes on American Politics*. New York: W. W. Norton.

Education Trust. (1996). *Education Watch: The 1996 Education Trust State and National Data Book*. Washington, DC: Author.

Education Week. (1998). *Quality Counts: The Urban Challenge* (Jan. 8). Bethesda, MD: Author.

Educational Testing Service. (1991). *The State of Inequality*. Princeton, NJ: Author.

Educational Testing Service. (1997). *Computers and Classrooms: The Status of Technology in U.S. Schools*. Princeton, NJ: Author.

Eldridge, D. (1997). *Teacher Talk: Multicultural Lesson Plans for the Elementary Classroom*. Needham Heights, MA: Allyn and Bacon.

Finn, P. (1999). *Literacy with an Attitude: Educating Working-Class Children in Their Own Self-Interest*. Albany, NY: SUNY Press.

Firestone, W., Goertz, M., Natriello, G. (1997). *From Cashbox to Classroom: The Struggle for Fiscal Reform and Educational Change in New Jersey*. New York: Teachers College Press.

Freedman, S. (1999). Suburbia Outgrows Its Image in the Arts. *New York Times*, (Feb. 28), 2–1.

Freire, P. (1970). *Pedagogy of the Oppressed*. New York: Herder and Herder.

Georgakas, D. and Surkin, M. (1998). *Detroit, I Do Mind Dying: A Study in Urban Revolution*. Cambridge, MA: South End Press.

Goodlad, J. (1984). *A Place Called School: Prospects for the Future*. New York: McGraw-Hill.

Haberman, M. (1996). The Pedagogy of Poverty Versus Good Teaching. In B. Ayres (Ed.), *City Kids, City Teachers* (pp. 118–130). New York: New Press.

Herman, E. and Chomsky, N. (1988). *Manufacturing Consent: The Political Economy of the Mass Media*. New York: Pantheon.

Hollins, E. (Ed.). (1999). *Pathways to Success in School: Culturally Responsive Teaching*. Mahwah, NJ: Lawrence Erlbaum.

Johnson, K. (1999). Separate but Unequal: Two Schools' Tales. *New York Times* (Jan. 14). p. A-1.

Judd, D. and Swanstrom, T. (1994). *City Politics: Private Power and Public Policy*. New York: Harper Collins.

King, C. and Barrett Osborne, L. (1997). *Oh, Freedom! Kids Talk about the Civil Rights Movements and the People Who Made It Happen*. New York: Knopf.

King, J. (Ed.). (1997). *Preparing Teachers for Cultural Diversity*. New York: Teachers College Press.

King, M.L, Jr., and King, C. S. (1992). *I Have a Dream: Writings and Speeches That Changed the World*. San Francisco: Harper.

Knapp, M. (1995). *Teaching for Meaning in High-Poverty Classrooms*. New York: Teachers College Press.

Kohl, H. (1990 reissue). *36 Children*. New York: New American Library.

Kohl, H. (1996). *I Won't Learn From You and Other Thoughts on Creative Maladjustment*. New York: The New Press.

Kohn, A. (1998). Only for My Kid—How Privileged Parents Undermine School Reform. *Phi Delta Kappan*, 79(8), 568–577.

Kotlowitz, A. (1991). *There Are No Children Here: The Story of Two Boys Growing Up in the Other America*. New York: Doubleday, Anchor Books.

Kozol, J. (1991). *Savage Inequalities: Children in America's Schools*. New York: Crown Publishers.

Kraft, B. (1995). *Mother Jones: One Woman's Fight for Labor*. Boston: Clarion Books.

Kretzmann, J. (1992). *Community Based Development and Local Schools: A Promising Partnership*. Evanston, IL: Center for Urban Affairs and Policy Research, Northwestern University.

Ladson-Billings, G. (1997 reprint). *The Dreamkeepers: Successful Teachers of African-American Children*. San Francisco: Jossey-Bass.

Lester, N. and Onore, C. (1990). *Learning Change: One School District Meets Language across the Curriculum*. Portsmouth, NH: Boynton/Cook.

Levin, M. (1998). *Teach Me! Kids Will Learn When Oppression Is the Lesson*. New York: Monthly Review Press.

Lucas, S. R. (1999). *Tracking Inequality: Stratification and Mobility in American High Schools*. New York: Teachers College Press.

Massey, D. and Denton, N. (1993). *American Apartheid: Segregation and the Making of the Underclass*. Cambridge, MA: Harvard University Press.

Meier, D. (1997). *Learning in Small Moments: Life in an Urban Classroooom*. New York: Teachers College Press.

Meier, D. (1995). *The Power of Their Ideas: Lessons for America from a Small School in Harlem*. Boston: Beacon Press.

Mishel, L. et al. (1999). *The State of Working America: 1998–1999*. Ithaca, NY: Cornell University Press.

National Center for Educational Statistics. (1996). *Urban Schools: The Challenge of Location and Poverty*. Washington, DC: Author.

National Center for Educational Statistics. (1998). *The Social Context of Education*. Washington, DC: Author.

New Jersey State Department of Education. (1994). *Comprehensive Compliance Investigation of the Newark Public Schools*. Trenton: Author.

Oakes, J. (1985). *Keeping Track: How Schools Structure Inequality*. New Haven, CT: Yale University Press.

Orfield, G. and Easton, S. (1996). *Dismantling Desegregation: The Quiet Reversal of Brown v. Board of Education*. New York: The New Press.

Orfield, G. and Yun, J.T. (1999). *Resegregation in American Schools* (manuscript). The Civil Rights Project, Harvard University, Cambridge, MA: Authors.

Parker, R. and Haskins, J. (1999 reprint). *Rosa Parks: My Story*. New York: Puffin Books.

Perry, T. and Delpit, L. (Eds.). (1998). *The Real Ebonics Debate: Power, Language, and the Education of African-American Children*. Boston: Beacon.

Philadelphia Children Achieving Challenge. (1996). *A First-Year Evaluation Report*. Philadelphia: Author.

Quint, S. (1995). *Schooling Homeless Children*. New York: Teachers College Press.

Rathbone, C. (1998). *On the Outside Looking In: One Year in an Inner-City School*. New York: Atlantic Monthly Press.

Rivera, F. and Erlich, J. (1998). *Community Organizing in a Diverse Society* (3rd ed.). Boston: Allyn and Bacon.

Rose, M. (1996). *Possible Lives: The Promise of Public Education in America*. New York: Penguin.

Schneidewind, N. (1984). *Open Minds to Equality: A Sourcebook of Learning Activities to Promote Race, Sex, Class, and Age Equity*. Englewood Cliffs, NJ: Prentice-Hall.

Schwarz, J. and Volgy, T. (1993). *The Forgotten Americans: Thirty Million Working Poor in the Land of Opportunity*. New York: Norton.

Shirley, D. (1997). *Community Organizing for Urban School Reform*. Austin: University of Texas Press.

Sleeter, C. (1996). *Multicultural Education as Social Activism*. Albany, NY: SUNY Press.

U.S. Bureau of the Census. (1995). *Census of the Population 1990*. Washington, DC: U.S. Government Printing Office.

U.S. Department of Education. (1993). *Prospects: The Congressionally Mandated Study of Educational Growth and Opportunity*. Washington, DC: U.S. Government Printing Office.

U.S. General Accounting Office. (1997). *School Finance: State Efforts to Reduce Funding Gaps between Poor and Wealthy Districts*. Washington, DC: U.S. Government Printing Office.

Weiner, L. (1999). *Urban Teaching: The Essentials*. New York: Teachers College Press.

Williams, B. (1996). *Closing the Achievement Gap: A Vision for Changing Beliefs and Practices in Education*. Alexandria, VA: Association for Supervision and Curriculum Development.

Wilson, W. J. (1997). *When Work Disappears: The World of the New Urban Poor*. New York: Vintage Books.

Zinn, H. (1999). *A People's History of the United States* (20th anniversary ed.). New York: Harper.

CHAPTER 5

Religious Diversity and Education

James K. Uphoff

A beautiful new mosque stands with its center dome and twin minarets vivid against the blue sky. Where in the United States is this religious center located? In Washington, DC, where many nations of the world send their diplomats? In New York City, the home of the United Nations? In Los Angeles? The answer to each of these questions is no.

The mosque is located on the flat, fertile farmland of northwest Ohio, just south of Toledo, deep in the heart of the midwestern United States. Another attractive mosque is located near Route I-75 just north of Cincinnati, Ohio. Unusual? Yes, but a vivid sign of the changing times as the kinds of religions in the United States become more diverse.

Watching local law enforcement officers chain and padlock a church door on the television news about fifteen years ago in the 1980s was unsettling to many people. Yet this scenario did happen in rural Nebraska, when a small, independent Protestant church decided to defy a state law requiring all teachers in the state to be certified. This church had recently created its own small school, which met in the church. However, the teaching staff did not meet the qualifications set by the law. The minister made national news as he, on behalf of the congregation, defied the law and all attempts of the authorities to reach a compromise.

In California's San Ramone School District, some parents raised objections to an education curriculum because it called for teachers and students to use decision-making techniques and because it was alleged to be teaching "secular humanism," considered by some people to be a type of religion ("Alleged 'Secular Humanism' Courses Attacked," 1986). The decision by the State of Kansas Board of Education in 1999 to remove all coverage of evolution from the state's tests and curriculum led Stephen Jay Gould to headline his August 23, 1999, viewpoint column in *Time*: "Dorothy, It's Really Oz." These examples are only the tip of a large iceberg of formal objections that have been made in school districts throughout the nation. More than ever before, school materials and teaching methods, standards, and requirements are being challenged on religious grounds as groups and individuals fight back against what they perceive as the antireligious nature of the public schools.

A January 14, 1995, headline in the Dayton, Ohio, Daily News read, "Prayerful Return? For some the abandoned activity never left the halls of learning" (Hundley, 1995). The issues of whether prayer or silence can be permitted in a public school and, if so, under what conditions remain very current in this first decade of the twenty-first century. Secretary of Education and former Governor of South Carolina, Richard Riley, has supported voluntary school prayer as long as "it's not coercive or intrusive on other children" (Winik, 1995, p. 6). He does not, however, support a constitutional amendment on school prayer.

A mid-decade cover story in *Newsweek* (Alter & Wingert, 1995) indicates that elements of religion are on the "front burner" of public interest and concern. Entitled "Shame. How do we bring back a sense of right and wrong?" the feature raises more questions about the role of religion in our diverse culture and our schools. Who determines what is right and wrong, and by what criteria are such shame-inducing decisions to be made?

The September 1999 issue of the *Phi Delta Kappan* (Vol. 81, No. 1) features a special section on "Religion and the Schools." Guest editor Gilbert Sewall observes, "Americans support teaching about religion in public schools. They overwhelmingly support character education in the schools. When it comes to linking the two, however, they are often uneasy and even quarrelsome" (Sewell, 1999, p. 12).

This chapter helps you better understand the religious element of cultural diversity. If the United States is to function as a cohesive unit, it must be able to accommodate the diversity within it. Teachers have a key role to play, but they can perform it only if they fully understand the play and the audiences who will attend.

To help teachers prepare for this theater, this chapter provides definitions of religion, a glimpse at the importance of religion, a brief review of relevant U.S. history, an examination of constitutional issues involved, facts and figures about the religious diversity within the United States, and a focus on the educational implications of all of these factors.

DEFINITIONS OF RELIGION

Before we can discuss religion, we must come to some agreement about what religion is. The word *religion* is a common one that seems easy to define but in fact is difficult to explain. Nearly everyone uses the term, but few have a well-developed idea of what we mean. Wilson (1982) contends, "Often, one's definition of 'religion' reveals much more about the point of view or prejudices of the definer than it does about religion itself" (p. 18). He feels that the definition can be either negative or positive, depending on the emotions it calls forth in the speaker.

Albanese (1981) states, "Everyone knows what religion is—that is, until one tries to define it. It is in the act of defining that religion seems to slip away" (p. 2). She believes that the difficulty exists because religion crosses many boundaries, even though the purpose of most definitions is to establish boundaries.

We provide a definition by describing examples, thus providing each of us with a more common picture on which to build our look at the educational implications of religious diversity. As we focus our camera on this concept, we need to use both a close-up and a wide-angle lens. These views give us first the narrow definition most commonly used and then the much broader definition used by the U.S. Supreme Court in several landmark decisions regarding church and state.

If we were to play a word-association game using the term *religion*, the responses would probably include at least some of the following: buildings of worship; traditions and festivals; names of organized groups; special objects, symbols, or literature; sets of beliefs; and specific types of persons or roles. Thus, such words as *church, temple, pagoda, shrine, confirmation, bar/bat mitzvah, Hindu, Shinto, Buddhist, Society of Mary, cross, Star of David, clerical collar, Upanishad, Koran, baptism, creed, priest, monk, nun, minister, rabbi, mullah,* and *evangelist* would be commonly stated by people using this narrowly focused view of religion.

The wide-angle view was described by the leaders of the Public Education Religion Studies Center (PERSC) in their book, *Questions and Answers* (Bracher, Panoch, Piediscalzi, & Uphoff, 1974):

> The broad definition envisions religion as any faith or set of values to which an individual or group gives ultimate loyalty. . . . Buddhism, Taoism, Ethical Culture, secularism, humanists, scientism, nationalism, money, and power illustrate this concept of religion. (p. 5)

The U.S. Supreme Court has for several decades been using this broader definition as it has made decisions. Thus, Madeline Murray O'Hare, an avowed atheist, was considered by some people to be a very religious person by this broad definition.

Several of the most recent church-state cases currently on appeal in the federal courts involve this broader definition. One federal judge found that secular humanism is a religion, that many textbooks discuss its beliefs, and that other religions such as Christianity do not have their own beliefs included in those same textbooks; thus, more than forty textbooks must be withdrawn from the public schools. Judge William Brevard Hand's ruling in *Smith et al.* v. *Board of School Commissioners of Mobile County et al.* of March 4, 1987, represented a direct use of the broader definition even though it was overturned on appeal to higher courts.

One important aspect of this dual definition is that many individuals use and live by both. Often referred to as crypto (hidden) religion, these people use a sectarian (narrow definition) mask to hide an ultimate concern. They often use the same symbols as people whose prime belief is a more traditional form of religion. For instance, such groups as the Ku Klux Klan use the Christian cross as a symbol of their "WASP-supremacy ultimate concern religion." Other people believe in the acquisition of power or wealth, doing everything they can to obtain them, even though they outwardly profess belief in the giving, sharing, and serving creeds of a particular church.

Thus, the broad definition, because it so clearly includes values and the valuing process, must also be used as we proceed through this chapter. We can understand the many educational implications of religious diversity in the United States and in the world at large only if we use both views. These views include the traditional notion of religion (being Jewish or Christian, for example) and the idea of religion as any strong faith.

Importance of Religion

For what idea, principle, cause, belief, or value would you be willing to give your life? As each of us answers this question of ultimate commitment, we state the importance of our religion. In the history of humanity, millions of people have answered this question through action.

Countless lives have been given in defense of religious beliefs. There has been no shortage of examples, from the earliest hunter who believed in the security of family and died while protecting the family, to those who blow themselves up as they conduct holy war.

It is our own system of values and beliefs that makes each example positive or negative. Such emotion-laden terms as *religious fanatic, heroic,* and *martyr* provide clues as to how we perceive a particular event.

If human beings are willing to die for a belief, then they are even more willing to suffer lesser penalties such as ridicule, separation, torture, imprisonment, fines, or restrictions on behalf of their beliefs. British and American women of the early twentieth century who fought for women's rights certainly suffered as a result of their beliefs. Today, parents who decide to school their children at home have often found themselves in court facing state charges for disobeying school-attendance laws. The Holocaust Museum in Washington, DC, highlights the number of non-Jews who literally risked and gave their own lives to save Jews from Hitler's forces.

Religion is an important element in the lives of many people; to some, it is the most important element. It has been the source of strength in times of trouble. Certainly this has been the case for African Americans in their history in the United States. African American historian Barbara Green (1984) writes of the relationship between the survival skills and the folklore of African Americans. The spirituals they sang provided them with comfort, hope, and strength. Green states, "The performance of work songs and spirituals was just as important as the songs themselves. Singing them sharpened memory skills; taught language skills, religious values, and survival strategy; and cultivated group identity" (p. 94).

Much of the civil rights movement of the last half of this century had a strong foundation within the churches and synagogues of the United States. People opposed to racial integration were often placed in the position of being opposed to their own church bodies or to religion in general. Churches became divided, and cryptoreligions developed.

The public schools often became the battleground for these contrasting belief systems. Governors who stood at the schoolhouse door to prevent integration were endorsed by some ministers and condemned by others. The schools were in the middle. Today, the schools are still in the middle. One example is when laws are passed requiring schools to teach sex education while many individuals and churches object with such vigor that they withdraw their children from school and establish new, private schools.

It should be no wonder, then, that public education as an arm of the state should have found itself frequently at odds with first one religious group and then another, as the United States has become ever more diverse and religiously pluralistic. Goodrich (1994) addressed this diversity in his article "Religion Is Alive and Diverse in US." Also, *Newsweek's* November 28, 1994, cover story was entitled "The search for the sacred: America's quest for spiritual meaning." Both publications strongly make the point that religion is very much a significant part of the lives of millions of people in the United States and thus worthy of being studied by their children.

We Are What We Were

Historically the United States has always had a number of different religions. The similar, yet very different, religions of the Native Americans were well in place when the Europeans arrived. These newcomers brought with them a collection of similar, yet very different, forms of Christianity. Several colonies adopted nearly exclusively a single form of this religion (for example, the Puritans and Congregationalists in Massachusetts, and the Anglicans and Episcopalians in Virginia), while others were settled by a variety of groups. Pennsylvania, for instance, became home to Quakers, Lutherans, Baptists, and many others.

Three different types of school systems developed, in part as a result of these patterns of religious settlement. The New England colonies developed public school laws (Massachusetts Laws of 1642 and 1647) that required an elementary school for every 50 families and a grammar school for every 100 families. However, since the government was essentially a theocracy, in which the church and state were essentially one, the name of those laws was "Ye Old Deluder Satan Act," and their purpose was to teach the children to read and write so they would be able to read the scriptures on their own and thus "ward off ye old deluder Satan." This public parochial school became the model for much of American education.

Because of the geographic size of the Southern colonies and the dominance by the Anglican Church of England, most schooling was done by traveling teachers who would stay for several months, visiting first one plantation and then another. Most children did not attend school; usually only boys from the wealthier families were so privileged. Apprenticeships were widely used for the less well-to-do. Formal education was much more a system of private schooling.

The middle colonies tended to have very diverse settlement patterns. No single religion dominated, but because religion was felt by many people to be a major reason for having formal education, little agreement among the various religious groups was possible. Therefore, a system of parochial schools resulted, with each group establishing its own schools.

Even amid this diversity, however, there was oneness of religion, a religious unity among Americans. Albanese (1981) says that religious unity refers to the "dominant and public cluster of organizations, ideas, and moral values which, historically and geographically, have characterized this country" (p. 10). Today, this idea is often referred to as the Judeo-Christian tradition. For some people, this ethic has become a civil religion, in which patriotism and nationalism become an ultimate concern, a cryptoreligion.

As each new wave of immigrants came into the United States, the oneness expanded to accommodate the new arrivals even as the established religions changed and adapted to the new setting. Some geographic areas became closely associated with a particular group, such as the Amish in Pennsylvania. Add to the problems associated with religious differences the difficulties of language, dress, and food and we can understand the assimilation problems experienced by immigrating groups. Most recently the new immigrants have come from non-Christian lands and are of a different race, thus making for a more difficult assimilation.

The process of assimilation did not always work smoothly. The religious oneness described above was nearly always patterned after the Massachusetts public school model—public parochial schools. Cincinnati's Bible War in 1869–1870 is one example of the assimilation process not working well. The public schools required the reading of the King James version of the Bible, which was objectionable to the large Catholic population, to Jews, and to others. Those in charge argued that the "common schools" were an appropriate place for the "common religion" to be taught. This religion was, however, a generalized Protestant version of Christianity and thus was not acceptable to all students (Michaelsen, 1970).

From the inception of the United States, the most fundamental question asked about religion and education has been, "To what extent should the public schools be an extension of the oneness of religion, an extension of the separateness of the many religions, or no extension of any kind of religion?" The many court cases in this century have been part of the process of trying to answer this question. The line separating church and state has always been unclear. Two centuries ago, the framers of the constitution addressed this question; legislative bodies and the courts have tried to clarify it; but it remains an issue very important to many people.

Constitutional Issues

The First Amendment to the U.S. Constitution says clearly: "Congress shall make no law respecting an establishment of religion, or prohibiting the free exercise thereof." The key word here is *Congress*, because not until the Fourteenth Amendment was adopted (1868) and gave to the citizens of the states all of the rights they had as citizens of the nation did the federal separation of church and state have any influence on the schools. In fact, not until the 1830s did the Commonwealth of Massachusetts repeal such laws as mandatory church membership as a requirement for holding a public office.

The constitutional separation of church and state has two key elements: no state support to create or maintain a religion (establishment), and no state laws against the practice of a religion (prohibition). Most constitutional cases regarding religion and the schools have dealt with the "establishment clause"; that is, the state (public school) cannot help to establish a religion by requiring prayer, Bible reading, or devotional moments of silent meditation or by permitting the use of school buildings or funds for religious instruction. Busing children to parochial schools for safety reasons and using public funds to purchase nonreligious textbooks are legal.

The Supreme Court gave strong support to the need for and appropriateness of teaching about religion in the public schools. On June 17, 1963, the Court gave its opinion on the cases of *Abington v. Schempp* and *Murray* (son of Madeline Murray O'Hare) *v. Curlett*, which dealt with required prayer and Bible reading in school. Associate Justice Tom Clark wrote the majority opinion, which included the following statement (cited in *School District of Abington Township v. Schempp*, 1963) (author's emphasis):

> In addition, it might well be said that one's education is not complete without a *study* of comparative religion or the history of religion and its relationship to the advancement of civilization. It certainly may be said that the Bible is worthy of *study* for its literary and historic qualities. Nothing we have said here indicates that such *study* of the Bible or of religion, when presented objectively as part of a secular program of education, may not be effected consistently with the First Amendment. (p. 225)

Because the headlines following this decision were inaccurate and misleading ("Prayer Banned—Bible Banned"), many educators as well as parents and other citizens were angry, perplexed, and concerned. Almost immediately the school curriculum guides and materials were subjected to self-censoring, first by educators and then by publishers. So much censorship occurred so rapidly that the American Association of School Administrators (1964) published a book in 1964 entitled *Religion in the Public Schools*. The association took a strong and clear position in support of the valid academic study of religion in the public schools when it stated:

A curriculum which ignored religion would itself have serious implications. It would seem to proclaim that religion has not been as real in men's lives as health, or politics, or economics. By omission it would appear to deny that religion has been and is important in man's history—a denial of the obvious. In day by day practice, the topic cannot be avoided. As an integral part of man's culture, it must be included. (pp. 53–55)

Even though the need for and appropriateness of teaching about religion has been strongly shown since 1963, not everyone in the nation concurs. Problems occur when the public feels that schools are teaching about the religions of other lands but are giving little attention to religions in the United States. The emotions that schools had hoped to avoid by focusing only on remote and thus less controversial peoples are now in the headlines and in the courts.

Other constitutional issues have addressed how much power the state actually has to regulate religious schools, to require attendance at an approved school (religious or public), and to provide aid (what kind, how much, etc.). A 1980s case, for example, that began in Dayton, Ohio, involved the issue of whether the state civil rights commission had the power to investigate a teacher's charge that she had been dismissed from a private Christian school because she exercised her civil right to question an administrative decision. The school contends that because the school is a religious institution, civil rights laws do not apply to how it treats its own personnel. This is one of a new type of church-state cases focusing on prohibiting the free-exercise-thereof clause of the First Amendment.

The founders of the United States had either experienced firsthand or knew about the unwelcome combination of church and state in Europe. Wars, inquisitions, and the absence of freedom were fresh in their minds as they developed the Constitution. The quality of their work is seen today in the fact that in the more than 200 years that have passed, the United States has become even more religiously diverse but has avoided the major problems of lasting and often violent interreligious conflicts too often found elsewhere in the world.

RELIGIOUS DIVERSITY IN THE UNITED STATES

Lessons from history tell us that religious, ethnic, and language diversity within a nation or other area often lead to many problems. Such examples as Ireland, India, Pakistan, Sri Lanka, and Belgium come to mind. Diversity, however, also exists within particular religions and even within particular denominations of a religion. Conflicts during the 1980s within the Southern Baptist Convention and a split in the Lutheran Church Missouri Synod—both separate Christian denominations—illustrate the point.

If we are to learn from history, we must be more knowledgeable about our own religious diversity and must learn how to respond to it more appropriately. This section examines the extent of religious diversity within the United States and within Christianity, the major religious group.

As a nation, the United States began with a diversity of peoples and their beliefs. The dominant common Western European heritage, although not one of peace and goodwill among themselves, was clearly Christian in a general way. Some early settlers were deeply religious and came to America in order to practice their religion; others came for different reasons, including economic gain, adventure, and escape from legal or other problems. It must be noted that some individuals who sought religious freedom were, in turn, unwilling to grant it to others; Rhode Island was founded by people whose religious beliefs were not welcome in neighboring Massachusetts.

Specific data on religious diversity in the United States are difficult to find. One must turn to a variety of sources and sometimes use information from different studies to gain even a fuzzy picture of how many religions are practiced today in the United States. There is always a danger that comparisons of religions are like comparisons between apples and oranges.

A massive 1980 survey of Judeo-Christian denominations (*The New Book of American Rankings*, 1984) found more than 228 different church groups. A few, 17 out of 111 who returned surveys, reported having more than 1 million adherents, and another 25 church bodies claimed between 100,000 and 1 million members. After Roman Catholics, who accounted for 42 percent of the total, the figures dropped dramatically to 14.5 percent for Southern Baptists and 10.3 percent for Methodists. A total of 108 'denominations' were listed for the other 33.2 percent, with no one group claiming more than 2.6 percent of the total.

Add to these data the fact that there are thousands of local churches not affiliated with any larger body, synod, or organization. Many of these independent churches grew in number of adherents during the 1970s and 1980s. Specific figures for the 1990s are not yet available, but some of the rapid growth of the independent churches may have slowed during this decade. Television evangelists, at least until their scandals of the late 1980s, experienced large and growing video congregations, which were also outside of the enumerations of the survey cited above.

Still other groups that stand partially or totally outside the Judeo-Christian realm (Unification Church of the Rev. Sun Myung Moon, the Scientologists, and the Hare Krishna movement, for example) experienced growth during the 1970s. Such groups tend not to be included in the data presented in various almanacs. Precise numbers for such groups are not available.

Gaustad's (1976) data indicate that as the United States has grown over the years, the percentage of the population claiming a religious affiliation has also increased. Another way to say this is that as the United States has become more diverse in the social and religious aspects of its peoples, a larger percentage of people have become affiliated with a religious body. Gaustad reports that in 1865, 26 percent claimed a religious affiliation. This percentage rose over the years to 44 percent in 1930 and 62 percent in 1970, the final year for these data.

Table 5.1, from *Statistical Abstract of the United States* (U.S. Bureau of the Census, 1998), summarizes data on religious preference, church membership, and attendance from 1980 to 1997 for the noninstitutional population of the United States eighteen years old and over. The table indicates that this population showed the following religious preferences in 1997: Protestant, 58 percent; Catholic, 26 percent; Jewish, 2 percent; and other, 6 percent. Although 89 percent of this population expressed a religious preference (11 percent expressed no preference), only 67 percent were church or synagogue members and only 40 percent actually attended churches or synagogues.

The 1991 *Yearbook of American and Canadian Churches* (Jacquet & Jones, 1991), reporting data from the Gallup organization, found that worship attendance by adults has remained remarkably steady over a fifty-year period, moving from 41 percent in 1939 to only 43 percent

Table 5.1 Religious Preference, Church Membership, and Attendance: 1980–1997

[In percent. Covers civilian noninstitutional population, 18 years old and over. Data represent averages of the combined results of several surveys during year or period indicated. Data are subject to sampling variability, see source]

Year	Religious Preference					Church/ Synagogue Members	Persons Attending Church/ Synagogue[1]	Age and Region	Church/ Synagogue Members, 1997
	PROTESTANT	CATHOLIC	JEWISH	OTHER	NONE				
1980	61	28	2	2	7	69	40	18–29 years old	63
1985	57	28	2	4	9	71	42	30–49 years old	66
1990	56	25	2	6	11	65	40	50–64 years old	71
1993	57	26	1	8	[2]8	68	40	65 years and over	75
1994	60	24	2	6	[2]8	68	42	East[3]	70
1995	58	25	2	(NA)	(NA)	69	43	Midwest[4]	73
1996	58	25	3	5	[2]9	65	38	South[5]	73
1997	58	26	2	6	[2]8	67	40	West[6]	51

NA Not available. [1]Persons who attended a church or synagogue in the last 7 days. [2]Includes those respondents who did not designate. [3]ME, NH, RI, NY, CT, VT, MA, NJ, PA, WV, DE, MD, and DC. [4]OH, IN, IL, MI, MN, WI, IA, ND, SD, KS, NE, and MO. [5]KY, TN, VA, NC, SC, GA, FL, AL, MS, TX, AR, OK, and LA. [6]AZ, NM, CO, NV, MT, ID, WY, UT, CA, WA, OR, AK, and HI.

Source: U.S. Bureau of the Census. (1998). Statistical Abstract of the United States: 1998 (118th ed.). Washington, DC: U.S. Government Printing Office.

in 1989 after a nearly twenty-year decline. However, the worship attendance of U.S. teens has grown significantly, from 50 percent in 1980 to 57 percent in 1989. Such figures are, however, called into question by a study by C. Kirk Hadaway (Keeler, 1994). The study suggests that the "real attendance rate is only half the reported rate" (p. 6C), a difference some are calling "The God Gap."

The December 17, 1990, issue of *Newsweek* included a seven-page story entitled "A Time to Seek—with babes in arms and doubts in mind, a generation looks to religion." Noting the clear trend of former baby boomers to return to religion, the article reports the following:

- At one time or another, roughly two-thirds of baby boomers dropped out of organized religion. But in recent years, more than one-third of the dropouts have returned.

- About 57 percent—43 million people—now attend church or synagogue.

- More than 80 percent of the boomers consider themselves religious and believe in life after death.

- The biggest group of returnees (about 60 percent) are married with children.

- The least likely to have returned are married couples without kids. (p. 51)

Data for Christians and Jews are much easier to obtain than is accurate and reliable information for other religions. Only the former tend to maintain records and statistics (many of which are less than complete and current). Most information for other religions is based on informed estimates. What follows, then, should be viewed as general patterns rather than as hard data.

"The century which began in the United States as a much-heralded 'Christian Century' appears at its conclusion to have been the 'Century of Religious Pluralism.' To be sure, the growth in religious pluralism was more characteristic of the last third of the century than of the first two-thirds" (Lindner, 1999, p. 9). Eileen Lindner, editor of the *Yearbook of American and Canadian Churches*, 1999, opens her commentary with these words. The data that follow indicate why she reached this conclusion.

Immigration reports provide a basis for enlightened conjecture as to how many adherents there are for each religion. *The World Almanac and Book of Facts: 1995* (1995) indicates that the total percentage of European immigrants to the United States went down from 33.8 percent in 1961 to only 17.8 percent for the following decade and down further to 10.4 percent for the 1981–1990 period. In sharp contrast is the number of immigrants from Asia. Figures for these immigrants went up dramatically, from 12.9 percent of total immigrants in the 1960s to 35.3 percent in the 1970s and 37.3 percent in the 1980s. The figures for African immigrants rose from 0.9 percent to 1.8 percent and to 2.4 percent in the 1980s. Those for immigrants from South and Central America and from Australia both declined a little. The continued emigration of the many refugees from Southeast Asia during the 1980s and 1990s maintained this pattern and probably increased the influx of persons from non–Christian-Judaic backgrounds, thus further increasing the religious diversity of the United States.

Holmes (1999) noted that in 1997, an estimated 26 million persons living in the United States were foreign born—the highest percentage of total population since 1930. He indicates that the Phillipines (1.1 million), China and Hong Kong (1.1 million), Vietnam (770,000), and India (748,000) were among the leading home-nations of many immigrants to the United States (p. 373). Each of these nations has a religion other than Christianity as its main belief system.

Other data that support these conclusions indicate that in 1957 there were only 10,000 Buddhists in the United States, but in 1970, 100,000 were here (U.S. Bureau of the Census, 1989). However, the Handbook of Denominations in the U.S. (Hill, 1990), published in 1990, shows 250,000 Buddhists in the United States. The 1998 edition of *Statistical Abstract of the United States* indicates a sizable increase in the number of Buddhists, citing a figure of 401,000 (p. 71).

Jacquet and Jones's (1991) *Yearbook of American and Canadian Churches* indicates that practicing Jews in the United States numbered 3,750,000, with a more inclusive count totaling 5,981,000 Jewish "adherents." This larger group made up about 2 percent of the total U.S. population, according to *Statistical Abstracts of the United States: 1994* (U.S Bureau of the Census, 1994). The U.S. Jewish population in 1960 numbered 5,367,000, thus giving a growth rate over thirty years of only about 11.4 percent (U.S. Bureau of the Census, 1989).

In contrast, U.S. believers of the Muslim faith were estimated to number 3,000,000 in the 1990 *Handbook of Denominations in the U.S.* (Hill, 1990). The 1998 *Information Please Almanac* gives a figure of almost 6,000,000 Muslim adherents within the United States (p. 408). Even though these figures are not as precise as those for Christianity and Judaism, they do clearly indicate a significant growth rate for followers of Islam.

Christianity remains the largest religion in the United States, and Judaism may have already been surpassed for its number-two ranking by Muslim followers. This increase in the numbers of Muslims has resulted from immigration from such areas as Lebanon, Iran, Egypt, India, and Pakistan, as well as from the growth of the Black Muslims.

Given the fact that U.S. schools and textbooks have paid little attention to the teachings of the Islamic faith, this growth will represent a challenge. According to Uphoff (1974), "William J. Griswold, a key investigator in a thorough study of U.S. textbooks and their treatment of Islam in history, reports that twenty-seven of forty-five texts examined either have nothing on the Muslim world, are biased, simplistic, and error-filled, or are scanty and not always dependable in their treatment of Islam" (p. 201).

Such lack of knowledge about the Islamic faith and those who follow it led to major problems following the outbreak of the Persian Gulf War in January 1991. The January 27, 1991, issue of the *Dayton Daily News* ran a front-page story with the following headlines: "Ignorance Turns to Violence: Arab-Americans the Target of Misplaced Anger in Cleveland." The February 4, 1991, issue of *Time* addressed similar violence and then informed its readers that

> the attacks are one measure of widespread ignorance about the
> Arab-American community. Few are aware, for example, of the degree
> to which Arab-Americans have flourished in this country, rising to the
> ranks of White House chief of staff and Senate majority leader. . . .
> Arab-Americans are better educated than the U.S. population as a
> whole, more likely to hold management or professional positions, and
> wealthier: an average household income of $22,973 is above the U.S.
> average of $20,973. (*Time*, 1991, pp. 18–19)

The ABC-TV news program "Nightline" focused its February 8, 1991, show on the backlash against Arab Americans. It reported the frequent use of such derogatory terms as *camel jockey* and said that slogans such as "Arabs Go Home!" were being used much more often along with more violent actions. The show also reported that hate crimes against Arab Americans numbered forty-one in all of 1990, but that a total of thirty-six had been documented in January 1991.

It is obvious that such actions clearly demonstrate ignorance about the religion of Islam and the people who practice it. The problem becomes even more serious when we realize that this religion has the same roots as Christianity and Judaism (all three trace their heritage back to Abraham) and that Islam's adherents make up a sizable proportion of the U.S. population.

A report on languages other than English spoken in the United States is another source of data for our conjecturing about the nation's religious diversity. According to the 1998 report (U.S. Bureau of the Census, 1998, p. 56), in 1990 the primary languages spoken at home by persons aged five and above were as follows:

- Vietnamese, spoken by 507,000

- Korean, 626,000

- Japanese, 428,000

- Arabic, 355,000

- Chinese, 1,249,000

- Other non-European, 1,580,000+

Spanish was the largest, with 17,339,000 speakers, but most of these children are within the Christian tradition, given their cultural heritage. Hundreds of thousands of children speaking languages other than English at home and coming from nations where religions other than Christianity and Judaism are practiced are now common in the United States and its schools.

The New Book of World Rankings (Kurian, 1991) has developed what it calls a homogeneity index to use when comparing nations on a scale of internal diversity. The book's introduction states:

> Political stability is often associated with linguistic and ethnic homogeneity. While developed societies in the West are moving toward pluralism and multi-culturalism, traditional societies in Asia and Africa are moving toward monocultures. Many governments are striving to create nations from heterogeneous populations and finding the task difficult. Because the primary loyalty of an individual in traditional societies is to his race, language, and religion, ethnicity becomes the basis for factional and separatist tendencies. (pp. 43–44)

The index includes 135 countries, with the highest ranking indicating the most homogeneity. North and South Korea are tied for first and second place, with a homogeneity percentage of 100. Others in the top ten include South Yemen, Portugal, Japan, Haiti, Puerto Rico, Hong Kong, and Germany. The United States ranks 82:135, with a homogeneity percentage of only 50. These data indicate that the United States is among the most diverse nations in the world in terms of ethnicity, race, language, and religion.

Diversity in the United States was recognized in September, 1999, when a study in Montgomery County, Ohio (Dayton), was released. This typical midwestern community found the changes from 1990 to 1998 to be as follows:

Hispanics = +29%; and Asians = +40%. These figures were in line with national data which predicted that the Hispanic population will become larger than the non-Hispanic African American population by the end of 2004. (Kissell & Gulliver, 1999, pp. 1, 5 A)

Changes have also taken place within the dominant Christian community of the United States. Membership in many mainline denominations has declined during the past ten to twenty years, while fundamentalist religions have experienced growth. The figures below illustrate these patterns of growth and decline (Jacquet & Jones, 1991):

Denominations with Their Highest Membership Figures between 1960 and 1970

Christian Church (Disciples of Christ) (1965)

Church of the Brethren (1960)

Episcopal Church (1965)

Evangelical Lutheran Church in America (1965)

Lutheran Church—Missouri Synod (1970)

Presbyterian Church (USA) (1965)

Reformed Church in America (1965)

United Church of Christ (1960)

United Methodist Church (1965)

Denominations with Their Highest Membership Figures in 1989

Assemblies of God

Christian and Missionary Alliance

Church of Jesus Christ of Latter-Day Saints

Church of the Nazarene

Jehovah's Witnesses

Roman Catholic Church

Salvation Army

Seventh-Day Adventists

Southern Baptist Convention

Lindner (1999) notes that, "For the last four years, the *Yearbook of American and Canadian Churches* has noted a flattening of the rate of change for both those churches with increasing membership as well as those with declining membership" (p. 9). But even within many mainstream churches, movement also occurred during the 1970s and 1980s. Hill (1990) describes it as "the infusion of unfamiliar styles of Christian practice and expression into existing denominations" (pp. 262–263). He talks about many people who remain happily Lutheran or Episcopalian or Roman Catholic "while embracing new forms of spirituality that are more often 'Spirit-filled' than 'pentecostal.'"

Hill (1990) contends that this movement was away from authority within a church and toward greater individuality. He sees a "moving from tradition to immediacy; from church as authoritative institution to free-form congregations and each individual; from prescribed worship to informal gatherings" (pp. 262–263). For example, when the two major Lutheran bodies merged into a single church in 1987, a small, but vocal number of congregations refused to join and became independent or created a new organization (Lindner, 1999, p. 62). More recently, when the now-merged body, The Evangelical Lutheran Church in America, voted to extend formal relationships with the Episcopal Church, many Lutherans fought this move vigorously ('Historic Episcopate Divides Synods,' 1999, pp. 42–43).

Combined with the other growing diversities of religious groups within the United States, schools now face a different public. This change gave public school leaders many more headaches because they had to deal more frequently with individuals and with individual congregations than with only the local ministerial association. There was more scrutiny of more aspects of public education by more people than ever before in the nation's history.

EDUCATIONAL IMPLICATIONS

The high level of religious diversity in the United States is a fact. The public schools, which at one time were a public extension of a generalized Protestant belief system, can no longer fill that role. On the other hand, these same schools must be sure that they do not move in the opposite direction, to a position of open hostility to religion.

The mission of the public schools is a broad one and may go beyond what some religious groups deem acceptable. For example, people who object to the teaching of critical-thinking skills (and there are some) will most likely have to find an alternative to public education. Although the public schools cannot be all things to all people, they must be sure to be fair to all, respect all, and be open to all.

Specific implications of this state of diversity are focused on the following eight aspects of education:

1. Curriculum resources such as textbooks, library books, films, and speakers
2. Subject matter to be included in the curriculum, whether elective or required, such as values clarification, sex and health education, and religion
3. School rules of all types, such as teacher qualifications, school attendance, discipline, and dress codes, whether from the federal, state, or local level
4. Student services, such as psychological counseling, testing, and health care
5. School calendar decisions, historically tied to Christmas and Easter
6. Scheduling of student activities that interfere with the religious observances of some students (e.g., athletic events on Friday nights)

7. Teaching methods that require student behaviors objectionable to some people, such as value clarification, decision-making, and thinking and debating skills

8. School financing, especially where local voters must approve new monies for the school budget, but even at the state level, where legislators are subject to intense political pressure.

The eight factors described here have too often caused significant controversies within a community, a state, or the entire nation. Headlines, television cameras, angry protesters, emotional meetings, and court cases have been too common. To avoid such negative situations, every educator must first become better informed about religion in general, and especially about its influence on human beings now and throughout history. The academic study of religion is vital for both teachers and students. Within the public schools, the best place for this type of study to occur is wherever it logically falls in the regular curriculum. In a home economics unit on food preparation, for example, it would be logical to include how some religions have given their adherents rules to follow regarding the handling and consumption of foods in their daily lives. During a unit on the Colonial period of American history, students could study the roles of the various churches and how each affected the geographic area in which it was dominant. The effects of beliefs on the decisions of individual leaders could be examined.

Curriculum resources need to be examined carefully. Earlier in this chapter the lack of appropriate treatment of Islamic peoples and beliefs in U.S. history textbooks was cited. An Associated Press story on May 28, 1986, carried the headline "Most High School Texts Neglect Religion, Group Says." The article quotes People for the American Way as follows: "Students aren't learning about America's rich and diverse religious heritage because textbook publishers are still afraid of offending anyone, from moral majoritarians to civil libertarians" ("Most High School Texts . . . ", 1986, p. 16).

Another report, by the well-respected Association for Supervision and Curriculum Development, refers to the "benign neglect" of religion by textbooks at all levels. It states that "an elementary student can come away from a textbook account of the Crusades, for example, with the notion that these wars to win the Holy Land for Christendom were little more than exotic shopping expeditions" ("Panel of Educators Ask End to 'Neglect' about Religions," 1987, p. 1+).

It is interesting that liberal and conservative political action groups, as well as educational groups, have arrived at the same conclusions regarding the inappropriate treatment of religion in school textbooks. This was exactly the basis used by Judge William Brevard Hand in his decision to ban dozens of books from use in schools.

In addition to becoming better educated about religion, educators must use appropriate teaching methods. The continuing controversy over the teaching of evolution and the call for the balancing inclusion of "creation science" illustrate the need to use effective and sensitive teaching methods. People who accept the story of creation in Genesis and teach it to their children are highly offended when their children are told by teachers that the parents are wrong. The anger of the parents is understandable.

How a teacher handles the teaching of evolution is crucial. Two possible exam questions illustrate how easy it is to avoid a direct confrontation with these children and their parents, and at the same time continue to teach the prescribed curriculum:

Poor It took millions of years for the earth to evolve to its present state. (True/False)

Better Evolutionists believe that it took millions of years for the earth to evolve to its present state. (True/False)

The first question requires the student to agree with a statement of "fact." The second question allows the student to answer that one group of people has a different set of beliefs than the child has, while at the same time protecting his or her own integrity. The difference is subtle, but powerful. The second question respects diversity of beliefs while teaching scientific information—that is, information about evolutionary theory. No child is forced to go against personal or family beliefs.

Such a change in teaching approaches will help reduce conflict between home and school. However, we need to be aware from the beginning that not everyone will be satisfied. Some people have such a narrow belief system that the public school system will never be able to satisfy them.

Teachers of all subject areas can benefit from the work done on teaching about religion by the National Council for the Social Studies (NCSS). The January 1981 issue of *Social Education* has as its theme "Teaching about Religion: Vistas Unlimited" and includes an article entitled "Instructional Issues in Teaching about Religion." This article calls for teachers to use a wide range of methodologies, including the use of music, skits, art, and role playing (Uphoff, 1981). It is next to impossible to teach students to think critically if they are limited to a single source of information, the textbook. A teacher's academic knowledge about religion as distinguished from personal, experiential knowledge is vital. The importance of the teacher's objectivity is also stressed, and specific teacher behaviors to bring this about are presented.

The National Council for the Social Studies (1984) published its official position in an article entitled "Including the Study about Religions in the Social Studies Curriculum: A Position Statement and Guidelines." The fourteen guidelines it recommends are specific and helpful. Two guidelines are:

1. Study about religions should stress the influence of religions on history, culture, the arts, and contemporary issues.

2. Study about religions should be descriptive, nonconfessional, and conducted in an environment free of advocacy.

Sources of further help on teaching about religion within the public schools of the nation are available as follows:

- *Religion and Education*, a professional journal published at Webster University is available by contacting Cathy Heidemann at Webster University, 470 Lockwood, St. Louis, MO 63119-3194 or by calling (314) 968-7135.

- The Religion and Public Education Resource Center contains all kinds of materials and curriculum guides. The center is located at the Butte County Office of Education IRC, Oroville, CA 95395, tel. (530) 538-7847. It is jointly operated by California State University: Chico and Professor Bruce Grelle. Its website address is: http://www.csuchico.edu/rs/reperc.html

- The Association for Supervision and Curriculum Development has one of its Network groups devoted to this general topic, The Religion and Public Education Network. Nominal dues of $10 can be sent to Dr. James Uphoff, CTL 023 Dunbar Library, Wright State University, Dayton, OH 45435. tel (937) 775-3651; james.uphoff@wright.edu
- The Freedom Forum First Amendment Center has published a guide entitled Finding Common Ground: A First Amendment Guide to Religion and Public Education. Call (615) 321-9588 for details.

SUMMARY

The United States is a religiously diverse nation and is becoming more so every day. If the United States is to avoid the fractionalization and inner turmoil that have destroyed other diverse nations, the public schools must lead the nation in being sensitive to the diversity itself and by helping students to learn about each other as well as about people in other parts of the world.

The old etiquette guide about not discussing religion or politics in mixed company has done more harm than good. It is not an appropriate policy for the schools of the United States as they prepare students for life in the twenty-first century.

Questions and Activities

1. What is the broad definition of religion developed by the Public Education Religion Studies Center? How is this definition of religion similar to and different from other definitions of religion with which you are familiar? With your own personal definition of religion?

2. What are the educational consequences of broad and narrow definitions of religion?

3. Prepare a report indicating the role religion has played in the history and culture of an ethnic group, such as Jewish Americans or African Americans. Helpful references are Irving Howe's *World of Our Fathers: The Journey of the East European Jews to America and the Life They Found and Made* (New York: Simon & Schuster, 1976); E. Franklin Frazier's *The Negro Church in America* (New York: Schocken Books, 1964); and *The Black Church in the African American Experience* (Durham, NC: Duke University Press, 1990) by C. Eric Lincoln and Lawrence H. Mamiya.

4. Uphoff points out that an increasing number of children now in U.S. schools have come from nations where religions other than Christianity and Judaism are common. This means that religious diversity is increasing in U.S. schools. What are the educational implications of the increasing religious diversity in U.S. schools?

5. Controversies have developed in many communities about the way Christmas is celebrated in the schools. In some communities, the school boards have established

policies that prevent teachers from using religious songs or symbols in holiday celebrations during the Christmas season. What is your opinion of such school board policies? Give reasons to support your position.

6. According to the author, why is it important for students to study religion in the public schools?

7. Why do textbooks tend to ignore religion? How can teachers supplement the textbook treatment of religion? What guidelines should teachers keep in mind when teaching about religion in public schools? What knowledge and sensitivities should they have?

8. To develop a better understanding of religious and cultural diversity in U.S. society, attend services at several religious institutions within your community or region, such as a synagogue, a Catholic church, an African American Baptist church, a Buddhist temple, and a mosque. How are the services and rituals at these institutions alike and different?

References

Albanese, C. L. (1981). *America: Religions and Religion.* Belmont, CA: Wadsworth Publishing Co.

"Alleged 'Secular Humanism' Courses Attacked." (1986). *Education Week,* 5(Oct. 15), 12.

Alter, J. and Wingert, P. (1995). Shame. How Do We Bring Back a Sense of Right and Wrong? *Newsweek* (Feb. 6), 20–25.

American Association of School Administrators. (1964). *Religion in the Public Schools.* (1964). New York: Harper and Row. pp. 53–55.

A Time to Seek. (1990). *Newsweek* (Dec. 17), 51.

Bracher, P., Panoch, J. V., Piediscalzi, N., and Uphoff, J. K. (1974). *Public Education Religion Studies: Questions and Answers.* Dayton, OH: Public Education Religion Studies Center, Wright State University.

Gaustad, E. S. (1976). *Historical Atlas of Religion in America* (rev. ed.). New York: Harper & Row.

Goodrich, L. J. (1994). Religion Is Alive and Diverse in US. *The Christian Science Monitor* (Jan. 10), 11–13.

Gould, Stephen Jay. Dorothy, It's Really Oz. (1999). *Time* (Aug. 23), 59.

Green, B. L. (1984). Solace, Self-Esteem, and Solidarity: The Role of Afro-American Folklore in the Education and Acculturation of Black Americans. *Texas Tech Journal of Education,* 2(1), 94.

Hill, S. S. (Ed.). (1990). *Handbook of Denominations in the U.S.* (9th ed.). Nashville, TN: Abington Press.

'Historic Episcopate' Divides Synods. (1999). *The Lutheran.* Chicago: ELCA, (July), 42–44.

Holmes, J. (1999). United States Population: A Profile of America's Diversity—The View from the Census Bureau, 1998. *The World Almanac and Book of Facts.* Mahwah, NJ: World Almanac Books, 373.

Hundley, W. (1995). Prayerful Return? For Some the Abandoned Activity Never Left the Halls of Learning. *Dayton Daily News* (Jan. 14), 6C.

Ignorance Turns to Violence. (1991). *Dayton (OH) Daily News* (Jan. 27), 18–19.

Information Please Almanac. (1998). Boston: Information Please, LLC.

Jacquet, C. H., Jr., and Jones, A. M. (Eds.). (1991). *Yearbook of American and Canadian Churches.* Nashville, TN: Abington Press.

Keeler, B. (1994). Study Says We Lie about How Often We Go to Church. *Dayton Daily News* (Jan. 20), 6C.

Kissell, M.R. and Gulliver, D. (1999). Valley Steadlily Becoming More Diverse, Stats Show. *Dayton Daily News* (Sept. 15), 1, 5A.

Kurian, G. T. (1991). *The New Book of World Rankings.* New York: Facts on File Publications.

Lester, W. (1999). Census Report Reflects Nation's Growing Diversity. *Dayton Daily News* (Sept. 15), 5A.

Lindner, E. W. (Ed.). (1999). *Yearbook of American and Canadian Churches.* Nashville, TN: Abingdon Press

Michaelsen, R. (1970). *Piety in the Public School.* New York: Macmillan.

Most High School Texts Neglect Religion, Group Says (1986). *The Journal Herald* (May 28), 16.

National Council for the Social Studies. (1985). Including the Study about Religion in the Social Studies Curriculum: A Position Statement and Guidelines. *Social Education, 49*(5), 413–414.

Panel of Educators Ask End to 'Neglect' about Religions. (1987). *New York Times 1*(9) (July. 2), 28.

Sewall, G. (Guest Ed.) (1999). Religion and the Schools. *Phi Delta Kappan, 81*(1) (Special Issue).

The New Book of American Rankings. (1984). New York: Facts on File Publications.

School District of Abington Township v. *Schempp.* (1963). 374 U.S., pp. 203, 2250.

The Search for the Sacred. (1994). *Newsweek* (Nov. 28), 52+.

The World Almanac and Book of Facts: 1995. (1995). New York: World Almanac.

Time (1991). The Fog of War (Feb. 4), 16–19.

Uphoff, J. K. (1974). Religious Minorities: In or Out of the Culturally Pluralistic Curriculum? *Educational Leadership, 32*(3), 199–202.

Uphoff, J. K. (1981). Instructional Issues in Teaching about Religion. *Social Education, 45*(1), 22–27.

U.S. Bureau of the Census. (1989). *Historical Statistics of the United States: Colonial Times to 1970,* Part 1. Washington, DC: U.S. Government Printing Office.

U.S. Bureau of the Census. (1994). *Statistical Abstract of the United States: 1994* (114th ed.). Washington, DC: U.S. Government Printing Office.

U.S. Bureau of the Census. (1998). *Statistical Abstract of the United States: 1998* (118th ed.). Washington, DC: U.S. Government Printing Office.

Wilson, J. F. (1982). *Religion: A Preface.* Englewood Cliffs, NJ: Prentice-Hall.

Winik, L. W. (1995). Who Is Responsible? *Parade* (Mar. 19), 6.

INTRODUCTION TO AMERICAN MUSLIMS: COUSINS AND STRANGERS

Islam is the world's fastest growing religion with more than 1.1 billion followers worldwide (Hajar, 2003). In 2000, there were about 5.8 million Americans who practiced Islam (Watanabe, 2001). Even though Islam is known and practiced throughout the world, it did not receive much attention in the United States until September 11, 2001. United States authorities have evidence that Osama Bin Laden and the Al Quaeda Network committed the terrorist attacks on that day. Bin Laden and the Al Quaeda Network are Islamic extremists. The events of September 11 heightened interest and concern about Islam and Muslims in the United States.

Since September 11, Americans have many questions about Islam, including: What kind of religion is Islam? Are extremists distorting Islam for their own political gain? Does the veil worn by many Muslim women symbolize their oppression or are the issues related to the veil complex? To help prevent misinformation and misunderstandings, educators should be able to respond to these and other questions about Islam and Muslims in the United States and throughout the world.

"American Muslims: Cousins and Strangers" is a condensed version of a chapter from *A New Religious America* by Diana L. Eck (2001). Eck is Professor of Comparative Religion and Indian Studies at Harvard University and Director of the Pluralism Project. This chapter provides an overview of Islam in the United States and discusses the relationship of U.S. Muslims to Muslims throughout the world. *Islam* is a religion based on the belief that there is only one God (Allah) and that Mohammed is the Prophet of Allah. *Muslims* are people who practice the religion of Islam. Although most Arabs are Muslims, Arabs make up no more than 20% of the estimated 1.1 billion Muslims in the world (Hajar, 2003).

This chapter describes how Muslims—who are members of different racial, ethnic, language and cultural groups—share a rich and complex religious tradition. Muslims, however, are a very diverse group. This chapter describes their complex differences, including the differences between Shi'ite and Sunni Muslims.

Islam has deep historic roots in the United States. This chapter describes the historic presence of Islam in the United States. It also describes the major issues, including discrimination and prejudice, that American Muslims have faced and still experience today.

The concepts, insights, and understandings that Eck describes in this chapter can enrich and inform your teaching. These understandings can assist you in helping Muslim students to function in the traditional cultures of their parents and their American peer culture. The information in this chapter about Islam and Muslims and can also serve as a departure point for teaching students to know, to care, and to act against discrimination directed toward Muslims and other religious, cultural, ethnic, and language groups.

References

Eck, D. L. (2001). *A New Religious America: How a "Christian Country" Has Become the World's Most Religiously Diverse Nation*. New York: HarperCollins.

Hajar, P. (2003). Arab Americans: Concepts, Strategies and Materials. In J. A. Banks, *Teaching Strategies for Ethnic Studies* (7th Edition). Boston: Allyn and Bacon.

Watanabe, T. (2001, October 15). For Muslims, War and Peace Open to Interpretation. *The Seattle Times*, p. 2.

Recommended Books

Barber, B. R. (1995). *Jihad vs. McWorld: How Globalism and Tribalism Are Reshaping the World*. New York: Ballantine Books.

Bayoumi, M. & Rubin, A. (Eds.) (2000). *The Edward Said Reader*. New York: Vintage.

Esposito, J. L. (1999). *The Islamic Threat: Myth or Reality* (3rd Edition). New York: Oxford University Press.

Eck, D. L. (2001). *A New Religious America: How a "Christian Country" Has Become the World's Most Religiously Diverse Nation*. New York: HarperCollins.

Esposito, J. L. (1998). *Islam: The Straight Path* (3rd Edition). New York: Oxford University Press.

Haddad, Y. Y. & Esposito, J. (Eds.) (2000). *Muslims on the Americanization Path?* New York: Oxford University Press.

Joseph, S. (Ed.) (2000). *Gender and Citizenship in the Middle East*. Syracuse: Syracuse University Press.

Zeliknow, P. D. & Zoellick, R. B. (Eds.) (1998). *America and the Muslim Middle East: Memos to a President*. Queenstown, MD: The Aspen Institute.

FEATURE:

American Muslims: Cousins and Strangers*

Diana L. Eck

When Siraj Wahaj, iman of Masjid al-Taqwa in Brooklyn, stood in the U.S. House of Representatives on June 25, 1991, and offered the first-ever Muslim invocation, he wove into his prayer one of the most oft-cited verses of the Qur'an: "Do you not know, O people, that I have made you into tribes and nations that you may know each other." The moment was historic, and the Islamic prayer for life in a pluralist society was arresting. Our religious and cultural differences should not be the occasion for division, but on the contrary the occasion for the biggest challenge of all: that "we may know each other."

As Muslims become increasingly articulate about their place in the American pluralist experiment, they bring this particular Qur'anic teaching to bear on the question of difference. The problem of pluralism in America is from this perspective a God-given challenge. Difference is built into the scheme of things. How we respond to it is up to us. The Qur'an offers us all a good place to start: we should come to know each other. But knowing each other is not easy in the American context. Misinformation about Islam and, even more, sheer ignorance of Islam, are common. Even while American Muslims create mainstream mosques and Islamic centers, register to vote, and become active participants in the American democratic process, newspapers bring to American homes the images of Islamic and other terrorist organizations, their rifle-toting leaders and their hideouts, creating a view of Islam as dangerous, subversive, highly political, and anti-American. When a terrorist attack occurs elsewhere in the world, American Muslims may well be the first to condemn the attack and to speak of terrorism as anti-Islamic, but their voices are usually not heard, let alone magnified by the popular press. American Muslims may also be among the first to feel the repercussions, as their mosques are pelted with stones.

In the media, Islam is too often painted with one brush, in bold and monochromatic tones. Ali Asani, one of my Muslim colleagues here at Harvard, knows how difficult the challenge to understanding is. "I think the levels of prejudice and the ignorance about Islam in this society are so deep that it's really going to be a long struggle to educate people in America about what Islam is, that Islam is not just this monolith, and that if Muslims do something it is not necessarily to be associated with their faith." In reality, we know that every tradition has its extremists. Many Muslims would say in no uncertain terms that militant extremist Muslims are to Islam what the radical Christian identity movements, the Christian militias, and the Aryan Nation are to Christianity: one end of a wide spectrum, one thread in a complex pattern of faith and culture.

---

* Source: Eck, D. L. (2001). A New Religious America: How a "Christian Country" Has Become the World's Most Religiously Diverse Nation. New York: HarperCollins.

As a guest of the community tonight, I note that my mind travels to the dozens of Muslim communities I have visited across the United States in the past few years. They too are coming together for the Night of Power in the huge old movie theater that is now the Muslim Community Center in Chicago, in the Bosnian mosque in Northbrook, Illinois, in the suburban mosque in Pompano Beach, Florida, in the big downtown Islamic Center in Los Angeles, and in the huge prayer room of the Santa Clara Islamic Center in the Silicon Valley.

ISLAM IN AMERICA: THE BEGINNING IN SHARON

The history of the Muslim community in Sharon, Massachusetts, is in some ways typical of a wide range of Muslim experience in America. This new facility is a branch, an expansion really, of the Islamic Center of New England in Quincy, located just south of downtown Boston and not far from the birthplace of America's sixth president, John Quincy Adams.

The community dates back to the early 1900s when immigrants came from Syria and Lebanon to work in the Quincy shipyards. There were more Christians than Muslims at first and more men than women. Before long, the Muslims came together for prayers and special observances. Seven families, in all, lived in the area of the shipyards. Mohammed Omar Awad volunteered as the imam, the leader of the prayers. In 1934 they formed a cultural, social, and charitable organization called the Arab American Banner Society. They met in a house on South Street in Quincy, organizing informal religious lessons for their children, gathering for Friday prayers, and celebrating the two big Muslims feast days, Eid al-Fitr at the end of the month of Ramadan and Eid al-Adha, the feast of sacrifice during the time of pilgrimage to Makkah. In 1962, after three decades of temporary housing, the leaders of this Muslim community decided to build a mosque on South Street. Almost as soon as the new building was dedicated in 1964, the community began to experience the impact of the new immigration. The small group of Muslims suddenly tripled in the decade between 1964 and 1974.

By the early 1980s the community took a giant step by hiring its first full-time imam, Talal Eid, who came from Lebanon and had been educated at the al-Azhar University in Cairo. He was jointly sponsored by the Quincy mosque community and the Muslim World League. Talal Eid has led the community now for over twenty years.

Like many other Muslim communities in the United States, the Muslim community of New England has experienced fear and pain along with growth. In March 1990 a three-alarm fire swept through the Quincy mosque, causing an estimated $500,000 worth of damages. The fire was attributed to arson, but the investigation was inconclusive and no one was arrested. The experience was unsettling for the community. Iman Eid recalls, "In the past, whenever a sad incident involving Muslims would take place in the Middle East or in any part of the world, people would focus on us. We received harassing calls and threatening letters. Angry people came over to demonstrate in front of the Islamic Center. And then there was the arson. If it's cloudy anywhere in the world, it will rain on us here." For a year after the arson, Muslims pulled together and poured their resources and energies into rebuilding what had been destroyed—the dome, much of the prayer hall, and the education wing.

Even before the fire, however, the Quincy community was bulging at the seams in the South Street mosque and had been looking for a larger home. In 1991 the group found a large building for sale in Milton—an estate that had housed a Jesuit center with more than seven acres of surrounding land. It seemed perfect for a new Islamic center. Before long, voices of resistance, apprehension, even suspicion were heard in Milton. Would there be too much traffic? Would there be enough parking? Would this be in keeping with the character of Milton? Dr. Mian Ashraf, a Boston surgeon and a prominent leader of the Muslim community, remembers the meeting with Milton neighbors. "They were worried we were going to destroy their neighborhood by bringing in a lot of people. A man from the newspaper asked me, 'Doctor, how many people are you expecting to come here to pray?' I said, 'Well you know on our great holy days, we will probably have thousands.' But of course there are only two such holy days a year. So the next day, the headline in the paper was 'Thousands of Muslims Coming for Prayers to Milton.' I was so upset."

Negotiations to buy the property went forward, but while the Islamic community was finalizing its mortgage arrangements, a group of Milton buyers purchased the property out from under them for one and a quarter million dollars in cash. Happily, the opportunity soon came to purchase a former horse farm in Sharon, a small town of 15,500 that is more than half Jewish. "I got a telephone call," said Dr. Ashraf, "The man said, 'Doctor, I have just the place for your Islamic center. I've been reading in the newspaper what they've been trying to do to you. You want to build a house for worship and I think I can help you.' He took me out to Sharon. He had fifty-five acres of peaceful land for sale. I fell in love with the place right away."

This time, the community came up with a plan to introduce themselves to the town of Sharon. To begin with, they gave an educational videotape on Islam to every neighbor on the road. "We told them, 'If you have any questions, come and talk to us. We'll have a meeting. We'll sit down. We'll answer your questions.'" Their proactive energy seemed to work, and the town of Sharon began to open its doors to the new Muslims. The rabbi of Temple Israel, Barry Starr, told Ashraf, "I think you are going to enrich our town. You're going to bring new things here." Starr called a meeting of the Sharon Clergy Association, and all of them had the opportunity to meet representatives of the Muslim commu-

nity. The clergy voted a unanimous welcome to the Islamic Center. They printed their endorsement in the local paper, under the headline, "*Sharon Welcomes Islamic Center.*" Two years later the new center was open for its first ever Eid al-Fitr, the feast day at the end of Ramadan.

The Islamic Center of New England is really a microcosm of Islam in America today, with its generations of history, its growing pains, its efforts to establish Islamic practice in a culturally diverse Islamic community, and its efforts to create Islamic institutions on American soil. Its saga of relations with non-Muslim neighbors is also a mirror of wider experience—from the threats and arson attack to the zoning battles and finally the successful effort to build new bridges of relations with other communities of faith.

THE MOST MISUNDERSTOOD: COUSINS AND STRANGERS

Islam, like Judaism and Christianity, traces its heritage to the prophet Abraham, and Muslims consider Jews and Christians their cousins as "people of the Book." It is strongly monotheistic, looks to Moses and Jesus as communicators of God's message to humankind, and has an ethic of equality and justice for all. The faith is simple, as stated clearly in the *shahadah*, the closest thing to a creed in Islam: "There is no God but God, and Muhammad is God's messenger." Bearing witness to this once, with deep conviction, makes one a Muslim, and walking the path of Islam means aligning one's whole life with this conviction.

Despite this kinship, Islam is the religious tradition about which many Americans have the most negative stereotype—extremist terrorism, saber-rattling jihad, and the oppression of women. In America the Muslim community feels misunderstood, maligned by the media, and subject to continuous low-level harassment. The resurgence of Islamic confidence and the rise of militant Islam throughout the world have shaped the public image of an Islam dominated by its most radical voices. It is no wonder that American Muslims place public education and information high on their list of priorities and that Muslim community leaders often spend countless hours interpreting Islam to non-Muslim neighbors.

Misunderstanding Islam is not new in the West. The growing Islamic world permeated and threatened the medieval lands of European Christendom from Spain and Italy to the Balkans. The direct and violent encounter of Christianity and Islam took place not only in the years of the Crusades and in the far-off Holy Land, but on the very soil of Europe. Europeans developed a centuries-long rhetoric of hostility and denigration toward the Islamic world. Not until the twelfth century was the Qur'an translated into Latin, and in the sixteenth century the first publication of the Arabic text of the Qur'an was ordered burned by the pope. In that same century, Luther spoke in favor of translating the Qur'an—but primarily so that people could see how full of lies it was. A seventeenth-century translation from French into English bore the subtitle *Newly Englished for the Satisfaction of All Who Desire to Look into the Turkish Vanities.* An 1884 book on Islam was called *Error's Chains.* And, from the Muslim side, the legacy of hostility associated with Christianity is also considerable. From the Crusades to colonialism, Muslims of the Middle East have also spoken of Christianity in the language of power, exploitation, and the sword. There is plenty of misunderstanding on both sides.

This heritage of Islamophobia was certainly prevalent at the time of the World's Parliament of Religions held in Chicago in 1893. The caliph in Turkey did not send Muslim representatives to the parliament, and the sole Muslim speaker was an American, Mohammed Russell Alexander Webb, the son of a newspaper publisher in upstate New York. Webb had attended private school and college and had worked as a journalist before being posted in 1887 as America's consul general to the Philippines. There he was exposed to Islam for the first time and converted to Islam.

His background made him well aware of the mistrust most Americans had of his newly adopted faith. "I am an American of the Americans. I carried with me for years the same errors that thousands of Americans carry with them today," said Webb at the 1893 parliament, speaking of the stereotypes and ignorance of Islam.

> Those errors have grown into history; false history has influenced your opinion of Islam. It influenced my opinion of Islam and when I began, ten years ago, to study the Oriental religions, I threw Islam aside as altogether too corrupt for consideration. But when I came to go beneath the surface, to know what Islam really is, to know who and what the prophet of Arabia was, I changed my belief very materially, and I am proud to say I am now a Mussulman.

Becoming a Muslim was a radical move for a nineteenth-century American. The image of Islam as the religion of the sword was prevalent, just as it is today: the horseman charging through the desert with upraised sword, Arab and Muslim identities conflated in a single image of violence. Webb addressed just this issue: "I have not returned to the United States to make you all Mussulmans in spite of yourselves . . . I do not propose to take a sword in one hand and the Koran in the other and go through the world killing every man who does not say, *La illala illala Mohammud resoul Allah*— 'There is no God but one and Mohammed is the prophet of God.'"

Despite the stereotypes, Webb articulated a deep-seated confidence that true knowledge of Islam would prevail. He concluded with an important challenge: "I have faith in the American intellect, in the American intelligence, and in the American love of fair play and will defy any intelligent man to understand Islam and not like it." This is a challenge Muslims in America have continued to issue: have a look at Islam, not as you have received it secondhand through the media, but as it really is. Once you see it through the eyes of Muslims of faith, you will no longer be able to sustain the negative images.

The first generation of Syrian and Lebanese Muslims established in 1952 the Federation of Islamic Associations. The primary purpose of the association was to "band together to combat the false and degrading propaganda leveled at them and to present to the American public a true and unadulterated picture of the true Moslem." If the founders of the FIA thought that educating non-Muslims was difficult in the 1950s, it is in some ways even more difficult today, as resurgent Islamist movements from the Middle East to Indonesia present images of a militant Islam easily magnified by the media. A new generation of American Islamic organizations developed in the 1990s, and each of these organizations tackles, in one way or another, the task of correcting misinformation about Islam.

The Institute of Islamic Information and Education in Chicago, located next to the large Muslim Community Center, publishes dozens of brochures and booklets, distributing more than 3.5 million copies free. Its founders, Dr. Amir Ali and his wife Euro-American convert Mary Ali, have dedicated themselves to correcting misinformation about Islam by providing readily accessible and accurate information. They operate an information line "Islam on the Phone," a computerized voice-mail service to answer questions about Islam. In Los Angles, the Islamic Center of Southern California has its own line of brochures introducing Islam. Its introductory brochure *What Is Islam?* is also printed in Spanish, *Qué es el Islam?*, for the increasing number of Hispanic seekers and converts. It explains the five pillars of Islam—profession of faith in One God and the Prophet Muhammad, five-times-a-day prayer, the obligation of almsgiving, the practice of fasting in Ramadan, and the pilgrimage to Makkah. It responds to the most commonly asked questions about Islam: How does Islam treat women? What is *jihad*? Who is Muhammad?

Perhaps the most focused effort to educate Americans about Islam is the nation-wide *Islam Awareness Week* sponsored by the Muslim Students Association. More than one hundred campus affiliates of the MSA organize a week-long program to generate awareness and understanding of Islam among their classmates. "Cogito Ergo Islam: I think, therefore, Islam" was the motto of the 2000 Islam Awareness Week at Stanford University. The events of the week included dozens of speakers and Friday prayer outside on the Stanford oval. At Harvard, the Harvard Islamic Society set up loudspeakers on the steps of the library, and a freshman *muezzin* issued the call to prayer out over Harvard Yard.

Jamal Badawi, a professor of management at Dalhousie University in Halifax, Nova Scotia, is one of the most sought-after speakers in North America. His dozens of tapes and books provide a clear approach to many facets of Islam—for Muslims and non-Muslims alike. He states that Islam is peace through submission to and commitment to God. It is aligning one's life with God. It is commitment to living under new management—God's management.

Allah is the Arabic term for God. Badawi notes that the God known by Christians and Jews is the same as Allah. Christians who worship in Arabic speak of God as Allah, too. Badawi goes on to say that, "In Christianity, there are people who have rejected the fruits of science and the critical study of the Bible. They are called fundamentalists. But Islam is not a closed system. For 650 years, Muslim scientists were the brightest, the most predominant scientific thinkers in the world. Islam does not reject the fruits of scientific thinking. Through the process of discrimination—we call it *ijtihad*— Islam is dynamic and is renewed in each century."

THE ROOTS: AFRICAN-AMERICAN ISLAM

The first major movement of Muslims to America came with the slave trade. Some 10 million

Africans were forcibly brought to North America to be sold as slaves in the eighteenth and nineteenth centuries, and many came from West Africa, which by this time, had been acquainted with Islam for more than a century. At least 10 percent of these slaves were Muslim, according to Allen Austin, whose groundbreaking book, *African Muslims in Antebellum America,* opens an important chapter in the history of America's many religious traditions.

The Muslims from West Africa were as diverse as the West African cultures from which they came—Mandingoes and Fula, Fulbe, and Fulani. The French scholar Sylviane Diouf writes, "A large proportion of the Muslims arrived in the New World already literate, reading and writing Arabic and their own languages transcribed in the Arabic alphabet." According to Austin and Diouf, the presence of literate Africans was vexing to those who bought and sold Africans as slaves. Indeed, because of their literacy, they did not fit the White stereotype of the African race as ignorant and uncivilized.

THE MIDDLE EAST IN THE MIDWEST

Between the fading traces of old African Islam in the mid-nineteenth century and the revival of a new African-American Islam in the 1930's another group of Muslims began arriving in the United States. Immigration from Syria, including much of what we know today as Jordan and Lebanon, began slowly in the 1870s and gained in intensity in the 1890s.

On the whole, these early Middle Eastern immigrants did not strike out for America because of political oppression or dire poverty in the homeland but simply because economic opportunity beckoned. Most intended to return home. When Alixa Naff studied this early Arab-American history she noted, "Almost without exception, the pioneers of the first phase and many in the second came with the intention of

returning home in no more than two or three years much wealthier and prouder than they came." But in the process of making a living in America, they gradually made a home here as well. As Naff writes, "It was in America, while pursing their goals, that immigrants became aware of the ideals of freedom, individual liberty, and equality of opportunity—ideals that at first had little relevance to their motivation for emigrating. As the Syrian immigrants became conscious of those ideals, however, they embraced them fervently."

Theirs was a chain migration, in which those who came first and succeeded in America sent money for the next family member or neighbor back home to come. This was the way my own Swedish family came to America two and three generations ago, just about the time these immigrants were arriving from Syria and Lebanon. One of the common means of making a living for the first wave of immigrants from the Middle East was peddling, especially in the rural Midwest where farm families had little access to stores and little time to travel to find the goods they needed. From their packs, peddlers unloaded an enticing spread of ribbons and rosaries, jewelry and buttons, notions, knives, and napkins. A new immigrant often hit the road within a few days of arriving, knowing little English but "Buy sumthin', ma'am." They immediately encountered both the hospitality and the hardship of America. When Naff interviewed those who remembered the pack-peddling days, she concluded, "Peddling must be held to the major factor in explaining the relatively rapid assimilation of Arabic-speaking immigrants before World War I."

At first, this late-nineteenth- and early-twentieth-century immigration brought many more Christians than Muslims. Syrian Orthodox congregations were established in Worcester, Massachusetts; Fort Wayne, Indiana; and Cedar Rapids, Iowa. About 10 percent of the immigrants were Muslims. While the Sunni population predominates among Muslims in Syria and Lebanon, the immigrants to the United States included a relatively higher proportion of Shi'ite Muslims and Druze. Shi'ites, who make up only about 15 percent of Muslims worldwide, hold that the Prophet Muhammad designated his son-in-law Ali and his descendants to be leaders of the community after his death, and the Druze are a small sect of Shi'ites found primarily in Syria and Lebanon. Sunnis, who make up about 85 percent of Muslims, place authority in the consensus of religious scholars to interpret the Qur'an and the Sunnah (custom) of the Prophet. In the first two decades of this century, we hear of Shit'ites in Fort Dodge, Iowa; Sunnis in Cedar Rapids, Iowa; and a Druze Association in Seattle, Washington. We can look in many places for the beginnings of organized Islam in the United States, but most of us would not think first of North Dakota.

In three small communities on the windswept plains of North Dakota, small groups of Muslims began to hold Friday prayers in the first years of the 1900s, the first evidence of communal Muslim prayer in the United States. In Ross, North Dakota, one of America's first purpose-built mosques was erected in 1920. By 1925 the Muslim population of the Ross-Stanley area was thirty to forty families. The headline from the *Fargo Forum* on August 8, 1937 was "Ross, N.D., Area Is Home for Some 50 Mohammedans."

Other early mosques, most in buildings adapted from other uses, sprang up in unlikely places, like Biddeford, Maine, where Albanian immigrants created a space for a mosque as early as 1915. In Highland Park, Michigan, an imam with a brother who was a construction contractor brought the small community together to build a mosque. It was dedicated in 1923 but closed amid internal controversy several years later. Perhaps the oldest mosque still in use is the building in Michigan City, Indiana, which was purchased by the Muslim community in 1925. One part of the building was designated for social events and religious instruction and the other part for prayer.

In the American heartland in Cedar Rapids, Iowa, is a building that is today called the Mother Mosque of North America. Its claim to fame is twofold: It was built from the ground up as a mosque, and the same Islamic community that built it is still thriving today, albeit in a larger building. According to Cedar Rapids old-timers, "This was the first place of worship specifically designated and built as a mosque in North America." Muslim history in Cedar Rapids goes back to 1895 when Hussein Ali Sheronick arrived from Lebanon. He made a living as a travelling peddler until he was able to open a dry goods store in Cedar Rapids in 1900. Other Muslims arrived, also single men who started out as peddlers—Ahmed Sheronick, Abdo Aossey, Hussein Igram, and later his cousin Hassan Igram. Sheronick's store served as home base for many of these pioneers, and the first gatherings for prayer were held in Sheronick's home. By 1914 some forty-five Muslims lived in Cedar Rapids.

By the 1920s the community was settled. The peddling days were over, and the Muslim pioneers had married and were beginning families. Regular prayers rotated among houses, and the community rented a hall for the Eid al-Fitr prayers and celebration at the end of Ramadan and the Eid al-Adha feast during the time of the pilgrimage to Makkah. In 1929 the community had its first imam, and by the early 1930s the Muslims of Cedar Rapids began to plan for a mosque. The fund-raising campaign, as American as apple pie, began with bake sales and Lebanese dinners for the wider Cedar Rapids community. The first of the annual fund-raising dinners attracted over six hundred ticket buyers. In 1934 the community formed the Rose of Fraternity Lodge, which became the official administrative and fund-raising body for the mosque. Representatives of the Rose Fraternity Lodge went from city to city during the Great Depression, appealing to Muslims in Toledo, Chicago, and Detroit for help with the project. Miraculously, they raised enough to build. The groundbreaking took place on March 10, 1935, and the 'Moslem Temple' opened on June 16, 1936.

After the mosque opened in 1936, young Abdullah Igram and Hussein Ali Sheronick were the first American-born Muslims to study the Qur'an there in Arabic. The first designated and registered Muslim cemetary opened there in 1949; the first publishing house, Igram Press, was established there in the 1950s. By this time the community also supported a mosque softball team and a women's group. The roots of activism can be found there as well. Abdullah Igram, when he served in World War II, was refused the right to have *Islam* inscribed on his dog tag as his religion but had to settle for *Other.* Igram was determined to secure recognition for Islam in America, and in 1952 he and other Muslims formed the Federation of Islamic Associations (FIA), declaring as their primary purpose to "band together to combat the false and degrading propaganda leveled at them and to present to the American public a true and unadulterated picture of the true Moslem." These early pioneers not only built Iowa's first mosque but also laid claim to the freedom of religious practices that is the real promise of America. For Igram and others, that meant not simply the freedom to practice one's faith quietly, but the freedom to organize and agitate for change when the practicing of one's faith was in some way hindered or obstructed.

The Igram family in Cedar Rapids arrived in the earliest wave of Middle Eastern immigration, which by 1914 had brought about a hundred thousand Arabic-speaking immigrants to the United States. A second and larger wave began about 1918, bringing Lebanese to the Detroit area, particularly to Dearborn, Michigan, to work in the Ford Motor Company plant, and to Quincy, Massachusetts, to work in the shipyards. After World War II a third period of immigration began, bringing Palestinians displaced from Israel, Egyptians and Iraqis leaving political turmoil at home, and Yugoslavian and Albanian Muslims fleeing communism. The fourth wave began with the changes to immigration law in the mid-1960s and brought educated professionals from throughout the Muslim world, some of whom settled in America to take the kinds of jobs for which they prepared as students and graduate students in American universities.

If Cedar Rapids is Muslim America's hometown, Detroit is surely its urban epicenter. Ironically, it was Henry Ford who discriminated so blatantly against Jews and blacks, who brought the Muslims to Detroit with the magnetic offer of five dollars a day for work in the new Ford Motor Company. Dearborn was originally the estate of Henry Ford, but eventually the whole of Dearborn was developed to house Ford employees. The Muslim population in those days was small, perhaps only 2 percent of the total, but it put down roots and built mosques and community centers. With each generation of immigrants, Dearborn kept growing. Today, with the post-1965 immigration, over a quarter million Arab Americans live in the metropolitan Detroit area. The largest part of the Muslim population is Lebanese, both old and new immigrants, followed by Iraqis, especially with the new influx following the Gulf War in 1991, Yemenis, and Palestinians. Of the eighty-seven thousand citizens of Dearborn today, about 25 percent are Arabs, most of them Muslims.

Driving down Warren Avenue through the heart of Dearborn, I found myself in what is now called Arabic Town, with groceries, restaurants, bakeries, music, and clothing stores catering to a Middle Eastern clientele. My host in Detroit was Bill Gepford, a minister at Littlefield Presbyterian Church in Dearborn who spent many years in the Middle East. At the time we met in 1996, he was likely the only full-time minister on any American church staff whose primary work was to build bridges between Christians and Muslims. The leafy neighborhood around his Presbyterian church is over half Muslim, and in the greater Detroit area as well he has his work cut out for him. "When the Arab population began to grow around 1976," he explained, "people took all the negative images they had of blacks and just put them wholesale on the Arabs."

We drove to the Islamic Institute of Knowledge a few blocks away, a Shi'ite center located in the heart of the Arab-American business district in a building that had been a bank. During the Gulf War the institute was defaced with anti-Arab graffiti, and people from the Presbyterian church came over to help the Muslim congregation scrub it off. The institute is one of half a dozen Muslim centers in Dearborn. Today in 2001, it has erected a new multimillion dollar mosque and school in the heart of Dearborn. Next we drove to the Islamic Center of America, dubbed the Joy Road Mosque, a Shi'ite mosque whose groundbreaking took place in 1962. The mosque is a hub of community activity—classes for all ages, meals in the dining hall, Thursday evening youth programs with pizza, even a Girl Scout and a Brownie troop.

Today new immigrants, mostly from Yemen and Iraq, have settled into the southern fringe of Dearborn, near the original Ford plant. This part of Dearborn is about 90 percent Arab American, and in the neighborhood school 98 percent of the children are said to be Arabic-speaking immigrants, mostly Muslims. The largest mosque in the area, the American Muslim Society, is also one of the oldest, dating to 1938. It is a strong, square, utilitarian brick building, like an old armory or school with a thriving weekend school in the basement, and three basketball courts.

The Arab Community Center for Economic and Social Services is one of the nation's most successful advocacy groups for Arab immigrants. Its dozens of pamphlets describe the beginnings: "Back in 1971, amid discussions of discrimination in the auto plants, the grape boycott and issues concerning newly arrived Arab immigrants, a community center was launched in a small storefront on Vernor Highway in Dearborn, Michigan. From that humble, grassroots start, The Arab Community Center for Economic and Social Services (ACCESS) has become the nation's premier Arab-America service and advocacy agency." Its annual cultural arts program is the largest Arab festival in the United States and brings other Dearborn communities together too—Latino, African, Asian, and Native American.

While the Arab-American identity is strong, Detroit's Muslim community is not defined by Arab identity alone. As an ACCESS activist put it, "Twenty years ago Muslim meant Arab. Now the Muslim Council is accepting and enacting the diversity of Islam-Pakistani, Lebanese, Yemeni, Arab. We are all here."

"All here" also means those of America's indigenous Islam-African-American Islam. Detroit has a special place in the history of America's Black Muslims. As we have seen, Muslims came from Africa on the steady stream of slave ships in the late eighteenth and early nineteenth centuries, and their religious life was largely submerged in America until it resurfaced in the 1930s—right here in Detroit.

AFRICAN-AMERICAN ISLAM: IN THE TWENTIETH CENTURY

The image of young African-American men in suits, white shirts, and bow ties, with impeccable posture, a look of confidence and strength on their faces, has now become familiar to most Americans. They are the members of the Nation of Islam's unarmed and highly disciplined Fruit of Islam, which closes crack houses, conducts drug patrols, and has proven so effective in security that it has been hired by housing authorities in Los Angeles, Chicago, Washington, and New York to provide security patrols for some of urban America's most distressed high-rise projects. Equally important, the self-respect and discipline of these young Muslim men has transformed their lives and given them leverage on some of America's most intractable problems.

The Nation of Islam has captured headlines, positive and negative, in the past twenty years, not least because of the charisma and rhetorical skills, as well as controversial views, of its leader, Louis Farrakhan, who is heir to the movement launched in the 1930s by Elijah Muhammad. But the Nation of Islam is not the largest of America's Black Muslim movements today. By far the majority are the followers of a loose coalition of mosques that follows the son of Elijah

Muhammad, W. D. Mohammed, who turned the movement his father had started back from black separatism toward orthodox Sunni Islam.

We could follow many strands as we investigate the black recovery of Islam in twentieth-century America. One began in Newark, New Jersey, in 1913, when a twenty-seven-year-old man named Timothy Drew, renamed Noble Drew Ali, established the Moorish Science Temple of America. It was not orthodox Islam by any means, but Noble Drew Ali was inspired by Islamic ideas, calling urban blacks of America's cities to a sense of dignity and belonging, rooted in what he called their Moorish past, which he also referred to as their Asiatic past. He traveled widely as a young man, and according to the lore surrounding him, the queen of England made him a noble, the sultan of Turkey gave him the name Ali, and the king of Morocco commissioned him to teach the Muslim faith to Americans of African descent.

The *Holy Koran of the Moorish Science Temple of America* is not the Qur'an revealed to Muhammad but is rather an eclectic composite of Christian, Muslim, and Eastern religious traditions. It calls readers to a life of dignity and love:

> Come all ye Asiatics of America and hear the truth about your nationality and birthrights, because you are not negroes. Learn of your forefathers' ancient and divine Creed. That you will learn to love instead of hate.

Here the call to American blacks is not to deny their racial identity but rather to resist the meanings of that identity in white America; yet the use of the term *Asiatic* to describe black origins falls into yet another, at that time romantic, racial stereotype.

The *Holy Koran* of Noble Drew Ali strongly emphasizes the essential divinity of the human soul, a view far more consonant with the spirituality of India than with either Christianity or Islam. The *Holy Koran* proclaims that Allah is known under many names. "You Brahmans call Him Parabrahm, in Egypt he is Thoth, and Zeus is His name in Greece, Jehovah is His Hebrew name, but everywhere His is the causeless cause, the root-less root from which all things have grown" (10:19). In this Koran, Jesus is said to have studied and taught in India, a view common to the Ahmadiyya movement, which came to America at about the same time.

Noble Drew Ali was the first to realize that a new people reclaiming their past needed a new name. In the Moorish Science Temple, they were not black or Negro but Moorish Americans. The men wore the Turkish fez, the women long dresses. Many took Muslim names. While they did not perform the ritual sequence of kneeling and prostrating in prayer, they did pray facing Makkah. The nationality card given to new members, which they carried, reportedly, with considerable pride, affirmed their Moorish-American heritage and bore, in addition to the crescent of Islam, clasped hands of unity and a statement that the bearer of the card honors all divine prophets, including Jesus, Muhammad, Buddha, and Confucius. Like these prophets, Noble Drew Ali was himself seen to have a divine mission.

Noble Drew Ali died in 1929, amid both mystery and rivalry within the movement. The Moorish Science Temple has continued through the decades since then but has been overshadowed by other African-American Islamic movements. Even today, however, there are a few local Moorish Science Temples and a Chicago headquarters. While the movement was not orthodox Islam, it was the first to recover an awareness of Islam in the struggle for a new black identity.

Recovering an awareness of Islam took another giant step with Wallace D. Fard and, later, his successor, Elijah Muhammad, both of whom apparently associated with the Moorish Science Temple before they launched what would be a new and decisive phase in the recovery of Black Islam. It began in Detroit in the 1930s. Wallace D. Fard, also called Wali Farad or Farrad Muhammad, is a mysterious figure who appeared as a peddler and itinerant evangelist in Detroit in 1930. He was said to be Turkish or perhaps Iranian, but he preached to black urban folk from the Bible and the Qur'an and claimed to have been sent from Makkah to restore blacks to their proper Muslim heritage as members of the "Lost-Found Nation of Islam." In Detroit he established the first Temple of Islam, which became known as Muhammad's Temple No. 1. The two-story red brick building is still standing today on Detroit's Linwood Avenue.

The times were ripe for a new message. The shift in the black population from the South to the urban North had created settlements of disaffected people in search of a new identity and suffering from the experience of northern urban racism. In this environment new black identity movements began to grow, including the Moorish-American identity propagated by Noble Drew Ali and the back-to-Africa movement focused on a return to Liberia advocated by Marcus Garvey, who founded the United Negro Improvement Association in 1917. The impact of the Great Depression made the situation of northern cities even worse, and we can well imagine the sense of disillusionment with Christianity and its pretense to a Christian society that the black urban poor must have experienced. It is probably no coincidence that Black Islam began in one of the cities that already had an established immigrant Arab Islamic population, though little research indicates a direct influence of Detroit's Muslim immigrants on the incipient Black Muslim movement.

In the climate of anti-immigrant nativism that followed World War I, racism was on the rise, anti-Semitism was on the rise, and more than a few Americans were attracted to a new spate of racial theories about the inherent superiority of the blue-eyed "Nordic race." Detroit's own Henry Ford was one of the most vocal, and he controlled the *Dearborn Herald*, the pages of which were filled with searing racial rhetoric. Neither Jews nor blacks were hired at the Ford

Motor Company. It is thus hardly surprising to find Fard in Detroit in the late 1920s turning the claims of blue-eyed superiority upside down, teaching that whites were "blue-eyed devils." In Fard's racial origins theory, the black man is the "original man," from which whites are a deviant, weak, hybrid race, created by a misguided scientist and destined for certain defeat in the apocalyptic confrontation of black and white. In this view, the nation of America does not include blacks, who have their own identity, their own nation—the Nation of Islam. Fard's new movement created cadres of discipline and identity—the Fruit of Islam corps for young men and the Muslim Girls Training Class for women.

In 1934 Fard passed the mantle of Messenger of Allah to Elijah Muhammad, his foremost disciple in the new Muslim cause, a man then in his thirties, born the son of a black Baptist minister in Georgia. Fard disappeared as mysteriously as he had come. Some say he returned to Makkah. His mysterious departure, like that of Noble Drew Ali, seems to have been part of his mythic persona. The transition of power after Fard's disappearance was clearly not without contention, for Elijah Muhammad had to leave Detroit under threat. He eventually established Temple No. 2 in Chicago's South Side, which became the home base of the Nation of Islam. According to historian C. Eric Lincoln, "Elijah Muhammad must be credited with the serious re-introduction of Islam to the United States in modern times, giving it the peculiar mystique, the appeal, and the respect without which it could not have penetrated the American bastion of Judeo-Christian democracy."

In building the Nation of Islam, Elijah Muhammad used everything available to him. He drew on the Bible, which he and the black urban poor knew well. He introduced the teachings of the Qur'an, which brought a new and authoritative voice. He drew upon the manuals and teachings of W. D. Fard, including the teaching of black dignity and the white man as devil. He adapted Islamic practice to the situation at hand, for instance, observing Ramadan in December, coinciding with the Christmas season. Perhaps the greatest change was reformulating the confession of faith, the *shahadah* affirm: "I believe that there is only one God (Allah) who came in the person of Master Fard, and (Elijah) Muhammad is the Messenger of Allah." This was more than an adaptation, however. For Muslims, this was wholly unorthodox Islam. Mainstream Islam insists that Allah takes no human form whatsoever. The very idea that anything or anyone can be compared with God constitutes heresy in Islam, for God is without peer, without comparison, without form. For orthodox Islam, the final messenger was and is Muhammad, and to speak of Elijah Muhammad as the messenger constituted a clear heresy. But in Detroit in the 1930s, no one was checking, and what attracted urban blacks to the movement was not internationally sanctioned orthodox Islam.

Orthodoxy, after all, has never been the measure of black religion in America. Experience has always won out over official doctrine. As Lincoln put it, "The salient tradition of Black religion has always been the sufficiency of its own insight." Christians in the new black Christian churches had little reason to respect or imitate the so-called orthodoxy or authenticity of the white churches that excluded them. Black Christians developed their own rhythms, forms, and structures. For new black Muslims as well, meeting standards of orthodoxy was not their first priority. Decades later, in the 1980s, Louis Farrakhan again responded to the question of orthodoxy in characteristic fashion:

> We believe in Muhammad, the Qur'an, God, the Honorable Elijah Muhammad and his mission and work among us. And now all of a sudden we have to come prove to somebody that we're Muslims. I don't care if none of you believe I'm a Muslim. You are not my judge. Take off the robes of Allah. They don't fit you well!

Continuing in this vein in 2000, Minister Farrakhan appointed the first woman, Minister Ava Muhammad, to be a regional representative of the Nation of Islam and to be imam of a mosque in Atlanta. This unprecedented move is yet another way in which Minister Farrakhan follows his own lights, not those of an imposed orthodoxy.

Elijah Muhammad preached not only Islam, but also self-help, hard work, and economic self-reliance. There was almost a Gandhian hue to his views of social transformation: that self-government begins in one's own life and in one's own neighborhood. Starting small businesses, selling newspapers, and opening credit unions were the economic manifestations. Giving up drugs, alcohol, and smoking became the expressions of personal transformation. This "Black Puritanism" came with a new surname: X. It meant ex-addict or ex-Negro or ex-slave. As scholar Lawrence Mamiya puts it, "It also signified that the new convert to Black Islam was 'undetermined,' no longer the predictable 'Negro' created by the white man."

The idea that blacks constitute a new nation without primary obligation to the America of racism was also integral to the movement. During World War II, Elijah Muhammad and about one hundred other members of the Nation of Islam were imprisoned for resisting the draft. Elijah Muhammad did not permit the bearing of arms, even by the Fruit of Islam, a position that was later challenged by Malcolm X's militancy and insistence on the right of blacks to defend themselves. There was agreement, however, on refusing to participate in the armed forces of a country that denied them equal rights and dignity. This tradition led Cassius Clay, who became Muhammad Ali after his conversion to Islam, to go to prison for refusing to serve in the military in the Vietnam War, saying, "No Vietnamese ever called me a nigger."

The ministry of Malcolm X brought nationwide attention to the Black Muslim movement. During the period from 1952 to 1965, Malcolm was a minister of the Nation of Islam and eventually its national representative, second only to Elijah Muhammad himself. His leadership and energy were responsible for the tremendous growth of the Nation in this period. He was a fine orator and a talented organizer. He was also a real missionary who preached in the streets of Harlem and launched the publication of *Muhammad Speaks*, a newspaper that he required young men in the movement to sell on the streets as part of their mission and ministry.

As is well known from his autobiography, Malcolm Little grew up in Omaha, where no one expected a young black to succeed, even though he was a fine student. His adviser suggested carpentry, not law, as an appropriate ambition. After dropping out of school, Malcolm became a shoeshine boy, a pimp, a pusher, and a small-time thief and eventually ended up in Norfolk State Prison in Massachusetts. There he encountered Islam through the testimony of a fellow prisoner and in 1948 wrote the critical letter that initiated his relationship with Elijah Muhammad. Malcolm turned the next four years in prison into a strenuous tutorial in English literacy and literature and in Islam and its relation to the issues of the day. By the time he was released in 1952, Malcolm X was ready for a lifelong ministry in the Nation. He was made Minister of Temple No. 11 in Boston and eventually of Temple No. 7 in Harlem. He became one of the strongest voices of the 1960s in articulating black power and black pride. He was known for expressing in clear terms the rage and frustration that were, by that time, seething in black urban America.

Malcolm's straight-talking manner eventually brought an end to his meteoric career in the Nation of Islam. He heard rumors about Elijah Muhammad's alleged sexual liaisons with several women and went to the source to confirm it, and when he was convinced it was indeed true, he was deeply upset. At that time, in December of 1963, Elijah Muhammad officially imposed a three-month period of silence on Malcolm X, claiming it was because of impetuous remarks about "chickens coming home to roost" that Malcolm had made at the time of President Kennedy's assassination. But it was clear to Malcolm that the silencing was a reprimand for his brewing critique of Elijah Muhammad.

In 1964 Malcolm X left the Nation of Islam and traveled to the Middle East and Africa, where he came into contact with leading spokesmen for orthodox Sunni Islam. The story of his hajj, his pilgrimage to Makkah, has gained almost mythic dimensions as it came to symbolize the shift to a new vision of Islam for African Americans—nonracist, nonseparatist, and truly universal. He wrote,

> There were tens of thousands of pilgrims from all over the world. They were of all colors, from blue-eyed blondes to black-skinned Africans. But we were all participating in the same ritual, displaying a spirit of unity and brotherhood that my experiences in America had led me to believe never could exist between the white and the non-white.

With a determination to transform the course of American Black Islam toward the mainstream of international Islam, Malcolm returned to the United States and launched a new mosque in New York, openly challenging what he now saw as the implicit racism of the Nation of Islam. He was assassinated on February 21, 1965—some say by members or agents of the Nation of Islam, but the case has never been proven.

The vision of a new future for the Black Muslim movement did not die with Malcolm X, however. In the long run, this became the new mainstream of African-American Islam, and it began under the leadership of none other than Elijah Muhammad's own son. When Elijah Muhammad died in 1975, twenty thousand members of the Nation of Islam came together in Chicago for his funeral. There they unanimously chose his son, W. D. Mohammed, as the successor to leadership. Within a year of taking the reins, W. D. Mohammed dissolved the structure of the Nation of Islam that his father had built over thirty years and began to follow Malcolm X down the road toward mainstream orthodox Islam. He turned from theories of black racial superiority to the Islamic foundations of human racial equality. He even welcomed whites into the Muslim family: "There will be no such category as a white Muslim or a black Muslim," he said in a speech a few months after his father's death in Chicago. "All will be Muslims. All children of God."

W. D. Mohammed signaled this transition toward universal orthodox Islam by dropping the term *minister* and taking the name *imam*, as did his clergy: The "temples" were now mosques or "masjids." The observance of Ramadan was brought into accord with the lunar calendar followed by Muslims throughout the world. In 1976 W. D. Mohammed fasted during the recognized month of Ramadan for the first time. He changed *Muhammad Speaks* to the weekly newspaper now published as the *Muslim Journal*. And to emphasize the turn from black separatism to black citizenship, the *Muslim Journal* bears the American flag on its masthead.

The movement has had several names, beginning with The World Community of Al-Islam in the West, then the American Muslim Mission. Then even that name was dropped. "We're just Muslims. Within Islam there is no division," says Mohammed. His words have special force in an American in which Indo-Pakistani Muslims and Arab Muslims are trying, for the first time, to come to know one another as "just Muslims." Imam W. D. Mohammed now has a considerable number of mosques that "follow his leadership," as they put it, but they are independent. A loosely structured national organization of these mosques now calls itself the Muslim American Society, and under its banner African-American Muslims gather in an annual national conference and in workshops on race, jobs, education, and the role of women. Some fifty Sister Clara Muhammad Schools are also operating, named for the wife of Elijah Muhammad who took on her own children's education as a young mother in Detroit and was so instrumental in starting Islamic education as an alternative to public schooling.

At the time Malcolm X was silenced and fell from favor, Louis Farrakhan was appointed national representative of the Nation of Islam. He also succeeded Malcolm X as minister of Temple No. 7 in Harlem, one of the most active centers of the Nation. In many ways, he was a protege of Malcolm X and came closest to duplicating the charisma and fiery frankness that made Malcolm X one of the most powerful black leaders of his time. Indeed, Malcolm X had been one of those who first moved young Louis Eugene Wolcott, a talented violinist and calypso singer, to become Louis X, a minister of the Nation of Islam.

Louis did not share the turn toward universal orthodox Islam made by Malcolm X and W. D. Mohammed. He did not think Islamic ideals alone were insurance against racism. Indeed, he saw in Islam some of the same hypocrisy and racism that he hated in America. By 1978 Louis Farrakhan had revived a remnant of the old Nation of Islam and become its chief minister. The enemy was still racism. Everywhere in the world, blacks are still at the bottom of the social order, he observed, no matter which religious tradition is prevalent.

Today African-American Islam is complex in composition and constitutes over 25 percent, some say as much as 40 percent, of all Muslims in America. Farrakhan and the Nation of Islam still receive most of the headlines but are a small minority in the total picture, with only about ninety affiliated mosques. By contrast, hundreds of mosques follow the less charismatic but more centrist and orthodox leadership of W. D. Mohammed. The world of African-American Islam is dynamic, however, and there have been signs of a milder and more universalistic voice coming from Louis Farrakhan, which some attributed to his recovery from a life-threatening illness and his determination to leave a lasting legacy as a Muslim leader. On the Nation's annual Savior's Day celebration on February 21, 1999, he was joined on the platform in Chicago by Imam W. D. Mohammed and a range of Muslim leaders from immigrant communities. The widely noted embrace of Imam Mohammed and Farrakhan was amplified by indications from both sides that they would like to resolve their differences and begin walking together on the path of Islam. If so, this chapter in Islam in America will be written in the years ahead.

AMERICA IS PART OF THE MUSLIM WORLD

Labor Day marks America's transition from summer to fall with barbecues, picnics, and weekends at the beach. For many American Muslims, however, Labor Day is convention time, and the huge annual convention of the Islamic Society of North America, ISNA for short, has become a ritual ingathering-part family fair, part conference, and part business. The convention has been held in Cincinnati, Kansas City, and St. Louis, but in recent years the group has out— grown virtually every major convention venue except Chicago. On Labor Day weekend in 1994, between twelve thousand and fourteen thousand Muslims attended, and Chicago mayor Richard Daley proclaimed September 2, 1994, Islam Appreciation Day

The Islamic Society of North America has its headquarters in Plainfield, Indiana, a town with a water tower and a Main Street like hundreds in Indiana. The modern brick mosque and its extensive office complex are alive with activity—a speaker's bureau, workshops for teachers, and planning for conferences. An extensive publications department produces informational pamphlets on Islam and the *Islamic Horizons* magazine. Matrimonial listings appear on the ISNA Web site, and the society provides information on Muslim marriage certificates and Islamic wills. Above all, it is a broad-spectrum organization designed to serve the needs of Muslims in America and to connect them to one another.

ISNA grew out of the Muslim Student Association organized in the 1960s by what were then international students from South Asia and the Middle East. Now they are middle-aged immigrants, American citizens with families of teenagers and college students of their own. The range of topics they discuss in these annual meetings gives us a quick roster of the concerns of Muslims in America. In Chicago, for example, they discussed Islam and the American judicial system, Islamic-banking systems, the coverage of Islam in the media, Islamic weekend and full-time schools, and Islamic political involvement. There were new issues as well, such as the use of the Internet for Islamic networking and information. The theme of the Chicago convention, "Our Youth, Our Family, Our Future," highlighted the tension between assimilation as Americans and the preservation of religious identity as Muslims, a tension that has been the story of immigrants to America for two hundred years. Thousands of Muslim teens attended, some in T-shirts and jeans, some of the girls wearing the head scarf and some not. During their own conference sessions, they engaged in energetic discussion with a few members of their parents' generation on what are called the "controversial and conflicting issues of entertainment and socializing: Who should set limits and how?"

Hosting the meeting of ISNA in Chicago were the Muslims of the greater metropolitan area— some five hundred strong, affiliated with about seventy mosques and Islamic centers. There are old Muslim communities, like the Bosnians who formed an Islamic society in the early part of this century and have built a striking new mosque in suburban Northbrook. There are more recent immigrants, primarily from India and Pakistan, who have converted an old movie theater into the Muslim Community Center, with thriving educational programs and a huge prayer hall where more than a thousand gather weekly under the glittering crystal chandeliers for congregational prayers. In the western suburb of Bridgeview is the Mosque Foundation of Chicago, a complex that includes a mosque and two full-time Islamic schools enrolling some four hundred students in the full range of twelve grades. Some two thousand Muslim families purchased an elementary school in Villa Park in 1983 and transformed it into an Islamic Center and a full-time school up to eighth grade. Across town close to the lakeshore stands America's first Islamic University. On the South Side are a dozen active African-American Islamic centers and the nationwide headquarters of both Louis Farrakhan's Nation of Islam and W. D. Mohammed's Sunni Islamic movement. The spectrum of Chicago's Islam spans the entire world.

The "Muslim world" is not somewhere else; Chicago is part of the Muslim world. In America the Islamic population is conservatively estimated to be about 6 million and growing. The so-called Muslim world can't be limited in our mind's eye to those nations with large Muslim populations from Indonesia, to India, to Iran, to Egypt and across north Africa to Morocco. Today there are mosques in Paris and Lyon, and more Muslims than Protestants in France. Storefront mosques are found in the Netherlands and Sweden and landmark mosques near the Tiber in Rome and in Regent's Park in London. They signal the rise of substantial Muslim communities and the marbling of religious communities old and new in most of the countries of the West. America's more than 1,400 mosques give a visible testimony to the presence of Islam.

Spectacular new mosques are adding a new dimension to America's skyline, such as the enormous mosque on 96th and Third in New York designed by Skidmore, Owings, and Merrill; the Islamic Society of Greater Toledo with domes and minarets visible across the cornfields; and the Islamic Center of Cleveland, glistening white at the end of a tree-lined approach road. The Phoenix area has two extraordinary mosques: Masjid Jauhartul is a replica of a mosque in Makkah, with a large courtyard at the center, and in nearby Tempe near Arizona State University is a mosque designed after the Dome of the Rock mosque in Jerusalem—octagonal with a central domed prayer room. Other new, spectacular

mosques include the Islamic Center of Virginia in Bon Air near Richmond; Masjid Abu-Bakr Al Siddiq in Metairie, Louisiana; the Islamic Center of Connecticut in Windsor; and the Pullman Islamic Center in Pullman, Washington.

The post-1965 Muslim immigrants have come in greatest numbers from India and Pakistan, but they have also come from Indonesia, Africa, and the Middle East. The story of Islamic expansion can be told in many American cities. In Houston, the booming oil industry and the space program brought Muslims to town. Today there are over two dozen Islamic centers, ten of which have joined together in the Islamic Society of Greater Houston. Formed in 1968, the ISGH dedicated itself to the dual task of providing for the religious needs of Houston's Muslims and explaining Islam to Houston's non-Muslims. As Houston and its Muslim population have grown, the ISGH divided the sprawling city into five zones and developed a cohesive Islamic plan for the urban environment. The main ISGH mosque now anchors these ten satellite mosques. In every zone, the Islamic centers began in suburban homes, storefronts, or transformed office buildings, and today they are busy building, moving from temporary quarters into new mosques. The Southwest Zone Mosque on Synott Road, for example, is a huge structure of warm terracotta colored bricks, with a copper dome and a tall minaret.

In Florida the Muslim community is also growing, with as many as fifteen thousand Muslims in Dade and Broward Counties alone. Masjid Miami was the first community in the area, converting a home into a mosque in 1976 in a largely Hispanic neighborhood near the Miami Airport. Today the two hundred people who attend Friday prayers spill out onto the patio and the lawn. Masjid Miami Gardens began in a former Pentecostal Church and has completed a new mosque in Opa Locka with a prayer room that accommodates five hundred. The Islamic Center of South Florida in Pompano Beach began as a small, largely Palestinian community and has grown in fifteen years to an ethnically diverse community of more than five hundred, holding its Eid prayers in a local park. Muslims in Fort Pierce hold prayers in a converted Presbyterian Church. All these Muslims in South Florida can locate their friends and their businesses in a Muslim telephone directory and can read area news in the *Muslim Chronicle*.

What is the shape and size of the American Muslim population today? In the mid-1990s the Islamic Research Institute found over 1,200 mosques in the United States. Today the number is closer to 1,400. About 80 percent of these mosques were founded in the last twenty-five years. Though each mosque could estimate the number of Muslims regularly attending prayers and the number on its mailing list, mosque affiliation is not an accurate gauge of the Islamic population. Of the some six million American Muslims today, we noted that about 25 to 40 percent are African Americans, and the rest are immigrants, both old and new. There is also a small but growing number of Euro-American converts to Islam.

What seems from a distance a unified tradition is, like all religious traditions, diverse and complex up close. Most American Muslims, and most Muslims in the world, are Sunni. A small percentage, certainly no more than 20 percent, are Shi'ite. The Shi'ites include both Iranian and Iraqi Muslims and are further subdivided to include Ismailis and the sectarian movements of Bohras and Nizaris. In many American communities, there are also mosques of the Ahmadiyyas, founded by a nineteenth-century leader to await the final return of the imam or *mahdi*. There are clearly many streams of Islam, and Muslims themselves have different interpretations of these many streams. The Ismailis and Ahmadiyyas, for example, are often seen as unorthodox by Sunni Muslims, and yet the very meaning of orthodoxy is contested.

Sufism, the interior path of spiritual life, is not a separate sect of Islam, but suffused through the entire tradition. Its form of meditative and ecstatic dance called *dhikr* is increasingly known through traveling performances of the Mevlevi order of "Whirling Dervishes," and its devotional poetry is popular in the West. Indeed the best-selling poet in America is currently Rumi, the thirteenth-century mystic whose breath-taking poetry is translated in multiple popular editions.

There are many Sufi movements in the United States. The Naqshbandi movement looks for leadership to Shaykh Muhammad Nazim al-Haqqani and seeks to build bridges of understanding among many schools of Islamic thought and spread the appreciation of the Sufi way of devotion among non-Muslims as well. The International Association of Sufism also creates a forum of dialogue, publishing a journal called *Sufism, An Inquiry*, and hosting an annual Sufism symposium. Part of the Association is the Sufi Women Organization that brings Sufi women together to advocate for women's rights and justice for women in society and within the Muslim community. Appealing primarily to Euro-Americans is The Sufi Order International founded by in 1910 Hazrat Inayat Khan, who described Sufism as the universal "religion of the heart." Today the worldwide movement, led by his son and successor Pir Vilayat Inayat Khan, has nearly 100 centers in the United States and sponsors Dances of Universal Peace in dozens of cities.

UNIVERSAL CALL

Islam is truly universal in its reach and cultural diversity. But the convergence of this diverse family on one soil is the special destiny of American Muslims. New Muslim immigrants come from countries as different from each other as India and Nigeria. Here they encounter Muslims already part of the American scene—the indigenous home-grown Black Muslim communities and the long-settled Arab-American communities like those in Cedar Rapids and Detroit. Imagine what this transcultural reach means for American Muslims who have grown up in an African-American Muslim community in Columbia, South Carolina, or in a Muslim family that has come to America from Hyderabad in India. Suddenly, their religious community spans the whole world, not just in the imagined world-wide community called the *ummah*, and not just in the once-in-a-lifetime experience of pilgrimage to Makkak, but in the week-to-week life of a local mosque.

The American experience of religious diversity is not new for most Muslim immigrants. After all, in nations like India or Indonesia religious diversity is taken for granted. But the internal cultural diversity within Islam itself is challenging. As my colleague Ali Asani, an Ismaili professor originally from Kenya, put it, "You have all these Muslims from different ethnic and cultural backgrounds coming together here who have never even been in touch with each other. In theory, you know that they exist, but when you encounter them on a day-to-day basis and practice your faith with Muslims who may have a different cultural expression, this is new. I think this is what being Muslim in America means—having to deal with the diversity, the pluralism within Islam itself.

The bottom line is quite clear: Islam is not to be confused with any particular culture and its ways but is a universal path of faith. In the United States, where Islam is too often identified with the Middle East, Muslims continually remind us, and one another, that "Islam is a universal call. It is not an Arab religion or an eastern or Middle Eastern cult."

Muslims take pride in the universalism of Islam—its insistence on human equality and dignity before God, on the irrelevance of nation and tribe when it comes to walking in the way of God. The Muslim communities of America have been challenged to put Islamic universal ideals into practice as nowhere else on earth. Worldwide, translocal Islam has always been ecumenical, but the very complexity of American Muslim communities has begun to generate ecumenical Islam at the local level as well. Islamic educator Shabbir Mansuri puts it strongly: "If

some people lose their identity with India, the language, the customs, they feel they have lost their tradition. But for us as Muslims ethnicity does not matter. In fact, we discourage a South Asian identity or an Arab identity. We discourage connection of ethnicity with identity. I left all that business behind when I left India and came to America. I am an American now."

Some American Muslims go even further in emphasizing the universal *ummah*, the community. I visited with the American-born principal of a full-time Muslim school who contended that even the Sunni-Shi'ite distinction has no future in the long-term development of Islam in America:

> I don't believe in Shi'ah-Sunni. I think it is an aberration for American Islam. Some of the things I say are not popular, but I firmly believe that there is no place for the Sunni-Shi'ah division for Muslims in America. The board of our school is half Sunni, half Shi'ah. Of the two assistant principals, one is Sunni and one is Shi'ah. Whatever happened 1400 years ago in the Middle East, happened then and was significant for a time. We can study it in our Islamic studies and history classes. We can understand it. We can even learn from it. But it is not relevant to the future of Islam in America.

First-generation immigrants rarely go this far, but this educator's views may well indicate a growing commitment to a community that has left some of the scars of ethnicity and sectarianism behind.

Most Muslim observers of the American scene admit that even if the first generation is not as committed to leaving ethnicity and division behind, the second generation will be. It is difficult to reproduce deep ethnic and sectarian identities half a world away from their sources; at least that is what optimists postulate. Hassan Hathout and his colleagues at the Islamic Center of Southern California put it this way:

Parents who are still torn apart between two cultures, the old and the new, should bear in mind that their children are the fruit of only one culture, the American. This does not mean that Islam is to be compromised or changed. But parents should not confuse ethnic habits and Islamic religion.

THE PILLARS OF ISLAM IN AMERICA

The Muslim community is sustained by five pillars of faith observed by Muslims everywhere. *Islam* means "submission" to God, aligning one's life with the path of faith. It comes from the Arabic word *salama*, which means both surrender and peace. It is this same word Muslims use in greeting one another, *salam alaikum*, literally, "peace be with you." The word *Muslim* comes from the same Arabic root and means one who surrenders or submits to what God has made plain. The proper response is not so much "believing" it but responding to it. Islam, in this sense, is not so much a noun but a verb, an action. The five pillars of faith undergird and support the lives of Muslims: the confession of faith, prayer, fasting, charity, and pilgrimage. These are foundational to many religious traditions, but in Islam they are lifted up as obligatory, for they are literally the pillars of a strong house of faith.

The first pillar is the affirmation of the *shahadah*: "There is no God but God, and Muhammad is God's messenger." Speaking these words with true commitment makes one a Muslim. It means bearing witness to the truth of God's oneness and the compelling authority of God's word and making it a reality in one's life. It does not mean that there is no God but Allah, as if Allah were other than what Christians and Jews mean by "God." It means that there is none worthy of worship except God, who is beyond our every description, beyond all our adjectives and names. Even so, virtually every chapter of the Qur'an begins with the *Bismillah*, "In the name of God, the Most Merciful, the Compassionate . . ." The invocation of God as merciful and compassionate is constantly reiterated.

Muhammad is the messenger, the prophet, who received the revelation of the Holy Qur'an and recited it to the people. He did not write it, for he was illiterate. But Muhammad is known as the trustworthy, the honest, messenger of God. Muslims do recognize other messengers, including Moses and Jesus. Indeed, in every place on earth God has spoken to humankind through messengers, but so much has gotten lost, gone awry, and been distorted. To Muhammad the whole of God's intention and message for humankind was once and for all time revealed. For this, Muslims love Muhammad, even revere him, even utter a blessing, "peace be upon him," when they speak his name, but they do not worship him. He is but the bearer of the message of God, and only God is worthy of worship.

Salat refers to the prayers offered five times a day—before dawn, at noon, mid-afternoon, sunset, and night. Every tradition includes some form of prayer and even regular daily cycles of prayer—for the orthodox, for the priests, or for the monastics. But no other tradition has so universally and elegantly ritualized a daily rhythm of prayer. Muslims speak not just of praying every day but of "establishing" prayer as a part of everyday life. In Islamic understanding, our human condition is not so much a matter of original sin but of perpetual forgetfulness. We do forget God and thus fail as well to remember who we are as human beings. To establish prayer in one's life is to stop the daily rush of life and commerce at regular intervals, to collect the mind and will in intention to prayer, and to perform the required prayers.

In places with large Muslim communities, the call to prayer, the *adhan*, can be heard throughout the neighborhood from the minaret:

God is most great. *Allahu Akbar.* God is most great. I witness that there is no God but God; I witness that Muhammad is His messenger. Come to prayer. Come to prosperity. *Allahu Akbar.* There is no God but God.

In the United States, the *adhan* is heard publicly in very few places, but if you pass by the storefront of the Muslim Community Center on Divisadero Street in downtown San Francisco you might hear the *muezzin* come out on the sidewalk to issue the call to prayer, or if you visit the Islamic Center of Washington, D.C., on Embassy Row, you will hear the call broadcast over loudspeakers, at least for community prayers on Friday noon. The first public call to prayer was probably made at the Islamic Center of America, the mosque I visited on Joy Road in Detroit, where Muslims have lived since the first decades of this century. When the community built the present mosque in 1952, they included a minaret also. From the shopping center across the street, from the Episcopal church next door, and from the homes in this Dearborn neighborhood, the sounds of the call to prayer can be heard along with chimes of the church bells.

Most American Muslims, however, do not have the prompting of a public call to prayer, but the hours of prayer are still built into the inner clock of each day. Sometimes prayer times are programmed into their watches or computers and the directions of prayer indicated on special compasses. Living a life structured by prayer is second nature. It is not a burden but a joy. And it is not rigid but flexible. If it is impossible to keep one of the prayers, it can be made up later. The point is not slavish obedience but establishing a rhythm of life in which remembering God has a place. And it makes a difference to know that at virtually every hour of the day there is a worldwide prayer wheel of millions of Muslims, facing Makkah in prayer.

Most of the daily prayer cycle is done individually, but some Muslims come to a mosque for one or more daily prayers, and certainly for noon prayers on Friday. On a regular weekday, several hundred men and a few women gather for midday prayers in the huge prayer hall of the Muslim Community Center, located in a former movie theater in downtown Chicago. The leader calls out the *adhan.* "God is great. *Allahu Akbar.*" The group assembles in lines, shoulder to shoulder, and all begin the prayer together—bowing, kneeling, touching the head to the floor, sitting back on the heels, rising again. The women, who line up at the back of the room, would resist any suggestion that this indicates second-class citizenship. After questions about head covering, no question is asked of Muslim women more often than how they experience praying at the back of the prayer hall. It is not the back of the bus, most would insist. "There is no lesser role for women in Islam," one woman at the MCC explains. "We ourselves don't want to be bowing to the ground in front of a row of men while we are praying. It would be embarrassing for us and distracting for them." Among many Muslim women with whom I have raised the question, prayer at the back is simply not an issue. Many would nonetheless prefer the prayer room to be divided down the middle, with men and women praying side by side on opposite sides of the hall. What is problematic, at least for some, is to be relegated to the basement or a separate room altogether and to be cut off from the sense of participation in the whole community.

The direction of Makkah is marked in a mosque by the arch called the *mihrab.* It is not an altar and bears no symbols of the faith. It is simply a marker of orientation, but it does indeed orient the whole community toward a symbolic center as surely as does the cross or the ark of the covenant. Muslims turn toward Makkah, the birthplace of Islam, not because it is a sacred place or because God is especially present there, for God is present everywhere. Rather, this is the place where Abraham worshiped, where Muhammad received the revelation of the Holy Qur'an, and where Muhammad himself worshiped. Centering upon

Makkah is the only location-oriented aspect of a worldwide community that has transcended nation and ethnicity. Facing Makkah is not a theological statement but a statement about the nature of a community that is both local and translocal.

While daily prayers are to be said wherever one happens to be, Friday midday prayers, called *jum'ah* prayers, are congregational. Friday is not a Sabbath or day of rest. It is a business day like any other, but it does require a longer break in the routine of work for prayers. Getting time off in the middle of working hours for Friday prayers has been difficult for many Muslims in America. In 1989, after hard work by the Muslim community, the District of Columbia passed a Religious Accommodation Act, making it explicit that employers in the district, including the government, must allow Muslims time off for *jum'ah* prayers. The subsequent federal guidelines on "Religious Expression in the Federal Workplace" have made attendance at Friday prayers a clear example of the need for workplace accommodation.

Fasting during the month of Ramadan is the third pillar of the House of Islam. It is observed throughout the world, and Greensboro, North Carolina, is no exception. Dr. Sayid Muhammed Sayeed, Secretary General of the Islamic Society of North America, often tells the story of the year his daughter Najeeba, an American-born Muslim, was a freshman at Guilford College in Greensboro. As Ramadan approached, both Najeeba and her parents were apprehensive about how it would be for her to observe the Ramadan fast far from home and in an overwhelmingly non-Muslim environment. Since she was the only Muslim student at a liberal arts college originally endowed by the Quakers, it promised to be a lonely spiritual regimen. The first day of Ramadan, Najeeba set her alarm clock and rose before dawn to head down to the dormitory kitchen for breakfast. She was surprised and delighted to find a dozen other girls in the dorm ready to join her for this predawn

meal. The others went on about their day, having a snack and soda when they felt like it, having lunch or not as they wished. But all of them knew that from sunrise until sunset Najeeba would not eat or drink anything. They also learned firsthand during that Ramadan season that Najeeba would not be alone in her fast. A fifth of the world's population would be observing the Ramadan fast as she did. She missed the evening meals at home during Ramadan, for they always had a special celebratory quality, but the support of her friends, many of whom had not had a Muslim friend before, made the fast of Ramadan easier. Her father and mother were relieved and moved by what had happened.

People like to be together as they break the fast each day at dusk, taking a glass of water and sharing some dates. The ritual fast breaking, called *iftar*, is followed by evening prayers and then a hearty and festive meal. Gathering for an *iftar* has become one of the ways in which Muslims make their presence in the workplace and in public contexts known during this pivotal time of religious observance. An *iftar* hosted on Capitol Hill has become a tradition for Muslim aides and staffers in the government, and in 1999 Madeleine Albright was the host for an *iftar* that took place at the U.S. State Department, an event that was repeated in 2000.

Muslims experience both the unity and diversity of the American community during Ramadan. "During the month, we often share the evening meal with other Muslims," says Shabbir Mansuri of Los Angeles. "One day last year, for instance, we shared the breaking of the fast with a Bosnian Muslim family in L.A. When we sat down to eat, it was delicious, but it was not my chicken curry. There was a cultural difference there, just as there is with Muslims originally from Turkey or Africa. But as soon as we finished eating, we went into the living room, and the young man in the family led us in prayer. Then the common bond came into being. He led the prayers in the Arabic of the Qur'an that I have known all my life. That's when we feel real community. That's when I felt truly at home."

Charity or almsgiving, *zakat*, is the fourth pillar of Islamic faith. If you were to enter the lobby of the Muslim Community Center in Chicago or the Islamic Center of Southern California in Los Angeles, you would find fliers and information sheets put out by many charitable organizations announcing needs for *zakat*: relief programs in Bosnia, refugees in Somalia, literacy programs in Africa, the Red Crescent disaster relief fund for Turkey. Just as prayer is integral to the life of the community, so is responsibility for the welfare of the whole community. *Zakat* is a form of tithing—a percentage, usually 2.5 percent, of one's entire wealth and assets. This is what one owes to others. As one Muslim graduate student explains, "Unless you pay *zakat* on your income and wealth, all your income and wealth becomes impure, in a sense. One of the meanings of *zakat* is related to purity. *Zakat* is what 'purifies' your wealth for your own use."

Zakat is not really charity, for it is based on the belief that human beings are entitled not to ownership, but only to stewardship of resources. It is not because one is pious that one gives, it is because wealth is really not one's own. It is the same understanding that in Jewish law prohibited harvesting the corners of the field so that the poor may do so and required the forgiveness of all debts at regular intervals. These are reminders that we are not owners but trustees. As one of the many brochures introducing Islam puts it, "This precept teaches that what belongs to the individual also belongs to the community in the ultimate sense."

Zakat cannot be used to build mosques or other Islamic institutions. It is for people, more specifically for Muslims, in need. The categories of people who should receive *zakat* include, according to the Qur'an, poor Muslims, new Muslims, Muslims in bondage, debt, or service to Allah, Muslim travelers, and Muslims who are employed to administer *zakat*. A contribution packet I picked up at one of the mosques in

Boston provides a worksheet for calculating one's assets in cash and accounts, gold and silver (including jewelry), and in business accounts. The distributor of *zakat*, in this case, is Care International, which operates an orphan sponsorship program and enables sponsors to specify from which country—from Afghanistan to Tajikistan—they would like to sponsor an orphan.

The obligation to give *zakat* reminds us that Islam has its own distinctive form of economics and economic ethics, and we must not pass by this fact without note. Islam prohibits usury: charging interest on money loaned or paying interest on money borrowed. How Muslims manage their financial affairs, buy homes, even rent cars in a world premised on credit and interest will amaze non-Muslims, most of whom have no idea that the prohibition on interest is part of Islamic faith. Fasting for the whole month of Ramadan may be far easier for non-Muslims to grasp than life without a credit card. Harvard's Islamic Legal Studies Program regularly sponsors conferences on Islamic banking, with hundreds of Muslim participants gathering to discuss the emerging worldwide Islamic banking system that carefully negotiates alternatives to interest-driven banking.

Pilgrimage to Makkah, called the Hajj, is the fifth pillar. It takes place in the month of Dhu al-Hijja, not long after the month of Ramadan. The pilgrimage to Makkah is required of Muslims once in a lifetime, if one is able, both physically and financially, to go. Every Muslim yearns to go, if not this year then next or sometime before one dies. For most Muslims, throughout most of Muslim history, it was a long and risky journey of many months by land or sea. It still is a long journey, even today, though most pilgrims come today by plane to the nearby airport of Jeddah in Saudi Arabia. In 2000, more than two million are estimated to have arrived in Jeddah for the Hajj.

The five pillars make it easy to remember the fundamentals of Islam, whether one is a college student in a class on religion or a Muslim eight-year-old studying at a weekend school in the American suburbs. They must not make our task of understanding Islam too simple, however, for there are many Muslims for whom this structure of life is not the definitive formula for Islamic life. They might not pray five times a day or ever go to the mosque. They might visit the shrines of Muslim saints for blessing and inspiration, or they might learn their grounding in Islam from the women's cultures of their grandmothers and aunts, women who have listened to Qur'anic recitation in their homes, who have taken seriously the notion that there is no priesthood in Islam, who know in their hearts that there are no intermediaries between human beings and God, and whose lives of faith are not at all set by the dictates of Islamic legal tradition.

As in the study of any tradition, our eyes should remain open to the amazing multiplicity of ways of faith, even when we have found some simple and convenient roads of entry into the tradition.

THE NEXT GENERATIONS

"If you lose your children, no number of mosques will help you." These words of Jamal Badawi are repeated in one form or another by Muslims all over America. Speaking at an annual meeting of the Islamic Society of North America, Badawi continued,

> Establishing of Islamic schools, in the environments in which we live, takes precedence over building mosques. You can have a huge, decorative, expensive mosque and lose your children, and end up having no one in the mosque to pray. I have seen it in Australia, where the early Afghan immigrants built mosques like monuments, some of which are now museums. Many of their children have already been lost.

Every mosque has a weekend school of one sort or another, with programs on Saturdays, Sundays, or both. As Mian Ashraf of the Islamic Center of New England put it, "We have a tendency to take Islam for granted, especially those of us who grew up in an Islamic environment before coming to America. But here you have to work at it. We're scared that we're going to lose our identity. Our kids are going into this melting pot, where they might not be able to maintain their religious values, and we'll lose them.

In an effort to reach out to young people, the leaders of the Islamic Society of Southern California prepared a book for American Muslim communities in which they write,

> One of the most detestable actions that could be conceived is to make coming to the Islamic Center an unpleasant experience to the young people. We hear it time and time again from parents across the country: "Our children hate to come to the Islamic Center." Some parents force their children to go to the Islamic Center. How short-sighted we are! Our children have to be convinced and motivated if we want them to make use of the institutions set up in the name of Islam for the future generations of Islam. This is the United States of America, and everybody knows parental authority ceases to function beyond a certain age.

The youth group in L.A. does not strictly segregate its activities by sex. It is clear, they say, that the marriage crisis among young Muslims is, in part, because Muslim girls and boys get to know non-Muslims better than Muslims if mosque activities are separate. As the leaders of this mosque see it, segregating Muslim boys and girls simply means that young people arrive at the age of marriage without getting to know other Muslims of the opposite sex at all. The summer camps in the San Bernardino mountains, the weekend conferences in Orange County, the social service activities—all are undertaken by young women and men together. So far, they say, dozens of successful marriages have come from the youth group alone.

Both the Islamic Center of Southern California and the Mosque Foundation at Bridgeview in Chicago are associated with full-time Islamic schools. Across the country, there are more than two hundred full-time Islamic schools, according to the Council of Islamic Schools of North America. A 1998 *New York Times* article reported twenty-three Islamic schools in New York City alone, and more in the planning stage. At Al Noor in Brooklyn, it was reported that the student body was capped at six hundred, and four hundred more had to be turned away. The large Islamic Cultural Center of New York in Manhattan is in the process of building a school in the lot next door that will accommodate a thousand students when it is completed. As Americans debate the question of vouchers for private education, the American Muslim community is keenly involved and interested, for an Islamic education system is clearly in the making.

The public–private school debate is lively within the Islamic community today in ways that to some extent revisit the earlier experience of both Catholics and Jews in America. Dr. Tauhidi takes his place in a long historical debate on parochial education in the United States when he says, "Muslims have to wake up and realize that they have to take care of their children. As the community gets stronger, we can make a contribution to society. But first the community, including the younger generation, must get stronger." Many Muslims despair of the drugs, the dating, and the saturation with entertainment culture that are so much part of the public school experience. These parents establish full-time Islamic schools to create a stronger environment of support for Muslim faith and practice.

But establishing full-time Islamic schools is not without its opponents, even within the Muslim community. A panel on the public–private school debate at the 1993 ISNA convention in Kansas City drew hundreds of participants and elicited strong views. "Will two or three hours of weekend school do it, when seventy hours a week are spent in the non-Islamic environment of the public schools or the TV?" asked Aminah Jundali, the mother of four children. "You put children in school eight hours a day, five days a week, and then you expect them to come out of that with an Islamic personality and Islamic values? That's almost an impossible task." A young high school girl responded in favor of public schooling. "It is even harder for us as girls, because we wear *hijab* to school and we stand out as different. Still, I want to go to the public school, because if we are not there as Muslims, how will other kids ever understand anything about Islam?"

Both sides in the debate realize that it is not an either-or issue. Full-time schools are being established, one after another, year after year. But it is also important to focus on critical issues for Muslims in the public schools. To this end, ISNA published a brochure that is sent by the thousands to public school teachers and administrators. *You've Got a Muslim Child in Your School* spells out some of the basics of Islam and specifies some of the restrictions.

> On behalf of the Islamic Society of North America, the largest organization of Muslims in the United States and Canada, we would like to request that in view of the above teachings of Islam, Muslim students in your school system should not be required to:
>
> 1. sit next to the opposite sex in the classroom,
>
> 2. participate in physical education, swimming or dancing classes. Alternative meaningful education activities should be arranged for them. We urge you to organize physical education and swimming classes separately for boys and girls in

accordance with the following guidelines:

    a. Separate classes should be held for boys and girls in a fully covered area.

    b. Only male/female instructors for the respective group.

    c. Special swimming suits which will cover all the private parts of the body down to the knee.

    d. Separate and covered shower facilities for each student.

3. participate in plays, proms, social parties, picnics, dating, etc. which require free mixing of the two sexes.

4. participate in any event or activity related to Christmas, Easter, Halloween, or Valentine's Day. All such occasions have religious and social connotations contrary to Islamic faith and teachings.

We also urge you to ensure that the following facilities are available to Muslim students in your school:

1. They are excused from their classes to attend off-campus special prayers on Fridays (approximately 1:00 to 2:00 P.M.).

2. They are excused for 15 minutes in the afternoon to offer a special prayer in a designated area on the Campus. This prayer is mandatory for all Muslims and often cannot be offered after the school hours.

3. All food items containing meat of a pig in any form and shape, as well as alcohol should be clearly labeled in the cafeteria.

4. At least one properly covered toilet should be available in each men's and women's room.

5. Muslim students are excused, without penalty of absence, for the two most important festivals of Islam: Eid al-Fitr and Eid al-Adha, in accordance with the lunar calendar.

For school boards and principals, a brochure like this may be received as a welcome and educational set of guidelines for a new situation. On the other hand, it might be received as an unwarranted intrusion into the secular atmosphere of the school. What is clear, however, is that the church–state issues in public education have changed forever and make the discussion of such issues as school-sponsored prayer, the posting of the Ten Commandments, and the teaching of creation science the arguments of yesterday.

HERE TO STAY: CREATING ISLAM IN AMERICA

"I am convinced that the resurgence of Islam will occur in America," said Mian Ashraf, a Boston surgeon and Muslim leader. "That's a big statement to make. Why do I think this is so? Because America is the only country in the world where education is very high. But also, America, to me, is the only place left in this world where you can today stand up and literally say anything you want to say. This is a tremendous opportunity for physical, mental, and emotional growth, and it should be nourished. But in order to take advantage of it, we're going to have to work for it."

Participation and engagement are essential to the texture of real pluralism. American Muslims are engaged in debate about how much to participate in the civic and political life of the country. In Islam the world is seen as divided into Dar al-Islam, the "House of Islam," and Dar al-Kufr, the "House of Unbelief." What these mean is itself a matter of ongoing discussion. Some say Dar al-Islam is a land under Muslim rule and law, while Dar al-Kufr is where Muslims live in a minority, under non-Muslim rule. In these terms, America is not Dar al-Islam. Yet in the view of many Muslims today, any land where Muslims can live safely and freely because the government is committed to religious freedom is a good place for Muslims to dwell. There Muslims can live as if it were Dar al-Islam. Living in this context is not a matter of living in isolated Muslim enclaves but being involved in the society. It is clear that Muslims, however they debate participation among themselves, are increasingly engaged participants in the American pluralist experiment.

Shabbir Mansuri puts the challenge succinctly: "As students and young professionals in the sixties and seventies, we talked about how we would eventually return to India or Pakistan. That's gone now. We're Americans and we're going to be buried here, so we should work within the system and participate in the process." In the past thirty years, America's Muslims have created a multitude of organizations to do just that. We have seen how Shabbir Mansuri's Council on Islamic Education organizes both Muslim and non-Muslim scholars to bring an accurate account of Islam to publishers of textbooks and teachers in public schools, and how the Islamic Society of North America provides a connective web for the concerns of Muslims to be discussed and addressed. The Council on American Islamic Relations monitors the civil rights of Muslims, while the American Muslim Council provides a forum for Muslim voices in the nation's capitol and educates Muslims on participating in the political process. All this is part of a growing American infrastructure enabling Muslims to participate more effectively in political and civil society. The Islamic infrastructure put in place in the past twenty years is by far the most extensive and also the most complex of any of those of the new immigrant religious groups.

Professional societies are active as well—the Association of Muslim Scientists and Engineers, the Association of Muslim Social Scientists, and the Islamic Medical Association of North - America, known by the acronym IMANA. The last, based in Downer's Grove, Illinois, is an association of Muslim doctors and medical professionals founded in 1967 to enable them to bring an Islamic perspective to the medical and ethical issues they face in American medicine. IMANA works with the international Red Crescent Society to provide medical emergency teams. It publishes the *Journal of Islamic Medical Ethics*, making clear that the Muslim voice is an important and articulate one on some of today's most gnarled ethical dilemmas.

Islam is here to stay in the United States and will become an increasingly visible part of all our lives. Nothing testifies to this more powerfully than the commitment of American-born Muslims, the so-called second generation, who have taken both their Islamic and American identities seriously and have established their own second-generation institutions. AMILA is an organization of young men and women in the San Francisco Bay Area with precisely this goal. The word *amila* means "work" in Arabic, but it has also become the acronym of an activist network of young Muslims who are fully involved in community and service activities, both for Muslims and for the wider society. *AMILA* means American Muslims Intent on Learning and Activism. They identify as Americans, recognize themselves as part of American society, and want to "contribute to the growth of humanity in America and to be influenced by those aspects of American customs and culture which do not contradict Islam." They are also Muslims; their "moral code and belief system are shaped by Islam." They are dedicated to learning about "both the Islamic outlook and the American reality." As for activism, they say, this "signifies our firm belief that wishes and dreams alone shall get us nowhere. Members of this organization are firmly committed to action." Their activism represents the kind of engagement that is the very fabric of pluralism in a free society. They work regularly at the Loaves and Fishes soup kitchen in San Jose, they are counselors at a Muslim youth camp in Santa Cruz, they sponsor an "Eid for Everyone" gift drive for Muslim children during the month of Ramadan, and they study political and civic issues and are involved in the Muslim Public Affairs Council.

Islam has a long history in the United States, but in the past thirty years has expanded exponentially to become one of the most active communities in the new religious landscape of America. As we will see as our story continues, the struggle for Islamic recognition in the American public square has been complicated by stereotypes, discrimination, ignorance, and outright fear. But history cannot be turned back, and America's vibrant new Muslim communities are here to stay. Now more than ever, all Americans need the instructive challenge of the Qur'an: that our differences require us to get to know each other.

Questions and Activities

1. Invite a representative from the local Islamic Center or Masjid (mosque) to speak to your students about Islam. Have students prepare questions for the visitor.

2. Ask students these questions about fasting to introduce a unit on Ramadan: If you were to fast for a day, what would you miss the most? Why? How would you have to change your schedule to accommodate fasting? Is it possible to change one's habits or perspectives by fasting? For example, do you think fasting would affect your feelings about people who are less fortunate?

3. Contact an Islamic Center during Ramadan and arrange to be a part of an Iftar gathering. Iftar is the evening meal taken after sunset to break the daily fast.

4. Have students research the importance of turbans and veils in different cultures and their significance to Muslims. Have students present their findings to the class.

5. Discuss the following scenario: Each year at the end of the school year, the school and PTA co-sponsor a graduation party. The party is held at a parent's home. This year the PTA would like to have a swim party. Several parents have swimming pools and have offered their homes for the party. You are concerned because several of your new students are Muslims and their parents weren't involved in planning the party. You don't know whether the Muslim parents will allow their children to attend a party where boys and girls swim together.

    What is the problem in this scenario?

    What would you do to try to resolve it?

6. Discuss the ways in which the school's expectations for attendance, punctuality, and participation may conflict with religious expectations for Muslim students. What is the school's responsibility in responding to religious diversity?

Glossary

Allah—The Arabic name for the One God.

Burka—A form of Muslim veiling. In its most conservative form, it completely covers the face of the person wearing it, leaving only a mesh-like screen to see through.

Eid al-Adha (Festival of Sacrifice)—A major Islamic celebration.

Eid al-Fitr (Festival of Breaking the Fast)—This is a festival at the end of Ramadan to celebrate completing the month of fasting.

Hajj—Annual pilgrimage to the city of Makkah in modern-day Saudi Arabia where the Kaba is located. The Kaba is the stone structure at the center of the Grand Mosque.

Hijab—The veil many Muslim women use to cover their hair. Some Muslim women cover their entire face.

Iman—The person who handles the services of the mosque and leads the people in prayer.

Islam—The religion based upon the belief that there is only one God (Allah).

Jihad—In Arabic means "effort." It is often used by Muslims to mean an effort for God. Mohammed is the Prophet of Allah.

Makkah (Mecca)—As the birthplace of Mohammed, Makkah is considered a sacred city. It is located in modern-day Saudi Arabia. Muslims pray five times daily in the direction of Makkah.

Masjid (Mosque)—A building for public worship by Muslims.

Medina—Located in western Saudi Arabia, it is considered one of the holiest cities of Islam.

Monotheism—The belief in One God.

Muezzin—A crier who announces prayer time. This is traditionally done from the minaret or tower of a masjid.

Muhammad—A righteous person and prophet who Muslims believe is the final messenger of God.

Muslims—People who practice the religion of Islam.

Polytheism—The belief in many gods.

Qur'an (Koran)—The sacred text of Islam containing God's revelation to Muhammad through the angel Gabriel.

Ramadan—The ninth month of the Islamic lunar calendar during which Muslims fast daily from dawn to sunset as part of an effort toward self-purification and betterment.

Effective teachers in multicultural classrooms are knowledgeable about and respond to both the challenges and opportunities experienced by female and male students.

Gender

Social, economic, and political conditions for women have improved substantially since the women's rights movement emerged as part of the civil rights movement of the 1960s and 1970s. However, gender discrimination and inequality still exist in schools and in society at large. In 1998, the median earnings for women who were full-time workers were 73 percent of those for men, up from 70.2 percent in 1988. The status of women in the United States within the last two decades has changed substantially. More women are now working outside the home than ever before, and more women are heads of households. In 1997, 83.6 percent of women worked outside the home, making up 46.2 percent of the total work force. In 1998, 21.7 percent of households in the United States were headed by women. A growing percentage of women and their dependents constitute the nation's poor. Some writers use the term *the feminization of poverty* to describe this development. In 1996, 61 percent of poor families in the United States were headed by women.

The three chapters in Part III of this book describe the status of women in the United States, the ways in which schools perpetuate gender discrimination, and strategies that educators can use to create equal educational opportunities for both female and male students. As Sadker and Sadker point out in Chapter 6, both males and females are harmed by sex stereotypes and gender discrimination. Tetreault, in Chapter 7, describes how school knowledge is dominated by male perspectives and how teachers can infuse their curricula with perspectives from both genders and thereby expand their students' thinking and insights. In Chapter 8, Butler discusses how women of color have often been ignored by the women's movement, which is predominately a White, middle-class phenomenon. She describes perspectives and content that will enable teachers to integrate their curricula with the experiences and cultures of women of color.

CHAPTER 6

Gender Bias: From Colonial America to Today's Classrooms

David Sadker and
Myra Sadker[1]

The anthropologist Margaret Mead once suggested that if fish were anthropologists, the last thing they would discover would be the water. We are all like those fish, swimming in a sea of sexism, but few of us "see" the water, the gender bias that engulfs us. So common (and vexing) is our bias myopia that the term *gender blindness* has been coined to capture this cultural shortsightedness (Bailey, Scantlebury, & Letts, 1997, p. 29). Gender blindness influences virtually every aspect of our lives, including how we teach and learn.

In *Failing at Fairness* (Sadker & Sadker, 1994a), Myra and I referred to the gender blindness we uncovered in schools as "a syntax of sexism so elusive that most teachers and students were completely unaware of its influence" (p. 2). It is still elusive, and many teachers still miss it. Teacher education and staff development programs do little to prepare teachers to "see" the subtle, unintentional, and damaging gender bias that shortchanges children. Many educators hold the costly misperception that gender bias is a "female" issue, one with little relevance for males. The violence and shootings in schools across the nation offer powerful reminders of the cost associated with the male sex-role stereotype. Unfortunately, many of today's boys and girls, unaware of the struggle that was waged to gain even rudimentary educational rights for females, disdain the term *feminist* and lack the perspective and tools necessary to confront the continuing challenges posed by sexism in school.

This chapter provides a context for understanding gender bias. It includes (1) a brief historical overview of women's struggle for educational opportunity; (2) an update of the progress made and the gains yet to be made in promoting gender equity in schools; (3) an analysis of gender bias in curriculum; (4) recent research findings concerning gender bias in

---

[1]In 1995, Myra Sadker died while undergoing treatment for breast cancer. This was one of many writings that she originally co-authored. For more about her life and work and her organization, Myra Sadker Advocates, visit her website: www.sadker.org

instruction; (5) a preview of some of the emerging trends and challenges concerning gender issues; and (6) a dozen suggestions for creating gender-equitable classrooms.

THE HIDDEN CIVIL RIGHTS STRUGGLE

The education of America's girls was so limited that less than one-third of the women in colonial America could even sign their names. For centuries, women fought to open the schoolhouse door. Although a woman gave the first plot of ground for a free school in New England, female children were not allowed to attend the school. In fact, women were commonly viewed as being mentally and morally inferior to men, relegated to learning only domestic skills. Not until the 1970s and 1980s did they win the right to be admitted to previously all-male ivy league colleges and universities, and not until the 1990s did they breach the walls of the Citadel and the Virginia Military Institute. It is rare indeed that such a monumental civil rights struggle—so long, recent, and impacting so many—has remained so invisible. Let us take a brief look at this hidden civil rights struggle, a struggle unknown to most people in the United States.

During the colonial period, dame schools educated very young boys and girls (with few exceptions, *White* boys and girls) in the homes of women who had the time and desire to teach. Girls lucky enough to attend such schools would learn domestic skills along with reading (so that they could one day read the Bible to their children). For the boys, such schools also taught them how to write and prepared them for further, more formal, education. Girls graduated to the kitchen and the sewing area, focusing on their futures as wives and mothers.

With a new democracy came new ideas, and the promise of greater educational opportunities for females. Elementary schools gradually opened their doors to females, and for the families financially able, secondary schools became possible in the form *of female seminaries*. Seminaries provided a protected and supervised climate melding religious and academic lessons. In New York, Emma Hart Willard battled to establish the Troy Female Seminary, and in Massachusetts, Mary Lyon created Mount Holyoke, a seminary that eventually became a noted women's college. Seminary often emphasized self-denial and strict discipline, considered important elements in molding devout wives and Christian mothers. By the 1850s, with help from Quakers such as Harriet Beecher Stowe, Myrtilla Miner established the Miner Normal School for Colored Girls in the nation's capital, providing new educational opportunities for African American women. While these seminaries sometimes offered a superior education, they were also trapped in a paradox they could never fully resolve: They were educating girls for a world not ready to accept educated women. Seminaries sometimes went to extraordinary lengths to reconcile this conflict. Emma Willard's Troy Female Seminary was devoted to "professionalizing motherhood" (and who could not support motherhood?). But en route to reshaping motherhood, seminaries reshaped teaching.

For the teaching profession, seminaries became the source of new ideas and new recruits. Seminary leaders such as Emma Hart Willard and Catherine Beecher wrote textbooks on how to teach and on how to teach more humanely than was the practice at the time. They denounced corporal punishment and promoted more cooperative educational practices. Since school was seen as an extension of the home and another arena for raising children, seminary graduates were allowed to become teachers—at least until they decided to marry. More than 80 percent of the graduates of Troy Female Seminary and Mount Holyoke became teachers. Female teachers were particularly attractive to school districts—not just because of their teaching effectiveness, but also because they were typically paid one-third to one-half the salary of male teachers.

By the end of the Civil War, a number of colleges and universities, especially tax-supported ones, were desperate for dollars. Institutions of higher learning experienced a serious student shortage due to Civil War casualties, and women became the source of much-needed tuition dollars. But female wallets did not buy on-campus equality. Women often faced separate courses and hostility from male students and professors. At state universities, such as the University of Michigan, male students would stamp their feet in protest when a woman entered a classroom, a gesture some professors appreciated.

While an economic necessity for many colleges, the idea of educating women was not a popular one, and some people even considered it dangerous. In *Sex in Education* (1873), Dr. Edward Clarke, a member of Harvard's medical faculty, argued that women attending high school and college were at medical risk. According to Dr. Clarke, the blood destined for the development and health of their ovaries would be redirected to their brains by the stress of study. Too much education would leave women with "monstrous brains and puny bodies . . . flowing thought and constipated bowels" (pp. 120–128). Clarke recommended that females be provided with a less demanding education, easier courses, no competition, and "rest" periods so that their reproductive organs could develop. The female brain was too small, and the female body too vulnerable, for such mental challenges. He maintained that allowing girls to attend places such as Harvard would pose a serious health threat to the women themselves, with sterility and hysteria potential outcomes. The famous psychologist G. Stanley Hall (1905) agreed with the Harvard doctor's prescription. It would take another century before Harvard and other prestigious men's colleges would finally admit women.

Dr. Clarke's constructed some powerful fears in women. M. Carey Thomas, future president of Bryn Mawr and one of the first women to earn a Ph.D. in the United States, wrote of the fears created by writers like Clarke. "I remember often praying about it, and begging God that if it were true that because I was a girl, I could not successfully master Greek and go to college, and understand things, to kill me for it" (cited in Sadker & Sadker, 2000, p. 438). In 1895, the faculty of the University of Virginia concluded, that "women were often physically unsexed by the strains of study" (cited in Sadker & Sadker, 2000, p. 438). Parents, fearing for the health of their daughters, would often place them in less demanding programs reserved for females, or would keep them out of advanced education entirely. Even today, the echoes of Clarke's warnings resonate—some people still see well-educated women as less attractive, or view advanced education as "too stressful" for females, or believe that education is more important for males than for females.

There were clear racist overtones in Clarke's writing. The women attending college were overwhelmingly White, and education delayed marriage and decreased childbearing. As a result, while women of color were reproducing at "alarming" rates, wealthy White women were choosing college rather than motherhood. The dangers to the White establishment were clear.

By the twentieth century, women were winning greater access to educational programs at all levels, although well into the 1970s gender-segregated programs were the rule. Although females attended the same schools as males, they often received a less valuable education. "Commercial courses" prepared girls to become secretaries, while "vocational programs" channeled them into cosmetology and other low-paying occupations. After World War II it was not unusual for a university to require a married woman to submit a letter from her husband granting her permission to enroll in courses before she would be admitted. With the passage of Title IX of the Education Amendments of 1972, females saw significant progress toward gaining access to educational programs, but not equality.

Title IX of the 1972 Education Amendments Act become law as the women's movement gained momentum. The opening section of Title IX states:

> No person in the United States shall, on the basis of sex, be excluded from participation in, be denied the benefits of, or be subjected to discrimination under any education program or activity receiving federal financial assistance.

While most people have heard of Title IX in relation to sports, Title IX reaches far beyond the athletic field. Every public school and most of the nation's colleges and universities are covered under Title IX, which prohibits discrimination in school admissions, in counseling and guidance, in competitive athletics, in student rules and regulations, and in access to programs and courses, including vocational education and physical education. Title IX also applies to sex discrimination in employment practices, including interviewing and recruitment, hiring and promotion, compensation, job assignments, and fringe benefits. Although enforcement of the law remains sporadic, while the law remains on the books there is still cause for optimism. But even this weakened entitlement of educational rights was targeted for elimination by the conservative political movement of the 1990s.

In *Backlash*, Susan Faludi (1991) documents the negative impact on women resulting from the conservative political gains of the 1980s and 1990s. Most of the federal educational programs designed to assist girls and women have been eliminated, and Title IX itself is often under attack. In high school and college, a "glass wall" still keeps women from the most lucrative careers and keeps men from entering traditionally "female" jobs. In certain vocational areas, such as engineering, physics, chemistry, and computer science, few women can be found. In nursing, teaching, library science, and social work, few men can be found. Even in high-status careers where tremendous progress has been made, like medicine and law, a second generation of bias persists. In both professions, women find themselves channeled into the least prestigious, least profitable specialties. Being aware of these historical threads, the channeling of females into certain specialties and the devaluation of their worth as students or employees, can help us to tease out the subtle (and not-so-subtle) biases that persist today.

By the mid 1990s, a militant cadre of political conservatives alleged that the feminist movement had gone too far and claimed that the real victims of sexism were males. After all, they point out, boys receive lower report card grades, are assigned in greater numbers to special education classes, are disciplined more, and are more likely to drop out of school. While many of their criticisms of educational research were politically motivated, they did remind us of the problems faced by males. While today's gender bias is typically less problematic than in the past, the bias is still virulent. Let's take a look at some of the salient statistics.

REPORT CARD: THE COST OF SEXISM IN SCHOOLS

Below is a report card you will not find in any elementary or secondary school, yet these statistics document the loss that both girls and boys suffer because of sex bias in society and in education. More than a quarter of a century after the passage of Title IX, gender inequities continue to permeate schools and shortchange our children (American Association of University Women, 1998a; American Psychological Association, 1999; Levante, 1996; Mid-Atlantic Equity Center, 1999; Sadker & Sadker, 1994a; Women's Educational Equity Act, 1999).

Academic

Girls

- In the early grades, girls score ahead of boys in verbal skills; their academic performance is equal to that of boys in math and almost equal to boys in science. However, as they progress through school, many of their high-stakes achievement test scores (such as the SATs) decline. Girls are the only group in our society to begin school with a testing advantage, yet they leave school with a testing disadvantage.

- Males outperform females on both the verbal and mathematics sections of the Scholastic Assessment Test (SAT). Gender differences on the American College Testing Program Examination (ACT) are less pronounced, with females ahead in verbal scores and males in mathematics.

- Female enrollment in mathematics and science courses has increased dramatically in recent years. However, boys still take more advanced courses, all three core science courses—biology, chemistry, and physics—and score higher on competitive tests, such as the Advanced Placement tests.

- Computer science and technology, exciting growth fields, reflect continuing gender (and racial) disparities. Boys not only enroll in more of these courses, but they also enroll in the more advanced courses. Girls are more likely to be found in word processing and clerical support courses.

- In spite of the performance decline on many standardized achievement tests, girls frequently receive better grades in school. This may be one of the rewards they receive for more quiet and docile classroom behavior. However, their silence may be at the cost of achievement, independence, and self-reliance.

- Females receive fewer academic contacts in class. They are less likely to be called on by name, are asked fewer complex and abstract questions, receive less praise or constructive feedback, and are given less direction on how to do things for themselves. In short, girls are more likely to be invisible members of classrooms.

- Girls who are gifted, especially in math and science, are less likely to participate in special or accelerated programs to develop their talent. Girls who suffer from learning disabilities are also less likely to be identified or enrolled in special-education programs than are learning-disabled boys.

- Girls who repeat grades are more likely to drop out of school than are boys. The overall dropout rate (percentage of girls sixteen to twenty-four years of age who are not in school and have not completed high school) is approximately 11 percent. That dropout rate is approximately twice as high for African American girls, three times higher for Latinas, and almost five times as high for American Indian females.

- By 1996, about 24 percent of the U.S. population, twenty-five years or older, had at least four years of college. That percentage included 24 percent of White females and 29 percent of White males; 14 percent of African American women and 12.5 percent of African American men; and 10 percent of Latinas and 11 percent of Latinos. (Data are not available for American Indians.) Only 16 percent of all women with disabilities are likely to have any college education, compared with 28 percent of men with disabilities.

- Although more women than men (approximately 56 to 44 percent) are college students, overall, women still lag behind men in earning Ph.Ds and professional degrees.

Boys

- Boys are more likely to be scolded and reprimanded in school, even when their misbehavior is equivalent to that of females. Males are more likely to be referred to school authorities for disciplinary action than are girls.

- Boys are far more likely to be identified as exhibiting learning disabilities, reading problems, and mental retardation. As a result, they are more likely to be enrolled in classes for the learning and emotional disturbed.

- Males receive lower report card grades from elementary school through college. In their elementary and high school years, they are more likely to be grade repeaters.

- Boys are disciplined more harshly, more publicly, and more frequently than are girls. They constitute 71 percent of school suspensions.

- The mismatch between boy norms and school norms contributes to the male dropout rate. As a result, boys are more likely to drop out of school than are girls.

- Boys enroll in fewer English, sociology, psychology, foreign language, and fine arts courses than do females.

- African American males are about half as likely as African American females to take Advanced Placement exams.

- Males lag behind females in a variety of extracurricular areas, including school government, literary activities, and the performing arts.

- The National Assessment of Educational Progress indicates that males perform significantly below females in writing achievement.

- Men are now the minority (about 44 percent) of students enrolled in both undergraduate and graduate institutions and as a group lag behind women in degree attainment at the associate, bachelor, and master's levels.

Psychological and Physical

Girls

- One in five girls report sexual or physical abuse, although these incidents are frequently not communicated to the authorities.
- Girls are sexually harassed more often than are boys and report more serious and more damaging consequences.
- About half of adolescent girls report having dieted, most in order to "look better."
- About one million U.S. teenage girls get pregnant each year, a higher relative percentage than in most Western nations. Between 1991 and 1996, teen birth rate for African Americans decreased by 17 percent, and by 9 percent for non-Hispanic Whites. The Hispanic birth rate has not declined.
- Teenage pregnancy is related to a constellation of factors, including poverty, low self-esteem, academic failure, and the perception of few life options. Forty-three percent of girls gave marriage or pregnancy as a reason for dropping out of school.
- One in four girls does not receive necessary health care.
- Both girls and boys believe that girls will have a more difficult time achieving their aspirations than will boys, and adolescent girls report higher levels of stress and depression and a lower level of confidence. Females exhibit lower self-esteem than do males during secondary and higher education.
- Despite extraordinary strides made by females in high school athletics, females exercise far less than do boys and receive only half the sports' budgets of male programs.

Boys

- Boys are taught stereotyped behaviors earlier and more harshly than are girls; there is a greater probability that such stereotyped behavior will stay with them for life.
- Society socializes boys into an active, independent, and aggressive role. But such behavior is incongruent with school norms and rituals that stress quiet behavior and docility. This results in a pattern of role conflict for boys, particularly during the elementary years.
- Hyperactivity is estimated to be nine times more prevalent in boys than in girls. Boys are more likely to be identified as having emotional problems, and statistics indicate a higher suicide rate among males.
- Conforming to the male sex-role stereotype takes a psychological toll. Boys who score high on sex-appropriate behavior tests also score highest on anxiety tests.
- Boys are underdiagnosed for depression and are more likely to be involved in alcohol or drug abuse.
- Males are less likely than females to be close friends with one another. When asked, most men identify women as their closest friends.

- In terms of school violence, three times as many boys as girls carry weapons, and twice as many have been threatened, injured with weapons, or in physical fights. In general, African American and Latino boys are more likely than others to be involved with crime and violence on school property.

- Male gang members outnumber females fifteen to one.

- In some areas of the country, it is more likely for a Black male between the ages of fifteen and twenty-five to die from homicide than it was for a U.S. soldier to be killed on a tour of duty in Vietnam.

- One in eight teenage dating relationships involves abuse. Until recently, programs focusing on adolescent sexuality and teen pregnancy were directed almost exclusively at females. Males were ignored, and this permissive "boys will be boys" attitude translated into sexual irresponsibility.

- Males are more likely to succumb to serious disease and be victims of accidents or violence. The average life expectancy of men is approximately eight years shorter than that of women.

Career and Family Relationships

Women

- On average, a female college graduate of any racial, ethnic, socioeconomic, or ability group still earns less than a White male with a college degree.

- Women overall earned 74 cents for every dollar earned by men; Latinas earned 54 cents, African American women earned 63 cents, White women earned 72 cents and Asian American women 80 cents (U.S. Bureau of the Census, 1997).

- More women than ever before are in the work force, but gender stereotypes still limit female options. Women comprise only 16.9 percent of electricians and electronic technicians, 11.1 percent of engineers, 2 percent of construction workers, 4 percent of mechanics, 2.5 percent of firefighters, and 4.1 percent of sheet metal workers.

- Within the few broad occupational categories in which women continue to be concentrated, further segregation also exists by race. For example, the occupations with the highest concentrations of African American women are nursing aides, cashiers, and secretaries; for Native American women it is welfare aides, childcare workers, and teacher's aides; and for White women it is administrative support workers, dental hygienists and assistants, and occupational therapists. In contrast, the three occupations with the highest concentrations of White men are executive and managerial workers, airplane pilots, and sales engineers.

- Women receive only about 16 percent of undergraduate and 11 percent of doctorate degrees in engineering, less than 2 percent of doctorate degrees in math and physical sciences, and 28 percent of undergraduate and 15 percent of doctorate degrees in computer and information sciences.

- Between 1970 and 1996, the percentage of women earning first professional degrees has increased dramatically. For example, in dentistry women increased from less than 10 percent to 36 percent; in medicine women increased from less than 10 percent to 41 percent; and in law women increased from less than 10 percent to 44 percent.
- Women are 73 percent of the elementary and secondary schoolteachers, but only 35 percent of the principals.

Men

- Even well-meaning teachers and counselors often advise boys to enter sex-stereotyped careers and limit their potential in occupations such as kindergarten teacher, nurse, or clerical worker.
- Many boys build career expectations that are higher than their abilities. This can result in later compromise, disappointment, and frustration.
- Current parenting patterns reinforce male stereotyping. Many families accept the notion that adolescent boys are naturally aggressive, withdrawn, and emotionally unexpressive, and they support these characteristics as normal development.
- As a result of the limited range of masculinity role models, boys tend to define themselves in opposition to others, either as nonfemale, nonhomosexual, or anti-authority (e.g., schools, parents). Adolescent boys, in particular, see female qualities as nonacceptable for males, contributing to an antigay and antifemale disposition.
- Both at school and at home, males are taught to hide or suppress their emotions; as husbands and fathers, they may find it difficult or impossible to show positive feelings toward their family and friends.
- Men and women vary in their beliefs about a father's role. Men emphasize the need for the father to earn a good income and to provide solutions to family problems. Women, on the other hand, stress the need for fathers to assist in caring for children and in responding to the emotional needs of the family. These differing perceptions of fatherhood increase family strain and anxiety.
- Few schools provide programs that encourage boys to understand and prepare for the parenting role. As a result, through absence and apathy, many men become not so much parents as "transparents."
- The male propensity for violence is too often manifested in family life by fathers and husbands who perpetrate physical abuse on spouses and children.

Research Summary

The report card reflects the volatile state of gender equity in and beyond school; while some gender barriers are crumbling, others seem impervious to change. During the past two decades, the gender gap has decreased in mathematics, biology, and chemistry, and in professional careers such as law and medicine. In fact, these rapid changes underscore the profound power of schools and society to radically alter age-old cultural norms (Hyde, Fenneman, & Lamon, 1990; Hyde & Lynn, 1988). Yet other areas have been resistant to change: computer science, technology, physics and engineering, for example, remain male domains, while elementary and preschool teaching positions are overwhelmingly female. To complicate matters further, an array of gender-related psychological and physical dynamics impact both males and females, in very different but often harmful ways. Gender equity has reached a new stage; just as the blatant bias and discrimination of the past becomes less frequent, subtle and pervasive bias continues to plague schools and to shortchange both girls and boys.

For the typical classroom teacher, gender equity emerges as a continuing challenge on at least two levels. First, gender is often the invisible issue in the curriculum, with the contributions and experiences of women absent. At other times, when the information is present, it is frightfully distorted. Second, female students typically receive less active instruction. Teachers focus more of their time and talent on male students. As a result, in the pages of books and in the voices of the classroom, females struggle to be heard (Hahn, 1996; Loewen, 1995). To help teachers tease out the subtle biases that persist in classrooms, we focus on two central areas of classroom life—student-teacher interaction and the curriculum.

GENDER BIAS IN TODAY'S CLASSROOMS: THE CURRICULUM

Today's curriculum, both "low-tech" books and "high-tech" computers, often set the pace and the tone of classroom instruction. Studies (Woodward & Elliot, 1990) suggest that students spend as much as 80 to 95 percent of classroom time using textbooks and that teachers make a majority of their instructional decisions based on the textbook. In recent years, the advent of the Internet and enhanced media options, such as cable and satellite television broadcasting, have come to offer students a greater array of curricular resources than ever before. Today, both print and electronic resources typically determine what is taught in U.S. classrooms, and what is not.

In the 1970s and the 1980s, textbook companies and professional associations, such as the American Psychological Association, issued guidelines for nonracist and nonsexist books, suggesting how to include and fairly portray different groups in the curriculum. As a result, textbooks became more balanced in their description of underrepresented groups; but problems of biased instructional material persist. In science textbooks, two-thirds to three-quarters of drawings are male, and not one of the five texts examined contained an image of a female scientist (Bazler & Simons, 1990). Seventy percent of music-related figures found in school textbooks were male (Koza, 1992). A 1989 language arts textbook had twice as many males as females represented and far more stories featuring male characters (Sadker & Sadker, 1994b, p. 72; Women's Educational Equity Act, 1999). In Addison-Wesley's 1991 *World History: Traditions and New Directions*, five times more men than women are pictured, the text index cites 41 women and 596 men, and only 1 page of text (in a 819-page book) discusses women. Prentice-Hall's *1992 History of the United States* by Daniel Boorstin and Brooks Mather Kelley offers four times more illustrations of males than females, and less than 3 percent of the text history relates the lives, experiences, and contributions of women (Sadker & Sadker, 1994b, pp. 130–131.) Unfortunately, bias is alive and flourishing in today's curriculum.

How can teachers detect such bias? Perhaps the first step is to be able to understand the different manifestations of bias. Following is a description of seven forms of bias that can be used to assess instructional materials. These forms of bias can be based not only on gender, race, or ethnicity, but they can also help identify prejudice against the elderly, people with disabilities, non-English speakers, gays and lesbians, and limited English speakers. In short, any group can be inaccurately portrayed through one or more of these seven forms of bias.

Invisibility

Women have made significant contributions to the growth and development of the United States, contributions mostly ignored in history textbooks. This form of bias (invisibility, or omission) characterizes not only history books, but also texts in reading, language arts, mathematics, science, spelling, and vocational education.

A 1970 study of history texts found that students had to read more than 500 pages before they found 1 page of information about women (Trecker, 1977). New history texts, published in the 1990s, continue to devote only 2 or 3 percent of book space discussing the experiences or contributions of women (Women's Educational Equity Act, 1999). When girls and women are systematically excluded from curricular material, students are deprived of information about half the nation's people. The result is that both boys and girls lower their opinions about the importance of females in creating the United States. For example, when asked to name twenty famous women from American history, most students cannot do it. Typically, they list fewer than five (Sadker & Sadker, 1994b). A similar case can be made for the invisibility of males in parenting and other roles nontraditional to their gender.

Linguistic Bias

The use of masculine terms and pronouns was one of the earliest forms of gender bias to be detected, and authors and publishers quickly set about to correct the language. As a result, newer texts are less likely to use terms such as *caveman*, *forefathers*, or *policeman*. Yet, some linguistic bias persists, especially in the use of selected adjectives. The conservative nineteenth-century diplomat Klemens von Metternich is described in one recent and popular high school history book as a man whose "charm" worked well with "elegant ladies"–adjectives and facts of dubious historical import, but not without prurient interest (Beck, Black, Krieger, Naylor, & Ibo Shabaka, 1999). The German use of the term *fatherland* to describe Germany while Russians use *motherland* to describe Russia are examples of gendered nouns that offer insights into different national consciousness; such gender and linguistic insights are frequently left unexplained in texts.

In addition to these subtle forms of linguistic bias that persists in newer textbooks, more overt linguistic bias continues to emerge in classroom life. Many economically strapped districts are forced to use texts that are ten, twenty, or even thirty years old, books replete with gender bias. And teachers themselves may unintentionally perpetrate linguistic bias through the materials they create for instruction, and in their spoken language. Too often teachers resort to the familiar sexist words of their own past, using pronouns such as *he* or nouns such as *mankind* to refer to all people, or using unnecessary modifiers, such as *female doctor*, which serve to promote sexist assumptions. Linguistic bias is certainly less common in today's classrooms, but it is far from extinct.

Stereotyping

Stereotyping persists when one gender is portrayed exhibiting one set of values, behaviors, and roles, and the other gender is in possession of a different set of values, behaviors, and roles. From traditional phonics reading texts to current computer software, boys routinely have been shown as ingenious, creative, brave, athletic, achieving, and curious, and men are seen as the movers and shakers of history, the scientists of achievement, and the political leaders. Not all the male action figures in the curriculum have been positive, since males are also portrayed as the evil doers in history, or as the violent and unruly ones at home.

Girls more often are portrayed as dependent, passive, fearful, docile, and even as victims, with a limited role in or impact on the world. In a study of seventy-seven basal readers published between 1980 and 1982, books that are still in use in some classrooms today, Britton and Lumpkin (1983) found a total of 5,501 careers depicted; 64 percent were attributed to Anglo males, 14 percent to Anglo females, 17 percent to males of color, and 5 percent to females of color.

The most common careers shown for Anglo males were soldier, farmer, doctor, and police officer. The most frequently shown role models for males of color were worker, farmer, warrior, Indian chief, and hunter. The most common careers for White women were mother, teacher, author, and princess. For females of color, mother and teacher also headed the list, followed by slave, worker, porter, and artist (Britton & Lumpkin, 1983). Unfortunately, even with instructional materials published more recently, gender stereotypes persist. A 1990s study of elementary mathematics software revealed that when gender-identifiable characters were present (about 40 percent of the time), only 12 percent of the characters were female. Reinforcing stereotypes, female characters were portrayed passively as mothers and princesses while male characters were shown as active and as "heavy equipment operators, factory workers, shopkeepers, mountain climbers, hang gliders, garage mechanics, and as a genie providing directions" (Hodes, 1995–1996).

Imbalance

Textbooks perpetuate bias by presenting only one interpretation of an issue, situation, or group of people, avoiding subtleties and complexities. Sometimes the reason for imbalance is to simplify a difficult issue or to squeeze a complex topic into limited book space. At other times, only one point of view is present to avoid potential controversy and to ensure that school board members, educational administrators, and teachers or parents are not offended.

The suffrage movement is one example of imbalance in history texts. The fight to enfranchise half the population and the efforts made by women like Elizabeth Cady Stanton are described as a time when women were "given" the vote (Sewall, 1992). Few texts report the bravery and sacrifices of the suffrage leaders that eventually "won" the right to vote.

Unreality

Textbooks the world over share this common form of bias called unreality. In this technique, controversial topics such as discrimination and prejudice are glossed over in favor of a more fanciful, favorable, and traditional view of national history or current issues. Like imbalance, this unrealistic portrayal is done to avoid offending adults who are the decision makers in purchasing textbooks. For example, almost 50 percent of all marriages in the United States end in divorce, and one-third of all children will live with a single parent during part of their lives (U.S. Department of Education, 1996). Some texts provide sensitive and accurate portrayals of these new demographic realities; others find these new realities difficult to confront. For example, one text reports: "In some cultures, the basic unit is the nuclear family, or a mother, father, and their children. This pattern is common in industrial nations such as the United States, Great Britain, and Germany" (Jacobs, LeVasseur, & Randolph, 1998). When difficult issues are papered over, students are denied the information they will need to confront and resolve real social challenges (Noddings, 1992).

Fragmentation

Did you ever read a textbook that separates the discussion of women into a disconnected chapter, or perhaps a separate section or insert? This is called fragmentation (or sometimes isolation) and communicates to readers that while women are an interesting diversion, their contributions do not constitute the mainstream of history or literature or the sciences. Fragmentation also occurs when groups are depicted as interacting only among themselves and as having little or no influence on society as a whole. For example, textbook discussions of feminism often talk about how women are affected by this contemporary movement, but there is little analysis of the impact of the women's movement on men, politics, or the business community.

Cosmetic Bias

Cosmetics can provide an illusion of an up-to-date, well-balanced textbook; yet beneath the superficial appearance, bias persists. Cosmetic bias emerges in a science textbook that features a glossy pullout of female scientists but includes precious little narrative of the scientific contributions of women. Another example is a music book with an eye-catching, multiethnic cover that projects a world of diverse songs and symphonies, yet behind the cover, traditional White male composers dominate the book. This illusion of equity is really a marketing strategy directed at potential adopters who *flip* the pages and might be lured into purchasing books that appear current, diverse, and balanced.

RECENT PROGRESS

The last thirty years have witnessed uneven progress in creating fairer textbooks. In the 1970s, professional associations and publishers created and distributed guidelines for creating nonsexist books (NCTE Committee, 1973). These guidelines recommended that the achievements of women be included in their textbooks; that women and girls be given the same respect as men and boys; that abilities, traits, interests, and activities should not be assigned on the basis of male or female stereotypes; and that sexist language be avoided. Today, most textbook publishers edit books for sexist language and work to include more equitable presentations of females and people of color. For example, a study of story problems in mathematics textbooks from the mid-1930s to the late 1980s found a greater proportion of story problems about women in textbooks used in the 1980s than in the 1970s or before (Nibbelink, Stockdale, & Mangru, 1986). A study of the Newbery Medal Award books in the 1970s and 1980s found the portrayal of women and girls less stereotypic, and the number of girls and women as the main character has increased substantially (Kinman & Henderson, 1985). A study of the illustrations in seven elementary science textbook series found that female children were represented with greater frequency than were male children, a change from previous findings (Powell & Garcia, 1985). Unfortunately, progress can be slow, and the contributions of women in most history texts are still minimized (Crocco, 1997; Davis, Ponder, Burlbaw, Garza-Lubeck, & Moss, 1986; Sadker & Sadker, 1994a). In short, today's instructional materials are less biased, but they are not yet bias-free. Teachers still must exercise care in selecting and using curriculum materials.

Educators who choose gender-fair materials can encourage positive growth in students. Bias-free materials in literature expand students' knowledge of changing sex roles and encourage greater flexibility in attitudes regarding appropriate behavior for females and males. In science and math, gender-fair materials provide females with encouragement to enter careers in traditionally male areas. Such a curriculum can teach boys to consider their future family roles, and the importance of involved and caring fathers. But gender-fair curricular materials by themselves are not sufficient to create a nonsexist educational environment. Attention must also be paid to the process of instruction.

GENDER BIAS IN TODAY'S CLASSROOMS: INSTRUCTION

The following scene, an updated general music class in action, reflects the subtle ways gender bias can permeate the instructional process (Carter, 1987).

As the bell rings, students take their seats. The girls are clustered in the front and on the right-hand side of the room, while the boys are predominantly on the other side of the room and in the back. This seating arrangement doesn't bother the students; they choose their own seats. It doesn't seem to bother their teacher, Mrs. Howe, who feels that students should have the right to sit where they choose (unless of course, there is racial segregation. Mrs. Howe has little patience for that). Everyone seems comfortable with the boys and girls creating their own seating areas.

Mrs. Howe starts the lesson by playing part of Mozart's Symphony Concatenate on the CD player. After about five minutes, she turns to the class with questions.

MRS. HOWE: Who can tell me the name of this composer?
(A few hands are raised when John shouts out "Ricky Martin." After the laughter dies down, Mrs. Howe calls on Mitch.)
MITCH: Haydn.
MRS. HOWE: Why do you think so?
MITCH: Because yesterday you played Haydn.
MRS. HOWE: Close. Enrique, what do you think?

ENRIQUE: I don't know.

MRS. HOWE: Come on, Enrique. During the last two weeks we have been listening to various classical period composers. Out of those we've listened to, who wrote this piece? (Silence)

MRS. HOWE: John, can you help Enrique out?

JOHN: Beethoven.

MRS. HOWE: No, it's not Beethoven. Beethoven was more a Romantic period composer. Think!

(Mrs. Howe finally calls on Pam, who has had her hand half-raised during this discussion.)

PAM: I'm not sure, but is it Mozart?

MRS. HOWE: Uh-huh. Anyone else agree with Pam?

MITCH (calls out): It's Mozart. It's similar to the Mozart concerto you played yesterday.

MRS. HOWE: Very good. Can you tell us if this is another concerto he wrote?

MITCH: Yes, it's a violin concerto.

MRS. HOWE: That's almost right. It's a special concerto written for two instruments. To help you figure out the other instrument, let's listen to more of the piece.

(Mrs. Howe plays more of the piece and calls on Mitch.)

MITCH: Another violin.

MRS. HOWE: Peter?

PETER: A cello.

MRS. HOWE: You're all close. It's another string instrument, but it's not another violin or a cello.

RUTH (calls out): What about a viola?

MRS. HOWE: Ruth, you know I don't allow shouting out. Raise your hand next time. Peter?

PETER: A viola.

MRS. HOWE: Very good. This is a special kind of concerto Mozart wrote for both the violin and viola called Symphony Concatenate. One reason why I want you to listen to it is to notice the difference between the violin and the viola. Let's listen to the melody as played first by the violin then the viola. Listen for the similarities and differences between the two.

This scenario demonstrates several important interaction patterns; in this gender-segregated classroom, Mrs. Howe called on the boys more often than on the girls and asked them more higher-order and lower-order questions. She gave male students more specific feedback, including praise, constructive criticism, and remediation. Research (M. Sadker

& D. Sadker, 1985) shows that from grade school to graduate school, most classrooms demonstrate similar instructional patterns.

One large study (Sadker & Sadker, 1984) conducted in the fourth, sixth, and eighth grades in more than 100 classrooms in 4 states and the District of Columbia found that teachers gave boys more academic attention than they gave girls. They asked them more questions and gave them more precise and clear feedback concerning the quality of their responses. In contrast, girls were more likely to be ignored or given vague evaluation of the academic quality of their work (D'Ambrosio and Hammer, 1996; Sadker & Sadker, 1994a). Other research shows that these same patterns are prevalent at the secondary and postsecondary levels (Sadker, Sadker, & Klein, 1991).

One reason boys get more teacher attention is that they demand it. More likely to shout out questions and answers, they dominate the classroom airwaves. However, when boys call out, teachers are likely to accept their comments. In contrast, when girls call out teachers are more likely to reprimand them by saying things like, "In this class, we raise our hands before talking."

Another factor allowing boys to dominate interaction is the widespread gender segregation that characterizes classrooms. Occasionally teachers divide their classrooms into gender-segregated lines, teams, work and play areas, and seating arrangements. More frequently, students gender-segregate themselves. Drawn to the sections of the classroom where the more assertive boys are clustered, the teacher is positioned to keep interacting with male students.

The conclusion of most interaction studies is that teachers give more attention (positive, negative, and neutral) to male students. However, some researchers emphasize that low-achieving males get most of the negative attention, while high-achieving boys get more positive and constructive academic contacts. But no matter whether they are high or low achievers, female students are more likely to be invisible and ignored (Brophy & Good, 1974; Sadker & Sadker, 1994b; Sadker & Sadker, 1994c).

The gender difference in classroom communications is more than a mere counting game of who gets the teacher's attention and who does not. Teacher attention is a vote of high expectations and commitment to a student. Decades of research show that students who are actively involved in classroom discussion are more likely to achieve and to express positive attitudes toward schools and learning (Flanders, 1970; Good & Brophy, 1994).

Most teachers do not choose to be biased in their treatment of students and are typically unaware of inequitable interaction. On the positive side, studies show that with resources, awareness, and training, teachers can eliminate gender bias instructional patterns and can achieve equity in how they teach female and male students. It is unfortunate that most schools of education still do not provide these resources, and that today's new teachers continue to be unaware of the research and skills needed for gender-fair instruction (Campbell & Sanders, 1997; Sadker, Sadker, & Shakeshaft, 1992).

TRENDS AND CHALLENGES

The 1990s witnessed the emergence of several fascinating, and disturbing, gender-related school issues. Gender equity became a political issue as conservative commentators attacked the validity of educational research, suggesting that if gender bias exists at all, it is the boys, not the girls, who are the real victims. For instance, a literature review of gender-related research studies collected by Wellesley College and funded by the AAUW was attacked as biased "advocacy research" (Sommers, 1995). Although the critics questioned only a few of the more than one thousand studies described in these reports, and most of their charges were flimsy at best, such criticism weakened public and political support for gender equity programs (Sadker, 1996). Many people who read about these criticisms were unaware that the commentators themselves were often not independent researchers, but were in fact funded by ultraconservative foundations. While decrying "advocacy research," they were in fact modeling it. In one case, the author of this chapter was telephoned by one such commentator and asked to photocopy and mail hundreds of pages of a fifteen-year-old research report. When the author suggested that the researcher go to a library and read the report, the conservative critic wrote a number of articles claiming that the research and the report documenting gender bias never existed (Kleinfeld, 1999).

At the same time, some writers, researchers, and political leaders, both conservative and liberal, called for the reestablishment of single-gender education, although for different reasons. Conservatives argued that sex-separate education was more effective than was coeducation, citing educational research that suggested for girls, at least, there was evidence to support such a position. Conservatives believed that single-gender environments led to more focus, less distraction, and higher academic performance. Liberal critics of coeducation were convinced that gender bias was so endemic, so real, and so damaging that the current school organization could never be responsive to the needs of girls. As a result, both liberals and conservatives found common ground and advocated for single-gender classes and schools. In fact, by the late 1990s, the state of California joined a number of local school districts across the nation experimenting with single-gender education, an experiment that would await a court test to determine the constitutionality of separate-but-equal single-gender schools (Sadker & Sadker, 1995).

While some people worked to separate the sexes, others feared for the safety of their students as gun violence erupted across the nation. Most instances of school cruelty and injury, such as physical violence, bullying, sexual harassment, antigay acts, and shootings, were being perpetrated by males. It was not difficult to link school shootings to the violence associated with the male stereotype. Even as these vicious incidents threatened to take schools back to a more primitive and dangerous past, the last decade of the twentieth century witnessed technological breakthroughs pushing schools into a brave new world, a world driven by computers. Once again, females found themselves on the wrong end of a new gender gap, this time in technological training and careers. Let's take a brief look at some of these newer gender issues (Sadker, 1999).

Single-Sex Schools and Classes

From the 1960s through the early part of the 1990s, there was a precipitous decline in U.S. single-sex secondary and postsecondary schools. The number of women's colleges dwindled from almost 300 to fewer than 100, and single-gender high school statistics reflected a similar decline. The widespread belief that single-sex education was an anachronism led many schools to become coeducational institutions, or to close their doors.

By the early 1990s, single-sex education was "in" again, and there was a resurgence of interest in girls' schools and women's colleges. Research findings suggested that for females, at least, single-sex education may indeed offer advantages, including increased academic achievement, self-esteem, and career salience, as well as a decrease in sex-role stereotyping (Cairns, 1990; Hollinger, 1993; Tyack & Hansot, 1990). One study found that students in girls' schools in the United States expressed greater interest in both mathematics and English, took more mathematics courses, did more homework, and had more positive attitudes toward academic achievement (Lee & Bryk, 1986). Girls in single-sex schools showed more interest in the feminist movement and were less sex-role stereotyped than were their peers in coeducational schools (Lee & Marks, 1990; Riordan, 1990; Sadker & Sadker,1995). As a result, some public schools established single-sex classes or schools, usually for girls, but sometimes, as in the case of California, for both girls and boys. While not all researchers believe that the findings on single-gender education were all that persuasive, or that single-gender schools were in fact a good idea, most agree that the research on male schools and classes showed little or no benefits for single-sex boys' schools (AAUW, 1998b).

Title IX

Widely known for its application to sports, Title IX of the 1972 Educational Amendments also prohibits sex discrimination in counseling, discipline, testing, admissions, medical facilities, the treatment of students, financial aid, and a host of educational activities. By now, some people might have hoped that Title IX would have eliminated sex bias, since it became the law of the land approximately three decades ago. In reality, despite some sparkling advances (women's soccer and increased college enrollments, to name two striking examples), Title IX requirements are often ignored. With no funding provided to promote awareness of Title IX, gender bias continues to be a daily part of the school lives of both students and teachers. Too often, sexist school practices persist because parents and students are either unaware of their rights under the law, or find it difficult to lodge a complaint with unresponsive or uninformed school administrators. The slow pace of federal enforcement and opposition from groups unfriendly to the provisions of gender equity legislation not only hamper current implementation of Title IX but also raise concerns for the future of the law.

Violence and the Male Stereotype

Research studies indicate that while most males do not perpetrate violence, most gendered violence is perpetrated by males (Foulis & McCabe, 1997; Schwartz, 1997). A more violent and physical disposition seems to begin for males at an early age. In the first three years of school, research indicates that young boys initiate most of the teasing and bullying incidents, that teachers and adults frequently ignore such incidents, and that both boys and girls are the targets of bullying and sexual harassment. For boys, the harassment takes the form of questioning and challenging their male sexuality. Typically, males respond with a physical reaction to such taunts, feeding the cycle of violence. Male taunts regarding sexuality underscore the deep homophobia in male youth (AAUW, 1993). For girls, the response to harassment or bullying is more likely to be verbal and ineffective (Froschl, Sprung, & Mullin-Ridler, 1998). For gay, lesbian, and bisexual students, taunts and physical attacks, usually from males, have become commonplace. In one survey, nine out of ten such youth reported verbal or physical attacks, and in 15 percent of the cases, the attacks were so severe that medical services were required (Safe Schools Coalition of Washington, 1995).

Males with traditional sex-role stereotypes and perceptions are more likely to harass or commit violence, more likely to see such acts as normal, and less likely to take responsibility for their actions (LeJeune & Folette, 1994; Perry et al., 1998). Males have perpetrated the majority of gun violence and shootings in U.S. schools. Educators and psychologists are investigating male socialization patterns, seeking not only reasons for this violence connection, but also strategies to prevent such incidents. In a very real sense, the male voice, more likely to be read in the curriculum and heard in the classroom, is now shouting to be heard on a national stage.

By the late 1990s, volumes about boys were cascading into book stores. These tomes varied dramatically in quality and approach. Some books called for greater parental understanding of the pressures boys faced and emphasized the need for more love and communication between adults and boys. Some authors indicted the cultural pressures on males for creating an unspoken "boy code," a set of rules and societal expectations that pushed boys into limited, unrealistic, and damaging roles (Pollack, 1998). Other books focused on boy "risk factors," condemning the contemporary tide of boy-initiated violence and decrying the "culture of cruelty" in male peer groups (Garbarino, 1999; Gillian, 1997; Kindlon & Thompson, 1999; Miedzian, 1992). Several books focused on thoughtful, practical strategies and advice for parents and educators concerned with raising caring males of integrity (Kivel, 1999; Salisbury & Jackson, 1995; Silverstein & Rashbaum, 1995). Unfortunately, a few books found it advantageous to lash out at females, in a sense perpetuating male aggression by charging that the feminist movement was the root cause of the problem boys face today. These books argued that inappropriate mothering, female teachers, and the drive for female rights interfered with natural male biology. Some authors maintained a testosterone-based explanation of gender differences, explaining that males and females were "wired" differently from birth, and that traditional male aggression and behavior must be recognized and can best be channeled only by other males (Gurian, 1997). As the sweeping targets and disparate reasonings found in these new books suggest, the rebirth of interest in the male role offers both promise and pitfalls.

Technology

The swift advent of computers, the Internet, and high-tech innovations has dramatically affected the nation's economy, culture, and schools. Many of today's students are preparing for, and some are already profiting from, these information-age changes. However, statistics reveal that the new technology is plagued by an old phenomenon: the gender gap. Females account for less than 20 percent of the student enrollment in advanced computer science courses, but they still dominate the data-entry courses, preparing them for employment in the lower-paying clerical fields (AAUW, 1998a). Girls are also less likely to use computers outside of school, and girls from all ethnic groups rate themselves considerably lower than boys on computer ability. Certainly this situation is not helped by current software products, which are more likely to reinforce gender stereotypes and bias than to reduce them. Without appropriate teacher training, more equitable software, and programs designed to build technological self-confidence and self-competence among girls, women workers in the twenty-first century are likely to see this technology gap grow into a costly income gap (AAUW, 1998a).

A DOZEN STRATEGIES FOR CREATING GENDER-FAIR CLASSROOMS

Some of these recent trends are discouraging, but they are not the final word. Teachers can make an enormous difference in the lives of their students. The following suggestions consist of ways to make your own classroom a nonsexist one (AAUW, 1998a; Sadker, Sadker, & Klein, 1986; 1994).

1. If the textbooks and software that you are given are biased, you may wish to confront this bias rather than ignore it. Discuss the issue directly with your students. It is entirely appropriate to acknowledge that instructional materials are not always perfect. By engaging your students in a conversation about curricular omission and stereotyping, you can introduce them to important social issues and help them to develop critical reading skills as well.

2. Supplementary materials can offset the influence of limited textbooks. School, university, and local libraries, as well as the Internet, can offer information on the lives and contributions of women and other underrepresented groups.

3. Have your students help you assemble bulletin boards, websites, and other instructional displays. Teach them about the forms of bias and make sure that the displays, projects, and products are bias-free.

4. Analyze your seating chart to determine whether there are pockets of race or gender segregation in your classroom. Make certain that you do not teach in one area of the room, investing your time and attention on one group of students while ignoring others. When your students work in groups, construct the groups to reflect diversity. Monitor student groups for equitable participation and decision making.

5. Role modeling is central to learning. Students are taught less by what adults say, and more by what adults do. This is particularly true in the classroom, where teachers' words are measured against their actions. A male teacher who cooks or weaves, or a female teacher active on the athletic fields or skillful with machines teach students believable and powerful lessons about the range of behaviors available to all of us. Teachers need to be sensitive as to the potent lessons their everyday behaviors teach.

   Educators can extend these lessons by inviting guest speakers to the classroom, speakers who can address interests and competencies that break stereotypic boundaries. For younger children, inviting male nurses and female physicians to the classroom widens the career horizons of both genders. Even for older children, an engineer or a graphic artist who describes the exact tasks involved in their jobs (specifics that often elude even adults!) can enlighten both girls and boys to the amazing possibilities of the work place.

6. Technology, although a new educational frontier, can be short-circuited by curricular and instructional biases. Teachers should schedule computer time equally for all students. A schedule is better than the democratic sounding "free-time" phrase, which can result in the very undemocratic domination of the keyboard by a few of the more aggressive students. Schedules create more equitable access. In addition to creating rules for computer access, software needs to be considered. Newer technologies are no guarantee that old and destructive biases will not reappear. Teachers and students need to make certain that new technology does not reinforce racial, ethnic, gender, or any form of destructive bias.

7. Positive reinforcement can be effective for increasing the amount of time boys and girls work and play in coeducational arrangements. In some studies (Holden, 1993; Petersen, Johnson, & Johnson, 1991; Schmuck & Schmuck, 1992) teachers made a consistent effort to praise girls and boys who were working and playing cooperatively together. When teachers praised in this way, the amount of time girls and boys spent working and playing cooperatively increased.

8. Peer tutoring and cooperative learning can encourage positive gender and racial relationships. Moreover, these techniques increase achievement not only for the students being helped, but for those doing the helping as well. Both peer tutoring and cooperative learning are much more powerful when students receive training in how to work constructively with others. Where such training is not given, boys tend to dominate cooperative learning groups.

9. Most teachers find it difficult to track their own questioning patterns while they are teaching. Try to have someone do this for you. Make arrangements to have a professional whose feedback you value (a supervisor, your principal, another teacher) come into your classroom and observe. Your observer can tally how many questions you ask boys and how many you ask girls; and how many questions you ask students of different racial and ethnic groups. Then you can consider the race and sex of your active students and silent students in your class. Determine whether one group is receiving more than its fair share of your time and attention.

10. Because teachers may find it difficult to have professional observers come into their classrooms on a regular basis, many have found it helpful to have students tally questioning patterns, counting who gets questions, and who is likely to be left out. Before you do this, you may want to explain to the class how important it is for all students to become involved in classroom discussion. Sharing your commitment to equity with your students is itself an important and genuine technique for promoting fairness in and beyond the classroom.

11. Do not tolerate harmful words, bullying, or harassment in your classroom. Do not say "Boys will be boys" to excuse sexist comments or behaviors. Nor are racist or anti-gay comments to be ignored, laughed at, or tolerated. As a teacher, you are the model and the norm setter: if you do not tolerate hurtful prejudice, your students will learn to honor and respect each other.

12. Because research on gender equity in education is occurring at a rapid pace, it is important to continue your reading and professional development in this area. Be alert for articles and other publications on the topic, and be careful that your own rights are not denied because of sex discrimination. Also, be discerning as you read related topics. Remember that research publications are less susceptible to political agendas than are the popular press or politically funded organizations.

Questions and Activities

1. The authors of this chapter list seven forms of gender bias that you can use when evaluating instructional materials: (1) linguistic bias, (2) stereotyping, (3) invisibility, (4) imbalance, (5) unreality, (6) fragmentation, and (7) cosmetic bias. In your own words, define each form of bias. Examine a sample K–12 textbook in your teaching area and determine whether it contains any of these forms of gender bias. Are there forms of bias reflected against any other groups? Share your findings with your classmates or workshop participants.

2. Give three examples of how teachers can supplement textbooks to eliminate the seven forms of gender bias identified in Activity 1 above. Now go on-line and search for equity websites that provide supplementary resources.

3. Why have centuries of female effort to gain educational access gone almost unnoticed and unrecognized? How has that experience differed from civil rights efforts undertaken by African Americans, Latinos, and other groups? How has it been similar?

4. In what ways do Mrs. Howe's interactions with the boys and girls during the music lesson indicate gender bias? How might you help Mrs. Howe change her behavior and to make it more gender-fair?

5. Observe lessons being taught in several classrooms that include boys and girls and students from different racial and ethnic groups. Create a seating chart and count the interactions given to each student. Did the ways the teachers interacted with males and female students differ? If so, in what ways? Did the teachers interact with students from various ethnic groups differently? If so, in what ways? Did you notice any ways that gender and ethnicity combined to influence the ways the teachers interacted with particular students? If so, explain.

6. How can you use technology to supplement classroom materials and promote gender equity? Can you find some useful equity websites for your students that augment information missing from textbooks?

7. Girls start out in school ahead of boys in speaking, reading, and counting. Boys surpass girls in math performance by junior high school. Why do you think this happens? Recent research indicates that the disparities in the academic achievement of boys and girls are declining. Why do you think this achievement gap is shrinking?

8. In what ways, according to the authors, are single-sex schools beneficial for females? Why do you think all-girls schools are making a comeback? Do you think this trend should be halted or supported? Why or why not?

9. After reading this chapter, do you think there are some ways you can change your behavior to make it more gender fair? If yes, in what ways? If no, why not?

10. How are the rights of gay and lesbian students related to gender equity issues? How does homophobia endanger the rights of all students? What can teachers do to create safe and effective classroom climates for all students?

11. Identify six classroom strategies that can encourage girls to develop both technological confidence and competence.

12. Check out the requirements of Title IX. Prepare a brief list to remind you of some of the ways the law is designed to insure gender equity. (The Internet is a good source for this information. Try http://womensequity@edc.org/;http://www.maec.org/ or http://phoenix.edc.org/WomensEquity/).

13. Consider how gender bias impacts males by creating questions based on the report card findings in this chapter. Interview boys of various ages and collect their insights about male and female roles. How aware are your interviewees about the dangers of the male stereotype? How do they describe their roles as adult men?

References

American Association of University Women Educational Foundation (AAUW). (1998a). *Gender Gaps: Where Schools Still Fail Our Children*. Washington, DC: Author.

American Association of University Women Educational Foundation (AAUW). (1998b). *Separated by Sex: A Critical Look at Single-Sex Education for Girls*. Washington, DC: Author.

American Association of University Women Foundation (AAUW). (1993). *Hostile Hallways: The AAUW Survey of Sexual Harassment in America's Schools*. Washington, DC: Author.

American Psychological Association. (1999). *APA Public Policy Office*. Is Youth Violence Just Another Fact of Life? In *Raising Children to Resist Violence: What You Can Do*. Washington, DC: Author.

Bailey, B. L., Scantlebury, K., and Letts, W. J. (1997). It's Not My Style: Using Disclaimers to Ignore Issues in Science. *Journal of Teacher Education 48*(1), 29–35.

Bazler, J., and Simons, D. (1990). Are Women Out of the Picture? *Science Teacher 57*(9), 24–26. [See also Potter, E. and Rosser, S. (1992). Factors in Life Science Textbooks That May Deter Girls Interest in Science. *Journal of Research in Science Teaching 57*(9), 669–686.]

Beck, R., Black, L. Krieger, L. Naylor, P., and Shabaka, D. (1999). *World History: Patterns of Interaction*. Evanston, IL: McDougal Littell.

Britton, G., and Lumpkin, M. (1983). Females and Minorities in Basal Readers. *Interracial Books for Children Bulletin, 14*(6), 4–7.

Brophy, J. and Good, T. (1974). *Teacher Student Relationships: Causes and Consequences*. New York: Holt, Rinehart and Winston.

Cairns, E. (1990). The Relationship between Adolescent Perceived Self-Competence and Attendance at Single-Sex Secondary School. *British Journal of Educational Psychology, 60*(3), 207–211.

Campbell, P. B. and Sanders, J. (1997). Uninformed, but Interested: Findings of a National Survey on Gender Equity in Preservice Teacher Education. *Journal of Teacher Education, 48*(1), 69–75.

Carter, R. (1987). Unpublished class paper. American University, Washington, DC. Used with permission.

Clarke, E. H. (1873). *Sex in Education: Or, a Fair Chance for Girls.* Boston: Houghton Mifflin.

Crocco, M. S. (1997). Making Time for Women's History: When Your Survey Course Is Already Filled to Overflowing. *Social Education, 6*(1), 32–37.

D'Ambrosio, M. and Hammer, P. S. (April 1996). Gender Equity in the Catholic Elementary Schools. Paper presented at the annual convention and exposition of the National Catholic Education Association, Philadelphia.

Davis, O. L., Jr., Ponder, G., Burlbaw, L., Garza-Lubeck, M., and Moss, A. (1986). *Looking at History: A Review of Major U.S. History Textbooks.* Washington, DC: People for the American Way.

Faludi, S. (1991). *Backlash: The Undeclared War against American Women.* New York: Crown.

Flanders, N. (1970). *Analyzing Teaching Behaviors.* Reading, MA: Addison-Wesley.

Foulis, D. and McCabe, M. P. (1997). Sexual Harassment: Factors Affecting Attitudes and Perceptions. *Sex Roles: A Journal of Research, 37*(9–10), 773–798.

Froschl, M., Sprung, B., and Mullin-Ridler, N. (1998). *Quit It! : A Teacher's Guide on Teasing and Bullying for Use with Students in Grades K–3.* New York: Equity Concepts; Wellesley, MA: Wellesley College Center for Research on Women; Washington, DC: NEA.

Garbarino, J. (1999). *Lost Boys: Why Our Sons Turn Violent and How We Can Save Them.* New York: Free Press.

Gilligan, J. (1997). *Violence: Reflections on a National Epidemic.* New York: Vintage.

Good, T. L. and Brophy, J. E. (1994). *Looking in Classrooms.* New York: Harper-Collins College Publishers.

Gurian, M. (1997). *The Wonder of Boys.* New York: Tarcher Putnam.

Hahn, C. L. (1996). Gender and Political Learning. *Theory and Research in Education, 24*(1), 8–35.

Hall, G. S. (1905). *Adolescence: Its Psychology and Relations to Physiology, Anthropology, Sociology, Sex, Crime, Religion, and Education.* New York: D. Appleton.

Hodes, C. L. (1995–1996). Gender Representations in Mathematics Software. *Journal of Educational Technology Systems, 24,* 67–73.

Holden, C. (1993). Giving Girls a Chance: Patterns of Talk in Co-Operative Group Work. *Gender & Education, 5,* 179–89.

Hollinger, D. (Ed.). (1993). *Single-Sex Schooling: Perspectives from Practice and Research.* Washington: DC: Office of Educational Research and Improvement, U.S. Department of Education.

Hyde, J., Fenneman, E., and Lamon, S. (1990). Gender Differences in Mathematical Performance: A Meta-Analysis. *Psychological Bulletin, 107,* 139–155.

Hyde, J. and Lynn, M. (1988). Gender Differences in Verbal Activity: A Meta-Analysis. *Psychological Bulletin, 104,* 53–69.

Jacobs, H., LeVasseur, M., and Randolph, B. (1998). *Western Hemisphere Geography, History, Culture* (Prentice-Hall World Explorer Program). Upper Saddle River, NJ: Prentice-Hall.

Kindlon, D. and Thompson, M. (1999). *Raising Cain.* New York: Ballantine Books.

Kinman, J. and Henderson, D. (1985). An Analysis of Sexism in Newbery Medal Award Books from 1977 to 1984. *The Reading Teacher, 38*(May), 885–889.

Kivel, P. (1999). *Boys Will Be Men: Raising Our Sons for Courage, Caring, and Community.* British Columbia, Canada: New Society Publishers.

Kleinfeld, J. (1999), Student Performance: Males Versus Females. *The Public Interest*, *134*(Winter), 3–20.

Koza, J. E. (1992). The Boys in the Band: Sexism and the Construction of Gender in Middle School Textbook Illustrations. *Educational Foundations*, *6*(3), 85–105.

Lee, V. and Bryk, A. (1986). Effects of Single-Sex Secondary Schools on Student Achievement and Attitudes. *Journal of Educational Psychology*, *78*(5), 381–395.

Lee, V. and Marks, H. (1990). Sustained Effects of the Single-Sex Secondary School Movement on Attitudes, Behaviors, and Values in College, *Journal of Educational Psychology*, *82*(3), 578–592.

LeJeune, C. and Folette, V. (1994). Taking Responsibility: Sex Differences in Reporting Dating Violence. *Journal of Interpersonal Violence*, *9*(1), 133–140.

Levante, R. (1996). New Psychology of Men. *Professional Psychology Research and Practice*, *27*, 259–265.

Loewen, J. (1995). *Lies My Teacher Told Me*. New York: The New Press.

Mid-Atlantic Equity Center. (1999). *Adolescent Boys: Statistics and Trends (A Fact Sheet)*. Chevy Chase, MD: Mid-Atlantic Equity Assistance Center.

Miedzian, M. (1992). *Boys Will Be Boys: Breaking the Link between Masculinity and Violence*. New York: Doubleday.

NCTE Committee on the Role and Image of Women in the Council and in the Profession. (1973). Guidelines for Publishers. *Elementary English*, *50*(7), 1019.

Nibbelink, W., Stockdale, S., and Mangru, M. (1986). Sex Role Assignments in Elementary School Mathematics Textbooks. *The Arithmetic Teacher*, *34*(Oct.), 19–21.

Noddings, N. (1992). Social Studies and Feminism. *Theory and Research in Social Education*, *20*(3), 230–241.

Perry, E. L., Schmidtke, J. M., and Kulik, C. T. (1998). Propensity to Sexually Harass: An Exploration of Gender Differences. *Sex Roles: A Journal of Research* *38*(5–6), 443–460.

Petersen, R. Johnson, D., and Johnson R. (1991). Effects of Cooperative Learning on Perceived Status of Male and Female Pupils. *Journal of Social Psychology*, *131*, 717–735.

Pollack, W. (1998). *Real Boys: Rescuing Our Sons From the Myths of Boyhood*. New York: Random House.

Powell, R. and Garcia, J. (1985). The Portrayal of Minorities and Women in Selected Elementary Science Series. *Journal of Research in Science Teaching* *22*(6) 519–533.

Riordan, C. (1990). *Girls and Boys in School: Together or Separate?* New York: Teachers College Press.

Sadker, D. (1996). Where the Girls Are? *Education Week*, Commentary (Sept. 4), 49–50.

Sadker, D. (1999). Gender Equity: Still Knocking at the Classroom Door. *Educational Leadership*, *56*(7), 22–26.

Sadker, D. and Sadker, M. (1985). Is the O.K. Classroom O.K.? *Phi Delta Kappan*, *66*(Jan.), 358–361.

Sadker, D. and Sadker, J. (1995). Separate—But Still Short-Changed. *The Washington Post*, Op/Ed Section (Nov. 1), A19.

Sadker, M. and Sadker, D. (1982a). *Sex Equity Handbook for Schools*. New York: Longman.

Sadker, M. and Sadker, D. (1982b; reprinted and updated, 1990). The Report Card. *Sex Equity Handbook for Schools*. New York: Longman. Reprinted Carnegie Foundation.

Sadker, M. and Sadker, D. (1984). *Year 3: Final Report: Promoting Effectiveness in Classroom Instruction.* Washington, DC: National Institute of Education. ED257819

Sadker, M. and Sadker, D. (1985). Sexism in the Classroom of the 80s, *Psychology Today* (Mar.), 54–57.

Sadker, M. and Sadker, D. (1994a; updated for this chapter). *Failing at Fairness: How America's Schools Cheat Girls.* New York: Scribners. (The Report Card copyright of David and Myra Sadker. All rights reserved; no part may be reproduced or transmitted without permission from the authors.)

Sadker, M. and Sadker, D. (1994). *Failing at Fairness: How America's Schools Cheat Girls.* New York: Scribners.

Sadker, M. and Sadker, D. (1994c). Sex Equity: Assumptions and Strategies. *International Encyclopedia of Education.* Oxford, U.K.: Pergamon Press, pp. 5441–5445.

Sadker, M. and Sadker, D. (2000). *Teachers, Schools, and Society.* Boston: McGraw Hill.

Sadker, M., Sadker, D., and Klein, S. (1986). Abolishing Misperceptions about Sex Equity in Education. *Theory into Practice, 25*(Autumn), 220–226.

Sadker, M., Sadker, D., and Klein, S. (1991). The Issue of Gender in Elementary and Secondary Education. In G. Grant (Ed.), *Review of Research in Education* (pp. 269–334). Washington, DC: American Educational Research Association.

Sadker, M., Sadker, D., and Shakeshaft, C. (1992). Sexuality and Sexism in School: How Should Educators Be Prepared? In S. S. Klein (Ed.), *Sex Equity and Sexuality in Education* (pp. 363–375). Albany, NY: SUNY Press.

Safe Schools Coalition of Washington. (1995). *1995 Seattle Teen Health Risk Survey,* Seattle: Author. (Reprinted from the *Third Annual Report of the Safe Schools Anti-Violence* Project)

Salisbury, J. and Jackson, D. (1995). *Challenging Macho Values: Practical Ways of Working with Adolescent Boys.* London: Falmer Press.

Schmuck R. and Schmuck, P. (1992). *Group Processes in the Classroom* (6th ed.). Dubuque, IA: William C. Brown.

Schwartz, M. D. (1997). *Sexual Assault on the College Campus: The Role of Male Peer Support.* Thousand Oaks, CA: Sage.

Scott, K. (1986). Effects of Sex-Fair Reading Materials on Pupils' Attitudes, Comprehension, and Interest. *American Educational Research Journal, 23*(spring), 105–116.

Sewall, G. (1992). Do Textbooks Shortchange Girls? *Social Studies Review: A Bulletin of the American Textbook Council,* (11), 3–9.

Silverstein, O. and Rashbaum, B. (1995). *The Courage to Raise Good Men.* New York: Penguin.

Smith, M., Kalvelage, J., and Schmuck, P. (1982). *Women Getting Together and Getting Ahead.* Washington, DC: Women's Educational Equity Act Program.

Sommers, C. H. (1995). *Who Stole Feminism? How Women Have Betrayed Women.* New York: Simon and Schuster.

Trecker, J. L. (1977). Women in U.S. History High-School Textbooks. In J. Pottker and A. Fishel (Eds.), *Sex Bias in the Schools: The Research Evidence* (pp. 146–161). Cranbury, CT: Associated University Presses.

Tyack, D. and Hansot, E. (1990). *Learning Together: A History of Coeducation in American Schools.* New Haven, CT.: Yale University.

U.S. Bureau of the Census. (1997). *Current Population Reports.* Washington, DC: U.S. Government Printing Office.

U.S. Department of Education. (1996). *Youth Indicators.* Washington, DC: U.S. Department of Education.

Women's Educational Equity Act. (1999). *1999 Fact Sheet on Women's and Girl's Educational Equity.* Newton, MA: Educational Development Corporation.

Woodward, A. and Elliot, D. L. (1990). Textbook Use and Teacher Professionalism. In D. L. Elliot and A. Woodward (Eds.), *Textbooks and Schooling in the United States.* 89th Yearbook of the National Society for the Study of Education (pp. 178–193). Chicago: University of Chicago Press.

CHAPTER 7

Classrooms for Diversity: Rethinking Curriculum and Pedagogy

Mary Kay Thompson Tetreault

> It's time to start learning about things they told you you didn't need
> to know . . . learning about me, instead of learning about them,
> starting to learn about her instead of learning about him. It's a
> connection that makes education education. (A student of European
> and African American ancestry)

This student's reflection on her education signals a twin transformation that is pushing us to rethink our traditional ways of teaching. The first is that students in our classrooms are increasingly more diverse and the second is that traditional course content has been enriched by the new scholarship on women, cultural studies, and multiculturalism. It is in the classroom that these transformations intersect, and it rests on the teacher to make education "education" for this student and for the majority who feel their education was not made for them—women of all backgrounds, people of color, and men who lack privilege because of their social class—by bringing the two together. The current challenges to classroom teachers are not only to incorporate multiple perspectives into the curriculum but also to engage in pedagogical practices that bring in the voices of students as a source for learning rather than managing or controlling them.

FEMINIST PHASE THEORY

One of the most effective ways I have found to set a frame for envisioning a gender-balanced, multicultural curriculum, while at the same time capturing the reforms that have occurred over the past thirty years, is feminist phase theory. Conceptually rooted in the scholarship on women, feminist phase theory is a classification system of the evolution in thought about the incorporation of women's traditions, history, and experiences into selected disciplines. The model I have developed identifies five common phases of thinking about women: *male-defined curriculum*, *contribution curriculum*, *bifocal curriculum*, *women's curriculum*, and *gender-balanced curriculum*. A gender-balanced perspective, one that is rooted in feminist scholarship, takes into account the experiences, perspectives, and voices of women as well as men. It examines the similarities and differences between women and men and also considers how gender interacts with such factors as ethnicity, race, culture and class.

The language of this system or schema, particularly the word *phase*, and the description of one phase and then another suggest a sequential hierarchy in which one phase supplants another. Before reviewing the schema, please refrain from thinking of these phases in a linear fashion; envision them as a series of intersecting circles, or patches on a quilt, or threads in a tapestry, which interact and undergo changes in response to one another. It is more accurate to view the phases as different emphases that coexist in feminist research. The important thing is that teachers, scholars, and curriculum developers ask and answer certain questions at each phase.

The following section identifies key concepts and questions articulated initially at each phase, using examples from history, literature, and science; it then discusses how the phases interact and undergo changes in response to one another. The final part of this chapter shows teachers grappling with the intersection of changes in the disciplines and changes in the student population and presents four themes of analysis: mastery, voice, authority and positionality. The chapter concludes with specific objectives, practices, and teaching suggestions for incorporating content about women into the K–12 curriculum in social studies, language arts, and science.

Male-Defined Curriculum

Male-defined curricula rest on the assumption that the male experience is universal, that it is representative of humanity, and that it constitutes a basis for generalizing about all human beings. The knowledge that is researched and taught, the substance of learning, is knowledge articulated by and about men. There is little or no consciousness in it that the existence of women as a group is an anomaly calling for a broader definition of knowledge. The female experience is subsumed under the male experience. For example, feminist scientists have cited methodological problems in some research about sex differences that draws conclusions about females based on experiments done only on males or that uses limited (usually White, middle class) experimental populations from which scientists draw conclusions about all males and females.

The incorporation of women into the curriculum has not only taught us about women's lives but has also led to questions about our lopsided rendition of men's lives, wherein we pay attention primarily to men in the public world and conceal their lives in the private world. Historians, for example, are posing a series of interesting questions about men's history: What do we need to unlearn about men's history? What are the taken-for-granted truths about men's history that we need to rethink? How do we get at the significant masculine truths? Is man's primary sense of self defined in relation to the public sphere only? How does it relate to boyhood, adolescence, family, life, recreation, and love? What do the answers to these questions imply about the teaching of history?

Feminist scholarship, like African American, Native American, Latino, and Asian American scholarship, reveals the systematic and contestable exclusions in the male-defined curriculum. When we examine it through the lens of this scholarship, we are forced to

Table 7.1   Male-Defined Curriculum

Characteristics of Phase	Questions Commonly Asked about Women in History*	Questions Commonly Asked about Women in Literature*	Questions Commonly Asked about Women in Science*
The absence of women is not noted. There is no consciousness that the male experience is a "particular know-ledge" selected from a wider universe of possible knowledge and experience. It is valued, emphasized, and viewed as the knowledge most worth having.	Who is the author of a particular history? What is her or his race, ethnicity, religion, ideological orientation, social class, place of origin, and historical period? How does incorporating women's experiences lead to new understandings of the most fundamental ordering of social relations, institutions, and power arrangements? How can we define the content and methodology of history, so it will be a history of us all?	How is traditional humanism, with an integrated self at its center and an authentic view of life, in effect part of patriarchal ideology? How can the objectivist illusion be dismantled? How can the idea of a literary canon of "great literature" be challenged? How are writing and reading political acts? How do race, class, and gender relate to the conflict, sufferings, and passions that attend these realities? How can we study language as specific *discourse*, that is specific linguistic strategies in specific situations, rather than as universal language?	How do scientific studies reveal cultural values? What cultural, historical, and gender values are projected onto the physical and natural world? How might gender be a bias that influences choice of questions, hypotheses, subjects, experimented design, or theory formation in science? What is the underlying philosophy of an androcentric science that values objectivity, rationality, and dominance? How can the distance between the subject and the scientific observer be shortened so that the scientist has some feeling for or empathy with the organism? How can gender play a crucial role in transforming science?

*New questions generated by feminist scholars.

reconsider our understanding of the most fundamental conceptualization of knowledge and social relations within our society. We understand in a new way that knowledge is a social construction, written by individual human beings who live and think at a particular time and within a particular social framework. All works in literature, science, and history, for example, have an author, male or female, White, or ethnic or racial minority, elite or middle class or occasionally poor, with motivations and beliefs. The scientist's questions and activities, for instance, are shaped, often unconsciously, by the great social issues of the day (see Table 7.1). Different perspectives on the same subject will change the patterns discerned.

Contribution Curriculum

Early efforts to reclaim women's rightful place in the curriculum were a search for missing women within a male framework. Although there was the recognition that women were missing, men continued to serve as the norm, the representative, the universal human being. Outstanding women emerged who fit this male norm of excellence or greatness or conformed to implicit assumptions about appropriate roles for women outside the home. In literature, female authors were added who performed well within the masculine tradition, internalizing its standards of art and its views on social roles. Great women of science, who have made it in the male scientific world, most frequently Marie Curie, for example, were added.

Examples of contribution history can be seen in U.S. history textbooks. They now include the contributions of notable American women who were outstanding in the public sphere as rulers or as contributors to wars or reform movements to a remarkable degree. Queen Liliuokalani, Hawaii's first reigning queen and a nationalist, is included in the story of the kingdom's annexation. Molly Pitcher and Deborah Sampson are depicted as contributors to the Revolutionary War, as is Clara Barton to the Civil War effort. Some authors have also included women who conform to the assumption that it is acceptable for women to engage in activities outside the home if they are an extension of women's nurturing role within the family. Examples of this are Dorothea Dix, Jane Addams, Eleanor Roosevelt, and Mary McLeod Bethune (Tetreault, 1986a).

The lesson to be learned from understanding these limitations of early contribution history is not to disregard the study of notable women, but to include those who worked to reshape the world according to a feminist reordering of values. This includes efforts to increase women's self-determination through a feminist transformation of the home, to increase education, political rights, and women's rights to control their bodies, and also to improve their economic status. A history with women at the center moves beyond paying attention to caring for the unfortunate in the public sphere to how exceptional women influenced the lives of women in general (see Table 7.2). Just as Mary McLeod Bethune's role in the New Deal is worth teaching to our students, so is her aggressive work to project a positive image of Black women to the nation through her work in Black women's clubs and the launching of the *Afro-American Woman's Journal.*

Bifocal Curriculum

In bifocal curricula, feminist scholars have made an important shift, from a perspective that views men as the norm to one that opens up the possibility of seeing the world through women's eyes. This dual vision, or bifocal perspective, generated global questions about women and about the differences between women and men. Historians investigated the separation between the public and the private sphere and asked, for example, how the division between them explains women's lives. Some elaborated on the construct by identifying arenas of female power in the domestic sphere. Literary critics aimed to provide a new understanding of a distinctively female literary tradition and a theory of women's literary creativity. They sought to provide models for understanding the dynamics of female literary response to male literary assertion and coercion. Scientists grapple with definitions of woman's and man's nature by asking how the public and private, biology and culture, and personal and impersonal inform each other and affect men and women, science, and nature.

Scholars have pointed out some of the problems with bifocal knowledge. Thinking about women and men is dualistic and dichotomized. Women and men are thought of as having

Table 7.2 Contribution Curriculum

Characteristics of Phase	Questions Commonly Asked about Women in History	Questions Commonly Asked about Women in Literature	Questions Commonly Asked about Women in Science
The absence of women is not noted. There is a search for missing women according to a male norm of greatness, excellence, or humanness. Women are considered exceptional, deviant, or other. Women are added into history, but the content and notions of historical significance are not challenged.	Who are the notable women missing from history and what did they and ordinary women contribute in areas or movements traditionally dominated by men, for example during major wars or during reform movements, like abolitionism or the labor movement? What did notable and ordinary women contribute in areas that are an extension of women's traditional roles, for example, caring for the poor and the sick? How have major economic and political changes like industrialization or extension of the franchise affected women in the public sphere? How did notable and ordinary women respond to their oppression, particularly through women's rights organizations? *Who were outstanding women who advocated a feminist transformation of the home, who contributed to women's greater self-determination through increased education, the right to control their bodies, to increase their political rights, and to improve their economic status? *What did women contribute through the settlement house and labor movements?	Who are the missing female authors whose subject matter and use of language and form meet the male norm of "masterpiece"? What primary biological facts and interpretations are missing about major female authors?	Who are the notable women scientists who have made contributions to mainstream science? How is women's different (and inferior) nature related to hormones, brain lateralization, and sociobiology? Where are the missing females in scientific experiments? What is the current status of women within the scientific profession? *How does adding minority women into the history of science reveal patterns of exclusion and recast definitions of what it means to practice science and to be a scientist? *How is the exclusion of women from science related to the way science is done and thought? *What is the usual pattern of women working in science? How is it the same as or different from the pattern of notable women? *How do our definitions of science need to be broadened to evaluate women's contributions to science? Do institutions of science need to be reshaped to accommodate women? If so, how?

*New questions generated by feminist scholars.

different spheres, different notions of what is of value in life, different ways of imagining the human condition, and different associations with nature and culture. But both views are valued. In short, women are thought of as a group that is complementary but equal to men; there are some truths for men and there are some truths for women. General analyses of men's and women's experiences often come dangerously close to reiterating the sexual stereotypes scholars are trying to overcome. Because many people believe that the public sphere is more valuable than the private sphere, there is a tendency to slip back into thinking of women as inferior and subordinate.

The generalized view of women and men that predominates in the bifocal curriculum often does not allow for distinctions within groups as large and as complex as women and men. Important factors like historical period, geographic location, structural barriers, race, paternity, sexual orientation, and social class, to name a few, clearly make a difference.

Other common emphases in the bifocal curriculum are the oppression of women and the exploration of that oppression. Exposés of woman-hating in history and literature are common. The emphasis is on the misogyny (the hatred of women) of the human experience, particularly the means men have used to advance their authority and to assert or imply female inferiority. The paradoxes of women's existence are sometimes overlooked with this emphasis on oppression. For example, although women have been excluded from positions of power, a few of them as wives and daughters in powerful families were often closer to actual power than were men. If some women were dissatisfied with their status and role, most women adjusted and resisted efforts to improve women's lot. Too much emphasis on women's oppression perpetuates a patriarchal framework presenting women as primarily passive, reacting only to the pressures of a sexist society. In the main, it emphasizes men thinking and women being thought about.

Women's scholarship from the 1970s through the 1990s (Collins, 1998; Goldberger, Tarule, Clinchy, & Belenky, 1996; Schmitz, Butler, Rosenfelt, & Guy-Sheftall, 1995) has helped us see that understanding women's oppression is more complex than we initially thought. We do not yet have adequate concepts to explain gender systems, founded on a division of labor and sexual asymmetry. To understand gender systems, it is necessary to take a structural and experiential perspective that asks from a woman's point of view where we are agents and where we are not; where our relations with men are egalitarian and where they are not. This questioning may lead to explanations of why women's experiences and interpretations of their world can differ significantly from men's.

Further, the concepts with which we approach our analysis need to be questioned. Anthropologists have pointed out that our way of seeing the world—for instance, the idea of complementary spheres for women (the private sphere) and men (the public sphere)—is a product of our experience in a Western, modern, industrial, capitalistic state with a specific history. We distort our understanding of other social systems by imposing our world view on them. Feminist critics are calling for rethinking, not only of categories like the domestic versus the public sphere, and production and reproduction, but also even of categories like gender itself.

Feminist scholars have helped us see the urgency of probing and analyzing the interactive nature of the oppressions of race, ethnicity, class, and gender (Collins, 1998). We are reminded that we can no longer take a liberal reformist approach that does not probe the needs of the system that are being satisfied by oppression. We have to take seriously the model of feminist scholarship that analyzes women's status within the social, cultural, historical, political, and economic contexts. Only then will issues of gender be understood in relation to the economic needs of both male dominance and capitalism that undergird such oppressions.

One of the most important things we have learned about a bifocal perspective is the danger of generalizing too much, of longing for women's history, instead of writing histories about women. We must guard against establishing a feminist version of great literature and then resisting any modifications or additions to it. We have also learned that the traditional disciplines are limited in their ability to shed light on gender complexities, and it becomes apparent that there is a need for an interdisciplinary perspective (see Table 7.3).

Women's Curriculum

The most important idea to emerge in women's scholarship is that women's activities, not men's, are the measure of significance. What was formerly devalued, the content of women's everyday lives, assumes new value as scholars investigate female rituals, housework, child-bearing, child rearing, female sexuality, female friendship, and studies of the life cycle. For instance, scientists investigate how research on areas of interest primarily to women— menstruation, childbirth, and menopause—challenge existing scientific theories. Historians document women's efforts to break out of their traditional sphere of the home in a way that uses women's activities, not men's, as the measure of historical significance. These activities include women's education, women's paid work, and volunteer work outside the home, particularly in women's clubs and associations. Of equal importance is the development of a collective feminist consciousness, that is, of women's consciousness of their own distinct role in society. Analyses begun in the bifocal phase continue to explore what sex and gender have meant for the majority of women.

As scholars look more closely at the complex patterns of women's lives, they see the need for a pluralistic conceptualization of women. Although thinking of women as a monolithic group provides valuable information about patterns of continuity and change in those areas most central to women's lives, generalizing about a group as vast and diverse as women leads to inaccuracies. The subtle interactions among gender and other variables are investigated. Historians ask how the particulars of race, ethnicity, social class, marital status, and sexual orientation challenge the homogeneity of women's experiences. Third World feminists critique hegemonic "Western" feminisms and formulate autonomous, geographically, historically, and culturally grounded feminist concerns and strategies (Mohanty, Russo, & Torres, 1991).

Questions about sex and gender are set within historical, ideological, and cultural contexts, including the culture's definition of the facts of biological development and what they mean for individuals. Researchers ask, for example, Why are these attitudes toward sexuality prevalent at this time in history? What are the ways in which sexual words, categories, and ideology mirror the organization of society as a whole? What are the socioeconomic factors contributing to them? How do current conceptions of the body reflect social experiences and professional needs?

Life histories and autobiographies shed light on societies' perceptions of women and women's perceptions of themselves. Women's individual experiences are revealed through

Table 7.3 Bifocal Curriculum

Characteristics of Phase	Questions Commonly Asked about Women in History	Questions Commonly Asked about Women in Literature	Questions Commonly Asked about Women in Science
Human experience is conceptualized primarily in dualist categories: male and female, private and public, agency and communion. Emphasis is on a complementary but equal conceptualization of men's and women's spheres and personal qualities. There is a focus on women's oppression and on misogyny. Women's efforts to overcome the oppression are presented. Efforts to include women lead to the insight that the traditional content, structure, and methodology of the disciplines are more appropriate to the male experience.	How does the division between the public and the private sphere explain women's lives? Who oppressed women, and how were they oppressed? *What are forms of power and value in women's world? *How have women been excluded from and deprived of power and value in men's sphere? *How do gender systems create divisions between the sexes such that experience and interpretations of their world can differ significantly from men's? *How can we rethink categories like public and private, productive and reproductive, sex and gender?	Who are the missing minor female authors whose books are unobtainable, whose lives have never been written, and whose works have been studied casually, if at all? How is literature a record of the collective consciousness of patriarchy? What myths and stereotypes about women are present in male literature? How can we critique the meritocratic pretensions of traditional literary history? How can we pair opposite-sex texts in literature as a way of understanding the differences between women's and men's experiences? How is literature one of the expressive modes of a female subculture that developed with the distinction of separate spheres for women and men? *How can feminist literary critics resist establishing their own great canon of literature and any additions to it?	How have the sciences defined (and misdefined) the nature of women? Why are there so few women scientists? What social and psychological forces have kept women in the lower ranks or out of science entirely? How do women fit into the study of history of science and health care? How do scientific findings, originally carried out on males of a species, change when carried out on the females of the same species? How do the theories and interpretations of sociobiology require constant testing and change to fit the theory for males and females with regard to competition, sexual selection, and infanticide? How does the science/gender system—the network of associations and disjunctions between public and private, personal and impersonal, and masculine and feminine—inform each other and affect men and women, science and nature? *What are the structural barriers to women in science?

*New questions generated by feminist scholars.

these stories and contribute to the fashioning of the human experience from the perspective of women.

Scholars find it necessary to draw on other disciplines for a clearer vision of the social structure and culture of societies as individuals encounter them in their daily life. Likewise, there are calls for new unifying frameworks and different ways to think of periods in history and literature to identify concepts that accommodate women's history and traditions. There is also a more complex conceptualization of historical time. The emphases in much history are on events, a unit of time too brief to afford a sense of structural change, changes in the way people think about their own reality, and the possibilities for other realities. *L'Ecole des Annales* in France (a group of historians who pioneered the use of such public records as birth, marriage, and death certificates in historical analysis) has distinguished between events and what they call the *longue durée* (Letters to the Editors, 1982). By the *longue durée* they mean the slow, glacial changes, requiring hundreds of years to complete, that represent significant shifts in the way people think.

Examples of areas of women's history that lend themselves to this concept are the structural change from a male-dominated to an egalitarian perspective and the transformation of women's traditional role in the family to their present roles as wives, mothers, and paid workers outside the home. Also important is the demographic change in the average number of children per woman of childbearing age from seven to fewer than two children between 1800 and 1990 (see Table 7.4).

Gender-Balanced Curriculum

This phase continues many of the inquiries begun in the women's curriculum phase, but it articulates questions about how women and men relate to and complement one another. Conscious of the limitations of seeing women in isolation and aware of the relational character of gender, researchers search for the nodal points at which women's and men's experiences intersect. Historians and literary critics ask if the private, as well as the public, aspects of life are presented as a continuum in women's and men's experience.

The pluralistic and multifocal conception of women that emerged in the women's curriculum phase is extended to human beings. A central idea in this phase is *positionality* (Alcoff, 1988; Haraway, 1997; Harding, 1991). Positionality means that important aspects of our identity (for example, our gender, our race, our class, our age, and so on) are markers of relational positions rather than essential qualities. Their effects and implications change according to context. Recently, feminist thinkers have seen knowledge as valid when it comes from an acknowledgment of the knower's specific position in any context, one always defined by gender, race, class, and other variables.

Scientists ask explicit questions about the invention and reinvention of nature. For example, they ask questions about the meanings of the behavior and social lives of monkeys and apes and male-female relations in animals and inquire about how such variables as age, species, and individual variation challenge current theories. They also explore contemporary technoscience—its stories and dreams, its facts and delusions, its institutions and politics, and its scientific advances. (Haraway, 1991; 1997).

Accompanying this particularistic perspective is attention to the larger context, for example, the interplay among situation, meaning, economic systems, family organization, and

Table 7.4 Women's Curriculum

Characteristics of Phase	Questions Commonly Asked about Women in History	Questions Commonly Asked about Women in Literature	Questions Commonly Asked about Women in Science
Scholarly inquiry pursues new questions, new categories, and new notions of significance that illuminate women's traditions, history, culture, values, visions, and perspectives.	What were the majority of women doing at a particular time in history? What was the significance of these activities?	What does women's sphere— for example, domesticity and family, education, marriage, sexuality, and love—reveal about our culture?	How do the cultural dualisms associated with masculinity and femininity permeate scientific thought and discourse?
A pluralistic conception of women emerges that acknowledges diversity and recognizes that variables besides gender shape women's lives—for example, race, ethnicity, and social class.	How can female friendship between kin, mothers, daughters, and friends be analyzed as one aspect of women's overall relations with others?	How can we contrast the fictional image of women in literature with the complexity and variety of the roles of individual women in real life as workers, housewives, revolutionaries, mothers, lovers, and so on?	How do women's actual experiences, as compared to the physician's analysis or scientific theory, challenge the traditional paradigms of science and of the health care systems?
Women's experience is allowed to speak for itself. Feminist history is rooted in the personal and the specific; it builds from that to the general.	What kind of productive work, paid and unpaid, did women do and under what conditions?	How do the particulars of race, ethnicity, social class, marital status, and sexual orientation, as revealed in literature, challenge the thematic homogeneity of women's experiences?	How does research on areas of primary interest to women, for instance, menopause, childbirth and menstruation/estrus, challenge existing scientific theories?
The public and the private are seen as a continuum in women's experiences.	What were the reproductive activities of women? How did they reproduce the American family?	How does literature portray what binds women together and what separates them because of race, ethnicity, social class, marital status, and sexual orientation?	How do variables other than sex and gender, such as age, species, and individual variation, challenge current theories?
Women's experience is analyzed within the social, cultural, historical, political, and economic contexts.	How did the variables of race, ethnicity, social class, marital status, and sexual preference affect women's experience?	How does the social and historical context of a work of literature shed light on it?	How do the experience of female primates and the variation among species of primates, for example, competition among females, female agency in sexuality, and infanticide, test the traditional paradigms?
Efforts are made to reconceptualize knowledge to encompass the female experience. The conceptualization of knowledge is not characterized by disciplinary thinking but becomes multidisciplinary.	What new categories need to be added to the study of history, for instance, housework, childbearing, and child rearing? How have women of different races and classes interacted throughout history? What are appropriate ways of organizing or periodizing women's history? For example, how will examining women's experiences at each stage of the life span help us to understand women's experiences on their own terms?		

political systems. Thus, historians ask how gender inequities are linked to economics, family organization, marriage, ritual, and politics. Research scientists probe how differences between the male and female body have been used to justify a social agenda that privileges men economically, socially, and politically. In this phase, a revolutionary relationship comes to exist between things traditionally treated as serious, primarily the activities of men in the public sphere, and those things formerly perceived as trivial, namely the activities of women in the private sphere.

This new relationship leads to a recentering of knowledge in the disciplines, a shift from a male-centered perspective to one that includes both females and males. This reconceptualization of knowledge works toward a more holistic view of the human experience. As in the previous stage, the conceptualization of knowledge is characterized by multidisciplinary thinking.

Feminist scholars have cautioned against moving too quickly from women's curricula to gender-balanced curricula. As historian Gerda Lerner (1982) once observed, our decade-and-a-half-old investigation of women's history is only a speck on the horizon compared to the centuries-old tradition of male-defined history. By turning too quickly to studies of gender, we risk short-circuiting important directions in women's studies and again having women's history and experiences subsumed under those of men. It remains politically important for feminists to defend women as women in order to counteract the male domination that continues to exist. French philosopher Julia Kristeva (cited in Moi, 1985), however, pushes us to new considerations when she urges women (and men) to recognize the falsifying nature of masculinity and femininity, to explore how the fact of being born male or female determines one's position in relation to power, and to envision more fluid gender identities that have the potential to liberate both women and men to a fuller personhood (see Table 7.5).

CHANGING TRADITIONAL WAYS OF TEACHING

Feminist scholarship has helped us understand that all knowledge, and therefore all classroom knowledge, is a social construction. This insight affirms the evolving nature of knowledge and the role of teachers and students in its ongoing construction. For me, the term *pedagogy* applies not just to teaching techniques but also to the whole classroom production of knowledge; it encompasses the full range of relationships among course materials, teachers, and students. Such broadened conceptualizations of pedagogy challenge the commonly held assumptions of the professor as a disinterested expert, the content as inherently "objective," and the method of delivery as irrelevant to the message (hooks, 1994). To educate students for a complex, multicultural, multiracial world, we need to include the perspectives and voices of those who have not been traditionally included—women of all backgrounds, people of color, and females and males who perceive their education as not made for them.

Feminist teachers are demonstrating how they transform courses through their attention to cultural, ethnic, and gender diversity and give concrete form to the complexity of the struggles over knowledge, access, and power (hooks, 1994; Maher & Tetreault, 1994; Weiler, 1988). In a study, *The Feminist Classroom*, Frances Maher and I (Maher & Tetreault, 1994)

Table 7.5 Gender-Balanced Curriculum

Characteristics of Phase	Questions Commonly Asked about Women in History	Questions Commonly Asked about Women in Literature	Questions Commonly Asked about Women in Science
A multifocal, gender-balanced perspective is sought that weaves together women's and men's experiences into multilayered composites of human experience. At this stage, scholars are conscious of positionality.	What is the knower's specific position in this historical context?	How does the author's specific position, as defined by gender, race, and class, affect this literary work?	What explicit questions need to be raised about the invention and reinvention of nature? What is the meaning of male-female relations in animals?
Positionality represents the insight that all women and men are located in historical contexts, contexts defined in terms of race, class, culture, and age, as well as gender, and that they gain their knowledge and their power from the specifics of their situations.	How is gender asymmetry linked to economic systems, family organizations, marriage, ritual, and political systems? How can we compare women and men in all aspects of their lives to reveal gender as a crucial historical determinant?	How can we validate the full range of human expression by selecting literature according to its insight into any aspect of human experience rather than according to how it measures up to a predetermined canon? Is the private as well as the public sphere presented as a continuum in women's and men's experiences?	How do variables such as age, species, and individual variation challenge current theories? What are the limits to generalizing beyond the data collected on limited samples to other genders, species, and conditions not sampled in the experimental protocol?
Scholars begin to define what binds together and what separates the various segments of humanity.	Are the private, as well as the public, aspects of history presented as a continuum in women's and men's experiences?	How can we pair opposite-sex texts in literature as a way of understanding how female and male characters experience "maleness" and "femaleness" as a continuum of "humanness"?	How have sex differences been used to assign men and women to particular roles in the social heirarchy?
Scholars have a deepened understanding of how the private as well as public form a continuum in individual experience. They search for the nodal points at which comparative treatment of men's and women's experience is possible.	How is gender a social construction? What does the particular construction of gender in a society tell us about the society that so constructed gender? What is the intricate relation between the construction of gender and the structure of power?	How do the variables of race, ethnicity, social class, marital status, and sexual orientation affect the experience of female and male literary characters? How can we rethink the concept of periodicity to accentuate the continuity of life and to contain the multitude of previously ignored	How have differences between the male and female body been used to justify a social agenda that privileges men economically, socially, and politically?
Efforts are made to reconceptualize knowledge to reflect this multilayered composite of women's and men's experience. The conceptualization of knowledge is not characterized by disciplinary thinking but becomes multidisciplinary.	How can we expand our conceptualization of historical time to a pluralistic one that conceives of three levels of history: structures, trends, and events? How can we unify approaches and types of knowledge of all social sciences and history as a means of investigating specific problems in relational history?	literary works, for example, instead of Puritanism, the contexts for and consequences of sexuality? How can we deconstruct the opposition between masculinity and femininity?	

show how all students may benefit from, and how some are even inspired by, college courses transformed by their professor's attention to cultural, ethnic, and gender diversity. We have found that the themes we used to analyze teaching and learning in seventeen classrooms on six campuses across the country apply to elementary and secondary classrooms as well. The four themes, *mastery*, *voice*, *authority* and *positionality*, all relate to issues present in today's classroom. Although all four deal with reconstituted relationships between new students and new disciplinary frameworks, the themes of mastery and authority focus on knowledge and its sources; voice and positionality on the students themselves.

Mastery has traditionally meant the goal of an individual student's rational comprehension of the material on the teacher's and expert's terms. Women (and other marginalized groups) must often give up their voices when they seek mastery on the terms of the dominant culture. We found classrooms undergoing a shift away from unidimensional sources of expertise to a multiplicity of new information and insights. Students were no longer mastering a specific body of material, nor were they emphasizing subjective experiences that risk excluding students from a wealth of knowledge. Rather, they were struggling through or integrating often widely various interpretations of texts, scientific research, and social problems. These teachers redefined mastery as interpretation, as increasingly sophisticated handling of the topics at hand, informed by but not limited to the students' links to the material from their own experience. For example, a Japanese American student reread an Emily Dickinson poem about silences and invisibilities to comment on her gender and ethnic marginality.

> I couldn't help thinking of the idea of a mute culture within a dominant culture. A "nobody" knowing she's different from the dominant culture keeps silent . . . . But to be somebody! How dreary! How public! So when you become a somebody and buy into the dominant culture, you have to live in their roles.
>
> A silly example: It's like watching a Walt Disney movie as a child where Hayley Mills and these other girls dance and primp before a party singing "Femininity," how being a woman is all about looking pretty and smiling pretty and acting stupid to attract men. As a child I ate it up, at least it seemed benign. But once your eye gets put out and you realize how this vision has warped you, it would split your heart to try and believe that again, it would strike you dead.

Students were stretched by such broadenings of interpretative frameworks and indeed became authorities for one another. A white male student in the same class said:

> I could read Dickinson a thousand times and probably never try to relate to that because it just would never make an impression on me, but having the girls in that class interested in that particular topic, "How does that relate to me as a woman?" then I sit back and I think that's a really good question. Although I'm male I can learn how women react to women's text as opposed to maybe the way I react to it or the teacher reacts to it.

The teachers in our study consciously used their *authority* to give students responsibility for their own learning (Finke, 1993). Students and professors became authorities for one another to the extent that they were explicit about themselves as social and political actors with respect to a text or an issue (Tetreault, 1991). The teachers also struggled with reconceptualizing the grounds for their own authority, both over the subject matter and with students, because their traditional positions as the sole representatives of expertise were called into question by these multiple new sources of knowledge. These professors shared a sense of their authority as being grounded in their own experiences and in their intellectual engagement with feminist scholarship and other relevant fields.

As important as the rethinking of the disciplines is the power of expression that these new forms of knowledge, coming from the students' questions as well as from new topics, give to women and to other previously silenced groups. We explored the effects on students through our theme of voice. *Voice* is frequently defined as the awakening of the students' own responses. However, we came to think of these classrooms as arenas where teachers and students fashion their voices rather than "find" them, as they produce relevant experiences to shape a narrative of an emerging self.

Our fourth theme is *positionality*, which is defined in the section on gender-balanced curriculum. Positionality helps us to see the multiple ways in which the complex dynamics of difference and inequality, which come from outside society, also operate powerfully inside the classroom itself. Much of our emphasis in the past three decades has been on the consequences of sexism and racism on females and on students of color. We have learned much about how universalizing the position of maleness leads to intellectual domination.

Some educators and theorists are arguing that we need to become conscious in similar ways about the effects of universalizing the position of Whiteness (Frankenberg, 1993; 1997; McIntosh, 1990; Morrison, 1993; Tatum, 1992). For example, how does the norm of Whiteness or maleness shape the construction of knowledge in classrooms? How do those assumptions contribute to the intellectual domination of groups? Why is it that when we think of the development of racial identity in our students, we think primarily of students of color rather than of White students? What happens in classrooms where Whiteness is marked, revealed as a position? In our culture, the presumptions of Whiteness or maleness act to constrict voice by universalizing the dominant positions, by letting them float free of "position."

Frances Maher and I revisited data presented in our book, *The Feminist Classroom*, to examine how assumptions of Whiteness shape the construction of knowledge as it is produced and resisted in the classroom (Maher & Tetreault, 1997). We saw how the dominant voices continue to call the tune—that is, to maintain the conceptual and ideological frameworks through which suppressed voices are distorted or not fully heard. We saw more clearly the ways in which a thorough pedagogy of positionality must entail an excavation of Whiteness in its many dimensions and complexities. Understanding all the ways in which positionality shapes learning is a long, interactive process.

The lessons that follow attempt to model teaching that is constructed to reveal the particular and the common denominators of human experience. These sample lessons are organized by the subject areas of language arts, science, and social studies, but they can be adapted to other subject areas as well.

Language Arts

Analyzing Children's Literature
Suggested Activities

Ask students to locate five of their favorite children's books, to read or reread them, and to keep a written record of their reactions to the books. Either on the chalkboard or on a sheet of newsprint, keep a record of the students' (and your) book choices. Divide the class into small groups according to the same or similar favorite books and have students share their written reactions to the books. Ask the groups to keep a record of the most noteworthy ideas that emerge from their small-group discussions. When you bring the small groups together, ask each group to present its noteworthy ideas. Ideas that emerge may be as follows:

> How differently they read the book now than at the time of their first reading
>
> The differences and similarities in so-called girls books and boys books
>
> The importance of multicultural or international perspectives
>
> What the stories reveal about the culture in which the stories are set.

A follow-up activity could be to interview grandparents, parents, teachers, and other adults about characters and stories they remember from childhood. Questions to ask include, How do they recall feeling about those stories? Have images of female and male behavior or expectations in children's stories changed? Is race or ethnicity treated similarly or differently?

Pairing Female and Male Autobiographies
Suggested Activities

Pairings of autobiographies and fiction by male and female authors can contribute greatly to students' multifocal, relational understanding of the human experience. Two pairings I have found to be particularly illuminating are *Black Boy* by Richard Wright (1945) and *Woman Warrior* by Maxine Hong Kingston (1976). Other interesting pairings are Maya Angelou's *I Know Why the Caged Bird Sings* (1969) and Mark Twain's *Huckleberry Finn* (Clemens, 1912); *The Autobiography of Frederick Douglass* (1994) and *Incidents in the Life of a Slave Girl* (Jacobs, 1988); *The Adventures of Tom Sawyer* (Twain, 1996) and *Little Women* (Alcott, 1995).

One professor we observed at Lewis and Clark College, Dorothy Berkson, uses teaching logs to demystify the process of interpretation by linking the students' emotional connections to texts with their intellectual analysis. She asks her students to select a passage that puzzles or engages them or triggers a strong emotional reaction. Believing that some of the best criticism starts with such reactions, she asks the students next to paraphrase the passage they have chosen, to understand what it means, or, in a sense, to master it. They are then asked to look at it again, to become conscious of what cannot be captured by paraphrase as well as any concerns or questions that escaped them before. They finally place the passage in the context of the entire text, using the following questions: "Where does it happen? Are there other passages that relate to it? that contradict it? that confirm it? that raise more questions about it?" Concluding with a summary of where this procedure has taken them, they turn in these logs at the end of each class. Returned to the students with Berkson's comments, the logs then become the basis for the students' formal paper. This process forces students to reengage with the text over and over again, to engage in continuous reinterpretation of the text rather than to think they have arrived at some final mastery.

Science

Fear of Science: Fact or Fantasy?
Suggested Activities:

Fear of science and math and the stereotyping of scientists contribute to the limited participation of some students, most often female, in math and science classes. Their inadequate participation limits their choice of most undergraduate majors that depend on a minimum of three years of high school mathematics. In *Aptitude Revisited: Rethinking Math and Science Education for America's Next Century*, David E. Drew (1996) argues that the people least encouraged to study mathematics and science in our society are those who have the least power—especially students from poverty, minority students, and young women. Policy makers, teachers, and even parents often steer certain students away from math and science for completely erroneous reasons. The result, Drew contends, is not simply an inadequately trained work force: this educational discrepancy is widening the gap between the haves and the have-nots in our society. He challenges the conventional view that science and math are too boring or too hard for many students to argue that virtually all students are capable of mastering these subjects.

The following exercise was designed by the Math and Science Education for Women Project at the Lawrence Hall of Science (Fraser, 1982).[1] The purpose of the exercise is to decrease female and male students' fear of science by enabling them to function as researchers who define the problem and generate solutions to it.

Ask students to complete the following sentence by writing for about fifteen minutes:

> When I think about science, I . . .

When they are finished, divide students into groups of five or six to discuss their responses to the cue. Ask each group to state the most important things it has learned. Discuss fear of science with the class and whether there is a difference in how girls and boys feel about science. What could be some reasons for these differences or similarities? When the findings from this exercise are clear, suggest to students that they broaden their research to include other students and teachers in the school. Have each group brainstorm questions that might appear on a science attitude questionnaire. Put the questions on the chalkboard. Analyze the questions and decide on the ten best questions.

Decide with the class what group of students and teachers you will research and how you will do it; for example, other science classes, all ninth-grade science classes, or the entire school during second period. Obtain permission to conduct the survey from the

---

[1]Adapted from *Fact or Fantasy* (adapted from *Spaces: Solving Problems of Access to Careers in Engineering and Science*). Sherry Fraser, Project Director. Lawrence Hall of Science, Regents of University of California. Used with permission.

administration and other teachers or classes involved in your research project. Have the class do the survey or questionnaire as a pilot activity. Analyze the questions for sex differences and make minor revisions before giving the survey and questionnaire to your research group. Distribute the survey or conduct interviews. Have the students decide how to analyze the information. Let each group decide how it will display findings and information. Current statistics of male and female scientists in biology, chemistry, physics, and other sciences can be found in the NSF Science and Engineering Indicators on the web at: http://www.nsf.gov/sbe/srs/sein98/start/htm

Another valuable resource is *Re-Engineering Female Friendly Science* by Sue Rosser (1997).

Have each group give (1) a report to class on what it found, using graph displays to convey the information; and (2) recommendations for decreasing science anxiety in the school. Place the entire student research project in the school library, main office, or gymnasium, where the rest of the school population can see the results. Have a student summarize and write an article for the school paper.

Doing Science

Suggested Activities

Evelyn Fox Keller's (1983) biography of Barbara McClintoch, *A Feeling for the Organism*, allows students to explore the conditions under which dissent in science arises, the function it serves, and the plurality of values and goals it reflects. Questions her story prompts are: What role do interests, individual and collective, play in the evolution of scientific knowledge? Do all scientists seek the same kinds of explanations? Are the kinds of questions they ask the same? Do differences in methodology between different subdisciplines ever permit the same kinds of answers? Do female and male scientists approach their research differently? This book is difficult reading for high school or college students, but it is manageable if they read carefully and thoroughly. The best way I have found to help them manage is to ask them to read a chapter or section and to come to class with their questions about the reading and to propose some answers.

Social Studies

My Family's Work History
Suggested Activities

Women and men of different social classes, ethnic groups, and geographic locations have done various kinds of work inside and outside their homes in agricultural, industrial, and postindustrial economies. Before introducing students to the history of work, I pique their interest by asking them to complete a Family Work Chart (see Table 7.6). When their charts are complete, the students and I build a work chronology from 1890 to the present. Our work chronology contains information gleaned from the textbook and library sources about important inventions, laws, demographics, and labor history.

I then reproduce the work chronology on a chart so they can compare their family's history. By seeing their families' histories alongside major events in our collective work history, students can see how their family was related to society. A sample of items from our chart looks like this (Chapman, 1979):

Table 7.6 Family Work Chart

			Work Experience	
			AFTER MARRIAGE	
	YEAR OF BIRTH	BEFORE MARRIAGE	WHILE CHILDREN WERE YOUNG?	WHEN CHILDREN WERE GROWN?
Your Maternal Side				
Mother				
Grandmother				
Grandfather				
Great-grandmother				
Great-grandfather				
Great-grandmother				
Great-grandfather				
Your Paternal Side				
Father				
Grandmother				
Grandfather				
Great-grandmother				
Great-grandfather				
Great-great-grandmother				
Great-great-grandfather				

This activity was developed by Carol Frenier. Reprinted with permission from the Education Development Center from Adeline Naiman, Project Director, *Sally Garcia and Family Resource Guide*, Unit 3 of *The Role of Women in American Society* (Newton, Mass.: Education Development Center, Inc., 1978), p. 62.

Historical Events	*Your Family History*
1890 Women are 17 percent of the paid labor force	
1915 Telephone connects New York and San Francisco	
1924 Restriction of immigration	

Students conclude this unit by writing about a major theme in their family's work history. They might focus on how the lives of the women in the family differed from the lives of the men. They might focus on how their family's race or ethnicity shaped their work history.

Integrating the Public and Private Spheres
Suggested Activities

Human life is lived in both the public and the private spheres in wartime as well as in peacetime. By asking students consciously to examine individuals' lives as citizens, workers, family members, friends, members of social groups, and individuals, they learn more about the interaction of these roles in both spheres. War is an extraordinary time when the nation's underlying assumptions about these roles are often put to the test. By having students examine the interaction of these roles in wartime, they can see some of our underlying assumptions about the roles and how they are manipulated for the purposes of war. Through researching the histories of their families, and by reading primary source accounts, viewing films, and reading their textbook, they will see the complexity and variety of human experiences in the United States during World War II.

Students research their family's history during World War II by gathering family documents and artifacts and by interviewing at least one relative who was an adult during World War II. Students draw up questions beforehand to find out how the individual's social roles were affected by the war. During the two weeks they are researching their family's history, two class periods are spent on this project. During the first period, students give oral reports to a small group of fellow students in read-around groups.

Appropriate readings and films on World War II are widely available. Studs Terkel's (1984) book *The Good War* is particularly useful because of the variety of people the author interviewed. For instance, students can read about the internment of Japanese Americans and can role play an account read. Their textbook may provide good background information. A moving account written by an author who was interned is *Desert Exile: The Uprooting of a Japanese-American Family* by Yoshiko Uchida (1982). My students answer two questions in this unit: World War II has been described as a 'good war.' From the materials you have examined, was it a good war for individuals' lives as citizens, workers, family members, friends, and members of social groups? How were their experiences similar to or different from those of your relatives?

SUMMARY

This chapter has illustrated how women's studies is challenging male domination over curricular content. The evolution of that challenge is illuminated by understanding the different emphases that coexist in male-defined, contribution, bifocal, women's and gender-balanced curricula. We now have a conceptual framework for a curriculum that interweaves issues of gender with ethnicity, culture, and class. This framework acknowledges and celebrates a multifocal, relational view of the human experience.

The idea of the phases of feminist scholarship as a series of intersecting circles, or patches on a quilt, or threads on a tapestry, suggests parallel ways to think about a class of students.

Each student brings to your classroom a particular positionality that shapes his or her way of knowing. Your challenge as a teacher is to interweave the individual truths with course content into complex understandings that legitimize students' voices.

This relational knowledge, with the authority of the school behind it, has the potential to help students analyze their own social, cultural, historical, political, and economic contexts. The goal of relational knowledge is to build a world in which the oppressions of race, gender, and class, on which capitalism and patriarchy depend, are challenged by critical citizens in a democratic society.

Questions and Activities

1. What is a gender-balanced, multicultural curriculum?
2. What is feminist phase theory?
3. Define and give an example of each of the following phases of the feminist phase theory developed and described by the author: (a) male-defined curriculum; (b) contribution curriculum; (c) bifocal curriculum; (d) women's curriculum; (e) gender-balanced curriculum.
4. What problems do the contribution and bifocal phases have? How do the women's curriculum and gender-balanced curriculum phases help solve these problems?
5. The author states that "knowledge is a social construction." What does this mean? In what ways is the new scholarship on women and ethnic groups alike? In what ways does the new scholarship on women and ethnic groups challenge the dominant knowledge established in society and presented in textbooks? Give examples.
6. Examine the treatment of women in a sample of social studies, language arts, mathematics, or science textbooks (or a combination of two types of textbooks). Which phase or phases of the feminist phase theory presented by the author best describe the treatment of women in the textbooks you examined ?
7. What is the longue durée? Why is it important in the study of social history, particularly women's history?
8. Research your family history, paying particular attention to the roles, careers, and influence of women in your family's saga. Also describe your ethnic heritage and the influence of ethnicity on your family's past and present. Share your family history with a group of your classmates or workshop participants.

References

Alcoff, L. (1988). Cultural Feminism versus Post-Structuralism: The Identity Crisis in Feminist Theory. *Signs*, 13(spring), 405–436.

Alcott, L. M. (1995). *Little Women*. New York: Scholastic, Inc.

American Association of University Women Educational Foundation. (1998). *Gender Gaps: Where Schools Still Fail Our Children*. Washington, DC: Author.

Angelou, M. (1969). *I Know Why the Caged Bird Sings.* New York: Bantam Books.

Chapman, A. (Ed.). (1979). *Approaches to Women's History.* Washington, DC: American Historical Association.

Clemens, S. (1912). *The Adventures of Huckleberry Finn.* New York: Collier.

Collins, P. H. (1998). *Fighting Words: Black Women and the Search for Justice.* Minneapolis: University of Minnesota Press.

Douglass, F. (1994). *The Autobiography of Federick Douglass.* New York: Penguin Books.

Drew, D. E. (1996). *Aptitude Revisited: Rethinking Math and Science Education for America's Next Century.* Baltimore: The John Hopkins University Press.

Finke, L. (1993). Knowledge as Bait: Feminism Voice, and the Pedagogical Unconscious. *College English, 55*(1), 7–27.

Frankenberg, R. (1993). *White Women Race Matters: The Social Construction of Whiteness.* Minneapolis: University of Minnesota Press.

Frankenberg, R. (Ed.). (1997). *Displacing Whiteness: Essays in Social and Cultural Criticism.* Durham, NC: Duke University Press.

Fraser, S. (1982). *Spaces: Solving Problems of Access to Careers in Engineering and Science.* Berkeley: University of California, Lawrence Hall of Science.

Goldberger, N., Tarule, J., Clinchy, B., and Belenky, M. (Eds.). (1996). *Knowledge, Difference, and Power.* New York: Basic Books.

Haraway, D. (1991). *Simians, Cyborgs, and Women.* New York: Routledge.

Haraway, D. (1997). *Modest-Witness@-Second Millennium.* New York: Routledge.

Harding, S . (1991). *Whose Science? Whose Knowledge? Thinking from Women's Lives.* Ithaca, NY: Cornell University Press.

hooks, b. (1994). *Teaching to Transgress: Education as the Practice of Freedom.* New York: Routledge.

Jacobs, H. (1988) *Incidents in the Life of a Slave Girl.* New York: Oxford.

Keller, E. F. (1983). *A Feeling for the Organism: The Life and Work of Barbara McClintoch.* San Francisco: W. H. Freeman.

Kingston, M. H. (1976). *Woman Warrior.* New York: Alfred Knopf.

Lerner, G. (1982). As stated at a conference on women's history.

Letters to the Editor. (1982). *Social Education, 46*(6), 378–380.

Maher, F. and Tetreault, M. K. (1994). *The Feminist Classroom.* New York: Basic Books.

Maher, F. and Tetreault, M. K. (1997). Learning in the Dark: How Assumptions of Whiteness Shape Classroom Knowledge. *Harvard Educational Review, 67*(2), 321–349.

McIntosh, P. (1990). White Privilege and Male Privilege. In M. L. Andersen and P. J. Collins (Eds.) (p. 70–81), *Race, Class and Gender,* Boston: Wadsworth Publishing Company.

Mohanty, C., Russo, A., and Torres, L. (1991). *Third World Women and the Politics of Feminism.* Bloomington: Indiana University Press.

Moi, T. (1985). *Sexual/Textual Politics.* New York: Methuen.

Morrison, T. (1993). *Playing in the Dark: Whiteness and the Literary Imagination.* New York: Vintage.

Rosser, S. V. (1997). *Re-Engineering Female Friendly Science.* New York: Teachers College Press.

Schmitz, B., Butler, J. E., Rosenfelt, D., and Guy-Sheftall, B. (1995). *Women's Studies and Curriculum Transformation.* New York: Macmillan.

Tatum, B . (1992). Talking about Race, Learning about Racism: The Application of Racial Identity Development Theory in the Classroom. *Harvard Educational Review, 62*(1), 1–24.

Terkel, S. (1984). *The Good War: An Oral History of World War II.* New York: Pantheon Books.

Tetreault, C. (1991). *Metacommunication in a Women's Studies Classroom.* Unpublished senior honors thesis, Vassar College. Poughkeepsie, NY.

Tetreault, M. K. T. (1986a). Integrating Women's History: The Case of United States History Textbooks. *The History Teacher, 19*(2), 211–262.

Tetreault, M. K. T. (1986b). It's So Opinioney. *Journal of Education, 168*(2), 78–95.

Twain, Mark. (1996). *The Adventures of Tom Sawyer.* New York: Oxford University Press.

Uchida, Y. (1982). *Desert Exile: The Uprooting of a Japanese-American Family.* Seattle: University of Washington Press.

Weiler, K. (1988). *Women Teaching for Change: Gender, Class, and Power.* South Hadley, MA: Bergin and Garvey.

Wright, R. (1945). *Black Boy.* New York: Harper and Brothers.

CHAPTER 8

Transforming the Curriculum: Teaching about Women of Color

Johnnella E. Butler

Many efforts to include women and issues of gender into what is called the mainstream curriculum focus on White, middle-class women from the United States and on women from other nations and cultures. Generally, we have taken the White, middle-class woman's experience as the norm when examining and talking about women's lives. When we want to know about women's lives that differ from that norm, we generally have explored the global experience (Gross, 1987), despite the tremendous number of texts both by and about women of color in the United States across disciplines (Collins, 1998).

Curiously, when we deal with cultures of other nations, we seem to grasp that before we can have a proper understanding of the women in these cultures, we must adopt a multicultural perspective. It seems less apparent to us that to understand the lives of women in the United States, a cross-ethnic, multiethnic perspective that takes into account the structures and representations of racism, classism, ethnocentrism, sexism, and heterosexism on the goals and life experiences and their effects on women is necessary. Such a perspective is based on the recognition of the interconnections of various aspects of human identity and the consequent interconnectedness among structures hostile to those identities. This chapter provides an approach for studying women of color in the United States that is rooted in the exploration of connections that reveal the dynamics of similarity or sameness and dissimilarity or difference.

To talk about, study, and analyze racism is often a very frustrating endeavor. On one end of the spectrum, many scholars argue that racism is a thing of the past and that we need to move on to class analyses, return with more vigor to gender analyses, or to analyses of other forms of difference through which power is negotiated. Other people who share this perspective also question the wisdom of examining the United States as a multicultural society, determining that such an examination invites a division. On the other end, many people argue that while race is indeed a social construction, both *institutional racism* (racism that is integral to our various structures of human social, political, cultural, and economic organization) and *individual racism* (racism that is manifested in individual behavior and supported by racist beliefs) shape the existence and actions of all people in the United States. While references to these various positions are too numerous and various to list here, Michael Omi and Howard Winant (1994) in *Racial Formation in the United States* provide an excellent grounding for understanding the origins and the evolution of these positions.

This chapter focuses on teaching about women of color in the United States and also describes an approach useful for studying and teaching about all women in U.S. society. The discussion is rooted in the method of critical and dialogical pedagogy developing in this country that is influenced by Brazilian educator and activist Paulo Freire (1997). I see feminist pedagogy as an evolution of this critical pedagogy, as well as of the pedagogy implicit in ethnic studies. *Transformation*, as described in this chapter, is offered as the philosophical perspective for such dialogues. The content, context of, and pedagogy for teaching about women of color in the United States is part of that dialogue.

Examples are provided throughout the chapter to keep the theory from seeming only abstract and unrelated to people involved in the teaching process—the student and the teacher. Although the chapter does not include suggested activities for kindergarten and grades 1 through 12, it does provide information and a conceptual framework, the appropriate starting points for such activities. The appendix of this book includes bibliographic resources for content about the lives of women of color. These resources also provide a starting point. Much work has yet to be done to make this information available to most teachers.

WHY WOMEN OF COLOR?

The phrase *women of color* came into use gradually during the 1970s. It immediately brings to mind differences of race and culture. It also makes clear that African American women are not the only women of color in a nation where the Black racial experience historically and legally operates both to define and obscure racial dynamics between Whites and other racialized ethnic groups (see, for example Brodkin, 1998). Moreover, in a democratically structured society with a great power imbalance signified by race and class privilege, labels representative of reality for people outside the realm of power are difficult to determine. The form of that power is both cultural and political and consequently further complicates labeling. Selecting the phrase *women of color* by many women of U.S. ethnic groups of color is part of their struggle to be recognized with dignity for their humanity, racial heritage, and cultural heritage as they work within the women's movement of the United States. The effort of women of color to name themselves is similar to attempts by African Americans and other ethnic groups to define with dignity their race and ethnicity and to counter the many stereotypical names bestowed on them. Because we tend to use the word *women* to be all-inclusive and general, we usually obscure both the differences and the similarities among women.

With the decline of the civil rights movement of the 1960s, the women's movement in the second half of the twentieth century got under way. Not long after, African American women began to articulate the differences they experienced as African American women, not only because of the racism within the women's movement or the sexism within the African American community, but also because of their vastly differing historical reality. One major question posed by Toni Cade's (1970) pioneering anthology, *The Black Woman*, remains applicable: "How relevant are the truths, the experiences, the findings of White women to Black women? Are women after all, simply women?" Cade answers the question then as it might still be answered today: "I don't know that our priorities are the same, that our concerns and methods are the same, or even similar enough so that we can afford to depend on this new field of experts (White, female). It is rather obvious that we do not. It is obvious that we are turning to each other" (p. 9).

This anthology served as a turning point in the experience of the African American woman. Previously, White males, for the most part, had interpreted her realities, her activities, and her contributions. *The Negro Family: The Case for National Action* (1965), which became known as the "Moynihan Report" because it was written by Daniel P. Moynihan, was the most notable example of this scholarship. It was widely publicized and well received by most U.S readers. Blaming African American social and economic problems on the Black family, Daniel Moynihan argues that Black families, dominated by women, are generally pathological and pathogenic. His scholarship directly opposes the scholarship of Billingsley and others, which demonstrates the organizational differences between Black and White family units, the existence of a vital African American culture on which to base solutions to the problems, and the effects of racism, sexism, classism, and ethnocentrism in shaping the Black reality and government policy and societal attitudes towards that reality (Billingsley, 1968; Ladner, 1973; McAdoo, 1981; Moynihan, 1965). Bambara's (1970) anthology responded directly to such attacks and resulting policy, calling for Black women's direct involvement in both defining the problems and fashioning the solutions.

Although we are beyond the point of the complete invisibility and complete distortion of women of color in the academic branch of the women's movement (women's studies), African American women must still demand to be heard, must insist on being dealt with from the perspective of the experiences of women of color, just as they did in 1970, as the blurb in the paperback *The Black Woman* (Bambara, 1970) implies: "Black Women Speak Out. A Brilliant and Challenging Assembly of Voices That Demand to Be Heard." By the latter part of the 1970s, the logic of a dialogue among women of color became a matter of course. We find, as in Cade's *The Black Woman*, Black women speaking to one another in publications such as *Conditions: Five, The Black Women's Issue*, and women of color speaking in the pioneering *This Bridge Called My Back: Writings by Radical Women of Color* (*Conditions: Five*, 1979; Moraga & Anzaldua, 1981). The academic community began to recognize U.S. women of color who identify with the Third World, both for ancestral heritage and for related conditions of colonization; in 1980 we see, for example, the publication of Dexter Fisher's anthology *The Third Woman: Minority Women Writers of the United States* (Fisher, 1980), another milestone giving greater access to the voices of U.S. women of color.

The most familiar ethnic groups of color are the Asian Americans, African Americans, Hispanic Americans, and Native Americans. Yet within each group there are cultural, class, and racial distinctions. These ethnic groups can be further delineated: Asian Americans consist of Chinese Americans, Japanese Americans, Filipino Americans, Korean Americans, in addition to the more recent immigrants from Southeast Asia. African Americans consist of the U.S. African American and the West Indian or African Caribbean immigrants. The number of African immigrants is most likely too small and diverse to consider as a group; however, their presence should be acknowledged. Hispanic Americans, or Latino Americans as some people prefer, are largely Puerto Rican, Chicano, and Cuban. The Native American is made up of many nations, such as Sioux, Apache, Navajo, and Creek.

The phrase *women of color* helps women of all these groups acknowledge both their individual ethnicity and their racial solidarity as members of groups that are racial minorities in the United States, as well as a majority as people of color in the world. The concept also acknowledges similarity in historical experiences and position in relation to the White American. In addition, the use of the phrase and the concept *women of color* implies the existence of the race and ethnicity of White women, for whom the word *women* most often is used to indicate an assumed norm for all women or excludes other women.

WHAT WE LEARN FROM STUDYING WOMEN OF COLOR

When we study women of color, we raise our awareness and understanding of the experiences of all women either implicity or directly. Quite significantly, because of the imbalanced power relationship between White women and women of color, information about one group tends to make more apparent the experiences of the other group. It is well known, for example, that ideals of beauty in the United States are based on the blond, blue-eyed model. Dialogue about the reactions to that model in the experience of women of color, both within their ethnic groups and as they relate to White women, ultimately reveals that White women often judge themselves by that model of beauty. White women also serve simultaneously as reminders or representatives of that ideal to women of color and, most frequently, to themselves as failures to meet the ideal.

Another way of stating this is that a way of understanding an oppressor is to study the oppressed. Thus, we come to another level of awareness and understanding when we study women of color. We see clearly that White women function both as women who share certain similar experiences with women of color and as oppressors of women of color. This is one of the most difficult realities to cope with and still maintain productive, generative dialogue among women while teaching and conducting scholarship. White women who justifiably see themselves as oppressed by White men find it difficult to separate themselves from the effects of and power shared with White men. White women share with White men an ethnicity, an ancestral heritage, racial dominance, and certain powers and privileges by virtue of class, race, and ethnicity, by race and ethnicity if not class, and always by virtue of White skin privilege (Brodkin, 1998; Frye, 1983; McIntosh, 1987; Roediger, 1991; 1994).

The growing scholarship on women of color gives us much to teach about women's lives, their joys and celebrations, and their oppressions. I cannot begin to relate the content you must deal with in order to know women's lives. However, the books in the appendix can provide a beginning guide for you to become familiar with the history and culture of women of color. When we study women of color, we raise our awareness and understanding of the experiences of all women either explicit or implicitly.

Once we realize that all women are not White, and once we understand the implications of this realization, we see immediately the importance of race, ethnicity, and class when considering gender. Interestingly, much scholarship that intends to illustrate and analyze class dynamics is blind to racial and ethnic dynamics. In similar fashion, much scholarship that illustrates and analyzes racial dynamics and class dynamics fails to see ethnic dynamics. Other scholarship gives short shrift to, or even ignores, class. We have begun to grapple with the connectedness of the four big -isms—racism, sexism, classism, and ethnocentrism.

Much scholarship in women's studies, however, fails to work within the context of race, class, ethnicity, and gender and their related "isms," which modulate each other to a greater or lesser extent. Elizabeth V. Spelman illustrates how the racist equating of Blackness with lustfulness in Western culture modulates sexism toward African American women (Spelman, 1982). One resulting stereotype is that the African American woman has a bestial sexuality and, as such, deserves or expects to be raped. This racism is also modulated by an ethnocentrism that further devalues the African American woman, thereby justifying the sexism.

Classism may also modulate this sexism if the perpetrator is of a higher class status than are most African American women. However, if this cannot be claimed, then racism, ethnocentrism, or both may elevate the status of other people over the African American woman institutionally or socially. Nonetheless, each is operative to some degree. Lower-class Whites or Whites of the same economic class as African Americans can invoke skin privilege to differentiate within the class common denominator. The categories of race, class, ethnicity, and gender are connected and interrelated; likewise, their related "-isms" and their correctives.

Attention to race makes us aware of the differing perspectives that women have about race and skin color—perceptions of what is beautiful, ugly, attractive, or repulsive, and what is ordinary or exotic, pure or evil, based on racist stereotypes, on the role that color plays in women's lives, and on the norms by which women judge themselves physically. Attention to race also brings us to a realization that White women, too, are members of a race with stereotypes about looks and behavior. Attention to race in women's lives, with the particular understanding that race has a function for White women as well, reveals the oppression of racism, both from the point of view of one oppressed and of one who oppresses or participates in oppression by virtue of privilege.

Attention to class reveals, among other things, that because of different historical experiences, class means different things to different groups. Not necessarily measured by financial status, neighborhood, and level of education, class status frequently is measured by various ways in which one approximates variations on the Anglo-American norm of middle to upper class. Simultaneously, our society insists on formally measuring class status by economic means. The market/consumer representation of people in the United States drives goals and concepts of self-worth and continues today in variations on the themes of representations that gained currency during the 1980s, such as those in the television show *Dynasty* and the Yuppie and Buppie popular culture images. Yet for the woman of color, as for the man of color, the dynamic of social class becoming a measure for success is particularly insidious, threatening to destroy the affirmation of ethnic strengths that may be closely related to a generative self-identity. For example, Chinese Americans who have reached a high education level may move from Chinatown in a conflicting effort to succeed and participate in U.S. society. Adherence to the Anglo-American norm dictates certain dress, foods, and life-style, as well as a sense of superiority of the Anglo values. Ties to family and friends may be questioned, and the very traditions and understandings that provided the source of strength for coping in the White world may be devalued and discarded rather than transformed and adapted to the U.S. context.

Ethnicity, as a category of analysis, reveals the cultural traditions, perspectives, values, and choices that shape women's lives and their position in society, ranging from hairstyles and jewelry adornment to modes of worship and ways of perceiving a divine force, from values to the perception of women's roles and the roles of men. Ethnicity, our cultural and historical heritage, shapes our perception of race and racism, sex and sexism, class and classism.

The element of power or lack of power has a great deal to do with the benefits or deficits of race and ethnicity. Similar to the example regarding classism, the ethnic traditions, kinships, and values that are sustaining in the context of an ethnic group that is a minority, and thus, powerless, may become deficits when interacting with the majority or dominant society. On the other hand, when one becomes secure in one's ethnic identity, deficits of powerlessness and the moves to various levels of success (access to limited power) can be negotiated through variations on those strengths. Kinship networks, for example, are of primary importance to people of color for cultural reasons and for survival. Women's friendships often have particular significance, specifically friendships of younger women with older women. The structure of the larger U.S. society does not make allowances for such friendships. Most of us do not live in extended families or in neighborhoods near relatives. Women of color frequently insist that they maintain such relationships over great distances. Time spent with family, especially extended family, must have priority at various times during the year, not just for tradition's sake, but for maintaining a sense of rootedness, for a dose of shared wisdom, a balanced perspective of who you are, and often, simply for that affirmation that Momma or Aunt Elizabeth loves you. Ethnic identity provides a basis on which women of color celebrate who they are and where they come from in the awareness that they are not simply victims of ethnocentrism and other -isms.

Ethnicity is important in women's lives. Most important, ethnicity reveals that besides the usually acknowledged European American ethnic groups, White Anglo-Saxon Protestants are an ethnic group. Even though it is an ethnicity that boasts a defining dominance that makes it unnecessary to name itself, it is an ethnicity. That it is an ethnicity to which many Whites have subscribed, rather than one to which they belong by lineage, frequently is cause for confusion. However, it is no less an ethnicity for this reason.

The presence of Anglo-American ethnicity within the ethnicity of ethnic groups of color is often cause for confusion. Nonetheless, U.S. ethnic groups of color manifest ethnicities that constantly balance, integrate, and synthesize the Western European Anglo-American with what has become, with syncretism over the years, Chinese American, Japanese American, African American, Chicano, Native American, and Puerto Rican American. In a similar fashion, the English who came here syncretized with the values that emanated from being on this continent and became English Americans. They maintained a position of power so that other Europeans syncretized to their English or colonial American culture eventually resulted in their being called Americans. The assumption that people living in the United States are called Americans and that those living in other nations in the hemisphere are Latin Americans, Caribbean Americans, or Canadians attests to this assumed and enforced position of power.

Religion is closely related to ethnicity. Its values are sometimes indistinguishable from ethnic values, and it defines women's experiences in similar ways. Ethnicity as a category of analysis reveals sources of identity and sources of sustenance and celebration as well as the cultural dynamics that shape women's experience. It makes apparent the necessity of viewing women pluralistically.

Once we view women pluralistically, gender roles begin to assume differing degrees of importance. By virtue of the modulation of the other categories, women may see gender, sexual identity, sexism, and homophobia to be of lesser or greater importance. Gender roles for women of color are more apparently designated, determined, or modulated by ethnicity, race, and sexism. Therefore, racism may assume primary importance as an oppressive force with which to reckon. The African American woman harassed in the workplace because she wears her hair in intricate braids and wears clothes associated with her African heritage receives harsh treatment because of racism, not sexism. Racism has also caused African American women to be denied the right to vote after White women gained suffrage rights. Gender, sexual identity, and race become related targets for discrimination as a result of ethnic and/or religious values; an individual's conceptualization of gender roles may be in conflict with that of her racial/ethnic group. Thus, while key aspects of women's identities are connected and interrelated, they can be so in conflict as well as in harmony.

WOMEN OF COLOR: THE AGENT OF TRANSFORMATION

In dealing with the commonalities and differences among women (a necessity in teaching about women of color), I am reminded that the title of Paula Giddings's work on African American women is taken from Anna J. Cooper's observation: "When and where I enter, then and there the whole . . . race enters with me" (Giddings, 1984, p. 82). Repeated in many forms by women of color, from the nineteenth-century struggle for the vote to present-day women's organizing, this truth ultimately contains the goal of transformation of the curriculum: a curriculum that reflects all of us, egalitarian, communal, nonhierarchical, and pluralistic. Women of color are inextricably related to men of color by virtue of ethnicity and traditions as well as by common conditions of oppression. Therefore, at minimum, their struggle against sexism and racism is waged simultaneously. The experiences and destinies of women and men of color are linked. This reality poses a special problem in the relationship between White women and women of color. Moreover, in emphasizing the commonalities of privilege between White men and women, the oppressive relationship between men of color and White men, women of color and White men, and men of color and White women—all implied in Anna J. Cooper's observation—the teaching about women of color provides the naturally pluralistic, multidimensional catalyst for transformation. As such, women of color are agents of transformation.

This section defines transformation and provides the theoretical framework for the pedagogy and methodology of transformation. The final section discusses aspects of the process of teaching about women of color, which, though closely related to the theoretical framework, manifest themselves in very concrete ways.

A review of feminist pedagogy over the past twenty years or so reveals a call for teaching from multifocal, multidimensional, multicultural, pluralistic, interdisciplinary perspectives. This call, largely consistent with the pedagogy and methodology implied thus far in this chapter, can be accomplished only through *transformation*. Although many theorists and teachers now see this point, the terminology has still to be corrected to illustrate the process. In fact, we often use the words *mainstreaming, balancing, integration,* and *transformation* interchangeably. Mainstreaming, balancing, and integration imply adding women to an established, accepted, and unchangeable body of knowledge. The experience of White, middle-class women has provided a norm in a way that White Anglo-American male ethnicity provides a norm. All other women's experience is added to and measured by those racial, class, ethnic, and gender roles and experiences.

Transformation, which does away with the dominance of norms, allows us to see the many aspects of women's lives. Understanding the significance of naming the action of treating women's lives through a pluralistic process—transformation—leads naturally to a convergence between women's studies and ethnic studies. This convergence is necessary to give us the information that illuminates the function and content of race, class, and ethnicity in women's lives and in relation to gender. In similar fashion, treating the lives of people of color through a pluralistic process leads to the same convergence, illuminating the functions and content of race, class, and gender in relation to lives of ethnic Americans and in relation to ethnicity.

We still need to understand exactly what is meant by this pluralistic, multidimensional, interdisciplinary scholarship and pedagogy; much of the scholarship on, about, and even frequently by women of color renders them systematically invisible, erasing their experience or part of it. White, middle-class, male, and Anglo-American are the imposed norms corresponding to race, class, gender, and ethnicity. In contrasting and comparing experiences of pioneers, White males and females when dealing with Native Americans, for example, often speak of "the male," "the female," and "the Indian." Somehow, those of a different ethnicity and race are assumed to be male. Therefore, both the female and the male Indian experience is observed and distorted. They must be viewed both separately and together to get a more complete view, just as to have a more complete view of the pioneer experience, the White male and White female experiences must be studied both separately and together. Thus, even in our attempts to correct misinformation resulting from measurement by one norm, we can reinforce measurement by other norms if we do not see the interaction of the categories, the interaction of the -isms, as explained in the previous section. This pluralistic process and eye are demanded in order to understand both the particulars and the generalities of people's lives.

Why is it so easy to impose these norms, effectively to erase the experience of others? I do not think erasing these experiences is always intentional. I do, however, think that it results from the dominance of the Western cultural norms of individuality, singularity, rationality, masculinity, and Whiteness at the expense of the communal, the plural, the intuitive, the feminine, and people of color. A brief look at Elizabeth Spelman's seminal work, "Theories of Race and Gender: The Erasure of Black Women," explains the important aspects of how this erasure comes about (Spelman, 1982, pp. 57–59). Then, a consideration of the philosophical makeup of transformation tells us both how our thinking makes it happen and how we can think to prevent it from happening.

Spelman gives examples of erasure of the Black woman, similar to the examples provided in this chapter. She analyzes concepts that assume primacy of sexism over racism. Furthermore, she rejects the additive approach to analyzing sexism, an approach that assumes a sameness of women modeled on the White, middle-class, Anglo-oriented woman. Spelman shows that it is premature to argue that sexism and racism are either mutually exclusive, totally dependent on one another, or in a causal relationship with one another. She discusses how women differ by race, class, and culture or ethnicity. Most important, she demonstrates that Black does not simply indicate victim. Black indicates a culture—in the United States, the African American culture. She suggests, then, that we present women's studies in a way that makes it a given that women are diverse, that their diversity is apparent in their experiences with oppression and in their participation in U.S. culture. To teach about women in this manner, our process must not be additive, that is, integrating, mainstreaming, or balancing the curriculum. Rather, *transformation* is the process that leads to this goal.

Essentially, transformation is the process of revealing unity among human beings and the world, as well as revealing important differences. Transformation implies acknowledging and benefiting from the interaction among sameness and diversity, groups and individuals. The maxim on which transformation rests may be stated as an essential affirmation of the West African proverb, "I am because we are. We are because I am." The communality, the human unity implicit in the proverb, operates in African traditional (philosophical) thought in regard to human beings and to other categories of life—categories of knowledge and ways of thinking and being (Davidson, 1969; Mbiti, 1975). Traditional African thought is in opposition to the European, Western pivotal axiom, on which integration, balancing, and mainstreaming rest (as expressed through the White, middle-class, Anglo norm in the United States)—"I think; therefore, I am," as expressed by Descartes.

Traditional African thought is in tune with a pluralistic, multidimensional process; the European Western axiom with a monolithic, one-dimensional process. Stated succinctly as "I am we," the West African proverb provides the rationale for the interaction and modulation of the categories of race, class, gender, and ethnicity; for the interaction and modulation of their respective -isms; for the interaction and modulation of the objective and subjective, the rational and the intuitive, the feminine and the masculine—all those things that we, as Westerners, see as either opposite or as standing rigidly alone. This view is the breakdown of what is variously called critical pedagogy, feminist pedagogy, or multifocal teaching, when the ends are the comprehension of and involvement with cultural, class, racial, and gender diversity toward the end, not of tolerance, but rather of an egalitarian world based on communal relationships within humanity. Elsa Barkley Brown gives us an insightful and useful discussion of teaching African American women's history in a way consistent with transformation as described here. This way of teaching creates "a polyrhythmic, 'nonsymmetrical,' nonlinear structure in which individual and community are not competing entities" (Brown, 1989, p. 926).

To realize this transformation, we must redefine categories and displace criteria that have served as norms in order to bring about the life context (norms and values) as follows:

1. Nonhierarchical terms and contexts for human institutions, rituals, and action
2. A respect for the interaction and existence of both diversity and sameness
   (a removal of measurement by norms perpetuating otherness, silence, and erasure)
3. A balancing of and interaction between the individual and the group
4. A concept of humanity emanating from interdependence of human beings on one another and on the world environment, both natural and human-created
5. A concept of humanity emanating from a sense of self that is not totally abstract and totally individually defined (I think; therefore, I am), but that is both abstract

and concrete, individually and communally defined (I am we; I am because we are; we are because I am).

Such a context applies to pedagogy and scholarship in the dissemination and ordering of knowledge in all disciplines and fields. Within this context (the context in which the world does operate and against which the Western individualistic, singular concept of humanity militates), it becomes possible for us to understand the popular music form rap as an Americanized, Westernized version of African praise singing, functioning, obviously, for decidedly different cultural and social reasons. It becomes possible to understand the syncretization of cultures that produced Haitian voudon, Cuban santería, and Brazilian candomblé from Catholicism and the religion of the Yoruba. It becomes possible to understand what is happening when a Japanese American student is finding it difficult to reconcile traditional Buddhist values with her American life. It becomes possible to understand that Maxine Hong Kingston's *Woman Warrior* (1976) is essentially about the struggle to syncretize Chinese ways within the United States, whose dominant culture devalues and coerces against syncretization, seeking to impose White, middle-class conformity.

Thinking in this manner is foreign to the mainstream of thought in the United States, although it is alive and well in Native American traditional philosophy, in Taoist philosophy, in African traditional philosophy, and in African American folklore. It is so foreign, in fact, that I realized that in order to bring about this context, we must commit certain so-called sins. Philosopher Elizabeth Minnich suggested that these sins might be more aptly characterized as heresies, because they are strongly at variance with established modes of thought and values.

The following heresies challenge and ultimately displace the ways in which the Western mind orders the world (For related discussions see Freire, 1969; 1973; Hord & Lee, 1995; Yancy, 1998; Young, 1990). These heresies emanate from the experiences of people of color, the nature of their oppression, and the way the world operates. Adopting them is a necessity for teaching about women of color. Using the heresies to teach women's studies, to teach about the lives of all women, becomes natural when we study women of color, and it leads to the transformation of the curriculum to a pluralistic, egalitarian, multidimensional curriculum.

> **Heresy #1** The goal of interaction among human beings, action, and ideas must be seen not only as synthesis, but also as the identification of opposites and differences. These opposites and differences may or may not be resolved; they may function together by virtue of the similarities identified and the tensions they generate as they move ultimately toward resolution.
>
> **Heresy #2** We *can* address a multiplicity of concerns, approaches, and subjects without a neutral or dominant center. Reality reflects opposites as well as overlaps in what are perceived as opposites. There exist no pure, distinct opposites. Human experience has multiple, interconnected centerings.
>
> **Heresy #3** It is not reductive to look at gender, race, class, and culture as parts of a complex whole. The more different voices we have, the closer we are to the whole.
>
> **Heresy #4** Transformation demands an understanding of ethnicity that takes into account the differing cultural continua (in the United States, Western

European, Anglo-American, African, Asian, Native American) and their similarities.

Heresy # 5 Transformation demands a relinquishing of the primary definitiveness of gender, race, class or culture, and ethnicity as they interact with theory, methodology, pedagogy, institutionalization, and action, both in synthesis and in a dynamic that functions as opposite and same simultaneously. A variation on this heresy is that although all -isms are not the same, they are connected and operate as such; likewise, their correctives.

Heresy #6 The Anglo-American, and ultimately the Western, norm must be seen as only one of many norms, and also as one that enjoys privilege and power that has colonized, and may continue to colonize, other norms.

Heresy #7 Feelings are direct lines to better thinking. The intuitive as well as the rational is part of the process of moving from the familiar to the unfamiliar in acquiring knowledge.

Heresy #8 Knowledge is identity and identity is knowledge. All knowledge is explicitly and implicitly related to who we are, both as individuals and as groups.

Engaging transformation through these eight heresies means addressing the connections among human beings, among human beings and the environment, and among experiences, categories of identity. It means using the intuitive and the congitive, displacing dominating norms, exploring the comparative and relational aspects of various norms as well as the conflictual aspects, and acknowledging the power of knowledge to define self, others, and experience. Transformation, then, provides the basis of a pedagogy that stems from teaching about the experience of women of color in a way that engages both how women of color are constructed as subject, with an implicit understanding of how the student is constructed as subject.

Such an approach may prove helpful in teaching other content to today's postmodern youth, whom Henry Giroux describes as "border youth," that is, youth for whom "plurality and contingency—whether mediated through the media or through the dislocations spurned by the economic system, the rise of new social movements or the crisis of representation— have resulted in a world with few secure psychological, economic, or intellectual markers. . . . [they] increasingly inhabit shifting cultural and social spheres marked by a plurality of languages and cultures" (Giroux, 1994, p. 355). As stated at the beginning of this chapter, the content, context of, and pedagogy for teaching about women of color in the United States is part of the needed dialogue between modernism and postmodernism. The fragmentation and dislocation of women of color in relation to what and how we teach frequently reflect and refract the objectification of the student when we teach as if we are filling empty repositories, fulfilling Freire's banking concept (1969).

As the agent of transformation, women of color as subject content in the humanities and social sciences provide an excellent point for engaging our modern/postmodern conflict. It provides also a philosophical perspective, transformation, for a generative pedagogy that fosters students as subjects, generates knowledge and understanding through building on the interconnections among student, teacher, and content, and engages the conflictive from the strength of the multiply-centered, relational context.

TEACHING ABOUT WOMEN OF COLOR

The first six heresies cited above essentially address content and methodology for gathering and interpreting content. They inform decisions such as the following:

1. Not teaching Linda Brent's *Incidents in the Life of a Slave Girl* (1973) as the single example of the slave experience of African American women in the nineteenth century, but rather presenting it as a representative example of the slave experience of African American women that occurs within a contradictory, paradoxical world that had free Black women such as Charlotte Forten Grimke and African American abolitionist women such as Sojourner Truth. The picture of Black women that emerges then becomes one that illuminates their complexity of experiences and their differing interactions with White people rather than an aberrant experience.

2. Not simply teaching about pioneer women in the West, but teaching about Native American women, perhaps through their stories, which they have passed on to their children and their children's children, using the word to advance those concepts crucial to cultural survival. The picture of settling the West becomes more balanced, suggesting clearly to students the different perspectives and power relationships. The Native American becomes a subject—one who acts and interacts, rather than an object of Whites, portrayed as the only subjects.

3. Not choosing a single biography each for children to read of a White woman, an Asian American woman, and an African American woman, but rather finding ways through biography, poetry, and storytelling to introduce children to different women's experiences—different according to race, class, ethnicity, and gender roles and sexual identity—as well as ways to discuss women's lives comparatively.

The last two heresies directly address process. After accurate content, process is the most important part of teaching. Students who learn in an environment that is sensitive to their feelings and that supports and encourages the pursuit of knowledge will consistently meet new knowledge and new situations with the necessary openness and understanding for human development and progress. If this sounds moralistic, we must remember that the stated and implied goal of critical pedagogy and feminist pedagogy, as well as of efforts to transform the curriculum with content about women and ethnicity, is to provide an education that more accurately reflects the history and composition of the world, that demonstrates the relationship of what we learn to how we live, and that implicitly and explicitly reveals the relationship between knowledge and social action. Process is most important, then, in helping students develop ways throughout their education to reach the closest approximation of truth toward the end of a better, more democratic human condition.

The key to understanding the teaching process in any classroom in which teaching about women of color from the perspective of transformation is a goal is recognizing that the content alters all students' perceptions of themselves. First, they begin to realize that we can never say *women* to mean all women, that we must particularize the word as appropriate to context and understanding (for example, White, middle-class women; Chinese American, lower-class women; middle-class, Mexican American women). Next, students begin to understand that using White, middle-class women as the norm will seem distortingly reductive. White women's ethnic, regional, class, and gender commonalities and differences soon become apparent, and the role in oppression of the imposed Anglo-American ethnic conformity stands out.

Student reactions may range from surprise, to excitement about learning more, to hostility and anger. In the volume *Gendered Subjects*, Margo Culley (1985) details much of what happens. Her opening paragraph summarizes her main thesis:

> Teaching about gender and race can create classrooms that are charged arenas. Students enter these classrooms imbued with the values of the dominant culture: they believe that success in conventional terms is largely a matter of will and that those who do not have it all have experienced a failure of will. Closer and closer ties between corporate America and higher education, as well as the "upscaling" of the student body, make it even harder to hear the voices from the margin within the academy. Bringing those voices to the center of the classroom means disorganizing ideology and disorienting individuals. Sometimes, as suddenly as the fragments in a kaleidoscope rearrange to totally change the picture, our work alters the ground of being for our students (and perhaps even for ourselves). When this happens, classrooms can become explosive, but potentially transformative arenas of dialogue. (p. 209)

Even though Culley's observation is now more than fifteen years old, reports from faculty in various workshops I have conducted nationwide suggest that it still holds.

"Altering the ground of being" happens to some extent on all levels. The White girl kindergarten pupil's sense of the world is frequently challenged when she discovers that heroines do not necessarily look like her. Awareness of the ways in which the world around children is ordered occurs earlier than most of us may imagine. My niece, barely four years old, told my father in a definitive tone as we entered a church farther from her home than the church to which she belongs, "Gramps, this is the Black church." We had not referred to the church as such, yet clearly that Catholic congregation was predominantly Black and the girl's home congregation predominantly White. Her younger sister, at age three, told her mother that the kids in the day school she attended were "not like me." She then pointed to the brown, back side of her hand. Young children notice difference. We direct what they do with and think of that difference.

Teaching young children about women of color gives male and female children of all backgrounds a sense of the diversity of people, of the various roles in which women function in U.S. culture, of the various joys and sorrows, triumphs and struggles they encounter. Seeds of awareness of the power relationships between male and female, among racial, ethnic, and class groups are sown and nurtured.

Teaching about women of color early in students' academic experience allows the voices of the margin to be heard and to become a part of the matrix of reality. Teaching about women of color reveals race, ethnicity, gender, and class as essential components of human identity and also questions ideology and ways of being. It encourages an openness to understanding, to difference and similarity, and to the foreign and the commonplace necessary to the mindset of curiosity about and fascination for knowledge that we all want to inspire in our students no matter what the subject. Moreover, it highlights connections among human beings and human experiences and reveals relationships among actions one to another.

Culley (1985) also observes that "anger is the energy mediating the transformation from damage to wholeness," the damage being the values and perspectives of the dominant culture that have shaped opinions based on a seriously flawed and skewed American history and interpretation of the present (p. 212). Certain reactions occur and are part of the process of teaching about women of color. Because they can occur at all levels to a greater or lesser extent, it is useful to look for variations on their themes.

It is important to recognize that these reactions occur within the context of student and teacher expectations. Students are concerned about grading; teachers, about evaluations by superiors and students. Frequently, fear of, disdain for, or hesitancy about feminist perspectives by some students may create a tense, hostile atmosphere. Similarly, fear of, disdain for, or hesitancy about studying people different from you (particularly by the White student) or people similar to you (particularly by the student of color or of a culture related to people of color) also may create a tense, hostile atmosphere. Student expectations of teachers, expectations modulated by the ethnicity, race, class, and gender of the teacher, may encourage students to presume that a teacher will take a certain position. The teacher's need to inspire students to perform with excellence may become a teacher's priority at the expense of presenting material that may at first confuse the students or challenge their opinions. It is important to treat these reactions as though they are as much a part of the process of teaching as are the form of presentation, the exams, and the content, for, indeed, they are. Moreover, they can affect the success of the teaching of the material about women of color.

Specifically, these reactions are part of the overall process of moving from the familiar to the unfamiliar. As Heresy #7 guides us, "Feelings are direct lines to better thinking." Affective reactions to content, such as anger, guilt, and feelings of displacement, when recognized for what they are, lead to the desired cognitive reaction—the conceptualization of the facts so that knowledge becomes useful as the closest approximation to the truth. As Japanese American female students first read accounts by Issei (first-generation) women about their picture-bride experiences, the students' reactions might at first be mixed. Raising the issue of Japanese immigration to the United States during the late nineteenth century may not only challenge the exotic stereotype of the Japanese woman, but it may also engender anger toward Japanese males, because of students' incomplete access to history. White students may respond with guilt or indifference because of the policy of a government whose composition is essentially White and Anglo-oriented and with which they identify. Japanese American male students may become defensive, desirous of hearing Japanese American men's stories about picture-bride marriages. African American male and female students may draw analogies between the Japanese American experience and the African American experience. Such analogies may be welcomed or resented by other students. Of course, students from varied backgrounds may respond to learning about Issei women with a reinforced or instilled pride in Japanese ancestry or with a new-found interest in immigration history.

Teacher presentation of Issei women's experience as picture brides should include, of course, lectures, readings, films, and videos about the experience of male Issei immigrants to the United States during the first quarter of the twentieth century—the cheap labor they provided, the impossibility of return to Japan due to low wages, the male-female ratio of Japanese Americans at the turn of the century, and the tradition of arranged marriage in Japan. Presentations should also anticipate, however, student reaction based on their generally ill-informed or limited knowledge about the subject. Discussion and analysis of the students' initial perspectives on Issei women, of how those perspectives have changed given the historical, cultural, and sociological information, allow for learning about and reading Issei women's accounts to become an occasion, then, for expressing feelings of guilt, shame, anger, pride, interest, and curiosity, and for getting at the reasons for those feelings.

Understanding those feelings and working with them to move the student from a familiar that may be comprised of damaging misinformation and even bigotry, to a balanced understanding, sometimes become major portions of the content, especially when anger or guilt is directed toward a specific group—other students, the teacher, or perhaps even the self. Then it becomes necessary for the teacher to use what I call pressure-release sessions. The need for such sessions may manifest itself in many ways. For example,

> the fear of being regarded by peers or by the professor as racist, sexist or "politically incorrect" can polarize a classroom. If the [teacher] participates unconsciously in this fear and emotional self-protection, the classroom experience will degenerate to hopeless polarization, and even overt hostility. He or she must constantly stand outside the classroom experience and anticipate such dynamics. . . . "Pressure release" discussions work best when the teacher directly acknowledges and calls attention to the tension in the classroom. The teacher may initiate the discussion or allow it to come about in whatever way he or she feels most comfortable. (Butler, 1985, p. 236)

The hostility, fear, and hesitancy "can be converted to fertile ground for profound academic experiences . . . 'profound' because the students' knowledge is challenged, expanded, or reinforced" (Butler, 1985, p. 236) by a subject matter that is simultaneously affective and cognitive, resonant with the humanness of life in both form and content. Students learn from these pressure-release sessions, as they must learn in life, to achieve balance and harmony in whatever pursuits, that paradoxes and contradictions are sometimes resolved and sometimes stand separately yet function together (recall Heresy #1).

Teaching about women of color can often spark resistance to the teacher or cause students to question subject veracity. For example, students usually are taught that the latter part of the nineteenth century and the turn of the century was a time of expansion for the United States—the Progressive Era. Learning of the experiences of Native American and Mexican women who were subjected to particular horrors as the United States pushed westward, or reading about restrictions on Chinese immigrant women who were not allowed to enter the United States with the Chinese men who provided what was tantamount to slave labor for the building of the railroads, students begin to realize that this time was anything but progressive or expansive.

Teaching about Ida Wells-Barnett, the African American woman who waged the antilynching campaigns at the end of the nineteenth century and well into the twentieth century, also belies the progress of that time. Ida Wells-Barnett brings to the fore the horror of lynchings of African American men, women, and children; the inhuman practice of castration that was part of the lynching of Black males; the stereotyped ideas of African American men and women, ideas that were, as Giddings (1984) reminds us, "older than the Republic itself—for they were rooted in the European minds that shaped America" (p. 31). Furthermore, Wells-Barnett's life work reveals the racism of White women in the suffragist movement of the early twentieth century, a reflection of the racism in that movement's nineteenth-century manifestation.

The ever-present interaction of racism and sexism, the stereotyping of African American men and women as bestial, the unfounded labeling of African American men as rapists in search of White women, and the horrid participation in all of this by White men and women in all stations of life make for difficult history for any teacher to teach and for any student to study. The threat to the perfect founding fathers and Miss Liberty versions are apparent. Such content is often resisted by African American and White students alike, perhaps for different reasons, including rage, anger, or shame that such atrocities were endured by people like them; indifference in the face of reality because "nothing like that will happen again"; and anger, guilt, or shame that people of their race were responsible for such hideous atrocities. Furthermore, all students may resent the upsetting of their neatly packaged understandings of U.S. history and of their world.

The teacher must know the content and be willing to facilitate the pressure-release sessions that undoubtedly will be needed. Pressure-release sessions must help students sort out facts from feelings and, most of all, must clarify the relevance of the material to understanding the world in which we live and to preventing such atrocities from recurring. Also, in teaching about the Issei women and about the life of Ida Wells-Barnett, teachers must never let the class lose sight of the vision these women had, how they dealt with joy and sorrow, the triumphs and struggles of their lives, the contributions to both their own people and to U.S. life at large.

In addition to variations on anger, guilt, and challenges to credibility in learning about women of color, students become more aware of the positive aspects of race and ethnicity and frequently begin to take pride in their identities. As Heresy #8 states, "Knowledge is identity and identity is knowledge. All knowledge is explicitly and implicitly related to who we are, both as individuals and as groups." The teacher, however, must watch for overzealous pride as well as for unadmitted uneasiness with one's ethnic or racial identity. White students, in particular, may react in a generally unexpected manner. Some may predictably claim their Irish ancestry; others may be confused as to their ethnicity, for they may come from German and Scottish ancestry, which early on assumed Anglo-American identity. Students of Anglo-American ancestry, however, may hesitate to embrace that terminology, for it might suggest to them, in the context of the experiences of women and men of color, an abuse of power and "all things horrible in this country," as one upset student once complained to me. Here, teachers must be adept not only at conveying facts, but also at explaining the effects of culture, race, gender, and ethnicity in recording and interpreting historical facts. Teachers also must be able to convey to students both the beautiful and the ugly in all of us. Thus, the African American teacher may find himself or herself explaining the cultural value of Anglo-American or Yankee humor, of Yankee precision in gardening, of Yankee thriftiness, of the conflicting values of the founding fathers, and how we all share, in some way, that heritage. At whatever age this occurs, students must be helped to understand the dichotomous, hierarchical past of that identity and to move toward expressing their awareness in a pluralistic context.

Now that we have explored the why of the phrase *women of color*, identified the essence of what we learn when we study women of color, discussed the theory of transformation and its heresies, and identified and discussed the most frequent reactions of students to the subject matter, in conclusion we focus on the teacher.

CONCLUSION

Teaching about women of color should result in conveying information about a group of people largely invisible in our curricula in a way that encourages students to seek further knowledge and ultimately to begin to correct and reorder the flawed perception of the world based on racism, sexism, classism, and ethnocentrism. To do so is no mean feat. Redefining one's world involves not only the inclusion of previously ignored content, but also the revision, deletion, and correction of accepted content in light of missing and ignored content. As such, it might require a redesignation of historical periods, a renaming of literary periods, and a complete reworking of sociological methodology to reflect the ethnic and cultural standards at work. This chapter, then, is essentially an introduction to the journey that teachers must embark on to begin providing for students a curriculum that reflects the reality of the past, prepares students to deal with and understand the present, and creates the basis for a more humane, productive, caring future.

The implications of teaching about women of color are far-reaching, involving many people in many different capacities. New texts need to be written for college-level students. Teacher education must be restructured to include not only the transformed content but also the pedagogy that reflects how our nation and the world are multicultural, multiethnic, multiracial, multifocal, and multidimensional. College texts, children's books, and other materials need to be devised to help teach this curriculum. School administrators, school boards, parents, and teachers need to participate in and contribute to this transformation in all ways that influence what our children learn.

For teachers and those studying to be teachers, the immediate implications of a transformed curriculum can seem overwhelming, for transformation is a process that will take longer than our lifetimes. Presently, we are in the formative stages of understanding what must be done to correct the damage in order to lead to wholeness. I suggest that we begin small. That is, decide to include women of color in your classes this year. Begin adding some aspect of that topic to every unit. Pay close attention to how that addition relates to what you already teach. Does it expand the topic? Does it present material you already cover within that expansion? Can you delete some accepted, repetitive material and still meet your objectives? Does the new material conflict with the old? How? Is that conflict a valuable learning resource for your students? Answering such questions will move you quickly from simply adding to re-visioning and transforming. Continue to do this each year. Gradually, other central topics will emerge about men of color, White men, White women, class, race, ethnicity, and gender. By beginning with studying women of color, the curriculum then will have evolved to be truly pluralistic.

This chapter pays the most attention to the student. The teacher, who embarks on this long journey, must be determined to succeed. Why? Because all the conflicting emotions, the sometimes painful movement from the familiar to the unfamiliar, are experienced by the teacher as well. We have been shaped by the same damaging, ill-informed view of the world as our students have. Often, as we try to resolve their conflicts, we are simultaneously working through our own. Above all, we must demand honesty of ourselves before we can succeed.

Another important task of the teacher is changing how, in our attempts to change the construction of the student as object, a receptacle of information, we have constructed the student as a distant, theoretical, abstract subject. John Shilb (1992) cogently describes what it means to change how we construct the student as subject:

> Changing how the student is constructed as subject entails a number of related teaching practices. It means considering how social differences can affect the interests, backgrounds, learning styles, and degrees of confidence that students bring to the classroom. It means examining how authority operates there as well as in the larger society, analyzing how traditional power relations might be rethought or merely reinforced when teachers and students meet. It means taking students' accounts of their own experiences as at least potentially legitimate avenues to knowledge. It means recognizing that learning can involve intuition and emotion, not just cold, hard logic. Overall, it means taking as a central classroom aim the empowerment of students as conscious, active subjects in the learning process, thereby enhancing their capacity to develop a more democratic world. (p. 65)

The difficulty of the process of transformation is one factor contributing to the maintenance of the status quo. Often, we look for the easiest way out. It is easier to work with students who are not puzzled, concerned, or bothered by what they are studying. We, as teachers, must be willing to admit that we do not know everything, but that we do know how to go about learning in a way that reaches the closest approximation of the truth. Our reach must always exceed our grasp, and, in doing so, we will encourage the excellence, the passion, the curiosity, the respect, and the love needed to create superb scholarship and encourage thinking, open-minded, caring, knowledgeable students.

Questions and Activities

1. When Butler uses the phrase *women of color*, to what specific ethnic groups is she referring? Why did this phrase emerge, and what purpose does it serve?

2. How can a study of women of color help broaden our understanding of White women? Of women in general?

3. In what ways, according to Butler, is ethnicity an important variable in women's lives? Give specific examples from this chapter to support your response.

4. How does racism, combined with sexism, influence the ways in which people view and respond to women of color?

5. What does the author mean by transformation and a *transformed curriculum?* How does a transformed curriculum differ from a mainstream or balanced curriculum?

6. How can content about women of color serve as a vehicle for transforming the school curriculum?

7. The author lists eight heresies, or assumptions, about reality that differ fundamentally from dominant modes of thought and values. Why does she believe these heresies are essential when teaching about women of color?

8. The author states that teaching about women of color may spark resistance to the teacher, the subject, or both. What examples of content does she describe that may evoke student resistance? Why, according to Butler, might students resist this content? What tips does she give teachers for handling student resistance?

9. Develop a teaching unit in which you incorporate content about women of color, using the transformation approach described in this chapter. Useful references on women of color are found in the Appendix ("Gender" section).

References

Bambara, T. C. (ed.). (1970). *The Black Woman: An Anthology.* New York: New American Library.

Billinglsey, A. (1968). *Black Families in White America.* Englewood Cliffs, NJ: Prentice-Hall.

Brent, L. (1973). *Incidents in the Life of a Slave Girl.* Edited by L. M. Child. New York: Harcourt.

Brodkin, K. (1998). *How Jews Became White Folks and What That Says about Race in America.* New Brunswick, NJ: Rutgers University Press.

Brown, E. B. (1989). African American Women's Quilting: A Framework for Conceptualizing and Teaching African American Women's History. *Signs: Journal of Women in Culture and Society, 14*(4), 921–929.

Butler, J. E. (1985). Toward a Pedagogy of Everywoman's Studies. In M. Culley and C. Portuges (Eds.), *Gendered Subjects: The Dynamics of Feminist* Teaching (pp. 230–239). Boston: Routledge and Kegan Paul.

Collins, P. H. (1998). *Fighting Words: Black Women and the Search for Justice.* Minneapolis: University of Minnesota Press.

Conditions, Five. (1979). The Black Woman's Issue, *2*(3) (autumn).

Culley, M. (1985). Anger and Authority in the Introductory Women's Studies Classroom. In M. Culley and C. Portuges (Eds.), *Gendered Subjects: The Dynamics of Feminist Teaching* (pp. 209–217). Boston: Routledge and Kegan Paul.

Davidson, B. (1969). *The African Genius.* Boston: Little, Brown.

Fisher, D. (Ed.). (1980). *The Third Woman: Minority Women Writers of the United States.* Boston: Houghton Mifflin.

Freire, P. (1969). *Pedagogy of the Oppressed.* New York: Seabury.

Freire, P. (1973). *Education for Critical Consciousness.* New York: Seabury.

Frye, M. (1983). On Being White: Toward a Feminist Understanding of Race and Race Supremacy. In M. Frye (Ed.), *The Politics of Reality: Essays in Feminist Theory* (pp. 110–127). Trumansburg, NY: The Crossing Press.

Giddings, P. (1984). *When and Where I Enter: The Impact of Black Women on Race and Sex in America.* New York: William Morrow.

Giroux, H. (1994). Slacking Off: Border Youth and Postmodern Education. *Journal of Advanced Composition, 14*(2), 347–366.

Gross, S. H. (1987). Women's History for Global Learning. *Social Education, 51*(3), 194–198.

Hord, F. L. and Lee, J. (1995). *I Am Because We Are: Readings in Black Philosophy.* Amherst: University of Massachusetts Press.

Kingston, M. H. (1976). *The Woman Warrior: Memories of a Girlhood among Ghosts.* New York: Random House.

Ladner, J. (Ed.). (1973). *The Death of White Sociology.* New York: Vintage.

Mbiti, J. (1975). *Introduction to African Religion.* London: Heinemann.

McAdoo, H. (Ed.). (1981). *Black Families.* Beverly Hills, CA: Sage Publications.

McIntosh, P. (1987). *Understanding Correspondence between White Privilege and Male Privilege through Women's Studies Work.* Unpublished paper presented at the National Women's Studies Association Annual Meeting, Atlanta, GA.

Moraga, C. and Anzaldua, G. (Eds.). (1981). *This Bridge Called My Back: Writings by Radical Women of Color.* Watertown, MA: Persephone Press.

Omi, M. and Winant, H. (1994). *Racial Formation in the United States, from the 1960s to the 1990s* (2nd ed.). New York and London: Routledge.

Roediger, D. R. (1991). *The Wages of Whiteness: Race and the Making of the American Working Class.* London and New York: Verso.

Roediger, D. R. (1994). *Towards the Abolition of Whiteness: Essays on Race, Politics, and Working Class History.* London and New York: Verso.

Shilb, J. (1992). Poststructuralism, Politics, and the Subject of Pedagogy. In M. Kecht (Ed.), *Pedagogy Is Politics: Literary Theory and Critical Teaching* (pp. 62–85). Urbana: University of Illinois Press.

Spelman, E. V. (1982). Theories of Gender and Race: The Erasure of Black Women. *Quest: A Feminist Quarterly, 5*(4), 36–62.

The Negro Family: The Case for National Action. (1965). Washington, DC: U.S. Department of Labor.

Yancy, G. (Ed.). (1998). *African American Philosophers: 17 Conversations.* New York: Routledge.

Young, R. (1990). *White Mythologies: Writing History and the West.* London and New York: Routledge.

Teachers in multicultural classrooms and schools should use teaching strategies that build on the cultures, languages, and experiences of their students.

194

Race, Ethnicity, and Language

T he drastic increase in the percentage of students of color and of language-minority students in the nation's schools is one of the most significant developments in education in the last several decades. The growth in the percentage of students of color and of language-minority students in the nation's schools results from several factors, including the new wave of immigration that began after 1968 and the aging of the White population. The nation's classrooms are experiencing the largest influx of immigrant students since the beginning of the twentieth century. The United States received nearly 1 million immigrants in 1996, most of whom come from nations in Asia and Latin America. However, 62,800 came from nations in the Russian Federation, which reflected the political and economic chaos that occurred in that part of the world when the Soviet Union splintered. Between 1990 and 1996, nearly 1 million immigrants entered the United States each year.

Demographers predict that if current trends continue, about 46 percent of the nation's school-age youths will be of color by the year 2020. In 1995, 35 percent of students in grades 1 to 12 in public schools were members of a minority group, an increase of 11 percentage points since 1976. They were a majority of the students in the state of California as well as in many major cities, such as Seattle, San Francisco, Chicago, and Washington, DC. Another important characteristic of today's students is the large percentage who are poor and who live in female-headed households. Today, about one out of every five students lives in a poor family.

While the nation's students are becoming increasingly diverse, most of the nation's teachers remain White (87.2 percent), female (72 percent), and middle class. The percentage of teachers of color remains low. During the 1993–1994 school year, teachers of color made up only 12.8 percent of the nation's teachers. The growing racial, cultural, and income gap between teachers and students underscores the need for all teachers to develop the knowledge, attitudes, and skills needed to work effectively with students from diverse racial, ethnic, social-class, and language groups. The four chapters in this part of the book present concepts, knowledge, and strategies that all teachers will find helpful in working with students from diverse groups.

CHAPTER 9

Educational Equality for Students of Color

Geneva Gay

Educational equality in the United States is popularly understood to mean the *physical access* of African Americans, Latinos, Asian Americans, and Native Americans to the same schools and instructional programs as middle-class European American students. The prevailing assumption is that when these groups become students in majority schools, equal educational opportunity is achieved. Until recently, little attention was given to the quality of the curriculum content and instructional processes as key factors in formulas for educational equity.

For people who accept a strictly *de jure* or legal conception of desegregation, the issue of educational inequality is largely resolved. After all, they argue, federal and state laws now exist prohibiting educational discrimination on the basis of race, color, creed, gender, nationality, and social class. For these people, the persisting discrepancies between the academic achievement, quality of school life, and other indicators of school success of students of color and European Americans are not a result of differences in educational opportunities at all. Rather, these problems are matters of personal abilities, aspirations, and responsibilities. Students of color and poverty do not do as well in school as their middle-class European American counterparts because of individual deficiencies, not because of discrepancies in opportunities perpetuated by schools that serve systematically to their detriment.

Legal mandates guaranteeing the accessibility of schooling to all students do not ensure quality unless the opportunities themselves are of equal status (Astin, 1985). And, under no circumstances can identical educational opportunities for very diverse groups and individuals (whether that diversity stems from class, gender, race, ethnicity, nationality, or personal traits) constitute equality. Their differentness demands variability in treatment so that students in each group can have the best chances to perform at maximum capabilities. Thus, equality of educational opportunities should be understood to mean *equity*, *parity*, and *comparability* of instructional treatment based on diagnosed needs of diverse individuals and groups. How can this be accomplished? Should the *processes of schooling* be given much more attention in efforts to achieve educational equality for students of color? Or, as Grant and Sleeter (1985) might ask, what should happen "after the school bell rings" for students of color if they are to receive

197

educational equality? Answers to these questions are contingent on a clear understanding of the various inequalities that now exist. These issues and inequities and some possible solutions to them are discussed in the subsequent sections of this chapter.

EDUCATIONAL ATTAINMENT FOR STUDENTS OF COLOR

Most elementary and secondary schools in the United States continue to be racially segregated (Orfield, Eaton, & The Harvard Project on School Desegregation, 1996). These demographic divisions have some profound implications for providing ethnically diverse students with equal access to high quality educational opportunities and outcomes.

Enrollment Distributions and Persistence Rates

In 1996 (most recent available data) students of color constituted the majority population in 70 of the nation's 130 largest school districts (with 36,000 students or more), and this distribution is increasing yearly (U.S. Department of Education, 1999a). The percentages of their representation range from 50.7 in Toledo, OH, to 96.9 percent in Brownsville, TX. In 37 of these districts, students of color are 75 percent or higher, with 6 districts having 95 percent or more (San Antonio TX; Detroit, MI; New Orleans, LA; Washington, DC; Santa Ana, CA; Brownsville, TX). In addition to the largest school districts with majority students of color, another 9 have 45.0 to 49.9 percent. In the 449 school districts with 15,000 or more (which comprise a total of almost 18 and one-half million) students of color are 54.7 percent. The percentage distributions among African Americans, Latinos, Asian Americans/Pacific Islanders, and Native American/Alaskans are 26.9 percent, 21.4 percent, 5.7 percent, and 0.7 percent, respectively (U.S. Department of Education, 1999a).

Furthermore, ethnically diverse students are not necessarily attending school with each other. Districts with the highest representations of students of color are either predominately African American or Latino. In 41 of the largest school districts with majority students of color, African American predominate. When the other districts are added in which students of color are not the majority, the number in which African Americans are the largest group increases to 75. Latinos are predominant in 25 of the 70 large school districts with majority students of color, and 8 of the other 130 largest in the United States. Asian Americans have the highest representation in only 6 large districts with majority students of color. These districts are Sacramento, CA; Seattle, WA; St. Paul, MN; Elk Grove, CA; the state of Hawaii; and San Francisco. African American, Latino, and Asian American students are almost equally represented in only 4 of the 130 largest school districts (e.g., Fairfax, VA; Montgomery County, MD; San Juan, CA; Cherry Creek, CO), but their composite totals do not comprise a majority in any of them. Native Americans/Alaskans are the largest group of color in only Anchorage, Alaska (with 11.3 percent of the enrollment). Their other relatively sizable representations are in Tulsa (8.2 percent), Minneapolis (6.3 percent), and Oklahoma City (5.3 percent) (U.S. Department of Education, 1999a). Students of color also are geographically distributed unequally throughout the United States: African Americans are clustered in the Southeast and the Great Lakes areas; Latinos in the Southwest; Asian Americans along the Pacific Coast; and Native Americans in the Great Plains, Pacific Northwest, and Alaska.

Yet, the ethnicity of teachers, administrators, and policy makers in these districts is the reverse. European Americans far outnumber educators of color in all school leadership and instructional positions. In fact, the numbers of school teachers and administrators of color declined steadily for about fifteen years. The percentage of African American teachers declined from 12.0 in 1970 to an all-time low of 6.9 percent in 1987. By 1996 this percentage had increased slightly, to 7.3. Latinos comprised 4.9 percent of all elementary and secondary teachers in the United States. The percentage of Native American/Alaskan and Native and Asian/Pacific Islander teachers is 0.9 and 1.1 percent, respectively (U.S. Department of Education, 1999a). Traditionally, urban schools (where most students of color attend) have had less money, fewer resources and poorer facilities, larger numbers of inexperienced teachers, greater management problems, and higher turnover rates among teachers, administrators, and students (see Chapter 4 for a more detailed discussion). All of these factors can have negative effects on the educational opportunities and outcomes of students of color.

The high school completion rates in 1997 for twenty-five to twenty-nine-year-old European Americans was 92.9 percent, compared to 86.9 percent for African Americans, and 61.8 percent for Latinos (U.S. Department of Education, 1999b). (No data were reported for the high school graduation rates of Native American/Alaskans or Asian Americans/Pacific Islanders.) These data indicate that dropout rates are declining for all ethnic groups except European Americans. Between 1990 and 1997, dropout rates for eighteen and nineteen-year-old African Americans declined from 16.6 to 14.9 percent, while those of European Americans remained approximately the same (11.1 percent and 11.2 percent, respectively). While the dropout rates of Latino eighteen to nineteen years olds declined from 34.2 percent in 1990 to 25.2 percent in 1997, they are still more than twice those of European Americans and one and one-third times those of African Americans. For all ethnic groups, males dropped out of school at rates higher than did females in 1997. This is a change for African Americans from 1990, when 17.6 percent of eighteen to nineteen-year-old females dropped out of school, compared to 15.5 percent of males. The patterns has reversed for Latinos since 1995, when the female dropout rates (35 percent) exceeded that for males (27 percent) by 8 percent (U.S. Department of Education, 1999a).

Another school attendance factor that contributes to the educational inequality of students of color is *school delay*. Defined by Nielsen (1986, p. 79) as "the discrepancy between the educational level reached by students and the normal level corresponding to their age," school-delay rates are substantially greater for African Americans, Latinos, and Native Americans than for European and Asian Americans. These three groups repeat grades more often and generally take longer to complete school. Since 1980 the percentage of students of color below modal grade (the grade in which most children of a certain age are enrolled) has increased substantially. African American males have the highest below-modal grade averages. By age thirteen almost one-half of African American males and one-third of Latinos have repeated a grade at least once (Miller-Lachmann & Taylor, 1995).

School delays have serious ramifications for the educational equality of students of color. They may initiate a cumulative process that ultimately results in the youth leaving school completely. Delayed students are more likely to be declared academically inadequate and assigned to special category, low academic, or vocational-track curricula. As these students fall behind their age group, they become stigmatized as slow learners and become socially isolated in schools. Teachers tend to have low expectations of achievement for delayed students.

Together, these situations increase failure rates and the chances that the affected students will become school dropouts.

SAT Test Scores

Even for students of color who remain in school their academic achievement levels are significantly lower than those of European Americans. These differences exist on all measures for every age group at all levels of schooling, in every region of the country, and at every socioeconomic level (Gougis, 1986; The College Board, 1999). Some Asian Americans (notably students of Japanese, Korean, and Chinese origins) are exceptions to these patterns.

One powerful and frequently referenced indication of achievement among high school students is performance on college entrance tests, especially on the American College Test (ACT) and the Scholastic Aptitude Test (SAT) scores. Typically, ACT scores are reported by gender but not ethnicity. For this reason they are not included in this discussion. Trends in SAT scores offer both encouraging and discouraging news about the achievement of students of color. The good news is that the combined verbal and math scores on the SAT increased from 1006 in 1989 to 1016 in 1999. Also, SAT takers are becoming more ethnically, racially, and economically diverse. According to the College Board, which administers the SAT, students of color comprised one-third of the test takers in 1999; this was an increase of 25 percent from 1989. The specific ethnic distribution included 11 percent African Americans, 9 percent Asian Americans, 4 percent Mexican Americans, 1 percent Puerto Ricans, and 3 percent other Latinos. For those students for whom English was not their first language, 39 percent were Asian Americans and 25 percent each Mexican Americans and Puerto Ricans (www.collegeboard.org).

The bad news is that long-established ethnic group patterns of performance on the SAT persist largely unchanged despite some improvements in the scores of groups of color. As the data in Table 9.1 show, the greatest gains for the decade between 1989 and 1999 occurred for Native Americans/Alaskans (a combined score of 42 points), Asian American/Pacific Islanders (30 points), and Puerto Ricans (28 points). The least gains were made by other Latinos (5 points) and African Americans (7 points). The distribution of these increases tended to favor verbal performance over math for some ethnic groups but not others. For example, the increase in verbal scores for Native Americans/Alaskans on the 1999 SAT was 2 points higher than for math, 5 points for African Americans, and 8 points for Puerto Ricans. By comparison, the math scores of European Americans was 9 points higher than their verbal, and the math and verbal score increases were equal for Mexican and Asian Americans (www.collegeboard.org). Even for Latinos, African, and Native Americans who do well on the SAT and other college admission tests the grades they achieve at predominately White colleges and universities are significantly lower than those for European and Asian Americans. This phenomenon holds true even for students who attend selective, highly prestigious institutions (The College Board, 1999), such as Harvard, Yale, and Stanford.

The gaps among ethnic groups on the SAT, when compared to each other, continue to be significant. Although the combined scores of African Americans increased by 32 points between 1989 and 1999, their performance is the lowest of all groups. In 1999 there was a 53-point gap between them and Puerto Ricans and Mexican Americans, the groups whose performance is closest to theirs. Differences in the combined scores of African Americans and Asian and European Americans were 202 and 199 points, respectively.

Table 9.1   Scholastic Aptitude Test (SAT) Scores by Selected Ethnic Groups for 1989 and 1999

Ethnic Groups	Verbal Scores			Math Scores		
	1989	1999	DIF.	1989	1999	DIF.
African Americans	428	434	+6	421	422	+1
Asian Americans/Pacific Islanders	483	498	+15	545	560	+15
European Americans	523	527	+4	515	528	+13
Mexican Americans	459	453	−6	462	456	−6
Native Americans/Alaskans	462	484	+22	461	481	+20
Puerto Ricans	437	455	+18	438	448	+10
Other Latinos	466	463	−3	466	464	−2

Sources: The Condition of Education, 1999; College Board Website, www.collegeboard.org.   (*The Conditions of Education* is a U.S. Government Publication.)

Despite having the highest combined score (1043), Asian Americans had the largest gap between verbal (498) and math (545) scores, a total of 47 points. However, this gap is decreasing over time. For African Americans the verbal-math difference was 12 points, favoring verbal; Mexican Americans, 3 points in favor of math; Puerto Ricans, 7 for verbal; Native Americans/Alaskans, 3 points for verbal; and a 9-point math advantage for European Americans. These scores represent major declines in the verbal-math performance gaps for all ethnic groups over the last ten years (U.S. Department of Education, 1999a; 1999b; www.collegeboard.org).

NAEP Report Cards

Performance on proficiency tests given by the National Assessment of Educational Progress (NAEP) is another high-stakes, high-status measure of student achievement. The scores on these tests suggest major discrepancies in the educational quality of different ethnic groups. NAEP presents achievement data for nine- , thirteen- , and seventeen-year-olds on a regular basis in eight skill areas. Known as "Report Cards," reading and mathematics proficiency is assessed every two years, science and writing every four years, and geography and U.S. history every six years. In 1997 for the first time students were tested in music, theater, and the visual arts, but only thirteen-year-olds were involved. Civics was tested in 1998 for all three age groups.

Achievement profiles are routinely presented by gender and for European, African, and Latino ethnic groups, but not necessarily for Native Indian/Alaskans and Asian/Pacific Islanders. The National Center for Education Statistics explains that because these latter groups comprise only 1 percent of U.S. school enrollments, they are not represented in sufficient numbers in national education studies to permit reliable and valid generalizations about their characteristics (U.S. Department of Education, 1995).

Achievement gaps between students of color and European Americans in some subjects narrow somewhat as grade levels increase, but not for others. However, the differences continue to be significant, and greater for African Americans more frequently than for Latinos. These patterns are graphic in the 1994 (latest available) NAEP proficiency tests in geography and U.S. history. Fourth-, eighth-, and twelfth-grade African Americans scored 50, 41, and 33 points, respectively, lower than did European Americans. The gaps for Latinos were 35, 31, and 23 points. In U.S. history the achievement patterns were similar, but the actual point differences were significantly smaller, both when students of color were compared to European Americans and to each other. European Americans performed better than did African Americans by 38 points in fourth grade (215/177 scores), 28 in eighth grade (267/239), and 27 in twelfth grade (292/265). Differences with Latinos were 35, 24, and 25 points, respectively. While Latinos scored 10 to 15 points across the grades higher than did African Americans in geography, there were only 2- to 4-point differences in their history scores. On a scoring scale that ranged from 0 to 500, these performance levels mean that students knew a variety of factual information but were unable to understand major concepts, integrate ideas, or engage successfully in complex problem solving or critical thinking (U.S. Department of Education, 1999a; 1999b).

Overall, African Americans performed better in history than in geography. The differences in their scores for the two subjects were larger than those for other ethnic groups. These were 9, 10, and 7 points for fourth, eighth, and twelfth grades. In both subjects, the performance of twelfth-grade African Americans was lower than that of eighth-grade European Americans. The patterns were not as definitive for European Americans and Latinos. Fourth- and eighth-grade European Americans performed better in geography, and twelfth graders did better in history. Fourth- and twelfth-grade Latinos scored higher in geography, and eighth graders in history. Their twelfth-grade geography scores were lower than those of eighth-grade European Americans, and equal in history (U.S. Department of Education, 1999a). These data are summarized in Table 9.2.

Table 9.2   NAEP Test Scores for Six Subjects by Ethnic Groups in a Single Year

Subject and Ethnic Group	9-Yr.-Olds	13-Yr.-Olds	17-Yr.-Olds
GEOGRAPHY, 1994[1]			
European Americans	218	270	291
African Americans	168	229	258
Latinos	183	239	268
U. S. HISTORY, 1994[1]			
European Americans	215	267	292
African Americans	177	239	265
Latinos	180	243	267

Table 9.2 Continued

CIVICS, 1998[2]			
European Americans	159	159	158
African Americans	132	133	131
Latinos	126	127	130
Asian Americans/Pacific Islanders	153	153	151
Native Americans	137	134	129
MUSIC, 1997[2]			
European Americans		158	
African Americans		130	
Latinos		127	
Asian Americans		152	
Native Americans/Alaskans		(No Scores Reported)	
VISUAL ARTS, 1997[2]			
European Americans		159	
African Americans		124	
Latinos		128	
Asian Americans		153	
Native Americans/Alaskans		(No Scores Reported)	
THEATER, 1997[2]			
European Americans		159	
African Americans		120	
Latinos		139	
Asian Americans		(No Scores Reported)	
Native Americans/Alaskans		(No Scores Reported)	

[1]Latest data available

[2]Scores reported in averages with the mean proficiency established at 150 for all age groups. The scores presented for music, visual arts, and theater are on the skill of responding, and data are available only for 13 year olds.

Sources: Digest of Education Statistics, 1998; The Condition of Education, 1999; National Center for Education Statistics Website, www.nces.ed.gov

Mathematics test scores between 1990 and 1996 showed an increase of 4 points for nine-year-old African Americans, 1 for Latinos, 2 for European Americans, 4 for Asian Americans, and 8 for Native Americans/Alaskans. Gains have also occurred for thirteen-year-olds in all five ethnic groups in all testing years since 1990, except for Asian/Pacific Islanders (see Table 9.3). In 1996 their math scores were 15 points lower than they were in 1992 (U.S. Department of Education, 1999b). The math proficiency of seventeen-year-old African Americans declined between 1990 and 1992 by 3 points and then remained the same for 1994 and 1996. A similar pattern existed for Latinos for the same periods. Their math score increased by 8 points in 1992 and have remained stable since. The math scores of seventeen-year-old European Americans increased between 1990 and 1992 by 2 points and another 1 point in 1996 (U.S. Department of Education, 1999a). Asian Americans/Pacific Islanders had the highest math scores of all ethnic groups; these scores increased by 8 points from 1990 to 1996 (from a total score of 311 to 319). No scores were reported for seventeen-year-old Native Americans/Alaskans in 1990 through 1994, but their 1996 score (297) was higher than both Latinos and African Americans (U.S. Department of Education, 1999b). Students in all ethnic groups at all three ages tested better in areas of mathematical knowledge (recalling and recognizing facts) and skills (performing computations and manipulations) than in applications (reasoning and problem solving).

Science proficiency of all ethnic groups (for whom data were available) has increased since 1990 (see Table 9.3). However, the gains are small across grade levels. The greatest gains occurred for seventeen-year-old Latinos and African Americans (7 points each) and for nine-year-old African Americans (6 points). The greatest increase for European Americans (6 points) occurred among seventeen-year-olds. Neither the performance of African American nor Latinos *in any age group* matched that of European Americans in 1996. The differences for nine-, thirteen-, and seventeen-year-old African Americans were 37, 40, and 47 points, respectively. The scores of Latinos were equally as disturbing, but not quite as extreme. Their 1996 science scores were lower than those of European Americans by 32 points for nine-year-olds, 34 for thirteen-year-olds, and 38 for seventeen-year-olds. Furthermore, the performance of none of these ages or ethnic groups, with the exception of seventeen-year-old European Americans, reached the level of proficiency (300 points) that NAEP has declared is necessary to analyze and interpret scientific data. The Center for Educational Statistics did not report any data on the science achievement of Asian Americans/Pacific Islanders and Native Americans/Alaskans. (U.S. Department of Education, 1999a; 1999b).

The reading achievement of nine-year-olds from all ethnic groups increased between 1990 and 1998—by 12 points for African Americans, 7 for Latinos, and 10 for European Americans. While some sizable improvement also was evident for thirteen-year-old European Americans (10 points), only minimal gain occurred for seventeen-year-olds (1 point), and for thirteen (1 point) and seventeen-year-old African Americans (3 points). The performance of thirteen-year-old Latinos increased by 6 points over the decade, but seventeen-year-olds made no gains. Differences in these ethnic groups' reading achievement between 1996 and 1998 accounted for most of the variance. In many instances 1996 was a year of declining scores, and 1998 was a time of recovery. For example, the scores of seventeen-year-old Latinos decline between 1990 and 1996 by 10 points and increased by the same amount in 1998. Even more troubling are the facts that the 1998 reading performance of seventeen-year-old African Americans (270 points) is lower than that of thirteen-year-old European Americans (272 points) and that

Table 9.3   NAEP Achievement by Subject, Age, and Ethnic Groups, 1990 and 1996/98

Subject and Ethnic Group	9-Yr.-Olds		13-Yr.-Olds		17-Yr.-Olds	
SCIENCE	1990	1996	1990	1996	1990	1996
European Americans	238	239	264	266	301	307
African Americans	196	202	226	226	253	260
Latinos	206	207	232	232	262	269
MATHEMATICS	1990	1996	1990	1996	1990	1996
European Americans	235	237	276	281	310	313
African Americans	208	212	249	252	289	286
Latinos	214	215	255	256	284	292
READING	1990	1998	1990	1998	1990	1998
European Americans	217	227	262	272	297	298
African Americans	182	194	242	243	267	270
Latinos	189	196	238	244	275	275
Asian Americans/Pacific Islanders[1]	—	225	—	271	—	289
Native Americans/Alaskans[1]	—	207	—	248	—	276
WRITING	1990	1998	1990	1998	1990	1998
European Americans	211	157[2]	262	158	293	156
African Americans	171	131	239	131	268	134
Latinos	184	134	246	131	277	135
Asian American/Pacific Islanders	—	164	—	159	—	152
Native Americans/Alaskans	—	138	—	132	—	129

[1]No scores reported for these ethnic groups in 1990

[2]1998 scores reported as mean proficiency; 150 was the mean score established for each age group tested.

Sources: The Condition of Education, 1999; Digest of Education Statistics, 1998; National Assessment of Educational Progress Website, www.naep.org; National Center for Educational Statistics Website, www.nces.ed.gov

of Latinos (275) is only slightly higher. These data are summarized in Table 9.3. All of these scores are well below the level that NAEP has identified (300 points) as the ability to understand relatively complicated information (U.S. Department of Education, 1999a; 1999b). As is the case with mathematics, the reading achievement of Asian American students was comparable to European Americans, except for seventeen-years-olds. The difference in their achievement was 9 points. Native Americans/Alaskans performed better than did African Americans and Latinos at all three age levels (U.S. Department of Education, 1999b). These patterns of ethnic group reading performance continue long-established trends.

Writing NAEP scores have vacillated somewhat between 1990 and 1996 for most ages. For instance, scores increased in 1992 for nine- and thirteen-year-olds for all ethnic groups, but declined for all seventeen-year-olds. The declines for the older students continued through 1996. From 1992 to 1996 the writing achievement declines for European Americans were 4, 1, and 8 points, respectively. The writing performance for nine- and thirteen-years-olds increased during the same period for everyone except thirteen-year-old Latinos, whose 1990 and 1996 scores (246 points) were identical. The scores of their African American peers increased by 3 points, and European Americans by 9 points. The gains of fourth-grade African Americans (11 points) and Latinos (7 points) were greater than those of European Americans (5 points), even though their total scores were lower (see Table 9.3) (U.S. Department of Education, 1999a; 1999b). As was the case with math, science, and reading, none of the ethnic groups reached the level of writing proficiency (a score of 300), which indicates that students can write effective responses containing supportive details and can synthesize information from specialized reading materials.

NAEP presented a report card in 1997 for the first time on performance in music, theater, and the visual arts. But only eighth graders were tested, and a 0 to 300 point scale was used. The pattern of performance by ethnic groups established in other years and subjects was largely replicated once again. The order of achievement, from highest to lowest, was European, Asian, Latino, and African Americans. Two exceptions were noted—African Americans performed higher than did Latinos in music, and data were presented for Asian Americans in music and visual arts, but not theater. Differences in the scores of the various ethnic groups were as low as 6 points (between European and Asian Americans in music), and as high as 39 points (between African and European Americans in theater). Other differences in the performance of European and African Americans were 28 points in music and 35 points in visual arts. The performances of Latinos and African Americans were close, separated by only 3 points in music and 4 points in visual arts. Differences in their performance in theater (19 points) were much more substantial (see Table 9.2) (U.S. Department of Education, 1999a; 1999b).

The civics report card, released in November 1999, indicates both continuity and variability in established patterns of achievement among ethnic groups. Because of changes in how test results were presented, the actual scores of students across age levels cannot be compared. An average of 150 was established for each age group tested, but the skills it symbolizes are quite different for nine-, thirteen-, and seventeen-year-olds. The civics tests also provide information on the achievement of more ethnic groups. Scores were presented for Asian/Pacific Islanders and Native Americans, as well as for African, Latino, and European Americans.

For all three ages tested in civics, European and Asian Americans continued the pattern established in other areas of achievement by performing better than other ethnic groups. African Americans deviated from their achievement patterns in other areas by not performing the lowest of all groups. They performed better than did Latinos and Native Americans in grades 4, 8, and 12. Latinos had the lowest performance of all ethnic groups in grades 4 and 8, but not in grade 12, where their civics scores were slightly higher than those of Native Americans. While the achievement levels of European and Asian Americans in civics were close (3 to 7 points difference across the three grades tested, and favoring European

Americans), they are substantial for other ethnic groups. Differences between the scores of African and European Americans for grades 4, 8, and 12, were 27, 26, and 27 points, respectively; for Latinos the differences were 33, 32, and 28 points; and for Native Americans the differences were 22, 25, and 29 points. (These data are summarized in Table 9.2.) For Asian, Native, and African Americans these achievement gaps increased slightly from eighth to twelfth grade, but declined for Latinos (www.naep.org; www.nces.ed.gov).

MIXED SIGNALS IN ACHIEVEMENT PATTERNS

The overall academic achievement profiles of students of color send mixed messages. The NAEP and the National Center for Education Statistics do not track and report the performance of Asian/Pacific Islanders and Native Americans/Alaskans as routinely and thoroughly as they do for European, African, and Latino Americans. This practice leaves the educational status of these groups ambiguous and difficult to treat with appropriate pedagogical precision. The situation is better for other ethnic groups, but not as good as it needs to be. For example, the achievement differences between females and males within ethnic groups routinely are not reported. Nor is detailed information provided on the demographics and representative validity of the individuals tested within ethnic groups.

What Are the Mixed Signals?

The fact that students of color in all three age groups tested made small but steady gains in science and mathematics achievement is encouraging. But it is disheartening and troublesome that this pattern is not true for reading and writing. In general, Latinos seem to be making more academic progress than are African Americans even though their dropout rates are higher. Consequently, the gaps between their achievement levels and those of European American students are decreasing somewhat, while those of African Americans remain about the same. Although recent improvements by students of color on standardized tests show that they are making some gains on low-level cognitive skills, such as decoding, computation, factual recognition, and recall, they are not developing high-level skills, such as making inferences, critical thinking, analyzing and synthesizing information, logical reasoning, and creative expression.

Another good-news, bad-news dilemma associated with the achievement profiles is that the data are largely not disaggregated. The test scores presented earlier in this discussion are composite profiles for large groups and large clusters of skills. As such, they do not identify what aspects of the various subjects and skills were easy or difficult for students taking the tests. Nor do they give any detailed information on how individuals within ethnic groups were distributed across the range of skills included in the various tests. For instance, it is impossible to discern from the scores whether comprehension, vocabulary, making inferences, or some other component skill of reading was most challenging for Mexican Americans, Puerto Ricans, or Cuban Americans. How individuals' membership in ethnic groups is assigned and where they are placed for analysis also may distort some of the achievement patterns. Data on the educational achievement of African Americans are never distributed by subcategories, such as the various Afro-Caribbean groups (i.e., Jamaican, Trinidadans, Guyanese). Nor is the performance of Asian American specified by component ethnic groups (such as Japanese, Chinese, Koreans, or Vietnamese), or Native Americans by particular tribal identity (i.e., Navajo, Cherokee, Yakima). Furthermore, no distinctions are made between the performance of immigrant and U.S.-born members of different ethnic groups, such as Nigerian, Ethiopian, and Kenyan among African Americans, and Japanese and Mexican immigrants as opposed to Japanese Americans and Mexican Americans.

All of these demographic details affect performance patterns and have serious implications for reforming instruction to improve educational equality for ethnically diverse students. For example, Asian Americans are often considered the model minority and are perceived to be high achievers in all aspects of schooling and on all measures of achievement. This positive stereotype overlooks the immense national origins diversity of Asian American ethnic groups; the serious language and social adjustment problems that some Southeast Asian new immigrants encounter; the great disparities in Asian American verbal and math achievement; the self-concept dilemmas of even many higher achieving Asian Americans; the special educational needs of individual students; and the high dropout rates among some Asian groups, such as Hmongs, Cambodians, and Vietnamese (Gibbs & Nahme-Huang, 1989; Igoa, 1995; Miller-Lachmann & Taylor, 1995; Pang, 1995; Pang & Cheng, 1998; Pang, Mizokawa, Morishima, & Olstad, 1985; Yu, Doi, & Chang, 1986). Osajima (1991) cautions that "beneath the awards and accomplishments lie struggles, conflicts, and uncertainties that manifest racism's hidden and subtle impacts. . . . The quiet demeanor of Asian students, which has heretofore only garnered praise, may in fact be problematic, for this survival mechanism could also leave them isolated with their doubts about identity and belonging" (pp. 130–131).

Understanding Mixed-Achievement Signals

How can the mixed results that are apparent in the achievement profiles of students of color be explained? One possible explanation is that teachers and instructional programs are still not acknowledging and responding to these students' unique cultural orientations, values, and learning styles. The failure to do so is negatively affecting their achievement outcomes. As Boateng (1990) explains, the "deculturalization" of students of color in schools interferes with their ability to focus on and master academic tasks.

Achievement patterns may be a direct result of the curriculum differentiations that exist for students of color and for European American students in elementary and secondary schools. These students are not necessarily enrolled in similar kinds of courses; nor are they receiving equal-status instruction. It is not surprising, then, that there is so much variance in their academic achievement. Another possibility is that all students are not receiving the best quality education possible. Rarely do students from any ethnic group receive scores on NAEP tests that symbolize advanced levels of proficiency such as the ability to do critical thinking and complex problem solving in math, science, geography, and history.

Other possible explanations of these variations in achievement may be found in students' attendance patterns and dropout rates. Many of the most problematic students of color may drop out of school before age seventeen. Those who remain should be more like their European counterparts and, therefore, have similar achievement levels. This possibility may be counteracted by disproportionately low percentages of high school students of color enrolled in academic courses of study. The combination of these possibilities give credence to the contention that the longer African American, Latino, and Native American youths stay in school, the further they fall behind academically. Ralph, Keller, and Crouse (1994) explained this phenomenon further by pointing out that even after eight additional years of schooling seventeen-year-olds who were at the 10th percentile in math and the 25th percentile in reading and science at age nine still have not attained achievement scores equal to those of the 95th percentile of their cohort at age nine.

Another explanation is that students of color know much more than standardized achievement test scores indicate. Despite their frequent use, these tests may not be valid measures to use in determining the academic abilities of culturally and ethnically different students. The lack of sensitivity of these techniques, in both their content and administration procedures, to the cultural nuances of students of color may have a negative effect on their total scores. In other words, the lack of culturally relevant content, test-taking skills, and other preferred performance styles may mediate against some ethnic groups doing well on the SAT and NAEP tests of academic proficiency. Measures of achievement that are culturally sensitive, employ diverse techniques, and access multidimensional sites of performance, such as curriculum content and classroom instructional interactions, may produce very different results.

The unequal curriculum and instruction systems that exist in U.S. schools undoubtedly account for many of the disparities in achievement among students of color and European Americans. This inequity has been firmly established by research. For example, in its *Mexican-American Education Study*, conducted between 1971 and 1974, the U.S. Civil Rights Commission (1971–1974) attributed quality and equality of educational experiences to the opportunities different students receive to participate in classroom interactions with teachers. It found that Mexican Americans were not receiving as many opportunities as were European Americans to participate in classroom interactions, as evidenced by fewer and lower-level questions asked of them, the time allowed to give responses, and the praise and encouragement teachers gave for students' efforts. Gay (1974) found similar results for African American students interacting with both African and European American teachers. Teachers, regardless of their own ethnic identity, tended to give preferential treatment and more quality opportunities to participate in the substance of instruction to European American students.

Other disparities in curriculum options and instructional interactions available to racially and ethnically different groups have been reported by Goodlad (1984), Oakes (1985), Persell (1977), and Harry (1992). The studies by these researchers indicate that students of color are disproportionally enrolled in special education and vocational programs. Furthermore, the placement of students of color in vocational courses occurs earlier, and the programs differ substantially in kind and content from those for European Americans. Students of color are often assigned to courses that train specifically for low-status occupations (e.g., cosmetology, mill and cabinet shop, building maintenance, television repair, retail sales, clerical jobs). By comparison, European American students enroll more often in courses that offer managerial training, business finance, and general industrial arts skills. To receive their training, youths of color must leave the school campus more often than do European Americans, thus isolating them from many of the social activities and "cultural capital" of the school (Oakes, 1985), which helps to socialize them into the test-taking modes and ethos.

The enrollment of students of color in high-stakes, high-status academic programs also is unequally distributed. They are highly underrepresented in college preparatory, gifted and talented, and gateway programs or courses to higher educational success, such as calculus, chemistry, and advanced placements. Although college-bound African American and Latino seniors are as likely as European Americans to have taken three or more years of mathematics, they are less likely to have taken algebra, geometry, trigonometry, and calculus and more likely to have taken general and business math (U.S. Department of Education, 1994). Students in low-income and predominately children-of-color schools have less access to microcomputers, have fewer qualified teachers trained in the use of computers, and tend to use microcomputers more for drill and practice in basic skills rather than for conceptual knowledge or programming instruction (College Entrance Examination Board, 1985; U.S. Department of Education, 1999b; Winkler, Stravelson, Stasz, Robyn, & Fiebel, 1984). In 1997 approximately 61 percent of high school European American students used computers at home, compared to 22 percent of African Americans and Latinos. These figures represent more than a 100-percent increase from 1993 for students of color, and a 75 percent increase for European Americans. Elementary students use computers at home less often, but the increase over time is similarly significant (U.S. Department of Education, 1999b).

The system of tracking routinely used to organize students for instruction is a very effective way to deny educational equality to students of color. These inequities include overrepresentation of Latinos, African Americans, and Native Americans, and poor students from all ethnic groups in low-track, low-status instructional programs. These programs tend to offer low-quality instruction and emphasize compliance-type behaviors and attitudes, classroom management, discipline, and procedural matters. High-track students are advantaged by participating in subjects and curricula perceived to be high status; by having better teachers, equipment, materials, and more provocative learning experiences; by being taught leadership and high-order intellectual skills such as critical thinking and problem solving; by receiving high expectations of achievement from teachers; and by having more instructional time allocated to academic tasks in high tracks (Goodlad, 1984; Grant & Sleeter, 1985; Morgan, 1977; Oakes, 1985; Oakes & Guiton, 1995; Persell, 1977; Verdugo, 1986). These disparities are discussed in greater detail in Chapter 4.

Because African Americans, Latinos, and Native Americans are overrepresented in low-track curriculum programs, they are consistently and systematically denied equal access to the substance of quality education. *In effect, tracking is a process for the legitimization of the social inequalities that exist in the larger society.* It serves the instrumental functions of social selection, creating castes among students and closing off paths for personal advancement for students in the lower levels (Morgan, 1977). Through this practice, students learn to accept the unequal patterns of social and political participation in society and all its institutions as the natural order of things.

In the final analysis, access to high-status knowledge and high quality of instructional interactions between students and teachers defines educational equality. These processes are what ultimately determine which students are educated for intellectual rigor, personal self-determination, and social empowerment, and which ones are trained for a life of institutional compliance, economic dependence, and the social underclass (College Entrance Examination Board, 1985). The current educational status of students of color in the United States suggests that too many of them are being educated for the underclass.

WHY EDUCATIONAL INEQUALITY EXISTS FOR STUDENTS OF COLOR

The various resources used in the educational process have a direct effect on the level and quality of student achievement. When different groups of students are exposed to qualitatively different resources, their achievements also differ. In the debate on educational equality, a crucial question is whether the resources used in teaching students of color are comparable to those used with European Americans on measures of accuracy, technical quality, relevance, and appropriateness. These resources include facilities, personnel, financing, instructional materials and programs, and environmental settings.

The relative value of instructional resources cannot be determined independently of environmental context, intended users, and expected outcomes. Even when students of color and European Americans receive similar educational resources the effects are not identical. Sometimes resources that benefit and facilitate the academic achievement of European Americans block or retard the educational development of students of color. How is this possible? One way is how school systems treat curricular and instructional options that are highly populated by students of color relative to performance expectations and resource allocations. They receive fewer laboratory facilities, fewer out-of-classroom learning experiences, less qualified teachers, and less commitment, concern, and effort from teachers (Oakes, 1985; Oakes & Guiton, 1995).

Despite being overrepresented in low-track, nonacademic, and special education programs, most students of color are enrolled in a wide spectrum of *regular* curriculum options, including general education, academic, and college preparatory courses. If educational resources are allocated by programs and if these programs receive a fair share of them, then how is it that students of color are denied comparable access? Several ways are possible. First, the sameness of educational resources for diverse individuals and groups does not constitute comparability of quality or opportunity. To believe that they do is to assume that African, Latino, Native, Asian, and European origin students are identical in personal, social, cultural, historical, and family traits.

Second, most graduates of typical teacher-education programs know little about the cultural traits, behaviors, values, and attitudes that different children of color bring to the classroom and how they affect students' responses to instructional situations. Most teachers do not know how to understand and use the school behaviors of these students, which differ from their own normative expectations, as aides to teaching. Therefore, they often misinterpret these students as deviant and treat them punitively. Because most teachers' cultural backgrounds and value orientations are highly compatible with middle-class and European American culture, they can use these cultural connections and shared frames of reference to facilitate the learning of White students. The absence of these cultural connections in routine classroom instruction for students of color places them at a learning disadvantage.

Third, like teacher education, most curriculum designs and instructional materials are Eurocentric. When attempting to learn academic tasks, European American students may not have the additional burden of working across irrelevant instructional materials and methods. More of their efforts and energies can be directed toward mastering the substance of teaching. Students of color are often placed in double academic jeopardy. They must divide their energies and efforts between coping with instructional materials and methods that are not culturally relevant to them and mastering the academic knowledge and tasks being taught. Because this division of efforts dissipates their concentration on learning tasks, they do not receive the same kinds of educational opportunities to learn the substance of teaching as do European Americans.

Fourth, the school environments in which students live and learn are not comparable for racially majority and minority students. When students and teachers arrive at school they do not leave their cultural backgrounds at home. This is not a problem for most European Americans, since school culture and rules of behavior are reflections and extensions of their home cultures. These students do not experience much social-code incompatibility or need for cultural style shifting to adjust to the behavioral rules and expectations of schools. The converse is true for students of color. Many of the social codes for succeeding in school are unfamiliar to them, or are diametrically opposed to the codes they have learned in their home cultures. When learning situations do not reflect the cultures of the students, gaps exist "between the contexts of learning and the contexts of performing" (John-Steiner & Leacock, 1979, p. 87). These gaps are greatest for students from ethnic cultures and communities that are not part of the mainstream culture, and such gaps can mediate against effective teaching and learning. Therefore, the causes of many of the disparities that are apparent in the educational attainment of different ethnic groups are situated in cultural, procedural, and contextual incompatibilities (Gay, 2000).

Most educators do not think to teach students of color the skills on how to survive and succeed in school—for example, how to study across ethnic learning styles, how to adjust talking styles to accommodate school expectations, how to interact appropriately with school administrators and classroom teachers, and how to identify and adapt to the procedural rules for functioning in different instructional classrooms. Instead, educators tend to operate on the assumption that school codes of behavior are universal and commonly understood and are acquired from simply living in the broader culture that surrounds schools. What most of these educators forget is that many students of color live only marginally in mainstream culture. Furthermore, their parents may not be able to pass on to them a legacy of how to "do" schooling successfully because they did not experience it themselves.

These differences in socialization mean that students of color may have to learn how to survive in school while simultaneously learning what is taught. If they fail to master the social codes, they may never get a chance to try the academic tasks. As Holliday (1985) suggests, mastery of the social protocols and managerial procedures of schooling is frequently a prerequisite to receiving opportunities to participate in substantive instructional interactions and for academic learning to occur. Also, the in-class success of students of color is often determined more by social-skill mastery (such as compliance to institutional expectations and having pleasant or accommodating personality traits) than by academic performance. In assessing the performance of students of color, some teachers give less credit to academic factors than to non-academic ones such as "being nice, cooperative, and not trouble makers," "feeling sorry for students," and "work being neat, if not of very high substantive quality." In comparison, the performance of European American students is assessed more on academic criteria ("he studies hard"; "she is a good thinker"; "they are very attentive in class"; "she asks provocative questions"; "his writing is clear and cogent").

Closely related to the issue of comparable quality material and pedagogical resources is the role of teacher attitudes, expectations, and competencies in perpetuating educational inequality for students of color. The essence of this issue is: How can teachers who have grown up in ethnically isolated communities and in a racist society teach students whom they do not know, may not value, and may even fear? This question is crucial in equations of educational equality, especially when most teachers are racially White, culturally Eurocentric, middle class, and female, and when their professional preparation is grounded almost exclusively in Eurocentric cultural orientations. Therefore, they enter the profession assuming that all students can be taught as if they were European Americans. Teachers of color who receive the same kind of professional socialization frequently begin their careers with the same kind of expectations, attitudes, and values. Research shows that "Teachers form expectations about children based directly upon race and social class . . . pupil test scores, appearance, language style, speed of task performance, and behavior characteristics which are themselves culturally defined. Moreover, teacher expectations are more influenced by *negative* information about pupil characteristics than positive data" (Persell, 1977, p. 112). Teachers transmit these attitudes and expectations in what they say and do in the classroom. Students respond in ways that become self-fulfilling prophecies. Many children of color come to believe that they are destined to fail, and they act accordingly. Most European and Asian American students internalize the high expectations teachers have of them, believe they are destined to succeed, and do succeed.

The behaviors of educators reflect their performance expectations of different students. For example, teachers who do not have high academic expectations for students of color tend to ask them low-level memory, recall, and convergent questions, do not praise or encourage them as often as they praise European Americans, use lower standards for judging the quality of their work, and do not call on them as frequently (Good & Brophy, 1994; Oakes, 1985; Oakes & Guiton, 1995). Guidance counselors who do not believe students of color can master high-level math and science skills do not schedule them into these classes. School administrators who expect greater discipline problems from students of color tend to treat their rule infractions with harsher punishment. In general, low expectations of educators cause them to feed African Americans, Latinos, Native Americans, and some Southeast Asians (notably Vietnamese and Cambodians) academic pabulum. These educators then wonder why these students do not do well on standardized measures of school achievement. Students of color for whom educators have low expectations are suspected of dishonesty and cheating when they defy these expectations by performing well. When low expectations produce low performance teachers make comments such as "What else can you expect?" Presumed high-achieving European American students who do not live up to expectations are described as underachievers, and low-performing students who exceed expectations are called over-achievers. These attitudes cause wide disparities in how educators interact with European Americans and students of color in the day-to-day operations of schools and thereby perpetuate educational inequalities.

A similar argument holds for the content and substance of student evaluations. All achievement tests are designed to determine what students know. Presumably these tests reflect what is taught in schools. This is a reasonable expectation, and there would be no issue of ethnic inequality if schools taught equally relevant curricula equally well to all students. But they do not. Although progress has been made in the last three decades to make school curricula more inclusive of ethnic and cultural diversity, most of the knowledge taught, and consequently the achievement tests, continues to be Eurocentric.

Even skill mastery is transmitted through Eurocentric contexts. For instance, achievement tests may embed skills in scenarios about situations that are not relevant to the cultural backgrounds and life experiences of students of color. These students then have to decipher the contexts in order to extrapolate the skill content. One example is asking immigrant students from the Caribbean who have never experienced snow to engage in problem solving from a composition on the challenges and dilemmas of a blizzard. They may know the skill, but unfamiliarity with the contextual scenario (problems associated with snow) interferes with their effectively demonstrating their ability to do problem solving. Most European Americans students do not have these kinds of contextual-interference problems. They are familiar with both the context and the performance format because these formats are extracted from cultural orientations the students share with schools. If they know the skill, they therefore are advantaged in demonstrating their mastery. This is not to say that students of color should not take achievement tests, that their school performance should not be evaluated, or that high levels of achievement should not be expected of them.

ACHIEVING EDUCATIONAL EQUALITY

The College Entrance Examination Board (1985) concluded its report, *Equality and Excellence*, with the observation that "excellence for Black students will not become a reality until they receive enriched curricular opportunities in elementary and secondary schools, sufficient financial assistance to pursue higher education opportunities, and instruction from well-qualified teachers" (p. 4). A more recent report, *Reaching the Top* (The College Board, 1999), declares that "the rapid changes that are occurring in the racial and ethnic composition of the nation bring a new sense of urgency" (p. 1) to improving the educational opportunities and outcomes of students of color. This need has become "a moral and pragmatic imperative" (p. 2) because, "when a great many individuals—and entire groups of people—do not have a genuine chance to develop their academic talents fully, our society is much poorer for their lack of educational opportunities . . . this is fundamentally unjust and potentially an enormous source of social divisiveness . . ." (The College Board 1999, p. 5). Gay (1994) suggests that *comparability in culturally relevant learning experiences for ethnically diverse students* is essential to achieving educational equality and high level achievement for them.

Redefining Access

To accomplish these goals, reform efforts should begin with a redefinition of educational equality for students of color as *access to a variety of instructional processes that are informed by and responsive to their cultural orientations and learning styles*. In operational terms, this means affirming that problems in learning are located not so much in the inabilities of students as in culturally unequal, insensitive, and hegemonic practices used in the schools they attend. It also means that schools should be more responsive to human variability, spend less time manipulating students of color to make them comply to institutional structures, and implement programs and processes that empower students through access to high-quality, high-status, and high-power knowledge, skills, and experiences (Fantini, 1979). Translating these conceptions of educational equality into practice requires reform in teacher preparation, curriculum design, classroom instruction, grouping of students for instruction, school climates, and how students' needs are diagnosed and their achievement assessed. All of these issues cannot be discussed in great detail here. Because of the crucial role teachers play in determining the quality of learning opportunities students receive in classrooms, more attention is given to their professional preparation.

Changing Tracking and Testing

All forms of tracking should be eliminated entirely. Even under the best of circumstances, tracking denies equal educational opportunities to students of color and to other students who populate the lower levels. It closes rather than opens pathways to social and academic advancement, and it commits some students early to a permanent educational and social underclass. Tracking should be replaced with flexible and frequently changed cooperative and heterogeneous groupings of students for specific instructional tasks or skill development purposes. For example, students grouped together to learn geographical directions should remain together only until that skill is mastered. Then other kinds of arrangements should be constructed to deal with new learning skills, tasks, and experiences.

Norm-referenced standardized tests for evaluating student achievement should be used infrequently, cautiously, and only in conjunction with other performance measures. More emphasis should be placed on evaluating students against their own records, with *range of improvement between different points of reference being the focus of attention,* as opposed to performance at isolated points in time. This requires that schools and classrooms use multiple techniques and procedures, including academic, social, psychological and emotional measures, as well as verbal, visual, observational, participatory, and kinetic means, to assess students' knowledge and skills. This variety is necessary to prevent any one technique that is highly advantageous to one ethnic group from being used to the exclusion of others.. Both the *content and process* of performance apprasial should be revised to incorporate more fully the cultural contributions, experiences, orientations, and styles of the full range of ethnic groups in the United States.

These approaches should always be *culturally contextualized and designed to serve diagnostic and developmental learning and teaching functions.* That is, they should be used to determine how and why students are proceeding with specific learning tasks, and the formats these approaches take should reflect the cultural orientations and nuances of the students being assessed. They should be administered frequently, and instructional programming should be changed according to the results obtained. Thus, students of color should be put on self-referenced and self-paced programs to complete their schooling. Narrative reports, developmental profiles, student-teacher-parent conferences, and anecdotal records should replace or complement letter and symbol grades for reporting student progress.

Curriculum Reform

School curricula, too, must be reformed if students of color are to be assured equal educational opportunities and outcomes. However, greater content quantity as the measure of educational quality is not the answer. More of the same irrelevant school subjects will not improve the educational quality and achievement quality of students of color. If Latinos, Native Americans, and African Americans are already failing science, simply taking more of it without multiculturalizing any of its content or techniques means that these students will have even greater opportunities to fail. If low-track students are already taking substantially different kinds of mathematics courses than are high-track students, then the gap in the substantive content they are learning widens as the high-track students take even more advanced courses and the low-track students take even more remedial math courses.

What schools consider to be essential knowledge and skills for all students to learn and how these skills are understood and taught need to be revised to incorporate cultural pluralism. These revisions should reflect the *comprehensive demographic, social, cultural, and linguistic realities of U.S. society and the world,* not just the technological, economic, and political sides of life. This means first, that school curricula should demonstrate and emulate the *interdisciplinary nature of human life, knowledge, values, skills, and experiences.* Second, they should teach and model the *interdependence of the world*—a world in which Whites are a small numerical minority, and one in which the control of natural resources, social aspirations, and power negotiations is gradually shifting from Western to non-Western, non-White nations. Third, a concerted effort should be made to achieve a *greater balance between technological developments and humanistic concerns,* where skills in ethics, morality, and aesthetics are as important as cognition. These kind of curricular reforms increase the likelihood that students of color will identify with and relate better to schooling and improve their performance.

Multicultural Teacher Education

Because teachers play such a central role in the kinds of educational opportunities students of color receive in classrooms, their re-education and training are fundamental to providing educational equality. This training should have four primary emphases. The first is *self-knowledge.* Teachers, counselors, and administrators need to become conscious of their own cultural values and beliefs, of how these affect their attitudes and expectations toward students from different ethnic groups and are habitually exhibited in school behaviors. They also need to understand the effects of their values and beliefs on students, relative to the students' self-concepts, academic abilities, educational opportunities, and achievement outcomes.

Spindler and Spindler (1993) offer a model for how teacher self-knowledge can be facilitated. Called "cultural therapy," it is "a process of bringing one's own culture, in its manifold forms—assumptions, goals, values, beliefs, and communicative modes—to a level of awareness that permits one to perceive it as a potential bias in social interaction and in the acquisition or transmission of skills and knowledge" (p. 28). Cultural therapy has elements of *self-reflection, self-monitoring, and self-transcendence.* This cultural consciousness is imperative "so that potential conflicts, misunderstandings, and blind spots in the perception and interpretation of behavior can be anticipated" (p. 28) and unequal power relationships in school and the larger society can be explicated. Cultural therapy can help teachers to identify, understand, and analyze reasons they may find the values and behaviors of ethnically different students objectionable, shocking, and irritating (Spindler & Spindler, 1993). Its ultimate goals are to empower teachers and to implement the principle that social reforms begin with individuals.

Merely telling teachers about how their cultural assumptions can lead to low expectations and negative consequences for students of color receiving educational equality will not suffice.

Nor will reading the impressive body of research that documents these effects. Instead, teachers need to *see and understand* how they behave toward culturally diverse students in their classrooms. This can be accomplished by projecting mirror images of or replaying their classroom behaviors back to them and training teachers how to be participant observers of their own classroom dynamics and how to use different techniques systematically to analyze their instructional behaviors. Inexpensive technology, such as camcorders, makes it possible to accomplish such training with ease and expediency. Audio- and videotapes of teaching behaviors are invaluable for showing teachers what they actually do in classrooms. They are much better than are outside observers, because recorders and cameras do not interpret or misrepresent what actually occurs. Training in ethnographic techniques, interactional analysis, questioning strategies, frame analysis, self-reflection, feedback mechanisms, and participatory action research can help teachers to look systematically at these recorded behaviors and to monitor their change efforts.

In addition to *learning how to culturally decode their attitudes and behaviors* from an insider's viewpoint, teachers need to learn how to analyze these attitudes and behaviors from the perspectives of "others," especially those of their students of color. These skills are not acquired automatically; they must be deliberately taught. Without training, most educators cannot see the cultural biases and prejudices of their routine school behaviors. Suggestions to the effect that they are not treating students of color and European Americans equally tend to be associated with deliberate and blatant acts of discrimination. Teachers do not understand how thoroughly and subtly cultural nuances permeate all of their behaviors and can generate negative effects in instructional actions toward students who do not share their cultural frames of reference.

These cultural influences need to be counteracted by developing skills *in critical consciousness and culturally relevant pedagogy* for use with ethnically diverse students. Several contributing authors to the *Handbook of Research on Multicultural Education* (Banks & Banks, 1995), to *Culture, Style, and the Educative Process* (Shade, 1989), and to *Teaching Diverse Populations* (Hollins, King, & Hayman, 1994) explain what this means specifically for Native, African, Latino, and Asian American students. Their explanations include teaching about the cultural heritages and contributions of ethnic groups of concern; social and interpersonal relationships between students and teachers that convey a sense of personal kindredness, interdependence, connectedness, and caring; using cultural frames of reference to make the content of teaching personally meaningful to ethnically diverse students; concern for the affective and moral as well as the cognitive development of students; and cultivating social and cultural consciousness, solidarity, and responsibility. Thus, culturally appropriate or responsive pedagogy "empowers students intellectually, socially, emotionally, and politically by using cultural referents to impart knowledge, skills, and attitudes" (Ladson-Billings 1992, p. 382).

A second emphasis in teacher re-education for educational equality is *understanding differences in cultural values and behavioral codes* between themselves as middle-class European Americans and students of color and how instructional processes can be restructured to better accommodate them. Teachers cannot begin to treat African, Latino, Native, Asian, and European American students equitably until they accept that they all have comparable human worth and that differences do not automatically mean inferiorities. This acceptance begins with acquiring knowledge about the cultural backgrounds, life experiences, interactional patterns, and learning styles of different ethnic groups to replace racial myths and stereotypes. Once teachers understand the structures and motivations behind these cultural behaviors, they can begin to design more culturally compatible instructional options and thereby improve the quality of the learning experiences for students of color. This is the logic behind Pai's (1990) and Gay's (1994) contentions that knowledge of cultural diversity is an essential foundation for equality and excellence in both the processes and outcomes of education. These ideas are further elaborated in research reported by Foster (1989; 1991), Allen and Boykin (1992), Au (1993), Lee (1993), and Losey (1997). The findings consistently indicate that *cultural connectedness* in the educational process improves the academic achievement of students of color.

The third focus of teacher re-education should be the development of *pedagogical skills* appropriate for use with students of color. The point of departure for this training should be understanding the specific traits of different teaching styles and ethnic learning styles. This knowledge should be combined with learning how to diversify teaching strategies culturally; to create more culturally diverse supportive environments for learning and demonstrating achievement; to reduce stress, tension, and conflict in ethnically pluralistic classrooms; to select materials that have high-quality interest appeal for different ethnic groups; and to develop and use learning activities that are meaningful, involving, enabling, and empowering for students of color. In other words, teachers need to learn how to ethnically integrate the structural arrangements and curricular materials for teaching, to culturally diversify their instructional and assessment strategies, and to make democratic the environments constructed for learning. These general skills can be made operational by helping teachers learn how to use specific instructional techniques with students of color, such as questioning, feedback and reinforcement, cooperative learning, inductive teaching, social-context learning, and auditory and visual learning.

The approaches used in teacher training to develop these skills should be four-dimensional—including *diagnosis*, *development and implementation*, *analytical debriefing and reflection*, and *refinement*—with teachers-in-training actively involved in each aspect. The training process should begin with a careful assessment of the value of and problems associated with using various instructional strategies with students of color. Examples of actual teaching behaviors should be used for this purpose. The training should then proceed to having teachers develop alternative curriculum designs and instructional strategies that incorporate cultural diversity and try them out in real or simulated teaching situations and under careful supervision. After these development efforts have been piloted or field tested, they should be examined thoroughly through the filters of some established cultural diversity design and implementation criteria in order to determine their strengths and weaknesses. Central to this analysis should be discerning features of the new teaching strategies that facilitate or continue to inhibit the improvement of educational opportunities and achievement for students of color. Finally, the insights gained from these experiences and analyses should be used to further refine the multicultural curriculum designs and instructional strategies.

A fourth emphasis in the retraining of teachers, counselors, and school administrators for educational equality is *public relations skill development*. Major reform is needed in how educators are prepared to communicate and interact with parents of color and to mobilize their community resources to help in the educational process. Currently, there is a strong tendency for educators to blame the school failure of students on the lack of involvement of their parents in school affairs. This buck-passing is counterproductive to improving the education of students. It is a form of blaming and indicting the victims and of educators abdicating their own responsibility for teaching youths of color.

Certainly, parents of color should be more actively involved in their children's education, but it is understandable why they are reluctant or unable to do so. The schools that are failing their children are the same ones that failed many of them when they were students. Educators usually approach parents about their children only when the children get into trouble with the school system. This punitive, adversarial posture is not conducive to cooperation among educators and parents of color. Furthermore, teachers and administrators do not fully understand or appreciate the fact that many parents do not have the time, the personal resources, or the technical skills to assist in the education of their children in ways the teachers typically expect. How can parents effectively supervise their children's homework or come to the schools on demand when they are unfamiliar with the latest pedagogical strategies used in schools and when they are working at hourly wage or low-salaried jobs that do not permit them to take time off without significant cost? How can non- or limited English-speaking mothers and fathers even understand their children's language arts assignment, least of all supervise and help them complete it? Professional development programs should help pre- and in-service educators understand these real-life social and cultural factors, the effects they have on parents' reactions to invitations and challenges to being educational partners, and how to develop novel, culturally sensitive strategies to overcome these obstacles.

This retraining process should include *culturally appropriate public-relations skill development* for use with different ethnic communities. It should be a part of all levels of professional preparation, undergraduate and graduate, pre-service and in-service. It should start with acquiring an accurate knowledge base about the cultural dynamics of different ethnic communities, who the power brokers are in these communities, and how interactions and relationships are negotiated. It should also include specific strategies and skills about how to establish credibility and trust with different ethnic communities and parents. Specifically, this might include such skills as identifying and accessing the informal community networks of influence; understanding different ethnic groups' interactional protocols and decorums; establishing consultancy relations with parents and community organizations; establishing equal-status relationships with parents of color and other community members; being cultural brokers or mediators across the cultural systems of homes and schools; diffusing the threat and intimidation often associated with schools for parents of color; translating educational jargon into language styles that are meaningful for parents from different ethnic, social, and linguistic backgrounds; and identifying neutral sites or zones where parents and educators can meet, consult, confer, and, collaborate.

All of these are elements of *cultural diplomacy* that classroom teachers, guidance counselors, and school administrators need to master in order to develop more constructive and cooperative relations with parents and communities of color. These elements, like the components of cultural therapy, literacy in ethnic and cultural diversity, and culturally responsive pedagogy, are fundamental to improving the quality of educational opportunities and outcomes for students of color.

CONCLUSION

Educational achievement among many students of color continues to be disturbingly low, even after more than four decades of deliberate legal reforms and funding policies designed to improve it. Some improvements are apparent but they are not significant enough to alter long-established patterns. Consistently across time, place, and indicators of achievement, African Americans have the lowest academic proficiency levels of all ethnic groups, followed in sequence by Latinos and Native Americans. These trends are unequivocal in the math, science, reading, writing, history, and geography report cards issued at two-, four-, and six-year intervals by the National Assessment of Educational Progress (NAEP). African Americans perform somewhat better in civics, with scores higher than those of Latinos. The fact that school attendance and graduation rates are increasing for all students of color makes their low academic achievement even more troubling. If staying in school has positive consequences for mediating educational, social, and economic disadvantaged conditions, as theory claims, then as graduation rates increase and dropout rates decline students of color should perform academically much better than they are.

The failure of most students of color to achieve significant educational improvements from year to year gives credence to the position taken by Miller-Lachmann and Taylor (1995) that while funds and laws are necessary variables in providing educational equality, they are not sufficient. Something significantly different in *instructional quality* must be done to provide better educational opportunities and outcomes for students of color. Culturally responsive pedagogy and multicultural education offer ideologies and strategies that can facilitate these changes.

When the cultures of students and teachers are not congruent, someone loses out. Invariably, who loses out are the students and also the effectiveness of their learning, especially if they are members of racially visible groups, such as African, Native, Latino, and Asian Americans. Not understanding, accepting, or using their culture as instructional tools means that these students do not have access to high-quality instructional opportunities and inter-actions comparable to those of their European American counterparts. It is not surprising, then, that disparities in achievement outcomes exist. These situations will be reversed only when educators accept the fact that culture is a crucial, if not the ultimate, mediating factor in the quality of educational opportunities students of color receive, and the levels of academic performance they achieve. As John Goodlad (1984) suggests, the central problem of both educational equality and excellence for today and tomorrow is "no longer access to school. It is access to knowledge for all" (p. 140). This access is not maximally possible for students of color unless their cultural orientations are used as filters for teaching and learning. Therefore, *culturally responsive pedagogy* must be used to better educate students from diverse ethnic and cultural backgrounds.

Questions and Activities

1. How do popular conceptions of educational equality differ from the view of this concept presented by Gay, the author of this chapter? What unfortunate assumptions, according to Gay, underlie these popular notions of educational equality?

2. In what ways did the educational status of students of color improve between 1990 and 1998? Why did the educational status of students of color improve during this period?

3. In what ways did the educational status of students of color decline during the 1990s? What are some reasons for this decline?

4. How does the reference to Asian Americans as the model minority oversimplify their educational status? Give specific examples from this chapter to support your response.

5. How do school and curriculum practices such as tracking, vocational courses, and special education classes deny students of color equal educational opportunities?

6. The author argues that students of color are often placed in double jeopardy in school, in part because of differences between their cultures and the culture of the school. Explain what the author means by this concept. How can teachers help reduce the problems students of color experience in the schools?

7. How does testing, according to the author, promote educational inequality for low-income students and for students of color? How can assessment programs be changed so they will contribute to educational equality for all students?

8. According to the author, how can curriculum reforms related to ethnic diversity contribute to educational equality?

9. Gay contends that educational equality for students of color cannot be achieved short of "massive schoolwide reform." What factors in the school environment and in teacher education does she think require reform? What specific recommendations does she make for attaining these reforms?

10. Explain why Gay believes that multicultural education has the potential for improving educational equality for students of color.

11. Construct a descriptive profile of the concept of educational equality as developed by the author of this chapter.

12. Observe for several days in a school that has a large percentage of students of color. Look for evidence of the existence of the inequities discussed in this chapter. In what ways do your observations substantiate Gay's conclusions about the problems that students of color experience in schools? What programs and efforts are being implemented in the school you observed to improve the educational status of students of color, and to what extent are they effective?

References

Allen, B. A. and Boykin, A. W. (1992). African-American Children and the Educative Process: Alleviating Cultural Discontinuity through Prescriptive Pedagogy. *School Psychology Review, 21*(4), 586–598.

Astin, A. A. (1985). *Achieving Educational Excellence: A Critical Assessment of Priorities and Practices in Higher Education.* San Francisco: Jossey-Bass.

Au, K. H. (1993). *Literacy Instruction in Multicultural Settings.* New York: Harcourt Brace.

Banks, J. A. and Banks, C. A. M. (Eds.). (1995). *Handbook of Research on Multicultural Education.* New York: Macmillan.

Boateng, F. (1990). Combatting Deculturalization of the African-American Child in the Public School System: A Multicultural Approach. In K. Lomotey (Ed.), *Going to School: The African American Experience* (pp. 73–84). Albany, NY: SUNY Press.

The College Board. (1999). *Reaching the Top: A Report of the National Task Force on Minority High Achievement.* New York: Author.

The College Entrance Examination Board. (1985). *Equality and Excellence: The Educational Status of Black Americans.* New York: Author.

Fantini, M. D. (1979). From School System to Educational System: Policy Considerations. In D. A. Wilkerson (Ed.), *Educating All of Our Children: An Imperative for Democracy* (pp. 134–153). Westport, CT: Mediax.

Foster, M. (1989). It's Cooking Now: A Performance Analysis of the Speech Events of a Black Teacher in an Urban Community College. *Language in Society, 18*(1), 1–29.

Foster, M. (Ed.). (1991). *Readings on Equal Education: Qualitative Investigations into Schools and Schooling,* Vol. 11. New York: AMS Press.

Gay, G. (1974, January). *Differential Dyadic Interactions of Black and White Teachers with Black and White Pupils in Recently Desegregated Social Studies Classrooms: A Function of Teacher and Pupil Ethnicity.* Washington, DC: Office of Education, National Institute of Education.

Gay, G. (1994). *At the Essence of Learning: Multicultural Education.* West Lafayette, IN: Kappa Delta Pi.

Gay, G. (2000). *Culturally Responsive Teaching: Theory, Research, and Practice.* New York: Teachers College Press.

Gibbs, J. T. and Nahme-Huang, L. (Eds.). (1989). *Children of Color: Psychological Interventions with Minority Youth.* San Francisco: Jossey-Bass.

Good, T. L. and Brophy, J. E. (1994). *Looking in Classrooms* (6th ed.). New York: Harper Collins.

Goodlad, J. I. (1984). *A Place Called School: Prospects for the Future.* New York: McGraw-Hill.

Gougis, R. A. (1986). The Effects of Prejudice and Stress on the Academic Performance of Black Americans. In U. Neisser (Ed.), *The Achievement of Minority Children: New Perspectives* (pp. 145–158). Hillsdale, NJ: Lawrence Erlbaum.

Grant, C. A. and Sleeter, C. E. (1985). Equality, Equity, and Excellence: A Critique. In P. G. Altbach, G. P. Kelly, and L. Weis (Eds.), *Excellence in Education: Perspectives on Policy and Practice* (pp. 139–159). Buffalo, NY: Prometheus Books.

Harry, B. (1992). *Cultural Diversity, Families, and the Special Education System: Communication and Empowerment.* New York, Teachers College Press, Columbia University.

Holliday, B. G. (1985). Towards a Model of Teacher-Child Transactional Processes Affecting Black Children's Academic Achievement. In M. B. Spencer, G. K. Brookins, and W. R. Allen (Eds.), *Beginnings: The Social and Affective Development of Black Children* (pp. 117–130). Hillsdale, NJ: Lawrence Erlbaum.

Hollins, E. R., King, J. E., and Hayman, W. C. (Eds.). (1994). *Teaching Diverse Populations: Formulating a Knowledge Base.* Albany, NY: SUNY Press.

Igoa, C. (1995). *The Inner World of the Immigrant Child.* New York: St. Martin's.

John-Steiner, V. P. and Leacock, E. (1979). Transforming the Structure of Failure. In D. A. Wilkerson (Ed.), *Educating All of Our Children: An Imperative for Democracy* (pp. 79–91). Westport, CT: Mediax.

Ladson-Billings, G. (1992). Liberatory Consequences of Literacy: A Case of Culturally Relevant Instruction for African American Students. *The Journal of Negro Education, 61*(3), 378–391.

Ladson-Billings, G. (1994). *The Dreamkeepers: Successful Teachers of African-American Children.* San Francisco: Jossey-Bass.

Lee, C. (1993). *Signifying as a Scaffold to Literary Interpretation: The Pedagogical Implications of a Form of African American Discourse.* Urbana, IL: National Council of Teachers of English.

Losey, K. M. (1997). *Listen to the Silences: Mexican American Interaction in the Composition Classroom and Community.* Norwood, NJ: Ablex.

Miller-Lachmann, L. and Taylor, L. S. (1995). *Schools for All: Educating Children in a Diverse Society.* New York: Delmar Publishers.

Morgan, E. P. (1977). *Inequality in Classroom Learning: Schooling and Democratic Citizenship.* New York: Praeger.

Nielsen, F. (1986). Hispanics in High School and Beyond. In M. A. Olivas (Ed.), *Latino College Students* (pp. 71–103). New York: Teachers College Press.

Oakes, J. (1985). *Keeping Track: How Schools Structure Inequality.* New Haven, CT: Yale University Press.

Oakes, J. and Guiton, G. (1995). Matchmaking: The Dynamics of High School Tracking Decisions. *American Educational Research Journal, 32*(1), 3–33.

Orfield, G. Eaton, S. E., and The Harvard Project on School Desegregation. (1996). *Dismantling Desegregation: The Quiet Reversal of Brown v. Board of Education.* New York: The New Press.

Osajima, K. (1991). Breaking the Silence: Race and the Educational Experiences of Asian-American College Students. In M. Foster (Ed.), *Readings on Equal Education: Qualitative Investigations into Schools and Schooling,* Vol. 11 (pp. 115–134). New York: AMS Press.

Pai, Y. (1990). *Cultural Foundations of Education.* New York: Merrill.

Pang, V. O. (1995). Asian Pacific American Students: A Diverse and Complex Population. In J. A. Banks and C. A. M. Banks (Eds.), *Handbook of Research on Multicultural Education* (pp. 412–424). New York: Macmillan.

Pang, V. O. and Cheng, L. R. C. (Eds.). (1998). *Struggling to Be Heard: The Unmet Needs of Asian Pacific American Children.* Albany, NY: SUNY Press.

Pang, V. O., Mizokawa, D. T., Morishima, J. K., and Olstad, R. G. (1985). Self-Concept of Japanese American Children. *Journal of Cross-Cultural Psychology, 16*(Mar.), 99–108.

Persell, C. H. (1977). *Education and Inequality: A Theoretical and Empirical Synthesis.* New York: Free Press.

Ralph, J., Keller, D., and Crouse, J. (1994). How Effective Are American Schools? *Phi Delta Kappan, 76*(2), 144–150.

Shade, B. J. R. (Ed.). (1989). *Culture, Style, and the Educative Process.* Springfield, IL: Charles C Thomas.

Spindler, G. and Spindler, L. (1993). The Processes of Culture and Person: Cultural Therapy and Culturally Diverse Schools. In P. Phelan and A. L. Davidson (Eds.), *Renegotiating Cultural Diversity in American Schools* (pp. 27–51). New York: Teachers College Press.

U.S. Civil Rights Commission. (1971–1974). *Mexican-American Educational Study,* Reports I–VI. Washington DC: U.S. Government Printing Office.

U.S. Department of Education. (1994). *NAEP 1992 Trends in Academic Progress.* Washington, DC: U.S. Government Printing Office.

U.S. Department of Education. (1995). *Characteristics of American Indian and Alaska Native Education.* Washington, DC: U.S. Government Printing Office.

U.S. Department of Education. (1999a). *Digest of Education Statistics, 1998.* Washington, DC: U.S. Government Printing Office.

U.S. Department of Education. (1999b). *The Condition of Education, 1999.* Washington, DC: U.S. Government Printing Office.

Verdugo, R. R. (1986). Educational Stratification and Hispanics. In M. A. Olivas (Ed.), *Latino College Students* (pp. 325–347). New York: Teachers College Press.

Winkler, J. D., Stravelson, R. J., Stasz, C., Robyn, A., and Fiebel, W. (1984). *How Effective Teachers Use Microcomputers in Instruction. Santa Monica,* CA: Rand Corporation.

www.collegeboard.org. Academic and Demographic Features of 1.2 Million SAT Takers in the High School Class of 1999. New York: The College Board. [Accessed 12/4/99]

www.naep.org. NAEP Civics, Reading, and Writing Achievement Level Results, Grades 4, 8, and 12. [Accessed 12/4/99]

www.nces.ed.gov. *NAEP 1998 Civics Report Card for the Nation.* Washington, DC: U.S. Department of Education, U.S. Governmental Printing Office. [Accessed 12/4/99]

Yu, E. S. H., Doi, M., and Chang, C. (1986, November). *Asian American Education in Illinois: A Review of the Data.* Springfield: Illinois State Board of Education.

CHAPTER 10

Approaches to Multicultural Curriculum Reform

James A. Banks

THE MAINSTREAM-CENTRIC CURRICULUM

The United States is made up of many different racial, ethnic, religious, language, and cultural groups. In the year 2000, people of color, such as African Americans, Latinos, and Asian Americans, made up 28 percent of the U.S. population. These groups are projected to make up 48 percent of the U.S. population by 2050 (Martin & Midgley, 1999). Despite the deepening ethnic texture within the United States, the U.S. school, college, and university mainstream curriculum is organized around concepts, paradigms, and events that reflect the experiences of Anglo-Saxon Protestant males (Banks, 1996). The dominant, mainstream curriculum has been challenged and fractured within the last thirty-five years, beginning with the civil rights movement of the 1960s and 1970s. Consequently, the mainstream curriculum and textbooks today are much more multiethnic and multicultural than they were when the civil rights movement began. Progress has been made, and it should be acknowledged. However, the reforms have been neither as extensive nor as institutionalized as is needed, and the process of curriculum transformation needs to continue. Curriculum transformation is a process that never ends because of the changes that are continuing within the United States and throughout the world.

A curriculum that focuses on the experiences of mainstream Americans and largely ignores the experiences, cultures, and histories of other ethnic, racial, cultural, language, and religious groups has negative consequences for both mainstream U.S. students and students of color. A mainstream-centric curriculum is one major way in which racism and ethnocentrism are reinforced and perpetuated in the schools, in colleges and universities, and in society at large.

A mainstream-centric curriculum has negative consequences for mainstream students because it reinforces their false sense of superiority, gives them a misleading conception of their relationship with other racial and ethnic groups, and denies them the opportunity to benefit from the knowledge, perspectives, and frames of reference that can be gained from

225

studying and experiencing other cultures and groups. A mainstream-centric curriculum also denies mainstream U.S. students the opportunity to view their culture from the perspectives of other cultures and groups. When people view their culture from the point of view of another culture, they are able to understand their own culture more fully, to see how it is unique and distinct from other cultures, and to understand better how it relates to and interacts with other cultures.

A mainstream-centric curriculum negatively influences students of color, such as African Americans, Latinos, and Asian Americans. It marginalizes their experiences and cultures and does not reflect their dreams, hopes, and perspectives. Students learn best and are more highly motivated when the school curriculum reflects their cultures, experiences, and perspectives. Many students of color are alienated in the school in part because they experience cultural conflict and discontinuities that result from the cultural differences between their school and community. The school can help students of color mediate between their home and school cultures by implementing a curriculum that reflects the culture of their ethnic groups and communities. The school can and should make effective use of the community cultures of students of color when teaching them such subjects as writing, language arts, science, and mathematics (Ladson-Billings, 1994; Perry & Delpit, 1998).

In the mainstream-centric curriculum, events, themes, concepts, and issues are viewed primarily from the perspective of middle-class Anglo-Americans and Europeans. Events and cultural developments such as the European explorations in the Americas and the development of American music are viewed from Anglo and European perspectives and are evaluated using mainstream-centric criteria and points of view (Bigelow & Peterson, 1998; Lundquist & Szego, 1998).

When the European explorations of the Americas are viewed from a Eurocentric perspective, the Americas are perceived as having been "discovered" by the European explorers such as Columbus and Cortés (Loewen, 1995; Zinn, 1999). The view that native peoples in the Americas were discovered by the Europeans subtly suggests that Indian cultures did not exist until they were "discovered" by the Europeans and that the lands occupied by the American Indians were rightfully owned by the Europeans after they settled on and claimed them.

When the formation and nature of U.S. cultural developments, such as music and dance, are viewed from mainstream-centric perspectives, these art forms become important and significant only when they are recognized or legitimized by mainstream critics and artists. The music of African American musicians such as Chuck Berry and Little Richard was not viewed as significant by the mainstream society until White singers such as the Beatles and Rod Stewart publicly acknowledged the significant ways their own music had been deeply influenced by these African American musicians. It often takes White artists to legitimize ethnic cultural forms and innovations created by Asian Americans, African Americans, Latinos, and Native Americans.

Public Sites and Popular History

Anglocentric history is not only taught in the nation's schools, colleges and universities, but is also perpetuated in popular knowledge in the nation's parks, museums, and other public sites. Loewen (1999) describes the ways in which public history in the nation's historic sites often distort history in order to present a positive image of Anglo-Americans. The title of his book is *Lies across America: What Our Historic Sites Get Wrong*.

I have seen several examples of markers in public sites that perpetuate Anglocentric views of American history. The first appears on a marker in a federal park on the site where a U.S. Army post once stood in the state of Washington in Fort Townsend. With the choice of words such as *settlers* (instead of invaders), *restive*, and *rebelled*, the author justifies the taking of the Indian's lands and depicts their resistance as unreasonable.

Fort Townsend

A U.S. Army Post was established on this site in 1856. In mid-nineteenth century the growth of Port Townsend caused the Indians to become restive. Settlers started a home guard, campaigned wherever called, and defeated the Indians in the Battle of Seattle. Indians rebelled as the government began enforcing the Indian Treaty of 1854, by which the Indians had ceded most of their territory. Port Townsend, a prosperous port of entry on Puget Sound, then asked protection of the U.S. army.

The second example is in Marianna, Arkansas, my home town, which is the city center for Lee County. The site commemorates the life and achievements of Confederate soldiers from Lee County and the life of Robert E. Lee, a general of the Confederate Army and a Southern hero. The marker reads in part, "In loving memory of Lee County's Confederate soldiers. No braver bled for a brighter land. No brighter land had a cause so grand." The final example is from a marker in the Confederate Park in Memphis, Tennessee, which commemorates the life of Jefferson Davis, President of the Southern Confederacy. The marker reads, in part: "Before the war Between the States, he served with distinction as a United States Congressman and twice as a United States Senator. He also served as Secretary of War of the U.S. He was a true American patriot." Describing Davis as a "true American patriot" is at best controversial.

EFFORTS TO ESTABLISH A MULTICULTURAL CURRICULUM

Since the civil rights movement of the 1960s, educators have been trying, in various ways, to better integrate the school curriculum with ethnic content and to move away from a mainstream-centric and Eurocentric curriculum (Banks, 1999). These have proven to be difficult goals for schools to attain for many complex reasons. The strong assimilationist ideology embraced by most U.S. educators is one major reason (Banks, 2001). The assimilationist ideology makes it difficult for educators to think differently about how U.S. society and culture developed and to acquire a commitment to make the curriculum multicultural. Individuals who have a strong assimilationist ideology believe that most important events and developments in U.S. society are related to the nation's British heritage and that the contributions of other ethnic and cultural groups are not very significant by comparison. When educators acquire a multicultural ideology and conception of U.S. culture, they are then able to view the experiences and contributions of a wide range of cultural, ethnic, language, and religious groups as significant to the development of the United States.

Ideological resistance is a major factor that has slowed and is still slowing the development of a multicultural curriculum, but other factors have also affected its growth and development. Political resistance to a multicultural curriculum is closely related to ideological resistance. Many people who resist a multicultural curriculum believe that knowledge is power and that a multicultural perspective on U.S. society challenges the existing power structure. They believe that the dominant mainstream-centric curriculum supports, reinforces, and justifies the existing social, economic, and political structure. Multicultural perspectives and points of view, in the opinion of many observers, legitimize and promote social change and social reconstruction.

During the 1980s and 1990s a heated debate occurred about the extent to which the curriculum should be Western and European-centric and to which it should reflect the cultural, ethnic, and racial diversity in the United States. At least three major positions in this debate can be identified. The Western traditionalists argue that the West, as defined and conceptualized in the past, should be the focus in school and college curricula because of the major influence of Western civilization and culture in the United States and throughout the world (Ravitch, 1990; Schlesinger, 1991). Afrocentric scholars contend that the contributions of Africa and of African peoples should receive major emphasis in the curriculum (Asante, 1991; Asante & Ravitch, 1991). The multiculturalists argue that although the West should receive a major emphasis in the curriculum, the West should be reconceptualized so that it reflects the contributions that people of color have made to the West (Zinn & Kirschner, 1995). In addition to teaching about Western ideals, the gap between the ideals of the West and its realities of racism, sexism, and discrimination should be taught (Dilg, 1999). Multiculturalists also believe that in addition to learning about the West, students should study other world cultures, such as those in Africa, Asia, the Middle East, and the Americas, as they were before the Europeans arrived (Gates, 1999).

Other factors that have slowed the institutionalization of a multicultural curriculum include the low level of knowledge about ethnic cultures that most educators have and the heavy reliance on textbooks for teaching. Teachers must have an in-depth knowledge about ethnic cultures and experiences to integrate ethnic content, experiences, and points of view into the curriculum. Many teachers tell their students that Columbus discovered America and that America is a "new world" because they know little about the diverse Native American cultures that existed in the Americas more than 40,000 years before the Europeans began to settle in the Americas in significant numbers in the sixteenth century. As Gary Howard (1999) states in the title of his cogent and informative book, *We Can't Teach What We Don't Know.*

Many studies have revealed that the textbook is still the main source for teaching, especially in such subjects as the social studies, reading, and language arts (Goodlad, 1984; Social Science Education Consortium, 1982). Some significant changes have been made in textbooks since the civil rights movement of the 1960s. More ethnic groups and women appear in textbooks today than in those of yesteryear (Garcia, 1993). However, the content about ethnic groups in some textbooks is presented from mainstream perspectives, contains information and heroes that are selected using mainstream criteria, and does not incorporate information about ethnic groups throughout the text in a consistent and totally integrated way (Sleeter & Grant, 1991). Information about ethnic groups in some textbooks is presented in special units, topics, and parts of the text. However, ethnic and cultural groups are integrated well into some of the most recent textbooks (Banks, Beyer, Contreras, Craven, Ladson-Billings, McFarland, & Parker,

2000). These textbooks are often ahead of teachers in terms of curriculum transformation. Many teaches need to acquire more content knowledge about ethnic groups in order to use these newer textbooks effectively.

LEVELS OF INTEGRATION OF MULTICULTURAL CONTENT

The Contributions Approach

I have identified four approaches to the integration of ethnic and multicultural content into the curriculum (see Figure 10.1). The contributions approach to integration (Level 1) is one of the most frequently used; it is often used extensively during the first phase of an ethnic revival movement. It is also frequently used when a school or district first attempts to integrate ethnic and multicultural content into the mainstream curriculum.

The contributions approach is characterized by the insertion of ethnic heroes/heroines and discrete cultural artifacts into the curriculum, selected using criteria similar to those used to select mainstream heroes/heroines and cultural artifacts. Thus, individuals such as Crispus Attucks, Benjamin Bannaker, Pocahontas, Booker T. Washington, and Cesar Chavez are added to the curriculum. They are discussed when mainstream American heroes/heroines such as

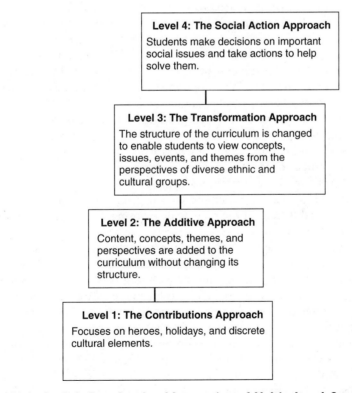

Level 4: The Social Action Approach
Students make decisions on important social issues and take actions to help solve them.

Level 3: The Transformation Approach
The structure of the curriculum is changed to enable students to view concepts, issues, events, and themes from the perspectives of diverse ethnic and cultural groups.

Level 2: The Additive Approach
Content, concepts, themes, and perspectives are added to the curriculum without changing its structure.

Level 1: The Contributions Approach
Focuses on heroes, holidays, and discrete cultural elements.

Figure 10.1   Banks's Four Levels of Integration of Multicultural Content

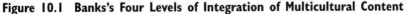

Patrick Henry, George Washington, Thomas Jefferson, Betsey Ross, and Eleanor Roosevelt are studied in the core curriculum. Discrete cultural elements such as the foods, dances, music, and artifacts of ethnic groups are studied, but little attention is given to their meanings and importance within ethnic communities.

An important characteristic of the contributions approach is that the mainstream curriculum remains unchanged in its basic structure, goals, and salient characteristics. Prerequisites for the implementation of this approach are minimal. They include basic knowledge about U.S. society and knowledge about ethnic heroes/heroines and their roles and contributions to U.S. society and culture.

Individuals who challenged the dominant society's ideologies, values, and conceptions and advocated radical social, political, and economic reform are seldom included in the contributions approach. Thus, Booker T. Washington is more likely to be chosen for study than is W. E. B. Du Bois, and Pocahontas is more likely to be chosen than is Geronimo. The criteria used to select ethnic heroes/heroines for study and to judge them for success are derived from the mainstream society and not from the ethnic community. Consequently, use of the contributions approach usually results in the study of ethnic heroes/heroines who represent only one important perspective within ethnic communities. The more radical and less conformist individuals who are heroes/heroines only to the ethnic community are often invisible in textbooks, teaching materials, and activities used in the contributions approach.

The heroes/heroines and holidays approach is a variant of the contributions approach. In this approach, ethnic content is limited primarily to special days, weeks, and months related to ethnic events and celebrations. Cinco de Mayo, Martin Luther King, Jr.'s Birthday, and African American History Week are examples of ethnic days and weeks celebrated in the schools. During these celebrations, teachers involve students in lessons, experiences, and pageants related to the ethnic group being commemorated. When this approach is used, the class studies little or nothing about the ethnic group before or after the special event or occasion.

The contributions approach (Level 1 in Figure 10.1) provides teachers with a way to integrate ethnic content into the curriculum quickly, thus giving some recognition to ethnic contributions to U.S. society and culture. Many teachers who are committed to integrating their curricula with ethnic content have little knowledge about ethnic groups and curriculum revision. Consequently, they use the contributions approach when teaching about ethnic groups. These teachers should be encouraged, supported, and given the opportunity to acquire the knowledge and skills needed to reform their curricula by using one of the more effective approaches described later in this chapter.

There are often strong political demands from ethnic communities for the school to put their heroes/heroines, contributions, and cultures into the school curriculum. These political forces may take the form of demands for heroes and contributions because mainstream heroes, such as Washington, Jefferson, and Lincoln, are highly visible in the school curriculum. Ethnic communities of color want to see their own heroes/heroines and contributions alongside those of the mainstream society. Such contributions may help give them a sense of structural inclusion, validation, and equity. Curriculum inclusion also facilitates the quests of marginalized ethnic and cultural groups for a sense of empowerment and efficacy. The school should help ethnic-group students acquire a sense of empowerment and efficacy. These factors are positively correlated with academic achievement (Coleman, Campbell, Hobson, McPartland, Mood, Weinfeld, & York, 1966).

The contributions approach is also the easiest approach for teachers to use to integrate the curriculum with ethnic content. However, this approach has several serious limitations. When the integration of the curriculum is accomplished primarily through the infusion of ethnic heroes/heroines and contributions, students do not attain a global view of the role of ethnic and cultural groups in U.S. society. Rather, they see ethnic issues and events primarily as an addition to the curriculum and consequently as an appendage to the main story of the development of the nation and to the core curriculum in the language arts, the social studies, the arts, and other subject areas.

Teaching ethnic issues with the use of heroes/heroines and contributions also tends to gloss over important concepts and issues related to the victimization and oppression of ethnic groups and their struggles against racism and for power. Issues such as racism, poverty, and oppression tend to be avoided in the contributions approach to curriculum integration. The focus tends to be on success and the validation of the Horatio Alger myth that all Americans who are willing to work hard can go from rags to riches and "pull themselves up by their bootstraps."

The success stories of ethnic heroes such as Booker T. Washington, George Washington Carver, and Jackie Robinson are usually told with a focus on their success, with little attention to racism and other barriers they encountered and how they succeeded despite the hurdles they faced. Little attention is also devoted to the process by which they become heroes/heroines. Students should learn about the process by which people become heroes/heroines as well as about their status and role as heroes/heroines. Only when students learn the process by which individuals become heroes/heroines will they understand fully how individuals, particularly individuals of color, achieve and maintain hero/heroine status and what the process of becoming a hero/heroine means for their own lives.

The contributions approach often results in the trivialization of ethnic cultures, the study of their strange and exotic characteristics, and the reinforcement of stereotypes and misconceptions. When the focus is on the contributions and unique aspects of ethnic cultures, students are not helped to view them as complete and dynamic wholes. The contributions approach also tends to focus on the life-styles of ethnic groups rather than on the institutional structures, such as racism and discrimination, that strongly affect their life chances and keep them powerless and marginalized.

The contributions approach to content integration may provide students with a memorable one-time experience with an ethnic hero/heroine, but it often fails to help them understand the role and influence of the hero/heroine in the total context of U.S. history and society. When ethnic heroes/heroines are studied separate and apart from the social and political context in which they lived and worked, students attain only a partial understanding of their roles and significance in society. When Martin Luther King, Jr., or Rosa Parks are studied outside the social and political context of institutionalized racism in the U.S. South in the 1940s and 1950s, and without attention to the more subtle forms of institutionalized racism in the North during this period, their full significance as social reformers and activists is neither revealed nor understood by students.

The Additive Approach

Another important approach to the integration of ethnic content to the curriculum is the addition of content, concepts, themes, and perspectives to the curriculum without changing its basic structure, purposes, and characteristics. The additive approach (Level 2 in Figure 10.1) is often accomplished by the addition of a book, a unit, or a course to the curriculum without changing it substantially. Examples of this approach include adding a book such as *The Color Purple* to a unit on the twentieth century in an English class, the use of the film *Miss Jane Pittman* during a unit on the 1960s, and the addition of a videotape on the internment of the Japanese Americans, such as *Rabbit in the Moon*, during a study of World War II in a class on U.S. history.

The additive approach allows the teacher to put ethnic content into the curriculum without restructuring it, a process that would take substantial time, effort and training and also a rethinking of the curriculum and its purposes, nature, and goals. The additive approach can be the first phase in a transformative curriculum reform effort designed to restructure the total curriculum and to integrate it with ethnic content, perspectives, and frames of reference.

However, this approach shares several disadvantages with the contributions approach. Its most important shortcoming is that it usually results in the viewing of ethnic content from the perspectives of mainstream historians, writers, artists, and scientists because it does not involve a restructuring of the curriculum. The events, concepts, issues, and problems selected for study are selected using mainstream-centric and Eurocentric criteria and perspectives. When teaching a unit entitled *The Westward Movement* in a fifth-grade U.S. history class, the teacher may integrate the unit by adding content about the Oglala Sioux Indians. However, the unit remains mainstream-centric and focused because of its perspective and point of view.

A unit called "The Westward Movement" is mainstream and Eurocentric because it focuses on the movement of European Americans from the Eastern to the Western part of the United States. The Oglala Sioux were already in the West and consequently were not moving westward. The unit might be called "The Invasion from the East" from the point of view of the Oglala Sioux. Black Elk, an Oglala Sioux holy man, lamented the conquering of his people, which culminated in their defeat at Wounded Knee Creek on December 29, 1890. Approximately 200 Sioux men, women, and children were killed by U.S. troops. Black Elk said, "The [Sioux] nation's hoop is broken and scattered. There is no center any longer, and the sacred tree is dead" (Neihardt, 1972, p. 230).

Black Elk did not consider his homeland "the West," but rather the center of the world. He viewed the cardinal directions metaphysically. The Great Spirit sent him the cup of living water and the sacred bow from the West. The daybreak star and the sacred pipe originated from the East. The Sioux nation's sacred hoop and the tree that was to bloom came from the South (Black Elk's Prayer, 1964). When teaching about the movement of the Europeans across North America, teachers should help students understand that different cultural, racial, and ethnic groups often have varying and conflicting conceptions and points of view about the same historical events, concepts, issues, and developments. The victors and the vanquished, especially, often have conflicting conceptions of the same historical event. However, it is usually the point of view of the victors that becomes institutionalized within the schools and the mainstream society. This happens because history and textbooks are usually written by people who won the wars and gained control of the society, and not by the losers—the victimized and the powerless. The perspectives of both groups are needed to help us fully understand our history, culture, and society.

The people who are conquered and the people who conquered them have histories and cultures that are intricately interwoven and interconnected. They have to learn each others' histories and cultures to understand their own fully. White Americans cannot fully understand their own history in the Western United States and in America without understanding the history of the American Indians and the ways their histories and the histories of the Indians are interconnected.

James Baldwin (1985) insightfully pointed out that when White Americans distort African American history, they do not learn the truth about their own history because the history of Blacks and Whites in the United States is tightly bound together. This is also true for African American history and Indian history. The history of African Americans and Indians in the United States is closely interconnected, as Katz (1986) documents in his book *Black Indians: A Hidden Heritage*. The additive approach fails to help students view society from diverse cultural and ethnic perspectives and to understand the ways that the histories and cultures of the nation's diverse ethnic, racial, cultural, and religious groups are interconnected.

Multicultural history enables students and teachers to understand America's complexity and the ways in which various groups within the United States are interconnected. Sam Hamod (cited in Reed, 1997) describes the way in which diverse ethnic perspectives enrich our understandings and lead to more accurate versions of U.S. society: "Our dual vision of 'ethnic' and American allows us to see aspects of the U.S. that mainstream writers often miss; thus, our perspectives often allow us a diversity of visions that, ironically, may lead us to larger truth—it's just that we were raised with different eyes" (p. xxii).

Content, materials, and issues that are added to a curriculum as appendages instead of being integral parts of a unit of instruction can become problematic. Problems might result when a book such as *The Color Purple* or a film like *Miss Jane Pittman* is added to a unit when the students lack the concepts, content background, and emotional maturity to deal with the issues and problems in these materials. The effective use of such emotion-laden and complex materials usually requires that the teacher help students acquire, in a sequential and developmental fashion, the content background and attitudinal maturity to deal with them effectively. The use of both of these materials in different classes and schools has resulted in major problems for the teachers using them. A community controversy arose in each case. The problems developed because the material was used with students who had neither the content background nor the attitudinal sophistication to respond to them appropriately. Adding ethnic content to the curriculum in a sporadic and segmented way can result in pedagogical problems, trouble for the teacher, student confusion, and community controversy.

The Transformation Approach

The transformation approach differs fundamentally from the contributions and additive approaches. In these two approaches, ethnic content is added to the mainstream core curriculum without changing its basic assumptions, nature, and structure. The fundamental goals, structure, and perspectives of the curriculum are changed in the transformation approach.

The transformation approach (Level 3 in Figure 10.1) changes the basic assumptions of the curriculum and enables students to view concepts, issues, themes, and problems from several ethnic perspectives and points of view. The mainstream-centric perspective is one of only several perspectives from which issues, problems, concepts, and issues are viewed. Richard White (1991), the Western historian, indicates how viewing the American West from a transformative perspective can offer new insights into U.S. history. He writes, "The first Europeans to penetrate the West arrived neither as conquerors nor as explorers. Like so many others history has treated as discoverers, they were merely lost" (p. 5).

It is neither possible nor desirable to view every issue, concept, event, or problem from the point of view of every U.S. ethnic group. Rather, the goal should be to enable students to view concepts and issues from more than one perspective and from the point of view of the cultural, ethnic, and racial groups that were the most active participants in, or were most cogently influenced by, the event, issue, or concept being studied.

The key curriculum issues involved in multicultural curriculum reform is not the addition of a long list of ethnic groups, heroes, and contributions, but the infusion of various perspectives, frames of references, and content from different groups that will extend students' understandings of the nature, development, and complexity of U.S. society. When students are studying the revolution in the British colonies, the perspectives of the Anglo revolutionaries, the Anglo loyalists, African Americans, Indians, and the British are essential for them to attain a thorough understanding of this significant event in U.S. history (see Figure 10.2). Students must study the various and sometimes divergent meanings of the revolution to these diverse groups to understand it fully (Gay & Banks, 1975).

In the language arts, when students are studying the nature of U.S. English and proper language use, they should be helped to understand the rich linguistic and language diversity in the United States and the ways that a wide range of regional, cultural, and ethnic groups have influenced the development of U.S. English. Students should also examine how normative language use varies with the social context, the region, and the situation. The use of Black English is appropriate in some social and cultural contexts and inappropriate in others (Perry & Delpit, 1998). This is also true of standard U.S. English. The United States is rich in languages and dialects. The nation has more than 20 million Latino citizens; Spanish is the first language for most of them. Most of the nation's approximately 30 million African Americans speak both standard English as well as some form of Black English or Ebonics (Perry & Delpit, 1998). The rich language diversity in the United States includes more than twenty-five European languages; Asian, African, and Middle-Eastern languages; and American Indian languages. Since the 1970s, languages from Indochina, spoken by groups such as the Hmong, Vietnamese, Laotians, and the Cambodians, have further enriched language diversity in the United States.

When subjects such as music, dance, and literature are studied, the teacher should acquaint students with the ways these art forms among U.S. ethnic groups have greatly influenced and enriched the nation's artistic and literary traditions. The ways that African American musicians such as Bessie Smith, W. C. Handy, and Leontyne Price have influenced the nature and development of U.S. music should be examined when the development of U.S. music is studied. African Americans and Puerto Ricans have significantly influenced the development of American dance. Writers of color, such as Langston Hughes, Toni Morrison, N. Scott Momaday, Carlos Bulosan, Maxine Hong Kingston, Rudolfo A. Anaya, and Piri Thomas, have not only significantly influenced the development of American literature, but have also provided unique and revealing perspectives on U.S. society and culture (Gillan & Gillan, 1994; Rico & Mano, 1995).

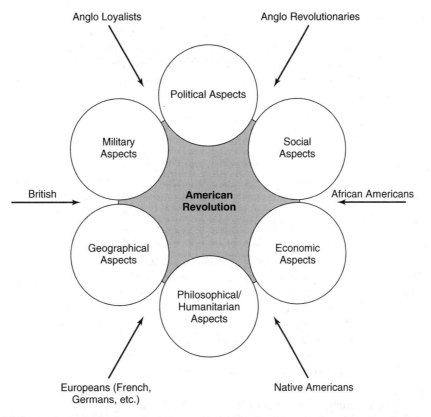

Figure 10.2   A Multicultural Interdisciplinary Model for Teaching the American Revolution

Source: James A. Banks and Geneva Gay, "Teaching the American Revolution: A Multiethnic Approach," *Social Education,* Vol. 39, No. 7 (November-December 1975): 462. Used with permission of National Council for Social Studies.

When studying U.S. history, language, music, arts, science, and mathematics, the emphasis should not be on the ways that various ethnic and cultural groups have contributed to mainstream U.S. society and culture. The emphasis should be on how the common U.S. culture and society emerged from a complex synthesis and interaction of the diverse cultural elements that originated within the various cultural, racial, ethnic, and religious groups that make up U.S. society. I call this process *multiple acculturation* and argue that even though Anglo-Saxon Protestants are the dominant group in the United States—culturally, politically, and economically—it is misleading and inaccurate to describe U.S. culture and society as an Anglo-Saxon Protestant culture (Banks, 2001). Other U.S. ethnic and cultural groups have deeply influenced, shaped, and participated in the development and formation of U.S. society and culture. African Americans, for example, profoundly influenced the development of the U.S. Southern culture, even though they had very little political and economic power. One irony of conquest is that those who are conquered often deeply influence the cultures of the conquerors.

A multiple acculturation conception of U.S. society and culture leads to a perspective that views ethnic events, literature, music, and art as integral parts of the common, shared U.S. culture. Anglo-Saxon Protestant culture is viewed as only a part of this larger cultural whole. Thus, to teach American literature without including significant writers of color, such as those named on page 234, gives a partial and incomplete view of U.S. literature, culture, and society.

The Social Action Approach

The social action approach (Level 4 in Figure 10.1) includes all the elements of the transformation approach but adds components that require students to make decisions and take actions related to the concept, issue, or problem studied in the unit (Banks & Banks, with Clegg, 1999). Major goals of instruction in this approach are to educate students for social criticism and social change and to teach them decision-making skills. To empower students and help them acquire *political efficacy*, the school must help them become reflective social critics and skilled participants in social change. The traditional goal of schooling has been to socialize students so they would accept unquestioningly the existing ideologies, institutions, and practices within society and the nation-state (Hahn, 1998).

Political education in the United States has traditionally fostered political passivity rather than political action. A major goal of the social action approach is to help students acquire the knowledge, values, and skills they need to participate in social change so that victimized and excluded ethnic and racial groups can become full participants in U.S. society and so the nation will move closer to attaining its democratic ideals. To participate effectively in democratic social change, students must be taught social criticism and must be helped to understand the inconsistency between our ideals and social realities, the work that must be done to close this gap, and how students can, as individuals and groups, influence the social and political systems in U.S. society. In this approach, teachers are agents of social change who promote democratic values and the empowerment of students. Teaching units organized using the social action approach have the components described below.

1. *A decision-problem or question.* An example of a question is: What actions should we take to reduce prejudice and discrimination in our school?

2. *An inquiry that provides data related to the decision problem.* The inquiry might consist of these kinds of questions:

    a.   What is prejudice?

    b.   What is discrimination?

    c.   What causes prejudice?

    d.   What causes people to discriminate?

    e.   What are examples of prejudice and discrimination in our nation, community, and school?

    f.   How do prejudice and discrimination affect the groups below? How does each group view prejudice? Discrimination? To what extent is each group a victim or a perpetuator of prejudice and discrimination?

    g. How has each group dealt with prejudice and discrimination? (Groups: White mainstream Americans, African Americans, Asian Americans, Hispanic Americans, Native Americans.)

The inquiry into the nature of prejudice and discrimination would be interdisciplinary and would include readings and data sources in the various social sciences, biography, fiction, poetry, and drama. Scientific and statistical data would be used when students investigated how discrimination affects the income, occupations, frequency of diseases, and health care within these various groups.

    3. *Value inquiry and moral analysis.* Students are given opportunities to examine, clarify, and reflect on their values, attitudes, beliefs, and feelings related to racial prejudice and discrimination. The teacher can provide the students with case studies from various sources, such as newspapers and magazines. The case studies can be used to involve the students in discussions and role-playing situations that enable them to express and to examine their attitudes, beliefs, and feelings about prejudice and discrimination.

Poetry, biography, and powerful fiction are excellent sources for case studies that can be used for both discussion and role playing. Countee Cullen's powerful poem "Incident" describes the painful memories of a child who was called "nigger" on a trip to Baltimore. Langston Hughes's poem "I, Too" poignantly tells how the "darker brother" is sent into the kitchen when company comes. The teacher and the students can describe verbally or write about incidents related to prejudice and discrimination they have observed or in which they have participated. The following case, based on a real-life situation, was written by the author for use with his students. After reading the case, the students discuss the questions at the end of it.

Trying to Buy a Home in Lakewood Island[1]

    About a year ago, Joan and Henry Green, a young African American couple, moved from the West Coast to a large city in the Midwest. They moved because Henry finished his Ph.D. in chemistry and took a job at a big university in Midwestern City. Since they have been in Midwestern City, the Greens have rented an apartment in the central area of the city. However, they have decided that they want to buy a house. Their apartment has become too small for the many books and other things they have accumulated during the year. In addition to wanting more space, they also want a house so that they can receive breaks on their income tax, which they do not receive living in an apartment. The Greens also think that a house will be a good financial investment.

---

[1] (Reprinted with permission from James A. Banks, *Teaching Strategies for Ethnic Studies*, 6th ed. Boston: Allyn and Bacon, 1997, pp. 234, 236)

The Greens have decided to move into a suburban community. They want a new house and most of the houses within the city limits are rather old. They also feel that they can obtain a larger house for their money in the suburbs than in the city. They have looked at several suburban communities and decided that they like Lakewood Island better than any of the others. Lakewood Island is an all-White community, which is comprised primarily of lower-middle-class and middle-class residents. There are a few wealthy families in Lakewood Island, but they are exceptions rather than the rule.

Joan and Henry Green have become frustrated because of the problems they have experienced trying to buy a home in Lakewood Island. Before they go out to look at a house, they carefully study the newspaper ads. When they arrived at the first house in which they were interested, the owner told them that his house had just been sold. A week later they decided to work with a realtor. When they tried to close the deal on the next house they wanted, the realtor told them that the owner had raised the price $10,000 because he had the house appraised since he put it on the market and had discovered that his selling price was much too low. When the Greens tried to buy a third house in Lakewood Island, the owner told them that he had decided not to sell because he had not received the job in another city that he was almost sure he would receive when he had put his house up for sale. He explained that the realtor had not removed the ad about his house from the newspaper even though he had told him that he had decided not to sell a week earlier. The realtor the owner had been working with had left the real estate company a few days ago. Henry is bitter and feels that he and his wife are victims of racism and discrimination. Joan believes that Henry is too sensitive and that they have been the victims of a series of events that could have happened to anyone, regardless of their race.

Questions: What should the Greens do? Why?

4. *Decision-making and social action* (synthesis of knowledge and values). Students acquire knowledge about their decision problem from the activities in 2, above. This interdisciplinary knowledge provides them with the information they need to make reflective decisions about prejudice and discrimination in their communities and schools. The activities in 3 enable them to identify, clarify, and analyze their values, feelings, and beliefs about prejudice and discrimination: The decision-making process enables the students to synthesize their knowledge and values to determine what actions, if any, they should take to reduce prejudice and discrimination in their schools. They can develop a chart in which they list possible actions to take and their possible consequences. They can then decide on a course of action to take and implement it.

Mixing and Blending Approaches

The four approaches for the integration of multicultural content into the curriculum (see Table 10.1) are often mixed and blended in actual teaching situations. One approach, such as the contributions approach, can be used as a vehicle to move to other, more intellectually challenging approaches, such as the transformation and social action approaches. It is unrealistic to expect a teacher to move directly from a highly mainstream-centric curriculum to one that focuses on decision-making and social action. Rather, the move from the first to higher levels of multicultural content integration is likely to be gradual and cumulative.

A teacher who has a mainstream-centric curriculum might use the school's Martin Luther King, Jr.'s, birthday celebration as an opportunity to integrate the curriculum with ethnic content about King, as well as to think seriously about how content about African Americans and other ethnic groups can be integrated into the curriculum in an ongoing fashion. The teacher could explore with the students these kinds of questions during the celebration:

1. What were the conditions of other ethnic groups during the time that King was a civil rights leader?

2. How did other ethnic groups participate in and respond to the civil rights movement?

3. How did these groups respond to Martin Luther King, Jr.?

4. What can we do today to improve the civil rights of groups of color?

5. What can we do to develop more positive racial and ethnic attitudes?

The students will be unable to answer all the questions they have raised about ethnic groups during the celebration of Martin Luther King, Jr.'s birthday. Rather, the questions will enable the students to integrate content about ethnic groups throughout the year as they study such topics as the family, the school, the neighborhood, and the city. As the students study these topics, they can use the questions they have formulated to investigate ethnic families, the ethnic groups in their school and in schools in other parts of the city, ethnic neighborhoods, and various ethnic institutions in the city such as churches, temples, synagogues, schools, restaurants, and community centers.

As a culminating activity for the year, the teacher can take the students on a tour of an ethnic community in the city. However, such a tour should be both preceded and followed by activities that enable the students to develop perceptive and compassionate lenses for seeing ethnic and cultural differences and for responding to them with sensitivity. A field trip to an ethnic community or neighborhood might reinforce stereotypes and misconceptions if students lack the knowledge and insights needed to view ethnic cultures in an understanding and caring way. Theory and research indicate that contact with an ethnic group does not necessarily lead to more positive racial and ethnic attitudes (Allport, 1979; Schofield, 1995). Rather, the conditions under which the contact occurs and the quality of the interaction in the contact situation are the important variables.

Table 10.1   Banks's Approaches for the Integration of Multicultural Content

Approach	Description	Examples	Strengths	Problems
Contributions	Heroes, cultural components, holidays, and other discrete elements related to ethnic groups are added to the curriculum on special days, occasions, and celebrations.	Famous Mexican Americans are studied only during the week of Cinco de Mayo (May 5). African Americans are studied during African American History Month in February but rarely during the rest of the year. Ethnic foods are studied in the first grade with little attention devoted to the cultures in which the foods are embedded.	Provides a quick and relatively easy way to put ethnic content into the curriculum. Gives ethnic heroes visibility in the curriculum alongside mainstream heroes. Is a popular approach among teachers and educators.	Results in a superficial understanding of ethnic cultures. Focuses on the life-styles and artifacts of ethnic groups and reinforces stereotypes and misconceptions. Mainstream criteria are used to select heroes and cultural elements for inclusion in the curriculum.
Additive	This approach consists of the addition of content, concepts, themes, and perspectives to the curriculum without changing its structure.	Adding the book *The Color Purple* to a literature unit without reconceptualizing the unit or giving the students the background knowledge to understand the book. Adding a unit on the Japanese American internment to a U.S. history course without treating the Japanese in any other unit. Leaving the core curriculum intact but adding an ethnic studies course, as an elective, that focuses on a specific ethnic group.	Makes it possible to add ethnic content to the curriculum without changing its structure, which requires substantial curriculum changes and staff development. Can be implemented within the existing curriculum structure.	Reinforces the idea that ethnic history and culture are not integral parts of U.S. mainstream culture. Students view ethnic groups from Anglocentric and Eurocentric perspectives. Fails to help students understand how the dominant culture and ethnic cultures are interconnected and interrelated.
Transformation	The basic goals, structure, and nature of the curriculum are changed to enable students to view concepts, events, issues, problems, and themes from the perspectives of	A unit on the American Revolution describes the meaning of the revolution to Anglo revolutionaries, Anglo loyalists, African Americans, Indians, and the British. A unit on 20th-century U.S. literature includes works by William Faulkner, Joyce	Enables students to understand the complex ways in which diverse racial and cultural groups participated in the formation of U.S. society and culture. Helps reduce racial and ethnic encapsulation.	The implementation of this approach requires substantial curriculum revision, in-service training, and the identification and development of materials written from the perspectives of various racial and cultural groups.

Table 10.1   Continued

Approach	Description	Examples	Strengths	Problems
	diverse cultural, ethnic, and racial groups.	Carol Oates, Langston Hughes, N. Scott Momoday, Saul Bellow, Maxine Hong Kingston, Rudolfo A. Anaya, and Piri Thomas.	Enables diverse ethnic, racial, and religious groups to see their cultures, ethos, and perspective in the school curriculum. Gives students a balanced view of the nature and development of U.S. culture and society. Helps to empower victimized racial, ethnic, and cultural groups.	Staff development for the institutionalization of this approach must be continual and ongoing.
Social Action	In this approach, students identify important social problems and issues, gather pertinent data, clarify their values on the issues, make decisons, and take reflective actions to help resolve the issue or problem.	A class studies prejudice and discrimination in their school and decides to take actions to improve race relations in the school. A class studies the treatment of ethnic groups in a local newspaper and writes a letter to the newspaper publisher suggesting ways that the treatment of ethnic groups in the newspapers should be improved.	Enables students to improve their thinking, value analysis, decision-making, and social-action skills. Enables students to improve their data-gathering skills. Helps students develop a sense of political efficacy. Helps students improve their skills to work in groups.	Requires a considerable amount of curriculum planning and materials identification. May be longer in duration than more traditional teaching units. May focus on problems and issues considered controversial by some members of the school staff and citizens of the community. Students may be able to take few meaningful actions that contribute to the resolution of the social issue or problem.

GUIDELINES FOR TEACHING MULTICULTURAL CONTENT

The following fourteen guidelines are designed to help you better integrate content about ethnic groups into the school curriculum and to teach effectively in multicultural environments.

1. You, the teacher, are an extremely important variable in the teaching of ethnic content. If you have the necessary knowledge, attitudes, and skills, when you encounter racist content in materials or observe racism in the statements and behavior of students you can use these situations to teach important lessons about the experiences of ethnic groups in the United States. An informative source on

racism is Gary Howard, *We Can't Teach What We Don't Know: White Teachers, Multiracial Schools*. New York: Teachers College Press, 1999. Another helpful source on this topic is Chapter 11 in this book.

2. Knowledge about ethnic groups is needed to teach ethnic content effectively. Read at least one major book that surveys the histories and cultures of U.S. ethnic groups. One book that includes historical overviews of U.S. ethnic groups is James A. Banks, *Teaching Strategies for Ethnic Studies*, 6th ed. (Boston: Allyn and Bacon, 1997).

3. Be sensitive to your own racial attitudes, behavior, and the statements you make about ethnic groups in the classroom. A statement such as "Sit like an Indian" stereotypes Native Americans.

4. Make sure that your classroom conveys positive images of various ethnic groups. You can do this by displaying bulletin boards, posters, and calendars that show the racial and ethnic diversity within U.S. society.

5. Be sensitive to the racial and ethnic attitudes of your students and do not accept the belief, which has been refuted by research, that "kids do not see colors." Since the pioneering research by Lasker (1929), researchers have known that very young children are aware of racial differences and that they tend to accept the evaluations of various racial groups that are normative within the wider society. Do not try to ignore the racial and ethnic differences that you see; try to respond to these differences positively and sensitively. Chapter 11 of this book provides thoughtful guidelines for avoiding the "colorblind" phenomenon. Also see Walter Stephan, *Reducing Prejudice and Stereotyping in Schools* (New York: Teachers College Press, 1999).

6. Be judicious in your choice and use of teaching materials. Some materials contain both subtle and blatant stereotypes of ethnic groups. Point out to the students when an ethnic group is stereotyped, omitted from, or described in materials from Anglocentric and Eurocentric points of view. A useful guide for teachers of young children is Louise Derman-Sparks and the A. B. C. Task Force (1989), *Anti-Bias Curriculum, Tools for Empowering Young Children* (Washington, DC: National Association for the Education of Young Children).

7. Use trade books, films, videotapes, and recordings to supplement the textbook treatment of ethnic groups and to present the perspectives of ethnic groups to your students. Many of these sources contain rich and powerful images of the experience of being a person of color in the United States. A large collection of books and videotapes are annotated in James A. Banks, *Teaching Strategies for Ethnic Studies*, 6th ed. (Boston: Allyn and Bacon, 1997).

8. Get in touch with your own cultural and ethnic heritage. Sharing your ethnic and cultural story with your students will create a climate for sharing in the classroom, will help motivate students to dig into their own ethnic and cultural roots, and will result in powerful learning for your students.

9. Be sensitive to the possible controversial nature of some ethnic studies materials. If you are clear about the teaching objectives you have in mind, you can often use a less controversial book or reading to attain the same objectives. *The Color*

Purple by Alice Walker (1982), for example, is a controversial book. A teacher however, who wants her students to gain insights about African Americans in the South can use *Roll of Thunder, Hear My Cry* by Mildred D. Taylor (1976) instead of *The Color Purple.*

10. Be sensitive to the developmental levels of your students when you select concepts, content, and activities related to ethnic groups. Concepts and learning activities for students in kindergarten and the primary grades should be specific and concrete. Students in these grades should study such concepts as similarities, differences, prejudice, and discrimination rather than higher-level concepts such as racism and oppression. Fiction and biographies are excellent vehicles for introducing these concepts to students in kindergarten and the primary grades. As students progress through the grades, they can be introduced to more complex concepts, examples, and activities.

(*If you teach in a racially or ethnically integrated classroom or school you should keep the following guidelines in mind.*)

11. View your students of color as winners. Many students of color have high academic and career goals. They need teachers who believe they can be successful and are willing to help them succeed. Both research and theory indicate that students are more likely to achieve highly when their teachers have high academic expectations for them.

12. Keep in mind that most parents of color are very interested in education and want their children to be successful academically even though the parents may be alienated from the school. Do not equate education with schooling. Many parents who want their children to succeed have mixed feelings about the schools. Try to gain the support of these parents and enlist them as partners in the education of their children.

13. Use cooperative learning techniques and group work to promote racial and ethnic integration in the school and classroom. Research indicates that when learning groups are racially integrated, students develop more friends from other racial groups, and race relations in the school improve. A helpful guide is Elizabeth G. Cohen's *Designing Groupwork: Strategies for the Heterogeneous Classroom,* 2nd ed. (New York: Teachers College Press, 1994).

14. Make sure that school plays, pageants, cheerleading squads, school publications, and other formal and informal groups are racially integrated. Also make sure that various ethnic and racial groups have equal status in school performances and presentations. In a multiracial school, if all of the leading roles in a school play are filled by White characters, an important message is sent to students and parents of color whether such a message was intended or not.

SUMMARY

This chapter describes the nature of the mainstream-centric curriculum and the negative consequences it has for both mainstream students and students of color. This curriculum reinforces the false sense of superiority of mainstream students and fails to reflect, validate, and celebrate the cultures of students of color. Many factors have slowed the institutionalization of a multicultural curriculum in the schools, including ideological resistance, lack of teacher knowledge of ethnic groups, and the heavy reliance of teachers on textbooks. However, the institutionalization of ethnic content into the school, college, and university curriculum has made significant progress within the last thirty years. This process needs to continue because curriculum transformation is a development that never ends.

Four approaches to the integration of ethnic content into the curriculum are identified in this chapter. In the *contributions approach*, heroes, cultural components, holidays, and other discrete elements related to ethnic groups are added to the curriculum without changing its structure. The *additive approach* consists of the addition of content, concepts, themes, and perspectives to the curriculum, with its structure remaining unchanged. In the *transformation approach*, the structure, goals, and nature of the curriculum are changed to enable students to view concepts, issues, and problems from diverse ethnic perspectives. The *social action approach* includes all elements of the transformation approach, as well as elements that enable students to identify important social issues, gather data related to them, clarify their values, make reflective decisions, and take actions to implement their decisions. This approach seeks to make students social critics and reflective agents of change. The final part of this chapter presents guidelines to help you teach ethnic content and to function more effectively in multicultural classrooms and schools.

Questions and Activities

1. What is a mainstream-centric curriculum? What are its major assumptions and goals?

2. Examine several textbooks and find examples of the mainstream-centric approach. Share these examples with colleagues in your class or workshop.

3. How does a mainstream-centric curriculum influence mainstream students and students of color?

4. According to Banks, what factors have slowed the development of a multicultural curriculum in the schools? What is the best way to overcome these factors?

5. What are the major characteristics of the following approaches to curriculum reform: the contributions approach; the additive approach; the transformation approach; the social action approach?

6. Why do you think the contributions approach to curriculum reform is so popular and widespread within schools, especially in the primary and elementary grades?

7. In what fundamental ways do the transformation and social action approaches differ from the other two approaches identified above?

8. What are the problems and promises of each of the four approaches?

9. What does the author mean by "multiple acculturation"? Do you think this concept is valid? Why or why not?

10. What problems might a teacher encounter when trying to implement the transformation and social action approaches? How might these problems be overcome?

11. Assume that you are teaching a social studies lesson about the westward movement in U.S. history and a student makes a racist, stereotypic, or misleading statement about Native Americans, such as, "The Indians were hostile to the White settlers." How would you handle this situation? Give reasons to explain why you would handle it in a particular way.

12. Develop a teaching plan in which you illustrate how you would teach a unit incorporating elements of the transformation and social action approaches to curriculum reform.

References

Allport, G. W. (1979). *The Nature of Prejudice* (25th anniversary ed.). Reading, MA: Addison-Wesley.

Asante, M. K. (1991). The Afrocentric Idea in Education. *Journal of Negro Education, 60*(2), 170–180.

Asante, M. K. and Ravitch, D. (1991). Multiculturalism: An Exchange. *The American Scholar, 60*(2), 267–276.

Baldwin, J. (1985). *The Price of the Ticket: Collected Nonfiction 1948–1985.* New York: St. Martin's Press.

Banks, J. A. (Ed.). (1996). *Multicultural Education, Transformative Knowledge and Action: Historical and Contemporary Perspectives.* New York: Teachers College Press.

Banks, J. A. (1997). *Teaching Strategies for Ethnic Studies* (6th ed.). Boston: Allyn and Bacon.

Banks, J. A. (1999). *An Introduction to Multicultural Education* (2nd ed.). Boston: Allyn and Bacon.

Banks, J. A. (2001). *Cultural Diversity and Education: Foundations, Curriculum and Teaching* (4th ed.). Boston: Allyn and Bacon.

Banks, J. A. and Banks, C. A. M., with Clegg, A. A., Jr. (1999). *Teaching Strategies for the Social Studies* (5th ed.). New York: Longman.

Banks, J. A., Beyer, B. K., Contreras, G., Craven, J., Ladson-Billings, G., McFarland, M.A., and Parker, W. C. (2000). *Adventures in Time and Place.* New York: McGraw-Hill School Division.

Bigelow, B. and Peterson, B. (1998). *Rethinking Columbus: The Next 500 Years.* Milwaukee, WI: Rethinking Schools.

Black Elk's Prayer from a Mountaintop in the Black Hills, 1931. (1964). In J. D. Forbes (Ed.), *The Indian in America's Past* (p. 69). Englewood Cliffs, NJ: Prentice-Hall.

Coleman, J. S., Campbell, E. Q., Hobson, C. J., McPartland, J., Mood, A. M., Weinfeld, F. D., and York, R. L. (1966). *Equality of Educational Opportunity.* Washington, DC: U.S. Government Printing Office.

Dilg, M. (1999). *Race and Culture in the Classroom: Teaching and Learning through Multicultural Education.* New York: Teachers College Press.

Garcia, J. (1993). The Changing Image of Ethnic Groups in Textbooks. *Phi Delta Kappan, 75*(1), 29–35.

Gates, H. L., Jr. (1999). *Wonders of the African World.* New York: Knopf.

Gay, G. and Banks, J. A. (1975). Teaching the American Revolution: A Multiethnic Approach. *Social Education, 39*(Nov.–Dec.), 461–465.

Gillan, M. M. and Gillan, J. (Eds.). (1994). *An Anthology of Contemporary Multicultural Poetry.* New York: Penguin.

Goodlad, J. I. (1984). *A Place Called School*. New York: McGraw-Hill.

Hahn, C. L. (1998). *Becoming Political: Comparative Perspectives on Citizenship Education*. Albany: State University of New York Press.

Howard, G. (1999). *We Can't Teach What We Don't Know: White Teachers, Multiracial Schools*. New York: Teachers College Press.

Katz, W. L. (1986). *Black Indians: A Hidden Heritage*. New York: Atheneum.

Ladson-Billings, G. (1994). *The Dreamkeepers: Successful Teachers of African American Children*. San Francisco: Jossey-Bass.

Lasker, B. (1929). *Race Attitudes in Children*. New York: Henry Holt.

Loewen, J. W. (1995). *Lies My Teacher Taught Me: Everything Your American History Textbook Got Wrong*. New York: The New Press.

Loewen, J. W. (1999). *Lies across America: What Our Historic Sites Get Wrong*. New York: The New Press.

Lundquist, B. and Szego, C. K. (Eds.). (1998). *Musics of the World's Cultures: A Source Book for Music Educators*. Reading (United Kingdom), University of Reading: International Society for Music Education (ISME).

Martin, P. and Midgley, E. (1999). Immigration to the United States. *Population Bulletin, 54*(2), 1–44. Washington, DC: Population Reference Bureau.

Neihardt, J. G. (1972). *Black Elk Speaks*. New York: Pocket Books.

Perry, T. and Delpit, L. (Eds.). (1998). *The Real Ebonics Debate: Power, Language, and the Education of African-American Children*. Boston: Beacon Press.

Ravitch, D. (1990). Diversity and Democracy: Multicultural Education in America. *American Educator,* (Spring), 16–48.

Reed, I. (Ed.). (1997). *MultiAmerica: Essays on Cultural Wars and Cultural Peace*. New York: Viking.

Rico, B. R. and Mano, S. (Eds.). (1995). *American Mosaic: Multicultural Readings in Context* (2nd ed.). Boston: Houghton Mifflin.

Schlesinger, A. M., Jr. (1991). *The Disuniting of America: Reflections on a Multicultural Society*. Knoxville, TN: Whittle Direct Books.

Schofield, J. W. (1995). Improving Intergroup Relations among Students. In J. A. Banks and C. A. M. Banks (Eds.), *Handbook of Research on Multicultural Education* (pp. 635–646). New York: Macmillan.

Sleeter, C. E. and Grant, C. A. (1991). Race, Class, Gender, and Disability in Current Textbooks. In M. W. Apple and L. K. Christian-Smith (Eds.), *The Politics of the Textbook* (pp. 78–110). New York: Routledge.

Social Science Education Consortium. (1982). *The Current State of Social Studies: A Report of Project SPAN*. Boulder, CO: Author.

Taylor, M. (1976). *Roll of Thunder, Hear My Cry*. New York: Dial.

Walker, A. (1982). *The Color Purple*. New York: Harcourt Brace.

White, R. (1991). *"It's Your Misfortune and None of My Own": A New History of the American West*. Norman: University of Oklahoma Press.

Zinn, H. (1999). *A People's History of the United States* (20th anniversary ed.). New York: Harper/Collins.

Zinn, H. and Kirschner, G. (1995). *A People's History of the United States: The Wall Charts*. New York: The New Press.

CHAPTER 11

The Colorblind Perspective in School: Causes and Consequences

Janet Ward Schofield

INTRODUCTION

Race matters, or at least it has historically in the United States. Racial group membership is the basis on which individuals were treated as the property of others and denied the basic rights of citizenship even after the formal abolition of slavery. The civil rights laws passed in the middle of the twentieth century were designed to do away with such group-based discrimination—to dismantle dual school systems, to ensure political rights, and to prevent discrimination in employment and housing, among other things.

However, the passage of these laws created a situation that Jones (1998) has called the "New American Dilemma"—a conflict between "the values embodied in the democratic principles of freedom and equality without regard to race, and . . . the belief that current as well as cumulative racial biases persist making it necessary to take race into account in order to realize the principles of freedom and equality" (p. 645). The first of these perspectives was given voice by Supreme Court Justice John Marshall Harlan in his famous call for a colorblind society in his dissenting opinion in *Plessy* v. *Ferguson*. A colorblind society is one in which racial or ethnic group membership is irrelevant to the way individuals are treated (Rist, 1974). People in favor of colorblind approaches to policy argue that taking cognizance of group membership in decision making is illegitimate since it is likely to lead either to discrimination against minority groups or to reverse discrimination in their favor. Neither of these actions is viewed as desirable. The people aligned with this side of the debate argue that since the laws that systematically disadvantaged African Americans were overturned decades ago a fair system is now in place and that this system can only be truly fair to the extent that it completely ignores group membership—treating individuals solely as individuals and striving to ignore race or ethnicity completely.

Yet, others, such as Levin (2000), argue that such an approach is the antithesis of fairness—that it is akin to a race between a well-nourished and well-trained athlete whom most of the spectators are rooting for and an individual who has just been released from an unjust prison term during which food was sparse and opportunities for exercise and training were denied. People taking this perspective agree with Justice Harry Blackmun, who wrote in the *Regents of the University of California* v. *Bakke* (1978) case that "in order to get beyond racism, we must first take account of race. In order to treat persons equally, we must treat them differently" (pp. 2806–2808). They contend that the reality of continuing racism (Jones, 1997; Sidanius & Pratto, 1999; Trent, Owens-Nicholson, Eatman, Burke, Daugherty, & Norman, 2000) as well as the continuing impact of prior discrimination, such as the striking difference in net worth among Blacks and Whites with similar incomes due at least in part in larger inheritances received by Whites (Jaynes & Williams, 1989), make policies designed specifically to promote the inclusion of African Americans in the economic and political life of the country both just and wise. Thus, they tend to support affirmative action and other related policies designed to do this by explicitly taking account of the relative participation rates of various groups—an approach at direct odds with the colorblind approach.

The New American Dilemma is complex and unlikely to be easily solved. Full consideration of it would of necessity involve philosophical and historical issues as well as issues of psychology, law, ethics, economics, and politics. Thus, this chapter does not try to solve this dilemma. Rather, it has a more modest but nonetheless important goal—to provide a glimpse of how the colorblind perspective works in reality in one of the most important institutions in our society—its schools.

I did not set out initially to explore this question. Rather, as a scholar deeply interested in the potential of interracial school settings for improving intergroup relations, I embarked on a longitudinal ethnographic study designed to illuminate the nature of peer relations in a desegregated school and the impact that school policies, structures, and culture have on those relations (Schofield, 1989). It just so happened that having chosen a particular school for study, as described below, I found myself in an environment that strongly endorsed the colorblind perspective. Furthermore, over time, it became apparent that the institution's endorsement of this perspective had important consequences that people at the school did not anticipate and often did not recognize. Thus, the causes and consequences of this perspective became the focus of the part of my research reported here.

I argue that two basic factors make understanding the implications of the colorblind perspective important. First, evidence suggests that this perspective is widespread in schools both within the United States and elsewhere, either as part of official policy or as an informal but nonetheless powerful social norm (Gillborn, 1992; Jervis, 1996; Rist, 1978; Sagar & Schofield, 1984; Sleeter, 1993). Second, the colorblind approach is also frequently espoused as a goal to be sought in many other realms, including employment practices and judicial proceedings. This research led me to conclude that although in many ways the colorblind perspective is appealing because it is consistent with a long-standing American emphasis on the importance of the individual, it easily leads to a misrepresentation of reality in ways that allow and sometimes even encourage discrimination against minority group members, as later parts of this chapter demonstrate.

THE RESEARCH SITE: WEXLER MIDDLE SCHOOL

In choosing a site for the research, I adopted a strategy that Cook and Campbell (1976) call "generalizing to target instances." The aim was not to study what happens in a typical desegregated school, if such an entity can even be said to exist. Rather, it was to explore peer relations under conditions that theory suggests should be relatively conducive to positive relations between Blacks and Whites.

Nearly fifty years ago in his classic book *The Nature of Prejudice*, Allport (1954) proposed that intergroup contact may reinforce previously held stereotypes and increase intergroup hostility unless the contact situation is structured in a way that (1) provides equal status for minority and majority group members, (2) encourages cooperation toward shared, strongly desired goals, and (3) provides institutional support for positive relations. These ideas, as elaborated and refined by more recent theoretical and empirical work (Amir, 1969; 1976; Cook, 1969; 1985; Hewstone & Brown, 1986; Pettigrew, 1986; 1998; Schofield, 1995; Schofield & Eurich-Fulcer, in press), constitute a useful foundation for understanding the likely outcomes of interracial contact. For example, although equal status may be neither an absolutely necessary prerequisite nor a sufficient condition for change, it does appear to be very helpful (Amir, 1969; 1976; Brewer & Brown 1998; Brown, 1995; Cohen, 1975; Cohen, Lockheed, & Lohman, 1976; Cook, 1978; 1985; Norvell & Worchel, 1981; Pettigrew, 1998; Riordan, 1978; Schofield & Eurich-Fulcer, in press; Stephan & Stephan, 1996). In addition, a substantial body of research suggests that cooperation toward mutually desired goals is indeed generally conducive to improved intergroup relations (Aronson, Blaney, Stephan, Sikes, & Snapp, 1978; Bossert, 1988/89; Cook, 1978; 1985; Johnson & Johnson, 1982; Johnson, Johnson, & Maruyama, 1984; Johnson, Maruyama, Johnson, Nelson, & Skon, 1981; Schofield, 1995; Sharan, 1980; Sherif, 1979; Slavin, 1995; Stephan & Stephan, 1996).

Wexler Middle School was constructed in a large industrial northeastern city to serve as a model of high quality integrated education. When it first opened, Wexler had a student body almost precisely 50 percent African American and 50 percent White, mirroring closely the proportion of Black and White students in the city's public schools. This school, which serves 1,200 children in sixth through eighth grades, was chosen for study because the decisions made in planning for it suggested that it would come reasonably close to meeting the conditions specified by Allport and the more recent theorists who have built on his work. The school's strong efforts to provide a positive environment for interracial education can be illustrated by examination of its staffing policy. The administration, faculty, and staff of the school are biracial, with about 25 percent of the faculty being African American. The top four administrative positions are filled by two Blacks and two Whites, clearly symbolizing the school's commitment to providing equal status for members of both groups.

The extent to which Wexler met the conditions specified by Allport and his intellectual heirs as conducive to the development of improved intergroup relations has been discussed at length elsewhere (Schofield, 1989). Here, I merely report the conclusion drawn in that discussion—that Wexler came considerably closer to these criteria than did most desegregated public schools. Yet, it fell seriously short of meeting them completely in a number of ways, many of which were the direct result of societal conditions over which Wexler had little or no control. For example, in spite of Wexler's commitment to a staffing pattern that would provide equal formal status for African Americans and Whites, the proportion of Black teachers on its staff was considerably lower than the proportion of Black students in the school because the school system did not want to put too high a proportion of its Black teachers in one school.

In addition, a large majority of Wexler's White students came from middle- or upper-middle-class homes. Although some of the African American children were middle-class, the majority came from either poor or working-class families. These social-class differences had implications for the status of Black and White students within the school. For example, in the eighth grade, which divided students into a "regular" and a "gifted" track, a much higher proportion of the White than African American students achieved scores on standardized tests that led to their placement in the gifted track. Even in the sixth or seventh grades, which had academically heterogenous classes, this difference influenced students' status (Schofield, 1980), although not in a way emphasized and formalized by a tracking policy. In sum, Wexler made stronger than usual efforts to foster positive relations between Blacks and Whites but fell markedly short of being a theoretically ideal milieu for the accomplishment of this goal.

DATA GATHERING

The analysis that follows is based on an intensive four-year study of peer relations at Wexler. The basic data-gathering strategy was intensive and extensive observation in Wexler's classrooms, hallways, playgrounds, and cafeteria. Observers used the full field-note method for recording the events they witnessed (Olson, 1976). A large number of events were observed because they were representative of the events that filled most of the school day at Wexler. However, an important subgroup of events was oversampled in relation to their frequency of occurrence because of their direct relevance to the study's focus. This strategy, which Glaser and Strauss (1967) call theoretical sampling, led to oversampling certain activities, such as affective education classes, designed to help students get to know each other, and meetings of Wexler's interracial student advisory group set up to handle the special problems students may face in a desegregated school. Over the course of the study, more than 500 hours were devoted to observation of students and staff at Wexler.

A wide variety of other data-gathering techniques ranging from sociometric questionnaires to experimental work was also used (Sagar & Schofield, 1980; Schofield, 1979; Schofield & Francis, 1982; Schofield & Sagar, 1977; Schofield & Whitley, 1983; Whitley & Schofield, 1984). Interviews were employed extensively. For example, randomly selected students participated in open-ended interviews twice a year. Teachers and administrators were also interviewed repeatedly. In addition, graffiti in the bathrooms and on the school walls were routinely recorded, school bulletins were collected, and careful note was taken of such things as wall decorations and public address system announcements.

Space does not allow full discussion of the many varied techniques used in collecting and analyzing the data on which this chapter is based. However, two general principles that guided the research must be mentioned. First, both data-gathering and analysis were as rigorous and systematic as possible. For example, sampling techniques were employed where appropriate; trained coders, who were unaware of the race and sex of particular respondents, coded the open-ended interviews using reliable systems developed for this research; and field notes were carefully indexed so that all notes relevant to a given topic could be examined.

Second, because it is often impossible to achieve extremely high levels of precision and control in field research, strong efforts were made to triangulate the data (Webb, Campbell, Schwartz, & Sechrest, 1966). Great care was taken to gather many different types of information bearing on the same issue, to minimize the potential problems with each data source, and to be sensitive in analyzing and interpreting the data to biases that could not be completely eliminated. The basic approach used in the analysis of the qualitative data is outlined in works such as Becker and Greer (1960), Bogdan and Taylor (1975), Campbell (1975), Miles and Huberman (1984), and Strauss and Corbin (1990). Fuller details on data-gathering and analysis are presented elsewhere, as is information on the strategies used to minimize observer reactivity and bias (Schofield, 1989; Schofield & Sagar, 1979).

THE COLORBLIND PERSPECTIVE AND ITS COROLLARIES

Wexler's faculty clearly tended to subscribe to the colorblind view of interracial schooling. Interviews with both African American and White teachers suggested that the majority of both groups tended to see Wexler as an institution that could help impart middle-class values and modes of behavior to lower-class students so that they could break out of the cycle of poverty and become middle-class persons themselves. Even though most of these lower-class students were African American, race was seen as quite incidental to the anticipated class assimilation process.

A Black administrator, with perhaps more candor than many similarly oriented White administrators and teachers, made her class assimilation goals explicit and, at the same time, made it clear just which students needed to be so assimilated:

> I really don't address myself to group differences when I am dealing with youngsters. . . . I try to treat youngsters, I don't care who they are, as youngsters and not as Black, White, green or yellow. . . . Many of the Black youngsters who have difficulty are the ones who . . . have come from communities where they had to put up certain defenses and these defenses are the antithesis of the normal situation . . . like they find in school. It is therefore [difficult] getting them to become aware that they have to follow these rules because [they] are here . . . not over there in their community. . . . I think that many of the youngsters [from the] larger community have a more normal set of values that people generally want to see, and therefore do not have [as] much difficulty in coping with their school situation. . . . [The Black children] do have difficulty in adjusting because they are just not used to it. Until we can adjustively counsel them into the right types of behavior . . . I think we're going to continue to have these types of problems.

The only thing atypical in the preceding remarks is the frank acknowledgment that the children perceived as lacking "the normal set of values that people generally want to see" are typically African American. More usually, this was implicit in remarks emphasizing the negative effects of growing up in a poor family or a low-income neighborhood.

As a reaction to the invidious distinctions that have traditionally been made in the United States on the basis of race, the colorblind perspective is understandable and, from a social policy standpoint, it seems laudable. However, this orientation was accompanied at Wexler by a number of other logically related beliefs, which taken together with it had some important though largely unrecognized negative consequences. These beliefs and their basis in the ongoing social reality at Wexler are discussed individually. Then the consequences of this belief system are discussed in some detail.

Race as an Invisible Characteristic

It is not a very great leap from the colorblind perspective, which says that race is a social category of no relevance to one's behaviors and decisions, to a belief that individuals should not or perhaps even do not notice each other's racial group membership. At Wexler, acknowledging that one was aware of another's race was viewed by many people as a possible sign of prejudice, as illustrated by the following excerpt from project field notes:

> When I was arranging the student interviews, I mentioned to Mr. Little [White] that I thought there was only one White girl in one of his classes. I asked if I was right about this and he said, "Well, just a minute. Let me check." After looking through the class roster in his roll book he said, "You know, you're right. I never noticed that. . . . I guess that's a good thing." Our data suggest that teachers not only denied that they noticed children's race when the researchers were present, but also did so among themselves. For example, when complying with a request to mark down the race of his students on a class roster for research purposes a White teacher remarked, "Did you ever notice those teachers who say, 'I never notice what they are?'"

Although there was less unanimity on the issue of whether students noticed the race of others than of whether teachers did, a substantial proportion of Wexler's faculty asserted that the students rarely noticed race. This point of view is exemplified by the following excerpt from an interview with an African American science teacher:

MS. MONROE: You know, I hear the things the students usually fight about. As I said before, it's stupid things like someone taking a pencil. It's not because [the other person] is Black or White. . . . At this age level . . . I don't think it's Black or White.

INTERVIEWER: There's something I'm wondering about. It is hard to believe, given the way our society is, that you can just bring kids together and they won't be very much aware.

MS. MONROE: They just go about their daily things and don't . . . I don't think they think about it really. . . . I see them interacting with one another on an adult basis. . . . They are not really aware of color . . . or race or whatever.

INTERVIEWER: You really don't see that as a factor . . . in their relationships?

MS. MONROE: No.

Although the faculty at Wexler saw themselves, and to a lesser extent their students, as oblivious to the race of others, a wide variety of data suggest that this view was not accurate. Most removed from the specific situation at Wexler but nonetheless pertinent is a substantial body of data from research on stereotyping and person perception. This work suggests that individuals tend to use preexisting categories in perceiving and responding to others (Brewer, 1988; Brown, 1995; Fiske & Neuberg, 1990). More specifically, research suggests that individuals spontaneously use the physical appearance of other people as a basis for categorizing them by race. Further, this categorization has an impact on how individuals are perceived and on how others respond to them (Devine, 1989; Dovidio, Gaertner, Voulidzic, Matoka, Johnson, & Frazier, 1997; Duncan, 1976; Fazio, Jackson, Dunton, & Williams, 1995; Katz, Wackenhut, & Hass, 1986; Katz, 1976; Malpass & Kravitz, 1969; Sagar & Schofield, 1980; Taylor, Fiske, Etcoff, & Ruderman, 1978).

The teachers and students at Wexler were to some extent self-selected members of an interracial institution and thus might conceivably be less prone to use race as a category for processing information about others than would the college student populations used in most studies on person perception cited above. However, given the importance of race as a social category in many aspects of life in the United States, it seems highly unlikely that the prevailing tendency at Wexler was for individuals not even to notice each other's race.

Interviews with students made it clear that many of them were very conscious of their race or of the race of other students, which is hardly surprising given the fact that interracial schooling was a new and somewhat threatening experience for many of them. The following excerpt from an interview in which the interviewer had not herself previously mentioned race suggests just how salient racial categories were to the children.

INTERVIEWER: Can you tell me who some of your friends are?

BEVERLY [AFRICAN AMERICAN]: Well, Stacey and Lydia and Amy, even though she's White.

Similarly, students' awareness of racial group membership is seen in an excerpt from field notes taken in a seventh-grade class with a higher-than-average proportion of African American students because the teachers had decided to put many lower-achieving children in a class by themselves.

Howard, a White male, leaned over to me (a White female observer) and said, "You know, it just wasn't fair the way they set up this class. There are sixteen Black kids and only nine White kids. I can't learn in here." I said, "Why is that?" Howard replied, "They copy and they pick on you. It just isn't fair."

Race as a Taboo Topic

Before discussing why the view that they and their students tended not even to notice race gained considerable popularity among Wexler's teachers in spite of everyday indications that this was often not the case, this section discusses two other phenomena closely related to the development of the colorblind perspective. The first was the development of a norm strong enough to be labeled a virtual taboo against the use of the words *white* and *black* in a context in which they referred to racial-group membership. Thus, for example, in almost 200 hours of observations in classrooms, hallways, and teachers' meetings during Wexler's first year, fewer than 25 direct references to race were made by school staff or students (Schofield, 1989). Any use of the words *black* and *white* in a context in which they referred to an individual or group was classified as a reference to race, as were racial epithets and words and phrases used almost exclusively within one group to express solidarity (e.g., "Hey, Brother") or the like.

The extremely infrequent reference to race was all the more surprising when one considers that our observations included a wide variety of formal and informal situations, ranging from workshops funded by the Emergency School Assistance Act, federal legislation that provided funds to desegregating schools to help them handle special problems that might arise as a result of desegregation, to informal student interactions on the playgrounds and in the hallways.

Students' awareness of the taboo is shown clearly in the following field notes, which recount a conversation with a White social worker whose work at Wexler on the extracurricular program was funded by a local foundation concerned with race relations. Perhaps not surprisingly under these circumstances, she showed much less reluctance than did most staff to deal in a straightforward manner with the issue of race.

> Ms. Fowler said that a short while ago she had heard from Martin [Black] that another child had done something wrong. The offense was serious enough so that she wanted to track down this individual. She asked Martin to describe the child who had committed the offense. Martin said, "He has black hair and he's fairly tall." He didn't give the race of the other person even though he went on to give a fairly complete description otherwise. Finally, Ms. Fowler asked, "Is he Black or White?" Martin replied, "Is it all right for me to say?" Ms. Fowler said that it was all right. . . . Martin then said, "Well, the boy was White."

Students were well aware that making references to race displeased many of their teachers and might also offend peers.

INTERVIEWER: You know, the other day I was walking around the school and heard a sixth-grade student describing a student from the seventh grade to a teacher who needed to find this student in order to return something she had lost. The sixth grader said the seventh grader was tall and thin. She described what the girl had been wearing and said her hair was dark, but she didn't say whether the girl was Black or White. . . . Why do you think she didn't mention that?

SYLVIA [AFRICAN AMERICAN]: The teacher might have got mad if she said whether she was White or Black.

INTERVIEWER: Do some teachers get mad about things like that?

SYLVIA: Some do . . . they holler. . . .

INTERVIEWER: Now, when you talk to kids who are Black, do you ever mention that someone is White or Black?

SYLVIA: No.

INTERVIEWER: What about when you're talking with kids who are White?

SYLVIA: Nope.

INTERVIEWER: You never mention race? Why not?

SYLVIA: They might think I'm prejudiced.

Social Life as a Web of Purely Interpersonal Relations

Consistent with the view that race is not, or at least should not be, a salient aspect of other individuals and with the practice of not speaking about race were tendencies to conceptualize social life as a web of interpersonal rather than intergroup relations and to assume that interpersonal relations are not much influenced by group membership. As one teacher put it:

> Peer-group identity here in middle school . . . has nothing to do
> with race. There's a strong tendency to group that exists independent
> of . . . racial boundaries. . . . We started in September with these
> students letting them know we weren't going to fool around with
> that. . . . You're a student and we don't care what color you are.

This tendency to minimize the potential importance of intergroup processes was illustrated clearly during an in-service training session, the stated purpose of which was to help teachers deal effectively with the racially heterogeneous student body. The facilitator, a White clinical psychologist employed by a local foundation, began by making some general statements about the importance of understanding cultural differences between students. Although the facilitator kept trying to nudge and finally to push the group to discuss ways in which the racially mixed nature of the student body influenced peer relations, appropriate curricular materials, and the like, the group ended up discussing issues such as the problems caused by individual children who acted out aggressively in the classroom, the difficulty that overweight children have in gaining peer acceptance, and the fact that children with disabilities were sometimes taunted by their classmates.

Contrasting sharply with the teachers' tendency to insist that they and their students reacted to each other exclusively as individuals and to de-emphasize the importance of intergroup as opposed to interpersonal processes was the students' willingness to discuss with interviewers the important role race played in Wexler's social life.

INTERVIEWER: I have noticed . . . that [in the cafeteria] very often White kids sit with White kids and Black kids sit with Black kids. Why do you think that this is?

MARY [WHITE]: Cause the White kids have White friends and the Black kids have Black friends. . . . I don't think integration is working. . . . Blacks still associate with Blacks and Whites still associate with Whites. . . .

INTERVIEWER: Can you think of any White kids that have quite a few Black friends or of any Black kids who have quite a few White friends?

MARY: Not really.

The tendency for students to group themselves by race in a variety of settings was very marked. For example, on a fairly typical day at the end of the school's second year of operation 119 White and 90 African American students attended the seventh-grade lunch period.

Of these more than 200 children, only 6 sat next to someone of the other race (Schofield & Sagar, 1977).

Of course, it is possible that race itself was not a factor in producing such interaction patterns, but something correlated with race such as socioeconomic status, academic achievement, or the opportunity for previous contact with each other. Such factors did appear to reinforce the tendency to prefer intragroup interactions and were often cited by teachers as the actual cause of the visually apparent tendency of students to cluster with those of their own race. Yet, the results of an experiment conducted at Wexler demonstrate that race itself was a real factor in peer relations. In this study, eighty male sixth graders were presented with carefully drawn pictures of a number of ambiguously aggressive types of peer interactions that were quite common at Wexler, such as poking another student with a pencil. For each type of interaction, some students were shown pictures in which both students were African American, others saw pictures in which both students were White, and others saw mixed race dyads with the Black student shown as either the initiator of the behavior or as the student to whom it was directed.

The results suggested that the race of the person initiating the behavior influenced how mean and threatening the behavior was interpreted as being (Sagar & Schofield, 1980) (see Table 11.1). Such a finding is, of course, inconsistent with the notion that students take

Table 11.1   Mean Ratings of Both White and Black Actors' Ambiguously Aggressive Behaviors by White and Black Subjects

Subject Group	Actor Race	Rating Scale: Mean/Threatening
White	White	8.28
	Black	8.99
Black	White	7.38
	Black	8.40

Note. Means are based on sums of paired 7-point scales indicating how well the given adjective described the behaviors, from 1 (not at all) to 7 (exactly). N = 40 in each group. Each subject rated two White and two Black actors (e.g., the perpetrator of the ambiguously aggressive act) and two White and Black targets. The 4 × 4 nature of the Latin square required treating the race permutations as four levels of a single factor. Significant F values on this factor provided justification for testing actor race, target race, and interaction effects with simple contrasts, using the error variance estimate generated by the ANOVA. The significant main effect of race permutations on the summed mean/threatening scales, $F(3,192) = 3.02$, $p < .05$, was found to reflect, as predicted, tendency for subjects to rate the behaviors by Black actors more mean/threatening than identical behaviors by White actors, $t(144) = 2.90$, $p < .01$. Means are not broken down by target race because no statistically significant main effects or interactions were found for this variable.

Source: From Sagar, H. A., and Schofied, J. W. (1980). Racial and Behavioral Cues in Black and White Children's Perceptions of Ambiguously Aggressive Acts. *Journal of Personality and Social Psychology, 39*(4) 590–598. Copyright 1980 by the American Psychological Association. Adapted with permission.

no notice of others' race. It is also incompatible with the idea that intergroup processes have no influence on students' reactions to their peers because the data suggest that the perception of an individual's behavior is influenced by the group membership of the person performing it.

THE FUNCTIONS AND CONSEQUENCES OF THE COLORBLIND PERSPECTIVE AND ITS COROLLARIES

Regardless of the fact that the colorblind perspective and its corollaries were not completely accurate views of the social processes occurring at Wexler, they appeared to influence the development of the social fabric at Wexler in ways that had a number of important consequences, some positive and some negative. The following discussion of the functions of this set of beliefs suggests why the colorblind perspective was attractive to teachers and how it affected both the education and social experiences of Wexler's students.

Reducing the Potential for Overt Conflict

One concern that typifies many desegregated schools, and that is often especially salient in newly desegregated situations, is a desire to avoid dissension and conflict that are or could appear to be race related (Sagar & Schofield, 1984). The adoption of colorblind policies is often seen as useful in achieving this goal because if such policies are implemented fully they can help protect the institution and people in positions of responsibility in it from charges of discrimination. This is not to say that such policies lead to equal outcomes for members of all groups. Indeed, when there are initial group differences on criteria relevant to success in a given institution, such policies are likely to lead to differential outcomes, a situation that some people would characterize as institutional racism (Jones, 1997). However, as noted earlier, the colorblind perspective is consistent with notions of fairness that have long held sway in the United States and thus that can be relatively easily defended. Policies that give obvious preference to either minority or majority group members are much more likely to spark controversy and conflict.

An example from Wexler illustrates how the operation of the colorblind perspective helps to minimize overt conflict in situations in which the outcomes for Blacks and Whites as a whole are extremely different. The suspension rate for African American students at Wexler was roughly four times that for White students. The strong correlation between race and socioeconomic background at Wexler made it predictable that the African American students' behavior would be less consistent than that of White students with the basically middle-class norms prevailing in the school. However, the colorblind perspective appeared instrumental in helping to keep Wexler's discipline policies from becoming a focus of contention. To my knowledge, the disparity in suspension rates was never treated as a serious issue that needed attention. When researchers asked faculty and administrators about it, some, perhaps not altogether candidly, denied having noticed it. Others argued that it was not a problem in the sense that individual students were generally treated fairly. In fact, teachers often emphasized strongly the effort they made to treat discipline problems with White and African American students in exactly the same way.

On the relatively rare occasions in which charges of discrimination were raised by students unhappy with the way a teacher had dealt with them, teachers tended to discount the complaints by reiterating their commitment to the colorblind perspective:

> MS. WILSON [WHITE]: I try not to let myself listen to it [the charge of discrimination]. Maybe once in a while I ask myself, "Well, why would he make that statement?" But I know in my mind that I do not discriminate on the basis of race. . . . And I will not have someone create an issue like that when I know I have done my best not to create it.

Only an occasional teacher, more often than not African American, suggested that the colorblind perspective actually worked to help create the disparity in suspension rates; this issue is addressed later in this chapter. Be this as it may, the colorblind perspective clearly fostered an atmosphere that minimized the chances that the disparity itself was likely to become the focus of either overt discontent or constructive action.

Minimizing of Discomfort or Embarrassment

Many of the faculty and students at Wexler had little prior experience in desegregated schools. Also, most of them lived in neighborhoods that were either heavily White or heavily African American. Thus, for many, there was an initial sense of awkwardness and anxiety, like the intergroup anxiety Stephan and Stephan (1985) discuss. Under such circumstances, avoiding mention of race and contending that it rarely influenced relations between individuals seemed to minimize the potential for awkward or embarrassing social situations. This is related to the aforementioned conflict-avoidance function of these beliefs, but it can be distinguished conceptually because feelings of awkwardness and embarrassment can but do not always lead to conflict. In fact, these beliefs and norms seemed to help maintain the veneer of politeness that Clement, Eisenhart, and Harding (1979) have argued is part of the etiquette of race relations in some desegregated situations.

One way to illustrate the ways in which the colorblind perspective and the associated beliefs and norms helped smooth social relations between Blacks and Whites is to compare the situation at Wexler to another sort of interaction that is often rather strained, at least initially—interaction between individuals who have visible disabilities and those who do not. In a fascinating analysis of this latter situation, Davis (1961) argues that the emotion aroused in the person without disabilities by the sight of a person with disabilities creates tension and an uncertainty about what is appropriate behavior; this tension interferes with normal interaction patterns. There is a tendency for the disability to become the focus of attention and to foster ambiguity about appropriate behavior. Davis argues that the initial reaction to this situation is often a fictional denial of the disability and of its potential effect on the relationship, that is, a tendency to pretend to ignore the existence of the disability, which at least temporarily relieves the interactants of the necessity of dealing with its implications.

Analogously, one can think of the racial-group membership of individuals in a biracial interaction, be they Black or White, as a sort of visually apparent disability. Like a disability, one's group membership may provoke an affective response in other people that predisposes them to avoidance or at least raises questions about appropriate behavior. Of course, just as some individuals will feel more awkward than will others when interacting with a person with a disability, so some individuals will more likely be more affected by interacting with someone of the other race. However, to the extent that either person is perceived as a potential threat to a smooth, relaxed, and pleasant interaction, one way of handling that threat is to pretend to be unaware of the attribute that creates it.

Although Davis (1961) argues that initial interactions between people with disabilities and other people are characterized by a fictional denial of the disability, he also suggests that with time this fiction is discarded because, being based on an obvious falsehood, it is inherently unstable and in the long run dysfunctional. Similarly, I argue that although the colorblind perspective and the accompanying taboo may have made the initial adjustment to Wexler easier, in the long run they tended to inhibit the development of positive relations between African American and White students. These students were vividly aware of differences and of tensions between them that were related to their group membership. Yet such issues could not be dealt with in a straightforward manner in the colorblind climate. Thus, anger sometimes festered and stereotypes built when fuller discussion of the situation might have made it easier for individuals to see each other's perspectives.

This is not to suggest that schools have the responsibility to function as giant T-groups or as therapeutic institutions. Rather, it is to say that the refusal of many of Wexler's faculty to recognize the fundamental role that race played in peer relationships meant that these people played a less constructive role than they might have in guiding students through a new and sometimes threatening experience. Jervis (1996) observed a similar phenomenon with similar results in her study of a multi-ethnic middle school.

Increasing Teachers' Freedom of Action

The colorblind perspective and its corollaries undoubtedly gained some of their appeal because they tended to simplify life for Wexler's staff and to increase their freedom of action. An example can illustrate both points. After being asked by one member of the research team about the outcome of a closely contested student council election, a White teacher disclosed that she had purposely miscounted votes so that a 'responsible child' (a White boy) was declared the winner rather than the 'unstable child' (an African American girl) who had actually received a few more votes. The teacher seemed ambivalent about and somewhat embarrassed by her action, but the focus of her concern was her subversion of the democratic process. She reported that she had looked at the two children as individuals and decided that one was a more desirable student council representative than the other. As far as I could tell from an extended discussion with her, she did not consciously consider the race of the students involved. Further, she did not appear to consider the fact that her action had changed the racial composition of the student council.

The failure to consider such issues clearly simplified the decision-making process because there was one less item, and an affect-laden one at that, to be factored into it. Related to this, such a colorblind approach increased teachers' freedom of action because actions that sometimes appeared acceptable if one were to think about them in a colorblind way often appeared much less acceptable from a perspective that was not colorblind. Indeed, the colorblind perspective and its corollaries fostered an environment that research suggests is conducive to discriminatory behavior, at least on the part of certain types of individuals. First, work by Snyder, Kleck, Strenta, and Mentzer (1979) demonstrates that people are more likely to act in accordance with feelings they prefer not to reveal when they can appear to be acting on some other basis than when no other obvious explanation for their behavior is available. Specifically, they found that individuals avoided people with physical disabilities when such avoidance could easily be attributed to preference for a certain kind of movie.

However, when the situation did not provide this sort of rationale for avoidance behavior, the tendency to avoid people with physical disabilities disappeared. Thus, by analogy, one might expect that an environment that minimizes the importance of race and even forbids overt consideration or discussion of the topic would free individuals whose basic tendency is to discriminate (a normatively unacceptable orientation at Wexler) to do so. The vast majority of Wexler's faculty espoused basically equalitarian racial attitudes and would quite rightly be insulted by the idea that they would intentionally discriminate against their African American students. Yet, the work of Gaertner and Dovidio (1981; 1986) demonstrates that one need not be an old-fashioned racist to discriminate against African Americans when the conditions are conducive to do so.

Specifically, Gaertner and Dovidio (1981; 1986) argue that a great many liberal White people are highly motivated to maintain an image of themselves as egalitarian individuals who neither discriminate against others on the basis of race nor are prejudiced. However, the desire to maintain such an image is coupled with some negative affect and with certain beliefs that predispose them to react negatively to African Americans. This predisposition is expressed primarily in circumstances that do not threaten an egalitarian self-concept. One important relevant circumstance is the availability of non-race-related rationales for the behavior in question (Dovidio & Gaertner, 1998; Gaertner & Dovidio, 1986). It is precisely this aspect of the situation that is influenced by the colorblind perspective and its corollaries. To the extent that they help remove awareness of race from conscious consideration, they make other explanations for one's behavior relatively more salient. Thus, they free the aversive racist to act in a discriminatory fashion. Further, to the extent that the taboo at Wexler inhibited individuals from challenging the behavior of other people as racist in outcome or intent, it removed a potential barrier to racist behavior because it minimized the probability that such behavior would pose a threat to a liberal self-concept.

Ignoring the Reality of Cultural Differences between Students

Although the colorblind perspective and its corollaries served some useful purposes, they also had several unrecognized negative effects, as indicated. One important negative consequence of this mind set was a predisposition to ignore or deny the possibility of cultural differences between White and Black children that influenced how they functioned in school. For example, the differential suspension rate for African American and White children may have stemmed partially from differences between the White and Black students in what Triandis and his colleagues (Triandis, 1994; Traindis, Vassiliou, Vassiliou, Tanaka, & Shanmugam,1972) call their "subjective culture." Specifically, data from the Sagar and Schofield (1980) experiment described earlier suggested that Black boys saw certain types of ambiguously aggressive acts as less mean and threatening and as more playful and friendly than did their White peers. These behaviors were ones that sometimes began conflicts between students that resulted in suspensions. Awareness of the differential meaning of such behaviors to White and African American students might at least have suggested ways of trying to reduce the disproportionate suspension of Black students.

Other research suggests that Black-White differences in culture are not limited to this one area (Hill, 1971; Irvine, 1990; Jones, 1986;1997). For example, Kochman (1981) has argued convincingly that Black and White students use widely differing styles in classroom discussion and that misunderstanding the cultural context from which students come can lead peers and teachers to misinterpret involvement for belligerence. Heath's (1982) research suggests that the types of questions teachers typically pose in elementary school classrooms are quite similar to those asked in White middle-class homes but differ substantially from those typically addressed to young children in poor Black homes. Thus, there is reason to think that in assuming a completely colorblind perspective teachers may rule out awareness and use of information that would be helpful in deciding how best to structure materials in ways that work well for the range of students they teach as well as in interpreting many aspects of their students' behavior.

Failing to Respond to and Capitalize on Diversity

There were numerous less subtle ways in which the colorblind perspective and the accompanying de-emphasis on the biracial nature of the school worked to the disadvantage of Wexler's students, and more often to the disadvantage of African American than of White students. One of the more obvious of these concerned the extent to which efforts were made to use instructional materials and pedagogical approaches that were likely to reflect the interests and life experiences of Wexler's African American students, an approach that has been called "using culturally responsive pedagogy" (Carter & Goodwin, 1994; Irvine, 1991; Nieto, 1992; Ramsey, 1987). Wexler operated as part of a school system that made some effort to use multicultural texts. In addition, some teachers, a disproportionate number of whom were African American, took special care to relate class work to the concerns and interests likely to be found in their Black students as well as their White ones.

The prevailing tendency, however, was to abjure responsibility for making sure instructional materials reflected the diversity of the student body. Interviews with teachers suggested that many saw no reason to try to locate or develop instructional materials that reflected African Americans' participation in and contributions to our society. For example, one math teacher who used a book in which all individuals in the illustrations were White contended that "math was math" and that an interview question about the use of biracial or multicultural materials was irrelevant to his subject matter. Perhaps more surprisingly, similar claims were made by other teachers, including some who taught reading, language arts, and social studies.

The colorblind perspective and its corollaries not only made it more likely that individual faculty members would ignore the challenge of trying to present all students with materials that related in motivating ways to their own experiences, but they actually led to a constriction of the education provided to students. For example, in a lesson on the social organization of ancient Rome, one social studies teacher discussed at length the various classes in Roman society, including the nobles and plebeians, but avoided all reference to slaves. Another teacher included George Washington Carver on a list of great Americans from whom students could pick individuals to learn about but specifically decided not to mention that Carver was Black for fear of raising racial issues. In the best of all worlds, there would be no need to make such mention, because children would have no preconceptions that famous people are generally White. However, in a school in which one White child was surprised to learn from a member of our research team that Martin Luther King, Jr., was African American, not White, it would seem reasonable to argue that highlighting the accomplishments of African Americans and making sure that students do not assume famous figures are White are reasonable practices.

Such constriction based on a desire to avoid racial problems is not unique at Wexler. For example, Scherer and Slawski (1979) report that a desegregated high school they studied eliminated the lunch hour and study halls to minimize the sort of loosely supervised contact between students that seemed to be likely to lead to conflict. However, the nature of the constriction at Wexler was influenced by the colorblind perspective and its corollaries. At Wexler, the tendency was to ignore or avoid certain topics. Such a tendency, while undeniably a low-risk one, failed to take advantage of the diversity of experiences and perspectives of Wexler's students as a resource for the educational process. Furthermore, in some cases, it literally distorted the education all students received as teachers attempted to avoid potentially controversial facts or issues.

CONCLUSIONS

Since Supreme Court Justice Harlan first spoke of a colorblind society as a goal to be striven for more than 100 years ago, the colorblind approach has often been held up as a needed antidote to the virulent racism in our society that traditionally consigned certain individuals to subordinate positions on the basis of their color and their color alone. However, this chapter takes the position that the colorblind perspective is not without some dangers. It may ease initial tensions and minimize the frequency of overt conflict. Nonetheless, it can also foster such phenomena as the taboo against ever mentioning race or connected issues and the refusal to recognize and deal with the existence of intergroup tensions. Thus, it fosters an environment in which aversive racists, who are basically well intentioned, are prone to act in a discriminatory manner. Further, it makes it unlikely that the opportunities inherent in a pluralistic institution will be fully realized or that the challenge facing such an institution of providing all its students with an effective education will be dealt with effectively.

Acknowledgments

The author expresses her deep appreciation to the students and staff of Wexler School. The research on which this chapter is based was funded by the author's contract with the National Institute of Education (Contract 400–76–0011). Other expenses relating to the chapter's preparation were covered by the Learning Research and Development Center, which is partly funded by NIE. However, all opinions expressed herein are solely those of the author, and no endorsement of the ideas by NIE is implied or intended.

Questions and Activities

1. According to the author, how does the social context influence the expression of racism and discrimination?

2. What is the *colorblind perspective*? Give some examples of it. On what major beliefs and assumptions is it based?

3. In what ways does the colorblind perspective contribute to racial discrimination and institutionalized racism in schools? Give specific examples.

4. How does the colorblind perspective often lead to what the author calls a "misrepresentation of reality"? Which realities are often misrepresented by the colorblind perspective?

5. Why did the teachers at Wexler deny that they were aware of the race of their students? What were some consequences of their denial? How was their denial inconsistent with many realities related to race in the school?

6. What did the interviews with Wexler students reveal about their conceptions of race? How did their conceptions of race differ from those of the teachers? Why?

7. Why do teachers often embrace the colorblind perspective? According to the author, what are its benefits and costs?

8. How does the colorblind perspective make it easier for liberal White teachers to discriminate? Give specific examples from this chapter and from your own observations and experiences in schools and in other settings and contexts.

9. How does the colorblind perspective negatively affect the development of a multicultural curriculum? What are the most promising ways to counteract the colorblind perspective? Give specific examples.

References

Allport, G. W. (1954). *The Nature of Prejudice*. Cambridge, MA: Addison-Wesley.

Amir, Y. (1969). Contact Hypothesis in Ethnic Relations. *Psychological Bulletin, 71*(5), 319–342.

Amir, Y. (1976). The Role of Intergroup Contact in Change of Prejudice and Ethnic Relations. In P. A. Katz (Ed.), *Towards the Elimination of Racism* (pp. 245–308). New York: Pergamon.

Aronson, E., Blaney, N., Stephan, C., Sikes, J., and Snapp, M. (1978). *The Jigsaw Classroom*. Beverly Hills, CA: Sage Publications.

Becker, H. S. and Greer, B. (1960). Participant Observations: Analysis of Qualitative Data. In R. N. Adams and J. J. Preiss (Eds.), *Human Organization Research* (pp. 267–289). Homewood, IL: The Dorsey Press.

Bogdan, R. C. and Taylor, S. J. (1975). *Introduction to Qualitative Research Methods: A Phenomenological Approach to the Social Sciences*. New York: Wiley.

Bossert, S. T. (1988/89). Cooperative Activities in the Classroom. In E. Z. Rothkopt (Ed.), *Review of Research in Education*, Vol. 15 (pp. 225–250). Washington, DC: American Educational Research Association.

Brewer, M. B., and Brown, R. J. (1998). Intergroup Relations. In D. T. Gilbert, S. T. Fiske, and G. Lindzey (Eds.), *The Handbook of Social Psychology* (4th ed.). New York: McGraw Hill.

Brown, R. (1995). *Prejudice: Its Social Psychology*. Oxford, England: Blackwell.

Campbell, D. T. (1975). Degrees of Freedom and the Case Study. *Comparative Political Studies, 8*(2), 178–193.

Carter, R. T. and Goodwin, A. L. (1994). Racial Identity and Education. In L. Darling-Hammond (Ed.), *Review of Research in Education* (pp. 291–336). Washington, DC: American Educational Research Association.

Clement, D. C., Eisenhart, M., and Harding, J. R. (1979). The Veneer of Harmony: Social-Race Relations in a Southern Desegregated School. In R. C. Rist (Ed.), *Desegregated Schools* (pp. 15–62). New York: Academic Press.

Cohen, E., Lockheed, M., and Lohman, M. (1976). The Center for Interracial Cooperation: A Field Experiment. *Sociology of Education, 49*, 47–58.

Cohen, E. G. (1975). The Effects of Desegregation on Race Relations. *Law and Contemporary Problems, 39*(2), 271–299.

Cook, S. W. (1969). Motives in the Conceptual Analysis of Attitude-Related Behavior. In W. J. Arnold and D. Levine (Eds.), *Nebraska Symposium on Motivation*, Vol. 17 (pp. 179–235). Lincoln: University of Nebraska Press.

Cook, S. W. (1978). Interpersonal and Attitudinal Outcomes in Cooperating Interracial Groups. *Journal of Research and Development in Education, 12*(1), 97–113.

Cook, S. W. (1985). Experimenting on Social Issues: The Case of School Desegregation. *American Psychologist, 40*, 452–460.

Cook, T. and Campbell, D. (1976). The Design and Conduct of Quasi-Experiments and True Experiments in Field Settings. In M. Dunnette (Ed.), *Handbook of Organizational Psychology* (pp. 223–281). Chicago: Rand McNally.

Davis, F. (1961). Deviance Disavowal: The Management of Strained Interaction by the Visibly Handicapped. In H. S. Becker (Ed.), *The Other Side: Perspectives on Deviance* (pp. 119–137). New York: The Free Press.

Devine, P. G. (1989). Stereotyping and Prejudice: Their Automatic and Controlled Components. *Journal of Personality and Social Psychology, 56*, 5–18.

Dovidio, J. F. and Gaertner, S. L. (1998). On the Nature of Contemporary Prejudice: The Causes, Consequences, and Challenges of Aversive Racism. In J. L. Eberhardt and S. T. Fiske (Eds.), *Confronting Racism: The Problem and the Response* (pp. 3–32). Thousand Oaks, CA: Sage.

Dovidio, J. F., Gaertner, S. L., Voulidzic, A., Matoka, A., Johnson, B., and Frazier, S. (1997). Extending the Benefits of Recategorization: Evaluations, Self-Disclosure, and Helping. *Journal of Experimental Social Psychology, 33*, 401–420.

Duncan, B. L. (1976). Differential Racial Perception and Attribution of Intergroup Violence. *Journal of Personality and Social Psychology, 35*, 590–598.

Fazio, R. H., Jackson, J. R., Dunton, B. C., and Williams, C. J. (1995). Variability in Automatic Activation as Unobtrusive Measure of Racial Attitudes: A Bona Fide Pipeline? *Journal of Personality and Social Psychology, 69*, 1013–1027.

Fiske, S. T., and Neuberg, S. L. (1990). A Continuum of Impression Formation, from Category-Based to Individuating Processes: Influences of Information and Motivation on Attention and Interpretation. In M. P. Zanna (Ed.), *Advances in Experimental Social Psychology*, Vol. 23 (pp. 1–74). New York: Academic Press.

Gaertner, S. L. and Dovidio, J. F. (1981). Racism among the Well-Intentioned. In E. Clausen and J. Bermingham (Eds.), *Pluralism, Racism, and Public Policy: The Search for Equality* (pp. 208–222). Boston: G. K. Hall.

Gaertner, S. L. and Dovidio, J. F. (1986). The Aversive Form of Racism. In J. F. Dovidio and S. L. Gaertner (Eds.), *Prejudice, Discrimination, and Racism* (pp. 61–89). Orlando, FL: Academic Press.

Gillborn, D. (1992). Citizenship, Race and the Hidden Curriculum. *International Studies in Sociology of Education, 2*(1) 57–73.

Glaser, B. G. and Strauss, A. L. (1967). *The Discovery of Grounded Theory: Strategies for Qualitative Research.* Chicago: Aldine.

Heath, S. B. (1982). Questioning at Home and at School: A Comparative Study. In G. Spindler (Ed.), *Doing the Ethnography of Schooling: Educational Anthropology in Action* (pp. 102–131). New York: Holt, Rinehart and Winston.

Hewstone, M., and Brown, R. (Eds.). (1986). *Contact and Conflict in Intergroup Encounters.* Oxford, England: Basil Blackwell.

Hill, J. (1971). *Personalized Education Programs Utilizing Cognitive Style Mapping.* Bloomfield Hills, MI: Oakland Community College Press.

Irvine, J. J. (1990). *Black Students and School Failure: Policies, Practices, and Prescriptions.* Westport, CT: Greenwood Press.

Irvine, J. J. (1991). *Culturally Responsive and Responsible Pedagogy: The Inclusion of Culture, Research, and Reflection in the Knowledge Base of Teacher Education.* Paper presented at the annual meeting of the American Association of Colleges for Teacher Education, Atlanta.

Jaynes, G. D., and Williams, R. M., Jr. (1989). *A Common Destiny: Blacks and the American Society.* Washington, DC: National Academy Press.

Jervis, K. (1996). How Come There Are no Brothers on That List?: Hearing the Hard Questions All Children Ask. *Harvard Educational Review, 66*(3).

Johnson, D. W. and Johnson, R. T. (1982). The Study of Cooperative, Competitive, and Individualistic Situations: State of the Area and Two Recent Contributions. *Contemporary Education: A Journal of Reviews, 1*(1), 7–13.

Johnson, D. W., Johnson, R. T., and Maruyama, G. (1984). Goal Interdependence and Interpersonal Attraction in Heterogeneous Classrooms: A Meta-Analysis. In N. Miller and M. B. Brewer (Eds.), *Groups in Contact: The Psychology of Desegregation* (pp. 187–212). Orlando, FL: Academic Press.

Johnson, D. W., Maruyama, G., Johnson, R. T., Nelson, D., and Skon, L., (1981). Effects of Cooperative, Competitive, and Individualistic Goal Structures on Achievement: A Meta-Analysis. *Psychological Bulletin, 89,* 47–62.

Jones, J. M. (1986). Racism: A Cultural Analysis of the Problem. In J. F. Dovidio and S. L. Gaertner (Eds.), *Prejudice, Discrimination, and Racism* (pp. 279–313). Orlando, FL: Academic Press.

Jones, J. M. (1997). *Prejudice and Racism* (2nd ed.). New York: McGraw-Hill.

Jones, J. M. (1998). Psychological Knowledge and the New American Dilemma of Race. *Journal of Social Issues, 54*(4), 645.

Katz, I., Wackenhut, J., and Hass, R. G. (1986). Racial Ambivalence, Value Duality, and Behavior. In J. F. Dovidio and S. L. Gaertner (Eds.), *Prejudice, Discrimination, and Racism* (pp. 35–59). Orlando, FL: Academic Press.

Katz, P. A. (1976). The Acquisition of Racial Attitudes. In P. Katz (Ed.), *Toward the Elimination of Racism* (pp. 125–156). New York: Pergamon Press.

Kochman, T. (1981). *Black and White Styles of Conflict.* Chicago: University of Chicago Press.

Levin, S. (2000). Social Psychological Evidence on Race and Racism. In M. Chang, D. Witt, J. Jones, and K. Hakuta (Eds.), *Compelling Interest: Examining the Evidence on Racial Dynamics in Higher Education.* Stanford, CA: Stanford University Press.

Malpass, R. S. and Kravitz, J. (1969). Recognition for Faces of Own and Other Races. *Journal of Personality and Social Psychology, 13,* 330–334.

Miles, M. B., and Huberman, A. M. (1984). *Qualitative Data Analysis: A Sourcebook of New Methods.* Newbury Park, CA: Sage Publications.

Nieto, S. (1992). *Affirming Diversity.* New York: Longman.

Norvell, N. and Worchel, S. (1981). A Reexamination of the Relation between Equal Status Contact and Intergroup Attraction. *Journal of Personality and Social Psychology, 41,* 902–908.

Olson, S. (1976). *Ideas and Data: Process and Practice of Social Research.* Homewood, IL: The Dorsey Press.

Pettigrew, T. (1986). The Intergroup Contact Hypothesis Reconsidered. In M. Hewstone and R. Brown (Eds.), *Contact and Conflict in Intergroup Encounters* (pp. 169–195). Oxford, England: Basil Blackwell.

Pettigrew, T. F. (1998). Intergroup Contact Theory. *Annual Review of Psychology, 49,* 65–85.

Ramsey, P. G. (1987). *Teaching and Learning in a Diverse World.* New York: Teachers College Press.

Riordan, C. (1978). Equal-Status Interracial Contact: A Review and Revision of the Concept. *International Journal of Intercultural Relations, 2*(2), 161–185.

Rist, R. C. (1974). Race, Policy and Schooling. *Society, 12*(1), 59–63.

Rist, R. C. (1978). *The Invisible Children: School Integration in American Society.* Cambridge, MA: Harvard University Press.

Sagar, H. A. and Schofield, J. W. (1980). Racial and Behavioral Cues in Black and White Children's Perceptions of Ambiguously Aggressive Acts. *Journal of Personality and Social Psychology, 39*(4), 590–598.

Sagar, H. A. and Schofield, J. W. (1984). Integrating the Desegregated School: Problems and Possibilities. In M. Maehr and D. Bartz (Eds.), *Advances in Motivation and Achievement: A Research Annual.* Greenwich, CT: JAI Press.

Scherer, J. and Slawski, E. J. (1979). Color, Class, and Social Control in an Urban Desegregated School. In R. C. Rist (Ed.), *Desegregated Schools* (pp. 117–153). New York: Academic Press.

Schofield, J. W. (1979). The Impact of Positively Structured Contact on Intergroup Behavior: Does It Last under Adverse Conditions? *Social Psychology Quarterly, 42*(3), 280–284.

Schofield, J. W. (1980). Cooperation as Social Exchange: Resource Gaps and Reciprocity in Academic Work. In S. Sharon, P. Hare, C. Webb, and R. Hertz-Lazarowitz, (Eds.), *Cooperation in Education.* Provo, UT: Brigham Young University Press.

Schofield, J. W. (1989). *Black and White in School: Trust Tension or Tolerance?* New York: Teachers' College Press.

Schofield, J. W. (1995). Improving Intergroup Relations among Students. In J. A. Banks and C. A. M. Banks (Eds.), *Handbook on Multicultural Education* (pp. 635–645). New York: Macmillan.

Schofield, J. W. and Eurich-Fulcer, R. (in press). When and How School Desegregation Improves Intergroup Relations. In R. Brown and S. Gaertner (Eds.), *Handbook of Social Psychology,* Vol.4. New York: Blackwell.

Schofield, J. W. and Francis, W. D. (1982). An Observational Study of Peer Interaction in Racially-Mixed 'Accelerated' Classrooms. *The Journal of Educational Psychology, 74*(5), 722–732.

Schofield, J. W. and Sagar, H. A. (1977). Peer Interaction Patterns in an Integrated Middle School. *Sociometry. 40*(2), 130–138.

Schofield, J. W. and Sagar, H. A. (1979). The Social Context of Learning in an Interracial School. In R. Rist (Ed.), *Inside Desegregated Schools: Appraisals of an American Experiment* (pp. 155–199). San Francisco: Academic Press.

Schofield, J. W. and Whitley, B. E. (1983). Peer Nomination Versus Rating Scale Measurement of Children's Peer Preferences. *Social Psychology Quarterly, 46*(3), 242–251.

Sharan, S. (1980). Cooperative Learning in Teams: Recent Methods and Effects on Achievement, Attitudes and Ethnic Relations. *Review of Educational Research, 50*(2), 241–272.

Sherif, M. (1979). Superordinate Goals in the Reduction of Intergroup Conflict: An Experimental Evaluation. In W. G. Austin and S. Worchel (Eds.), *The Social Psychology of Intergroup Relations* (pp. 257–261). Monterey, CA: Brooks/Cole Publishing Company.

Sidanius, J. and Pratto, F. (1999). *Social Dominance: An Intergroup Theory of Social Hierarchy and Oppression*. Port Chester, NY: Cambridge University Press.

Slavin, R. E. (1995). *Cooperative Learning: Theory, Research and Practice* (2nd ed.). Boston: Allyn and Bacon.

Sleeter, C. E. (1993). How White Teachers Construct Race. In C. McCarthy and W. Crichlow (Eds.), *Race Identity and Representation in Education*. (pp. 157–171). New York: Routledge.

Snyder, M. L., Kleck, R. E., Strenta, A., and Mentzer, S. J. (1979). Avoidance of the Handicapped: An Attributional Ambiguity Analysis. *Journal of Personality and Social Psychology, 12*, 2297–2306.

Stephan, W. G. and Stephan, C. W. (1985). Intergroup Anxiety. *Journal of Social Issues, 41*(3), 157–175.

Stephan, W. G. and Stephan, C. W. (1996). *Intergroup Relations*. Boulder, CO: Westview Press.

Strauss, A. and Corbin, J. (1990). *Basics of Qualitative Research*. Newbury Park, CA: Sage Publications.

Taylor, S., Fiske, S., Etcoff, N., and Ruderman, A. (1978). Categorical and Contextual Basis of Person Memory and Stereotyping. *Journal of Personality and Social Psychology, 36*(7), 778–793.

Trent, W., Owens-Nicholson, D., Eatman, T., Burke, M., Daugherty, J., and Norman, K. (2000). Justice, Equality of Educational Opportunity, and Affirmative Action. In M. Chang, D. Witt, J. Jones, and K. Hakuta (Eds.), *Compelling Interest: Examining the Evidence on Racial Dynamics in Higher Education*. Stanford, CA: Stanford University Press.

Triandis, H. C. (1994). *Culture and Social Behavior*. New York: McGraw-Hill.

Triandis, H. C., Vassiliou, V., Vassiliou, G., Tanaka, Y., and Shanmugam, A. (Eds.). (1972). *The Analysis of Subjective Culture*. New York: Wiley.

Webb, E. J., Campbell, D. T., Schwartz, R. D., and Sechrest, L. (1966). *Unobtrusive Measures: Nonreactive Research in the Social Sciences*. Chicago: Rand McNally.

Whitley, B. E. and Schofield, J. W. (1984). Peer Preference in Desegregated Classrooms: A Round Robin Analysis. *Journal of Personality and Social Psychology, 46*(4), 799–810.

CHAPTER 12

Language Diversity and Education

Carlos J. Ovando

> *Language is a shared and sharing part of culture that cares little about formal classifications and much about vitality and connection, for culture itself perishes in purity or isolation. (Carlos Fuentes, 1988, p. 27)*

> *In nature's talent show we are simply a species of primate with our own act, a knack for communicating information about who did what to whom by modulating the sounds we make when we exhale. (Steven Pinker, 1994, p. 19).*

Language diversity has a strong influence on the content and process of schooling practices for both language-minority and language-majority students in the United States. As a system of communication linking sound, written or visual symbols, and meaning, language is an indispensable bridge for sharing knowledge, skills, values, and attitudes within and across cultures. It has tremendous power as the paramount instrument of cognitive development, and it can open or close the door to academic achievement. How, then, is the educational inequality often experienced by language-minority students related to the extent of their ability to understand, speak, read, and write standard English?

To present an overview of how language diversity is related to educational outcomes, this chapter is organized into three sections. The first section considers what language is and how children and adults acquire their first and second languages. The second section surveys varieties of nonstandard English as well as non-English-language diversity in the United States. The third section discusses classroom adaptations to meet the needs of language-minority students.

THE SOCIOCULTURAL NATURE OF LANGUAGE AND LANGUAGE ACQUISITION

Language is a powerful and transformative part of culture. Like culture, language is learned, it is shared, and it evolves and changes over time. It is much more than a set of words and grammar rules. It is a forceful instrument for giving individuals, groups, institutions, and cultures their identity. Through language, we communicate our values, attitudes, skills, and aspirations as bearers of culture and as makers of future culture.

Language can be analyzed from many different points of view. At the physical level, it is a system of sounds and movements made by the human body and decoded by the listener's auditory system. From the cognitive point of view, it is a tool for the expression of thought. From the anthropological point of view, language is an intricate and pervasive component of culture. From the semiotic point of view, language can also be studied as a system of signs and symbols that have socially determined meanings (Shaumyan, 1987).

From the pedagogical point of view, what has been learned by someone who is said to have gained communicative competence in a particular language? To begin with, there are the more familiar components of language that have to be developed:

1. Phonetics and phonology—the sound system.

2. Morphology—how units of meaning are formed into words.

3. Syntax—the grammar of sentence formation.

4. Lexicon—the vocabulary.

Beyond these four components, however, there are other culture-related domains that must be mastered in order for communicative competence to be achieved. These five domains illustrate the subtleties and sociocultural aspects of the process of learning a language:

1. Discourse—how the language is organized in speech and writing beyond the sentence level; for example, how paragraphs or conversations are structured.

2. Appropriateness—the way language use is adjusted according to the social situation; for example, "Hit the lights, will ya?" versus "Would you mind turning the lights off, please?"

3. Paralinguistics—distance between speakers, intonation, volume and pitch of speech, gestures, facial expressions, and other body language.

4. Pragmatics—the interaction of discourse, appropriateness, and paralinguistics; for example, pragmatics involve implicit and explicit cultural norms for when it is and is not appropriate to talk, how speech is paced, the correct way to listen, when to be direct and when to be indirect, how to take turns in conversation, and how to adapt language according to roles, social status, attitudes, settings, and topics.

5. Cognitive-academic language proficiency (Cummins, 1979; 1981; 1991; 2000)—mastery of the language skills needed to learn and develop abstract concepts in such areas as mathematics, science, and social studies (Ovando & Collier, 1998).

Even such a cursory listing of the components and domains of language clearly suggests that language acquisition is a complicated, subtle, culture-specific, and lifelong process. Educators thus need to realize that the difference between English and Spanish, for example, or even between standard English and Black English, is much more than a difference in phonology, morphology, syntax, and lexicon (Ogbu, 1999; Perry & Delpit, 1998). It has often been said that learning basic communication in one's first language is a simple process—child's play, so to speak. When examined carefully, however, full development of one's first language—including literacy skills and knowledge about the structure and function of the language—is a complex process requiring years to reach communicative competence. When teachers understand this, they are more likely to develop respect for and sensitivity to students who arrive in the classroom speaking anything other than standard English. For non-English speakers, in particular, teachers should be realistic about the years of language development that will be needed for speakers to move from basic communication in English to full communicative competence.

Languages grow and develop as tools of communication within a given environment. In this sense, there is no such thing as "right" or "wrong" language, only language that is appropriate or inappropriate in a given context. Languages and language varieties develop and thrive because they meet the needs of communities. If a given community of speakers finds it necessary to maintain a language because it satisfies spiritual, social, intellectual, technical, scientific, economic, or political needs, then the chances that this particular linguistic community will survive are greatly enhanced. Thus, for example, Yupik (an Eskimo Aleut language) is alive in Akiachak, Alaska, despite the powerful influence of English, because Yupik fulfills the people's need for continuity with their heritage. Within the domain of English itself, the United States teems with a variety of linguistic microcultures representing a diversity of experiences—American Indian varieties of English, creoles, Black English, and a broad array of regional accents, vocabularies, and styles (Ovando, 1999).

Because through multicultural education we seek to promote equity and excellence across such variables as race, ethnicity, nationality, gender, social class, regional groups, religion, exceptionality, literacy background, age, and language background, it is vital for educators to understand the function that language can play in either helping or inhibiting the educational fulfillment of individuals. As Hymes (1981) states:

> The law of the land demands that equal educational opportunity not be denied because of language. "Language" has been understood most readily in terms of "languages," such as Spanish, and structurally definable varieties of a language, such as Black English Vernacular. If one defines "language," as I do, in terms of ways of speaking, as involving both structure and ways of using structure, there are even deeper implications, implications not yet legally explored. One's language affects one's chances in life, not only through accent, but also through action. Access to opportunities in the form of access to schools, jobs, positions, memberships, clubs, and homes, may depend on ways of using language that one has no chance to master, or chooses not to master. (pp. vii–viii)

Within and outside the school setting, it is important to consider how people come to acquire and value the particular types of first and second languages they prefer to use in formal and informal situations. Therefore, I now turn to research on first and second language acquisition and its application in classrooms. I focus here on the process by which non-English speakers acquire English language skills.

First and Second Language Acquisition

For the past thirty years, linguists and cognitive psychologists have made considerable progress in understanding first and second language acquisition. It would be impossible to provide a complete overview of this complex field of study here (see Cummins, 2000; Minami & Ovando, 1995, for more extensive examinations of this field). This section fo-cuses on aspects of language acquisition that relate closely to the effective education of language-minority students.

The research indicates that language learning is an instinctual (Pinker, 1994) and developmental process that involves predictable stages. We acquire our first language as children, in the context of natural, interesting, and meaningful interactions within our social and physical environment. In such an environment, children are exposed on a daily basis to peer and adult language models in a context that gives meaning to language. Because of this strongly contextualized environment, speakers tend to learn communication shortcuts such as incomplete responses and many nonverbal cues.

Although it is now more commonly called social or playground language, Cummins (1981) initially referred to this type of language as basic interpersonal communicative skills (BICS). Doing research with English-language learners in Canada, Cummins suggested that an average non-English-speaking student could learn to communicate at this level in English after about two years of instruction in an acquisition-rich environment similar to that of a child learning a first language (Cummins, 1981; 2000). This ability to get along in the world conversationally enables English-language learners to make everyday conversational contact with their English-speaking peers. Such contact, in turn, plays a pivotal role in the acculturation of these students, especially to the school culture. In addition, face-to-face communication serves as a platform for beginning to build a self-concept in social relationships. In other words, the acquisition of social language serves a powerful and important sociolinguistic function in the lives of those who are learning their second language.

Even though a student of limited English proficiency may seem to be making rapid progress in the acquisition of English, having a command of social language does not necessarily equip that student for the more cognitively demanding tasks of the curriculum. Cognitive tasks require a second developmental level, beyond conversational language, that consists of the language used in school and in many facets of adult life. Here, the context is less clear. This level of communication depends on a speaker's (or writer's) ability to manipulate the vocabulary and syntax and discourse style with precision (Ovando, 1983). Cummins has referred to this type of language competence as cognitive academic language proficiency (CALP). Again, research by Cummins (1981) indicates that, as measured by standardized tests, children with little or no prior schooling experience attain the cognitive-academic language proficiency of a native English speaker in about five to seven years. For the past ten years, Cummins's research (initially reported in 1981) has been replicated and expanded in a series of studies by Collier and Thomas (see Collier, 1995, and Thomas & Collier, 1999, for a synthesis of their work). Affirming Cummins's earlier research, they conclude (cited in Collier, 1995):

> In our studies we have found that in U.S. schools where all
> instruction is given through the second language (English),
> non-native speakers of English with no schooling in their first
> language take 7–10 years or more to reach age and grade-level

> norms of their native English-speaking peers. Immigrant students
> who have had 2–3 years of first language in their home country
> before they come to the U.S. take at least 5–7 years to reach typical
> native-speaker performance. (p. 8)

Just because children speak little or no English does not mean that they come to school as blank slates. These children bring to the classroom a wealth of home experiences and of skills and competence in their home language. All of this provides a basis for future learning. Again, Cummins (1981) concludes that prior acquired knowledge and skills in the home language transfer to the new language. This transfer is known as the common underlying proficiency (CUP). Thus, for example, a Filipino student who already knows in Tagalog how to manipulate the language involved in the solution of word problems will be able to transfer those skills into the second language as she acquires new mathematical vocabulary in English. In other words, knowledge acquired through the student's first language is not only useful but also crucial in the continuous cognitive development of the student in the second language (Ramírez, 1991). In fact, ample research evidence suggests that cognitive and academic development in the first language can have a very positive effect on second-language schooling (see Collier, 1995, for a synthesis of the research on the role of the first language on second-language schooling). Of importance to language-minority educators is Cummins's (1981) conclusion on the instructional use of both the home language (L1) and English (L2):

> The results of research on bilingual programs show that
> minority children's L1 can be promoted in school at no cost to the
> development of proficiency in the majority language. . . . The data
> clearly show that well-implemented bilingual programs have had
> remarkable success in developing English academic skills and have
> proved superior to ESL-only programs in situations where direct
> comparisons have been carried out. (p. 28)

Tracking and expanding on the work of Cummins, Collier (1995) reports:

> In our examination of large datasets across many different
> research sites, we have found that the most significant student
> background variable is the amount of formal schooling students
> have received in their first language. Across all program treatments,
> we have found that non-native speakers being schooled in second
> language for part or all of the school day typically do reasonably
> well in the early years of schooling (kindergarten through second or
> third grade). But from fourth grade on through middle school and
> high school, when the academic and cognitive demands of the
> curriculum increase rapidly with each succeeding year, students with
> little or no academic and cognitive development in their first
> language do less and less well as they move into the upper grades.
>   What about students schooled bilingually in the U.S.? It still
> takes a long time to demonstrate academic proficiency in second
> language comparable to a native speaker. But the difference in

student performance in a bilingual program, in contrast to an
all-English program, is that students typically score at or above
grade level in their first language in all subjects areas, while they are
building academic development of second language. When students
are tested in their second language, they typically reach and surpass
native speakers' performance across all subject areas after 4–7 years
in a quality bilingual program. Because they have not fallen behind
in cognitive and academic growth during the 4–7 years that it takes
to build academic proficiency in second language, bilingually
schooled students typically sustain this level of academic
achievement and outperform monolingually schooled students in
the upper grades. (p. 9)

Thus, native language support in a quality bilingual program can provide academic development through comprehensible instruction. This development can then be applied to students' academic and language growth in English.

LANGUAGE VARIETY IN THE UNITED STATES

As a language laboratory, the United States is truly remarkable. Of the scores of American Indian languages that existed prior to European contact, about 175 have survived the overwhelming assimilative powers of English in the United States, and about 35 such languages have survived in Canada (Krauss, 1995). Languages other than English used by the colonizers of North America—such as Spanish and French—not only have survived but also continue to serve as lively communicative and cultural instruments in various regions of the country. The successive waves of immigrants to the United States have added to the nation's linguistic richness (Ovando, 1999). Today, the country's language assets range from such languages as Navajo—still spoken in the same communities in which it was spoken hundreds of years ago—to Hmong, spoken by refugees from the highlands of Laos, Thailand, and Cambodia.

In addition to the mix of languages, language contact in the United States has produced many indigenous language varieties known as pidgins, creoles, and dialects. A *pidgin* is a type of language that evolves through contact between groups speaking different languages. It mixes components of the contact languages and has its own grammar system. A *creole* is the adoption of a pidgin as the accepted language of a community. As Anttila (1972) puts it, "this happened often on the plantations of the New World, where slaves from different language backgrounds were forced to use a pidgin among themselves, and between themselves and the masters. After escape, freedom, or revolution the pidgin was all they had, and it had to become the first language of the community" (p. 176). Three examples of creole varieties in the United States are Gullah, a creole of English and West African origin that is spoken on the Sea Islands, from the Carolinas to northern Florida; Louisiana French Creole, which coexists with two local varieties of French and another local variety of English; and Hawaiian Creole, which has been influenced by Hawaiian, Japanese, Chinese, Portuguese, English, and Ilocano. Complementing the rich indigenous creole traditions of the United States is Black English, which is spoken by a large segment of the

African American population. To gain a better understanding of these indigenous language varieties, the next section examines more closely the nature of Gullah, Louisiana French Creole, Hawaiian Creole, and Black English.

Gullah

Gullah originated among African Americans who settled in South Carolina in the 1700s. Nichols (1981) has estimated that in the early 1980s there were about 300,000 African Americans who spoke Gullah in an area including South Carolina, Georgia, and parts of lower North Carolina and northern Florida. Gullah is different from standard English in a number of ways. For example, its West African ancestry is reflected in certain vowel sounds and some vocabulary items, such as *goober* for "peanut," *cooter* for "turtle," and *buckra* for "White man" (Nichols, 1981, p. 75). There are structural differences as well. Instead of using "he" and "she," the neuter pronoun *ee* is used for both males and females. *Fuh* is used to indicate an infinitive clause, as in "I came *fuh* get my coat." Progressive action can be indicated by *duh* plus the verb: "Greg *duh* hide" instead of "Greg is hiding" (Nichols, 1981, pp. 73–75).

Most members of the Gullah-speaking community are not strictly creole speakers. Instead, individuals "show greater or lesser use of creole features along a continuum of language use ranging from creole to a dialect of English" (Nichols, 1981, p. 73). Not surprisingly, there is a strong association of Gullah use with age and amount of formal schooling. The very old and the very young tend to use Gullah more extensively. School-age children tend to switch back and forth between Gullah—referred to as "country talk"—and the prestige variety of standard English, especially for the benefit of teachers, who usually do not understand Gullah.

Gullah has been analyzed extensively by linguists, and much is known about its phonology, grammar, vocabulary, and sociolinguistic usage. The language has also been popularized through literature such as the stories of Ambrose González and the novels and Gullah sketches of Pulitzer Prize winner Julia Peterkin (Nichols, 1981). Yet children who speak Gullah have been stigmatized in the schools, and there has not been a vigorous effort to incorporate their language into the curriculum in order to create bridges to standard English. Although some teachers are addressing literacy development for these children through such means as the language-experience approach, by and large Gullah-speaking children may not be receiving equal educational opportunities in classrooms in which standard English is the accepted medium of instruction.

Louisiana French Creole

Like Gullah, Louisiana French Creole exhibits a linguistic structure that sets it apart from English. Its speakers may have difficulty understanding English, and vice versa. Louisiana French Creole, a contemporary of Gullah, seems to have evolved among West African slaves who were introduced to southern Louisiana by French colonists and needed a common language to communicate with each other. Louisiana French Creole has structural similarities to English-related creoles such as Gullah. For example, the pronoun *li* is used for both "he" and "she." Also, as in Gullah, the verb "to be" is not used in equative clauses. In contrast to Gullah, however, most of the Louisiana French Creole vocabulary is derived from French rather than from English, with some use of African vocabulary items (Nichols, 1981).

Although Acadian and standard French are officially affirmed in the school curriculum in Louisiana, Louisiana French Creole traditionally has not had the same status. Like Gullah-speaking children, children who speak Louisiana French Creole therefore run the risk of not receiving equal educational opportunities. Furthermore, they and their parents may interpret the neglect of their primary language as a devaluation of their sociolinguistic background in the eyes of school personnel and society at large.

Hawaiian Creole

Hawaiian Creole is a relative newcomer to the family of indigenous creoles in U.S. society. Its use dates back to the late nineteenth century. In contrast to Louisiana French Creole, there is considerably more careful scholarly documentation about its origin, structure, and function (Nichols, 1981). Hawaiian Creole evolved as a pidgin during the late nineteenth century, when plantations were being developed and the Hawaiian Islands came under the influence of English speakers from the United States mainland. Similar to Gullah, Hawaiian Creole is English-related, and its lexicon is predominantly English, with the aforementioned influence from Hawaiian, Japanese, Chinese, Portuguese, and Ilocano. This rich linguistic mixture in the Hawaiian Islands has led language scholars to view Hawaiian English "in terms of three coexistent systems—a pidgin, Creole, and dialect of English—none of which occurs in unadulterated forms but only in combinations of different proportions" (Nichols, 1981, p. 48).

Whether Hawaiian English is a dialect of English or a creole language is a complex issue. As is true to some extent of Gullah, its degree of similarity to English ranges along a continuum, depending on the community and the context. For example, linguists note a highly decreolized language variety in the more urbanized population centers such as Oahu and more creolized traditional patterns in the more remote islands of Kauai and Hawaii (Nichols, 1981).

In any event, Hawaiian Creole is a lively language that plays a key social and academic role in the lives of many Hawaiian children. Like Gullah and Louisiana French Creole, Hawaiian Creole, or Pidgin English, as it is known by island residents, is a highly stigmatized language variety that until the 1970s was singled out by educational policy makers as a cause of the many academic problems experienced by Hawaiian students. According to Nichols (1981), the policy at that time was to decreolize the students' language. Because this posture was not successful in achieving the elimination of Hawaiian Creole, however, education policies since then have tended toward acceptance of the language in the lives of the students. Yet there has remained a sense that it is a "deficient language" and thus in need of correction (p. 86). The attempt in Hawaii to eradicate Hawaiian Creole confirms once more that when a cultural component as important as a language is threatened, its users tend to protect and defend it. This is what happened in the islands, where speakers of Hawaiian Creole began to view its use as an important symbol of solidarity in their community.

Black English

Speaking a standard dialect certainly has advantages in certain settings, but it can also present a dilemma for a person in terms of local community norms. Not everyone needs to speak a standard

> dialect for all social occasions. Furthermore, there are consequences
> that go along with the use of both a standard and local dialect.
> (Wolfram, 1987, p. 10)

Although Black English is a dialect of English rather than a creole, it shows parallels with creole languages in its historical development. Black English reflects influences from British and American English as well as English-based pidgin from sixteenth-century West Africa. In situations involving language contact, it is important to understand the nature of social relationships both within and outside the involved communities. The inhumanity of master-slave relationships was certainly not conducive to an egalitarian communicative process. But it was in this socially strained context that Black English and standard English coexisted and influenced each other. From the late 1700s until the early 1900s, approximately 90 percent of the African American population lived in the Southern states (Whatley, 1981). With such a high concentration of speakers, Black English was able to mature into a highly sophisticated and rule-governed "subsystem within the larger grammar of English" (Whatley, 1981, p. 64).

Unlike Gullah, Louisiana French Creole, and Hawaiian Creole, Black English spread throughout the United States. In the twentieth century, many African Americans began to migrate to the large urban centers of the North. Through this connection between Black communities in the rural South and the industrial North, Black English continued to evolve. As Whatley observes, "Funerals, homecoming celebrations at churches, and family reunions took northerners 'down home' at least annually" (Whatley, 1981, p. 94). Strong regional and familial ties between South and North generated much cross-fertilization of old and new communication patterns.

On the other hand, *de facto* segregation in the large urban centers of the North tended to insulate African American and White communities from each other. That meant that, given the social distance created between the speakers of Black English and standard English, the two languages had minimal influence on one another. Thus, Black English continued to develop its own structures, functional patterns, and styles.

Despite its presence throughout the United States, many people have a highly distorted perception of Black English. As Whatley points out, most people's understanding of Black English is based on its portrayal by Hollywood and the electronic media. The world of entertainment has given us a highly stylized, stereotyped version of Black speech—jiving, copping, playing the dozens, boasting, preaching, and fussing, for example. This, however, is just the tip of the linguistic iceberg. There are many aspects of Black English other than those represented in the media (Whatley, 1981).

As is true of any language, there is great speech variation among speakers of Black English. Also, speech behavior is highly contextualized. That is, individuals tend to assess the communicative situation and respond accordingly. Most speakers of English use a variety of styles of language in their daily lives, these variations being determined by degrees of formality and social status. Within the African American experience, praising, fussing, teasing, lying, preaching, jiving, boasting, and joking are carefully determined by the age, gender, and status of speakers. For example, the eldest members of the African American community tend to have greater latitude and prestige in language use, and children are the lowest-ranking members of the speech community (Whatley, 1981). This does not mean, of course, that African

American children are not allowed to interact with adults in creative and expressive ways. What it does mean is that there is a speech protocol that is sensitive to such variables as age, social status, gender, and formal and informal settings (Smitherman, 1999).

Because of African Americans' historical status as an oppressed minority, Whites have tended to perceive Black English as "a mass of random errors committed by Blacks trying to speak English" (Labov, Cohen, Robins, & Lewis, 1968, p. 366). The language varieties used by African Americans, however, are valid linguistic systems (Perry & Delpit, 1998; Smitherman, 1999). They have an internal linguistic infrastructure and a set of grammar rules just as any other language does. For example, the use of the verb "to be" follows different rules in Black English than in standard English. Speakers of standard English tend to contract forms of "to be," as in the sentence "She's tall" instead of "She is tall." Black English deletes "is" entirely, so that the sentence becomes "She tall." Black English also has a use for "be" that standard English does not. The sentences "He always be walkin' on a desert on TV" and "He jus' be walkin' dere sometime" use what linguists call the "invariant be." This use of the verb refers to action that takes place habitually over a period of time, and for this there is no exact standard English equivalent (Whatley, 1981).

Multiple negation is perhaps one of the most stigmatized aspects of Black English for speakers who enter the formal school system. Yet there is no logical basis for such stigmatization. Acceptance or nonacceptance of the double negative as a socially correct form is essentially a historical accident. According to language scholars, multiple negation was an integral part of the English language up to the time of Shakespeare. Also, it is useful to know that although Latin is credited with having influenced the "correctness" of single negation in English, other Romance languages, such as Spanish, French, and Italian, use the double negative as part of their standard speech patterns (Whatley, 1981).

A fair curricular process is one that builds on the sociocultural and linguistic backgrounds that students bring with them. Yet the use of Black English has had negative consequences for Black students. Many African American youth have not prospered in U.S. schools, and in the process of searching for the reasons, some educators have singled out their communication patterns as an important contributor to their academic failure. In the past, a common perception among educators, although not necessarily articulated, was that speakers of Black English are language-deficient. From this point of view, the use of Black English is seen as detrimental to a student's cognitive development. Thinking skills, however, can be demonstrated in any language; they are not the exclusive domain of standard English. Consider as an example the following conversation between two young speakers of Black English (Whatley, 1981, p. 99):

A: Do you know 'bout factors and all that stuff?

B: Yeah, I know all that.

A: Well, how come you only made a 50 on that test?

B: That test was tough—she ain't no good teacher anyway.

A: But you have been in the other math class, the one dat ain't done factors like we have.

B: Yeah, but I can do spelling—and you can't.

Whatley (1981) interprets the above playful interaction as follows:

> It is clear in this boasting episode that child A had collected highly specific information to support his boast, and he set child B up to a challenge by asking a seemingly innocent question. The strategies and information to support these were planned in advance. Child A wins this sequence, because child B must shift topic and begin another boast. (p. 30)

Although these children are not using standard English, they are certainly not language-deficient. If anything, the pair reflect a high level of creativity and spontaneity with language behavior, which is highly desirable for cognitive development. The children's language is different from standard English, but the language they use is not deficient. Their linguistic behavior and vocabulary inventory serve their communication needs extremely well.

Gullah, Louisiana French Creole, Hawaiian Creole, and Black English have much in common. They are rule-governed and they are legitimate linguistic expressions, just as standard English is. They are a link to our past, and they have a right to exist and to be accepted. Yet they are not given much recognition in the larger society. Rather, they are viewed by many people as aberrant and inferior language varieties. Consequently, a great unfounded fear exists on the part of educators that affirmation of such languages among students will perpetuate school failure. Because teaching practices are not always linguistically enlightened, language can become a primary source of inequality for students who come to school with a speech variety that marks them for stigmatization.

Cognitive psychologists, educators, and anthropologists, on the other hand, tell us that we build our cognitive repertoire on prior knowledge, experiences, attitudes, and skills (Ogbu, 1999; Perry & Delpit, 1998; Pinker, 1994; Wertsch, 1985). It is a layering process. Rather than destroy what was there before, the goal for educators should be to build on and add to what is already present in the lives of students. Creative bridges using the early socialization patterns of the home language and culture can be useful in motivating students to learn. These students will come to see their teachers as professionals who understand the value of their nonstandard languages. Such teachers, while respecting the structure and function of the home language, will help to build another layer of linguistic skill that will enable these students to negotiate the prestige variety of English in the larger society, and thus to have more options in their lives.

Language use in society is also about issues of power and identity, Therefore, the creation of culturally and linguistically compatible classroom practices can lead to much political controversy (Ovando & McLaren, 2000). Responding to the alarming school failure, absenteeism, and suspension rates of African American students attending Prescott Elementary School, the African American Task Force in Oakland, California, recommended to the School Board that Black English be used in schools. Task force members argued that Black English would serve as a springboard to affirm African American students' linguisitic and cultural experiences, to develop competency in Standard English, and to enhance academic achievement. Affirming the Task Force's recommendation, the School Board unanimously endorsed the Ebonics Resolution on December 21, 1996.

Criticized by the media and key African American leaders as a concession that would lower academic standards, the war of words that followed the passage of the resolution was intense. This prompted the editors of *Rethinking Schools* to write:

> The irrational and racist discourse that followed the school board's approval of the Ebonics Resolution has made it almost impossible to have a careful conversation about the important educational, political, and linguistic issues embedded in the resolution. (Perry & Delpit, 1998, p. xii)

The Demographics of Students from Non-English-Language Backgrounds

As a result of shifting demographics, the number of English-language learners in U.S. schools is increasing. Since the passage of the 1968 Title VII Bilingual Education Act and the landmark U.S. Supreme Court Decision *Lau* v. *Nichols* (Waugh & Koon, 1974), which provided a legal basis for equitable treatment of students from a non-English-speaking background in U.S. schools, educational policy for non-English-language communities has put linguistic minorities in the national spotlight. Many foreign-born children come to U.S. schools speaking only the language of their home country. Their families may be voluntary immigrants or involuntarily uprooted refugees, such as the Hmong. They may reside in the United States legally or as undocumented immigrants. There are also U.S.-born language-minority students. This group includes speakers of American Indian languages. It also includes groups who have maintained over generations the use of colonial and early immigration languages such as Spanish, French, German, and Swedish. And today it includes the offspring and subsequent generations of immigrants of virtually every nationality. Upon entering school, these students may fall anywhere along a broad continuum of language status. A child may be entirely monolingual in the non-English language, bilingual in the home language and English, or dominant in English with only a few fragmentary skills in his or her ancestral language.

The diversity of languages in the United States is truly amazing. In Anchorage, Alaska, students speaking more than 100 different languages, from virtually every region of the world, have been identified in the local school district's bilingual education program. As of 1992, the Los Angeles School District, whose identified language-minority students spoke at least 80 different languages, offered bilingual instruction in Spanish, Cantonese, Vietnamese, Korean, Filipino, and Armenian. With its large language-minority population, California has become the Ellis Island of the 1990s. California has an ethnic minority population between 40 and 50 percent; over 50 percent of its school population consist of ethnic minorities.

Other data show that during the ten years between 1980 and 1990, U.S. society became increasingly multiracial, multicultural, and multilingual. The demographic trend shows that in these ten years the total population of the United States grew by 9.8 percent. However, groups in which the most language-minority students are found were growing at a much faster rate. The American Indian population (including Eskimo and Aleut) grew by 37.9 percent, Asian and Pacific Islanders by 107.8 percent, Hispanic Americans by 53 percent, and "Others" by 45.1 percent (NABE, n.d., p. 1). Increased immigration from Latin America and Asia and the high fertility rates within these populations are among the major factors contributing to this demographic shift.

The upswing in immigration has resulted in large numbers of school entrants whose first language is not English (Minami & Ovando, 1995). Summarizing census data concerning demographic changes from 1980 to 1990, the *New York Times* of April 28, 1993 (Barringer, 1993) reported that the number of U.S. residents for whom English is a foreign/second language had increased nearly 40 percent, to 32 million. The U.S. Department of Education (1992) estimated that in 1990–1991, approximately 2.3 million children lived in language-minority households, made substantial use of minority languages, and were of limited proficiency in English. According to the Stanford Working Group (1993), the number of such children is much greater, perhaps as many as 3.3 million children between the ages of five and seventeen. Language-minority children are now the fastest-growing group in schools in the United States (McKeon, 1992). Spanish-speaking households are the fastest-growing sector among language-minority groups. The U.S. Census (cited in Matin & Midgley, 1999) projects that by 2025 Hispanics will be 18 percent of the U.S. population. They will outnumber African Americans, who are projected to make up 13 percent of the population.

While these figures are useful in giving at least an imperfect glimpse at the approximate number of children from language-minority homes, they do not begin to scratch the surface when it comes to figuring out who is eligible for bilingual services and how long they are to be served. Thus, as Ulibarri (1986) suggests,

> Differences in estimates of the limited-English-proficient population derive from efforts to count the number of children according to different definitions and interpretations of eligibility for services. At issue are the criteria for determining which language minority children are in need of English and native language related services. Thus, the problem is not simply one of differences in number of eligible children, but one in which the actual definition of who is eligible also varies. (p. 57)

Although there is great variation depending on a student's background and schooling opportunities, a disproportionate number of English-language learners do not achieve well academically. In fact, they are all too often overrepresented at the bottom of the test score ladder. Despite the research-based knowledge we have gained over the past thirty years about how individuals learn their first and second languages and about how acculturative and assimilative forces work with immigrants and indigenous groups, there is still a wide gap between theory and practice. Consider, for example, the strong resistance that bilingual instruction has encountered in educational circles despite the evidence indicating that English-language learners who develop a strong sociocultural, linguistic, and cognitive base in their primary language tend to transfer those attitudes and skills to the other language and culture. Moreover, the chronically poor track record that schools have had in educating American Indians suggests that the schooling of most language minorities has generally been surrounded by political and ideological controversy at the expense of sustained and well-founded curricular development.

ADDRESSING LANGUAGE NEEDS IN THE MULTICULTURAL CLASSROOM

The debate about the schooling of language-minority students has to do essentially with the kind of citizens we want and need in our society. Should the school curriculum affirm cultural and linguistic pluralism through an additive process? Or should the schools pursue an ideologically conservative agenda of assimilating language minorities into mainstream U.S. society by subtracting their ancestral cultures and languages?

These questions raise some pointed and difficult issues regarding the nature and extent of cultural and linguistic pluralism in the United States. Rather than thinking in either/or terms of pluralism or assimilation, however, perhaps it would be useful to view U.S. society as a dynamic and complex cultural and linguistic organism—one that is constantly evolving and changing in accordance with the nature of circumstances. With this framework, we can envision a constructive pluralism in which cultural and linguistic maintenance, diversification, and assimilation are taking place simultaneously under varying circumstances. Within such an environment of constructive pluralism, it cannot be acceptable to blame the student's genetic, environmental, cultural, or linguistic background for his or her lack of academic success in the English-dominated classroom. Programs and practices can be implemented to redress some of the past inequities experienced by all language-minority students—English-background students who come to our schools speaking stigmatized nonstandard versions of English as well as students whose primary language is not English. Given the political climate at the beginning of the twenty-first century, however, trying to implement such programs can be like trying to paddle a canoe against a powerful tide while being buffeted from the sides by strong, cold winds. Not to do so, on the other hand, suggests abdicating responsibility for the basic tenets of sound multicultural education.

A good place to start in designing quality programs for language-minority students is by examining effective teaching and learning classroom climates for students in general, taking into account the important school reform movements currently evolving. Summarizing and endorsing the case for constructivist classrooms in the educational reform efforts of the 1990s, Fosnot (1993) states that

> constructivism is not a theory about teaching. It's a theory about knowledge and learning. Drawing on a synthesis of current work in cognitive psychology, philosophy, and anthropology, the theory defines knowledge as temporary, developmental, socially and culturally mediated, and thus, non-objective. Learning from this perspective is understood as a self-regulated process of resolving inner cognitive conflicts that often become apparent through concrete experience, collaborative discourse, and reflection. (p. vii)

Fosnot identifies five key principles of such constructive pedagogy: (1) posing problems of emerging relevance to learners; (2) structuring learning around "big ideas" or primary concepts; (3) seeking and valuing students' points of view; (4) adapting curriculum to address students' suppositions; and (5) assessing student learning in the context of teaching (Fosnot, in Brooks & Brooks, 1993, pp. vii–viii).

These principles provide an important reminder of certain basic pedagogical practices that may have validity for all students, regardless of language background; such practices should not be overlooked in the attempt to create a "special" program for language-minority students. Nevertheless, a variety of language issues in classroom instruction are unique to addressing the needs of language-minority students.

One issue pertaining to the education of speakers of nonstandard varieties of English, such as Black English, Appalachian English, and Hawaiian Creole, is whether their home languages should be used formally in the classroom. Also, should students be trained to be *bidialectical*, that is, to be able to switch from their home variety of English to standard English according to the situation? Some educators interpret bidialectalism as a waste of educational effort, suggesting that students need to discard their home language and replace it with standard English, preferably by the time they leave kindergarten. Yet most linguists remind us that suppressing such dialects is confusing and detrimental to the academic and social well-being of students.

As evidenced by the repeated attempts over the last fifty years to eradicate nonstandard varieties of English from the schools, such efforts have not been positively correlated with achievement gains among language-minority students (Ovando & Collier, 1998). The use of nonstandard English itself cannot be singled out as the cause for school failure. As Torrey puts it, "teachers should not judge children's language abilities by their schoolyard grammar" (Torrey, 1983, p. 627). Instead, among the sources of poor academic performance are the school's reaction and approach to nonstandard English. A more positive pedagogical position, states Torrey (1983), is one that

> affirms the importance of home dialect and its appropriate use
> within the community in which it is spoken while at the same time
> students are taught the standard variety. Affirming home language
> means that students may produce utterances in the classroom in
> native dialect without being told that they are wrong or that what
> they say is vulgar or bad. Instead, the teacher analyzes with the
> students the differences between their dialect and the standard
> variety: grammatical patterns, pronunciation, vocabulary items,
> varying social contexts, and so on. (p. 627)

The challenge for English-language learners, of course, is not that they speak a stigmatized variety of English, but rather that their first language is one other than English. A variety of important instructional approaches have been developed to meet the unique needs of these students. Such curricular approaches support the idea that creating bridges between the world of the language-minority student and the world of the school will produce positive cognitive, linguistic, and cultural outcomes. In 1980, for example, the California Office of Bilingual Education launched the Case Studies Project, based on leading theories of cognitive development, second-language acquisition, and cross-cultural communication. An integrated curriculum incorporating home language instruction, communication-based sheltered English, and mainstream English has produced excellent results in reading, language arts, and mathematics for language-minority students. Five principles serve as the pedagogical platform for the Case Studies Project (Crawford, 1999, p. 161):

1. Language development in the home language as well as in English has positive effects on academic achievement.

2. Language proficiency includes proficiency in academic tasks as well as in basic conversation.

3. [English Language Learners] should be able to perform a certain type of academic task in [their] home language before being expected to perform the task in English.

4. Acquisition of English language skills must be provided in contexts in which the student understands what is being said.

5. The social status implicitly ascribed to students and their languages affects student performance. Therefore, majority and minority students should be in classes together in which cooperative learning strategies are used. English speakers should be provided with opportunities to learn the minority languages, and teachers and administrators should model using the minority languages for some noninstructional as well as instructional purposes.

A two-way bilingual program is specifically designed to give both languages equal status. The English-speaking children learn the minority language at the same time that the language-minority students are learning English. Collier (1995) found the following five elements to be important for effective two-way bilingual instruction. It is interesting and important to note the important role of sociocultural issues and community involvement among these elements for a successful bilingual program.

> (1) integrated schooling, with English speakers and language minority students learning academically through each other's languages; (2) perceptions among staff, students, and parents that it is a "gifted and talented" program, leading to high expectations for student performance; (3) equal status of the two languages achieved, to a large extent, creating self-confidence among language minority students; (4) healthy parent involvement among both language minority and language majority parents, for closer home-school cooperation; and (5) continuous support for staff development, emphasizing whole language approaches, natural language acquisition through all content areas, cooperative learning, interactive and discovery learning, and cognitive complexity for all proficiency levels. (pp. 15–16)

Bilingual programs by definition include an English-as-a-second-language (ESL) component, since a main goal is to develop the language-minority student's proficiency in English. Many communities, however, do not or are unable to provide bilingual instruction for all language-minority students. This occurs for a variety of reasons, involving such factors as politics, the availability of bilingual teachers, and demographics. In such situations, English-language learners are provided with ESL instruction alone, without any significant instruction in their home language. Among the skills important to the ESL teacher are (1) a sound knowledge of theory and methods of language acquisition; (2) an understanding of the relationships among culture and language, identity, and adjustment to the new school environment; and (3) the ability to design instruction in such a way that students are helped to become as proficient as possible in content areas such as math, science, and social studies at the same time that they are learning English.

Regarding the knowledge of language acquisition, the ESL teacher strives to enable the English-language learner to develop phonology, morphology, syntax, and vocabulary primarily through real communicative activities rather than through such approaches as lecture and drills (Heath, 1986). Crawford (1987) describes such language-rich instruction as follows:

(a) Content is based on the students' communicative needs;
(b) instruction makes extensive use of contextual clues; (c) the
teacher uses only English, but modifies speech to students' level and
confirms student comprehension; (d) students are permitted to
respond in their native language when necessary; (e) the focus is on
language function or content, rather than grammatical form;
(f) grammatical accuracy is promoted, not by correcting errors
overtly, but by providing more comprehensible instruction; and
(g) students are encouraged to respond spontaneously and
creatively. (p. 43)

With respect to cultural knowledge, effective ESL teachers do not necessarily need to speak the first languages of their students, but they do need to have as broad an understanding as possible of the history, folklore, traditions, values, attitudes, and current sociocultural situation of the cultural groups with which they work. This knowledge gives the teacher a better understanding of the behavior of ESL students as they adjust to life in the United States, and, equally important, it shows the students and their parents that the teacher values the family's cultural background and recognizes that students come to school not as blank slates, but rather as unique individuals with a rich background.

We must also consider the role of the ESL teacher in enabling English-language learners to develop cognitive-academic language proficiency. Two such curricular and instructional approaches are communication-based sheltered English classes and the Cognitive Academic Language Learning Approach (CALLA). Sheltered English is an immersion type of methodology that "shelters" English-language learners from "input beyond their comprehension, first in subjects that are less language-intensive, such as mathematics, and later in those that are more so, such as social studies" (Crawford, 1987, p. 177). In sheltered English classes, teachers, who may be familiar with the students' first languages and cultures, adjust subject matter content and methodology for students who represent a variety of linguistic backgrounds and who are at about the same level of competence in the target language (Richard-Amato, 1988). As reflected in the Case Studies design, sheltered English classes require that

teachers change their speech register by slowing down; limiting
their vocabulary and sentence length; repeating, emphasizing, and
explaining key concepts, and using examples, props, visual clues,
and body language to convey and reinforce meaning carried by the
language of instruction. (cited in Crawford, 1999, p. 132)

Like sheltered English, CALLA is a content-based ESL instructional model originally developed by Chamot and O'Malley (1986) in response to the lack of academic success of English-language learners. The model supports the notion that by adding academic content to the ESL curriculum and following a specific set of instructional strategies, English-language learners can be prepared for grade-level content classrooms (Chamot & O'Malley, 1994). Buttressed by cognitive theory, research, and ongoing classroom use, CALLA is aimed at English-language learners who are at the advanced beginning and intermediate levels of English-language proficiency. As developed by Chamot and O'Malley (1994), CALLA is compatible with such instructional approaches as language across the curriculum, language experience, whole language, process writing, cooperative learning, and cognitive instruction.

Reflecting the bilingual and ESL principles discussed throughout this section, the California Commission on Teacher Credentialing (1993) has adopted a design for the preparation of teachers who serve English-language learners. The design includes two credential variations—a Cross-Cultural, Language, and Academic Development (CLAD) emphasis for nonbilingual contexts, and the Bilingual Cross-Cultural, Language, and Academic Development (BCLAD) emphasis for bilingual contexts. The CLAD/BCLAD credentials include the following six domains of knowledge and skills in which teachers must show competence: (1) language structure and first- and second-language development; (2) methodology of bilingual, English-language development and content instruction; (3) culture and cultural diversity; (4) methodology for primary language instruction; (5) the culture of emphasis; and (6) the language of emphasis. (Culture and language of emphasis refer to the particular group with whom the teacher is preparing to work, such as Vietnamese, Korean, or Chinese.)

Whether we are talking about speakers of nonstandard varieties of English or non-English speakers, and whether we are talking about bilingual programs, ESL programs, or mainstream classrooms, two common threads run through this entire section on how to address language needs in the multicultural classroom. First, the language that children bring to the classroom must be respected and used as valuable cognitive tools and as bridges to the development of the language skills that will enable them to succeed academically. Second, all language-minority students need opportunities to develop the complex language skills they will use in literacy-related school activities and throughout their lives as lifelong learners and thinking, active citizens. In other words, it is not enough for students to be able to converse with their peers only on the playground or in the halls, or to be able to recite a few rules about standard English. They need to be able to use the context-reduced language associated with extracting meaning from the printed word, for synthesizing and evaluating materials, and for writing. The importance of the development of such high-level skills is illustrated in Collier's (1987) research on non-English-speaking students who entered school in the United States at seventh grade and who were not provided with native-language content instruction. Even though they may have had a solid academic background in their home language, in the U.S. school system they tended to fall behind in standardized test norms, except in mathematics, by the time they reached the eleventh grade. Collier (1987) points out that

> as they master enough BICS and develop a wide enough range of
> vocabulary in English to move into deeper development of CALP
> in second language, they have in the meantime lost
> 2–3 years of CALP development at their age-grade level. This puts
> them significantly behind in mastery of the complex material
> required for high school students. (p. 12)

The Sociolinguistic Context of Classroom Language Development

An important principle to keep in mind when working with language-minority students—either English-speaking or non-English-speaking—is that their cognitive development must be launched from within the existing sociolinguistic context. There is no such thing as an exportable model that works everywhere without adaptation. As Heath (1986) points out, language arts curricula are based on an assumption of a path of language development that is the same for all children, regardless of their ethnic origin. Yet the research that establishes such lines of development is based predominantly on middle-class English-speaking families. Only in the last two decades have ethnographers working in language-minority communities begun to identify culturally different patterns of language socialization experienced by children. One implication of this variation in language development is that the academic success of language-minority students may hinge to some degree on how these children are able to manipulate language in a variety of contexts and for different purposes, rather than on the specific language they use.

In describing the nature of language earlier in this chapter, we list the culturally influenced domains of language beyond phonology, morphology, syntax, and vocabulary—such things as body language, degrees of formality, organizational styles, styles of speech, and appropriate speaking and listening etiquette. Related to these domains is Heath's research on genres. Regarding the specific linguistic elements that are essential for academic success in school regardless of language background, Heath (1986) has summarized the research on genre, which she defines as the

> kind of organizing unit into which smaller units of language, such as conversations, sentences, lists, or directives may fit. Each cultural group has fundamental genres that occur in recurrent situations; and each genre is so patterned as a whole that listeners can anticipate by the prosody or opening formulae what is coming—a joke, a story, or a recounting of shared experiences. Moreover, each sociocultural group recognizes and uses only a few of the total range of genres that humans are capable of producing. (pp. 168–170)

Heath (1986) then argues that in order to function well in formal U.S. school settings, students must be able to use a variety of genres typical of U.S. pedagogy, such as label quests, meaning quests, recounts, accounts, event casts, and stories. Label quests are activities in which adults ask children to say their name or to identify an item—"What's that?" or "What kind of _____ is that?" Meaning quests are activities in which an unstated or partly stated meaning is inferred from an oral or written language source. For example, a teacher might ask, "What did the author mean when she wrote, 'Andy kicked the book out of his way'?" In recounts, the child retells an experience that is already known to the teller and the listener. The speaker may be prompted with guiding questions by the adult. Accounts are activities in which the child provides new information to the listener. Accounts are often judged by their logical sequence and their truthfulness. Such accounts are the predecessors of research and creative writing assignments in the upper grades. Event casts are running narratives of events occurring or about to occur. For example, making a gelatin dessert may be accompanied by the mother's sequenced narrative (Heath, 1986).

Heath (1986) indicates that such genres exist in mainstream U.S. school-based activities in a predictable and consistent manner, but that genres may or may not be consistently present in the same way in the language-minority child's home context. Heath suggests that it is the school's responsibility to help students acquire these genres by working closely with the ethnolinguistic community. Teachers can thereby broaden cross-culturally the base of linguistic experiences to maximize their students' opportunities for acquiring such genres. Language-minority students should have access first to these genres in their dominant language. Also, parents who have a limited grasp of English should be encouraged to use their primary language rather than English with their children. Given their limited command of the English language, they will not be able to use English across the variety of suggested genres and thus will limit the quality and range of linguistic interaction with their children. Instead, such parents ideally should concentrate on engaging their children in conversations in their home language that are interesting and also representative of the variety of genres—written and oral—that schools require. Heath suggests that teachers in a creative partnership with ethnolinguistic communities should make a sustained and creative effort to expose students to these school-valued genres, at the same time capitalizing on community genres available.

As noted earlier, there is no single model for addressing the cognitive, linguistic, and cultural needs of all language-minority students. But the principles and designs, and their practical implications discussed here, can help educators who are genuinely interested in putting into practice in their classrooms what we have learned over the past thirty years or so about how children acquire their first and second languages, about how they develop cognitively in their primary and secondary languages, and about how they adjust socioculturally to the dominant culture.

Language diversity, as a powerful and ubiquitous ingredient of the U.S. multicultural mosaic, enriches the lives of the people who use these languages. It also enriches the lives of monolingual English speakers as they live, study, and work with people of non-English-language background. As educators, we have much power to ensure that the valuable and varied sociolinguistic experiences of language minorities do not continue to be translated into negative cognitive, cultural, and linguistic outcomes. As suggested in this chapter, we now have some of the conceptual, programmatic, and curricular tools with which to begin the job.

Unfortunately, bilingual education has become entangled in the politics of the English Only movement. With the passage of Proposition 227 on June 2, 1998, Californians voted to eliminate bilingual education. This draconian initiative puts a very negative spin on biculturalism, bilingualism, and biliteracy in U.S. society. It also denigrates the positive value that first-language instruction can have on academic achievement for language-minority students. Finally, it rejects the accumulated knowledge base generated for the past twenty-five years by linguists, cognitive psychologists, and bilingual educators; this knowledge supports the idea that quality-controlled bilingual programs do yield positive outcomes (Crawford, 2000; Ovando & Collier, 1998; Ovando & Pérez, 2000).

SUMMARY

This chapter stresses the power that language issues have to affect schooling outcomes for language-minority students. The first section discusses how language is interwoven with cultural styles and values. Thus, language comprises more than grammar rules, vocabulary, and a sound system. To have communicative competence in a language requires not only these things but also many others, such as the appropriate facial and body gestures, the use of varying levels of formality in the appropriate contexts, correct styles of conversation, and the ability to express abstract concepts.

By studying language learning among children, psycholinguists and cognitive psychologists have determined that it is a developmental process involving predictable stages. Researchers such as Cummins and Collier and Thomas have identified two levels of language proficiency that are particularly important in designing educational programs for language-minority students: social language skills, which take approximately two years to develop, and cognitive academic language proficiency, which may take five to seven years or longer to acquire. Equally important is the common underlying proficiency (CUP) proposed by Cummins—the notion that skills learned in the first language will transfer to the second language. This concept is one of the major underpinnings for the value of bilingual instruction.

The second section of the chapter surveys the extent of language variety in the United States. An examination of nonstandard English and creole languages emphasizes that language changes fulfill sociohistorical needs. Likewise, the language varieties resulting from these changes have their own grammatical and phonological rules and appropriate cultural styles, and they are valid means of expression rather than "deficient" language systems. This section also documents that the proportion of students from non-English-speaking backgrounds continues to increase in the United States, and these students are present in significant numbers throughout the United States.

The final section of the chapter describes some principles for the instruction of language-minority students. In the case of speakers of nonstandard English, the home language cannot be blamed for school failure. On the contrary, one cause for language-related school failure is the educator's negative attitude toward the home language. Through an additive process, the value of the home language can be affirmed, while models are also provided for use of the standard language in appropriate contexts.

For students who come from non-English-speaking backgrounds, an active, hands-on teaching style rather than a lecture style is needed, with frequent checking for understanding. Concepts, a knowledge base, and thinking skills ideally should be developed in the home language through bilingual instruction, which, of course, includes an ESL component. Regarding ESL instruction, social communicative skills—which may be acquired fairly rapidly—are not sufficient for academic success. Schools must continue to provide support for language-minority students to help them achieve cognitive-academic language proficiency in English.

Finally, there is a need for the continued development and maintenance of social and cultural bridges between the language-minority student's home life and school life. An awareness of how language is used in the home community will enable educators to be sensitive to school genres that are different. Efforts to equalize the social and linguistic status of majority and minority students within the school setting will produce positive results for all students in the classroom and, ultimately, in society.

Questions and Activities

1. What are some of the major characteristics of a language? What role does language play in the maintenance of a culture?

2. How can teachers draw on the home experiences of non-English speakers and speakers of nonstandard varieties of English to help these students develop competence in standard English?

3. What are some common misconceptions about Black English and how can they be overcome? How can a knowledge of the nature of Black English be helpful to teachers of African American students?

4. What special problems do language-minority students experience in schools? What programs and practices can schools implement to help these students experience educational success?

5. Prepare a debate on the pros and cons of bilingual education.

6. Interview officials in a nearby school district to get a profile of local language diversity. Find out how many different languages are spoken by the students in the district and what programs are being implemented to address the needs of these students.

7. Identity some principles for working effectively with language-minority students. What support and training might teachers need to implement these principles in the classroom? Interview an ESL teacher, a bilingual teacher, or a teacher who has many nonstandard English speakers in his or her classroom. Discuss what concepts, principles, and methods this teacher uses for students' language and academic development.

References

Anttila, R. (1972). *An Introduction to Historical and Comparative Linguistics.* New York: Macmillan.

Barringer, F. (1993). Immigration in 80's Made English a Foreign Language for Millions. *New York Times* (April 28), A1, A10.

Brooks, J. G. and Brooks, M. G. (Eds.) (1993). *In Search of Understanding: The Case for Constructivist Classrooms.* Alexandria, VA: ASCD.

California Commission on Teacher Credentialing. (1993, May 19). CLAD/BCLAD: *California's New Design for the Preparation and Credentialing of Teachers of Limited-English-Proficient Students.* Sacramento: Author.

Chamot, A. U. and O'Malley, J. M. (1986). *A Cognitive Academic Language Learning Approach: An ESL Content-Based Curriculum.* Washington, DC: National Clearinghouse for Bilingual Education.

Chamot, A. U. and O'Malley, J. M. (1994). *The CALLA Handbook: Implementing the Cognitive Academic Language Learning Approach.* Reading, MA: Addison-Wesley.

Collier, V. P. (1987). Age and Rate of Acquisition of Cognitive-Academic Second Language Proficiency. Paper presented at the American Educational Research Association Meeting (April 23), Washington, DC.

Collier, V. P. (1995). Second Language Acquisition for School: Academic, Cognitive, Sociocultural and Linguistic Processes. Paper presented at the Georgetown University Round Table (GURT).

Crawford, J. (1987). Bilingual Education: Language, Learning, and Politics. *Education Week: A Special Report* (April 1), 43.

Crawford, J. (1999). *Bilingual Education: History, Politics, Theory and Practice* (4th ed.). Los Angeles: Bilingual Education Services.

Crawford, J. (2000). Language Politics in the United States: The Paradox of Bilingual Education. In C. J. Ovando and P. McClaren (Eds.), *The Politics of Multiculturalism and Bilingual Education* (pp. 106–125). Boston: McGraw-Hill.

Cummins, J. (1979). Cognitive/Academic Language Proficiency, Linguistic Interdependence, the Optimal Age Question, and Some Other Matters. *Working Papers on Bilingualism, 9,* 1–43.

Cummins, J. (1981). The Role of Primary Language Development in Promoting Educational Success for Language Minority Students. In California State Department of Education, *Schooling and Language Minority Students: A Theoretical Framework.* Los Angeles: National Evaluation, Dissemination, and Assessment Center, California State University.

Cummins, J. (1991). Interdependence of First- and Second-Language Proficiency in Bilingual Children. In E. Bialystok (Ed.), *Language Processing in Bilingual Children* (pp. 70–89). New York: Cambridge University Press.

Cummins, J. (2000). Beyond Adversarial Discourse: Searching for Common Ground in the Education of Bilingual Students. In C. J. Ovando and P. McLaren (Eds.), *The Politics of Multiculturalism and Bilingual Education: Students and Teachers Caught in the Cross Fire* (pp. 126–147). Boston: McGraw-Hill.

Fosnot, C. T. (1993). Preface. In J. G. Brooks and M. G. Brooks (Eds.), *In Search of Understanding: The Case for Constructivist* Classrooms (pp. vii–viii). Alexandria, VA: ASCD.

Fuentes, C. (1988). *Myself with Others: Selected Essays.* New York: Farrar, Straus & Giroux.

Heath, S. B. (1986). Sociocultural Contexts of Language Development. In California State Department of Education, *Beyond Language: Social & Cultural Factors in Schooling Language Minority* Students (pp. 143–186). Los Angeles: National Evaluation, Dissemination, and Assessment Center, California State University.

Hymes, D. H. (1981). Foreword. In C. A. Ferguson and S. B. Heath (Eds.), *Language in the USA* (pp. v–ix). New York: Cambridge University Press.

Krauss, M. (1995, February 3). Keynote Address: *Endangered Languages: Current Issues and Future Prospects.* Dartmouth College, Hanover, NH.

Labov, W., Cohen, P., Robins, C., and Lewis, J. (1968). *A Study of the Non-Standard English of Negro and Puerto Rican Speakers in New York City, Report on Cooperative Research Project 3288.* New York: Columbia University.

Martin, P. and Midgley, E. (1999). Immigration to the United States. *Population Bulletin, 54*(2), 1–44. Washington, DC: Population Reference Bureau.

McKeon, D. (1992). Introduction. In *TESOL Resource Packet* (p. i). Alexandria, VA: TESOL.

Minami, M. and Ovando, C. J. (1995). Language Issues in Multicultural Contexts In J. A. Banks and C. A. M. Banks (Eds.), *Handbook of Research on Multicultural Education* (pp. 427–444). New York: Macmillan.

National Association for Bilingual Education (NABE). (n.d.). *Fact Sheet Need for Additional Funding for the Federal Bilingual Education Act.* Washington, DC: Author.

Nichols, P. (1981). Creoles of the USA. In C. A. Ferguson and S. B. Heath (Eds.), *Language in the USA* (pp. 69–91). New York: Cambridge University Press.

Ogbu, J. U. (1999). Beyond Language: Ebonics, Proper English, and Identity in a Black-American Speech Community. *American Educational Research Journal, 36*(2), 147–184.

Ovando, C. J. (1983). Bilingual/Bicultural Education: Its Legacy and Its Future. *Phi Delta Kappan, 64*(8), 564–568.

Ovando, C. J. (1999). Bilingual Education in the United States: Historical Development and Current Issues. Paper presented at the annual meeting of the American Educational Research Association, Montreal, Canada.

Ovando, C. J. and Collier, V. P. (1998). *Bilingual and ESL Classrooms: Teaching in Multicultural Contexts* (2nd ed.). New York: McGraw-Hill.

Ovando, C. J. and McLaren, P. (2000). *The Politics of Multiculturalism and Bilingual Education: Students and Teachers Caught in the Cross Fire.* Boston: McGraw-Hill.

Ovando, C. J. and Pérez, R. (2000). The Politics of Bilingual Immersion Programs. In C. J. Ovando and P. McLaren (Eds.), *The Politics of Multiculturalism and Bilingual Education: Students and Teachers Caught in the Cross Fire* (pp. 148–165). Boston: McGraw-Hill.

Perry, T. and Delpit, L. (1998). *The Real Ebonics Debate.* Boston: Beacon Press.

Pinker, S. (1994). *The Language Instinct.* New York: William Morrow.

Ramírez, D. (1991). Study Finds Native Language Instruction Is a Plus. *NABE News, 14*(5), 1.

Richard-Amato, P. A. (1998). *Making It Happen: Interaction in the Second Language Classroom.* New York: Longman.

Shaumyan, S. (1987). *A Semiotic Theory of Language.* Bloomington: Indiana University Press.

Smitherman, G. (1999). *Talkin That Talk: Language, Culture, and Education in Africa America.* New York: Routledge.

Stanford Working Group. (1993). *Federal Education for Limited-English-Proficient Students: A Blueprint for the Second Generation.* Palo Alto, CA: Stanford University.

Thomas, W. P. and Collier, V. P. (1999). Evaluation That Informs School Reform of Programs for Language Minority Students. Paper presented at the American Educational Research Association Meeting, Montreal, Canada.

Torrey, J. W. (1983), Black Children's Knowledge of Standard English. *American Educational Research Journal, 20*(4), 627–643.

Ulibarri, D. M. (1986). Issues in Estimates of the Number of Limited English Proficient Students. In *A Report of the Compendium of Papers on the Topic of Bilingual Education of the Committee on Education and Labor House of Representatives, 99th Congress, 2D Session.* Washington, DC: U.S. Government Printing Office.

U.S. Department of Education. (1992). *The Condition of Bilingual Education: A Report to the Congress and the President.* Washington, DC: U.S. Government Printing Office.

Waugh, D. and Koon, B. (1974). *Breakthrough for Bilingual Education.* Washington, DC: U.S. Commission on Civil Rights.

Wertsch, J. V. (1985). *Vygotsky and the Social Formation of Mind.* Cambridge, MA: Harvard University Press.

Whatley, W. (1981). Language among Black Americans. In C. A. Ferguson and S. B. Heath (Eds.), *Language in the USA* (pp. 92–107). New York: Cambridge University Press.

Wolfram, W. (1987). *American Tongues: An Instructional Guide.* New York: The Center for New American Media.

Students with special challenges as well as those with unique gifts should receive thoughtful attention and action by teachers.

Exceptionality

Expanded rights for students with disabilities was one major consequence of the civil rights movement of the 1960s and 1970s. The Supreme Court's Brown decision, issued in 1954, established the principle that to segregate students solely because of their race is inherently unequal and unconstitutional. This decision, as well as other legal and social reforms of the 1960s, encouraged advocates for the rights of students with disabilities to push for expanded rights for them. If it were unconstitutional to segregate students because of their race, it was reasoned, segregating students because of their disabilities could also be challenged.

The advocates for the rights of students with disabilities experienced a major victory in 1975, when Congress enacted public Law 94–142, The Education for All Handicapped Children Act. This act was unprecedented and revolutionary in its implications. It requires free public education for all children with disabilities, nondiscriminatory evaluation, and an individualized education program (IEP) for each student with a disability. The act also stipulates that each student with a disability should be educated in the least restricted environment. This last requirement has been one of the most controversial provisions of Public Law 94–142. Most students who are classified as having disabilities—about 90 percent—have mild disabilities. Consequently, most students with disabilities—about two-thirds—spend at least part of the school day in regular classrooms. Students with disabilities who are taught in the regular classroom are mainstreamed; this process is called mainstreaming.

Exceptionality intersects with factors such as gender and race or ethnicity in interesting and complex ways. Males and students of color are more frequently classified as special education students than are females and White mainstream students. Nearly twice as many males as females are classified as special education students. Consequently, males of color are the most likely group to be classified as mentally retarded or learning disabled. The higher proportion of males and students of color in special education programs is related to the fact that mental retardation is a socially constructed category (see Chapter 1).

Students with disabilities as well as gifted students are considered exceptional. Exceptional students are those who have learning or behavioral characteristics that differ substantially from most other students and that require special attention in instruction. Concern for U.S. students who are gifted and talented increased after the Soviet Union successfully launched Sputnik in 1957. A Gifted and Talented Children's Education Act was passed by Congress in

1978. However, the nation's concern for the gifted is ambivalent and controversial. In 1982, special funding for gifted education was consolidated with twenty-nine other educational programs. The controversy over gifted education stems in part from the belief by many people that it is elitist. Others argue that gifted education is a way for powerful mainstream parents to acquire a unique education for their children in the public schools. The fact that few students of color are classified as gifted is another source of controversy. Despite the controversies that surround programs for gifted and talented youths, schools need to find creative and democratic ways to satisfy the needs of these students.

The three chapters in this part describe the major issues, challenges, and promises involved in creating equal educational opportunities for students who are exceptional—those with disabilities as well as those who are intellectually gifted and talented.

CHAPTER 13

Educational Equality for Students with Disabilities

William L. Heward and
Rodney A. Cavanaugh

Children differ from one another. Look in any classroom in any school and you will immediately notice differences in children's height, weight, style of dress, hair and skin color, and other physical characteristics. Look a bit closer and you will see some obvious differences in children's language and their academic and social skills. Closely observe the interactions between students, curriculum, and instruction, and you will begin to see how individual children respond differently to the curriculum content and to the instructional methods.

Children also differ from one another in ways that are usually not apparent to a casual observer. Differences in the educational opportunities children receive and the benefits they derive from their time in school are two examples. The educational implications of gender, race, social class, religion, ethnicity, and language diversity not only influence how children may respond to curriculum and instruction but also affect the structure and design of educational systems in general.

While gender, social class, race, ethnicity, and language differences increasingly characterize U.S. classrooms and influence equitable access to the benefits of educational programs, every classroom can also be characterized by students' *skill diversity*. Some children learn quickly and easily apply what they learn to new situations. Other children must be given repeated practice to master a simple task and then may have difficulty successfully completing the same task the next day. Some children are popular and have many friends. Others are ostracized because they have not learned how to be friendly. Some children can run fast; others cannot run at all.

The skill differences among most children are relatively small, allowing most children to benefit from the general education program offered by their schools. When the physical, social, and academic skills of children differ to such an extent that typical school curricula or teaching methods are neither appropriate nor effective, however, equitable access to and benefits from educational programs are at stake.

Since 1975, federal legislation has mandated educational equality for learners with disabilities through individualized programs of special education. Like the rest of the chapters in this book, this chapter is not about surface or educationally irrelevant differences among individual children. Nor does it propose that teachers are casual observers. Teachers must have the knowledge and skills to recognize and to be instructionally responsive to the diversity their students represent. This chapter extends the concept of diversity to include children with disabilities, and it lays the foundation for teachers to examine educational equity for learners with diverse skills.

This chapter briefly outlines the history of exclusion and educational inequality experienced by many students with disabilities in our nation's schools. It also examines the progress made during the past twenty-five years, paying particular attention to the Individuals with Disabilities Education Act (IDEA), federal legislation that requires that all children, regardless of the type or severity of their disabilities, be provided with appropriate educational programs. We look at the key features of this landmark law, the outcomes of its implementation, and the major barriers that still stand in the way of true educational equity for students with disabilities. But first, let us take a closer look at the concept of disability and examine when skill diversity necessitates special education.

WHO ARE STUDENTS WITH DISABILITIES?

When the term *exceptional* is used to describe students, it includes both children who have difficulty learning and children whose performance is advanced. The performance of children who are exceptional differs from the norm (either above or below) to such an extent that individualized programs of special education are necessary to meet their diverse needs. *Exceptional* is an inclusive term that describes not only students with severe disabilities but also those who are gifted and talented. This chapter focuses on children with disabilities—those students for whom learning presents a significant challenge.

The term *disability* refers to the loss or reduced function of a certain body part or organ; impairment is often used synonymously with disability. A child with a disability cannot perform certain tasks (e.g., walking, speaking, seeing) in the same way in which nondisabled children do. A disability does not constitute a handicap, however, unless the disability leads to educational, personal, social, vocational, or other difficulties for the individual. For example, a child with one arm who can function in and out of school without special support or accommodations is not considered handicapped. Similarly, a child who may not read as fluently as his or her classmates, but whose progress in the grade-level curriculum is commensurate with his or her peers, is not handicapped.

Handicap refers to the challenges a person with a disability experiences when interacting with the environment. Some disabilities pose a handicap in some environments but not in others. The child with one arm may be handicapped when playing with nondisabled classmates on the playground, but having the use of only one arm might not pose an academic handicap in the classroom. Individuals with disabilities also experience handicaps that have nothing to do with their disabilities, but instead are the result of negative attitudes and inappropriate behavior of others who needlessly restrict their access and ability to participate fully in school, work, or community activities.

Children not currently identified as handicapped, but who are considered to have a higher-than-normal chance of developing a handicap, are referred to as *at risk*. This term is used with infants and preschoolers who, because of difficulties experienced at birth or conditions in the home environment, may be expected to have developmental problems as they grow older. Some educators also use the term to refer to students who are having learning problems in the regular classroom and are therefore "at risk" of being identified as handicapped and in need of special education services. Physicians also use the terms *at risk* or *high risk* to identify pregnancies in which there is a higher-than-usual probability of the baby's being born with a physical or developmental disability.

A physical, behavioral, or cognitive disability is considered a handicap when it adversely affects the educational performance of a student. Students with disabilities are entitled to special education and related services because their physical or behavioral attributes conform to one or more of the following categories of disability:

- Mental retardation or developmental disabilities (Beirne-Smith, Patton, & Ittenbach, 1998)
- Learning disabilities (Mercer, 1997)
- Behavior disorders or emotional disturbance (Kauffman, 1997)
- Communication (speech and language) disorders (Shames, Wiig, & Secord, 1998)
- Hearing impairments (Moores, 1996)
- Visual impairments (Barraga & Erin, 1992)
- Physical and other health impairments (Hill, 1999)
- Severe and multiple disabilities (Snell & Brown, 2000)
- Autism (Koegel & Koegel, 1995)
- Traumatic brain injury (Savage & Wolcott, 1994)

It is beyond the purpose and scope of this chapter to describe the defining characteristics and educational implications of each type of disability. Interested readers should refer to the sources identified in the References in the Appendix to obtain information about each area.

Regardless of the terms used to refer to students who exhibit diversity in academic, vocational, and social skills, it is incorrect to believe that there are two distinct kinds of students—those who are exceptional and those who are typical. All children differ from one another to some extent. Exceptional students are those whose skill diversity is significant enough to require a specially designed program of instruction in order to achieve educational equality.

Students with disabilities are more like other students than they are different from them. All students are alike in that all students can benefit from an appropriate education, an education that enables students to do things they were previously unable to do and to do them with greater independence and enjoyment.

Disability as a Social Construct?

The proposition that some (perhaps all) disabilities are social constructs merits attention in any discussion of educational equity for exceptional children (Coleman, 1966; Danforth, 1995; Sleeter, 1986). The issue is perhaps particularly relevant to a text about multicultural education (Huebner, 1994).

The establishment of membership criteria in any group is, by definition, socially constructed because the criteria have been created by human beings (Banks, 2000). How educational communities respond to the cultural-, ethnic-, gender-, and class-specific attributes children bring to the classroom is more important than how they perceive the establishment of membership criteria for a particular group. Education's response to the diversity children represent will influence their achievement as well as the professional and societal judgments about that achievement.

Children who are poor or whose ethnicity is not White European American are generally underrepresented in programs for children who are gifted and talented and overrepresented in programs for children who experience learning difficulties (Correa & Heward, 2000). There is evidence that some children's so-called disabilities are primarily the result of culture, class, or gender influences that are at odds with the culture, class, or gender that has established a given category of disability and the assessment procedures used to make those determinations (Grossman, 1995). As is discussed later in this chapter, a significant focus of special education litigation and legislation has dealt directly with these inequities.

Deconstructing the traditional sociopolitical view of exceptionality, changing social group membership, or passing legislation will not, however, eliminate the real challenges students with disabilities experience in acquiring fundamental academic, self-help, personal-social, and vocational skills. While the criteria for determining the presence or absence of a disability may be hypothetical social constructions, the handicaps created by educational disabilities are not (Fuchs & Fuchs, 1995a).

Be wary of the conception of disabilities as merely socially constructed phenomena, that all children who are identified as disabled would achieve success and behave well if others simply viewed them more positively. This romantic ideology is seldom, if ever, promoted by individuals with disabilities themselves or by their parents and families.

School-aged learners with disabilities, those who have pronounced difficulty acquiring and generalizing new knowledge and skills, are real children, with real needs, in real classrooms.

Our discussion of students with disabilities and of the role special education plays in addressing their needs assumes that a child's physical, behavioral, or cognitive skill diversity is influenced by, but also transcends, other variables such as ethnicity and social class. We also assume that the educational challenges students with disabilities experience represent real and significant barriers to their ability to experience independence and personal satisfaction across a wide range of life experiences and circumstances. Many factors will contribute to educational equality for children with disabilities. Among the most important of these factors is carefully planned and systematically delivered instruction with meaningful and future-oriented curricula.

How Many Students with Disabilities Are There?

It is impossible to know for certain how many students with disabilities there are in U.S. schools. Four reasons for this uncertainty are:

1. State and local school systems use different criteria for identifying exceptional students.

2. The relative resources and abilities of different school systems to provide preventive services so that students, who may be at-risk, do not become students who eventually receive special education.

3. The imprecise nature of assessment and the large part that subjective judgment plays in interpretation of assessment data.

4. A student might be identified as disabled at one time and as not disabled (or included in another disability category) at another time.

In spite of the difficulty these and other factors pose in determining the actual number of students with disabilities, data are available showing how many students with disabilities receive special education services in the United States. Each year, the U.S. Department of Education, Office of Special Education and Rehabilitation Services (OSERS), submits a report to Congress on the education of children with disabilities. The most recent information available is for the 1996–1997 school year (U.S. Department of Education, 1998).

Consider these eight statements about students with disabilities and the extent to which they receive special education in the United States:

- More than 5.7 million children with disabilities, or 7.7 percent of the resident population from birth to age twenty-one, received special education services during the 1996–1997 school year.

- The number of children and youth who receive special education has increased every year since a national count was begun in 1976, with an overall increase of 51 percent since 1976–1977.

- New early intervention programs have been major contributors to the increases since 1986. During 1996–1997, 559,902 preschoolers (aged three to five) and 187,384 infants and toddlers (birth through age two) were among those receiving special education.

- Children with disabilities in special education represent approximately 10.8 percent of the entire school-age population.

- The number of children who receive special education increases from age three through age nine. The number served decreases gradually with each successive year after age nine until age seventeen. After age seventeen, the number of students receiving special education decreases sharply.

- Of all school-age children receiving special education, 91 percent are reported under four disability categories: learning disabilities (51.1 percent), speech and language impairment (20.1 percent), mental retardation (11.4 percent), and emotional disturbance (8.6 percent).

- The percentage of school-age students receiving special education under the learning disabilities category has grown dramatically (from 23.8 percent to 51.1 percent), while the percentage of students with mental retardation has decreased by more than half (from 24.9 percent to 11.4 percent) since the federal government began collecting and reporting child count data in 1976–1977.

- About twice as many males as females receive special education.

- The vast majority—approximately 85 percent—of school-age children receiving special education have "mild disabilities."

Classification of Students with Disabilities

The classification and labeling of exceptional students have been widely debated for many years. Some educators believe the classification and labeling of exceptional students serve only to stigmatize and exclude them from the mainstream of educational opportunities (Reschly, 1996; Reynolds & Heistad, 1991; Stainback & Stainback, 1991). Others argue that a workable system of classification is necessary to obtain the special educational services and programs that are prerequisite to educational equality for exceptional students (Kauffman, 1998; MacMillan, Gresham, Bocian, & Lambros, 1998). Here is a summary of the most common arguments given for and against the labeling of students who are exceptional (Heward, 2000):

Possible Advantages of Labeling

- Labeling recognizes meaningful differences in learning or behavior and is a first and necessary step in responding responsibly to those differences.
- Labeling helps professionals communicate with one another and to classify and assess research findings.
- Funding and resources for research and other programs are often based on specific categories of exceptionality.
- Labels allow disability-specific advocacy groups (e.g., parents of children with autism) to promote specific programs and to spur legislative action.
- Labeling helps make the special needs of exceptional children more visible to policy makers and the public.

Possible Disadvantages of Labeling

- Because labels usually focus on disability, impairment, and performance deficits, some people may think only in terms of what the individual cannot do instead of what he or she can do or might be able to learn to do.
- Labels may cause other people to react to and hold low expectations of a child based on the label, resulting in a self-fulfilling prophecy.
- Labels may stigmatize the child and lead peers to reject or ridicule the labeled child.
- Labels may negatively impact the child's self-esteem.
- Labels that describe a child's performance deficit often mistakenly acquire the role of explanatory constructs (e.g., "Sherry acts that way because she is emotionally disturbed.").
- Labels suggest that learning problems are primarily the result of something wrong within the child, thereby reducing the systematic examination of and accountability for instructional variables as the cause of performance diversity. This is an especially damaging outcome when the label provides educators with a built-in excuse for ineffective instruction (e.g., "Jalen hasn't learned to read because he's _____."
- Special education labels have a certain permanence; once labeled, a child has difficulty ever achieving the status of simply being just another kid.
- Labels may provide a basis for keeping students out of the regular classroom.

- The classification of exceptional children is costly and requires the expenditure of much professional and student time that could be better spent in planning, delivering, and receiving instruction.

There are strong arguments both for and against the classification and labeling of exceptional students. Research conducted to assess the effects of labeling has been of little help, with most of the studies contributing inconclusive and contradictory evidence (MacMillan, 1988). Two important issues are how the use of categorical labels affects a child's access to special education services and the quality of instruction that he or she receives as a result of classification.

Eligibility for Special Education

Under current law, to receive an individualized program of special educational services to meet his or her needs, a student must first be identified as having a disability, that is, must be labeled and then, with few exceptions, further classified into one of the categories, such as learning disabilities or visual impairment. So, in practice, membership in a given disability category, and therefore being exposed to the potential disadvantages that label carries with it, is prerequisite to receiving the special education services necessary to achieve educational equality.

Kauffman (1998) points out the reality of labels as a necessary first step in serving students with important differences in behavior and learning: "Although universal interventions that apply equally to all, regardless of their behavioral characteristics or risks of developing disorders, can be implemented without labels and risk of stigma, no other interventions are possible without labels. Either all students are treated the same or some are treated differently. Any student who is treated differently is inevitably labeled" (p. 12).

Impact on Instruction

The classification of students according to the various categories of exceptionality is done largely under the presumption that students in each category share certain physical, behavioral, and learning characteristics that hold important implications for planning and delivering educational services. It is a mistake, however, to believe that once a child has been identified by a certain disability category, his or her educational needs and the manner in which those needs should be met have also been identified.

Regardless of what labels may or may not do for children with disabilities, labels do not teach. Although written three decades ago, the advice of Becker, Engelmann, and Thomas (1971) is still pertinent today: "For the most part the labels are not important. They rarely tell the teacher who can be taught in what way. One could put five or six labels on the same child and still not know what to teach him or how" (pp. 435–436).

HISTORY OF EDUCATIONAL EQUALITY FOR STUDENTS WITH DISABILITIES

If a society can be judged by the way it treats people who are different, our educational system does not have a distinguished history. Students who are different, whether because of race, culture, language, gender, or disability, have often been denied equal access to educational opportunities. For many years, educational opportunity of any kind did not exist for many students with disabilities. Students with severe disabilities were completely excluded from public schools. Before 1970, many states had laws permitting local school districts to deny access to children whose physical or intellectual disability caused them, in the opinion of school officials, to be unable to benefit from instruction.

Most students with disabilities were enrolled in school, but perhaps half of the nation's children with disabilities were denied an appropriate education through what Turnbull and Turnbull (1998) call "functional exclusion." The students were allowed to come to school but were not participating in an educational program designed to meet their special needs. Students with mild learning and behavior problems remained in the regular classroom but were given no special help. If they failed to make satisfactory progress in the curriculum, they were called "slow learners"; if they acted-out in class, they were called "disciplinary problems" and were suspended from school.

For students who did receive a program of differentiated curriculum or instruction, special education usually meant a separate education in segregated classrooms and special schools isolated from the mainstream of education. These children were labeled *mentally retarded, crippled, or emotionally disturbed.* Special education often meant a classroom specially reserved for students who could not measure up in the regular classroom. The following passage exemplified what was too often a common occurrence (Aiello, 1976):

> I accepted my first teaching position in a special education class in a basement room next door to the furnace. Of the fifteen "educable mentally retarded" children assigned to work with me, most were simply nonreaders from poor families. One child had been banished to my room because she posed a behavior problem to her fourth-grade teacher. My class and I were assigned a recess spot on the opposite side of the play yard, far away from the "normal" children. I was the only teacher who did not have a lunch break. I was required to eat with my "retarded" children while the other teachers were permitted to leave their students. (p. 14)

As society's concepts of equality, freedom, and justice have expanded, education's response to students with disabilities has changed slowly but considerably over the past several decades. Educational opportunity has gradually shifted from a pattern of exclusion and isolation to one of integration and participation. But change has not come easily, nor has it occurred by chance. Judiciary and legislative authority has been necessary to begin to correct educational inequities for children with disabilities.

Recent efforts to ensure educational equality for students with disabilities can be viewed as an outgrowth of the civil rights movement. All of the issues and events that helped shape society's attitudes during the 1950s and 1960s affected the development of special education for exceptional students, particularly the 1954 landmark case of *Brown* v. *Board of Education of Topeka* (1954). This case challenged the practice, common in 1954, of segregating schools according to the race of the children. The U.S. Supreme Court ruled that education must be available to all children on equal terms, and that it is unconstitutional to operate segregated schools under the premise that they are separate but equal.

The *Brown* decision that public school education should be provided to African American and White children on equal terms initiated a period of intense questioning by parents of children with disabilities who wondered why the same principles of equal access to education did not also apply to their children. Numerous cases challenging the exclusion and isolation of children with disabilities by the schools were brought to court by parents and advocacy groups. At issue in these cases were numerous questions, including (1) the fairness of intelligence testing and the legitimacy of placing children in special education classes solely on the basis of those tests, (2) intelligence testing and other assessment instruments that were not administered in a child's native language or were otherwise culturally biased, and (3) arguments by schools that they could not afford to educate exceptional students. One of the most influential court cases in the development of educational equality for exceptional students was the 1972 *Pennsylvania Association for Retarded Children* v. *Commonwealth of Pennsylvania* (1972). The association (PARC) brought the class-action suit to challenge a state law that enabled public schools to deny education to children they considered "unable to profit from public school attendance."

The attorneys and parents who represented PARC argued that it was neither rational nor necessary to assume that the children were uneducable. Because the state could neither prove that the children were uneducable nor demonstrate a rational basis for excluding them from public school programs, the court decided that the children were entitled to a free public education. Other court cases followed with similar rulings—children with disabilities, like all other people in the United States, are entitled to the same rights and protection under the law as guaranteed in the Fourteenth Amendment, which declares that people may not be deprived of their equality or liberty on the basis of any classification such as race, nationality, or religion. For a summary of these court cases, see Heward (2000).

The term *progressive integration* (Reynolds, 1989) has been used to describe the history of special education and the gradual but unrelenting progress of ensuring equal educational opportunity for all children. Of the many court cases involving education for children with disabilities, no case resulted in sweeping educational reform. With each instance of litigation, however, the assembly of what was to become the Individuals with Disabilities Education Act (IDEA) became more complete. Together, all of these developments contributed to the passage of a federal law concerning educational equality for students with disabilities.

THE INDIVIDUALS WITH DISABILITIES EDUCATION ACT: A LEGISLATIVE MANDATE FOR EDUCATIONAL EQUALITY FOR STUDENTS WITH DISABILITIES

Public Law 94–142 (1975), originally titled the Education for All Handicapped Children Act, but since amended as the Individuals with Disabilities Education Act (IDEA), was reluctantly signed by President Gerald Ford, who expressed concern that the federal government was promising more than it could deliver. Shortly after its passage, PL 94–142 was called "blockbuster legislation" (Goodman, 1976) and hailed as the law that "will probably become known as having the greatest impact on education in history" (Stowell & Terry, 1977, p. 475).

These predictions have proven accurate; IDEA is a landmark piece of legislation that has changed the face of education in the United States. This law has affected every school in the

United States and has changed the roles of regular and special educators, school administrators, parents, and many other people involved in the educational process. Its passage marked the culmination of the efforts of a great many educators, parents, and legislators to bring together in one comprehensive bill this country's laws regarding the education of children with disabilities. The law reflects society's concern for treating people with disabilities as full citizens, with the same rights and privileges that all other citizens enjoy.

The purpose of IDEA is to

> assure that all children with disabilities have available to them . . . a
> free appropriate public education which emphasizes special
> education and related services designed to meet their unique needs,
> to assure that the rights of children with disabilities and their
> parents or guardians are protected, to assist states and localities to
> provide for the education of all children with disabilities, and to
> assess and assure the effectiveness of efforts to education children
> with disabilities. (IDEA, 20 U.S. C. § 1400[c])

Major Components of the Individuals with Disabilities Education Act (IDEA)

IDEA is directed primarily at the states, which are responsible for providing education to their residents. The majority of the many rules and regulations defining how IDEA operates are related to six major principles that have remained unchanged since 1975 (Turnbull & Cilley, 1999; Turnbull & Turnbull, 1998).

Zero Reject

Schools must educate *all* children with disabilities. This principle applies regardless of the nature or severity of the disability; no child with disabilities may be excluded from a public education. This requirement of the law is based on the proposition that all children with disabilities can learn and benefit from an appropriate education, and that schools, therefore, do not have the right to deny any child access to equal educational opportunity. The mandate to provide special education to all students with disabilities is absolute between the ages of six and seventeen. If a state provides educational services to children without disabilities between the ages three to five and eighteen to twenty-one, it must also educate all children with disabilities in those age groups. Each state education agency is responsible for locating, identifying, and evaluating all children, from birth to age twenty-one, residing in the state with disabilities or who are suspected of having disabilities. This requirement is called the *child find system*.

Nondiscriminatory Identification and Evaluation

IDEA requires that students with disabilities be evaluated fairly. Assessment must be nondiscriminatory. This requirement of IDEA is particularly important because of the disproportionate number of children from non-White and non-English-speaking cultural groups who were identified as having disabilities, often solely on the basis of a score from standardized intelligence tests. Both intelligence tests that have been used most often in the identification of students with learning problems had been developed based on the performance of White, middle-class children. Because of their Anglocentric nature, the tests are often considered to be unfairly biased against children from diverse cultural groups who have had less of an opportunity to learn the knowledge sampled by the test items (Mercer, 1973). IDEA states clearly that the results of one test cannot be used as the sole criterion for placement into a special education program. Ortiz and Garcia (1988) have developed a prereferral process for preventing inappropriate placements of culturally diverse students in special education.

In addition to nondiscriminatory assessment, testing must be multifactored to include as many tests and observational techniques as necessary to fairly and appropriately identify an individual child's strengths and weaknesses. A child who has been referred for a multifactored assessment for a learning disability, for example, must be evaluated by several individuals across several different social and academic areas. The school psychologist may administer several different tests in order to obtain reliable data about the child's ability and achievement levels. The school counselor may observe the child in various academic settings as well as non-academic settings such as the playground and lunchroom. Observational data from the child's teachers and samples of the child's work should be compiled. A speech and language therapist, occupational therapist, rehabilitation counselor, or social worker may also be included in the assessment process. Parental input and the child's own perceptions of his or her needs complete a thorough and well-rounded multifactored assessment. The result of these efforts should be an accurate picture of the child's current levels of performance, with clear indications as to what type of educational program will be most appropriate.

Free, Appropriate Public Education

All children with disabilities, regardless of the type or severity of their disability, shall receive a free, appropriate public education. This education must be provided at public expense—that is, without cost to the child's parents. An *individualized education program* (IEP) must be developed and implemented for each child with a disability. The law is specific in identifying the kind of information an IEP must include and who is to be involved in its development. Each IEP must be created by a *IEP team* consisting of (at least) the child's parents (or guardians), at least one regular education teacher of the child, at least one special education teacher, a representative of the local school district, and, whenever appropriate, the child. For suggestions on how students with disabilities can participate in the IEP process, see Martin, Marshall, Maxson, and Jerman (1993), Peters (1990), and Van Reusen and Bos (1990; 1994). Many IEP teams also include professionals from various disciplines such as school psychology, physical therapy, and medicine.

The IEP is the foundation of the special education and related services a child with a disability receives. A carefully and collaboratively prepared IEP specifies the skills the child needs to learn in relation to his or her present levels of performance, the procedures that will be used to occasion that learning, and the means of determining the extent to which learning has taken place (Bateman & Linden, 1998). Although IEP formats vary widely across school districts, and schools may go beyond the requirements of the law and include additional information, all IEPs must include the following seven components:

1. A statement of the child's present levels of educational performance, including

   i. How the child's disability affects the child's involvement and progress in the general curriculum; or

   ii. For preschool children, as appropriate, how the disability affects the child's participation in appropriate activities;

2. A statement of measurable annual goals, including benchmarks or short-term objectives, related to

   i. Meeting the child's needs that result from the child's disability to enable the child to be involved in and progress in the general curriculum; and

   ii. Meeting each of the child's other educational needs that result from the child's disability;

3. A statement of the special education and related services and supplementary aids and services to be provided to the child, or on behalf of the child, and a statement of the program modifications or support for school personnel that will be provided for the child

   i. To advance appropriately toward attaining the annual goals;

   ii. To be involved in and progress in the general curriculum and to participate in extracurricular and other nonacademic activities; and

   iii. To be educated and participate with other children with disabilities and nondisabled children in [such] activities;

4. An explanation of the extent, if any, to which the child will not participate with nondisabled children in the regular class and in the activities described in paragraph (3);

5. A statement of

   i. Any individual modifications in the administration of State or district-wide assessments of student achievement that are needed in order for the child to participate in such assessment; and

   ii. If the IEP team determines that the child will not participate in a particular State or district-wide assessment of student achievement (or part of an assessment), a statement of

      A. Why that assessment is not appropriate for the child; and

      B. How the child will be assessed;

6. The projected date for the beginning of the services and modifications described in paragraph (3) and the anticipated frequency, location, and duration of those services and modifications; and

7. A statement of

    i. How the child's progress toward the annual goals described in paragraph (2) will be measured; and

    ii. How the child's parents will be regularly informed (through such means as periodic report cards), at least as often as parents are informed of their nondisabled children's progress, of

        A. Their child's progress toward the annual goals; and

        B. The extent to which that progress is sufficient to enable the child to achieve the goals by the end of the year. (20 U.S.C. Section 1414 [d] [1] [A])

IEPs for students age fourteen and older must also include information on how the child's transition from school to adult life will be supported.

Essentially, the IEP is a system for spelling out where the child is, where he or she should be going, how he or she will get there, how long it will take, and how to tell when he or she has arrived. Although the IEP is a written document signed by both school personnel and the child's parents, it is not a legally binding contract. That is, parents cannot take their child's teachers or the school to court if all goals and objectives stated in the IEP are not met. However, schools should be able to document that the services described in the IEP have been provided in a systematic effort to meet those goals. IEPs must be reviewed by the IEP team at least annually.

Of all the requirements of IDEA, the IEP is "probably the single most unpopular aspect of the law, not only because it requires a great deal of work, but because the essence of the plan itself seems to have been lost in the mountains of paperwork" (Gallagher, 1984, p. 228). Properly including all of the mandated components in an IEP is no guarantee that the document will guide the student's learning and teacher's teaching in the classroom, as intended by IDEA. Although many educators agree that the idealized concept of the IEP is "grand and has great potential" (Morse, 1985, p. 182), inspection and evaluation of IEPs often do not reveal consistency between what is written on the document and the instruction that students experience in the classroom (e.g., Nevin, McCann, & Semmel, 1983; Smith, 1990).

Several tools have been developed that IEP teams can use to create IEPs that go beyond compliance with the law and actually serve as a meaningful guide for the "specially designed instruction" a student with disabilities needs. For example, Giangreco, Cloninger, and Iverson (1998) have developed and field-tested an IEP process called *Choosing Outcomes and Accommodations for Children (COACH)*, which guides child-study teams through the assessment and planning stages of IEP development in a way that results in goals and objectives directly related to functional skills in integrated settings.

Least Restrictive Environment

IDEA mandates that students with disabilities be educated in the *least restrictive environment* (LRE). Specifically, the law states that

> to the maximum extent appropriate, children with disabilities,
> including children in public or private institutions or other care

> facilities, [will be] educated with children who are not disabled, and that special classes, separate schooling or other removal of children with disabilities from the regular educational environment [may occur] only when the nature or severity of the disability is such that education in regular classes with the use of supplementary aids and services cannot be achieved satisfactorily. (20 U.S.C. Section 1412[a][5])

The LRE requirement has been one of the most controversial and least understood aspects of the IDEA. During the first few years after its passage, some professionals and parents erroneously interpreted the law to mean that all children with disabilities, regardless of type or severity of their disabilities, had to be placed in regular classrooms. Instead, the LRE principle requires that each child with a disability be educated in a setting that most closely resembles a regular class placement and in which his or her individual needs can be met. Although some people argue that any decision to place a child with a disability in a special class or school is inappropriate, most educators and parents realize that a regular classroom placement can be overly restrictive if the child's academic and social needs are not met. Two students who have the same disability should not necessarily be placed in the same setting. LRE is a relative concept; the least restrictive environment for one student with a disability would not necessarily be appropriate for another.

Children with disabilities need a wide range of special education and related services. Today, most schools provide a *continuum of services*—that is, a range of placement and service options to meet the individual needs of students with disabilities. The continuum is often symbolically depicted as a pyramid, with placements ranging from least restrictive (regular classroom placement) at the bottom to most restrictive (special schools and residential programs) at the top (see Figure 13.1). The regular classroom is at the bottom of the pyramid and is widest to show that the greatest number of exceptional students should be placed there. Moving up from the bottom of the pyramid, each successive placement option represents an environment in which increasingly more restrictive, specialized, and intensive instructional and related services can be offered. The more severe a child's disability, the greater the need for specialized services. As noted, however, the majority of students who receive special education services experience mild disabilities; hence, the pyramid grows smaller at the top to show that more restrictive settings are required for fewer students.

Placement of a student with disabilities should not be viewed as all-or-nothing at any one level on the continuum. The IEP team should consider the extent to which the student can effectively be integrated in each of three dimensions of school life—the general academic curriculum, extracurricular activities (e.g., clubs), and other school activities (e.g., recess, meal times). The LRE "provision allows for a 'mix and match' where total integration is appropriate under one dimension and partial integration is appropriate under another dimension" (Turnbull & Cilley, 1999, p. 41).

In addition, placement must not be regarded as permanent. The continuum concept is intended to be flexible, with students moving from one placement to another as dictated by their individual educational needs. The IEP team should periodically review the specific goals and objectives for each child—they are required to do so at least annually—and make new placement decisions if warranted.

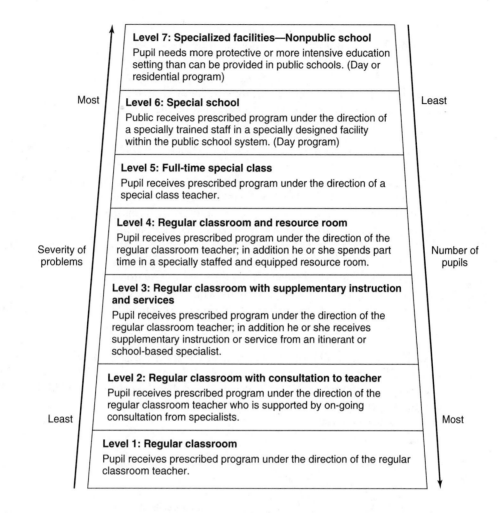

Figure 13.1   Continuum of Educational Services for Students with Disabilities

Source: From Montgomery County Public Schools, Rockville, MD. Reprinted with permission.

Although the continuum-of-services model represents well-established practice in special education, it is not without controversy. A number of specific criticisms have been leveled at this tradition of providing services to exceptional students (e.g., Taylor, 1988). Some critics have argued that the continuum overly legitimizes the use of restrictive placements, implies that integration of persons with disabilities can take place only in least-restrictive settings, and may infringe on the rights of people with disabilities to participate in their communities. Maynard Reynolds (1989), who was among the first to propose the continuum of services concept, believes it is time to make some changes in the model—specifically, to do away with the two most restrictive placements.

> In this writer's view, we are prepared now to lop off the top two levels of the continuum; . . . it is now well demonstrated that we can deliver special education and related services within general school buildings and at a continuum level no higher than the special class. Thus, we can foresee the undoing or demise of special schools (day and residential) as delivery mechanisms for special education— at least in the United States. (pp. 7–11)

Not all special educators agree with Reynolds. The relative value of providing services to students with disabilities outside of the regular classroom, and especially in separate classrooms and schools, is a hotly contested issue in special education (Fuchs & Fuchs, 1994; 1995b; Kauffman & Hallahan, 1995; O'Neil, 1995; Shanker, 1995; Taylor, 1995).

Note that in the first three placement options, students with disabilities spend the entire school day in regular classes with their nondisabled peers. Nearly three out of four students with disabilities receive at least part of their education in regular classrooms with their nondisabled peers (see Figure 13.2). Many of these students, however, spend a portion of each school day in a resource room, where they receive individualized instruction from a specially trained teacher. Approximately one of every five students with disabilities is educated in a separate classroom in a regular public school. Special schools and residential facilities provide the education for less than 4 percent of children with disabilities, usually students with the most severe disabilities.

Neither IDEA nor the regulations that accompany it specify exactly how a school district is to determine LRE. After reviewing the rulings on litigation in four LRE suits that have reached the U.S. Courts of Appeals, Yell (1995) concluded that the courts have held that IDEA does not require the placement of students with disabilities in the regular classroom, but fully supports the continuum of services.

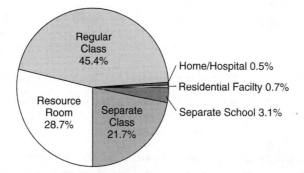

Figure 13.2 Percentage of All Students with Disabilities Ages Three through Twenty-One in Six Educational Placements

Notes: Separate school includes both public and private separate school facilities. Residential facility includes both public and private residential facilities.

Source: Based on data from U.S. Department of Education (1998). *Twentieth Annual Report to Congress on the Implementation of the Individuals with Disabilities Education Act.* Washington, DC: U. S. Government Printing Office.

Due Process Safeguards

IDEA acknowledges that students with disabilities are people with important legal rights. The law makes it clear that school districts do not have absolute authority over exceptional students. Schools may not make decisions about the educational programs of children with disabilities in a unilateral or arbitrary manner.

Due process is a legal concept that is implemented through a series of procedural steps designed to ensure fairness of treatment among school systems, parents, and students. Specific due process safeguards were incorporated into IDEA because of past educational abuses of children with disabilities (Meyen, 1978). In the past, special education placements were often permanent, void of periodic reviews, and made solely on the basis of teacher recommendations. Further, students with severe and profound disabilities were automatically excluded from public school programs, and placed in residential programs, where the quality of instructional programs often was very poor. The fact that children from minority cultural groups were disproportionately placed into special education programs was another factor in mandating the due process procedures.

Key elements of due process as it relates to special education are the parents' right to:

- Be notified in writing before the school takes any action that may alter the child's program (testing, reevaluation, change in placement)
- Give or withhold permission to have their child tested for eligibility for special education services, reevaluated, or placed in a different classroom or program
- See all school records about their child
- Have a hearing before an impartial party (not an employee of the school district) to resolve disagreements with the school system
- Receive a written decision following any hearing
- Appeal the results of a due process hearing to the state department of education (school districts may also appeal)

Ann and Rud Turnbull (1990), who are special educators and parents of a young man with disabilities, describe due process as the legal technique that seeks to achieve fair treatment, accountability, and a new and more equal "balance of power" between professionals, who have traditionally wielded power, and families, who have felt they could not affect their children's education.

Parent and Student Participation and Shared Decision Making

IDEA recognizes the benefits of active parent and student participation. Parents not only have a right to be involved in their child's education, but parents also can help professionals select appropriate instructional goals and can provide information that will help teachers be more effective in working with their children. As noted, parents (and, whenever appropriate, students) are to take an active role as full members of the IEP team; their input and wishes must be considered in determining IEP goals and objectives, placement decisions, and related services needs (e.g., sign language interpreting, special transportation). Of course, parents cannot be forced to do so and may waive their right to participate.

Section 504 of the Rehabilitation Act of 1973

Another important law that extends civil rights to people with disabilities is Section 504 of the Rehabilitation Act of 1973. This regulation states, in part, that "no otherwise qualified handicapped individual shall, solely by reason of his handicap, be excluded from the participation in, be denied the benefits of, or be subjected to discrimination in any program or activity receiving federal financial assistance." This law, worded almost identically to the Civil Rights Act of 1964 (which prohibited discrimination based on race, color, or national origin), promises to expand opportunities to children and adults with disabilities in education, employment, and various other settings. It calls for provision of "auxiliary aides for students with impaired sensory, manual, or speaking skills"—for example, readers for students who are blind, interpreters for students who are deaf, and people to assist students with physical disabilities in moving from place to place. This requirement does not mean that schools, colleges, and employers must have *all* such aids available at *all* times; it simply demands that no person with disabilities may be excluded from a program because of the lack of an appropriate aid.

Architectural accessibility for students, teachers, and other people with physical and sensory impairments is an important feature of Section 504; however, the law does not call for a completely barrier-free environment. Emphasis is on accessibility to programs, not on physical modification of all existing structures. If a chemistry class is required for a premedical program of study, for example, a college might make this program accessible to a student with physical disabilities by reassigning the class to an accessible location or by providing assistance to the student in traveling to an otherwise inaccessible location. All sections of all courses need not be made accessible, but a college should not segregate students with disabilities by assigning them all to a particular section, regardless of disability. Like the IDEA, Section 504 calls for nondiscriminatory placement in the "most integrated setting appropriate" and has served as the basis for many court cases over alleged discrimination against individuals with disabilities, particularly in their right to employment.

Americans with Disabilities Act

The Americans with Disabilities Act (PL 101–336) was signed into law on July 26, 1990. Patterned after Section 504 of the Rehabilitation Act of 1973, the Americans with Disabilities Act (ADA) extends civil rights protection to persons with disabilities in private sector employment, all public services, and in public accommodations, transportation, and telecommunications. A person with a disability is defined in the ADA as a person (1) with a mental or physical impairment that substantially limits that person in a major life activity (e.g., walking, talking, working, self-care); (2) with a record of such an impairment (such as a person who no longer has heart disease but is discriminated against because of that history); or (3) who is regarded as having such an impairment (a person with significant facial disfiguration due to a burn who is not limited in any major life activity but is discriminated against). The major provisions of the ADA are as follows:

- Employers with fifteen or more employees may not refuse to hire or promote a person because of a disability if that person is qualified to perform the job. Also, the employer must make reasonable accommodations that will allow a person with a disability to perform essential functions of the job. Such modifications in job requirements or situation must be made if they will not impose undue hardship on the employer.

- All new vehicles purchased by public transit authorities must be accessible to people with disabilities. All rail stations must be made accessible, and at least one car per train in existing rail systems must be made accessible.

- It is illegal for public accommodations to exclude or refuse persons with disabilities. Public accommodations are the everyday businesses and services such as hotels, restaurants, grocery stores, parks, and so on. All new buildings must be made accessible, and existing facilities must remove barriers if the removal can be accomplished without much difficulty or expense.

- Companies offering telephone service to the general public must offer relay services to individuals who use telecommunications devices for the deaf (such as TDDs) twenty-four hours a day, seven days a week.

EDUCATIONAL EQUALITY FOR STUDENTS WITH DISABILITIES: SOME PROGRESS AND REMAINING CHALLENGES

What impact has IDEA had? The most obvious effect is that many more students with disabilities are receiving special education and related services than before the law's passage. But this is what the law requires and is only one aspect of its impact.

Educational equality for students with disabilities is also evidenced in the ways that today's schools function as complex human services agencies. Since the passage of the IDEA, there has been a dramatic increase in the number of both special education teachers and support staff. Providing the related services necessary to meet the diverse needs of students with disabilities requires that the number of nonclassroom professionals be nearly equal to that of special education teachers. School psychologists, social workers, speech and language therapists, occupational therapists, physical therapists, audiologists, recreational therapists, adaptive physical educators, vocational specialists, and mental health professionals all lend support and expertise to the education of learners with special needs.

Perhaps the law has had its most dramatic effect on students with severe disabilities, many of whom had been completely denied the opportunity to benefit from an appropriate education. No longer can schools exclude students with disabilities on the premise that they are ineducable. IDEA is based on the presumption that all students can benefit from an appropriate education, and it states clearly that the local school has the responsibility to make the modifications in curriculum content and teaching method dictated by the unique needs of each student. In essence, the law requires schools to adapt themselves to the needs of students rather than allowing schools to deny educational equality to students who do not fit the school.

Most people would agree that IDEA has contributed positively to the education of students with disabilities, but significant barriers remain to full educational equality for exceptional students in the United States. We briefly examine five of these issues. If a truly appropriate educational opportunity is to be a reality for students with disabilities, U.S. schools must work hard to (1) bridge the research-to-practice gap with regard to effective instruction, (2) improve cooperation and collaboration between special and regular educators, (3) provide more and better early intervention programs for young children with disabilities, (4) increase the success of young adults with disabilities as they make the transition from school to adult life, and (5) ensure relevant, individualized education to students with disabilities from culturally and linguistically diverse backgrounds.

Effective Instruction

Educational equality for students with disabilities is required by IDEA. The letter of the law can be met by following the mandates for multifactored evaluations, IEPs, due process, and placements in the least restrictive environment. None of these mandated processes, however, teach. True educational equality for children with disabilities can be achieved only through effective instruction.

Special education is not a slowed-down, watered-down version of general education. It is a systematic, purposeful approach to teaching students with disabilities the academic and social skills they will need to live independent, satisfying, and productive lives, and to do it more effectively and efficiently than could be accomplished by general education alone.

Effective teaching is much more than simply assigning something to learn. One role of all teachers, but especially special educators, is to ensure that the instruction they deliver is measurably effective in meeting the needs of their students. When this occurs, the education that students with disabilities receive will be truly special.

Special education can be nothing more, or less, than the quality of instruction provided by teachers. Teachers, of course, are ultimately responsible for providing effective instruction to exceptional students. With this responsibility comes several obligations. With the support of the school administration, teachers must (1) use direct assessment and observation of students' performance as a means of designing instruction and evaluating its effectiveness (Bushell & Baer, 1994; Greenwood & Maheady, 1997); (2) use empirically validated methods of instruction (Gardner et al., 1994; Lovitt, 1995); (3) teach so that newly learned skills are useful outside of the classroom (Horner, Dunlap, & Koegel, 1988); (4) change an instructional program when it does not promote achievement and success (Howell, Fox, & Morehead, 1993); (5) consult with their regular education colleagues and their students' parents (Heron & Harris, 2000); (6) be an advocate for the needs of exceptional learners in the school as a whole; and (7) command a professional knowledge base that can generate multiple solutions to the diverse needs of their learners (Lovitt, 1996).

Teachers must demand effectiveness from their instructional approaches. For many years conventional wisdom has fostered the belief that it takes unending patience to teach children with disabilities. I believe this view is a disservice to students with special needs and to the educators—both special and general education teachers—whose job it is to teach them. Teachers should not wait patiently for exceptional students to learn, attributing lack of progress to some inherent attribute or faulty process within the child, such as mental retardation, learning disability, attention-deficit disorder, or emotional disturbance. Instead, the teacher should use direct and frequent measures of the student's

performance as the primary guide for modifying instruction in
order to improve it effectiveness. This, I believe, is the real work of
the educator. (Heward, 2000, p. xxv)

Although the IDEA does not state that the job of a teacher is to change behavior, that is what good teachers do. When a teacher helps a child who previously could not add, spell, compose, tie her shoes, apply for a job, or make a friend, behavior has been changed. Effective instruction does not change children's behavior by chance. Effective instruction is deliberate in its intent. Chance has no place in assuring children's equal opportunity to lead productive, independent, and satisfying lives.

In order to remove chance from the equation for children with disabilities, special education must bridge the research-to-practice gap regarding instructional practice in the classroom (Carnine, 1997). Contrary to the contentions of some people, special-education research has produced a significant and reliable knowledge base about effective teaching practices (Lloyd, Weintraub, & Safer, 1997). No knowledgeable person will argue that research has discovered everything that is important to know about teaching exceptional students. There are many questions to be answered, the pursuit of which will no doubt lead to other questions yet to be asked.

While there is a significant gap between what is relatively well understood and what is poorly understood or not understood at all, the more distressing gap may be between what research has discovered about teaching and learning and what is practiced in many classrooms. For example, scientific research has helped us discover a great deal about the features of early reading instruction that can reduce the number of children who later develop reading problems (Grossen, 1997) and the components of secondary special education programs that can increase students' success in making the transition from school-to-work (Wehman, 1998), but the beginning reading instruction and transition plans implemented for many students with disabilities do not reflect that knowledge.

Regular and Special Education Partnership

Traditionally, regular and special education have been viewed as separate disciplines, each serving a different student population. Today, general and special education teachers are becoming partners in meeting the needs of all learners. The concept of "your kids" and "my kids" is gradually being replaced by "our kids."

Some people argue that special and regular education should merge their respective talents and methods to create an approach more efficient than the dual system commonly practiced. Creating a general education system that services the needs of all students by combining the most effective practices of regular and special education was originally referred to as the "regular education initiative" (Reynolds, Wang, & Walberg, 1987; Stainback & Stainback, 1987; Wang & Walberg, 1988). Other people argue that such a merger would not be in the best interests of exceptional students until teacher training and professional practice improve and child-centered curricula become more common (Kauffman, Gerber, & Semmel, 1988; Lieberman, 1985; Mesinger, 1985).

Mainstreaming has traditionally been thought of as the process of integrating students with disabilities into regular schools and classes. Today, the term *inclusive education* is changing not only the language of special education reform, but its intent as well. Inclusive education can be successful only with full cooperation of and collaboration among those people responsible for the educational programs of students with disabilities (Giangreco, Cloninger, Dennis, & Edelman, 1994; Putnam, 1993; Stainback & Stainback, 1992). Although IDEA does not specifically mention mainstreaming or inclusion, it creates a presumption in favor of the regular classroom by requiring that educational services be provided in the least restrictive environment, which in turn necessitates cooperation between general and special educators.

The effects of IDEA on general education are neither entirely clear nor without controversy. This dissonance is further complicated by the tone and content of many discussions about how special education can or should reform while ensuring that the best interests of students with disabilities are appropriately served (Fuchs & Fuchs, 1994; 1995a; 1995b; Taylor, 1995). What is clear, however, is that the entire educational community has the responsibility to do the best job it can in meeting the needs of children with diverse skills. In the final analysis, issues of labeling, classification, placement, and teaching assignments are secondary to the quality of instruction that takes place in the classroom (Keogh, 1990; Lovitt, 1996).

Improved collaboration between special education and general education is important not only for the more than 5 million students with disabilities in U.S. schools. In addition to the 10 percent to 12 percent of school-age children with disabilities who receive special education, it is estimated that another 10 percent to 20 percent of the student population have mild to moderate learning or behavior problems that interfere with their ability to progress and succeed in the general education program (Will, 1986). Both special and regular educators must develop strategies for working together and sharing their skills and resources to prevent these millions of students, who are at-risk, from becoming failures of our educational system.

Early Intervention

The years from birth to school age are critical to a child's learning and development. The typical child enters school with a large repertoire of intellectual, language, social, and physical skills on which to build. Unfortunately, for many children with disabilities, the preschool years represent a long period of missed opportunities. Without systematic instruction, most young children with disabilities do not acquire many of the basic skills their nondisabled peers seemingly learn without effort. Parents concerned about their child's inability to reach important developmental milestones have often been told by professionals, "Don't worry. He'll probably grow out of it before too long." Many children with disabilities, as a result, fall further and further behind their nondisabled peers, and minor delays in development often become major delays by the time the child reaches school age.

Twenty-five years ago, there were virtually no early intervention programs for children with disabilities from birth to school age; today, early childhood special education is the fastest-growing area in the field of education. As with special education of school-age exceptional students, federal legislation has played a major role in the development of early intervention programs. By passing Public Law 99–457, the Education of the Handicapped Act Amendments of 1986, Congress reaffirmed the basic principles of the original PL 94–142 and added two major sections concerning early intervention services.

Only about 70 percent of the preschoolers aged three to five with disabilities were being served under the incentive provisions of the IDEA (which did not require states to provide a free, public education to children with disabilities under the age of six years). PL 99–457 requires each state to show evidence of serving all three- to five-year-old children with disabilities in order to receive any preschool funds.

The second major change brought about by PL 99-457 is that incentive grants are available to states for developing systems of early identification and intervention for infants and toddlers with disabilities from birth to age two. The services must be planned by a multidisciplinary team that includes the child's parents and must be implemented according to an *individualized family services plan (IFSP)* that is similar in concept to the IEP for school-aged students with disabilities.

Nearly every special educator today now realizes the critical importance of early intervention for both children who are at risk and who have disabilities, and most also agree that the earlier intervention is begun, the better. Fortunately, many educators are working to develop the programs and services so desperately needed by the increasing numbers of babies and preschoolers, especially as a result of prenatal exposure to drugs and alcohol (Carta, 2000; Howard, Williams, & McLaughlin, 1994). These programs are necessary to give these children a fighting chance to experience educational equality when they enter school.

Transition from School to Adult Life

If the degree of educational equality afforded to students who are exceptional is to be judged, as we think it should, by the extent to which students with disabilities can function independently in everyday environments, then we still have a long way to go. Follow-up studies of young adults who have graduated or left public school secondary special education programs have produced disquieting results. Data from the National Longitudinal Transition Study (Blackorby & Wagner, 1996), an on-going study of more than 8,000 youths with disabilities after they left secondary special education programs, show an unemployment rate of 36.5 percent after being out of school for three to five years. And much of the work for those who do find jobs is part-time and at or below minimum wage. The probability of a person with moderate or severe disabilities finding real work in the community is much lower. One study of 117 young adults with moderate, severe, or profound mental retardation found an unemployment rate of 78.6 percent (Wehman, Kregel, & Seyfarth, 1985). Of the 25 who had jobs, only 14 were in the community; 11 were working in sheltered workshops. Only 8 of those working earned more than $100 per month.

Employment problems are not the only difficulties faced by adults with disabilities. In a statewide follow-up study of graduates of secondary special education programs in Iowa, Sitlington, Frank, and Carson (1993) found only 5.8 percent of 737 students with learning disabilities, 5 of 142 students with mental retardation (3.5 percent), and just 1 of 59 students with behavior disorders could be judged as having made a "successful adult adjustment" (p. 230) one year after they had completed high school. A national survey found that 56 percent of Americans with disabilities indicated that their disabilities prevented them from doing many everyday activities taken for granted by nondisabled people, such as getting around the community, attending cultural or sporting events, and socializing with friends outside their homes (U.S. Department of Education, 1986, p. xiv).

Education cannot be held responsible for all of the difficulties faced by adults with disabilities, but the results of these and other studies make it evident that many young people leave public school special education programs without the skills necessary to function in the community. Many educators today see the development of special-education programs that will effectively prepare exceptional students for adjustment and successful integration in the adult community as the ultimate measure of educational equality for students with disabilities.

Special Education in a Diverse Society

Both special and general educators face major challenges in providing relevant, individualized education to students with disabilities from culturally diverse backgrounds (Baca & Cervantes, 1998; Correa & Heward, 2000). Many students with disabilities experience discrimination or experience inadequate educational programs because their racial, ethnic, social class, or gender is different from the majority. Students from culturally and linguistically diverse backgrounds are often under- or overrepresented in educational programs for exceptional children (Artiles & Trent, 1994; Artiles & Zamora-Durán, 1997; Correa, Blanes-Reyes, & Rapport, 1995; Kauffman, Hallahan, & Ford, 1998). For example:

- Asian Pacific students are generally underrepresented in disability categories and overrepresented in gifted and talented programs.

- African American students comprise about 16.3 percent of the general school population but more than 31 percent of students classified with mild mental retardation and 23.7 percent of students with severe emotional disturbance.

- Latinos are overrepresented in programs for students with learning disabilities and speech language impairments.

- Native Americans are in classes for students with learning disabilities in disproportionately high numbers, whereas their representation in classes for students who are gifted is consistently low (Chinn & Hughes, 1987; Ford, 1998).

- Ethnically diverse students constitute about 32.5 percent of the general school population but only about 22.6 percent of all students who are identified as gifted and talented.

- Approximately one-half million migrant students live in the United States, but only 10.7 percent of them with mild disabilities appear to be identified (Smith & Luckasson, 1995).

While a student's ethnicity or language should never be the basis for inclusion in or exclusion from special education programs, increased numbers of students from culturally and linguistically diverse backgrounds will require that educators attend to three important issues.

First, the adequacy of assessment and placement procedures must be assured. Multifactored assessments must be conducted in ways that will be appropriately sensitive to the students' culture and language to ensure that a special education placement is a function of the student's documented needs rather than of biased referral and assessment practices.

Second, providing appropriate support services that are responsive to the cultural and linguistic needs of the student may enhance the child's educational program. For example, bilingual aides, in-service training for teachers, and multicultural education for peers may be necessary to ensure that the child's education is meaningful and maximally beneficial.

Third, teachers and other school staff may need to learn about the values and standards of behavior present in the child's home. Since most teachers are White (Ladson-Billings, 1994), learning not only to understand but also to respect and appreciate the child's culture as it is reflected in his or her home will be important to understanding the child's behavior in the classroom and in communicating with parents.

Good intentions or token attempts at cultural sensitivity, of course, will do little to provide an appropriate individualized educational program for students with disabilities from culturally diverse backgrounds. The instructional materials educators use and the methods they employ while teaching must be responsive to the differing cultural background of their students.

Does this mean that a teacher with students from four different cultural backgrounds needs four different methods of teaching? The answer is both "no" and "yes." For the first answer, it is our view that systematic instruction benefits children from all cultural backgrounds. When students with disabilities must also adjust to a new or different culture or language, it is especially important for the teacher to plan individualized activities, convey expectations clearly, observe and record behavior precisely, and give the child specific, immediate feedback during instruction. When coupled with a respectful attitude, these procedures will increase the motivation and achievement of most students.

Good teachers must also be responsive to changes (or lack of change) in individual students' performance. It thus can also be argued that the effective teacher needs as many different ways of teaching as there are students in the classroom. Cultural diversity just adds another dimension to the many individual characteristics students present each day. While the basic methods of systematic instruction apply to all learners, teachers who will be most effective in helping children with disabilities from culturally diverse backgrounds achieve will be those who are sensitive to and respectful of their students' heritage and values.

As with all children with disabilities, the teacher of culturally diverse students must be flexible in teaching style, establish a positive climate for learning, and use a variety of approaches to meet individual student needs. Through careful assessment and observation of behavior, and the use of appropriate materials and community resources, the teacher can do a great deal to help culturally and linguistically diverse children with disabilities and their families experience success in school.

SUMMARY

The task of providing educational equality for students with markedly diverse skills is enormous. By embracing the challenge, U.S. schools have made a promise to exceptional students, to their parents, and to society. Progress has been made, but, as we have seen, significant challenges must still be overcome if the promise is to be kept. The views of our society are changing and continue to be changed by people who believe that our past practice of excluding people with disabilities was primitive and unfair. As an institution, education reflects the attitudes of society.

Common expressions of humanity and fair play ought to dictate that all children are entitled to educational equality; but the history of exclusion and inequality for students with disabilities tells us that humanity and fair play have not driven a great deal of educational policy for children with disabilities in the absence of legislation or litigation. While much progress has been made in achieving educational equality for students with disabilities, much work remains to be done.

Educational equality for children with disabilities must ultimately be assessed by the effects of the schooling those children receive. If educational equality means simply having access to curriculum and instruction in schools and classrooms attended by students without disabilities, it has largely been attained. But equal access alone does not guarantee equal outcomes. Special education must ultimately be judged by the degree to which it is effective in helping individuals with disabilities to acquire, maintain, and generalize skills that will appreciably improve their lives. New skills are needed that will promote real participation and independence in the changing school, workplace, and community environments of the twenty-first century.

Providing educational equality for students with disabilities does not mean either ignoring a child's disability or pretending that it does not exist. Children with disabilities do have differences from children who do not have disabilities. But, as stated at the beginning of this chapter, students who are exceptional are more like than unlike other students. Every exceptional student must be treated first as an individual, not as a member of a labeled group or category.

There is a limit to how much educational equality can be legislated. In many cases it is possible to meet the letter of the law but not necessarily the spirit of the law. Treating every student with a disability as a student first and as an individual with a disability second may be the most important factor in providing true educational equality. This approach does not diminish the student's exceptionality, but instead it might give us a more objective and positive perspective that allows us to see a disability as a set of special needs. Viewing exceptional students as individuals tells us a great deal about how to help them achieve the educational equality they deserve.

Questions and Activities

1. Why are both children who are learning disabled and those who are gifted considered exceptional?

2. In what ways are students with disabilities similar to and different from other students?

3. Name ten categories of disability. Identify community and school resources from which teachers can receive help when working with students with these disabilities.

4. What are the advantages and disadvantages of labeling and classifying students with disabilities? Be sure to consider the views of educators, parents, and students.

5. Interview a local special education school administrator to determine: (a) how many students in the district receive special education services; (b) how many of these students are bilingual, males, females, and/or are students of color; (c) how many students are in each of the ten categories of disability; and (d) how many

special education students are mainstreamed, the portion of the school day in which they are mainstreamed, and the classes in which mainstreamed students participate.

6. How did the civil rights movement influence the movement for educational equality for students with disabilities?

7. What is an IEP and how can it benefit students with disabling conditions? Visit a special education classroom and talk with the teacher about how an IEP might influence regular classroom teachers when students are mainstreamed.

8. Do you think all students with disabilities should be educated in regular classrooms? Why or why not? How does the concept of least restrictive environment (LRE) influence alternative placements for students with disabilities?

9. Why are collaboration and teaming between special educators and general classroom teachers so critical to the quality of education experienced by children with disabilities?

10. In your view, which of the challenges currently facing the education of exceptional students is the most critical? What suggestions would you make for meeting that challenge?

References

Aiello, B. (1976). Up from the Basement: A Teacher's Story. *New York Times* (April 25), 14.

Artiles, A. J. and Trent, S. C. (1994). Overrepresentation of Minority Students in Special Education: A Continuing Debate. *The Journal of Special Education, 27,* 410–437.

Artiles, A. J. and Zamora-Durán, G. (1997). *Reducing Disproportionate Representation of Culturally Diverse Students in Special and Gifted Education.* Reston, VA: Council for Exceptional Children.

Baca, L. M. and Cervantes, H. T. (1998). *The Bilingual Special Education Interface* (3rd ed.). Upper Saddle River, NJ: Merrill/Prentice-Hall.

Banks, J. A. (2000). *Cultural Diversity and Education: Foundations, Curriculum, and Teaching.* (4th ed.) Boston: Allyn and Bacon.

Barraga, N. C. and Erin, J. N. (1992). *Visual Handicaps and Learning* (3rd ed.). Austin, TX: PRO-ED.

Bateman, B. D. and Linden, M. L. (1998). *Better IEPs: How to Develop Legally Correct and Educationally Useful Programs* (3rd ed.). Longmont, CO: Sopris West.

Becker, W. C., Engelmann, S., and Thomas, D. R. (1971). *Teaching: A Course in Applied Psychology.* Chicago: Science Research Associates.

Beirne-Smith, M., Patton, J. R., and Ittenbach, R. (1998). *Mental Retardation: Foundations of Educational Programming* (5th ed.). Upper Saddle River, NJ: Merrill/Prentice-Hall.

Blackorby, J. and Wagner, M. (1996). Longitudinal Postschool Outcomes of Youth with Disabilities: Findings from the National Longitudinal Transition Study. *Exceptional Children, 62,* 399–413.

Brown v. *Board of Education of Topeka.* (1954). 347 U.S. 483.

Bushell, D., Jr., and Baer, D. M. (1994). Measurably Superior Instruction Means Close, Continual Contact with the Relevant Outcome Data. Revolutionary! In R. Gardner III, D. M. Sainato,

J. O. Cooper, T. E. Heron, W. L. Heward, J. Eshleman, and T. A. Grossi (Eds.), *Behavior Analysis in Education: Focus on Measurably Superior Instruction* (pp. 3–10). Pacific Grove, CA: Brooks/Cole.

Carnine, D. (1997). Bridging the Research to Practice Gap. *Exceptional Children, 63,* 513–521.

Carta, J. J. (2000). Perspectives on Educating Young Children Prenatally Exposed to Illegal Drugs. In W. L. Heward, *Exceptional Children: An Introduction to Special Education* (6th ed.), (pp. 167–168). Upper Saddle River, NJ: Prentice-Hall/Merrill.

Chinn, P. C. and Hughes, S. (1987). Representation of Minority Students in Special Education Classes. *Remedial and Special Education, 8,* 41–46.

Coleman, J. S. (1966). *Equality of Educational Opportunity.* Washington, DC: U.S. Government Printing Office.

Correa, V. I., Blanes-Reyes, M., and Rapport, M. J. (1995). Minority Issues. In H. R. Turnbull and A. P. Turnbull. (Eds.), *A Compendium Report to Congress.* Lawrence, KS: Beach Center.

Correa, V. I. and Heward, W. L. (2000). Special Education in a Culturally Diverse Society. In W. L. Heward, *Exceptional Children: An Introduction to Special Education* (6th ed.) (pp. 82–114). Upper Saddle River, NJ: Merrill/Prentice Hall.

Danforth, S. (1995). Toward a Critical Theory Approach to Lives Considered Emotionally Disturbed. *Behavioral Disorders, 20*(2), 136–143.

Ford, D. Y. (1998). The Underrepresentation of Minority Students in Gifted Education: Problems and Promises in Recruitment and Retention. *Journal of Special Education, 32,* 4–14.

Fuchs, D. and Fuchs, L. S. (1994). Inclusive Schools Movement and the Radicalization of Special Education Reform. *Exceptional Children, 60,* 294–309.

Fuchs, D. and Fuchs, L. S. (1995a). What's "Special" about Special Education? *Phi Delta Kappan, 76*(7), 531–540.

Fuchs, D. and Fuchs, L. S. (1995b). Sometimes Separate Is Better. *Educational Leadership, 52*(4), 22–25.

Gallagher, J. J. (1984). The Evolution of Special Education Concepts. In B. Blatt and R. J. Morris (Eds.), *Perspectives in Special Education: Personal Orientations* (pp. 210–232). Glenview, IL: Scott, Foresman.

Gardner, R. III, Sainato, D. M., Cooper, J. O., Heron, T. E., Heward, W. L., Eshleman, J., and Grossi, T. A. (Eds.), (1994). *Behavior Analysis in Education: Focus on Measurably Superior Instruction.* Monterey, CA: Brooks/Cole.

Giangreco, M. F., Cloninger, C., Dennis, R., and Edelman, S. (1994). Problem-Solving Methods to Facilitate Inclusive Education. In J. S. Thousand, R. A. Villa, and A. I. Nevin (Eds.), *Creativity and Collaborative Learning* (pp. 322–346). Baltimore: Paul H. Brookes.

Giangreco, M. F., Cloninger, C. J., and Iverson, V. S. (1998). *Choosing Options and Accommodations for Children: A Guide to Educational Planning for Students with Disabilities* (2nd ed.). Baltimore: MD: Paul H. Brookes.

Goodman, L. V. (1976). A Bill of Rights for the Handicapped. *American Education, 12*(6), 6–8.

Greenwood, C. R. and Maheady, L. (1997). Measurable Change in Student Performance: Forgotten Standard in Teacher Preparation? *Teacher Education and Special Education, 20,* 265–275.

Grossen, B. (1997). *30 Years of NICHD Research: What We Now Know about How Children Learn to Read.* Santa Cruz: Center for the Future of Teaching and Learning. [http://www.cftl.org/]

Grossman, H. (1995). *Special Education in a Diverse Society.* Boston: Allyn and Bacon.

Heron, T. E. and Harris, K. C. (2000). *The Educational Consultant: Helping Professionals, Parents, and Mainstreamed Students* (4th ed.). Austin, TX: PRO-ED.

Heward, W. L. (2000). *Exceptional Children: An Introduction to Special Education* (6th ed.). Upper Saddle River, NJ: Prentice-Hall/Merrill.

Hill, J. L. (1999). *Meeting the Needs of Students with Special Physical and Health Care Needs.* Upper Saddle River, NJ: Merrill/Prentice Hall.

Horner, R. H., Dunlap, G., and Koegel, R. L. (1988). *Generalization and Maintenance: Life-Style Changes in Applied Settings.* Baltimore, MD: Paul H. Brookes.

Howard, V. F., Williams, B. F., and McLaughlin, T. F. (1994). Children Prenatally Exposed to Alcohol and Cocaine: Behavioral Solutions. In R. Gardner III, D. M. Sainato, J. O. Cooper, T. E. Heron, W. L. Heward, J. Eshleman, & T. A. Grossi (Eds.), *Behavior Analysis in Education: Focus on Measurably Superior Instruction* (pp. 131–146). Pacific Grove, CA: Brooks/Cole.

Howell, K. W., Fox, S. L., and Morehead, M. K. (1993). *Curriculum-Based Education.* Pacific Grove, CA: Brooks/Cole.

Huebner, T. A. (1994). Understanding Multiculturalism. *Journal of Teacher Education, 45*(5), 375–377.

Kauffman, J. M. (1997). *Characteristics of Emotional and Behavioral Disorders of Children and Youth* (6th ed.). Upper Saddle River, NJ: Merrill/Prentice Hall.

Kauffman, J. M. (1998). Commentary: Today's special education and its messages for tomorrow. *Journal of Special Education, 32*(3), 127–137.

Kauffman, J. M., Gerber, M. M., and Semmel, M. I.. (1988). Arguable Assumptions Underlying the Regular Education Initiative. *Journal of Learning Disabilities, 21,* 6–11.

Kauffman, J. M. and Hallahan, D. K. (1995). *The Illusion of Full Inclusion: A Comprehensive Critique of a Current Special Education Bandwagon.* Austin, TX: PRO-ED.

Kauffman, J. M., Hallahan, D. P., and Ford, D. Y. (Guest Eds.). (1998). Special section: Disproportionate Representation of Minority Students in Special Education. *Journal of Special Education, 32,* 3–54.

Keogh, B. K. (1990). Narrowing the Gap between Policy and Practice. *Exceptional Children, 57,* 186–190.

Koegel, R. L. and Koegel, L. (1995). *Teaching Children with Autism.* Baltimore, MD: Brookes.

Ladson-Billings, G. (1994). What We Can Learn from Multicultural Education Research. *Educational Leadership, 51,* 22–27.

Lieberman, L. (1985). Special Education and Regular Education: A Merger Made in Heaven. *Exceptional Children, 51,* 513–516.

Lloyd, J. W., Weintraub, F. J., and Safer, N. D. (1997). A Bridge between Research and Practice: Building Consensus. *Exceptional Children, 63,* 535–538.

Lovitt, T. C. (1995). *Tactics for Teaching* (2nd ed.). Englewood Cliffs, NJ: Prentice-Hall.

Lovitt, T. C. (1996). What Special Educators Need to Know. In W. L. Heward, *Exceptional Children: An Introduction to Special Education* (5th ed.) (pp. 84–86). Englewood Cliffs, NJ: Prentice-Hall/Merrill.

MacMillan, D.L. (1988). New EMRs: Chapter One. In G. A. Robinson (Ed.), *Best Practices in Mental Disabilities* (p. 24). Des Moines: Iowa State Department of Public Instruction. (ERIC Document Reproduction Services No. ED304 828)

MacMillan, D. L., Gresham, F. M., Bocian, K. M., and Lambros, K. M. (1998). Current Plight of Borderline Students: Where Do They Belong? *Education and Training in Mental Retardation and Developmental Disabilities, 33,* 83–94.

Martin, J. E., Marshall, L. H., Maxson, L., and Jerman, P. (1993). *Self-Directed IEP.* Colorado Springs: University of Colorado Press.

Mercer, C. D. (1997). *Students with Learning Disabilities* (5th ed.). Upper Saddle River, NJ: Merrill/Prentice Hall.

Mercer, J. R. (1973). *Labeling the Mentally Retarded.* Berkeley: University of California Press.

Mesinger, J. F. (1985). Commentary on a Rationale for the Merger of Special and Regular Education or, Is It Time for the Lamb to Lie Down with the Lion? *Exceptional Children, 51,* 510–512.

Meyen, E. L. (Ed.).(1978). *Exceptional Children and Youth: An Introduction.* Denver: Love.

Moores, D. F. (1996). *Educating the Deaf: Psychology, Principles, and Practices* (4th ed.). Boston: Houghton Mifflin.

Morse, W. C. (1985). *The Education and Treatment of Socioemotionally Impaired Children and Youth.* Syracuse, NY: Syracuse University Press.

Nevin, A., McCann, S., and Semmel, M. I. (1983). An Empirical Analysis of the Regular Classroom Teacher's Role in Implementing IEPs. *Teacher Education and Special Education, 6,* 235–246.

O'Neil, J. (1995). Can Inclusion Work? A Conversation with Jim Kauffman and Mara Sapon-Sevin. *Educational Leadership, 52*(4), 7–11.

Ortiz, A. A. and Garcia, S. (1988) A Prereferral Process for Preventing Inappropriate Referrals of Hispanic Students to Special Education. In A. Ortiz and B. A. Ramírez (Eds.), *Schools and the Culturally Diverse Exceptional Student: Promising Practices and Future Directions* (pp. 6–18). Reston, VA: Council for Exceptional Children.

Pennsylvania Association for Retarded Children v. Commonwealth of Pennsylvania. (1972). 343 F., Supp. 279.

Peters, M. T. (1990). Someone's Missing: The Student as an Overlooked Participant in the IEP Process. *Preventing School Failure, 34* (Summer), 32–36.

Public Law 94–142: The Education of All Handicapped Children Act. (1975). Section 612(5)B.

Putnam, J. W. (1993). *Cooperative Learning and Strategies for Inclusion: Celebrating Diversity in the Classroom.* Baltimore, MD: Paul H. Brookes.

Reschly, D. J. (1996). Identification and Assessment of Students with Disabilities. *Future of Children, 6*(1), 40–53.

Reynolds, M. C. (1989). An Historical Perspective: The Delivery of Special Education to Mildly Disabled and At-Risk Students. *Remedial and Special Education, 10,* 6–11.

Reynolds, M. C. and Heistad, D. (1991). Classification and Labeling. In J. W. Lloyd, N. N. Singh, and A. C. Repp (Eds.), *The Regular Education Initiative: Alternative Perspectives on Concepts, Issues, and Models* (pp. 29–42). Sycamore, IL: Sycamore.

Reynolds, M. C., Wang, M. C., and Walberg, H. J. (1987). The Necessary Restructuring of Special and Regular Education. *Exceptional Children, 53,* 391–398.

Savage, R. C. and Wolcott, G. F. (Eds.). (1994). *Educational Dimensions of Acquired Brain Injury.* Austin, TX: PRO-ED.

Shames, G. H., Wiig, E. H., and Secord, W. A. (1998). *Human Communication Disorders* (5th ed.). Boston: Allyn and Bacon.

Shanker, A. (1995). Full Inclusion Is Neither Free nor Appropriate. *Educational Leadership, 52*(4), 18–21.

Sitlington, P. L., Frank, A. R., and Carson, R. (1993). Adult Adjustment among High School Graduates with Mild Disabilities. *Exceptional Children, 59,* 221–233.

Sleeter, C. E. (1986). Learning Disabilities: The Social Construction of a Special Education Category. *Exceptional Children, 53*(1), 46–54.

Smith, D. D. and Luckasson, R. (1995). *Introduction to Special Education: Teaching in an Age of Challenge* (2nd ed.). Boston: Allyn and Bacon.

Smith, S. W. (1990). Individualized Education Programs (IEPs) in Special Education—from Intent to Acquiescence. *Exceptional Children, 57,* 6–14.

Snell, M. E. and Brown, F. (Eds.). (2000). *Instruction of Students with Severe Disabilities* (5th ed.). Upper Saddle River, NJ: Merrill/Prentice Hall.

Stainback, S. and Stainback, W. (1987). Integration versus Cooperation: A Commentary on Educating Children with Learning Problems: A Shared Responsibility. *Exceptional Children, 54,* 66–68.

Stainback, S. and Stainback, W. (1992). *Curriculum Considerations in Inclusive Classrooms: Facilitating Learning for All Students.* Baltimore, MD: Paul H. Brookes.

Stainback, S. and Stainback, W. (Eds.). (1991). *Teaching in the Inclusive Classroom: Curriculum Design, Adaptation and Delivery.* Baltimore MD: Brookes.

Stowell, L. J. and Terry, C. (1977). Mainstreaming: Present Shock. *Illinois Libraries, 59,* 475–477.

Taylor, S. J. (1988). Caught in the Continuum: A Critical Analysis of the Principle of Least Restrictive Environment. *The Journal of the Association for Persons with Severe Handicaps, 13,* 41–53.

Taylor, S. J. (1995). On Rhetoric: A Response to Fuchs and Fuchs. *Exceptional Children, 61,* 301–302.

Turnbull, A. P. and Turnbull, H. R. (1990). *Families, Professionals, and Exceptionality: A Special Partnership* (2nd ed.). New York: Macmillan.

Turnbull, H. R. and Turnbull, A. P. (1998). *Free Appropriate Public Education: The Law and Children with Disabilities* (5th ed.). Denver: Love.

Turnbull, R and Cilley, M. (1999). *Explanations and Implications of the 1997 Amendments to IDEA.* Upper Saddle River, NJ: Merrill/Prentice Hall

U. S. Department of Education. (1986). *Eighth Annual Report to Congress on the Implementation of the Education of All Handicapped Children Act.* Washington, DC: U.S. Government Printing Office.

U.S. Department of Education. (1998). *Twentieth Annual Report to Congress on the Implementation of the Individuals with Disabilities Education Act.* Washington, DC: U.S. Government Printing Office.

Van Reusen, A. K. and Bos, C. S. (1990). IPLAN: Helping Students Communicate in Planning Conferences. *Teaching Exceptional Children*, *22*(4), 30–32.

Van Reusen, A. K. and Bos, C. (1994). Facilitating Student Participation in Individualized Education Programs through Motivation Strategy Instruction. *Exceptional Children*, *60*, 466–475.

Wang, M. C. and Walberg, H. J. (1988). Four Fallacies of Segregationism. *Exceptional Children*, *55*, 497–502.

Wehman, P., Kregel, J., and Seyfarth, J. (1985).Employment Outlook for young Adults with Mental Retardation. *Rehabilitation Counseling Bulletin*, *5*, 343–354.

Will, M. C. (1986). Educating Children with Learning Problems: A Shared Responsibility. *Exceptional Children*, *52*, 411–415.

Yell, M. L. (1995). Least Restrictive Environment, Inclusion, and Students with Disabilities: A Legal Analysis. *Journal of Special Education*, *28*, 389–404.

CHAPTER 14

School Inclusion and Multicultural Issues in Special Education

Luanna H. Meyer, Jill Bevan-Brown,
Beth Harry, and Mara Sapon-Shevin

Before the passage of Public Law 94–142 by Congress in 1975, children with disabilities could be excluded from the public school system altogether if they were not performing academically at the level of their age-peers. If they did attend public school, there was no obligation that schools adapt curricula and instruction to meet their educational needs so that they might ultimately graduate with qualifications for meaningful adult roles.

The advent of the legislation now known as the Individuals with Disabilities Education Act (IDEA) changed the situation dramatically: IDEA requires that all children, regardless of the severity or extent of their disability, be provided with a free and appropriate education. Various due process protections are included in the law to ensure that schools not only cannot deny access but must also adapt curricula to meet diverse student needs, with no exceptions.

Throughout its history, special education has signified access to equality of educational opportunity as well as a commitment to meeting individualized student needs. Special education has also intersected with movements within general education—such as multicultural education—focused on pedagogical reform to address the diverse student population in today's schools. The relationship between special and general education is a complex one that can provide a measure of the extent to which our public education system is succeeding in its responsibility for equality of educational opportunity.

This chapter highlights this relationship and challenges the reader to acknowledge and promote future directions in both multicultural education and special education that do not compromise this fundamental responsibility.

THE SPECIAL EDUCATION MANDATE TO EDUCATE ALL CHILDREN

Special education has come to occupy "the high ground of many contemporary educational debates," located at "the forefront of pedagogical innovation and judicial reform" (Richardson, 1994, p. 713). Following the passage of national legislation, special education rose to the

327

challenge of developing diverse instructional strategies that resulted in significant educational achievement even in children once labeled "uneducable" (Horner, Meyer, & Fredericks, 1986). Furthermore, this evolution of effective specialized services in public education emerged at a time when general education continued, for the most part, to maintain the myth of homogeneity—a "one size fits all" approach. Special educators became the reformers, willing to address the complexities of educating children as they are, not as they are supposed to be. This is the generous and idealistic interpretation of the history of special education.

Special Education as Segregation from the Mainstream

There is another view, which Richardson (1994) describes as the consequence of the impact of compulsory education in linking three worlds of children—the typical, the delinquent, and the special. With the advent of compulsory education, students who had previously been excluded or absent voluntarily began to come to school. Richardson (1994) points to data from the state of California—a leader in the early special education movement before the passage of national legislation—that illustrates well the scenario that followed compulsory attendance requirements in general education. In 1947, a "separation of races" clause that had existed unchallenged since 1883 was under attack as the basis for segregating Mexican Americans in school. The California court ruled that because Mexican Americans were not one of the "great races of man" they could not be segregated. Richardson argues that this judicial decision became the impetus for the establishment of segregated, special education classes in California for students diagnosed as educably mentally retarded (EMR). At the same time, there was a dramatic increase in school use of long-term suspensions for behavior problems as the student population increased and became more diverse as a result of compulsory attendance requirements (Divergent Youth, 1963; Richardson, 1994). The original function of special education to provide programs for students with intellectual disabilities was also expanded to include a new behavioral category—educationally handicapped (EH)—rapidly populated by the same children previously excluded from school.

Special education in these early days was synonymous with special classes, which appeared to be the contemporary placement for many children who had previously been excluded from school. Thus, Richardson (1994) argues, special education emerged not primarily to meet individual needs but, instead, to provide a mechanism to continue to send some children to school elsewhere, apart from the mainstream. Dunn (1968) argued this same point in his influential article, "Special Education for the Mildly Retarded: Is Much of It Justifiable?" He highlighted the disproportionate overrepresentation of children of color in segregated special classes and noted the increase of these segregated programs in the 1950s and 1960s, just as the *Brown* v. *Board of Education* decision was otherwise challenging racial segregation. Dunn also presented evidence that the special education classes were not so very special: Children in those segregated programs did less well academically than did similar children who had remained in general education without special education services. Special education was being used, Dunn (1968) charged, to achieve socially acceptable racial segregation. His scathing critique, widely discussed for many years, was accompanied by continued evidence that children of color were disproportionately represented in special education programs.

Mercer (1973) studied the phenomenon labeled the "six-hour retarded child" used to describe the irony of children who had been diagnosed as EMR in school while doing just fine outside the school day and in their communities. She argued that both school structure and the nature of diagnostic measures (such as IQ) used to identify mental retardation were culturally biased in favor of Anglo children and against children of color. Hence, Anglo children would be conservatively diagnosed as EMR by these biased measures, resulting in more accurate identification of those children in need of special education. In contrast, the majority of children of color labeled EMR through existing measures were not retarded at all but were mislabeled. To remediate this situation, Mercer (1979) developed and validated the *System of Multicultural Assessment (SOMPA)*, which became the model for culture-free cognitive assessment. Her pioneering work was also instrumental in the design of certain procedural safeguards incorporated into IDEA, with key provisions requiring nondiscriminatory assessment and the use of both intellectual and adaptive behavior evaluations to establish eligibility for special education services. Of course, a continuing dilemma for the diagnostic category of mild mental retardation was also an issue for categories such as learning disabilities and emotional disturbance: These are the "soft" disability categories for which diagnosis is primarily determined by professional judgment influenced heavily by existing classroom ecologies (Adelman & Taylor, 1993).

Special Education as Racial Discrimination

As attacks on the concept and practice of "Educable Mental Retardation" became more pronounced, a shift in the pattern of diagnosis occurred. The population of students labeled EMR (more recently referred to as "mildly mentally retarded") declined dramatically during the 1970s and 1980s, while the percentage of children labeled as learning disabled (LD) or educationally handicapped (EH) grew just as dramatically. Nationally, the EH category became that of Serious Emotional Disturbance (SED), with patterns of identification and referral that were just as troubling (Webb-Johnson, 1999). Smith (1983) noted that African Americans continued to be overrepresented in EMR classes in some parts of the United States; where there were decreases in the EMR category, a corresponding increase in disproportionate labelling as LD occurred. Increasingly, the overrepresentation of children of color in EMR classes was paralleled by similar patterns in LD and EH/SED programs (Argulewicz, 1983; Finn, 1982; MacMillan, Jones, & Meyers, 1976; Oswald, Coutinho, Best, & Singh, 1999; Tucker, 1980).

Meier, Stewart, and England (1989) reported the results of a large-scale study conducted in nearly 200 school districts examining the effects of socioeconomic status and race on educational opportunities. They found widespread evidence of "second-generation discrimination," including various sorting practices resulting in overrepresentation of African American students in special education classrooms as well as in punishment and suspension statistics. In contrast, "a white student was 3.2 times more likely to be assigned to a gifted class than is a black student" (Meier et al., 1989, p. 5). In their study of New York City referral patterns, Gottlieb, Alter, Gottlieb, and Wishner (1994) found that only 15 percent of LD students in a 1992 sample actually fit the clinical disability, while the majority were poor children with low achievement and low scores on cognitive measures. What was happening, they argued, was that special education was being asked to accept "regular education fallout" (p. 458). They added, "The current state of urban education, so woefully underfunded relative to its needs, provides students little access to intensive resources outside of special education" (Gottlieb et al., 1994, p. 459).

Most recently, Oswald, Coutinho, Best, and Singh (1999) analyzed the extant data reported by nearly 4,500 U.S. school districts in the fall of 1992 for a survey of compliance with civil rights requirements. They found that African American students were two times as likely to be identified as EMR and just as likely to be identified as SED compared to their non-African American peers. These authors maintain that the issue is further complicated by national problems of general underidentification of students in both disability categories. A major purpose for their analysis, however, was to control for the effects of poverty and other demographic variables that are also known to be associated with mild developmental delay and emotional and behavioral problems—perhaps legitimately so, signifying actual special education needs. Ethnic minority status is known to be associated with greater poverty in the United States. Knowing that overrepresentation of ethnic minorities in special education statistics might actually be a function of the impact of poverty would lead to one set of intervention implications. What Oswald and his colleagues found, however, was that even after the effects of demographic variables were accounted for, identification in special education was still significantly influenced by ethnicity.

Finding that ethnic minorities are disproportionately represented in special education even after controlling for the effects of demographic variables such as poverty suggests that discriminatory educational practices are responsible. Given that the vast majority of teachers and administrators in the U.S. educational system are White, evidence of widespread referral of ethnic minority children away from the mainstream (whether into special education or exclusion through suspension) represents a significant challenge to equality of educational opportunity.

Eliminating Racial Bias in Educational Practice

Oswald and his colleagues (1999) conclude that "further work is warranted to determine the impact of other factors not included in these models, such as educators who mistake cultural difference for cognitive or behavioral disabilities during the prereferral, referral, assessment, or eligibility process" (p. 203). Patton (1998) believes that the fundamental school structures of general and special education represent the dominant, Anglo-European culture such that our knowledge base and educational practices inevitably devalue the contributions of African Americans at all levels. He challenges the research community to adopt qualitatively different knowledge-producing approaches that are "culturally and interculturally competent" (p. 27). In Aotearoa, New Zealand, similar concerns have been raised regarding the place of Maori in school and society, in a nation formally committed to Maori-Anglo biculturalism but reflecting predominantly Anglo culture infrastructures. The call for culture-specific research approaches for indigenous people to counter traditional research methodologies, seen as disempowering non-European groups, focuses on "decolonizing methodologies" and the validation of Maori knowledge (Smith, 1999). The education of Maori children in New Zealand includes emphasis on the availability of immersion Kura Kaupapa Maori schools from early years through university level, in educational units and institutions where only Te Reo Maori is spoken. Tertiary degrees are taught entirely in the indigenous language and are based on indigenous Maori knowledge rather than on a translation of western knowledge into Te Reo; beginning in 2000, even doctoral degree-level-Maori education was available.

Artiles (1998) locates competence within one's culture and emphasizes that we must deepen our understanding about how teachers deal with student diversity in the classroom. The message of contemporary work on multicultural education is not primarily fixed on remediation of racial discrimination and adopting unbiased educational practices in schools and classrooms, although this is a part of what needs to be done whenever such discrimination and bias exists. Current multicultural education theory and practice highlight pedagogy in cultural context and prescribe a future classroom and school whereby culturally diverse learners find educational practices that value their individual behavioral styles and culture-specific knowledge base (Banks & Banks, 2001).

Hence, work by Cronin (1998), Townsend (1998), and Webb-Johnson (1999) examining and intervening with the clash in cultural repertoire between teacher and child represents an important step in resolving the place of African American and other ethnically diverse students in today's classrooms. But even more fundamental reform at the preservice teacher education level will be required if the result is to be an educational system that no longer discriminates by institutionalizing "dominant" Western cultural structures, values, and practices. Research by Artiles and Trent (1994) and their colleagues examines the process of learning to teach in culturally diverse schools (Artiles & McClafferty, 1998; Artiles & Trent, 1997; Trent, Artiles, & Englert, 1998). Theirs is a data-based approach, whereby strategies are ultimately informed by evidence regarding outcomes rather than by professional opinion about what teachers need to know and do.

Bevan-Brown (1998; 1999) developed a data-based approach called a Cultural Audit Process. It is based on a Maori cultural input checklist and framework. Teachers can use this form to ensure that their educational practices are culturally appropriate. Bevan-Brown bases her definition of "cultural appropriateness" for Maori on the following criteria: Partnership, Participation, Active Protection, Empowerment and Tino Rangatiratanga, Equality and Accessibility, and Integration. These criteria are derived from existing tradition and entitlements (i.e., the Treaty of Waitangi between Maori and English signed in the nineteenth century) and her consultation research with families/whanau and local iwi (tribes).

The Maori Cultural Input Framework (see Figure 14.1) plots these criteria against the various components of programs and services offered at schools. Educators are challenged to describe specific actions (and action planning for vacant cells) to address each intersection on the framework. Specific questions guide these entries; for example, for the Content by Equality and Accessibility cell, the question asked is, "How is the Maori content in programmes accorded equal value and status as other curriculum content?" A sample set of "real-life" examples helps clarify appropriate entries so that for the sample question the example response given is "School report and the IEP form contains a section on the learner's effort and progress in the Maori language and cultural activities."

By aggregating individual teacher responses and structuring collaborative planning across teachers and the principal within the school, a Maori Cultural Input Action Plan is also developed for the entire school including specification of objectives, planned strategies to achieve objectives, and who is responsible and by what target date. Ongoing research with both the teacher and the school as units of analysis will provide a basis for evaluating the effectiveness of such proactive planning.

Maori Cultural Input Framework Criteria

	Partnership	Participation	Active Protection	Empowerment and Tino Rangatiratanga	Equality and Accessibility	Integration
Environment						
Personnel						
Policy						
Process						
Content						
Resources						
Assessment						
Administration						

(Row labels listed under *Program Components and Services*)

Figure 14.1 A Cultural Audit Process for School and Educators

Source: Created by the authors.

PARENT PARTICIPATION AND MULTICULTURAL SPECIAL EDUCATION

The importance of parental involvement is not unique to special education. However, parental involvement is particularly crucial for children with disabilities for two reasons. First, students with disabilities are more vulnerable because their performance and behavior may be misinterpreted through the use of inappropriate and incorrect assessments. Students with cognitive and language impairments may not be able to report negligent or abusive practices to their parents. Parental input is essential to ensure professional understanding of the student as well as to protect the student. Second, the historical fact that students with significant disabilities were traditionally excluded from schools necessitated greater specification of student rights and, consequently, of parental rights to ensure adequate provision of educational services to which a child is entitled.

For children of color, parental involvement becomes even more critical given the overrepresentation of these children in special education services. Parental involvement can function as a protection against the misinterpretation of cultural behavioral differences by dominant culture professionals. At the same time, low-income and ethnic minority parents are the least likely to participate in aspects of their children's schooling (Harry, 1992).

This section of the chapter analyzes how parental participation plays out for these families—or fails to work for them—in special education. Understanding why these parents are apparently disempowered by the special education system helps us develop alternative strategies enabling families to advocate effectively for their children's needs. The focus of the discussion is on families from diverse cultures, expected to fit within a special education (and general education) structure designed to match dominant cultural values.

The Structure of Parent Participation in the Context of Special Education

IDEA (Individuals with Disabilities Education Act) specifies a series of due-process requirements for a parent-professional "partnership" that should be reflected in special education, throughout the steps of referral, evaluation, placement, and instruction of a student with a disability (Turnbull & Turnbull, 1990). Policy makers, practitioners, researchers, and theorists in special education attempted to implement an equitable parent-professional foundation for the prescription of services to meet children's individual needs, with the best of intentions. Unfortunately, the designers of the special education model established a culturally biased structure that is firmly rooted in Western European cultural values. Many difficulties in implementing that model occur because the model is not always well suited to a multicultural population. Furthermore, the team of specialists involved at every stage of the special education process is most likely to be White and from a middle-class background, and thus culturally discontinuous with most of the people receiving special education services. Some of the special education cultural tensions include:

1. The focus in special education on deficit behavior and on one person as the target of intervention is not a cultural universal.

Pacific Island and Native American peoples may find many principles and practices of IDEA foreign culturally, including the structure of the IEP and the focus on the individual and his or her behaviors and skills in a formal, professional planning structure. In an interview with the parent of a child in Kohanga Reo, an immersion Maori preschool, a parent explains:

> After identifying the problem, the first step is always to talk about it, you know, and with Maori people they would rather communicate with their elders first, their whanau [family] . . . they would rather do that than have to be sitting in an office with these specialists who . . . it's frightening, it's daunting for parents to come into that situation . . . . The other thing too [is that] it's not appropriate to talk about yourself, not even your own problems as Maori people. The kumera doesn't go around talking about how sweet it is . . . that's why we do things in the whanau.

2. The formal prescriptions for due process are grounded in Anglo legal traditions, so that written consent and legalistic entitlements actually disempower culturally diverse families.

IDEA specifies that parents must consent to the initial evaluation; if they disagree with the results of that evaluation, they may seek an independent evaluation that must be paid for by the district if the results do not concur. Parents must also formally participate in the annual IEP process and must sign their concurrence to the intervention plan developed for their child at the formal IEP meeting. At one level, these seem like reasonable due-process guarantees that parent rights will be respected from referral to placement as well as throughout special education placement.

However, these very formalistic notions of legal accountability differ considerably from the interaction styles of most families. Research on such parent conferences reveals that it is very common for professionals to hold low expectations of parent involvement at these meetings (Evans, Salisbury, Palombaro, & Berryman, 1994). Observations of meetings reveal that parents are not generally expected to participate actively and that the agenda is usually structured to relegate the parent to the position of passive recipient of professional opinions and signatory to their recommendations (Bennett, 1988; Harry, 1992; Mehan, Hartwick, & Meihls, 1986). Harry, Allen, and McLaughlin (1995) report the comments of an African American mother: "They lay it out [the IEP]. If you have a question, you can ask them. Then you sign it."

Maori parents would expect to bring the whanau [family] to such a meeting, and the whanau might comprise a group even larger than the professional team. Everyone in the whanau would be involved in setting goals, because intervention to meet the child's needs would also be seen as intervention with the entire whanau. In an interview with a parent at a Kura Kaupapa Maori, an immersion elementary school, one parent said:

> This was one of the main reasons why we came together . . .
> so that any issues arising came back and we could deal with them
> together . . . . We don't just look at the individual. It is the whanau
> katoa . . . we have specifics with culture, we have specifics with
> language . . . . [We need to] get services that look at us holistically,
> that look at whanau; . . . they look at these kids in isolation.

3. Further complications arise from the cultural discontinuity in parent participation, such that ethnic minority parents are confronted by a dominant culture special education profession.

The special education structure of written communication and formal face-to-face conferences assigns a passive role to parents unless they possess the professional language and monocultural, legalistic skills integral to the process. The distinct middle-class quality of these events is a source of discomfort for many low-income and working-class parents.

In her well-known guide for parents, Coyne Cutler (1993), herself a parent, exhorts parents to develop various skills to advocate for their children in the following ways: making effective telephone calls and writing formal letters to school principals and other professionals, reviewing school records, and keeping records themselves. The productive assertiveness and confrontation framework in which these activities are suggested illustrate how difficult such advocacy would be for a parent whom professionals perceive as having low social status and less education, and whose literacy skills or experience with schools and bureaucracies are not adequate to these tasks.

Add to this the virtual certainty that the majority of the educational team (if not the entire team) will be themselves White and middle class, while most parents of children with disabilities are neither White nor middle class. Neither within nor outside these two sets of events is there any avenue for the voice of parents who do not use the language of the system. Logistical barriers to participation such as lack of transportation and child-care needs may be much more surmountable in comparison to the numerous barriers related to the structure and process of the special education system itself. Bennett (1988), for example, used ethnographic data with Caribbean Hispanic families to illustrate how school personnel determined what could be discussed at the IEP conference, and, in so doing, effectively excluded a parent's concern with classroom climate as a factor in her child's education. Studies by Figler (1981), Harry (1992), and Harry et al. (1995) of the perspectives of Puerto Rican and African American families offer vivid pictures of the progressive alienation of parents, who gradually withdrew from interaction with professional educators in the face of legal and formal diagnostic frameworks described here that were incompatible with the more personal and less technological cultural frameworks more familiar to the parents. These studies also identified a pattern of deferential parental behavior that masked the parents' real reactions to the process.

Dominant-culture professionals can also assume cognitive universals that have become institutionalized in the diagnostic process to identify disability but that actually represent culture-specific behavior. As a Maori mother explained:

> One of the big barriers . . . is those people who train up to be specialists [who] don't know anything about Te Reo [Maori language] and how the speaking of the language and the living of the language in Kohanga [immersion preschool]; this specialist would do these games and always asking the same question what isn't there. And I kept saying to her he doesn't understand what you're saying, he's come through Kohanga. We don't speak about what's not there, we speak about what is there, . . . it's the culture of the language, the structure of the language and how you implement it, the way you say things. Maori people do not ask what isn't there, what they are is what is in front of you, what you see, what you do know, they don't ask you what don't you know. This is what I kept telling this specialist and she was really young and she just kept brushing me off; . . . it was culturally inappropriate for her to be asking questions like that.

Improving Practices in Supporting Parent Participation

Effective practices ensuring representation of family members of color will require strategies that begin with trust between parents and professionals. Such strategies are not likely to be illustrated solely through the more narrow framing of participation required by law, such as attendance at formal meetings and signatures at selected meetings arranged by professionals. Furthermore, where formal meetings are held, perhaps the structure and composition of the group meeting should shift toward including the child's family members—whoever the family feels is relevant to the educational process rather than restricting attendance to selected "advocates."

We have also suggested elsewhere that ongoing communications between home and school could become a valued role performed by teacher aids who themselves come from the school community and thus are more likely to share cultural membership with the family (Meyer, Park, Grenot-Scheyer, Schwartz, & Harry, 1998). Harry (1992) described how one school district increased the participation of Puerto Rican parents by hiring a family liaison whose primary job was to personalize and clarify the entire special education process for parents. Similarly, Evans, Okifuji, and Thomas (1995) describe the role of school partners who were paraprofessional staff hired by their urban school district to serve as mediators and go-betweens, to advocate for both parents and teachers, and to interpret each group's needs. However it is achieved, only ongoing communication between the family and the school will enable a true partnership to emerge.

The educational community must, however, address the cultural discontinuity between the teacher—most often White and middle class as well as English speaking—and the family—increasingly ethnically diverse and speaking a first language other than English. Harry (1992) and Harry, Grenot-Scheyer, et al. (1995) have reported on some strategies that professionals can and do use even where such cultural discontinuities exist in order to carry out exemplary parent-teacher conferences. Successful conferences are the result of sensitive responding of individual professionals or teams to the concerns expressed by parents during those meetings. Of course, truly exemplary conferences must be based on a systemic structure that incorporates parental participation, rather than relying on the good will and personality characteristics of individual professionals and the initiative of parents (Correa, 1987; Goldstein & Turnbull, 1982; Malmberg, 1984; Thompson, 1982). More research is needed to identify the specifics of successful conference communication strategies and how to teach them to educators as part of their professional preparation (Harry & Kalyanpur, 1994). We also maintain that educators who choose to work in culturally diverse schools will have to make a commitment to biculturalism themselves and develop a rich personal cultural repertoire that goes beyond the monocultural experiences with which they entered the educational profession.

QUALITY INCLUSIVE SCHOOLING: BUILDING SCHOOL COMMUNITIES

IDEA has been a bold social experiment, signaling our acceptance of the responsibility to educate all children. Yet, while we adhere to the principles of compulsory education for all children, our ambivalence regarding its practice evidences itself in varied strategies for labeling and separating children who seem to fall outside the margins of a hypothetical mainstream that still fails to accommodate diversity. The persistent overrepresentation of children of color in special education is possible because disability itself can be a social judgement, most likely made about culturally diverse children and their families by the dominant school cultures.

As long as predominant models of special education involve segregation from the mainstream, special education can become a vehicle for legitimizing continued segregation of children whose behavior differs from dominant cultural norms. The intentions of special education are noble, but its practice can further delay the evolution of a public school system with the capacity to serve all children as they are. Recognizing that students are diverse in many ways and that diversity should be celebrated rather than denied has implications for how educational programs are organized and services delivered. Inclusive schools are purposely heterogeneous and attempt to meet individual educational needs within a shared, common social context, without the requirement or expectation that a child must go elsewhere for services (Meyer, 1997; Roach, 1994).

The movement for quality inclusive schooling in special education and general education began with a focus on enabling students with disabilities to attend their neighborhood schools and classrooms with their peers (Will, 1986). However, the inclusive schooling movement is now centered within the broader agenda of de-tracking and merging previously fragmented and categorical services for children (Cohen, 1994/1995; Meyer, 1997; Roach, 1994; Sapon-Shevin, 1994). From this broader perspective, inclusion entails a system that responds sensitively and constructively to racial, ethnic, religious, and all other student differences within a cohesive school community—accepting that children are different rather than expecting them to be the same (Ayres, 1993; Sapon-Shevin, 1999). Requiring schools to accommodate all children in the general education classroom is seen as the basis for creating multicultural schools to replace monocultural schools that exclude and separate children into groups of those who belong and those who do not. How we treat students with disabilities can, in practice, be how we treat children who are culturally different from the mainstream; and the messages schools give about who belongs in the mainstream classroom reveals our larger, lifelong agenda about who really belongs in our communities.

Ramsey's (1998) goals for teaching from a multicultural perspective represent the kinds of interpersonal and intrapersonal attitudes and behaviors also regarded as critical to quality inclusive schooling. These goals include teaching children to appreciate and value the contributions of others, to see themselves as members of a larger society, to respect different perspectives, and to accept responsibility for their social environment and society. Teaching children to be knowledgeable about difference, supportive of others, and active in changing structures that are oppressive to various groups can begin within inclusive classrooms. We now have a rich data base demonstrating the benefits to individual children (those with and without disabilities), professional school personnel, and the community as a function of the development of quality inclusive schooling (Meyer & Park, 1999). We also have documentation of effective strategies to meet the educational needs of students with the most significant disabilities enrolled in quality inclusive programs with their nondisabled peers (Meyer & Park, 1999).

Delivering Special Education within the Context of General Education

In inclusive schools, special services to meet the needs of individual children are delivered within the general education classroom and context. For example, Shakira may need speech therapy. Rather than sending her down the hall for a fifteen-minute pull-out individual speech therapy session, the speech therapist plans with the general education classroom teacher how to meet Shakira's speech needs within the regular classroom. The speech therapist would most likely come into the classroom and work with Shakira and a small group of children—who can also be positive models for her and for the speech therapist, who might otherwise lose touch with how children Shakira's age actually do speak and converse. The speech therapist may also coach the teacher on how to work with Shakira during her usual reading group activities. Because Shakira is African American, the speech therapist must be sensitive to issues of her dialect of English as she plans what speech patterns do and do not require remediation. Shakira must be viewed as a person with multiple identities, and these identities must be dealt with in an integrated fashion within the classroom and social context (Vygotsky, 1978).

All individuals are multifaceted. Banks (see Chapter 1) emphasizes that all persons bring with them to any interaction a racial identity, an ethnic background, their age, their religion, their social class, as well as other group identities. Mee Wong is a ten-year-old girl. She is also Korean, lives in the city, has two working-class parents, and is a practicing Buddist. Having a learning disability may be part of her identity, but it does not define who she is. All of her characteristics help define who she is and must be respected in the classroom. Having a learning disability should not preclude her from participation in the schooling experiences of her peer group (including attending the general education classroom) any more than being Buddhist should exclude her from interactions with her peers in the neighborhood.

Grant and Sleeter (in Chapter 3) explain that race, social class, and gender are used to construct major groups of people in society. Because all students are members of all three status groups, each group and the interactions among these groups affect students' perceptions and actions. When issues of disability are added to these categories, the number of interactions and spheres of influence increases exponentially. Adapting a Christmas craft activity for Joshua, who has cerebral palsy and uses a communication board, may not be an appropriate or adequate response to his individual identity when we know that Joshua is Jewish and does not celebrate Christmas. If we define Joshua according to only one dimension of his identity, we cannot meet his needs and treat him with respect. Shamika is African American, lives with her mother, and has difficulty reading. When she is given books at her level, we must be thoughtful about not limiting reading materials to books that portray only European American, two-parent families. We should create classroom environments in which children are comfortable revealing all aspects of their backgrounds and experiences that matter to them.

Classrooms must support the diversity of students by responding to each of their identities and by not stereotyping students according to unidimensional and narrow notions of who they are. Social context is critical for virtually all learning, and a child's experiences are the foundation of mastery of everything new (Tharp & Gallimore, 1989; Vygotsky, 1978). Putting our educational theories about social contexts for learning into action requires that we model the realities of children's personal and social lives throughout their academic lives in the general education classroom.

Sapon-Shevin (1992; 1999) has detailed the ways in which teachers can structure their classrooms so that students learn about racial, cultural, family, gender, religious, and skill differences as part of the curriculum. This information need not be limited to learning facts about other groups, but can be extended so that students are actively working to understand and combat prejudices and stereotypes they encounter in school and society. Work by Derman-Sparks and the ABC Task Force (1989) and by Cronin (1998) and others provide examples of how even very young children can be empowered through antibias curricula to challenge injustices and inequities in society. Inclusive classroom communities must also model social and academic interactions between and among children and adults that build capacities for lifelong competence in multicultural communities outside school. Cooperative learning strategies enable students to achieve academic mastery within the context of positive, collaborative social interactions that reflect student diversity. These alternatives to tracking and ability grouping can be adapted to enable the inclusion of the full range of differences in the classroom, and they also can signal powerful messages about individual responsibility to work together in order to achieve goals (Meyer & Fisher, 1999; Sapon-Shevin, Ayres, & Duncan, 1994).

Meyer, Minondo, Fisher, Larson, Dunmore, Black, and D'Aquanni (1998) describe the range of possible social relationships in children's lives evident in their research that can be fostered by educational practices and the organization of schooling. Their work highlights the importance of attention to the implementation of inclusive schooling, which is much more than the physical presence of students with disabilities in the classroom or even the provision of special education services within the general education environment. They found that when teachers communicated through actions and words that children with disabilities were not fully included, children mirrored those social patterns in their peer interactions. Thus, when the teacher always refers to "helping" the student with disabilities rather than working together, and fails to identify meaningful opportunities for academic participation for the student with disabilities, children without disabilities are most likely to see their peers with disabilities as students to be ignored, helped, or treated "specially," much as one would interact with a very young child or even a plaything (Evans, Salisbury, Palombaro, Berryman, & Hollowood, 1992). When classroom practices support full participation in the range of academic and social activities occurring in school, students with even the most severe disabilities experience social lives that include being part of the group in some contexts as well as enjoying regular and best friendships (Meyer, Minondo, et al., 1998; Schnorr, 1997). Figure 14.2 provides some examples of how teachers can assess their practices to support different social outcomes for children in inclusive classrooms.

Inclusive Classrooms, Inclusive Pedagogy

An inclusive classroom requires not only that a full range of students are represented and respected within the classroom context, but also that the teaching strategies respond to and include those differences. Narrow, inflexible teaching practices that assume all students learn best in the same way and bring the same experiences, background, learning style, and interests to the task are neither inclusive nor sensitive to student needs. Inclusive pedagogy can be described in terms of both the content of what is taught and the process.

Banks (Chapter 10) discusses the ways in which the "mainstream-centric curriculum" can be modified to incorporate multiple perspectives; he describes four levels of integration of multicultural content (see Chapter 10 for a more extensive discussion of these levels). In keeping with Banks's levels of integration, issues of ability-disability can be seen to have been incorporated into the practices of teaching and learning at each level as well, with substantial differences in the extent to which the status quo is accepted or challenged.

The *Contributions* level focuses on heroes, on holidays, and on discrete cultural elements. This approach is reflected in having the class read a book about Helen Keller and then teaching a unit on blindness. Students may come to appreciate that persons who are blind can make important contributions, but this level does not challenge the more fundamental notions of segregation and exclusion of *most* people who are blind and who are not seen as making exemplary contributions.

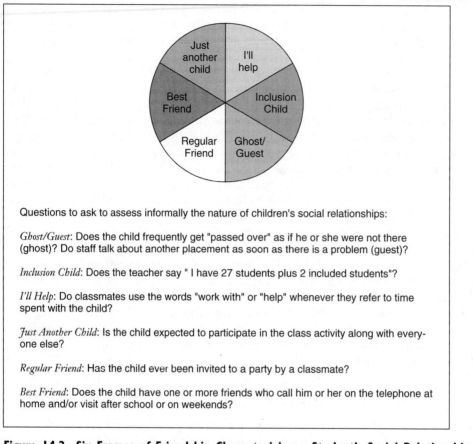

Questions to ask to assess informally the nature of children's social relationships:

Ghost/Guest: Does the child frequently get "passed over" as if he or she were not there (ghost)? Do staff talk about another placement as soon as there is a problem (guest)?

Inclusion Child: Does the teacher say " I have 27 students plus 2 included students"?

I'll Help: Do classmates use the words "work with" or "help" whenever they refer to time spent with the child?

Just Another Child: Is the child expected to participate in the class activity along with everyone else?

Regular Friend: Has the child ever been invited to a party by a classmate?

Best Friend: Does the child have one or more friends who call him or her on the telephone at home and/or visit after school or on weekends?

Figure 14.2   Six Frames of Friendship Characterizing a Student's Social Relationships at School

Source: L. H. Meyer, H. Park, M. Grenot-Scheyer, I.S. Schwartz, & B. Harry (Eds.) (1998). *Making Friends: The Influences of Culture and Development* (p.216). Baltimore: Paul H. Brookes. Reprinted with permission of the publisher.

At the *Additive* level, teachers "put ethnic content into the curriculum without restructuring it" (Banks, 2001, p. 232). A special education parallel to the Additive approach is to mainstream students with special education needs while leaving the curriculum of the classroom intact. Special activities may be implemented for the students with disabilities, but these activities are not integrated into the main life and curriculum of the classroom. Operationally, this level alone would result in an island in the mainstream, consisting of a special education student or small group working with a special educator (or teacher aid) on a separate activity while classmates are engaged in the larger group, *real* academic activity. Early exemplars of integration differed from today's inclusive efforts in their fundamental practices of creating small tutorials within the general education classroom rather than modifying ongoing instructional activities to enable the student with disabilities to participate fully.

The *Transformational* approach "changes the basic assumptions of the curriculum and enables students to view concepts, issues, events, and themes" from the perspectives of diverse ethnic and cultural groups (Banks, 2001, p. 233). This approach from an inclusive perspective involves not only having students with special needs become part of the classroom, but also rethinking and reinventing the curriculum so that it is inclusive and multilevel. All students—across a diverse range of abilities and needs—would be engaged in educational experiences appropriate to their level but as part of a common topic, focus, and lesson (Putnam, 1998).

The *Social Action* approach "includes all the elements of the transformation approach but adds components that require students to make decisions and take actions related to the concept, issue, or problem studied in the unit" (Banks, 2001, p. 236). This requires both reshaping and reinventing the nature of general education classrooms and making them multilevel and inclusive as well as thinking about how schools and teaching can be part of a broader social goal of changing arbitrary and limiting notions of ability, expectations, and the need for segregation. This level has implications for school-based and systemwide decisions about outcomes evaluation, diplomas, testing of students, and curriculum design. Portfolio assessment of student outcomes—as opposed to using a uniform psychometric test—is one example of flexible educational practices that can better accommodate the richness of the repertoires of all students and their achievements (Kleinart, Kearns, & Kennedy, 1997). Other examples of fundamental change at this level are the National Council of the Teachers of Mathematics (1993) standards that reconceptualize broader outcomes such as critical thinking and problem solving. These goals relate meaningfully to the use of mathematics in life and can be readily adapted to represent the wide range of mathematics skill levels of students found in any given classroom. Thus, students with and without disabilities might be working on their problem-solving skills in mathematics, but each student would have an individually appropriate learner objective, and the instructional unit would be adapted to accommodate differences rather than assuming everyone is learning at the same level.

Inclusive Pedagogy

Inclusive pedagogy can be described as a set of teaching practices and structures that acknowledge student differences and are responsive to that diversity. Banks's (2001) transformation and social action levels represent inclusive pedagogy. Cooperative learning and other strategies to support multilevel instruction are examples of pedagogy that can be structured inclusively (Kagan, 1998; Putnam, 1998; Sapon-Shevin, Ayres, & Duncan, 1994). In cooperative learning structures, students work together to achieve common goals. Social skills (listening, compromising, asking questions, encouraging) are taught both formally and informally, and the task is structured so that students must work together in order to achieve a successful outcome. A cooperatively structured math lesson, for example, may involve students generating and then solving their own multistep math problems. A student with a disability who cannot write could contribute to the task as the checker for the group, doing the problem on a calculator and confirming the group's answer. Tasks can be structured so that students generate problems related to their own lives and experiences. Because students are working together, student differences can contribute to successful task completion, rather than being viewed as obstacles to some standard curriculum.

Multilevel instruction involves structuring lessons so that different modalities, different content areas, and different levels of performance can be accommodated within current educational practices (Putnam, 1998). A thematic unit on families could be constructed involving math activities (graphing family demographics), language (writing biographies of family members, taking oral histories), and exploring music and arts activities related to different cultures. All students could be involved in reading, writing, and mathematics activities appropriate to their level and interests, so that even a student with the most profound disabilities could be meeting his or her educational objective in such a unit.

For example, a student with multiple disabilities might be working on operating a switch to activate a computer, small appliances, or a tape recorder. Depending on the student's communication goals, two needs could be met within the context of this hypothetical thematic unit on the family. First, the student could be telling a biography of a family member by listing some descriptive facts about a brother or sister—this might be part of a communication goal for that student involving describing important personal characteristics and using an augmentative communication system to write the list. Second, the student could be working on operating a switch to activate a tape recording of that list read out by a classmate. When it is the student's turn to read the biography to the class, he or she must operate the switch to start the recording and then again to stop it at the end. There are numerous examples of successfully including students with special needs through adaptations to good instruction and educational best practices for all students (Fisher, Bernazzani, & Meyer, 1998; Hedeen, Ayres, & Tate, in press; Meyer, Williams, Harootunian, & Steinberg, 1995; Ryndak, Morrison, & Sommerstein, 1999; Salisbury, Palombaro, & Hollowood, 1993; Sapon-Shevin, Ayres, & Duncan, 1994; Smith, 1997).

Inclusive School Supports and Teacher Education

Before the advent of quality inclusive schooling, the delivery of special education services occurred in separate schools, classrooms, and/or resource rooms. Both general and special educators were professionally prepared to teach their respective students in separate environments. Teacher education, curricula, classroom organization, instructional practices, and structures of educational teaming to support students have evolved for two parallel systems—one general and one special—over a period of decades. Winn and Blanton (1997) describe the major implications for changes in teacher education and school collaboration that will be needed if inclusive schools are to become a reality. Early movements toward the integration of students with disabilities into general education were characterized by attempts to transplant specialized, special education approaches into the mainstream (Meyer & Park, 1999). In contrast, the contemporary inclusive schooling movement recognizes that fundamental school reform will be required for both special and general education—indeed, merger toward one unified system of education—if quality inclusive schooling is to become a reality (Gartner & Lipsky, 1987; Meyer, 1997; Pugach & Johnson, 1995).

Goessling (1998) describes the changes that were required in thinking and practice by both general and special educators in fourteen different elementary schools following the decision to provide special education services within K–8 classrooms. She contrasts the traditions (e.g., homogeneity vs. heterogeneity), language (e.g., scope and sequence vs. goals and objectives), rituals (report cards vs. IEPs), and symbols (worksheets vs. graphs of student performance) of general versus special education programs as background to the restructuring efforts undertaken by the fourteen schools in her sample. For example, the traditional pull-out system of service delivery in special education had been supplanted by a more collaborative consultation model, with all special education services provided within the context of general education activities and lessons. Her research report chronicles the "process of assimilation" for the special education teachers in particular as they moved from special education into general education. Their presence within the general education classroom had an impact on them as well as on the culture of general education itself (Goessling, 1998):

> This research indicated that these fourteen teachers of students
> with severe disabilities were assimilated into the culture of general
> education and that their presence in general education could bring
> about changes within the culture of general education itself. . . .
> The presence of students with severe disabilities appeared to
> influence the push forward of school restructuring efforts and
> helped create schools that were less bureaucratic and more
> personalized and caring. . . . Perhaps there will be another study in
> a few years that does not discuss the cultural assimilation of special
> education teachers into general education, but rather the creation of
> a third school culture that incorporates the best of both. (p. 249)

The model of the Methods and Resource (M&R) teacher developed as an alternative to the traditional special education teacher exemplifies specialized school support personnel who are staffed to assist the learning of all students, working in collaboration with the classroom teacher. Porter and Stone (1998) describe the role and responsibilities of the M&R teacher and the school-based student services team structure that evolved in New Brunswick, Canada, once the school district had made the commitment to quality inclusive schooling. School district officials recognized that significant restructuring of teachers roles and responsibilities was needed to operationalize inclusion. This model does not involve placing students with disabilities into the mainstream without support services, nor does the model deny that some students do have disabilities that require significant services. The model does change the nature of those support services and creates a new "special education" support teacher role charged to work collaboratively with the classroom teacher to meet the diverse needs of all students—not only those with a disability label.

A major argument advanced in support of quality inclusive schooling is capacity building: schools and teachers within those schools would be committed to and capable of delivering effective instruction to all children, not only to those judged to be typical or tracked according to various criteria (Gartner & Lipsky, 1987; Roach, 1994; Sapon-Shevin, 1994). Yet, the evidence is that today's teachers are not confident of their abilities to manage and accommodate the diverse range of student characteristics in their classrooms. Gottlieb et al. (1994) reported that 63 percent of the teachers who referred children out of the classroom to special education said they did not know what resources would enable them to teach those children within their classrooms. Only 16 percent believed they could be trained with the skills to enable them to teach children whom they had referred. Only 10 percent of the referring general education teachers could even describe a curricular adaptation they might make to accommodate the child. It is no wonder, then, that Gottlieb and his colleagues conclude that without "massive staff development efforts," the mainstreaming movement was unlikely to improve children's academic status (Gottlieb et al., 1994, p. 462).

Similarly, in their 1994 study in New York City—again showing disproportionate referrals to special education for students whose needs were not much different from the needs of other students—referring classroom teachers had made only one attempt to address the learner's needs before seeking placement elsewhere. That one attempt did not involve making curricular adaptations, modifying instruction, or even seeking additional professional technical assistance from within their school or district; the teachers called the students' home and asked the parent to fix the problem! Given stressed economic circumstances and both cultural and language differences from that of the school professional staff, it is difficult to envision what parents would be expected to do to address academic learning and behavioral difficulties their children were experiencing in school.

Who then will staff the quality inclusive schools and classrooms of the future? What are the implications of teaching staff in schools who were themselves prepared in teacher education programs tracked for either special or general education? We believe that just as cultural diversity demands preparation in multicultural education for all teachers, individual learning differences (including disabilities) and multiple intelligences (Gardner, 1993) demand the preparation of a new generation of teachers with a repertoire of values and strategies that match the demands of inclusive classrooms. The National Association of State Boards of Education (1992) recognized the implications of inclusion for teacher preparation programs and called for the development of new directions in teacher education consistent with the merger of general and special education. Historically, many preservice teacher education programs have included dual certification options in both general and special education, but a truly merged program incorporating multicultural education as well as both special and general education preparation is still a rarity (Winn & Blanton, 1997).

One example of a merged and unified inclusive teacher education program, at Syracuse University, is described by Meyer, Mager, Yarger-Kane, Sarno, and Hext-Contreras (1997). This program was implemented in 1990. Its graduates are in strong demand, and graduate follow-up indicates that they enter the teaching profession with the commitment and professional repertoire for successful inclusion (Meyer et al., 1997). The recent collection by Blanton, Griffin, Winn, and Pugach (1997) provides examples of different versions of teacher education programs that are designed to better prepare tomorrow's teacher for the realities and ideals of today's inclusive schools and classrooms. It is our contention that quality inclusive schooling entails significant reform not only for the compulsory sector of schooling, but for higher education and the preparation of professional educators as well.

DIVERSITY AND CARING COMMUNITIES: OUTCOMES FOR THE SOCIAL GOOD

We believe that the existence and perpetuation of pull-out solutions to student differences inevitably generates (and reflects) some perhaps unintended but real negative side effects:

1. As long as the belief persists that general education classrooms are homogenous, the cycle of referral for differences will continue and will, ultimately, exceed the resources of marginalized systems.

Our current dual system of general and special education encourages the school to conceptualize homogeneous typical groupings as the only functional structures for teaching and learning. Systems that allow and even encourage narrowing of commitment and capacity to serve diverse needs, that expect children to fit curriculum rather than adapting schooling to meet children's needs, and that institutionalize the identification of difference through segregation and tracking will increasingly reduce tolerance for differences and restrict the range of those who are viewed as being typical and who are seen as belonging. This is particularly dysfunctional now, when new immigrant groups, increased poverty, and proportionately greater numbers of culturally and linguistically diverse students and families are facts of life in the United States. The inevitable result will be an increasing cycle of referrals that will ultimately exceed the resources of the various special systems that are both marginalized and devalued by the mainstream society.

2. In the long run, efforts to reduce class size and restrict general education enrollment to smaller groups of students ready to learn will fail. Instead, as children leave the mainstream, resources will follow, and the cycle will repeat.

Gottlieb and his colleagues (1994) note that the current system of special education reduces any need for the general education system to develop meaningful instructional and student support programs and services for children in the general education classrooms. Teachers seemed to believe that the only mechanism available to them to reduce class size and the instructional challenges confronting them in the short run was to fully access referrals to special education—which, in large urban areas, continued to mean placement in a separate educational environment. But as children do leave the general education enrollment, resources must be provided to them at their new destination—and those resources must come from somewhere. Increasingly, resources have declined in general education as our many entitlement programs have increased. While the relationship may not be a simple one, we believe that declining resources will be spread ever more thinly—and ultimately, that those resources will come from the same budget and require subsequent increases in class size in general education.

A major argument advanced by proponents of quality inclusive schooling is that our educational system cannot afford separate and fragmented systems. Children with disabilities must return to the general education classroom and attend school with their peers. But the resources supporting those children must return as well—and those resources must be restructured and capacities enhanced to better serve all children, those with and without disabilities.

3. When children with and without disabilities grow up in isolation from one another, they sacrifice much. Children will "Do as I do, and not as I say," and if we model segregation and rejection from a social system as central to our democratic institution as the public schools, we will have a great deal to answer for when those exclusionary models play out in the domains of daily living.

When children with disabilities are segregated from their nondisabled peers, they lose social context as a major teaching and learning environment. They become increasingly dependent on teacher-directed, highly structured learning and on adults in particular as the source of all new knowledge and support. On the other hand, they give up peer groups and participation in their neighborhood and community. Increasingly, as natural supports are prevented and thwarted from developing, persons with disabilities become more and more dependent on costly professional and paid services to fill the void.

More than fifty years ago, Adorno, Frenkel-Brunswik, Levinson, and Sanford (1950) advanced their theory that one's attitudes toward persons who are viewed as different was part of a consistent pattern that affected all aspects of the individual's behavior and beliefs. Their studies of racial prejudice and political conservatism were premised on the theory that cultural acceptance would be associated with democratic principles, and that the promotion of cultural acceptance would thus have broad benefits for the social good. The movement for diversity in education makes a similar point while acknowledging the futility of ignoring a pluralism that now dominates the population of U.S. school children. Learning to accept individual differences and to celebrate diversity as an enriching experience are broad principles consistent with democratic values and the creation of caring schools that support children's growth and development.

In addition to multicultural education, various other general education reform movements emphasize the need for caring school communities. Berman (1990) builds a case for such school communities if we are to address the basic societal needs of our democracy for the "nurturing in young people of a sense of social responsibility and social efficacy" (p. 1); he notes with irony that "We teach reading, writing, and math by doing them, but we teach democracy by lecture" (p. 2). In her writings, Noddings (1992) has long emphasized that the creation of educational environments that support learning involves the creation of caring communities, where teachers supplement the emphasis on academic excellence with relational ethics and moral education. She emphasizes that teachers must model caring throughout their teaching and interactions with students, a concern that can be traced to John Dewey's writings.

Wells and Crain (1994) note that a thirty-year research literature on school desegregation has most often focused on the immediate effects of racial integration on individual students—their achievement, their self-esteem, and their intergroup relations. These researchers argue that another perspective focused on life chances of African American students requires a longer-term outlook. According to a sociological perspective referred to as *perpetuation theory*, "the goal of desegregation is also to break the cycle of segregation and increase access to high status institutions and the powerful social networks within them" (p. 531). What is the purpose of our educational system and public education in the United States? Is it exclusively intended to meet the needs of each individual child? We think not. At least in part, our educational system was conceptualized as a pathway to a democratic community and the betterment of all its citizenry. Our challenge is, of course, to examine the rhetoric and practices within education with the goal of reaching a better balance between meeting unique needs and building community.

Questions and Activities

1. Why, according to the authors, are students of color and low-income students overrepresented in special education classes and programs?

2. Why is it especially important for parents of color and low-income parents to be involved in special education programs for their children? What are some effective ways in which these parents can become involved in special education programs?

3. Why do parents, especially low-income parents and parents of color, often find it difficult to participate meaningfully in special education programs even though laws exist to ensure their participation?

4. In what ways do the research and assessment work by Jane R. Mercer reveal that special education is a social construction? Give specific examples from this chapter to support your response.

5. According to the authors, what are some of the major characteristics of quality *inclusive* schools? On what major assumptions and beliefs are they based? How do inclusive schools exemplify and foster the idea of "the school as a community" described by the authors?

6. What do the authors mean by "inclusive pedagogy"? Give specific examples of this concept.

7. The authors believe that special education students should be educated in the same schools and classrooms as general education students. What problems and opportunities does this practice pose for classroom teachers? What changes might need to occur within teacher education to prepare teachers for inclusive classrooms? What guidelines, tips, and insights do the authors provide that may help teachers deal with the challenges and problems posed by inclusive education?

8. The authors maintain that a commitment to the principles and practices of inclusive education will benefit not only special education students, but will also lead to classrooms and schools that reflect diversity and can thus better serve all students with and without disabilities. How might fully inclusive schools prepare our children for fully inclusive communities?

References

Adelman, H. S. and Taylor, L. (1993). *Learning Problems and Learning Disabilities: Moving Forward.* Pacific Grove, CA: Brooks/Cole.

Adorno, T. W., Frenkel-Brunswik, E., Levinson, D. J., and Sanford, R. N. (1950). *The Authoritarian Personality*, Vols. 1 & 2. New York: John Wiley & Sons.

Argulewicz, E. N. (1983). Effects of Ethnic Membership, Socioeconomic Status, and Home Language on LD, EMR, and EH Placements. *Learning Disabilities Quarterly, 6*, 195–200.

Artiles, A. J. (1998). The Dilemma of Difference: Enriching the Disproportionality Discourse with Theory and Context. *The Journal of Special Education, 32*, 32–36.

Artiles, A. J. and McClafferty, K. (1998). Learning to Teach Culturally Diverse Learners: Charting Change in Preservice Teachers' Thinking about Effective Teaching. *The Elementary School Journal, 98*, 189–220.

Artiles, A. J. and Trent, S. C. (1994). Overrepresentation of Minority Students in Special Education: A Continuing Debate. *The Journal of Special Education, 27*, 410–437.

Artiles, A. J. and Trent, S. C. (1997). Forging a Research Program on Multicultural Preservice Teacher Education in Special Education: A Proposed Analytic Scheme. In J. W. Lloyd, E. J. Kameenui, and D. Chard (Eds.), *Issues in Educating Students with Disabilities* (pp. 275–304). Mahwah, NJ: Lawrence Erlbaum.

Ayres, B. J. (1993). *Equity, Excellence, and Diversity in the "Regular" Classroom*. Unpublished Doctoral Dissertation, Syracuse University, Syracuse, NY.

Banks, J. A. (2001). Approaches to Multicultural Curriculum Reform. In J. A. Banks and C. A. McGee Banks (Eds.), *Multicultural Education: Issues and Perspectives* (4th ed.) (pp. 225–246). New York: John Wiley & Sons.

Banks, J. A. and Banks, C. A. McGee. (Eds.). (2001). *Multicultural Education: Issues and Perspectives* (4th ed.). New York: John Wiley & Sons.

Bennett, A. T. (1988). Gateways to Powerlessness: Incorporating Hispanic Deaf Children and Families into Formal Schooling. *Disability, Handicap and Society, 3*(2), 119–151.

Berman, S. (1990). The Real Ropes Course: The Development of Social Consciousness. *ESR Journal: Educating for Social Responsibility, 1*, 1–18.

Bevan-Brown, J. (1998). *A Cultural Audit for Teachers: Looking Out for Maori Learners with Special Needs. SET: Special Education 2000*. Wellington, New Zealand: New Zealand Council for Educational Research.

Bevan-Brown, J. (1999). Catering for Maori Learners with Special Needs. Paper presented at the 23rd Annual International Conference of the Association for Persons with Handicaps, Seattle.

Blanton, L. P., Griffin, C. C., Winn, J. A., and Pugach, M. C. (Eds.). (1997). *Teacher Education in Transition: Collaborative Programs to Prepare General and Special Educators*. Denver, CO: Love Publishing.

Cohen, F. (1994/1995). Prom Pictures: A Principal Looks at Detracking. *Educational Leadership, 52*(4), 85–86.

Correa, V. I. (1987). Involving Culturally Diverse Families in the Educational Process. In S. H. Fradd and M. J. Weismantel (Eds.), *Meeting the Needs of Culturally and Linguistically Different Students: A Handbook for Educators* (pp. 130–144). Boston: College Hill.

Coyne Cutler, B. (1993). *You, Your Child, and "Special" Education: A Guide to Making the System Work*. Baltimore, MD: Paul H. Brookes.

Cronin, S. (1998). Culturally Relevant Antibias Learning Communities: Teaching Umoja. In L. H. Meyer, H. S. Park, M. Grenot-Scheyer, I. S. Schwartz, and B. Harry (Eds.), *Making Friends: The Influences of Culture and Development* (pp. 341–351). Baltimore, MD: Paul H. Brookes.

Derman-Sparks, L. and the ABC Task Force. (1989). *Anti-Bias Curriculum: Tools for Empowering Young Children*. Washington, DC: National Association for the Education of Young Children.

Divergent Youth. (1963). [Report of the Senate Fact Finding Committee on Education: Subcommittee on Special Education]. Washington, DC: U.S. Government Printing Office.

Dunn, L. (1968). Special Education for the Mildly Retarded: Is Much of It Justifiable? *Exceptional Children, 35*, 5–22.

Evans, I. M., Okifuji, A., and Thomas, A. D. (1995). Home-School Partnerships: Involving Families in the Educational Process. In I. M. Evans, T. Cicchelli, M. Cohen, and N. P. Shapiro (Eds.), *Staying in School: Partnerships for Educational Change* (pp. 23–40). Baltimore, MD: Paul H. Brookes.

Evans, I. M., Salisbury, C. L., Palombaro, M. M., Berryman, J., and Hollowood, T. M. (1992). Peer Interactions and Social Acceptance of Elementary-Age Children with Severe Disabilities in an Inclusive School. *Journal of the Association for Persons with Severe Handicaps, 17*, 205–212.

Figler, C. S. (1981). *Puerto Rican Families with and without Handicapped Children*. Paper presented at the Council for Exceptional Children Conference on the Exceptional Bilingual Child, New Orleans. (ERIC Document Reproduction Service No. ED 204 876)

Finn, J. D. (1982). Patterns in Special Education Placement as Revealed by the OCR Surveys. In K. A. Heller, W. H. Holtzman, and S. Mesrick (Eds), *Placing Children in Special Education: A Strategy for Equity* (pp. 322–381). Washington, DC: National Academy Press.

Fisher, M., Bernazzani, J. and Meyer, L. H. (1998). Participatory Action Research: Supporting Social Relationships in the Cooperative Classroom. In J. Putnam (Ed.), *Cooperative Learning and Strategies for Inclusion: Celebrating Diversity in the Classroom* (2nd ed.) (pp. 137–165). Baltimore, MD: Paul H. Brookes Publishing.

Gardner, H. (1993). *Multiple Intelligences: The Theory in Practice*. New York: Basic Books.

Gartner, A. and Lipsky, D. K. (1987). Beyond Special Education: Toward a Quality System for All Students. *Harvard Educational Review, 57*, 367–395.

Goessling, D. P. (1998). Inclusion and the Challenge of Assimilation for Teachers of Students with Severe Disabilities. *Journal of the Association for Persons with Severe Handicaps, 23*, 238–251.

Goldstein, S. and Turnbull, A. P. (1982). The Use of Two Strategies to Increase Parent Participation in IEP Conferences. *Exceptional Children, 48*, 360–361.

Gottlieb, J., Alter, M., Gottlieb, B. W., and Wishner, J. (1994). Special Education in Urban America: It's Not Justifiable for Many. *Journal of Special Education, 27*, 453–465.

Harry, B. (1992). *Cultural Diversity, Families, and the Special Education System: Communication for Empowerment*. New York: Teachers College Press.

Harry, B., Allen, N., and McLaughlin, M. (1995). Communication vs. Compliance: African American Parents' Involvement in Special Education. *Exceptional Children, 61*, 364–377.

Harry, B., Grenot-Scheyer, M., Smith-Lewis, M., Park, H.-S., Xin, F., and Schwartz, I. (1995). Developing Culturally Inclusive Services for Individuals with Severe Disabilities. *Journal of the Association for Persons with Severe Handicaps, 20*, 99–109.

Harry, B. and Kalyanpur, M. (1994). The Cultural Underpinnings of Special Education: Implications for Professional Interactions with Culturally Diverse Families. *Disability, Handicap, and Society, 9*(2), 145–166.

Hedeen, D. L., Ayres, B. J., and Tate, A. (in press). Getting Better, Happy Day, Problems Again! The Ups and Downs of Supporting a Student with Autism in Her Home School. In M. Grenot-Scheyer, M. Fisher, and D. Staub (Eds.), *At the End of the Day: Stories of Ordinary Lives of Children and Youth in Inclusive Schools and Communities*. Baltimore, MD: Paul H. Brookes Publishing.

Horner, R. H., Meyer, L. H., and Fredericks, H. D. B. (Eds.). (1986). *Education of Learners with Severe Handicaps: Exemplary Service Strategies*. Baltimore, MD: Paul H. Brookes Publishing.

Kagan, S. (1998). New Cooperative Learning, Multiple Intelligences, and Inclusion. In J. W. Putnam (Ed.), *Cooperative Learning and Strategies for Inclusion* (2nd ed.). Baltimore, MD: Paul H. Brookes Publishing.

Kleinert, H. L., Kearns, J. F., and Kennedy, S. (1997). Accountability for All Students: Kentucky's Alternate Portfolio Assessment for Students with Moderate and Severe Cognitive Disabilities. *Journal of the Association for Persons with Severe Handicaps, 22*, 88–101.

MacMillan, D. L., Jones, R. L., and Meyers, C. E. (1976). Mainstreaming the Mildly Retarded: Some Questions, Cautions and Guidelines. *Mental Retardation, 14*, 3–10.

Malmberg, P. A. (1984). *Development of Field Tested Special Education Placement Committee Parent Education Materials*. Unpublished Doctoral Dissertation, Virginia Polytechnic Institute and State University, Blacksburg.

Mehan, H., Hartwick, A., and Meihls, J. L. (1986). *Handicapping the Handicapped: Decision-Making in Students' Educational Careers*. Stanford, CA: Stanford University Press.

Meier, K. J., Stewart, J., and England, R. E. (1989). *Race, Class, and Education: The Politics of Second-Generation Discrimination*. Madison: The University of Wisconsin Press.

Mercer, J. R. (1973). *Labeling the Mentally Retarded: Clinical and Social System Perspectives on Mental Retardation*. Berkeley: University of California Press.

Mercer, J. R. (1979). *System of Multicultural Pluralistic Assessment: Technical Manual*. Cleveland, OH: The Psychological Corporation.

Meyer, L. H. (1997). Tinkering around the Edges? *Journal of the Association for Persons with Severe Handicaps, 22*, 80–82.

Meyer, L. H. and Fisher, M. (1999). Participatory Research on Strategies to Support Inclusion. *SET 1999: Special Education*. Wellington, New Zealand: New Zealand Council for Educational Research.

Meyer, L. H., Mager, G. M., Yarger-Kane, G., Sarno, M., and Hext-Contreras, G. (1997). Syracuse University's Inclusive Elementary and Special Education Program. In L. P. Blanton, C. C. Griffin, J. A. Winn, and M. C. Pugach (Eds.), *Teacher Education in Transition: Collaborative Progams to Prepare General and Special Educators* (pp. 18–38). Denver, CO: Love Publishing.

Meyer, L. H., Minondo, S., Fisher, M., Larson, M. J., Dunmore, S., Black, J. W., and D'Aquanni, M. (1998). Frames of Friendship: Social Relationships among Adolescents with Diverse Abilities. In L. H. Meyer, H.-S. Park, M. Grenot-Scheyer, I. S. Schwartz, and B. Harry (Eds.), *Making Friends: The Influences of Culture and Development* (pp. 189–221). Baltimore, MD: Paul H. Brookes Publishing.

Meyer, L. H. and Park, H.-S. (1999). Contemporary Most Promising Practices for People with Disabilities. In J. S. Scotti and L. H. Meyer (Eds.), *Behavioral Intervention: Principles, Models, and Practices* (pp. 25-45). Baltimore, MD: Paul H. Brookes Publishing.

Meyer, L. H., Park, H. S., Grenot-Scheyer, M., Schwartz, I., and Harry, B. (1998). Participatory Research: New Approaches to the Research to Practice Dilemma. *Journal of the Association for Persons with Severe Handicaps, 23*, 165–177.

Meyer, L. H., Williams, D. R., Harootunian, B., and Steinberg, A. (1995). An Inclusion Model to Reduce At-Risk Status among Middle School Students: The Syracuse Experience. In I. M. Evans, T. Chicchelli, M. Cohen, and N. Shapiro (Eds.), *Staying in School: Partnerships for Educational Change* (pp. 83–110). Baltimore, MD: Paul H. Brookes Publishing.

National Association of State Boards of Education. (1992). *Winners All: A Call for Inclusive Schools*. Alexandria, VA: Author.

National Council of Teachers of Mathematics. (1993). *Curriculum and Evaluation Standards for School Mathematics*. Reston, VA: Author.

Noddings, N. (1992). *The Challenge to Care in Schools: An Alternative Approach to Education*. New York: Teachers College Press.

Oswald, D. P., Coutinho, M. J., Best, A. M., and Singh, N. N. (1999). Ethnic Representation in Special Education: The Influence of School-Related Economic and Demographic Variables. *The Journal of Special Education, 32*, 194–206.

Patton, J. M. (1998). The Disproportionate Representation of African Americans in Special Education: Looking Behind the Curtain for Understanding and Solutions. *The Journal of Special Education, 32*, 25–31.

Porter, G. L. and Stone, J. A. (1998). The Inclusive School Model: A Framework and Key Strategies for Success. In J. W. Putnam (Ed.), *Cooperative Learning and Strategies for Inclusion: Celebrating Diversity in the Classroom* (2nd ed.)(pp. 229–248). Baltimore, MD: Paul H. Brookes Publishing.

Pugach, M. C. and Johnson, L. J. (1995). *Collaborative Practitioners, Collaborative Schools*. Denver, CO: Love Publishing.

Putnam, J. (Ed.). (1998). *Cooperative Learning and Strategies for Inclusion: Celebrating Diversity in the Classroom* (2nd ed.). Baltimore, MD: Paul H. Brookes Publishing.

Ramsey, P. G. (1998). *Teaching and Learning in a Diverse World: Multicultural Education for Young Children* (2nd ed.). New York: Teachers College Press.

Richardson, J. G. (1994). Common, Delinquent, and Special: On the Formalization of Common Schooling in the American States. *American Educational Research Journal, 31*, 695–723.

Roach, V. (1994). The Superintendent's Role in Creating Inclusive Schools. *The School Administrator, 52*(4), 64–70.

Ryndak, D. L., Morrison, A. P., and Sommerstein, L. (1999). Literacy before and after Inclusion in General Education Settings: A Case Study. *Journal of the Association for Persons with Severe Handicaps, 24*, 5–22.

Salisbury, C. L., Palombaro, M. M., and Hollowood, T. M. (1993). On the Nature and Change of an Inclusive Elementary School. *Journal of the Association for Persons with Severe Handicaps, 18*, 75–84.

Sapon-Shevin, M. (1992). Celebrating Diversity, Creating Community: Curriculum That Honors and Builds on Differences. In S. Stainback and W. Stainback (Eds.), *Curriculum Considerations in Inclusive Classrooms: Facilitating Learning for All Students* (pp. 19-36). Baltimore, MD: Paul H. Brookes Publishing.

Sapon-Shevin, M. (1994). *Playing Favorites: Gifted Education and the Disruption of Community*. Albany: State University of New York Press.

Sapon-Shevin, M. (1999). *Because We Can Change the World: A Practical Guide to Building Cooperative, Inclusive Classroom Communities*. Boston: Allyn and Bacon.

Sapon-Shevin, M., Ayres, B., and Duncan, J. (1994). Cooperative Learning and Inclusion. In J. Thousand, R. Villa, and A. Nevin (Eds.), *Creativity and Collaborative Learning: A Practical Guide to Empowering Students and Teachers* (pp. 45–58). Baltimore, MD: Paul H. Brookes Publishing.

Schnorr, R. F. (1997). From Enrollment to Membership: "Belonging" in Middle and High School Classes. *Journal of the Association for Persons with Severe Handicaps, 22*, 1–15.

Smith, G. R. (1983). Desegregation and Assignment of Children to Classes for the Mildly Retarded and Learning Disabled. *Integrated Education, 21*, 208–211.

Smith, L. T. (1999). *Decolonizing Methodologies: Research and Indigenous Peoples*. London: Zed Books.

Smith, R. M. (1997). Varied Meanings and Practice: Teachers' Perspectives Regarding High School Inclusion. *Journal of the Association for Persons with Severe Handicaps, 22*, 235–244.

Tharp, R. G. and Gallimore, R. (1989). *Rousing Minds to Life: Teaching, Learning and Schooling in Social Context*. Cambridge, MA: Cambridge University Press.

Thompson, T. M. (1982). An Investigation and Comparison of Public School Personnel's Perception and Interpretation of P. L. 94–142. *Dissertation Abstracts International, 43*, 2840A.

Townsend, B. L. (1998). Social Friendships and Networks among African American Children and Youth. In L. H. Meyer, H. S. Park, M. Grenot-Scheyer, I. S. Schwartz, and B. Harry (Eds.), *Making Friends: The Influences of Culture and Development* (pp. 225–241). Baltimore, MD: Paul H. Brookes.

Trent, S. C., Artiles, A. J., and Englert, C. S. (1998). From Deficit Thinking to Social Constructivism: A Review of Theory, Research, and Practice in Special Education. *Review of Research in Education, 23* (pp. 277–307). Washington, DC: American Educational Research Association.

Tucker, J. A. (1980). Ethnic Proportions in Classes for the Learning Disabled: Issues in Nonbiased Assessment. *The Journal of Special Education, 14*, 93–105.

Turnbull, A. P. and Turnbull, H. R. (1990). *Families, Professionals, and Exceptionality* (2nd ed.). Columbus, OH: Merrill.

U.S. Department of Education, Office of Civil Rights. (1994). *1992 Elementary and Secondary Civil Rights Compliance Report*. Washington, DC: U.S. Government Printing Office.

Vygotsky, L. S. (1978). *Mind in Society: The Development of Higher Psychological Processes*. M. Cole, V. John-Steiner, S. Scribner, and E. Souberman (Eds. and Trans.). Cambridge, MA: Harvard University Press.

Webb-Johnson, G. C. (1999). Cultural Contexts: Confronting the Overrepresentation of African American Learners in Special Education. In J. S. Scotti and L. H. Meyer (Eds.), *Behavioral Intervention: Principles, Models and Practices* (pp. 449–464). Baltimore, MD: Paul H. Brookes.

Wells, A. S. and Crain, R. L. (1994). Perpetuation Theory and the Long-Term Effects of School Desegregation. *Review of Educational Research, 64*, 531–555.

Will, M. (1986). Educating Children with Learning Problems: A Shared Responsibility. *Exceptional Children, 52*, 411–415.

Winn, J. and Blanton, J. (1997). The Call for Collaboration in Teacher Education. In L. P. Blanton, C. C. Griffin, J. A. Winn, and M. C. Pugach (Eds.), *Teacher Education in Transition: Collaborative Progams to Prepare General and Special Educators* (pp. 1–17). Denver, CO: Love Publishing.

CHAPTER 15

Teaching Gifted Students in a Multicultural Society

Rena F. Subotnik and
Gess LeBlanc

Children with breathtakingly fast problem-solving acuity can be found in every neighborhood, school, and community. This chapter discusses how these exceptional individuals function within schools and deal with societal expectations regarding their success. It also discusses why some gifted children may not achieve to their full potential. Issues involving the identification and nurturing of gifted students from diverse racial, cultural, ethnic, and language groups are also discussed.

WHAT ARE THE PURPOSES OF GIFTED EDUCATION?

Schooling that focuses on the development of talent should help gifted children learn how to attain recognition and success in the mainstream culture. It should also nurture abilities valued in communities' nonmainstream cultures and by gifted children themselves (Maker & Schiever, 1989; Williams, 1989). Although every child with exceptional gifts deserves consideration for special talent development programming, barriers to fulfilling this societal obligation include misguided identification processes, inappropriate curriculum, and inadequate counseling. These obstacles can be reduced by using the scholarship generated in the multicultural and gifted education literature, vigilant community support, and the advocacy of informed educators.

A common misconception is that gifted students do not require special attention in order to be successful in school. In fact, because they tend to learn more quickly and comprehensively, they need instruction presented at a differentiated speed and level of comprehension in order to be challenged. Far too frequently, gifted students spend hours in school covering material they already know and answering simplistic questions about complex issues. Gifted students who complete assignments ahead of classmates may be sent to the library for unsupervised reading or research, allocated more seat work, or asked to help fellow students. Although these stop-gap options are not intrinsically problematic and in some cases are effective, gifted students deserve to have at least some portion of both the school curriculum and the teacher's attention focused on their educational needs. Gifted students who are in a minority in terms of ability, social-class status, race, ethnicity, and/or language have special needs for teacher support and recognition.

THE GIFTED EDUCATION MOVEMENT: A BRIEF HISTORY

Until the 1920s, most people in the United States did not enroll in high school, and certainly not in college. Secondary and postsecondary education was therefore geared to the academically able, most often from among the White privileged classes. On the elementary school level, exceptional youngsters were double-promoted (i.e., skipped a grade). In the early 1920s, Lewis Terman developed a test designed to measure intelligence based on the work of French psychologist Alfred Binet; he named it the Stanford-Binet Intelligence Test. To validate his hypothesis that a high IQ would predict adult genius, he established a longitudinal study of nine- to eleven-year-olds who scored in the 99th percentile and above on the Stanford-Binet (IQ 140+) (Terman & Oden, 1925). Followed up in adulthood, these high-IQ individuals proved not to be geniuses, but exceptionally productive individuals compared to peers from their same fairly high social and economic background. Most became prominent academics, writers, lawyers, and business executives.

If Terman (Terman & Oden, 1925) could be considered the "father" of the movement in the United States to recognize and serve high-IQ gifted children, the "mother" would be Leta Hollingworth (Silverman, 1995; 1998). Much of Hollingworth's efforts were channeled into creating educational environments designed to meet the educational and psychological needs of these learners (Hollingworth, 1927). Based on the powerful influence of Terman's and Hollingworth's work in the psychological and education communities, several experimental programs, including the Hunter College Elementary School and the Speyer School in New York City, were developed using the Stanford-Binet to identify gifted children.

By 1947, Terman and his colleagues realized that IQ was not a sufficient predictor of exceptional achievement (Subotnik, Kassan, Summers, & Wasser, 1993; Terman & Oden, 1947). None of his study subjects had achieved true eminence; many could even be classified as adult underachievers. Clearly, other variables were important to the fulfillment of great potential. Concurrently, a rising negative reaction to sorting by virtue of intelligence thwarted the widespread replication of gifted programs (Chapman, 1988).

Psychologists J. P. Guilford (1967) and E. P. Torrance (1965) pursued investigations into the measurement of creativity, with the goal of persuading the scholarly community that IQ and creativity were not directly related. They argued that if high IQ was viewed as the sole predictor of creative productivity, many gifted individuals would be overlooked by special programs designed for talent development.

In the 1970s, the impact of the civil rights movement and the advent of special-education legislation led theorists and researchers in the field to focus on discovering and nurturing gifted children who had been underserved because of poverty, racism, sexism, or disabilities. The commitment to identifying and supporting gifted students outside the mainstream, middle-class, White culture was generally absent until that time. However, it is important to note that scholars of color have written about exceptional individuals within their race. W. E. B. Du Bois (1903), for example, termed the Black intelligensia the "Talented Tenth."

In 1972 Commissioner Sidney Marland entered into the public record the definition of giftedness proposed by the United States Office of Education (USOE) for use by state and local agencies in developing policies for serving gifted children. Children capable of high performance include those with demonstrated achievement and/or potential ability in any of the following areas, singly or in combination:

1. general intellectual ability
2. specific academic aptitude
3. creative or productive thinking
4. leadership ability
5. visual and performing arts
6. psychomotor ability. (pp. 10–11)

As a result of the continued struggle to recognize the special needs of gifted students, particularly those from groups underrepresented in special programs, a follow up to the Marland Report was commissioned in the 1990s. This document, *National Excellence: A Case for Developing America's Talent* (Ross, 1993), featured the following declaration: "Outstanding talents are present in children and youth from all cultural groups across all economic strata, and in all areas of human endeavor" (p. 26). This key statement was derived from the recognition that participants in special programs for the gifted remained disproportionately White and middle class, and from the emerging conceptions of giftedness developed in the last two decades.

CURRENT CONCEPTIONS OF GIFTEDNESS

Scholars and educators have proposed a variety of theoretical frameworks that seek to expand the conception of giftedness beyond the notion of high IQ. Definitions by Renzulli (1986), Sternberg (1986), and Gardner (1993) are the most widely discussed in the field; they are briefly described in the following paragraphs.

Based on a biographical review of eminent creators, Renzulli (1986) claimed that earlier notions of giftedness ignored the important roles of motivation, drive, and persistence in the manifestation of talent. IQ had served a purpose, according to Renzulli, in drawing attention to "school-house" giftedness, but it could not explain the derivation of seminal ideas and beautiful creations. Further, he argued that creativity and persistence were more important than very high IQ. He feared that exceptionally able children were being excluded from special services because programs focused exclusively on school-house giftedness rather than on the development of talent that is most valuable to our society.

Finally, Renzulli proposed that we reframe our thinking about gifted individuals and focus on gifted behaviors that can be enhanced by opportunities in schools. Given appropriately stimulating environments, students who apply above-average ability, creativity, and motivation (the three rings) to carry out creative tasks are exhibiting gifted behaviors. These students should then be provided with the educational resources to carry out those tasks. Renzulli and his colleagues designed a wide array of identification tools and schemes for curriculum differentiation built on the principles of the three-ring definition.

Sternberg's (1986) triarchic theory of intellectual giftedness also includes three components. The first subtheory addresses gifted individuals' executive skills in planning, learning, and carrying out given tasks. The second subtheory speaks to gifted individuals' insight into novel ideas and situations. The third subtheory incorporates contextual and practical decision-making skills, such as knowing when it is better to pursue or drop a project, to widen or narrow one's focus, or think reflectively rather than quickly. Sternberg believes that the three components of intelligence described in the triarchic theory can be taught. Gifted individuals, according to the theory, know how to capitalize on their strengths and use their executive skills, creativity, and practical intelligence to solve real-life problems.

Gardner (1983; 1993) proposed a theory of multiple intelligences that acknowledges a variety of human capacities and propensities. Each intelligence uses the manipulation of symbol systems to solve problems or create ideas or products. The seven intelligences in Gardner's framework are the linguistic, logical mathematical, spatial, musical, bodily kinesthetic, interpersonal, and intrapersonal. The least familiar concept in multiple intelligence theory is intrapersonal intelligence, which Gardner defines as the capacity to develop accurate insights about one's own thinking, feeling, and behaving.

According to Gardner, the intelligences are raw biological potentials that need to be identified and nurtured so that people can maximize their intellectual abilities to meet vocational and avocational goals. Additionally, Gardner notes that in his model an intelligence is not synonymous with a learning style. Instead, each of the seven intelligences should be viewed as a construct similar in nature to more general theories of intelligence (Gardner, 1996). Two principles are key to the application of the multiple intelligence theory approach. One is the recognition that intelligences are manifested and valued differentially in different cultures and community settings (Baldwin, 1994). The second important point is that the best way to identify children's intelligences is to provide naturalistic scenarios for exploring each domain. Children's propensities can then be noted and developed (Gardner, 1993).

The instruments needed to carry out an identification program based on Sternberg's or Gardner's theories are not yet widely available. However, their ideas are circulating in the education community and serving as stimuli to renew discussion of such important questions as "What is giftedness?" and "How is it manifested?"

IDENTIFICATION OF GIFTED STUDENTS

There are no federally mandated definitions of giftedness. The identification of students for special programming is tied to local definitions adopted by the school, school district, or state. Most U.S. school systems focus on serving gifted children who, because of their exceptional intellectual, creative, or academic abilities, need modification of the regular curriculum. Recognition is also given to giftedness in leadership and in visual and performing arts, although much less frequently. This policy is based on the belief that assessment of talent in leadership and in the visual and performing arts is too subjective, whereas standardized tests are available for use in the identification of intellectual, academic, and creative aptitude. Ironically, portfolios and auditions commonly used in the arts and leadership studies could open new ways to identify and serve gifted students even in academic domains (Subotnik, 2000).

In spite of these new paradigms of intelligence and giftedness, standardized test scores remain pervasive among the requirements for placement in gifted programs. In addition, the more removed a gifted child is from middle- to upper-middle-class mainstream culture, the less likely it is for the student to be identified and served by the educational system (Oden, Kelly, Ma, & Weikart, 1992). As a result, Ford (1996) challenges us to shift the point of reference away from middle- and upper-middle-class standards of giftedness by comparing individuals with those of similar cultural and economic backgrounds.

Why do standardized tests weigh so heavily in the labeling process? Some psychometricians believe that of all the ways we have to predict success in school or college, carefully designed tests are the most valid. Indeed, a very high score on such an instrument should be noted. Conversely, however, low scores do not necessarily reflect a person's lack of potential or ability. In fact, critics such as Helms (1992) point out that tests of general intelligence may be viewed as instruments that merely assess a White style of thinking. Clearly, other data need to be collected to make fair and accurate judgments about talent and educational needs.

For financial and political reasons, school districts set aside a limited number of seats in programs no matter how many students need special services. Test scores are used in order to cull pools of potential candidates to a manageable size because such instruments are publicly perceived as more objective than are teacher recommendations or grade point averages. Our goal should be to provide for all children who would benefit from admission to a special program or set of services (Barkan & Bernal, 1991; Callahan & McIntyre, 1994; Ford, 1994b; Kerr, Colangelo, Maxey, & Christensen, 1992; Louis, Subotnik, Breland, & Lewis, in press; Subotnik & Coleman, 1996).

A multicultural perspective can provide a more intellectually legitimate identification scheme by highlighting abilities and skills that are universally valued and indicating how those abilities are manifested in various cultures and communities (Baldwin, 1991; Frasier, 1991a; Kirschenbaum, 1988; Tonemah, 1991; 1992). According to Frasier and her colleagues (1991a; 1991b; Frasier, Garcia, & Passow, 1995; Frasier & Passow, 1994), a clear statement of the characteristics and behaviors associated with giftedness might include intense motivation, extraordinary quantitative or communication skills, superior memory capacity, exceptional problem-solving abilities, and high-level creativity. These characteristics may be expressed differently based on the form of analogical reasoning and symbol systems held valuable by the subculture (Oden, Kelly, Ma, & Weikart, 1992).

In response to the array of literature on alternative forms of assessment, Frasier and Passow (1994) contend that formulating special constructs, watering down criteria, or seeking different areas of talent are not the way to increase the representation of African American, Latino, and American Indian children in gifted programs. They argue that we must attend to how cultural differences and environmental contexts affect performance on the measures that are used. Some scholars have also argued that the disproportionate underrepresentation of African American, Latino, and American Indian children reflects the destructive elitism of identifying and labeling children as gifted (Borland, 1996; Margolin, 1996; Sapon-Shevin, 1996). We believe that some individuals possess extraordinary talents, not necessarily shared by all. Such individuals exist within all racial, cultural, ethnic, and language groups and are deserving of recognition and support.

More equitable and accurate identification can be made by focusing on outstanding performance in one or two domains rather than across many. A small number of elementary age students may indeed demonstrate great potential across all subject areas, in leadership, athletics, and performing arts. However, most gifted students exhibit profiles of distinct strengths. Talent profiles become even more distinct in adolescence, when standards of excellence are achieved as a result of heavy investment in study, practice, or leadership experience. Gifted teens will spend significant time in some domains of talent and not others. A policy that addresses specific strengths rather than global giftedness is more education-ally sound and allows for more children to be recognized. (Gardner, 1993; House & Lapan, 1994; Kay & Subotnik, 1994; Miserandino, Subotnik, & Ou, 1995; Roedell, Jackson, & Robinson, 1980).

Some of the data sources that may go into labeling a child as gifted are described below. Each has advantages and disadvantages.

Achievement Tests

Each year, most public school students take a battery of tests used to compare their academic standing with those of students in the same grade throughout the country. Results of these tests can pinpoint students who are significantly above the national norm. Raw scores are translated into percentiles or stanines, and children who score above a predetermined cutoff, such as the 91st percentile or the 9th stanine, may become candidates for further assessment.

Ceiling effects are one drawback inherent in the use of achievement tests for the identi-fication of gifted students. If tests are not challenging enough, too many scores get bunched at the very top percentiles. The use of off-level tests, those appropriate for students at higher grade levels, can provide teachers and admissions committees with clearer insights into students' maximum capabilities.

Another drawback to using achievement tests as an identification tool is their excessive dependence on reading ability for success. Even the mathematics portion of tests depend heavily on reading ability. The scores of children who have learning disabilities or who are English Language Learners (ELL) may not reflect their true aptitude for mathematics or aural comprehension of language (Barkan & Bernal, 1991). Finally, lack of exposure and practice in test-taking skills may depress the achievement test scores of children whose schools do not provide such training (Ford, 1994b).

Individual Intelligence Tests

Individually administered IQ tests remain the most widely used instruments for admission to gifted programs. Test items draw on students' problem-solving skills, such as reproducing block patterns. They also draw on educational and cultural experiences, such as vocabulary, memory for facts, and basic arithmetic. Individual IQ tests are expensive to administer and tend to underestimate the intellectual potential of children who are economically disadvantaged or who are English Language Learners. Test bias can also occur because of poor tester-testee rapport and variability in exposure to vocabulary and experiences appearing on the test.

Most scholars today recommend more dynamic forms of assessment (Borland & Wright, 1994; Ford & Harris, 1994; Frasier, 1991b; Helms, 1992). Dynamic assessment involves exposing children to a new task and demonstrating problem-solving methods for them and then noting how well children can apply the demonstrated skill or concept to a similar challenge (Feuerstein, 1973).

Behavior Checklists

Useful information can be collected about a specific student from teachers, parents, peers, and the student himself or herself. These instruments are not effective, however, unless they clearly delineate the behaviors and characteristics that define the gifts and talents being sought. The work developed by Gardner and his colleagues (1993) to describe childhood behaviors associated with each of the multiple intelligences should add a lot more power to the use of behavior checklists.

Teacher Recommendations

Teachers' reliability as identifiers of gifted students is influenced by their understanding of the school district's definition of giftedness. Without a set of descriptions of desired student characteristics, teachers tend to nominate academically able students who are obedient, attractive, bright, and socially adept, while missing students who are shy, bored, less popular, and of a lower socioeconomic level (Gallagher & Gallagher, 1994). Teachers are often too focused on addressing children's deficits to notice strengths, particularly with their African American, Latino, and American Indian students (Banks, 1995; Callahan & McIntyre, 1994; House & Lapan, 1994). Furthermore, as Boutte & McCoy (1993) suggest, factors such as ethnicity, gender, past achievement, and speech characteristics influence teacher attitudes regarding the competence of their students. If the identifying characteristics are made explicit and teachers are culturally and racially sensitive and informed, teachers can become more valuable sources of referrals (Borland & Wright, 1994).

Parent Nomination

Depending on their cultural background, parents may over- or underrate their children's abilities (Callahan & McIntyre, 1994; Ford, 1994b; Scott, Perou, Urbano, Hogan, & Gold, 1992). However, a well-designed questionnaire filled out by parents can provide invaluable assistance to teachers and administrators by describing children's interests and accomplishments outside of school (Borland & Wright, 1994; Ford, 1993a; 1994b; Frasier, 1991b).

Peer Nominations

Peers are an excellent source of information about possible candidates for special programming. School districts, such as the Seattle Public Schools, have devised instruments that ask for the names of schoolmates who best fit one or more of the following categories: (1) learns quickly and easily, (2) has creative ideas, (3) is concerned with fairness, and (4) tells the wildest stories (see Renzulli, Reis, & Smith, 1981). Obviously, these data are valid only if students have spent a period of time together in school. If school attendance patterns change from year to year, it delays peer nomination procedures until new students are at least fairly well integrated into the school population. Additionally, since these descriptive categories are associated with children who are outspoken in class and who exhibit a level of interpersonal intelligence (Gardner, 1983), or social giftedness (Smith, 1995), shy or introverted children may not be identified by their peers.

Self Nomination

Some students, because of their reticent personality, lack of social skills, interests that take place outside both the school and home, or cultural disinclination to draw attention to themselves (Callahan & McIntyre, 1994; Frasier, 1991a; Kitano, 1991), will not be noticed by parents, peers, or teachers. Self-nomination provides such individuals with the opportunity to describe their activities to specialists who can use the information for possible placement in a gifted program. The information derived directly from children may be especially enlightening in terms of identifying those gifted African American children whose academic effort is not commensurate with their ability, despite an achievement orientation (Ford, 1993b).

Work Samples

Direct examples of creative work that go beyond academic expectations are sometimes used for placement into special programs (Tonemah, 1991; 1992). These products are direct reflections of youngsters' creative ability and motivation and in this way have more content validity than do tests purported to measure *potential* to be creatively productive. This work can take the form of science projects, art work, dance or music performances, games, or essays. Portfolios can be used even with preschool-age children and can include both teacher- and student-selected materials (Coleman, 1994; Wright & Borland, 1993). To reduce bias in judgments of submitted products, it is important to use more than one rater.

In conclusion, a responsible and effective identification procedure uses as much information as possible to help raters make decisions about serving students. Furthermore, opportunities for placement in programs should be continuous and ongoing from kindergarten through grade twelve (Ford & Harris, 1994). Too often, placement decisions are made based on available space rather than on educational need (Louis et al., in press; Subotnik & Coleman, 1996). Generally it is better to err in the direction of inappropriately admitting a student into a program than to leave out a student on the basis of a single test-score cutoff.

ADDRESSING GIFTED STUDENTS' INTELLECTUAL CHARACTERISTICS IN SCHOOL SETTINGS

Gifted children and adults from all socioeconomic, ethnic, cultural and language backgrounds exhibit some or all of the following intellectual characteristics: accelerated pace of learning, superior memory and concentration, exceptional capacity for seeing relationships and patterns, and intense motivation (Frasier & Passow, 1994). Each individual has a unique profile of strengths drawn from this list. The characteristics become most visible when applied to a specific area, such as mathematics, music, creative writing, or chess.

Accelerated Pace of Learning

The primary characteristic of giftedness noticed by classroom teachers and parents is the speed with which these children learn. Students who learn mathematical concepts, vocabulary, and reading skills after minimal exposure are using their extraordinary ability to memorize, strategize, and concentrate. If a class dwells on a simple concept for too long, the gifted child may become bored and disruptive. It is not uncommon, however, for a stellar mathematics student to be a competent but uncreative writer. In fact, some gifted students have serious academic problems that require special planning and may be due to learning disabilities. Teachers who work with intellectually and academically gifted students learn to compact portions of the curriculum according to the profile of strengths presented by the students.

Capacity for Seeing Relationships and Patterns

Teachers have the opportunity to draw their students' attention to concepts and patterns that are central to one or more academic disciplines (e.g., power, beauty, change) so that students can make generalizations, solve complex problems, and devise creative insights. In addition, students who are skilled at seeing relationships and patterns can be taught two or more concepts at once, increasing the complexity of the lesson as well as saving time for enrichment. In beginning foreign language instruction, for example, both gender notations and tense can be taught together instead of separately (VanTassel-Baska, 1994).

Gifted specialists encourage students to view themselves as producers rather than as simply consumers of knowledge (Passow, 1985). The producer sees relationships where they did not exist before and translates those insights into products that give pleasure, satisfy a need, or generate new ideas. Creative children want to try different ways to solve problems (e.g., a new way to learn the multiplication tables, take attendance, sell cereal, breed fruit flies, end racism). Although we may admire our most creative students, their nontraditional approach to classroom life can sometimes be troublesome, particularly in a large heterogeneous class.

Class assignments can be designed to promote the notion of student-as-producer by requiring the inclusion of some original dimension to every major assignment. For example, a research report should not simply describe the history of the scholarship on the topic but should also incorporate the student's reactions to the literature described. Science reports would not only delineate the procedures of the experiment, but also encompass a section on follow-up questions or alternative hypotheses.

Intense Motivation

Gifted students tend to be extremely curious about many topics and concepts to which they are exposed, such as music composition, historical examples of racism, computer programming, or product invention. Once a child becomes captivated by a project, it may be difficult to tear him or her away to do anything else, even to eat or sleep. Such a child may become disgruntled when an interesting point in class is passed over by classmates who are satisfied with a superficial explanation. Scheduling, when possible, should include blocks of time in the class or resource room for students to pursue in-depth discussion or projects.

AFFECTIVE CHARACTERISTICS

Many gifted children have an extraordinary ability to read people and situations. They may not know how to handle what they see or hear, nor will they necessarily use the ability for the benefit of other people. Some of the ways gifted children manifest this sensitivity include high expectations for themselves and others, low tolerance for lags between intellectual and physical development, and concern with inconsistencies between ideal and real behavior. Problematic behavior derived from these attending characteristics (not requiring outside therapy or medication) are best handled in individual or small-group counseling sessions with other gifted students led by counselors familiar with the constellation of problems found most typically among gifted students from varied backgrounds.

High Expectations of Self and Others

At the elementary school level, many gifted children learn effortlessly, and if not adequately challenged will lower their personal standards and submit hastily conceived work (Ford, 1992; Matthew, Golin, Moore, & Baker, 1992). Others may refuse to participate in cooperative groups with classmates who are satisfied to achieve competence and not mastery of a particular task or assignment (Parker, 1997). In the course of private conversations gifted students may tell you that they find it exhausting to work on behalf of the other group members to achieve personal standards.

High expectations can be placed on others in the social realm as well. Gifted students tend to be extraordinarily concerned with issues of fairness and are devastated when friends fail to live up to the principles of behavior they hold up for themselves in relationships. Furthermore, African American, Latino, and American Indian children may encounter teacher and societal expectations that far underestimate their capabilities (Banks, 1995), causing painful confusion. Peer counseling groups and other support systems should be in place that prevent inaccurate and harmful perceptions from being internalized (Ford, 1994a; 1994b; Kitano, 1995; Noble, Subotnik, & Arnold, 1999).

Impatience with Lags in Physical Development

Many gifted children try to engage in activities and solve problems normally associated with older children. Primary-age gifted children are particularly prone to frustration when they can visualize problem solutions but do not have the agility or vocabulary to carry them out. For example, a first grader may want to explore the properties of a paper geodesic dome model but may not be able to manage the necessary cutting. The same holds true for the youngster who dreams up elaborate stories for a book but does not yet have the motor coordination to write. A friend from a sixth-grade classroom, the teacher, or teacher assistant can lend a literal helpful hand by doing the necessary cutting or writing.

Gifted adolescents may be extremely well read in topics such as gun control or racist militia groups but do not have the emotional maturity to achieve more than an intellectual understanding of the topic. Discussing their thoughts with uninterested age mates or with adults uncomfortable with the paradox of intellectual precocity and emotional immaturity can be problematic. Peer groups organized by school counselors or educators that can bring together gifted students for sessions around these topics can be very effective in reducing students' sense of isolation.

Noticing Inconsistencies between Ideal and Real Behavior

Gifted children can also be victims of a phenomenon called existential depression, or carrying the burden of the world on their shoulders (Webb, Meckstroth, & Tolan, 1986). Becoming aware of hypocrisies such as racism found in everyday life can leave such a child numb or cynical. Frank discussions with compassionate teachers and counselors are essential to supporting the self-concept of sensitive adolescents, particularly those who have been the direct recipients of the debilitating effects of racism. Activism and idealism modeled by a parent, teacher, or friend can help channel these concerns constructively.

SUGGESTIONS FOR CURRICULAR AND INSTRUCTIONAL MODIFICATIONS

Identification processes must be justified by providing high-quality services designed to foster the intellectual, academic, and creative strengths of participating students and *retaining* students in those programs (Ford, 1994b). The regular curriculum was designed to be a basic foundation for all students. Differentiating the regular curriculum for use with gifted students requires a combination of acceleration, enrichment, and the use of interdisciplinary themes; the proportions should be determined by the individual student's academic and talent profiles and interests (VanTassel-Baska, 1994).

Acceleration

Although the term *acceleration* is often associated with grade skipping, it can also be used to mean moving more rapidly through the year's required curriculum to create more time for higher-level enrichment activities. The teacher must first assess the skill and knowledge levels of the students, allowing those who have already mastered the initial topics to begin at a more advanced stage. Continuous monitoring for mastery is, of course, necessary. Some subjects, like mathematics, foreign language, grammar, and reading skills are more conducive to this kind of acceleration because of their sequential nature (VanTassel-Baska, 1994).

Many school subjects are taught as a series of incremental steps toward the acquisition of a higher goal. Acceleration works best when a goal is presented to the students at the beginning of a series of lessons. This advance organizer operates like the frame of a jigsaw puzzle. If the goal is figuring out the picture, the student and teacher can work together to determine the minimum amount of puzzle pieces the student needs to ensure success.

Another method of acceleration is to reduce the number of practice exercises a student must successfully complete to demonstrate mastery. If, after instruction, a child can do the last ten problems in the unit, he or she should not have to do the first forty. Reis and Purcell (1993) refer to this technique as curriculum compacting.

Gifted children from underrepresented groups have a special need for appropriately paced curriculum, as underachievement has been shown to be the result of insufficient challenge and a paucity of exercise in academic discipline and study skills (Frasier & Passow, 1994; Miserandino et al., 1995; Oden et al., 1992). Academic talent, therefore, needs to be recognized and served as early as possible (Borland & Wright, 1994; Ford, 1992; Matthew et al., 1992).

Enrichment

Enrichment should be an essential component of schooling for all students. Since children can best demonstrate their talents in a highly stimulating environment, an enriched curriculum not only provides exciting academic experiences, but it also creates additional opportunities for identification of gifted students (Frasier & Passow, 1994).

Curriculum can be enriched for students from all backgrounds in a number of ways. One important way is to introduce content that extends the regular curriculum through multicultural education (Ford, 1994b). Two examples include the study of biographies of female and culturally diverse scientists, mathematicians, or writers whose work contributed to the skills and knowledge learned in the science, mathematics, and language arts curriculum; and the collection of stories from various ethnic community newspapers covering a topic under examination in social studies. Enrichment topics and ideas are usually generated from the available expertise of teachers, community or parent mentors, or the students themselves.

Developing new skills traditionally not taught in the regular curriculum is another enrichment technique. Advanced research topics such as survey development, interviewing, finding primary resources, organizing case studies, and elementary statistics can be introduced to young students for use in establishing their "careers" as producers of knowledge. According to Renzulli (1986), students who respond to enriched curriculum by proposing independent or small-group projects are exhibiting gifted behaviors.

Barkan and Bernal (1991) question why all bright U.S. school children are not trained to be bilingual. Schools in Europe, Canada, and Latin America expect graduates to be competent in more than one language. If bilingualism were viewed as a positive and valued outcome of schooling, the stigma placed on English Language Learners in the United States could be transformed into an advantage, especially if exposure to dual language use began in the primary years.

Providing enrichment to gifted students in the regular classroom requires that the teacher answer three questions:

1. What topics from the regular curriculum are most conducive to extension and enrichment?

2. How much time for enrichment can be derived from acceleration or compacting of the regular curriculum?

3. What are the talents, interests, and availability of the students, staff members, parents, and community members who might be involved in independent projects that are outgrowths of the enrichment experience?

Contracts for time to work on independent projects can be negotiated with clearly established time limitations and criteria for evaluation. The expected outcome of enrichment is for students to synthesize their newly gained knowledge and skills into the design and completion of an individual or small-group investigation to be evaluated by experts within the school and the community (Renzulli, 1994).

Interdisciplinary Themes and Concepts

Teachers rarely use interdisciplinary frameworks in planning curricula for the gifted. This is unfortunate because the technique capitalizes on the gifted child's ability to see relationships and make generalizations. The real world, of course, is not divided up into academic subject areas. When we develop an impression of an event, place, or person, we do not think in terms of subtraction, verbs, spelling, or data-retrieval charts. Instead, we find ourselves intrigued because that object, person, or event is, among other things, *beautiful, revolutionary, adaptive,* or *powerful.* Teachers can take advantage of students' ability to organize their thinking around major concepts by pointing them out when they appear in the regular curriculum. For example, the concept of power can be explored in the social studies through the balance of power in the U.S. system of government, in science by the generation of electricity, in language arts by persuasive language, in art by political cartoons or posters, and in mathematics by symbol systems (e.g., powers of 10) that allow us to describe elegantly very large or small numbers.

ADMINISTRATIVE OPTIONS

Once identified, gifted students can be served by the schools in a variety of ways, depending on local policy. The options differ by the degree to which gifted students are segregated from their regular classroom peers. Ironically, while advocates for gifted education struggle to create and maintain options for gifted children to work with ability peers, the education establishment is pursuing the placement of all children in the regular classroom. Placement decisions, however, are best made on an individual child's needs rather than on politics or philosophy. Some gifted children can thrive in the regular classroom with a teacher who is prepared and able to differentiate the curriculum where necessary and where there are one or more gifted classmates for shared group work and discussion. Other gifted children require too many academic adjustments and experience too much social isolation to warrant placing them in a regular classroom.

Specialized Schools

Some states such as North Carolina have established residential schools for extremely talented students from all over the state. Metropolitan areas with large school-age populations have also created schools for highly intellectually or artistically gifted children. Because even students within these special schools have varied profiles of talent and academic strengths, regular (and even remedial) to very advanced classes must be offered in nearly all academic subjects. Special resource teachers make arrangements for individual students to work in their areas of strength with community, corporate, or university mentors. A drawback to this arrangement, however, is that some students suffer from lowered academic self-concepts within classes that are composed entirely of academically talented peers (Marsh,

Chessor, Craven, & Roche, 1995). Comparisons to their peers can lead to underachievement and related negative outcomes.

Special Groupings within Schools

When there are enough identified gifted students on a grade level to form a class, they may be grouped together for most of their school subjects: science, mathematics, language arts, foreign language, and social studies. Music, art, industrial arts, and physical education may be shared with other students in the building. Separate classes within a school can either be a boon to the school or a divisive force. Gifted classes with appropriately trained teachers, students identified in a nonarbitrary manner—with continuous opportunities for the admission of new members—may set a dynamic tone throughout the school. When the program is weak, however, staff and students outside the program may see the special class as an excuse for placating powerful parents or politicians.

Pull-Out Programs

The pull-out model is the most common administrative option for gifted children (Cox, Daniel, & Boston, 1985). A trained specialist meets with small groups of identified students for from one to five hours per week to focus on the unique interests and talents of the individual students rather than on the required curriculum. Students generally learn research and intellectual skills needed to conduct small-group and individual investigations and to make contact with adults in the community who can serve as mentors. Gifted students remain in contact with their age peers for most of their time in school.

Many regular classroom teachers resent the disruptions caused by children leaving the classroom to attend sessions with specialists. Other problems that stem from the pull-out arrangement include doubling up of homework from both special and regular classes and the difficulty of maintaining continuity in the special program when there are week-long breaks between sessions.

The special school, special class, and pull-out options allow gifted children to be inoculated against school and peer culture that subverts studiousness and the pursuit of academic excellence. In the case of females and ethnic and cultural groups underrepresented in science, homogeneous grouping has encouraged enrollment in advanced coursework (Casserly, 1980; Miserandino et al., 1995; Smith, LeRose, & Clasen, 1991) and realistic preparation for the competition encountered in postsecondary institutions (Seymour & Hewitt, 1994).

Conversely, segregated programs tend to reduce academic self-concept among participants when they compare themselves to equally talented peers (Marsh, Chessor, Craven, & Roche, 1995). Such comparisons can be devastating, particularly when encountered for the first time in adolescence.

Regular Classroom with Consulting Teacher

Many school districts and counties hire a gifted specialist to serve the entire system. The specialist arranges in-service courses, organizes curriculum-writing teams, and visits with individual teachers who seek advice. If the person provides quality service, regular classroom teachers can derive help and ideas for meeting the needs of gifted children within their classroom. The strength of this arrangement lies in the social integration of gifted students into the mainstream school culture. The drawbacks include the additional strain on teachers to specialize their curriculum and instructional strategies and the academic isolation of gifted students. Without modification, gifted students are often left to fend for themselves (Archambault, Westberg, Brown, Hallmark, Emmons, & Zhang, 1993).

INFLUENCES ON THE FULFILLMENT OF TALENT POTENTIAL

Being identified as gifted and placed in a program are no guarantees that a student will fulfill his or her potential. In addition to the role of task commitment and motivation addressed by Renzulli (1986), other factors can negatively influence the productivity of a gifted child, including lack of support from parents, teachers, peers, one's subculture, or counselors.

Parents

Parents with high ambitions for their gifted child will ensure that the child receives the highest-quality education possible. However, most parents prefer to have a bright but not gifted child with good social skills. The special child's needs can be intrusive on family life in many ways: reduction of attention to nongifted siblings, parental intimidation by their child's superior intellect, and fear that the gifted child will reject family culture to some degree if not altogether (Baldwin, 1987; Davis, 1977; Evans, 1996), particularly if their child will be a minority, ethnically or socioeconomically, in a special program (Callahan & McIntyre, 1994; Ford, 1994b; Kitano, 1991).

Successful programs must include an effective parent participation component (Ford, 1994b; Kerr et al., 1992; Maker & Schiever, 1989). Parents, particularly those distrustful of schools as an institution or concerned about removing their child from familiar contexts, need to be included in the discussion of program goals and must be convinced of the importance of their emotional support to their child's continuing participation in the gifted program (Oden et al., 1992; Scott et al., 1992). Since parents are sometimes hesitant to support a school's plan for working with their gifted child, some researchers suggest the use of mentors who serve as liaisons between the family and the school system (Torrance, Goff, & Satterfield, 1998).

It is also essential to avoid making assumptions about parental values based on socioeconomic status, race, or ethnicity. Variability is great among members of ethnic groups based on language, socioeconomic status, country of origin, generations in the United States, and the degree to which one subscribes to mainstream values (Kitano, 1991). Additionally, parents' understanding of what constitutes giftedness influences the ways in which they encourage their children. In this way, the family environment creates an educational setting that directly impacts on the achievement of the gifted child (Baker, Bridges, & Evans, 1998). Factors that are of major importance to the nurturing of giftedness by parents include expectations for achievement, language modeling, academic guidance, and intellectuality of the home (Frasier, 1991a; VanTassel-Baska, 1989). These characteristics are not exclusive to any one cultural, racial, or ethnic group.

Teachers

Teachers can help a gifted child by providing a source of support in schools that insufficiently recognize intellectual or academic achievement. Teachers can excite and stimulate children by modeling intellectual curiosity and can help students feel comfortable with their intellectual strengths. Teachers can actively recruit children who may be reluctant to be labeled as gifted due to concerns about standing out from peers or community members (Kitano, 1991). Teachers can help students build positive peer and social relationships to combat any negative consequences that may result from being identified as gifted (Ford, 1995). Teachers can seek out high-achieving role models from the African American, Latino, and American Indian communities to serve as guides and mentors in the classroom (Ford, 1994b; Maker & Schiever, 1989). On the secondary and middle school levels, teachers must ensure that challenging courses are available so that students in rural or inner-city schools can enroll in gatekeeper courses to the college-bound tracks, like algebra and calculus (Miserandino et al., 1995; Oakes, 1990; Oden et al., 1992; Seymour & Hewitt, 1994). Study groups in advanced courses have been shown to be effective in raising achievement, particularly with gifted African American students (Olszewski-Kubilius, Grant, & Seibert, 1994; Treisman, 1992).

Peer Group Membership

When children believe they must choose between a drive for excellence and a desire for friendship, they experience tremendous stress (Ford, 1992; Griffin, 1992; Kerr, 1994). Arguments for the segregation of gifted students into homogeneous groups are particularly salient in systems where the school culture is not supportive of academic brilliance (Subotnik & Olszewski-Kubilius, 1997). Homogeneous grouping into special schools, classes, or pull-out programs is especially effective for African American, Latino, and American Indian children if there is a critical mass of gifted ethnic peers also participating. Being a minority within a gifted program can to some degree be as stressful as being isolated intellectually in an age peer group (Cooley, Cornell, & Lee, 1991; Ford & Harris, 1994; Maker & Schiever, 1989).

Subculture

To succeed both in school and at home, language-minority students are challenged with becoming bilingual, bicultural, and learning how to "play the game" in the mainstream culture (Baldwin, 1991; Barkan & Bernal, 1991; Clark, 1991; Ford, 1994b; Fordham & Ogbu, 1986; Kitano, 1991; Ogbu, 1995). This means, for example, that a Mexican American youngster brought up speaking Spanish must also learn to operate comfortably in English and, most important, to know when each language is most appropriately used. Inability to function as a so-called border crosser (Giroux & McLaren, 1994) can impinge on successful competition for jobs, scholarships, and university entrance. Conversely, masterful border crossing can lead to brilliant new insights derived from perspectives not shared by mainstream classmates.

Feuerstein (1973), a pioneering Israeli psychologist, explained the inordinate numbers of intelligent non-European Israelis being labeled as retarded because of their lack of familiarity with Western-oriented academic tasks. Gifted children baffled by an unfamiliar school system need to be shown how it functions; they need, for example, test-taking skills (Ford, 1994b;

Oden et al., 1992; Olszewski-Kubilius, Grant, & Seibert, 1994). Teachers and school counselors can provide invaluable assistance by sensitively helping students know when to call on their cultural and ethnic ways of speaking, thinking, playing, and learning, and when to call on their proficiency with mainstream forms of expression and problem solving.

Counseling Needs

Gifted African American, Latino, and American Indian children are subject to several psychological stresses that are different from those of their White peers. Methods for addressing and even alleviating these stresses have been derived from research with high-achieving African American, Latino, and American Indian adults (Banks & Banks, 1995; Griffin, 1992; Kerr, 1994; Kitano, 1995; Ponterotto, Casas, Suzuki, & Alexander, 1995) and can serve to enhance the methodology of all counselors. Evans (1997), for example, has identified certain critical components of counselor training programs such as antiracism and consciousness raising whose goals are to prepare counselors to work effectively with students from a variety of cultural backgrounds.

Gifted children may not allow themselves the possibility of occasional failure and mistakes (Griffin, 1992; Kitano, 1995), particularly when they are a minority in an educational situation like a gifted program (Ford & Harris, 1999). They need assistance in learning to anticipate and resist internalizing messages of inferiority (Ford, 1993a; Kitano, 1995; Noble, Subotnik, & Arnold, 1999). Examples of resilience in the face of adversity can then be highlighted and encouraged (Ford, 1994a; Noble et al., 1999; Wang & Gordon, 1994). Most important, with proper guidance, gifted African American, Latino, and American Indian children can transform adversity into creative productivity by learning that adversity is the emotional source of much of humanity's greatest ideas and inventions (Ochse, 1990; Simonton, 1994).

An Ecological Approach

Several influences on talent development have been discussed in this chapter. It is important to note, however, that each of these influences acts simultaneously on the gifted child. Consistencies among influences (i.e. between parents and teachers) result in a greater likelihood of talent fulfillment, while inconsistencies result in less supportive environments. As a means of taking into account the various simultaneous influences that impact on the fulfillment of the gifted child's talents, *some* researchers have suggested the adoption of an ecological approach to the study of giftedness—particularly as giftedness is applied to multicultural settings (Baker, Bridges, & Evans, 1998). The ecological approach, as proposed by Urie Bronfenbrenner (1986), is a means of conceptualizing human development. In this approach, one must take into consideration the various contexts that simultaneously effect human development: one's level of socioeconomic status impacts on the type of neighborhood one lives in, which influences the type of schooling one receives, which influences one's academic/cognitive development. If we extend this approach to issues of giftedness, we must accept that the fulfillment of talent potential is not the result of singular factors in isolation (parents or teachers), or the result of additive influences (parents plus teachers), but rather the result of a dynamic relationship that exists among all of the factors.

For example, it is clear that parents play a large role in nurturing their children's talents. Often times such nurturing (music lessons, art supplies, computer software) requires spending money that is not always available. As a result, while some parents may both recognize and value their child's talents, they may not have the economic resources to support them. Additionally, while definitions of giftedness include an array of talents, many parents give priority (due to limited resources) to those talents most clearly linked to academic success (e.g., problem-solving skills that translate into better math grades). To be able to nurture talents that do not directly translate into better grades is a privilege not shared by all parents. As a result, while factors such as the intellectuality of the home may not be associated with any particular cultural or ethnic group, one's socioeconomic status is a constraint on one's ability to provide a home environment that is sufficiently intellectually stimulating to the gifted child. Therefore, it is important to take into account the many factors that not only influence the fulfillment of potential but to understand that no single influence can be held accountable for the failure to maximize that potential.

CONCLUSION

Great thinkers derive their ideas from nontraditional viewpoints. The greatest gift we can give to children is exposure to the multiple perspectives derived from the myriad cultures and ethnic and language groups that make up the U.S. population. The greatest gift we can give ourselves as educators is to reformulate our traditional views of identifying and serving gifted children so that we can alleviate the tragedy of lost talent that persists to this day.

Questions and Activities

1. What were some of the social and political factors that led to the development of gifted education in the United States?

2. What sources of data are used to identify gifted students in your community? Identify some of the problems associated with each source.

3. Form a group with several of your classmates. Research and report on ways students gifted in various areas such as language arts, mathematics, and science can be served in the regular classroom.

4. What are the characteristics associated with gifted children, regardless of their ethnicity or socioeconomic status? How might these characteristics be expressed in different cultural or economic milieus?

5. What resources and training will you need to teach gifted students?

6. Write a brief paper on how the concept of ability grouping is applied to teaching gifted students in regular classrooms, pull-out programs, specialized classes, and specialized schools. What are some benefits and disadvantages of each setting?

7. Using a lesson that you would normally teach, give examples of how the concepts of acceleration and enrichment can be applied in your classroom. What benchmarks

would you use to determine when acceleration was appropriate? How would you identify the students who would participate in enrichment activities? Give examples of acceleration and enrichment activities that can be used with the lesson.

8. Educators have a special responsibility to identify and provide services to gifted students who are bilingual, culturally and ethnically diverse, and from low-income homes. Research the policies of your local gifted programs to see whether there exists a commitment to identifying and serving gifted children from diverse racial, ethnic, cultural and language groups.

References

Archambault, F. X., Westberg, K. L., Brown, S. W., Hallmark, B. W., Emmons, C. L., and Zhang, W. (1993). *Regular Classroom Practices with Gifted Students: Results of a National Survey of Classroom Teachers*. Research Monograph 93102. Storrs, CT: National Research Center on the Gifted and Talented.

Baker, J. A., Bridges, R., and Evans, K. (1998). Models of Underachievement among Gifted Preadolescents: The Role of Personal, Family, and Schools Factors. *Gifted Child Quarterly, 42*(1), 5–15.

Baldwin, A. Y. (1987). Undiscovered Diamonds: The Minority Gifted Child. *Journal for the Education of the Gifted, 10*(4), 271–285.

Baldwin, A. Y. (1991). Ethnic and Cultural Issues. In N. Colangelo and G. A. Davis (Eds.), *Handbook of Gifted Education* (pp. 416–427). Boston: Allyn and Bacon.

Baldwin, A. Y. (1994). The Seven Plus Story: Developing Hidden Talent among Students in Socioeconomically Disadvantaged Environments. *Gifted Child Quarterly, 38*(2), 80–84.

Banks, J. A. (1995). Multicultural Education: Historical Development, Dimensions, and Practice. In J. A. Banks and C. A. M. Banks (Eds.), *Handbook of Research on Multicultural Education* (pp. 3–24). New York: Macmillan.

Banks, J. A. and Banks, C. A. M. (Eds.). (1995). *Handbook of Research on Multicultural Education*. New York: Macmillan.

Barkan, J. H. and Bernal, E. M. (1991). Gifted Education for Bilingual and LEP Students. *Gifted Child Quarterly, 35*(3), 144–147.

Borland, J. H. (1996). Gifted Education and the Threat of Irrelevance. *Journal for the Education of the Gifted, 19*(2), 129–147.

Borland, J. H. and Wright, L. (1994). Identifying Young, Potentially Gifted, Economically Disadvantaged Students. *Gifted Child Quarterly, 38*(4), 164–171.

Boutte, G. S. and McCoy, B. (1993). Racial Issues in Education: Real or Imagined? *Young Children, 49*(1), 19–23.

Bronfenbrenner, U. (1986). Ecology of the Family as a Context for Human Development: Research Perspectives. *Developmental Psychology 22*, 723–742.

Callahan, C. M. and McIntyre, J. A. (1994). *Identifying Outstanding Talent in American Indian and Alaska Native Students*. PIP 94–1219. Washington, DC: U.S. Government Printing Office.

Casserly, P. L. (1980). Factors Affecting Female Participants in Advanced Placement Programs in Mathematics, Chemistry, and Physics. In L. H. Fox, L. Brody, and D. Tobin (Eds.),

Women and the Mathematical Mystique (pp. 138–163). Baltimore, MD: The Johns Hopkins University Press.

Chapman, P. D. (1988). *Schools as Sorters*. New York University Press.

Clark, M. L. (1991). Social Identity, Peer Relations, and Academic Competence of African American Adolescents. *Education and Urban Society, 24*(1), 41–52.

Coleman, L. J. (1994). Portfolio Assessment: A Key to Identifying Hidden Talents and Empowering Teachers of Young Children. *Gifted Child Quarterly, 38*(2), 65–69.

Cooley, M. R., Cornell, D. G., and Lee, C. (1991). Peer Acceptance and Self Concept of Black Students in a Summer Gifted Program. *Journal for the Education of the Gifted, 14*(2), 166–177.

Cox, J., Daniel, N., and Boston, B. (1985). *Educating Able Learners: Programs and Promising Practices*. Austin: University of Texas Press.

Davis, G. (1977). Bitters in the Brew of Success. *Black Enterprise, 8*, 31–35.

Du Bois, W. E. B. (1903). The Talented Tenth. In *The Negro Problem: A Series of Articles by Representative Negroes of Today*. New York: James Pratt.

Evans, K. M. (1996). Counseling Gifted Women of Color. In K. D. Arnold, K. D. Noble, and R. F. Subotnik (Eds.), *Remarkable Women: Perspectives on Female Talent Development* (pp. 351–366). Cresskill, NJ: Hampton.

Evans, K. M. (1997). Multicultural Training Needs for Counselors of Gifted African American Children. *Multicultural Education, 5*(1), 16–19.

Feuerstein, R. (1973). *Instrumental Enrichment*. Baltimore, MD: University Park Press.

Ford, D. Y. (1992). Determinants of Underachievement as Perceived by Gifted, Above Average, and Average Black Students. *Roeper Review, 14*(3), 130–136.

Ford, D. Y. (1993a). An Investigation of the Paradox of Underachievement among Gifted Black Students. *Roeper Review, 6*(2), 78–84.

Ford, D. Y. (1993b). Support for the Achievement Ideology and Determinants of Achievement as Perceived by Gifted, Above Average, and Average Black Students. *Journal for the Education of the Gifted, 16*(3), 280–298.

Ford, D. Y. (1994a). Nurturing Resilience in Gifted Black Youth. *Roeper Review, 17*(2), 80–85.

Ford, D. Y. (1994b). *The Recruitment and Retention of African American Students in Gifted Education Programs: Implications and Recommendations*. Research Monograph No. 9406. Storrs, CT: National Research Center on the Gifted and Talented.

Ford, D. Y. (1995). *Counseling Gifted African American Students: Promoting Achievement, Identity, and Social and Emotional Well-Being*. Counseling Research-Based Decision Making Series 9506.

Ford, D. Y. (1996). *Reversing Underachievement among Gifted Black Students: Promising Practices and Programs*. New York: Teachers College Press.

Ford, D. Y. and Harris J. III. (1994). Reform and Gifted Black Students: Promising Practices in Kentucky. *Journal for the Education of the Gifted, 17*(3), 216–240.

Ford, D. Y. and Harris, J. J. III. (1999). *Multicultural Gifted Education*. New York: Teachers College Press.

Fordham, S. and Ogbu, J. (1986). Black Students' School Success: Coping with the Burden of 'Acting White.' *The Urban Review, 18*(3), 176–203.

Frasier, M. M. (1991a). Response to Kitano: The Sharing of Giftedness between Culturally Diverse and Non-Diverse Gifted Students. *Journal for the Education of the Gifted, 15*(1), 20–30.

Frasier, M. M. (1991b). Disadvantaged and Culturally Diverse Gifted Students. *Journal for the Education of the Gifted, 14*(3), 234–245.

Frasier, M. M., Garcia, J. H., and Passow, A. H. (1995). *A Review of Assessment Issues in Gifted Education and Their Implications for Identifying Gifted Minority Students.* Research Monograph 95204. Storrs, CT: National Research Center on the Gifted and Talented.

Frasier, M. M. and Passow, A. H. (1994). *Toward a New Paradigm for Identifying Talent Potential.* Research Monograph 94112. Storrs, CT: National Research Center on the Gifted and Talented.

Gallagher, J. J. and Gallagher, S. A. (1994). *Teaching the Gifted Child* (4th ed.). Boston: Allyn and Bacon.

Gardner, H. (1983). *Frames of Mind.* New York: Basic Books.

Gardner, H. (1993). *Multiple Intelligences: The Theory into Practice.* New York: Basic Books.

Gardner, H. (1996). Multiple Intelligences: Myths and Messages. *International Schools Journal, 15*(2), 8–22.

Giroux, H. A. and McLaren, P. (1994). *Between Borders: Pedagogy and the Politics of Cultural Studies.* New York: Routledge.

Griffin, J. B. (1992). Catching the Dream for Gifted Children of Color. *Gifted Child Quarterly, 36*(3), 126–130.

Guilford, J. P. (1967). *The Nature of Human Intelligence.* New York: McGraw-Hill.

Helms, J. E. (1992). Why Is There No Study of Cultural Equivalence in Standardized Cognitive Ability Testing? *American Psychologist, 47,* 1083–1101.

Hollingworth, L. (1927). *Gifted Children: Their Nature and Nurture.* New York: Macmillan.

House, E. R. and Lapan, S. (1994). Evaluation of Programs for Disadvantaged Gifted Students. *Journal for the Education of the Gifted, 17*(4), 441–466.

Kay, S. I. and Subotnik, R. F. (1994). Talent beyond Words: Unveiling Spatial, Expressive, Kinesthetic and Musical Talent in Young Children. *Gifted Child Quarterly, 38*(2), 70–74.

Kerr, B. A. (1994). *Smart Girls Two: A New Psychology of Girls, Women, and Giftedness.* Dayton: Ohio Psychology Press.

Kerr, B. A., Colangelo, N., Maxey, J., and Christensen, P. (1992). Characteristics of Academically Talented Minority Students. *Journal of Counseling and Development, 70*(5), 606–670.

Kirschenbaum, R. J. (1988). Methods for Identifying the Gifted and Talented American Indian Student. *Journal for the Education of the Gifted, 11*(3), 53–63.

Kitano, M. K. (1991). A Multicultural Educational Perspective on Serving the Culturally Diverse Gifted. *Journal for the Education of the Gifted, 15*(1), 4–19.

Kitano, M. K. (1995). Lessons from Gifted Women of Color. *Journal of Secondary Gifted Education, 6*(2), 176–187.

Louis, B. Subotnik, R. F., Breland, P. (in press). Identification vs. Admissions Practices: Implications for Policies and Practices in Gifted Education. *Educational Psychology Review.*

Maker, C. J. and Schiever, S. W. (1989). *Cultural Issues in Gifted Education: Defensible Programs for Cultural and Ethnic Minorities.* Austin, TX: Pro-Ed.

Margolin, L. (1996). A Pedagogy of Privilege. *Journal for the Education of the Gifted, 19*(2), 164–180.

Marland, S. P., Jr. (1972). *Education of the Gifted and Talented,* Vol. 1: Report to the Congress of the United States by the United States Commissioner of Education. Washington, DC: U.S. Government Printing Office.

Marsh, H. W., Chessor, D., Craven, R., and Roche, L. (1995). The Effects of Gifted and Talented Programs on Academic Self-Concept: The Big Fish Strikes Again. *American Educational Research Journal, 32*(2), 285–319.

Matthew, J. L., Golin, K. G., Moore, M. W., and Baker, C. (1992). Use of SOMPA in the Identification of Gifted African American Children. *Journal for the Education of the Gifted, 15*(4), 344–356.

Miserandino, A., Subotnik, R. F., and Ou, K. (1995). Identifying and Nurturing Mathematical Talent in Urban School Settings. *Journal of Secondary Gifted Education, 6*(4), 245–257.

Noble, K. D., Subotnik, R. F., and Arnold, K. D. (1999). To Thine Own Self Be True: A New Model for Female Talent Development. *Gifted Child Quarterly, 43*, 140–149.

Oakes, J. (1990). *Multiplying Inequalities: The Effects of Race, Social Class, and Tracking on Opportunities to Learn Mathematics and Science.* Santa Monica, CA: Rand.

Ochse, R. (1990). *Before the Gates of Excellence: Determinants of Creative Genius.* New York: Cambridge University Press.

Oden, S., Kelly, M. A., Ma, Z., and Weikart, D. P. (1992). *Challenging the Potential: Programs for Talented Disadvantaged Youth.* Ypsilanti, MI: High Scope.

Ogbu, J. (1995). Understanding Cultural Diversity and Learning. In J. A. Banks and C. A. M. Banks (Eds.). *Handbook of Research in Multicultural Education* (pp. 582–593). New York: Macmillan.

Olszewski-Kubilius, P., Grant, B., and Seibert, C. (1994). Social Support System and the Disadvantaged Gifted: A Framework for Development Programs and Services. *Roeper Review 17*(1) 20–25.

Parker, W. D. (1997). An Empirical Typology of Perfectionism in Academically Talented Children. *American Educational Research Journal, 34*(3), 545–562.

Passow, A. H. (1985). Intellectual Development of the Gifted. In F. R. Link (Ed.), *Essays on the Intellect* (pp. 23–43). Alexandria, VA: ASCD.

Ponterotto, J. G., Casas, J. M., Suzuki, L. A., and Alexander, C. M. (Eds.). (1995). *Handbook of Multicultural Counseling.* Thousand Oaks, CA: Sage.

Reis, S. M. and Purcell, J. H. (1993). An Analysis of Context Elimination and Strategies Used by Elementary Classroom Teachers in the Curriculum Compacting Program. *Journal for the Education of the Gifted, 16*, 147–170.

Renzulli, J. (1986). The Three Ring Conception of Giftedness: A Developmental Model for Creative Productivity. In R. J. Sternberg and J. E. Davidson (Eds.), *Conceptions of Giftedness* (pp. 53–92). New York: Cambridge University Press.

Renzulli, J., Reis, S. M., and Smith, L. H. (1981). The Revolving Door Identification Model. Mansfield Center, CT: Creative Learning Press.

Renzulli, J. S. (1994). *Schools for Talent Development: A Practical Plan for Total School Improvement.* Mansfield Center, CT: Creative Learning Press.

Roedell, W. C., Jackson, N. E., and Robinson, H. B. (1980). *Gifted Young Children.* New York: Teachers College Press.

Ross, P. O. (1993). *National Excellence: A Case for Developing America's Talent.* PIP 93–1201. Washington, DC: Office of Educational Research and Improvement.

Sapon-Shevin, M. (1996). Beyond Gifted Education: Building a Shared Agenda for School Reform. *Journal for the Education of the Gifted, 19*(2), 194–214.

Scott, M. S., Perou, R., Urbano, R., Hogan A., and Gold, S. (1992). The Identification of Giftedness: A Comparison of White, Hispanic, and Black Families. *Gifted Child Quarterly, 36*(3), 131–139.

Seymour, E. and Hewitt, N. M. (1994). *Talking about Leaving: Factors Contributing to High Attrition Rates among Science, Mathematics, and Engineering Undergraduate Majors.* Boulder: University of Colorado Bureau of Sociological Research.

Silverman, L. K. (1995). Why Are There So Few Eminent Women? *Roeper Review, 18*(1), 5–13.

Silverman, L. K. (1998). Through the Lens of Giftedness. *Roeper Review, 20*(3), 204–210.

Simonton, D. K. (1994). *Greatness: Who Makes History and Why?* New York: Guilford.

Smith, D. (1995). Social Giftedness—Its Characteristics and Identification. *Gifted Education International, 11*(1), 24–30.

Smith, J., LeRose, B., and Clasen, R. E. (1991). Underrepresentation of Minority Students in Gifted Programs: Yes It Matters. *Gifted Child Quarterly, 35*(2), 81–83.

Sternberg, R. J. (1986). A Triarchic Theory of Intellectual Giftedness. In R. J. Sternberg and J. E. Davidson (Eds.), *Conceptions of Giftedness* (pp. 223–243). New York: Cambridge University Press.

Subotnik, R. F. (2000). Developing Young Adolescent Performers at Juilliard: An Educational Prototype for Elite Level Talent Development in the Arts and Sciences. In C. F. Van Lieshout and P. G. Heymans (Eds.), *Talent, Resilience, and Wisdom across the Life Span* (pp. 249–276). Hove, UK: Psychology Press.

Subotnik, R. F. and Coleman, L. J. (1996). Establishing the Foundations for a Talent Development School: Applying Principles to Creating an Ideal. *Journal for the Education of the Gifted, 20,* 175–189.

Subotnik, R. F., Kassan, L., Summers, E., and Wasser, A. (1993). *Genius Revisited: High IQ Children Grown Up.* Norwood, NJ: Ablex.

Subotnik, R. F. and Olszewski-Kubilius, P. (1997). Distinctions between Children's and Adults' Experiences of Giftedness. *Peabody Journal of Education, 72*(3&4), 101–116.

Terman, L. M. and Oden, M. (1925). *Genetic Studies of Genius: Mental and Physical Traits of a Thousand Gifted Children.* Stanford, CA: Stanford University Press.

Terman, L. M. and Oden, M. (1947). *Genetic Studies of Genius: The Gifted Child Grows Up.* Stanford, CA: Stanford University Press.

Tonemah, S. A. (1991). Philosophical Perspectives of Gifted and Talented American Indian Education. *Journal of American Indian Education, 31*(1), 3–9.

Tonemah, S. A. (1992). American Indian Students and Alaska Native Students. In P. Cahape and C. B. Howley (Eds.), *Indian Nations at Risk: Listening to the People* (pp. 81–85). Charleston, WV: ERIC Clearinghouse on Rural Education and Small Schools.

Torrance, E. P. (1965). *Rewarding Creative Behavior: Experiments in Classroom Creativity.* Englewood Cliffs, NJ.: Prentice-Hall.

Torrance, E. P., Goff, K., and Satterfield, N. B. (1998). *Multicultural Mentoring of the Gifted and Talented.* Waco, TX: Prufrock Press.

Treisman, U. (1992). Studying Students Studying Calculus: A Look at the Lives of Minority Mathematics Students in College. *The College Mathematics Journal, 23*(5), 362–372.

VanTassel-Baska, J. (1989). The Role of Family in the Success of Disadvantaged Gifted Learners. In J. VanTassel-Baska and P. Olszenski-Kubilius (Eds.), *Patterns of Influence on Gifted Learners: The Home, the Self, the School* (pp. 60–80). New York: Teachers College Press.

VanTassel-Baska, J. (1994). *Comprehensive Curriculum for Gifted Learners* (2nd ed.). Boston: Allyn and Bacon.

Wang, M. C. and Gordon, E. W. (Eds.). (1994). *Educational Resilience in Inner-City America: Challenges and Prospects.* Hillsdale, NJ: Lawrence Erlbaum.

Webb, J. T., Meckstroth, E. A., and Tolan, S. S. (1986). *Guiding the Gifted Child* (2nd ed.). Columbus: Ohio Psychology Publishers.

Williams, L. R. (1989). Diverse Gifts: Multicultural Education in Kindergarten. *Childhood Education, 66*(1), 2–3.

Wright, L. and Borland, J. H. (1993). Using Early Childhood Developmental Portfolios in the Identification and Education of Young, Economically Disadvantaged, Potentially Gifted Students. *Roeper Review, 15*(4), 205–210.

The cultures of the students and of the community are major factors that influence successful school reform efforts.

School Reform

Reforming schools so that all students have an equal opportunity to succeed requires a new vision of education and social actors who are willing to advocate for and participate in change. The two chapters in Part VI discuss effective ways to conceptualize and implement school reform within a multicultural framework. In Chapter 16, Sonia Nieto presents and analyzes five conditions that will promote student achievement within a multicultural perspective. According to Nieto, school should (1) be antiracist and antibiased; (2) reflect an understanding and acceptance of all students as having talents and strengths that can enhance their education; (3) be considered within the parameters of critical pedagogy; (4) involve those people most intimately connected with teaching and learning; and (5) be based on high expectations and rigorous standards for all learners.

Cherry A. McGee Banks, in Chapter 17, discusses ways to involve parents in schools. She argues that parent involvement is an important factor in school reform and student achievement and that parents can be a cogent force in school reform. Parents, perhaps more than any other group, can mobilize the community to support school reform. Parents have first-hand knowledge about the school's effectiveness and can be vocal advocates for change. As consumers of educational services, parents can raise questions that are difficult for professional educators and administrators to raise, such as: "What is the proportion of males in special education classes?" and "What is the ethnic breakdown of students enrolled in higher-level math and science classes?"

Banks argues that parents are more willing to work for school reform when they are involved in schools. They are more likely to become involved in schools when parent involvement opportunities reflect their varied interests, skills, and motivations. Banks suggests ways to expand traditional ideas about parent involvement and to increase the number and kinds of parents involved in schools.

CHAPTER 16

School Reform and Student Learning: A Multicultural Perspective

Sonia Nieto

Learning is the primary purpose of schooling. Given this reality, it makes sense that student learning be at the center of school reform efforts. This means that school policies and practices need to be developed with an eye toward how they affect the learning and academic achievement of students. But some school policies, especially as espoused in the reform movement that began with the publication of *Our Nation at Risk* (National Commission on Excellence in Education, 1983), have been little more than bureaucratic shuffling or the imposition of city, state, and federal policies that pay scant attention to whether and to what extent students learn. These reform efforts often end up punishing schools, teachers, districts, and ultimately students who have not measured up to norms of success predetermined by people outside the schools. Longer school days and years, strict retention policies, placing schools "on probation," and more high-stakes testing (that is, tests used as the sole or primary criterion for such crucial decisions as placement in ability groups and college admission), and less attention to pedagogy and curriculum have been the result. Students who are most at risk of receiving an inadequate education are often the ones most jeopardized by such reform efforts.

This chapter begins with the assumption that student learning can be positively influenced by changes in school policies and practices that affirm students' identities and that are part of systemic school reform measures. Given the social nature of schooling, it is impossible to ascribe a fixed causal relationship between student learning and schooling. Many complex forces influence student learning, including personal, psychological, social, cultural, community, and institutional factors (Erickson, 1993; Nieto, 2000). That is, we cannot simply say that eliminating tracking will help all students succeed, or that native language instruction is the factor that will guarantee success for all language-minority students. Neither can we state that making pedagogy more culturally relevant is always the answer. These changes may in fact substantially improve educational outcomes for many more students than are now achieving academic success. However, taken in isolation, these changes fail to reflect the complex nature of student learning.

A comprehensive view of student learning that takes into account the myriad influences on achievement can help explain why some students succeed academically while others do not. For example, in one study of dropouts, it was found that 68 percent of the Puerto Rican students who had never been in bilingual programs dropped out of school, while only 39 percent of those who had been in bilingual classrooms for at least part of their school experience dropped out (Frau-Ramos & Nieto, 1993). The difference in dropout rates was dramatic, but a 39 percent dropout rate is still unacceptably high. It suggests that other conditions also were involved, including students' perceptions of fitting in and their previous educational preparation; teachers' limited knowledge of their students' backgrounds and their negative attitudes about diversity; and school policies and practices that led some students to feel like outsiders. In this case, although bilingual education was significant in mediating the school retention of some students, it was insufficient to ensure that all students would succeed academically.

Culturally responsive education, an approach based on using students' identities and backgrounds as meaningful sources of their education, can go a long way in improving the education of students whose cultures have been maligned, denied, or omitted in school curricula (Au & Kawakami, 1994; Gay, 2000; Irvine, 1997; Ladson-Billings, 1994). This approach offers crucial insights for understanding the lack of achievement of students from culturally subordinated groups. However, by itself, culturally responsive pedagogy cannot guarantee that all students will learn. There are, for instance, cases in which culturally marginalized students have been successfully educated *in spite* of what might be considered culturally incompatible settings. As a case in point, Catholic schools might seem at first glance to be culturally inappropriate for some children because bilingual programs are seldom offered, classes are usually overcrowded, and formal environments stress individual excellence rather than cooperation. Yet many students of African American and Latino backgrounds who attend Catholic schools have been academically successful (Bryk, Lee, & Holland, 1993; Irvine & Foster, 1996).

In the case of Catholic schools, we need to look beyond just cultural responsiveness to explain student academic success. Because of generally restricted resources, Catholic schools tend to offer *all* students a less differentiated curriculum, less tracking, and more academic classes, in addition to having clear, uncomplicated missions and strong social contracts (Bryk, Lee, & Holland, 1993; Irvine & Foster, 1996). What at first glance might appear to be incongruous in terms of cultural compatibility can be explained by school structures that imply similarly high expectations for all students. This example illustrates the complex relationship of academic success to a multiplicity of conditions, and it again indicates that there is no one simple solution to academic failure.

In this chapter, I explore the meaning of school reform with a multicultural perspective and consider implications for student learning. I begin by defining school reform with a multicultural perspective, including how a school's policies and practices implicitly illustrate a school's beliefs about who is deserving of the benefits of education. As a result, certain school policies and practices may exacerbate inequalities that exist in society. I then describe a set of five interrelated conditions for successful school reform within a multicultural perspective. Although it is arbitrary to consider these conditions as separate issues because they are intimately interconnected, for the purpose of expediency, I explain the five conditions separately, with implications for increasing student achievement.

SCHOOL REFORM WITH A MULTICULTURAL PERSPECTIVE

Many people assume that multicultural education is little more than isolated lessons in sensitivity training or prejudice reduction, or separate units about cultural artifacts or ethnic holidays. Sometimes, it is used to mean education geared for inner-city schools or, more specifically, for African American students. If conceptualized in this limited way, multicultural education will have little influence on student learning.

When conceptualized as broad-based school reform, multicultural education can have a major influence on how and to what extent students learn. When it focuses on conditions that can contribute to student underachievement, multicultural education allows educators to explore alternatives to systemic problems that lead to academic failure for many students and it fosters the design and implementation of productive learning environments, diverse instructional strategies, and a deeper awareness of how cultural and language differences can influence learning.

To approach school reform with a multicultural perspective, we need to begin with an understanding of multicultural education within its *sociopolitical context* (Nieto, 2000). A sociopolitical context underscores that education is part and parcel of larger societal and political forces, such as inequality based on stratification due to race, social class, gender, and other differences. Given this perspective, decisions concerning such practices as rigid ability tracking, high-stakes testing, native-language instruction, curriculum reform, and the use of innovative pedagogical approaches are all influenced by broader social policies.

As Freire (1985) states, every educational decision, whether made at the classroom, city, state, or national level, is imbedded within a particular ideological framework. Such decisions can be as simple as whether a classroom should be arranged in rows with all students facing the teacher, or in tables with groups of students to encourage cooperative work, or in a variety of ways depending on the task at hand. Alternatively, these decisions can be as far-reaching as eliminating tracking in an entire school system, or teaching language-minority students by using their native language and English, or by using English only. Imbedded within each educational decision are assumptions about the nature of learning, about what particular students are capable of achieving, about whose language is valued, and about who should be at the center of the educational process. Even seemingly innocent decisions carry an enormous amount of ideological and philosophical baggage, which is in turn communicated to students either directly or indirectly.

As stated more extensively elsewhere, I define multicultural education within a sociopolitical context as (Nieto, 2000)

> a process of comprehensive school reform and basic education for
> all students. It challenges and rejects racism and other forms of
> discrimination in schools and society and accepts and affirms the
> pluralism (ethnic, racial, linguistic, religious, economic, and gender,
> among others) that students, their communities, and teachers
> reflect. Multicultural education permeates the schools' curriculum
> and instructional strategies, as well as the interactions among
> teachers, students, and families, and the very way that schools
> conceptualize the nature of teaching and learning. Because it uses

> critical pedagogy as its underlying philosophy and focuses on
> knowledge, reflection, and action (*praxis*) as the basis for social
> change, multicultural education promotes democratic principles of
> social justice. (p. 305)

This definition of multicultural education assumes a comprehensive school reform effort rather than superficial additions to the curriculum or one-shot treatments with a focus on diversity, such as workshops for teachers or assembly programs for students. As such, I use this definition as a lens to view conditions for systemic school reform that can improve the learning of all students.

CONDITIONS FOR SYSTEMIC SCHOOL REFORM WITH A MULTICULTURAL PERSPECTIVE

Failure to learn does not develop out of thin air; it is scrupulously created through policies, practices, attitudes, and beliefs. In a very concrete sense, the results of educational inequality explain by example what a society believes its young people are capable of achieving and what they deserve. For instance, offering only low-level courses in schools serving culturally diverse and poor youngsters is a clear message that the students are not expected to achieve to high levels; in like manner, considering students to be at risk simply because of their ethnicity, native language, family characteristics, or social class is another unequivocal sign that some students have been defined by conventional wisdom as uneducable based simply on their identity.

As a result, we cannot think about education reform without taking into account both micro- and macrolevel issues that may affect student learning. Microlevel issues include the cultures, languages, and experiences of students and their families and how these are considered in determining school policies and practices (Cummins, 1996; Nieto, 1999). Macrolevel issues include the racial stratification that helps maintain inequality, and the resources and access to learning that schools provide or deny (Darling-Hammond, 1996; Kozol, 1991). In addition, how students and their families view their status in schools and society must be considered. Ogbu (1994), for instance, has argued that school performance gaps persist because the forces of racial stratification and the unequal treatment of dominated groups, as well as the responses of dominated groups to these experiences, also continue.

Conditions such as inequitable school financing (Darling-Hammond, 1995; Kozol, 1991), unrepresentative school governance (Meier & Stewart, 1991), and large class size (Mosteller, 1995) may play a powerful role in promoting student underachievement. For example, Ascher and Burnett (1993) found that disparities among rich and poor states, and among rich and poor districts in the same state, actually increased in the 1980s. Yet reform strategies such as longer school days, more rigorous graduation standards, and increased standardized testing often do not take such issues into account. We can safely conclude that equalizing just two conditions of schooling—funding and class size—would probably result in an immediate and dramatic improvement in learning for students who have not received the benefits of these two conditions.

School reform strategies that do not acknowledge such macrolevel disparities are bound to be inadequate because they assume that schools provide all students with a level playing field. The conditions described below, while acknowledging these disparities, nevertheless provide hope for school systems where such changes as equitable funding or small class size may not occur in the near future. Rather than wait for these changes to happen, schools and teachers can begin to improve the conditions for successful student learning. Five such conditions are described below (these conditions are slightly revised and described in greater detail in Nieto, 1999). These conditions, along with changes in funding and resource allocation, would help create schools where all students have a better chance to learn.

School Reform Should Be Antiracist and Antibiased

An antiracist and antibias perspective is at the core of multicultural education. This is crucial because too often people believe that multicultural education automatically takes care of racism; but this is far from the reality (Weinberg, 1990). In fact, multicultural education without an explicit antiracist focus may perpetuate the worst kinds of stereotypes if it focuses on only superficial aspects of culture and the addition of ethnic tidbits (see Chapter 10).

In contrast, being antiracist means paying attention to all areas in which some students may be favored over others, including the curriculum and pedagogy, sorting policies, and teachers' interactions and relationships with students and their communities. Educators committed to multicultural education with an antiracist perspective need to examine closely both school policies and the attitudes and behaviors of its staff to determine how these might be complicitous in causing academic failure. The kind of expectations that teachers and schools have for students (Nieto, 1994b), whether native-language use is permitted or punished (Cummins, 1996), how sorting takes place (Oakes, Wells, Jones, & Datnow, 1997), and how classroom organization, pedagogy, and curriculum may influence student learning (Haberman, 1991; Lee, Bryk, & Smith, 1993) each need to be considered.

To become antiracist, schools need to examine as well how the curriculum may perpetuate negative, distorted, or incomplete images of some groups while exalting others as the makers of all history. Unfortunately, many textbooks and children's books are still replete with racist and sexist images and with demeaning portrayals of people from low-income communities. Although the situation is improving, and the stereotypes that exist are certainly not as blatant as they once were, there are still inaccuracies and negative portrayals (Harris, 1997; Loewen, 1995; Willis, 1998).

In a related vein, most of the women and men presented as heroes or heroines in the standard curriculum—whether from dominant or nondominant cultures—are "safe"; that is, they do not pose a challenge to the status quo. Other people who have fought for social justice are omitted or made safe by downplaying their contributions. A now-classic article by Kozol (1975) graphically documents how schools bleed the life and soul out of even the most impassioned and courageous heroes, such as Helen Keller and Martin Luther King, Jr., in the process making them boring and less-than-believable caricatures. A more recent article by Kohl (1993) demonstrates how Rosa Parks, the mother of the civil rights movement, has been made palatable to the mainstream by portraying her not as a staunch civil rights crusader who consciously battled racist segregation, but rather as a tired woman who simply did not want to give up her seat on the bus (Kohl, 1993). Taking another example, few children learn about the slave revolt led by Nat Turner (Aptheker, 1943/1987), although most learn that "Abraham Lincoln freed the slaves." These are examples of at best misleading, and at worst racist, representations.

Through this kind of curriculum, students from dominant groups learn that they are the norm, and consequently they often assume that anyone different from them is culturally or intellectually disadvantaged. On the other hand, students from subordinated cultures may internalize the message that their cultures, families, languages, and experiences have low status, and they learn to feel inferior (Cummins, 1996). The result may be what has been called "stereotype stigma," or the devaluation faced by Blacks and other people of color in our society (Steele, 1999). All students suffer as a result of these messages, but students from dominated groups are the most negatively affected.

The issue of institutional power is also at play here. The conventional notion of racism is that it is an individual bias toward members of other groups. This perception conveniently skirts the issue of how institutions themselves, which are much more powerful than individuals, develop harmful policies and practices that victimize American Indians, African Americans, Latinos, poor European Americans, females, and other people from powerless groups (Winant, 1994). The major difference between *individual racism* and *institutional racism* is the wielding of power, because it is primarily through the power of the people who control institutions such as schools that oppressive policies and practices are reinforced and legitimated (Tatum, 1997; Weinberg, 1990). That is, when racism is understood as a systemic problem, not just as an individual dislike for a particular group of people, we can better understand its negative and destructive effects.

I do not wish to minimize the powerful effect of individual prejudice and discrimination, which can be personally very painful, nor to suggest that individual discrimination occurs only in one direction, for example, from Whites to African Americans. No group monopolizes prejudice and discrimination; they occur in all directions, and even within groups. But interethnic hostility, personal prejudices, and individual biases, while certainly hurtful, do not have the long-range and life-limiting effects on entire groups of people that *institutional* racism and bias have. Testing practices, for example, may be institutionally discriminatory because they label students from culturally and socially dominated groups as inferior as a result of their performance on these tests (Figueroa & Garcia, 1994). Rather than critically examining the tests themselves, the underlying purpose of such tests, or their damaging effects, the students themselves are often blamed (Neill, 1997).

An antiracist perspective is also apparent in schools when students are permitted, and even encouraged, to speak about their experiences with racism and other biases. Many White teachers feel great discomfort when racism is discussed in the classroom. They are uncomfortable for several reasons: their lack of experience in confronting such a potentially explosive issue, the conspiracy of silence about racism (as if not speaking about it will make it disappear), the guilt they may feel being a member of the group that has benefited from racism, and the generally accepted assumption that we live in a colorblind society (Schofield, 1986; also see Chapter 11), or a combination of these reasons (Fine, 1991; Kailin, 1999; Sleeter, 1994; Tatum, 1997). Yet when students are given time and support for expressing their views, the result can be powerful because their experiences are legitimated and used in the service of their learning (Jervis, 1996).

Donaldson (1996) describes how urban high school students used the racism they and their peers experienced in school as the content of a peer education assembly program. The result was a powerful and critical examination of the impact that race can have on their education. A similar result was documented by Zanger (1993), when she brought together a group of high-achieving Latino and Latina Boston high school students to talk about their experiences with discrimination. In the subsequent dialogue, students discussed such meaningful issues as their feelings of exclusion and subordination and their cultural invisibility in the school. They also proposed specific solutions that have profound implications for school policies and practices, including the kinds of program options that schools offer for learning English. In the words of one young woman (cited in Zanger, 1993):

> I think we should try to learn English, but not lose our
> Spanish. They want us to learn English and lose our cultural
> backgrounds. And I think there's a way they can work up on our
> *already* [existing] culture. And build it to be strong and better than
> what they are and we are. Two things combined can be very good. I
> mean we take the Spanish culture and a little bit of the English
> culture, we can be great students, we can be great people, we can be
> great leaders of this country. (p. 175; emphasis added)

Another example comes from an extensive study that took place over a one-year period in which numerous students, staff, and parents in California schools were consulted and interviewed (Poplin & Weeres, 1992). The researchers found that, in spite of the fact that racism was rarely discussed in their classes, most students described racist incidents in school and could easily relate them to racism in the larger society. In addition, and probably not coincidentally, most young people expressed an intense interest in knowing about one another's cultures and backgrounds, but they learned very little about these in school. Similarly, a study by Kiang and Kaplan (1994) explored the views of Vietnamese students on their exclusion in discussions about racial conflict after a violent clash between African American and White students. Not only did the students feel left out of these momentous discussions, but more important, they also felt that their involvement might help improve the race relations and the quality of life in the school.

In my own research on the views of academically successful students concerning their schooling, racism and other examples of discrimination on the part of fellow students and teachers were mentioned (Nieto, 1994a). Manuel, a Cape Verdean student who moved to the United States at age eleven, described how it felt to be the butt of jokes from his peers: "When American students see you, it's kinda hard [to] get along with them when you have a different culture, a different way of dressing and stuff like that. So kids really look at you and laugh, you know, at the beginning" (p. 414). Avi, a Jewish American young man, discussed a number of incidents of anti-Semitism, including one in which a student walked by him and whispered, "Are you ready for the Second Holocaust?" Other students talked about discrimination on the part of teachers. Marisol, a Puerto Rican student, and Vinh, who was Vietnamese, specifically mentioned language discrimination as a major problem. In Marisol's case, it happened when a teacher did not allow her to use Spanish in the classroom. For Vinh, it concerned teachers' attitudes about his language. He explained: "Some teachers don't understand about the language. So sometimes, my language, they say it sounds funny" (p. 414).

As these examples make clear, an antiracist perspective is essential in schools if all students are to be given equitable environments for learning. An antiracist perspective is a vital lens through which to analyze a school's policies and practices, including the curriculum, pedagogy, testing and tracking, discipline, faculty hiring, student retention, and attitudes about and interactions with parents.

School Reform Should Reflect an Understanding and Acceptance of All Students as Having Talents and Strengths That Can Enhance Their Education

It has been amply documented that many educators believe that students from culturally subordinated groups have few experiential or cultural strengths that can benefit their education (Haberman, 1991; Ryan, 1972). Such students, generally low-income children of all groups and children of color specifically, are considered to be "walking sets of deficiencies" (Nieto, 1994b). They may be considered "culturally deprived," a patronizing term popularized in the 1960s to shift the blame for student failure from schools and society to students and their families (Reissman, 1962). Students may be thought of as culturally deprived simply because they speak a language other than English as their native language, or because they have just one parent or live in poverty. Sometimes, they are labeled in this way just because of their race or ethnicity.

Rather than begin with this kind of deficit view, it makes more sense to begin with a more positive and, in the end, more realistic and hopeful view of students and their families. School reform measures based on the assumption that children of all families bring cultural and community strengths to their education would go a long way in providing more powerful learning environments for a greater number of youngsters. Moll and Gonzalez's (1997) research on incorporating "funds of knowledge" into the curriculum, that is, using the experiences and skills of all families to encourage student learning, is a more promising and productive way of approaching families than is the viewpoint that they have only deficits that must be repaired.

If we begin with the premise that children and their families have substantial talents that can inform student learning, a number of implications for improving schools follow. Instead of placing the blame for failure to learn solely on students, teachers need to become aware of how their own biases can act as barriers to student learning. Teachers also need to consider how their students best learn and how their own pedagogical practices need to change as a result. This implies that teachers need to learn culturally responsive ways of teaching all of their students (Irvine, 1997; Ladson-Billings, 1994).

Teachers also need to consider how the native language of students influences their academic achievement. For this to happen, they need to "unlearn" some of the conventional myths surrounding native language use (McLaughlin, 1992). For instance, it is common practice in schools to try to convince parents whose native language is other than English that they should speak only English with their children. This recommendation makes little sense for at least three reasons. First, these parents often speak little English themselves, and their children are thus provided with less than adequate models of English. Second, this practice often results in cutting off, rather than stimulating, communication between parents and children. In this regard, a nationwide survey of more than 1,000 families for whom English was a second language found evidence of serious disruptions of family relations when young children learned English in school and lost their native language (NABE No-Cost Study on Families, 1991). Likewise, if young people are encouraged to learn English at the expense of their native language, rather than in conjunction with it, they may lose meaningful connections that help maintain close and loving relations with family members (Wong Fillmore, 1991).

A more reasonable recommendation, and one that would honor the contributions parents can make to their children's education, is to encourage rather than discourage them to speak their native language with their children, to speak it often, and to use it consistently. In schools, this means that students would not be punished for speaking their native languages; rather, they would be encouraged to do so, and to do so in the service of their learning. A rich communicative legacy, both in school and at home, would be the result.

Another example of failing to use student and community strengths can be found in the curriculum. Young children are frequently presented with images of community helpers who may be unrelated to their daily lives. A perspective that affirms the talents and experiences of students and their families can expand the people and roles included in the curriculum. Not only would children study those community helpers traditionally included, such as police officers, mail carriers, and teachers, but they could also learn about local merchants, community social service activists, and street vendors. These people are also community helpers, although they have not generally been sanctioned as such by the official curriculum.

A further consideration concerning the talents and strengths of students and their families is what Cummins (1996) has called the "relations of power" in schools. In proposing a shift from "coercive" to "collaborative" relations of power, Cummins argues that traditional teacher-centered transmission models can limit the potential for learning, especially among students from communities whose cultures and languages are devalued by the dominant canon. For instance, the previously cited in-depth study of schools by Poplin and Weeres (1992) found that students frequently reported being bored and seeing little relevance in the school curriculum to their lives and futures. The researchers concluded that as the curriculum, texts, and assignments became more standardized, students became even more disengaged in their learning (Poplin & Weeres, 1992). That is, the more school experiences were unrelated to their own community experiences, the less relevant schooling became for students.

Their findings suggest that using students and their families as collaborators in developing the curriculum would help promote student learning. By encouraging collaborative relations of power, schools can begin to recognize other sources of legitimate knowledge that have been overlooked; this practice can, in turn, positively affect the degree to which students learn.

School Reform Should Be Considered within the Parameters of Critical Pedagogy

According to Banks (1997), the main goal of a multicultural curriculum is to help students develop decision-making and social-action skills. Consequently, when students learn to view situations and events from a variety of viewpoints, critical thinking, reflection, and action are promoted. The connection between critical pedagogy and a multicultural perspective has recently been explored, and it is a promising avenue for expanding and informing both of these philosophical frameworks (May, 1999; Sleeter & McLaren, 1995; Walsh, 1996). Critical pedagogy is an approach through which students and teachers are encouraged to view what they learn in a critical light; in the words of Freire (1970), by learning to read both "the word and the world." According to Freire, the opposite of a critical or empowering approach is "banking education," where students learn to regurgitate and passively accept the knowledge they are given. A critical education, on the other hand, expects students to seek their own answers, to be curious, and to question.

Most students do not usually have access to a wide range of viewpoints, but such access is essential if they are to develop the critical judgment and decision-making skills they will need to become productive members of a democratic society. Because a critical perspective values diverse viewpoints and encourages critical thinking, reflection, and action, students are empowered as learners because they are expected to become problem solvers. Critical pedagogy is based on using students' present reality as a foundation for their further learning, rather than on doing away with or belittling what they know and who they are. Critical pedagogy acknowledges cultural and linguistic diversity instead of suppressing it.

Shor's (1992) analysis concerning critical pedagogy is instructive. He begins with the assumption that because no curriculum can be truly neutral, it is the responsibility of schools to present students with the broad range of information they will need to learn to read and write *critically* and in the service of social change. But critical pedagogy is not simply the transfer of knowledge from teacher to students, even though it may be knowledge that has heretofore not been made available to them. A critical perspective does not simply operate on the principle of substituting one truth for another; instead, students are encouraged to reflect on multiple and contradictory perspectives in order to understand reality more fully. For instance, learning about the internment of Americans of Japanese descent and Japanese residents in the United States during World War II is not in itself critical pedagogy; it only becomes so when students analyze different viewpoints and use them to understand the inconsistencies they uncover (Daniels, 1971). They can then begin to understand the role played by racist hysteria, economic exploitation, and propaganda as catalysts for the internment, and they can judge this action vis à vis the stated ideals of our nation.

Without a critical perspective, reality is often presented to students as if it were static, finished, and flat; underlying conflicts, problems, and inherent contradictions are omitted. As we have seen, textbooks in all subject areas generally exclude information about unpopular perspectives, or the perspectives of disempowered groups in society. Few of the books to which students have access present the viewpoints of people who have built our country, from enslaved Africans to immigrant labor to other working-class people, even though they have been the backbone of society (Zinn, 1995).

Likewise, the immigrant experience, shared by many groups in the United States, is generally treated, if at all, as a romantic and successful odyssey instead of as a more complicated process that has been also a wrenching experience of loss. Moreover, the European immigrant experience is generally presented in our history books as the sole model for all immigrants, although the historical context, the racial politics and hostility, and the economic structures awaiting more recent immigrants are very different and more complicated than was true for the vast majority of Europeans who arrived during the late nineteenth and early twentieth centuries (Carnoy, 1994).

Using critical pedagogy as a basis for school reform renders very different policies for schools than do traditional models of school reform. Even more important than just increasing curricular options, critical pedagogy helps to expand teachers' and schools' perspectives about students' knowledge and intellectual capabilities. Using a critical perspective, students can learn to become agents of their own learning and use what they learn in productive and critical ways. The knowledge they learn can be used to explore the reasons for certain conditions in their lives and to design strategies for changing them.

A number of eloquent accounts of critical pedagogy in classrooms are compelling examples of the positive and empowering influence that teachers' guidance can have on student learning. For instance, Mercado (1993), working collaboratively with a middle-school teacher and her students, designed a project in which the young people became researchers about conditions in their Bronx neighborhood. Students learned a variety of sophisticated academic skills at the same time that they learned to think more deeply about the reasons for the situations such as drug abuse, homelessness, teenage pregnancy, and intergenerational conflicts. In many cases, students used their research skills in social-action projects to improve their community.

Peterson (1991), for instance, wrote about how he uses critical pedagogy with his elementary school students to teach literacy, debunk myths, and provide a rich environment for learning. He describes how class meetings become "problem-posing" exercises (Freire, 1970) as students list the concerns or problems they want to discuss and then decide which one to tackle on a particular day. He describes the five-step plan they use by listing a series of questions students need to answer:

1. What is the problem?

2. Are you sure about it?

3. What can we do about it?

4. Try it.

5. How did it work? (p. 166)

Peterson (1991) does not propose this process as a panacea. Instead, he states, "While many of the problems poor and minority children and communities face cannot be easily or immediately 'solved,' a 'problem-posing' pedagogy can encourage a questioning of why things are the way they are and the identification of actions, no matter how small, to begin to address them" (p. 166).

More recently, Patty Bode, a gifted art teacher who incorporates a multicultural perspective in her teaching, reflected on her experience with a first-grade child who was concerned about unfair representation in some of the books she was reading. In "A Letter from Kaeli" (Nieto, 1999), Patty discussed how she had received in her mailbox at school the following letter, using inverted spelling, from a first-grade student:

> Dear !!!!!! mis Boudie
> Ples! halp. my moom was spcing to me abut wite piple leving
> bran and blak piple out of books.
> Love Kaeli

> [Dear Ms. Bode,
> Please help! My mom was speaking to me about White people
> leaving Brown and Black people out of books.
> Love, Kaeli] (p. 125)

In the letter she sent to Kaeli as a response, Patty wrote, in part, "I am glad you asked for help. This is a problem that we need to help each other with. We need to ask our friends and teachers and families for help so we can work together. . . . I think we should work on this problem in art class" (p. 126). As a result, when Kaeli's class came to the art room, she read her letter aloud. She also showed her classmates the book that was the basis for her letter to Patty. It was a book about the human body that had been published fairly recently by a prominent publishing house. Out of the many illustrations in the book, Kaeli found only a small number of pictures of Brown and Black people. When the students discussed why this might be a problem, Patty recounted that

> In their first-grade voices and six-year-old vocabulary, they discussed "fair" and "unfair," "discrimination," "stereotypes," and more. Through their dialogue, they decided—without my prompting—that it was OK for some books to exclusively depict Black people or Brown people or White people or others if it was a story about a specific family or event. But books that claimed to be about the "HUMAN BODY" or about "PEOPLE OF THE WORLD" needed to be much more balanced to pass the scrupulous eye of this first grade class. (p. 127)

After engaging in a number of art activities—color theory, self-portraits, face shapes—the students discussed terminology and why some terms for people of different ethnic, racial, and social groups might be more appropriate than others. As a result of this discussion, the students concluded that "using words like *Black* or *African American*, *White* or *European American*, *Latino* or *Hispanic*, and *Asian* or *Chinese-American* were important decisions that required lots of thinking" (p. 127). Patty also gave the students examples of various books for analysis. At this point, the students decided that the publishers should receive some letters of information from them and some of their artwork to display good examples of fair pictures. Erika, one of the first-grade students, wrote the following letter, again in inverted spelling:

> Dear publisher,
>   Make your books faire! And if you don't me and my famyuliy will never by or read your unfaire books. we want fairenes.
> From, Erika
> [Make your books fair! And if you don't, me and my family will never buy or read your unfair books. We want fairness.] (p. 128)

In a powerful description of the impact of this kind of pedagogy and curriculum on students, Patty went on to describe what happened when she prepared a bulletin board around the theme of diversity in textbook representation:

> I filled the walls of the artroom with photographs of children's faces. I spent a great deal of time choosing images of children to reflect the enormous variety of ethnicity and race that our society holds. One European American boy looked at the photo display and said, "Ms. Bode, you left out the White people." (p. 127)

Patty asked him to count the number of people he thought were of different backgrounds (an activity through which he realized that this was not always easy to do), and to his surprise, he discovered that the bulletin board actually included many Whites. When Patty asked him why he had thought that European Americans were missing from the display, he answered "Maybe it's 'cuz I'm used to seeing more of them." (p.128)

Patty's reflection ended with the following words:

> This unit proved to be a good reminder to me that it is the responsibility of the entire community to work for social justice. One individual or one group should not be burdened to fight for their rights in solitude nor exempt from the responsibility of democracy. It requires careful observation, attentive listening, and critical thought to facilitate sociopolitical consciousness effectively within a first grade classroom. (pp. 128–129)

Experiences such as Patty Bode's reinforce the idea that critical multicultural education should not be reserved for the college classroom, or just for classes in history or English. Even an art class for six-year-olds is fertile ground for planting the seeds of critical thinking and social justice. Other accounts of critical pedagogy in action, written mostly by classroom teachers, are contained in recent publications by Rethinking Schools (Bigelow et al., 1994) and the Network of Educators on the Americas (Lee et al., 1998). In these powerful accounts, which discuss specific curricular and pedagogical innovations, critical pedagogy is the force behind student learning.

THE PEOPLE MOST INTIMATELY CONNECTED WITH TEACHING AND LEARNING (TEACHERS, PARENTS, AND STUDENTS) NEED TO BE MEANINGFULLY INVOLVED IN SCHOOL REFORM

Fine (1994), describing the massive school reforms in Philadelphia that began in 1988, wrote "Democratic change is frustrating, loud, but possible" (p.10). In fact, research on involvement by parents, students, and teachers has consistently indicated that democratic participation by people closest to learners can dramatically improve student learning. This is especially true in urban schools and in schools that serve poor, African American, Latino, and immigrant students (Henderson & Berla, 1995; Olsen et al., 1999). Yet these are the people who are most often excluded from discussions and implementation of school reform measures.

Cummins (1996) reviewed programs that included student empowerment as a goal and concluded that students who are encouraged to develop a positive cultural identity through interactions with their teachers experience a sense of control over their own lives and develop the confidence and motivation to succeed academically. In the case of teachers, an extensive review of research (Lee, Bryk, & Smith, 1993) reported that teachers who have more control over classroom conditions consider themselves more efficacious. An analysis of a number of effective parent involvement programs found that all the programs reviewed shared the following components: a commitment to involve low-income parents, family empowerment as a major goal, and a stated desire to reduce the gap between home and school cultures by designing programs that respond to and build on the values, structures, languages, and cultures of students' homes (Fruchter, Galletta, & White, 1993).

School reform measures that stress the meaningful involvement of teachers, parents, and students look quite different from traditional approaches. They begin with the assumption that these groups have substantial and insightful perspectives about student learning. Rather than thinking of ways to bypass their ideas, school reformers actively seek the involvement of students, families, and teachers in developing, for instance, disciplinary policies, curriculum development, and decisions concerning tracking and the use of tests. Similarly, allowing time in the curriculum for students to engage in critical discussions about issues such as whose language is valued in schools can help to affirm the legitimacy of the discourse of all students.

At the same time, these kinds of discussions also acknowledge the need to learn and become comfortable with the discourse of the larger society (Delpit, 1995). In addition, involving parents in curriculum development enriches the curriculum, affirms what families have to offer, and helps students overcome the shame they may feel about their cultures, languages, and values, an all-too-common attitude for students from culturally subordinated groups (Nieto, 2000; Olsen, 1997).

School Reform Needs to Be Based on High Expectations and Rigorous Standards for All Learners

Many students cope on a daily basis with complex and difficult problems, including poverty, violence, racism, abuse, families in distress, and lack of health care and proper housing. In addition to such situations, many students come to school with conditions that some teachers and schools consider as placing them at risk for learning, including speaking a language other than English or simply belonging to a particular racial or ethnic group. These conditions arc sometimes used as a rationalization by teachers and schools for low expectations of what students are capable of learning. Just the opposite should be the case. That is, in our society we have always expected schools to provide an equal and equitable education for all students, not just for those who have no problems in their lives or who fit the image of successful students due to race, class, or language ability. The promise of an equal education for all students of all backgrounds in the United States has yet to be realized, as is evident from a number of critiques of the myth of our schools as "the great equalizer" (Bowles & Gintis, 1976; Katz, 1975; Spring, 1989). Nevertheless, the ideal of equitable educational opportunity is worth defending and vigorously putting into practice.

It is undeniably true that many students come to our schools with unimaginably difficult problems, and the school cannot be expected to solve them all. Neither can we dismiss the heroic efforts of many teachers and schools who, with limited financial and other material resources, teach students who live in dire circumstances under what can best be described as challenging conditions. Nevertheless, the difficult conditions in which some students live need not be viewed as insurmountable barriers to their academic achievement. It is too often the case that society's low expectations of students, based on these situations, pose even greater obstacles to their learning. For example, if students do not speak English, teachers may assume that they cannot learn; or if they do not have consistent experiences with or access to libraries, museums, or other cultural institutions considered essential for preparing students for schools, teachers may assume that these children are not even ready to learn.

If we are serious about giving all students more options in life, particularly students from communities denied the necessary resources with which to access these options, then we need to begin with the assumption that these students are academically capable, both individually and as a group. Too many students have been dismissed as uneducable simply because they were not born with the material resources or family conditions considered essential for learning. The conventional attitude that students who do not arrive at school with such benefits are incapable of learning is further promoted by assertions of race-based genetic inferiority (Herrnstein & Murray, 1994).

Numerous examples of dramatic success in the face of adversity are powerful reminders that great potential exists in all students. Consider, for example, the case of Garfield High School in East Los Angeles, California. Here, the mostly Mexican American students taught by Jaime Escalante, the protagonist of the popular film *Stand and Deliver*, were tremendously successful in learning advanced mathematics. In fact, when they took the Advanced Placement (AP) calculus test, they did so well that the test makers assumed they had cheated. As a result, they had to take it a second time, and this time their performance was even better.

The success of the Algebra Project in Cambridge, Massachusetts (Moses, Kamii, Swap, & Howard, 1989) is another example. In this project, young people who had previously been denied access to algebra because they were thought to be incapable of benefiting from it became high achievers in math. When they went on to high school, 39 percent of the first graduating class of the project were placed in honors geometry or honors algebra classes; incredibly, none of the graduates was placed in a lower-level math course. The success of the project was explained by the authors: "Teachers and parents in the Open Program came to believe that ability grouping in mathematics seriously impaired the capacity of middle school students of color and females to learn as well as they might" (p. 45). The Algebra Project has now spread to other school systems throughout the United States.

Central Park East Elementary School in East Harlem, New York, a school with a student body made up overwhelmingly of Latino and African American students, provides another example of academic success among youngsters who might not have been thought capable of succeeding (Meier, 1995). The school, which accepts students from the neighborhood and not from elite or favored groups, has documented astonishing success: an in-depth study of the first seven graduating classes of the school revealed that 90 percent earned high school diplomas, and two-thirds went on to college, nearly double the rate for the city as a whole.

Conditions in students' lives that might be considered barriers to learning, such as speaking a language other than English or being a member of a specific racial or ethnic group, need not be problems or roadblocks, although they have generally been defined as such by the general population. These conditions may in fact *enrich* the lives of students, giving them a strong identity and cultural resources that can support their learning (Kiang, 1995). Although students' identities are often perceived to be handicaps to learning by an assimilationist society that encourages cultural and linguistic homogeneity, numerous success stories of students who use their cultural values and traditions as strengths have been reported in the educational research literature (Corson, 1995; Deyhle & Swisher, 1997; Igoa, 1995; Nieto, 2000; Soto, 1997; Zentella, 1997). This result leads us to the inevitable conclusion that before fixing what they may consider to be problems in students, schools and society need to change their own perceptions of students and view them as capable learners.

CONCLUSION

There is no simple formula for increasing student learning. A step-by-step blueprint for school reform is both unrealistic and inappropriate because each school differs from all others in its basic structure, goals, and human dimensions. Moreover, inequitable conditions such as school funding and the distribution of resources for learning also help explain why some students are successful and others are not. However, certain conditions can dramatically improve the learning of many students who are currently marginalized from the center of learning because of school policies and practices based on deficit models. If we begin with the assumptions that students cannot achieve at high levels, that their backgrounds are riddled with deficiencies, and that multicultural education is a frill that cannot help them to learn, we will end up with school reform strategies that have little hope for success.

This chapter presented and analyzed five conditions to promote student achievement within a multicultural perspective:

1. School reform should be antiracist and antibiased.
2. School reform should reflect an understanding and acceptance of all students as having talents and strengths that can enhance their education.
3. School reform should be considered within the parameters of critical pedagogy.
4. The people most intimately connected with teaching and learning (teachers, parents, and students themselves) need to be meaningfully involved in school reform.
5. School reform needs to be based on high expectations and rigorous standards for all learners.

This chapter began with assumptions based on student, family, and teacher strengths, and on the possibility that a comprehensive and critical approach to multicultural education can provide a critical framework for rethinking school reform. Given these assumptions, we have a much more promising scenario for effective learning and for the possibility that schools can become places of hope and affirmation for students of all backgrounds and situations.

Questions and Activities

1. What does the author mean by "culturally responsive education"? Why does she think it is important? According to the author, is culturally responsive education sufficient to guarantee academic success for students of color and low-income students? Why or why not?

2. What does it mean to say that multicultural education takes place within a sociopolitical context? What social, political, and economic factors must be considered when multicultural education is being implemented? How can a consideration of sociopolitical factors help multicultural school reform to be more effective?

3. What five conditions does the author believe are needed to improve students' academic achievement? How are these factors interrelated?

4. How does the author distinguish *individual* and *institutional racism*? Why does she think this distinction is important? Give examples of each type of racism from your personal experiences and observations.

5. What is an antiracist perspective? Why does the author believe that an antiracist perspective is essential for the implementation of multicultural education? Give specific examples of antiracist teaching and educational practices with which you are familiar.

6. The author briefly describes Moll's concept of incorporating community knowledge into the curriculum. How does this concept help teachers to implement "culturally sensitive" teaching?

7. What is critical pedagogy? How, according to the author, can it be used to enrich and strengthen multicultural education?

8. What positive contributions can parents and students make to creating an effective multicultural school? Give specific examples.

References

Aptheker, H. (1943/1987). *American Negro Slave Revolts*. New York: International Publishers.

Ascher, C. and Burnett, G. (1993). *Current Trends and Issues in Urban Education*. New York: ERIC Clearinghouse on Urban Education, Teachers College, Columbia University.

Au, K. A. and Kawakami, A. J. (1994). Cultural Congruence in Instruction. In E. R. Hollins, J. E. King, and W. C. Hayman (Eds.), *Teaching Diverse Populations: Formulating a Knowledge Base* (pp. 5–24). New York: State University of New York Press.

Banks, J. A. (1997). *Teaching Strategies for Ethnic Studies* (6th ed.). Boston: Allyn and Bacon.

Bigelow, B., Christensen, L., Karp, S., Miner, B., and Peterson, B. (Eds.). (1994). *Rethinking Our Classrooms: Teaching for Equity and Justice*. Milwaukee: Rethinking Schools.

Bowles, S. and Gintis, H. (1976). *Schooling in Capitalist America: Educational Reform and the Contradictions of Economic Life*. New York: Basic Books.

Bryk, A. S., Lee, V. E., and Holland, P. B. (1993). *Catholic Schools and the Common Good*. Cambridge, MA: Harvard Educational Review.

Carnoy, M. (1994). *Faded Dreams: The Politics and Economics of Race in America*. New York: Cambridge University Press.

Corson, D. (1995). Realities of Teaching in a Multiethnic School. In O. García and C. Baker (Eds.), *Policy and Practice in Bilingual Education: Extending the Foundations* (pp. 70–84). Clevedon, England: Multilingual Matters.

Cummins, J. (1996). *Negotiating Identities: Education for Empowerment in a Diverse Society*. Ontario: California Association for Bilingual Education.

Daniels, R. (1971). *Concentration Camps, U.S.A.: Japanese Americans and World War II*. New York: Holt.

Darling-Hammond, L. (1995). Inequality and Access to Knowledge. In J. A. Banks and C. A. M. Banks (Eds.), *Handbook of Research on Multicultural Education* (pp. 465–483). New York: Macmillan.

Darling-Hammond, L. (1996). The Right to Learn and the Advancement of Teaching: Research, Policy, and Practice for Democratic Education. *Educational Researcher, 25*(6), 5–17.

Delpit, L. (1995). *Other People's Children: Cultural Conflict in the Classroom.* New York: The New Press.

Deyhle, D. and Swisher, K. (1997). Research in American Indian and Alaska Native Education: From Assimilation to Self-Determination. In M. W. Apple (Ed.), *Review of Research in Education*, Vol. 22 (pp. 113–194). Washington, DC: American Educational Research Association.

Donaldson, K. (1996). *Through Students' Eyes.* New York: Bergin & Garvey.

Erickson, F. (1993). Transformation and School Success: The Politics and Culture of Educational Achievement: In E. Jacob and C. Jordan (Eds.), *Minority Education: Anthropological Perspectives* (pp. 27–51). Norwood, NJ: Ablex Publishing Corporation.

Figueroa, R. A. and E. García. (1994). Issues in Testing Students from Culturally and Linguistically Diverse Backgrounds. *Multicultural Education, 2*(1), 10–19.

Fine, M. (1991). *Framing Dropouts: Notes on the Politics of an Urban Public High School.* Albany: State University of New York Press.

Fine, M. (Ed.) (1994). *Chartering Urban School Reform: Reflections on Public High Schools in the Midst of Change.* New York: Teachers College Press.

Frau-Ramos, M. and Nieto, S. (1993). "I Was an Outsider": An Exploratory Study of Dropping Out among Puerto Rican Youths in Holyoke, Massachusetts. In R. Rivera and S. Nieto (Eds.), *The Education of Latino Students in Massachusetts: Issues, Research, and Policy Implications* (pp. 147–169). Boston: Gastón Institute.

Freire, P. (1970). *Pedagogy of the Oppressed.* New York: Seabury Press.

Freire, P. (1985). *The Politics of Education: Culture, Power, and Liberation.* South Hadley, MA: Bergin & Garvey.

Fruchter, N., Galletta, A., and White, J. L. (1993). New Directions in Parent Involvement. *Equity and Choice, 9*(3), 33–43.

Gay, G. (2000). *Culturally Responsive Teaching: Theory, Research, and Practice.* New York: Teachers College Press.

Haberman, M. (1991). The Pedagogy of Poverty versus Good Teaching. *Phi Delta Kappan, 73*, 290–294.

Harris, V. J. (Ed.). (1997). *Using Multiethnic Literature in the K–8 Classroom.* Norwood, MA: Christopher-Gordon.

Henderson, A. T. and Berla, N. (1995). *A New Generation of Evidence: The Family Is Crucial to Student Achievement.* Washington, DC: Center for Law and Education.

Herrnstein, R. J. and Murray, C. (1994). *The Bell Curve: Intelligence and Class Structure in American Life.* New York: The Free Press.

Igoa, C. (1995). *The Inner World of the Immigrant Child.* New York: Lawrence Erlbaum Associates, Publishers.

Irvine, J. J. (Ed.). (1997). *Critical Knowledge for Diverse Teachers and Learners.* Washington, DC: American Association of Colleges for Teacher Education.

Irvine, J. J. and Foster, M. (Eds.). (1996). *Growing up African American in Catholic Schools.* New York: Teachers College Press.

Jervis, K. (1996). "How Come There Are No Brothers on That List?": Hearing the Hard Questions All Children Ask. *Harvard Educational Review, 66*(3), 546–576.

Kailin, J. (1999). How White Teachers Perceive the Problem of Racism in Their Schools: A Case Study of "Liberal" Lakeview. *Teachers College Record, 100*(4), 724–750.

Katz, M. B. (1975). *Class, Bureaucracy, and the Schools: The Illusion of Educational Change in America*. New York: Praeger.

Kiang, P. N. (1995). Bicultural Strengths and Struggles of Southeast Asian Americans in School. In A. Darder (Ed.), *Culture and Difference: Critical Perspectives on the Bicultural Experience in the United States* (pp. 201–225). Westport. CT: Bergin & Garvey.

Kiang, P. N. and Kaplan, J. (1994). Where Do We Stand? Views of Racial Conflict by Vietnamese American High-School Students in a Black-and-White Context. *The Urban Review, 26*(2), 95–119.

Kohl, H. (1993). The Myth of "Rosa Parks the Tired." *Multicultural Education, 1*(2), 6–10.

Kozol, J. (1975). Great Men and Women (Tailored for School Use). *Learning Magazine* (Dec.), 16–20.

Kozol, J. (1991). *Savage Inequalities: Children in America's Schools*. New York: Crown.

Ladson-Billings, G. (1994). *The Dreamkeepers: Successful Teachers of African American Children*. San Francisco: Jossey-Bass Publishers.

Lee, E., Menkart, D., and Okazawa-Rey, M. (1998). *Beyond Heroes and Holidays: A Practical Guide to K–12 Anti-Racist, Multicultural Education and Staff Development*. Washington, DC: Network of Educators on the Americas [NECA].

Lee, V. E., Bryk, A. A., and Smith, J. B. (1993). The Organization of Effective Secondary Schools. In L. Darling-Hammond (Ed.), *Review of Research in Education*, Vol. 19 (pp. 171–267). Washington, DC: American Educational Research Association.

Loewen, J. W. (1995). *Lies My Teacher Taught Me: Everything Your American History Textbook Got Wrong*. New York: The Free Press.

May, S. (Ed.). (1999). *Rethinking Multicultural and Antiracist Education: Towards Critical Multiculturalism*. London: Falmer Press.

McLaughlin, B. (1992). *Myths and Misconceptions about Second Language Learning: What Every Teacher Needs to Unlearn*. Santa Cruz, CA: National Center for Research on Cultural Diversity and Second Language Learning.

Meier, D. (1995). *The Power of Their Ideas: Lessons for America from a Small School in Harlem*. Boston: Beacon Press.

Meier, K. J. and Stewart, J., Jr. (1991). *The Politics of Hispanic Education: Un Paso Pa'lante y Dos Pa'tras*. New York: State University of New York Press.

Mercado, C. I. (1993). Caring as Empowerment: School Collaboration and Community Agency. *Urban Review, 25*(1), 79–104.

Moll, L. and Gonzalez, N. (1997). Teachers as Social Scientists: Learning about Culture from Household Research. In P. M. Hall (Ed.), *Race, Ethnicity, and Multiculturalism*, Vol. 1 (pp. 89–114). New York: Garland.

Moses, R. P., Kamii, M., Swap, S. M., and Howard, J. (1989). The Algebra Project: Organizing in the Spirit of Ella. *Harvard Educational Review, 59*(4), 24–47.

Mosteller, F. (1995). The Tennessee Study of Class Size in the Early School Grades. *The Future of Children, 5*(2), 113–127.

NABE No-Cost Study on Families. (1991). *NABE News, 14*(4), 7, 23.

National Commission on Excellence in Education. (1983). *A Nation at Risk: The Imperative for Educational Reform*. Washington, DC: Author.

Neill, M. (1997). Transforming Student Assessment. *Phi Delta Kappan, 79*(1), 34–40, 58.

Nieto, S. (1994a). Lessons from Students on Creating a Chance to Dream. *Harvard Educational Review, 64*(4), 392–426.

Nieto, S. (1994b). What Are Our Children Capable of Knowing? *The Educational Forum, 58*(4), 434–440.

Nieto, S. (1999). *The Light in Their Eyes: Creating Multicultural Learning Communities*. New York: Teachers College Press.

Nieto, S. (2000). *Affirming Diversity: The Sociopolitical Context of Multicultural Education* (3rd ed.). New York: Longman.

Oakes, J., Wells, A. S., Jones, M., and Datnow, A. (1997). Detracking: The Social Construction of Ability, Cultural Politics, and Resistance to Reform. *Teachers College Record, 98*(3), 482–510.

Ogbu, J. U. (1994). Racial Stratification and Education in the United States: Why Inequality Persists. *Teachers College Record, 96*(2), 264–298.

Olsen, L. (1997). *Made in America: Immigrant Students in Our Public Schools*. New York: The New Press.

Olsen, L., Jaramillo, A., McCall-Perez, Z., White, J., and Minicucci, C. (1999). *Igniting Change for Immigrant Students: Portraits of Three High Schools*. Oakland, CA: California Tomorrow.

Peterson, R. E. (1991). Teaching How to Read the World and Change It: Critical Pedagogy in the Intermediate Grades. In C. E. Walsh (Ed.), *Literacy as Praxis: Culture, Language, and Pedagogy* (pp. 156–182). Norwood, NJ: Ablex.

Poplin, M. and Weeres, J. (1992). *Voices from the Inside: A Report on Schooling from Inside the Classroom*. Claremont, CA: Claremont Graduate School, Institute for Education in Transformation.

Reissman, F. (1962). *The Culturally Deprived Child*. New York: Harper & Row.

Ryan, W. (1972). *Blaming the Victim*. New York: Vintage Books.

Schofield, J. W. (1986). Causes and Consequences of the Colorblind Perspective. In J. F. Dovidio and S. L. Gaertner (Eds.), *Prejudice, Discrimination and Racism* (pp. 231–253). New York: Academic Press.

Shor, I. (1992). *Empowering Education: Critical Teaching for Social Change*. Chicago: University of Chicago Press.

Sleeter, C. E. (1994). White Racism. *Multicultural Education, 1*(4), 5–8, 39.

Sleeter, C. E. and McLaren, P. L. (1995). *Multicultural Education, Critical Pedagogy, and the Politics of Difference*. New York: State University of New York Press.

Soto, L. D. (1997). *Language, Culture, and Power: Bilingual Families and the Struggle for Quality Education*. Albany: State University of New York Press.

Spring, J. (1989). *The Sorting Machine Revisited: National Educational Policy since 1945*. White Plains, NY: Longman.

Steele, C. M. (1999). Thin Ice: "Stereotype Threat" and Black College Students. *The Atlantic Monthly* (Aug.), 44–54.

Tatum, B. D. (1997). *"Why Are All The Black Kids Sitting Together in the Cafeteria?" and Other Conversations About Race*. New York: HarperCollins.

Walsh, C. E. (Ed) (1996). *Education Reform and Social Change: Multicultural Voices, Struggles, and Visions*. Mahwah, NJ: Erlbaum Associates, 1996.

Weinberg, M. (1990). *Racism in the United States: A Comprehensive Classified Bibliography*. Westport, CT: Greenwood Press.

Willis, A. (Ed.) (1998). *Teaching and Using Multicultural Literature in Grades 9–12: Moving Beyond the Canon*. Norwood, MA: Christopher-Gordon.

Winant, H. (1994). *Racial Conditions: Politics, Theory, Comparisons*. Minneapolis: University of Minnesota Press.

Wong Fillmore, L. (1991). When Learning a Second Language Means Losing the First. *Early Childhood Research Quarterly, 6*, 323–346.

Zanger, V. V. (1993). Academic Costs of Social Marginalization: An Analysis of Latino Students' Perceptions at a Boston High School. In R. Rivera and S. Nieto (Eds.), *The Education of Latino Students in Massachusetts: Issues, Research and Policy Implications* (pp. 167–187). Boston: Gastón Institute.

Zentella, A. C. (1997). *Growing up Bilingual: Puerto Rican Children in New York*. Malden, MA: Blackwell.

Zinn, H. (1995). *A People's History of the United States*. (rev. ed.). New York: Harper & Row.

CHAPTER 17

Families and Teachers Working Together for School Improvement

Cherry A. McGee Banks

Barbara and Andy Parkwood sat silently as they drove home from their parent conference with Ms. Stevens, their son's fifth-grade teacher. East Lake Elementary School, where their son attends school, has a good reputation. Many of its students test into the accelerated program when they enter middle school. The Parkwoods were very pleased when their son was placed in Ms. Steven's room because she was a veteran teacher and considered one of the best teachers at East Lake.

Barbara finally broke the silence and said, "I don't think the kids in Ms. Steven's room will be ready for middle school next year. She's spending too much time on topics that aren't really important." "Yea," said Andy, "there was an article in last night's newspaper about how some schools are pushing multicultural education. I don't know why she thinks it is important to teach the kids about our differences. When it comes down to it, we're really all the same." "That's what I was trying to tell her," said Barbara. "All she's doing is making people like us feel guilty about things that happened long before we were born." "I don't think she heard a word you said," said Andy. "Her mind's made up and she doesn't care what we think." "Well," said Barbara, "she hasn't heard the last of me. I don't know what I can do, but I'm not going to let this drop. Ms. Stevens should be teaching the basics, not about diversity."

This hypothetical incident raises questions about how and when parents should be involved in schools. For example: How involved should parents be in determining curriculum, instruction, and staffing? What does it mean for parents to be partners with teachers and administrators? What roles should parents and teachers play in that partnership? How important is it for parents and teachers with different points of view and from different backgrounds to work together?

These are the kinds of questions Ms. Stevens will need to answer to reach out effectively to parents and family members. She will also need people skills, confidence in her ability to work with parents, and a clear understanding of how and why students benefit when parents and teachers are partners. Teachers who are unsure of the importance of parents and teachers working together and are uncomfortable reaching out to critical parents have difficulty collaborating with parents and may get a skewed view of parents' opinions, concerns, and interests.

When confronted with concerns like those raised by Barbara and Andy Parkwood, Ms. Stevens and other teachers may conclude that most parents do not support multicultural education. As a result, they may censor themselves. This would be unfortunate because there is wide public support for multicultural education. In 1994, Louis Harris conducted a national survey on cultural diversity in the school curriculum. Approximately nine out of ten people, including 91 percent of the Whites surveyed, indicated support for key aspects of multicultural school curriculum (National Conference, 1994).

While many people in the United States recognize the importance of multicultural education, few have a realistic understanding of the size of the different minority groups. For example, a 1997 survey conducted by the Gallup organization found that more than half of the people surveyed thought that Blacks made up at least 30 percent of the population and Hispanics made up about 20 percent of the population. In 2000, Blacks and Hispanics made up 12 and 11 percent of the nation's population respectively (Martin & Midgley, 1999; Pollard & O'Hare, 1999). Even though the demographic profile of our nation is shifting, Whites are and will continue into the foreseeable future to make up the largest percentage of the population. It is important for teachers to be able to communicate these and other facts about diversity to parents.

To be an effective communicator, teachers have to be good listeners. Ms. Stevens needs to be able to hear and respectfully respond to Barbara and Andy Parkwood's concerns about multicultural education. The Parkwoods may not have an accurate understanding of multicultural education or how their son and the community benefit when diversity is addressed in the classroom. Ms. Stevens can be a resource for them. She can share information with them, invite them to read the texts and materials used in her class, arrange for them to talk with parents who understand her goals, and invite them to take an active role in improving East Lake Elementary School. Barbara and Andy Parkwood, like most parents, want teachers to respect and work with them. Difficulties frequently arise when communication breaks down and when there is a lack of trust and respect.

In addition to differences of opinion, teachers must be aware of possible cultural boundaries that could limit their communication with parents. Cultural boundaries that result from differences in religion, language, and ethnic characteristics can make communication between parents and teachers difficult and strained. When you consider that some parents have to cross multiple cultural boundaries to work with teachers, it is not surprising that they are not actively involved in schools. However, the school loses an important voice for school improvement when culturally different parents are not involved. They can give teachers a unique and important view of their children as well as help their children use the resources and opportunities that are available from the school.

In a comprehensive review of research on parent involvement, Henderson & Berla (1994) found compelling evidence that parent involvement improves student achievement. Parent involvement is also associated with improvements in attendance and social behavior. However, to capitalize on the diverse strengths of parents, parent involvement strategies should be broadly conceptualized. Parents should be given an opportunity to contribute to school improvement by working in different settings and at different levels of the educational process (Mannan & Blackwell, 1992). For example, some parents may want to focus their energies on working with their own children at home. Other parents may want to work on decision-making committees. Still others may be able to provide in-class assistance to teachers.

Parents and other family members can also work with teachers to reform schools. Many tasks involved in restructuring schools, such as setting goals and allocating resources, are best achieved through a collaborative problem-solving structure that includes parents, educators, and family and community members (Mannan & Blackwell, 1992).

Family and community members can form what Goodlad (1984) calls "the necessary coalition of contributing groups" (p. 293). Educational reform needs their support, influence, and activism. Schools are highly dependent on and vulnerable to citizens who can support or impede change. Family members and community leaders can validate the need for educational reform and can provide an appropriate forum for exploring the importance of education. They can also extend the discussion of school improvement issues beyond formal educational networks and can help generate interest in educational reform in the community at large. Family members and community leaders can help provide the rationale, motivation, and social action necessary for educational reform.

WHY IS PARENT AND FAMILY INVOLVEMENT IMPORTANT?

Parent involvement is important because it acknowledges the importance of parents in the lives of their children, recognizes the diversity of values and perspectives within the community, provides a vehicle for building a collaborative problem-solving structure, and increases the opportunity for all students to learn in schools.

Parents, however, are not the only adults who support and contribute to the care of children. The role of grandparents and other family members as primary care givers is becoming more significant. In 1997, 1.3 million children lived with their grandparents, who were their primary caregivers. This was a decrease from 1995, when 1.4 million children lived with grandparents (U.S. Bureau of the Census, 1998).

Students, parents, and teachers all benefit when parents and family members are involved in schools (Comer, Ben-Avie, Haynes, & Joyner, 1999). When parents help their students at home, students perform better in school (Booth & Dunn, 1996). Although we do not know exactly why students show improvements when their parents are involved in their education, we know that parental involvement increases the number of people who are supporting the child's learning. Such involvement also increases the amount of time the child is involved in learning activities.

Parent involvement allows parents and teachers to reinforce skills and provides an environment that has consistent learning expectations and standards. Parents also become more knowledgeable about their child's school, its policies, and the school staff when they are involved in schools. Perhaps most important, parent involvement provides an opportunity for parents and children to spend time together. During that time, parents can communicate a high value for education, the importance of effort in achievement, and high positive regard for their children.

Parents and family members are often children's first and most important teachers. Students come to school with knowledge, values, and beliefs they have learned from their parents and in their communities. Parents directly or indirectly help shape their children's value system, orientation toward learning, and view of the world (Stratton, 1995). Most parents want their children to succeed in school. Schools can capitalize on the high value most parents put on education by working to create a school environment that respects the students' home and community (Hidalgo, Bright, Sau-Fong, Swap, & Epstein, 1995). When schools conflict with their students' home and community, they can alienate students from their families and communities.

To create a harmonious environment between the school, home and community, teachers need to understand their students' community and home life. Teachers need to know the educational expectations parents have for their children, the languages spoken at home, the family's values and norms, as well as how children are taught in their homes and communities. Parents also need information about the school. They need to know what the school expects their children to learn, how they will be taught, and the required books and materials their children will use in school. Most important, parents need to know how teachers assess students and how they can support their children's achievement.

Teachers and principals who know parents treat them with greater respect and show more positive attitudes toward their children (Berger, 1995). Teachers generally see involved parents as concerned individuals who support the school. Parents who are not involved in schools are frequently seen as parents who do not value education.

Historical Overview

While parent involvement in education is not new, its importance and purpose have varied over time. In the early part of the nation's history, families were often solely responsible for educating children. Children learned values and skills by working with their families in their communities.

When formal systems of education were established, parents continued to influence their children's education. During the colonial period, schools were viewed as an extension of the home. Parental and community values and expectations were reinforced in the school. Teachers generally came from the community and often personally knew their students' parents and shared their values.

At the beginning of the twentieth century, when large numbers of immigrants came to the United States, schools were used to compensate for the perceived failures of parents and communities. Schools became a major vehicle to assimilate immigrant children into U.S. society (Banks, 1997). In general, parents were not welcomed in schools. Students were taught that their parents' way of speaking, behaving, and thinking were inferior. In his 1932 study of the sociology of teaching, Waller (1965) concluded that parents and teachers lived in a state of mutual distrust and even hostility. There were, however, some notable exceptions.

One such exception was Benjamin Franklin High School in East Harlem, New York. Principal Leonard Covello instituted a program of intergroup education at Franklin in the

1930s. Parents were welcome at Franklin, and teachers encouraged students to appreciate their parents' language, values, and customs. These and other aspects of intergroup education were designed to reduce prejudice and increase cross-cultural understanding and appreciation.

Over time society changed and education became more removed from the direct influence of parents. Responsibility for transmitting knowledge from generation to generation was transferred from the home and community to the school. Education was seen as a job for trained professionals. Schools were autonomous institutions staffed by people who were often strangers in their students' home communities. Teachers did not necessarily live in their students' neighborhoods, know the students' parents, or share their values. Schools were given more and more duties that traditionally had been the responsibility of the home and community. Schools operated under the assumption of *in loco parentis*, and educators were asked to assume the role of both teacher and substitute parent.

In a pluralist society, what the school teaches as well as who and how the school teaches can create tensions between parents and schools. Issues ranging from what the school teaches about the role of women in our society to mainstreaming students with disabilities point to the need for teachers, parents, and community leaders to work together (Schneider & Coleman, 1993). However, parents and teachers do not always agree on meaningful ways to involve parents in the educational process (Cibulka & Kritek, 1996).

The Changing Face of the Family

Parent and family diversity mirrors student diversity. Involving parents in schools means that teachers have to be prepared to work with a range of parents, including single parents, parents with special needs, low-income parents, parents with disabilities, and parents who do not speak English. Working with parents from diverse backgrounds requires a sensitivity to and an understanding of their world (Chavkin & Gonzalez,1995; Kagan, 1995; Schneider & Coleman, 1993).

It is especially important that teachers are sensitive to and understand the changing nature of the ethnic and racial make-up of their students and their students' parents. In addition to the five major ethnic groups, the ethnic landscape of U.S. schools includes an increasing number of Arab, Jewish, Eastern European, and African students (Pollard & O'Hare, 1999). In 1998, 5 percent of Black Americans were foreign-born. Most came from the Caribbean (Pollard & O'Hare, 1999). For many of these individuals their ethnic identity has primacy over their racial identity. Such individuals, for example, would identify themselves as Cuban Americans or Puerto Ricans, not as Blacks or Whites. If they stated their racial identity, it might conflict with physical characteristics that traditionally are used to identify race in the United States. For example, a Cuban American with brown skin may consider himself White.

The lines between racial groups are becoming blurred. Some students and parents are members of more than one racial group. Even though marriage between people from different races is still an exception, more and more people are marrying interracially. As a result, the number of students with parents or grandparents of different races is increasing. In 1997, there were 1.26 million interracial couples, compared to 651, 000 in 1980 (U.S. Bureau of the Census, 1998). By 1998, approximately 5 percent of U.S. married couples were interracial. Among all the racial groups, American Indians were the most likely to marry someone outside their racial group (Pollard & O'Hare, 1999). Asians also tend to marry at a high rate outside their racial group. In 1990, 40 percent of Asians were married to non-Asians. Interracial marriage for African Americans increased from 6 percent in 1980 to about 9 percent in 1998 (Pollard & O'Hare, 1999).

The increase in interracial marriage has resulted in an increase of interracial children. Between 1977 and 1997, the number of babies born to interracial couples increased from less than 2 percent of the total births to about 5 percent. In 1997, interracial births were the third largest racial or ethnic category of U.S. births. In California, the number of interracial births surpassed Asian, Black, and American Indian births. Of all the ethnic and racial groups, interracial births were highest for American Indians. Approximately 50 percent of American Indians born in 1997 were biracial. About 20 percent of births to Asian women and 5 percent of births to African American women were biracial (Pollard & O'Hare, 1999).

Diversity in parent and community groups can be a tremendous asset to the school. However, it can also be a source of potential conflicts and tensions. Some parents are particularly difficult to involve in their children's education. They resist becoming involved for several reasons (Harry, 1992; Walker, 1996). In a national survey, parents indicated that a lack of time was the primary reason they were not involved in their children's schools (Clark, 1995). The pressures to earn a living and take care of a home and children can result in a great deal of stress. At the end of the day, some parents just want to rest. Other parents do not believe they have the necessary educational background to be involved in their children's school. They feel intimidated by educators and believe that education should be left to teachers. Still others feel alienated from their children's schools because of negative experiences they had in school or because they believe the school does not support their values (Berger, 1995; Clark, 1995; Rasinski, 1990).

Three groups of parents are frequently underrepresented in school involvement activities. They include parents with special needs, single-parent families, and low-income families. These three groups are not the only groups that are underrepresented in parent involvement activities. However, their experiences and needs illustrate particular problem areas. The specific groups of parents discussed should not be viewed as an indication that only parents from these groups are difficult to involve in schools or that all parents from these groups infrequently participate in schools. Parents from all groups share many of the concerns discussed below. There are examples of parents from each of the groups discussed who are actively involved in schools.

Parents with Special Needs

Families with special needs include a wide range of parents. They are found in all ethnic, racial, and income groups. Chronically unemployed parents, parents with long-term illnesses, abusive parents, and parents with substance-abuse problems are examples of parents with special needs. Although parents with special needs have serious problems that the school cannot address, teachers should not ignore the importance of establishing a relationship with them. Knowing the difficulties students are coping with at home can help teachers create environments that are supportive during the time students are in school (Swadener & Niles, 1991). Schools can help compensate for the difficult circumstances students experience at home. The school, for some students, is the only place during the day where they are nurtured.

Abusive parents require special attention from the school. Most schools have policies on how to treat suspected cases of child neglect and abuse. The policies should be written and available to all school personnel. All states require schools to report suspected cases of child abuse.

Working with special-needs families requires district or building support. Although some special-needs parents may resist the school's help, they need to know that their problems can negatively affect their children's success in school. Working with these parents can show students who are in difficult home environments that they are not alone. Most parents want to feel that they are valued and adequate human beings and that they can help their children succeed. They are willing to be involved in school, but they do not want to be humiliated (Berger, 1995). Some parents with special needs will be able to be actively involved in schools, but many will be unable to sustain on-going involvement. An important goal for working with parents with special needs is to keep lines of communication open. Try to get to know the parents. Do not accept a stereotypical view of them without ever talking to them. Encourage parents to be involved whenever and however they feel they are able to participate. Be prepared to recommend appropriate community agencies to the family. Try to develop a clear understanding of your student's home environment so that you can provide appropriate intervention at school.

Members of the community who are involved in school may be willing to serve as intermediaries between the school and uninvolved parents. In an ethnography of an inner-city neighborhood, Shariff (1988) found that adults shared goods and services and helped each other. Educators can build on the sense of extended family that may exist in some neighborhoods to form or connect with community support groups for students whose parents cannot be involved in school. However, regardless of the circumstances students confront at home, teachers have a responsibility to help them perform at their highest level at school.

Single-Parent Families

One of the most significant social changes in the United States in the last thirty years is the increase in the percentage of children living with one parent. In 1997, 32 percent of U.S. households with children under eighteen were headed by a single parent. The number of single-parent families is particularly significant in the African American community. In 1997, 64 percent of African American families with children under eighteen were headed by one parent (U.S. Bureau of the Census, 1998). Twenty-six percent of White and 36 percent of Hispanic families with children under eighteen were headed by one parent (U.S. Bureau of the Census, 1998).

Most children who live with one parent are from divorced homes or are the children of unwed mothers. In 1997, approximately 50 percent of all marriages in the United States ended in divorce (U.S. Bureau of the Census, 1998). The number of years from the dissolution of the first marriage until remarriage for women varies tremendously by race. Within one year after a divorce 21.9 percent of White women are remarried, compared to 10.9 percent for Black women. Five years after divorcing 53 percent of White women are remarried, compared to 25 percent for Black women (U.S. Bureau of the Census, 1998).

Single-parent families share many of the same hopes, joys, and concerns about their children's education as two-parent families. However, because these parents have a lower rate of attendance at school functions, single parents are frequently viewed as not supporting their children's education. When teachers respond sensitively to their needs and limitations, they can be enthusiastic partners with teachers. Four suggestions for working with single parents are listed below. Many of these suggestions apply to other groups of parents as well.

1. Provide flexible times for conferences, such as early mornings, evenings, and weekends.

2. Provide baby-sitting service when activities are held at the school.

3. Work out procedures for acknowledging and communicating with noncustodial parents. For instance, under what circumstances are noncustodial parents informed about their children's grades, school behavior, or attendance? Problems can occur when information is inappropriately given to or withheld from a noncustodial parent.

4. Use the parent's correct surname. Students will sometimes have different names from their parents.

Low-Income Families

In 1995, 21 percent of the children in the United States lived in poverty (Population Reference Bureau, 1998). A family of four in 1996 with a total income less than $16,036.00 was considered living below the poverty level (U.S. Bureau of the Census, 1998). The poverty level is an official governmental estimate of the income necessary to purchase a minimally acceptable standard of living. Poverty in the United States increased from 12.8 percent in 1989 to 15.1 percent in 1993. In 1996, the percentage of people living in poverty decreased to 13.7 percent (U.S. Bureau of the Census, 1998).

Even though the number of individuals of color in the highest income brackets has more than doubled since 1980, race continues to be a salient factor in poverty (Pollard & O'Hare, 1999). In 1996, 11.2 percent of Whites were below the poverty level, compared to 28.4 percent of Blacks and 29.4 percent of Hispanics. Most minorities earn less than Whites do. However, Asians earn more than all ethnic groups. In 1996, their median income in current dollars was $43,276.00 per year, compared to $37,161.00 per year for Whites, $23,482.00 for Blacks, and $24,906.00 for Hispanics (U.S. Bureau of the Census, 1998).

The poverty rate for children is also rising. In 1996, the poverty rate for children dropped to 19.8 percent from a high of 22 percent in 1993. However, the current percentage of children living in poverty is still higher than it was in the 1970s and 1980s. In 1970, 14.9 percent of children lived below the poverty level; in 1980, the percentage was 17.9 (U.S. Bureau of the Census, 1998). The number of children living in poverty is related to the number of female-headed households. The median family income in 1996 was $49,707.00 for married couples, compared to $19,911.00 for female-headed households (U.S. Bureau of the Census, 1998).

Low-income parents are often among the strongest supporters of education. They see education as a means to a better life for their children. However, they are often limited in their ability to buy materials and to make financial commitments that can enable their children to participate in activities such as field trips or extracurricular programs. Many of the suggestions listed for single-parent families also apply to low-income families. Schools can provide workbooks and other study materials for use at home as well as transportation for school activities and conferences. The school can also support low-income families by establishing community service programs. For example, students can help clean up neighborhoods and distribute information on available social services. The schools can provide desk space for voter registration and other services.

Perhaps the most important way for schools to work with low-income parents is to recognize that low-income parents can contribute a great deal to their children's education. Even though their contributions may not be in the form of traditional parent involvement, they can be very beneficial to teachers and students. The values and attitudes parents communicate to their children and their strong desire for their children to have a better chance in life than they had are important forms of support for the school.

TEACHER CONCERNS WITH PARENT AND FAMILY INVOLVEMENT

Even though teachers often say they want to involve parents, many are suspicious of parents and are not sure what parents expect from them. Some teachers think parents may disrupt their routine, may not have the necessary skills to work with students, may be inconvenient to have in the classroom, and may be interested only in helping their own child, not the total class. Even teachers who would like to involve parents are not sure they have the time or the skill and knowledge to involve parents. Many teachers believe that they already have too much to do and that working with parents would make their overburdened jobs impossible.

Many of these concerns result from a limited view of the possibilities for parent involvement. Frequently, when parents and teachers think of parent involvement, they think it means doing something for the school generally at the school or having the school teach parents how to become better parents. In today's society, a traditional view of parent involvement inhibits rather than encourages parents and teachers to work together. Traditional ideas about parent involvement have a built-in gender- and social-class bias and are a barrier to many males and low-income parents.

When parent involvement is viewed as a means of getting support for the school, parents are encouraged to bake cookies, raise money, or work at the school as unpaid classroom, playground, library, or office helpers. This form of parent involvement is generally directed to mothers who do not work outside the home. However, the number of mothers available for this form of involvement is decreasing. In 1997, 71.1 percent of married women with children under six-years-old worked full-time outside the home (U.S. Bureau of the Census, 1998).

The parent-as-helper idea is geared toward parents who have the skills, time, and resources to become school helpers. Not all parents want to or feel they can or should do things for the school. Whether parents are willing to come to school is largely dependent on the parent's attitude toward school. This attitude results in part from their own school experiences.

Cultural perspectives play an important role in the traditional approach to parent involvement. Bullivant (1993) points out the importance of understanding a social group's cultural program. To be effective, parent and community involvement strategies should reflect what Bullivant calls the core of the social group's cultural program, which consists of the knowledge and conceptions embodied in the group's behaviors and artifacts and the values subscribed to by the group.

When teachers do not understand a group's cultural program, they may conceptualize parent involvement as a means to help deficient parents become better parents (Linn, 1990). This view of parent involvement is often directed toward culturally different and low-income parents (Jennings, 1990). Instead of helping parents and teachers work cooperatively, this attitude can create barriers by suggesting that parents are the cause of their children's failure in school. Teachers are presented as more skilled in parenting than are parents. Parents and teachers may even become rivals for the child's affection (Lightfoot, 1978).

Involvement efforts based on "the parent in need of parenting skills" assumes that there is one appropriate way to parent and that parents want to learn it. Both "the parent as helper" and "the parent in need of parenting skills" are conceptualizations derived from questionable assumptions about the character of contemporary parents and reflect a limited cultural perspective.

STEPS TO INCREASE PARENT AND FAMILY INVOLVEMENT

Teachers are a key ingredient in parent and family involvement. They play multiple roles, including facilitator, communicator, and resource developer. Their success in implementing an effective parent-community involvement program is linked to their skill in communicating and working with parents and community groups. Teacher attitude is also very important. Parents are supportive of the teachers who they believe like their children and want their children to succeed. Teachers who have a negative attitude toward students will likely have a similar attitude toward the students' parents. Teachers tend to relate to their students as representatives of their parents' perceived status in society. Teachers use such characteristics as class, race, gender, and ethnicity to determine students' prescribed social category.

Below are five steps you can take to increase parent-community involvement in your classroom. These steps involve establishing two-way communication, enlisting support from staff and students, soliciting support from the community, developing resource materials for home use, and broadening the activities included in parent involvement.

Establish Two-Way Communication between the School and Home

Establishing two-way communication between the school and home is an important step in involving parents. Most parents are willing to become involved in their children's education if you let them know what you are trying to accomplish and how parents can help. Teachers should be prepared to engage in outreach to parents and not to wait for them to become involved. Actively solicit information from parents on their thoughts about classroom goals and activities. When you talk with parents and community members, be an active listener. Listen for their feelings as well as for specific information. Listed below are seven ways you can establish and maintain two-way communication with parents and community members.

1. If possible, have an open-door policy in your classroom. Let parents know they are welcome. When parents visit, make sure they have something to do.

2. Send written information home about school assignments and goals so that parents are aware of what is going on in the classroom. Encourage parents to send notes to you if they have questions or concerns.

3. Talk to parents by phone. Let parents know when they can reach you by phone. Call parents periodically and let them know when things are going well. Have something specific to talk about. Leave some time for the parent to ask questions or make comments.

4. Report problems to parents, such as failing grades, before it is too late for them to take remedial action. Let parents know what improvements you expect from their children and how they can help.

5. Get to know your students' community. Take time to shop in their neighborhoods. Visit community centers and attend religious services. Let parents know when you will be in the community and that you are interested in talking to them.

6. If you teach in an elementary school, try to have at least two in-person conferences a year with parents. When possible, include the student in the conference. Be prepared to explain your curriculum to parents and have books and materials that students use available for them to examine. Let the parents know in specific terms how their student is doing in class. Find out how parents feel about their children's levels of achievement, and let them know what you think about their children's achievement levels. Give the parents some suggestions on what their children can do to improve and how they can help.

7. Solicit information from parents on their views on education. Identify their educational goals for their children, ways they would like to support their children's education, and their concerns about the school. There are a number of ways to get information from parents, including sending a questionnaire home and asking parents to complete it and return it to you, conducting a telephone survey, and asking your students to interview their parents.

Enlist the Support of Other Staff Members and Students

Teachers need support from staff, students, the principal, and district-level staff to enhance their parent-involvement activities. They have some flexibility in their classrooms, but they are not able to determine some factors that influence their ability to have a strong parent-involvement program. For example, when teachers are consulted about the type and amount of supplies purchased for their classroom, they can decide if they want to have enough supplies on hand to be able to send paper, pencils, and other materials home for parents to use with their children. Also, if teachers are allowed to modify their schedules, they can find free time to telephone parents, write notes, and hold morning or evening conferences with parents. Additionally, school climate also influences parent involvement, but school climate is not determined by one individual; it is influenced by individuals including students, teachers, the principal, and the school secretary.

Your students can help solicit support for parent and community involvement from staff and other students. Take your class on a tour of the school. Ask the class to think about how their parents would feel if they came to the school. Two obvious questions for students are: Is there a place for visitors to sit? Are there signs asking visitors to go directly to the office? Ask your students to list things they could do to make the school a friendlier place for parents.

Invite your building principal to come to your classroom and discuss the list with your students. Divide the class into small groups and have them discuss how they would like their parents involved in their education. Ask them to talk to their parents and get their views. Have each group write a report on how parents can be involved in their children's education. Each group could make presentations to students in the other classrooms in the building on how they would like to increase parent involvement in their school.

If funds or other support is needed from the district office for parent-involvement activities, have the students draw up a petition requesting funding and solicit signatures from teachers, students, and parents. When all the signatures are gathered, they can be delivered to an appropriate district administrator.

Building principals and district administrators can give you the support you need to:

1. Help create and maintain a climate for positive parent-community involvement. This can include supporting flexible hours for teachers who need to be out of the classroom to develop materials or to work with parents. Teachers can be given time out of the classroom without negatively affecting students. Time can be gleaned from the secondary teacher's schedule by combining homerooms one day a week, by team-teaching a class, or by combining different sections of a class for activities such as chapter tests. At the elementary school level, team teaching, released time during periods when students are normally out of the classroom for specialized subjects such as music and art, or having the principal substitute in the classroom are ways to provide flexible hours for teachers.

2. Set up a parent room. The parent room could be used for a number of functions, including serving as a community drop-in center where parents could meet other parents for a cup of coffee, or as a place for parents to work on school activities without infringing on the teachers' lounge. It could also be used as a waiting room for parents who need to see a student or a member of the school staff.

3. Host parent nights during which parents can learn more about the school, the curriculum, and the staff.

4. Send a personal note to students and to their parents when a student makes the honor roll or does something noteworthy.

5. Develop and distribute a handbook that contains student names and phone numbers, PTA or other parent-group contact names, and staff names and phone numbers.

6. Ask the school secretary to make sure visitors are welcomed when they come to the school and are given directions as needed.

7. Encourage students to greet visitors and help them find their way around the building.

Enlist Support from the Community

To enlist support from the community, you need to know something about it. The following are some questions you should be able to answer.

1. Are there any drama, musical, dance, or art groups in the community?

2. Is there a senior-citizen group, a public library, or a cooperative extension service in the community?

3. Are employment services such as the state employment security department available in the community?

4. Are civil rights organizations such as the Urban League, Anti-Defamation League, or NAACP active in the community?

5. What is the procedure for referring people to the Salvation Army, Goodwill Industries, or the State Department of Public Assistance for emergency assistance for housing, food, and clothing?

6. Does the community have a mental-health center, family counseling center, or crisis clinic?

7. Are programs and activities for youth, such as Boys and Girls Clubs, Campfire, Boy Scouts, Girl Scouts, YMCA, and the YWCA, available for your students?

As you learn about the community, you can begin developing a list of community resources and contacts that can provide support to families, work with your students, and provide locations for students to perform community service projects. Collecting information about your students' community and developing community contacts should be viewed as a long-term project. You can collect information as your schedule permits and organize it in a notebook. This process can be shortened if several teachers work together. Each teacher could concentrate on a different part of the community and share information and contacts.

Community groups can provide support in several ways. They can develop big sister and big brother programs for students, provide quiet places for students to study after school and on weekends, donate educational supplies, help raise funds for field trips, set up mentor programs, and tutor students.

Community groups can also provide opportunities for students to participate in community-based learning programs. Community-based learning programs provide an opportunity for students to move beyond the textbook and experience real life. They give students an opportunity to see how knowledge is integrated when it is applied to the real world. It puts them in touch with a variety of people and lets them see how people cope with their environment.

Community-based learning also enhances career development. It can help students learn about themselves, gain confidence, and better understand their strengths and weaknesses. Students can learn to plan, make decisions, negotiate, and evaluate their plans. Here are some examples of community work. Students can:

- Paint an apartment for an ill neighbor
- Clean alleys and backyards for the elderly
- Write letters for people who are ill
- Read to people who are unable to read
- Prepare an empty lot as a play area for young children
- Plant a vegetable garden for the needy
- Collect and recycle newspapers

Develop Learning Resources for Parents to Use at Home

Many of the learning materials teachers use with students at school can be used by parents at home to help students improve their skills. The materials should be in a format suitable for students to take home and should provide clear directions for at-home completion. Parents could let the teacher know how they liked the material by writing a note, giving their child a verbal message for the teacher, or by calling the school. Clark (1995) has written a series of math home-involvement activities for kindergarten through eighth grade. The activities are included in a booklet and are designed to help students increase their math skills. Parents are able to use the creative activities to reinforce the skills their children learn at school. These kinds of materials are convenient for both parents and teachers to use.

It is important for teachers to have resources available for parents to use. This lets parents know that they can help increase their children's learning and that you want their help. Simply telling parents they should work with their children is not sufficient. Parents generally need specific suggestions. Once parents get an idea of what you want them to do, some will develop their own materials. Other parents will be able to purchase materials. You can suggest specific books, games, and other materials for parents to purchase and where these learning materials are available.

Some parents will not have the financial resources, time, or educational background to develop or purchase learning materials. With your principal's help or help from community groups, you can set up a learning center for parents. The learning center could contain paper, pencils, books, games, a portable typewriter, a portable computer, and other appropriate resources. The learning center could also have audiocassettes on such topics as instructional techniques, classroom rules, educational goals for the year, and readings from books. Parents and students could check materials out of the learning center for use at home.

Broaden the Conception of Parent and Community Involvement

Many barriers to parent-community involvement can be eliminated by broadly conceptualizing parent-community involvement. Parents can play many roles, depending on their interests, skills, and resources. It is important to have a variety of roles for parents so that more parents will have an opportunity to be involved. It is also important to make sure that some roles can be performed at home as well as at school. Below are five ways parents and community members can be involved in schools. Some of the roles can be implemented by the classroom teacher. Others need support and resources from building principals or central office administrators.

Parents Working with Their Own Children

Working with their own children is one of the most important roles parents can play in the educational process. Parents can help their children develop a positive self-concept and a positive attitude toward school as well as a better understanding of how their effort affects achievement. Most parents want their children to do well in school and are willing to do whatever they can to help them succeed. Teachers can increase the support they receive from their students' homes by giving parents a better understanding of what is going on in the classroom, by letting parents know what is expected in the classroom, and by suggesting ways they can support their child's learning.

You can work with parents to support the educational process in these three ways:

1. Involve parents in monitoring homework by asking them to sign homework papers.

2. Ask parents to sign a certificate congratulating students for good attendance.

3. Give students extra points if their parents do things such as sign their report card attend conferences or read to them.

Some parents want a more active partnership with the school. These parents want to help teach their children. Below are three ways you can help parents work with their children to increase their learning:

1. Encourage parents to share hobbies and games, discuss news and television programs, and talk about school problems and events with their children.

2. Send information home on the importance of reading to children and include a reading list. A one-page sheet could be sent home stating, "One of the best ways to help children become better readers is to read to them. Reading aloud is most helpful when you discuss the stories, learn to identify letters and words and talk about the meaning of the words. Encourage leisure reading. Reading achievement is related to the amount of reading kids do. It increases vocabulary and reading fluency. " Then list several books available from the school library for students to check out and take home.

3. You can supply parents with materials they can use to work with their children on skill development. Students can help make math games, crossword puzzles, and other materials that parents can use with them at home.

Professional Support Person for Instruction

Many parents and community members have skills that can be shared with the school. They are willing to work with students as well as teachers. These people are often ignored in parent and community involvement programs. A parent or community member who is a college professor could be asked to talk to teachers about a topic that interests him or her or to participate in an in-service workshop. A bilingual parent or community member could be asked to help tutor foreign-language students or to share books or magazines written in their language with the class. Parents who enjoy reading or art could be asked to help staff a humanities enrichment course before or after school or to recommend materials for the course. Parents and community members who perform these kinds of duties could also serve as role models for your students and would demonstrate the importance of education in the community. Review the list below and think of how you could involve parents and community members in your classroom. Parents and community members can:

- Serve as instructional assistants
- Correct papers at home or at school
- Use carpentry skills to build things for the school
- Tutor during school hours or after school
- Develop or identify student materials or community resources

- Share their expertise with students or staff
- Expand enrichment programs offered before, after, or during school, such as Great Books and art appreciation
- Sew costumes for school plays
- Type and edit a newsletter

General Volunteers

Some parents are willing to volunteer their time but they do not want to do a job that requires specific skills. When thinking of activities for general volunteers, be sure to include activities that can be performed at the school as well as activities that can be performed at home. Some possible activities include:

- Working on the playground as a support person
- Working in the classroom as a support person
- Working at home preparing cutouts and other materials that will be used in class
- Telephoning other parents to schedule conferences

Decision Makers

Some parents are interested in participating in decision making in the school. They want to help set school policy, select curriculum materials, review budgets, or interview prospective staff members. Roles for these parents and community members include school board member, committee member, and site council member. Serving on a site council is an excellent way for parents to participate in decision making. Site councils are designed to increase parent involvement in schools, empower classroom teachers, and allow the people who implement educational decisions to make them.

The Comer (1995) model is an effective way to involve parents, classroom teachers, and other educators in decision making. Comer believes schools can be more effective when they are restructured in ways that encourage and support cooperation among parents and educators. Comer did much of his pioneering work on parent involvement and restructuring schools in Prince George County, Maryland. There he implemented two committees—the School Planning and Management Team (SPMT) and the Student Staff Services Team (SSST).

The SPMT included the school principal, classroom teachers, parents, and support staff. Consensus was used to reach decisions. The committee also had a no-fault policy, which encouraged parents not to blame the school and educators not to blame parents. The SPMT provided a structure for parents and educators to create a common vision for their school, reduce fragmentation, and develop activities, curriculum, and in-service programs. It also developed a comprehensive school plan, designed a schoolwide calendar of events, and monitored and evaluated student progress. The SPMT met at least once a month. Subcommittees of the SPMT met more frequently.

The second committee that Comer implemented was the Student Staff Services Team (SSST). The SSST was composed of the school principal, guidance counselor, classroom teachers, and support staff, including psychologists, health aides, and other appropriate personnel. Teachers and parents were encouraged to join this group if they had concerns they believed should be addressed. The SSST brought school personnel together to discuss individual student concerns. The SSST brought coherence and order to the services that students receive.

Summary

Parent and community involvement is a dynamic process that encourages, supports, and provides opportunities for teachers, parents, and community members to work together to improve student learning. Parent and community involvement is also an important component of school reform and multicultural education. Parents and community groups help provide the rationale, motivation, and social action necessary for educational reform.

Everyone benefits from parent-community involvement. Students tend to perform better in schools and have more people supporting their learning. Parents know more about what is going on at school, have more opportunities to communicate with their children's teacher, and are able to help their children increase their learning. Teachers gain a partner in education. Teachers learn more about their students through their parent and community contacts and are able to use that information to help increase their students' performance.

Even though research has consistently demonstrated that students have an advantage in school when their parents support and encourage educational activities, not all parents know how they can support their child's education or feel they have the time, energy, or other resources to be involved in schools. Some parents have a particularly difficult time supporting their children's education. Three such groups are parents who have low incomes, single parents, and parents with special needs. Parents from these groups are often dismissed as unsupportive of education, but they want their children to do well in school and are willing to work with the school when the school reaches out to them and responds to their needs.

To establish an effective parent-community involvement program, you should establish two-way communication with parents and community groups, enlist support from the community, and have resources available for parents to use in working with their children. Expanding how parent-community involvement is conceptualized can increase the number of parents and community members able to participate. Parents can play many roles. Ways to involve parents and community members include parents working with their own children, parents and community members sharing their professional skills with the school, parents and community groups volunteering in the school, and parents and community members working with educators to make decisions about school.

Questions and Activities

1. Compare the role of parents in schools during the colonial period to that of students today. Identify and discuss changes that have occurred and changes you would like to see occur in parent involvement.

2. Consider this statement: Regardless of the circumstances students experiences at home, teachers have a responsibility to help them perform at their highest level at school. Do you agree? Why or why not?

3. Interview a parent of a bilingual, ethnic minority, religious minority, or low-income student to learn more about the parent's views on schools and the educational goals for his or her children. This information cannot be generalized to all members of these groups, but it can be an important departure point for learning more about diverse groups within our society.

4. Consider this statement: All parents want their children to succeed in school. Do you agree with the statement? Why or why not?

5. Interview a classroom teacher and an administrator to determine his or her perceptions of parent-community involvement.

6. Write a brief paper on your personal views of the benefits and drawbacks of parent-community involvement.

7. Form a group with two other members of your class or workshop. One person in the group will be a teacher, the other a parent, and the third an observer. The teacher and the parent will role play a teacher-parent conference. After role playing the conference, discuss how it felt to be a parent and a teacher. What can be done to make the parent and teacher feel more comfortable? Was the information shared at the conference helpful? The observer can share his or her view of the parent and teacher interaction.

References

Banks, J. A. (1997). *Teaching Strategies for Ethnic Studies* (6th ed.). Boston: Allyn and Bacon.

Berger, E. H. (1995). *Parents as Partners in Education: Families and Schools Working Together* (4th ed.). New York: Merrill.

Booth, A. and Dunn, J. F. (Eds.). (1996). *Family-School Links: How Do They Affect Educational Outcomes?* Mahwah, NJ: Lawrence Erlbaum.

Bullivant, B. M. (1993). Culture: Its Nature and Meaning for Educators. In J. A. Banks and C. A. M. Banks, *Multicultural Education: Issues and Perspectives* (2nd ed.) (pp. 29–47). Boston: Allyn and Bacon.

Chavkin, N. F. and Gonzalez. (1995). *Forging Partnerships between Mexican American Parents and the Schools*. Charleston, WV: Clearinghouse on Rural Education and Small Schools, Appalachia Educational Laboratory.

Cibulka, J. A. and Kritek, W. J. (Eds.). (1996). *Coordination among Schools, Families, and Communities: Prospects for Educational Reform*. Albany: State University of New York Press.

Clark, C. S. (1995). Parents and Schools. *CQ-Researcher*. *5*(3). 51–69.

Comer, J. (1995). *School Power: Implication of an Intervention Project*. New York: Free Press.

Comer, J. P., Ben-Avie, M., Haynes, N. M., and Joyner, E. T. (1999). *Child by Child: The Comer Process for Change in Education*. New York: Teachers College Press.

Goodlad, J. I. (1984). *A Place Called School: Prospects for the Future*. New York: McGraw-Hill.

Harry, B. (1992). Restructuring the Participation of African-American Parents in Special Education. *Exceptional Children 59*(2), 123–131.

Henderson, A. T. and Berla, N. (Eds.). (1994). *A New Generation of Evidence: The Family Is Critical to Student Achievement*. Washington, DC: National Committee for Citizens in Education.

Hidalgo, N. M., Bright, J. A., Sau-Fong S., Swap, S. M., and Epstein, J. L. (1995). Research on Families, Schools, and Communities: A Multicultural Perspective. In J. A. Banks and C. A. M. Banks (Eds.), *Handbook of Research on Multicultural Education* (pp. 498–524). New York: Macmillan.

Jennings, L. (1990). Parents as Partners. *Education Week* (Aug. 1), 23, 35.

Kagan, S. L. (1995). Meeting Family and Community Needs: The Three C's of Early Childhood Education. Paper presented at the Australia and New Zealand Conference on the First Years of School. Tasmania, Australia.

Lightfoot, S. L. (1978). *Worlds Apart: Relationships between Families and Schools.* New York: Basic Books.

Linn, E. (1990). Parent Involvement Programs: A Review of Selected Models. *Equity Coalition 1*(2), 10–15.

Mannan, G. and Blackwell, J. (1992). Parent Involvement: Barriers and Opportunities. *The Urban Review*, 24(1), 219–226.

Martin , P. and Midgley, E. (1999). Immigration to the United States. *Population Bulletin*, 54(2), 1–44. Washington, DC: Population Reference Bureau.

National Conference. (1994). *Taking America's Pulse: A Summary Report of the National Conference Survey on Inter-Group Relations.* New York: Author.

Pollard, K. M. and O'Hare, W. P. (1999). America's Racial and Ethnic Minorities. *Population Reference Bulletin*, 54(3), 1–48. Washington, DC: Population Reference Bureau.

Rasinski, T. (1990). Reading and the Empowerment of Parents. *The Reading Teacher, 42,* 226–231.

Schneider, B. and Coleman, J. S. (Eds.). (1993). *Parents, Their Children, and Schools.* Boulder, CO: Westview Press.

Shariff, J. W. (1998). Free Enterprise and the Ghetto Family. In J. S. Wurzel, (Ed.), *Toward Multiculturalism: A Reader in Multicultural Education.* Yarmouth, ME: Intercultural Press.

Stratton, J. (1995). *How Students Have Changed: A Call to Action for Our Children's Future.* Arlington, VA: American Association of School Administration.

Swadener, B. B. and Niles, K. (1991). Children and Families "At Promise": Making Home-School-Community Connections. *Democracy and Education*, 13–18.

U. S. Bureau of the Census. (1998). *Statistical Abstract of the United States, 1998* (118th ed.). Washington, DC: U. S. Government Printing Office.

Walker, V. S. (1996). *Their Highest Potential: An African American School Community in the Segregated South.* Chapel Hill: The University of North Carolina Press.

Waller, W. (1965). *The Sociology of Teaching.* New York: Wiley.

Wright, J. W. *The Universal Almanac, 1991.* New York: Andrews and McMeel.

Multicultural Resources

Issues and Concepts

Banks, J. A. (Ed.). (1996). *Multicultural Education, Transformative Knowledge, and Action: Historical and Contemporary Perspectives*. New York: Teachers College Press.

Banks, J. A. (1997). *Educating Citizens in a Multicultural Society*. New York: Teachers College Press.

Banks, J. A. (1999). *An Introduction to Multicultural Education* (2nd ed.). Boston: Allyn and Bacon.

Banks, J. A. (2001). *Cultural Diversity and Education: Foundations, Curriculum, and Teaching* (4th ed.). Boston: Allyn and Bacon.

Banks, J. A. & Banks, C. A. M. (Eds.). (1995). *Handbook of Research on Multicultural Education*. New York: Macmillan.

Cortés, C. E. (2000). *The Children Are Watching: How the Media Teach about Diversity*. New York: Teachers College Press.

Dilg, M. (1999). *Race and Culture in the Classroom: Teaching and Learning through Multicultural Education*. New York: Teachers College Press.

Garcia, R. L. (1998). *Teaching for Diversity*. Bloomington, IN: Phi Delta Kappa Foundation.

Gay, G. (2000). *Culturally Responsive Teaching: Theory, Research, and Practice*. New York: Teachers College Press.

Grant, C. A. (Ed.). (1999). *Multicultural Research: A Reflective Engagement with Race, Class, Gender, and Sexual Orientation*. Philadelphia: Falmer.

Howard, G. (1999). *We Can't Teach What We Don't Know: White Teachers, Multiracial Schools*. New York: Teachers College Press.

May, S. (Ed.). (1999). *Critical Multiculturalism: Rethinking Multicultural and Antiracist Education*. Philadelphia: Falmer.

McLaren, P. (1997). *Revolutionary Multiculturalism: Pedagogies of Dissent for the New Millennium*. Boulder, CO: Westview.

Nieto, S. (1999). *The Light in Their Eyes: Creating Multicultural Learning Communities*. New York: Teachers College Press.

Sleeter, C. E. & Grant, C. A. (1999). *Making Choices for Multicultural Education: Five Approaches to Race, Class, and Gender* (3rd ed.). Columbus, OH: Merrill/Prentice-Hall.

Social Class

Anyon, J. (1997). *Ghetto Schooling: A Political Economy of Urban Educational Reform*. New York: Teachers College Press.

Ayers, W. & Ford, P. (Eds.). (1996). *City Kids, City Teachers: Reports from the Front Row*. New York: The New Press.

Blank, R. M. (1997). *It Takes a Nation: A New Agenda for Fighting Poverty*. New York: Russell Sage Foundation.

Collins, C., Leondar-Wright, B., & Sklar, H. (1999). *Shifting Fortunes: The Perils of the Growing American Wealth Gap*. Boston: United for a Fair Economy.

Conley, D. (1999). *Being Black, Living in the Red: Race, Wealth, and Social Policy in America*. Berkeley: University of California Press.

Cose, E. (1993). *The Rage of a Privileged Class*. New York: HarperCollins.

Gans, H. (1995). *The War against the Poor: The Underclass and Antipoverty Policy*. New York: Basic Books.

Hernandez, D. J. (Ed.). (1999). *Children of Immigrants: Health, Adjustment, and Public Assistance*. Washington, DC: National Academy Press.

Kozol, J. (1991). *Savage Inequalities: Children in America's Schools*. New York: Crown Publishers.

Lucas, S. R. (1999). *Tracking Inequality: Stratification and Mobility in American High Schools*. New York: Teachers College Press.

Middlebrooks, S. (1999). *Getting to Know City Kids: Understanding Their Thinking, Imagining, and Socializing*. New York: Teachers College Press.

Quint, S. (1994). *Schooling Homeless Children: A Working Model for America's Public Schools*. New York: Teachers College Press.

Wang, M. C. & Gordon, E. W. (Eds.). (1994). *Educational Resilience in Inner-City America*. Hillside, NJ: Lawrence Earlbaum.

Wilson, W. J. (1999). *The Bridge over the Racial Divide: Rising Inequality and Coalition Politics*. Berkeley: University of California Press.

Zweigenhaft, R. L. & Domhoff, G. W. (1998). *Diversity in the Power Elite*. New Haven, CT: Yale University Press.

Religion

Bowker, J. (1997). *World Religions: The Great Faiths Explored and Explained*. New York: DK Publishing, Inc.

Carpenter, J. A. (1999). *Revise Us Again: The Reawakening of American Fundamentalism*. New York: Oxford University Press.

Cone, J. H. (1990). *A Black Theology of Liberation* (20th anniv. ed.). Maryknoll, NY: Orbis Books.

Corbett, J. M. (2000). *Religion in America* (4th ed.). Upper Saddle River, NJ: Prentice-Hall.

Doniger, W. (1999). *Merriam-Webster's Encyclopedia of World Religions*. Springfield, MA: Merriam-Webster.

Garber, J. B. (1999). *One Nation under God? Religion and American Culture*. New York: Routledge.

Housden, R. (1999). *Sacred America: The Emerging Spirit of the People*. New York: Simon & Schuster.

Nord, W. & Haynes, C. (1998). *Taking Religion Seriously across the Curriculum*. Alexandria, VA: Association for Supervision and Curriculum Development.

Orfield, G. & Lebowitz, H. (1999). *Religion and Civil Rights: New Visions for a More Diverse Society*. New York: The Century Foundation.

Sears, J. T. with Carper, J. C. (Eds.). (1998). *Curriculum, Religion, and Public Education*. New York: Teachers College Press.

Sewall, G. T. (Ed.). (1999). Religion and the Schools. *Phi Delta Kappan, 81*(1), 1–96. (special issue)

Smith, J. Z. & Green, W. S. (Eds.). (1995). *The Harper/Collins Dictionary of Religion*. San Francisco: Harper/Collins/San Francisco.

Swatos, W. H., Jr., & Wellman, J. K., Jr. (Eds.). (1999). *The Power of Religious Publics: Staking a Claim in American Society*. Westport, CT: Praeger.

Turpin, J. (1990). *Women in Church History: 20 Stories for 20 Centuries*. Cincinnati: St. Anthony Messenger Press.

Yoo, D. K. (Ed.). (1999). *New Spiritual Homes: Religion and Asian Americans*. Honolulu: The University Press of Hawaii.

Gender

American Association of University Women Foundation. (1998). *Gender Gaps: Where Schools Still Fail Our Children*. Washington, DC: Author.

Andersen, M. L. & Collins, P. H. (Eds.). (1998). *Race, Class, and Gender: An Anthology* (3rd ed.). Belmont, CA: Wadsworth Publishing Company.

Anderson, K. (1996). *Changing Women: A History of Racial Ethnic Women in Modern America*. New York: Oxford University Press.

Barton, A. C. (1998). *Feminist Science Education*. New York: Teachers College Press.

Benedek, E. (1995). *Beyond the Four Corners of the World: A Navajo Woman's Journey*. New York: Knopf.

Boyd, H. & Allen, R. L. (Eds.). (1995). *Brotherman: The Odyssey of Black Men in America—An Anthology*. New York: Ballantine Books.

Collins, P. H. (1998). *Fighting Words: Black Women and the Search for Justice*. Minneapolis: University of Minnesota Press.

Cott, N. F., Boydston, J., Braude, A., Ginzberg, L., & Ladd-Taylor, M. (Eds.). (1996). *Roots of Bitterness: Documents of the Social History of American Women* (2nd ed.). Boston: Northeastern University Press.

DuBois, E. C. & Ruiz, V. L. (1994). *Unequal Sisters: A Multicultural Reader in U.S. Women's History* (2nd ed.). New York: Routledge.

Frankenberg, R. (1993). *White Women, Race Matters: The Social Construction of Whiteness*. Minneapolis: University of Minnesota Press.

Garcia, A. M. (Ed.). (1997). *Chicana Feminist Thought: The Basic Historical Writings*. New York: Routledge.

Gillespie, M. & Clinton, C. (Eds.). (1998). *Taking Off the White Gloves: Southern Women and Women Historians*. Columbia: University of Missouri Press.

Goldberger, N., Tarule, J., Clinchy, B., & Belenky, M. (Eds.). (1996). *Knowledge, Difference, and Power: Essays Inspired by Women's Ways of Knowing*. New York: Basic Books.

Gurian, M. (1996). *The Wonder of Boys: What Parents, Mentors and Educators Can Do to Shape Boys into Exceptional Men*. New York: Putnam.

Guy-Sheftall, B. (Ed.). (1995). *Words of Fire: An Anthology of African-American Feminist Thought*. New York: The New Press.

Harding, S. (1998). *Is Science Multicultural? Postcolonialisms, Feminisms, and Epistemologies*. Bloomington: Indiana University Press.

Harfo, J. & Bird, G. (Eds.). (1997). *Reinventing the Enemy's Language: Contemporary Native Women's Writing in North America*. New York: Norton.

Katz, J. (Ed.). (1995). *Messengers of the Wind: Native American Women Tell Their Life Stories*. New York: Ballantine Books.

Kimmel, M. (2000). *The Gendered Society*. New York: Oxford University Press.

Maccoby, E. E. (1998). *The Two Sexes: Growing up Apart, Coming Together*. Cambridge, MA: Harvard University Press.

Maher, F. A. & Tetreault, M. K. (1994). *The Feminist Classroom*. New York: Basic Books.

Mankiller, W., Mink, G., Navarro, M., Smith, B., & Steinem, G. (Eds.). (1998). *The Reader's Companion to U.S. Women's History*. Boston: Houghton Mifflin.

Morales, A. L. (1998). *Remedios: Stories of Earth and Iron from the History of Puertoriqueñas*. Boston: Beacon Press.

Orenstein, P. (1994). *School Girls: Young Women, Self-Esteem, and the Confidence Gap*. New York: Doubleday.

Pattatucci, A. M. (Ed.). (1998). *Women in Science: Meeting Career Challenges*. Thousand Oaks, CA: Sage.

Pollack, W. (1998). *Real Boys: Rescuing Our Sons from the Myths of Boyhood*. New York: Henry Holt.

Sadker, M. & Sadker, D. (1994). *Failing at Fairness: How America's Schools Cheat Girls*. New York: Scribner's.

Sarasohn, E. S. (Ed.). (1998). *Issei Women: Echoes from Another Frontier*. Palo Alto, CA: Pacific Books Publishers.

Schofield, J. W. (1995). *Computers and Classroom Culture*. New York: Cambridge University Press.

Zinn, M. B. & Dill, B. T. (Eds.). (1994). *Women of Color in U.S. Society*. Philadelphia: Temple University Press.

Race, Ethnicity, and Language

August, D. & Hakuta, K. (Eds.). (1998). *Educating Language-Minority Children*. Washington, DC: National Academy Press.

Banks, J. A. (1997). *Teaching Strategies for Ethnic Studies* (6th ed.). Boston: Allyn and Bacon.

Banks, J. A. & Banks, C. A. M. (Eds.). (1995). *Handbook of Research on Multicultural Education*. New York: Macmillan.

Beykont, Z. F. (Ed.). (2000). *Lifting Every Voice: Pedagogy and Politics of Bilingualism*. Cambridge, MA: Harvard Education Publishing Group.

Bialystok, E. & Hakuta, K. (1994). *In Other Words: The Science and Psychology of Second-Language Acquisition*. New York: Basic Books.

Crawford, J. (1999). *Bilingual Education: History, Politics, Theory, and Practice* (4th ed.). Los Angeles: Bilingual Educational Services.

Faltis, C. J. (1997). *Joinfostering: Adapting Teaching for the Multilingual Classroom* (2nd ed.). Upper Saddle River, NJ: Merrill/Prentice-Hall.

Garcia, E. (1999). *Student Cultural Diversity: Understanding and Meeting the Challenge*. Boston: Houghton Mifflin.

Gordon, E. W. (1999). *Education and Justice: The View from the Back of the Bus*. New York: Teachers College Press.

Hess, D. J. (1995). *Science and Technology in a Multicultural World*. New York: Columbia University Press.

Miller, L. S. (1995). *An American Imperative: Accelerating Minority Educational Achievement*. New Haven, CT: Yale University Press.

Moreno, J. F. (Ed.). (1999). *The Elusive Quest for Equality: 150 Years of Chicano/Chicana Education*. Cambridge, MA: Harvard Educational Review.

Natriello, G. (Ed.). (1999). Education and Race. *Teachers College Record, 100*(4), 703–899. (special issue)

Ovando, C. J. & Collier, V. P. (1998). *Bilingual and ESL Classrooms: Teaching in a Multicultural Context* (2nd ed.). Boston: McGraw-Hill.

Ovando, C. J. & McLaren, P. (Eds.). (2000). *The Politics of Multiculturalism and Bilingual Education*. Boston: McGraw-Hill.

Perry, T. & Delpit, L. (Eds.). (1998). *The Real Ebonics Debate: Power, Language, and the Education of African-American Children*. Boston: Beacon Press.

Romero, M., Hondagneu-Sotelo, P., & Ortiz, V. (Eds.). (1997). *Challenging Fronteras: Structuring Latina and Latino Lives in the U.S.* New York: Routledge.

Smith, V. (Ed.). (1998). *Not Just Race, Not Just Gender: Black Feminist Readings*. New York: Routledge.

Smitherman, G. (1999). *Talkin That Talk: Language, Culture, and Education in Africa America*. New York: Routledge.

Stephan, S. (1999). *Reducing Prejudice and Stereotyping in Schools*. New York: Teachers College Press.

Suárez-Orozco, C. & M. (1995). *Transformations: Migration, Family Life, and Achievement Motivation among Latino Adolescents*. Stanford, CA: Stanford University Press.

Exceptionality

Artiles, A. J. & Duran, G. Z. (Eds.). (1997). *Reducing Disproportionate Representation of Culturally Diverse Students in Special and Gifted Education*. Reston, VA: Council for Exceptional Children.

Baca, L. M. & Cervantes, H. T. (1997). *The Bilingual Special Education Interface*. Englewood Cliffs, NJ: Prentice-Hall.

Bireley, M. (1995). *Crossover Children: A Sourcebook for Helping Children Who Are Gifted and Learning Disabled* (2nd ed.). Reston, VA: Council for Exceptional Children.

Carrasquillo, A. L. & Rodriguez, V. (1995). *Language Minority Students in the Mainstream Classroom*. Bristol, PA: Taylor & Francis.

Colangelo, N. & Davis, G. D. (1991). *Handbook of Gifted Education*. Boston: Allyn and Bacon.

Cumins, J. (1984). *Bilingualism and Special Education: Issues in Assessment and Pedagogy*. Bristol, PA: Taylor & Francis.

Ford, D. Y. & Harris, J. J. III. (1999). *Multicultural Gifted Education*. New York: Teachers College Press.

Gallagher, J. J. (1994). *Teaching the Gifted Child* (4th ed.). Boston: Allyn and Bacon.

George, D. (1995). *Gifted Education: Identification and Provision*. Bristol, PA: Taylor & Francis.

Golomb, C. (Ed.). (1995). *The Development of Artistically Gifted Children: Selected Case Studies*. Hillsdale, NJ: Lawrence Erlbaum.

Grossman, H. (1994). *Special Education in a Diverse Society*. Boston: Allyn and Bacon.

Harry, B. (1992). *Cultural Diversity, Families, and the Special Education System*. New York: Teachers College Press.

Heward, W. L. (2000). *Exceptional Children: An Introduction to Special Education* (6th ed.). Upper Saddle River, NJ: Prentice-Hall/Merrill.

Lombardi, T. P. (Ed.). (1999). *Inclusion: Policy and Practice*. Bloomington, IN: Phi Delta Kappa.

Mercer, C. D. & Mercer, A. R. (1998). *Teaching Students with Learning Problems* (5th ed.). Upper Saddle River, NJ: Prentice-Hall/Merrill.

Meyer, L. H., Park, H., Grenot-Scheyer, M., Schwartz, I., & Harry, B. (Eds.). (1998). *Making Friends: The Influences of Culture and Development*. Baltimore, MD: Paul H. Brookes Publishing Co.

Putnam, J. W. (Ed.). (1993). *Cooperative Learning and Strategies for Inclusion: Celebrating Diversity in the Classroom*. Baltimore, MD: Brookes Publishing Company.

Sapon-Shevin, M. (1999). *Because We Can Change the World: A Practical Guide to Building Cooperative, Inclusive Classroom Communities*. Boston: Allyn and Bacon.

Shapiro, A. (Ed.). (1999). *Everybody Belongs: Changing Negative Attitudes toward Classmates with Disabilities*. New York: Garland.

School Reform

Cohen, E. G. & Lotan, R. A. (Eds.). (1997). *Working for Equity in Heterogeneous Classrooms: Sociological Theory in Practice*. New York: Teachers College Press.

The College Board. (1999). *Reaching the Top: A Report of the National Task Force on Minority High Achievement*. New York: Author.

Comer, J. P. (1997). *Waiting for a Miracle: Why Schools Can't Solve Our Problems—And How We Can*. New York: Dutton.

Comer, J. P., Ben-Avie, M., Haynes, N. M., & Joyner, E. T. (1999). *Child by Child: The Comer Process for Change in Education*. New York: Teachers College Press.

Darling-Hammond, L. (1997). *The Right to Learn: A Blueprint for Creating Schools That Work*. San Francisco: Jossey-Bass.

Derman-Sparks, L. & Phillips, C. B. (1997). *Teaching/Learning Anti-Racism: A Developmental Approach*. New York: Teachers College Press.

Gardner, H. (1999). *The Disciplined Mind: What All Students Should Understand*. New York: Simon & Schuster.

Hidalgo, N. M., Bright, J. A., Sau-Fong, S., Swap, S. M., & Epstein, J. L. (1995). Research on Families, Schools, and Communities: A Multicultural Perspective. In J. A. Banks & C. A. M. Banks (Eds.), *Handbook of Research on Multicultural Education* (pp. 498–524). New York: Macmillan.

Levine, D. U. & Lezotte, L. W. (1995). Effective Schools Research. In J. A. Banks & C. A. M. Banks (Eds.), *Handbook of Research on Multicultural Education* (pp. 525–547). New York: Macmillan.

Mehan, H., Villanueva, I., Hubbard, L., & Linta, A. (1996). *Constructing School Success*. New York: Cambridge University Press.

Meier, D. (1995). *The Power of Their Ideas: Lessons for America from a Small School in Harlem*. Boston: Beacon Press.

Miller, L. S. (1995). *An American Imperative: Accelerating Minority Educational Advancement*. New Haven, CT: Yale University Press.

National Commission on Teaching and America's Future. (1996). *What Matters Most: Teaching for America's Future*. Woodbridge, VA: Author.

Oakes, J., Quartz, K. H., Ryan, S., & Lipton, M. (2000). *Becoming Good American Schools: The Struggle for Civic Virtue in Educational Reform*. San Francisco: Jossey-Bass Publishers.

Perkins, D. (1995). *Outsmarting IQ: The Emerging Science of Learnable Intelligence*. New York: The Free Press.

Powell, A. B. & Frankenstein, M. (Eds.). (1997). *Ethnomathematics: Challenging Eurocentrism in Mathematics Education*. Albany: State University of New York Press.

Rethinking Our Classrooms: Teaching for Equity and Justice. (1994). Milwaukee: Rethinking Schools.

Sleeter, C. E. (1996). *Multicultural Education as Social Activism*. Albany: State University of New York Press.

Varenne, H. & McDermott, R. (1998). *Successful Failure: The School America Builds*. Boulder, CO: Westview Press.

Glossary

African Americans United States residents and citizens who have an African biological and cultural heritage and identity. This term is used synonymously and interchangeably with *Blacks* and *Black Americans*. These terms are used to describe both a racial and a cultural group. According to the U.S. Census, there were 32,718,000 African Americans in the United States in 1998. This figure excludes African Americans of Hispanic origin.

The number of African Americans increased by 25 percent between 1980 and 1998 to about 12 percent of the U.S. population. The U.S. Census (1998) projects that African Americans will make up 14 percent of the nation's population by 2050; they will be outnumbered by Hispanic Americans. Today, African Americans make up 12 percent of the U.S. population, while Hispanics make up 11 percent. An excellent one-volume encyclopedia on African Americans is *Africana: The Encyclopedia of the African and African American Experience* (Appiah & Gates, 1999).

Afrocentric curriculum A curriculum approach in which concepts, issues, problems, and phenomena are viewed from the perspectives of Africans and African Americans. This curriculum is based on the assumption that students learn best when they view situations and events from their own cultural perspectives (Asante, 1991; 1998).

American Indian See *Native American*.

Anglo-Americans Americans whose biological and cultural heritage originated in England, or Americans with other biological and cultural heritages who have assimilated into the dominant or mainstream culture in the United States. This term is often used to describe the mainstream United States culture or to describe most White Americans.

Antiracist education A term used frequently in the United Kingdom and Canada to describe a process used by teachers and other educators to eliminate institutionalized racism from the schools and society and to help individuals to develop nonracist attitudes. When antiracist educational reform is implemented, curriculum materials, grouping practices, hiring policies, teacher attitudes and expectations, and school policy and practices are examined and steps are taken to eliminate racism from these school variables. A related educational reform movement in the United States that focuses more on individuals than on institutions is known as *prejudice reduction*.

Asian Americans and Pacific Islanders Americans who have a biological and cultural heritage that originated on the continent of Asia or in the Pacific region. The largest groups of Asian Americans in the United States in 1997 were (in descending order) Chinese, Filipinos, Asian Indians, Vietnamese, Koreans, and Japanese.

Other groups include Laotians, Thai, Cambodians, Pakistanis, and Indonesians. Asians are the fastest-growing ethnic group in the United States. They increased 379 percent between 1980 and 1997. There were about 10 million Asian Americans in the United States in 1997. The U.S. Census projects that Asians will make up 8 percent of the nation's population by 2050 (Pollard & O'Hare, 1999).

Cultural assimilation Takes place when one ethnic or cultural group acquires the behavior, values, perspectives, ethos, and characteristics of another ethnic group and sheds its own cultural characteristics.

Culture The ideations, symbols, behaviors, values, and beliefs that are shared by a human group. Culture can also be defined as a group's program for survival and adaptation to its environment. Pluralistic nation-states such as the United States, Canada, and Australia are made up of an overarching culture, called a *macroculture*, that all individuals and groups within the nation share. These nation-states also have many smaller cultures, called *microcultures*, that differ in many ways from the macroculture or that contain cultural·components manifested differently than in the macroculture. (See Chapters 1 and 2 for further discussions of *culture*.)

Disability The physical or mental characteristics of an individual that prevent or limit him or her from performing specific tasks.

Discrimination The differential treatment of individuals or groups based on categories such as race, ethnicity, gender, sexual orientation, social class, or exceptionality.

Ethnic group A microcultural group or collectivity that shares a common history and culture, common values, behaviors, and other characteristics that cause members of the group to have a shared identity. A sense of peoplehood is one of the most important characteristics of an ethnic group. An ethnic group also shares economic and political interests. Cultural characteristics, rather than biological traits, are the essential attributes of an ethnic group. An ethnic group is not the same as a *racial group*. Some ethnic groups, such as Puerto Ricans in the United States, are made up of individuals who belong to several different racial groups. White Anglo-Saxon Protestants,

Italian Americans, and Irish Americans are examples of ethnic groups. Individual members of an ethnic group vary considerably in the extent to which they identify with the group. Some individuals have a very strong identity with their particular ethnic group, whereas other members of the group have a very weak identification with it.

Ethnic minority group An ethnic group with several distinguishing characteristics. An ethnic minority group has distinguishing cultural characteristics, racial characteristics, or both, which enable members of other groups to identify its members easily. Some ethnic minority groups, such as Jewish Americans, have unique cultural characteristics. African Americans have unique cultural and physical characteristics. The unique attributes of ethnic minority groups make them convenient targets of racism and discrimination. Ethnic minority groups are usually a numerical minority within their societies. However, the Blacks in South Africa, who are a numerical majority in their nation-state, are often considered a sociological minority group by social scientists because they have little political and economic power.

Ethnic studies The scientific and humanistic analysis of behavior influenced by variables related to ethnicity and ethnic-group membership. This term is often used to refer to special school, university, and college courses and programs that focus on specific racial and ethnic groups. However, any aspects of a course or program that includes a study of variables related to ethnicity can accurately be referred to as ethnic studies. In other words, ethnic studies can be integrated within the boundaries of mainstream courses and curricula.

Eurocentric curriculum A curriculum in which concepts, events, and situations are viewed primarily from the perspectives of European nations and cultures and in which Western civilization is emphasized. This approach is based on the assumption that Europeans have made the most important contributions to the development of the United States and the world. Curriculum theorists who endorse this approach are referred to as *Eurocentrists* or *Western traditionalists*.

European Americans See *Anglo-Americans*.

Exceptional Used to describe students who have learning or behavioral characteristics that differ substantially from most other students and that require special attention in instruction. Students who are intellectually gifted or talented as well as those who have disabilities are considered exceptional.

Gender Consists of behaviors that result from the social, cultural, and psychological factors associated with masculinity and femininity within a society. Appropriate male and female roles result from the socialization of the individual within a group.

Gender identity An individual's view of the gender to which he or she belongs and his or her shared sense of group attachment with other males or females.

Global education Concerned with issues and problems related to the survival of human beings in the world community. International studies is a part of global education, but the focus of global education is the interdependence of human beings and their common fate, regardless of the national boundaries within which they live. Many teachers confuse global education and international studies with ethnic studies, which deal with ethnic groups within a national boundary, such as the United States.

Handicapism The unequal treatment of people who are disabled and related attitudes and beliefs that reinforce and justify discrimination against people with disabilities. The term *handicapped* is considered negative by some people. They prefer the term *disabled. People with disabilities* is considered a more sensitive phrase than is *disabled people* because the word *people* is used first and given emphasis.

Hispanic Americans Americans who share a culture, heritage, and language that originated in Spain. Most of the Hispanics living in the United States have cultural origins in Latin America. Many Hispanics in the United States prefer to use the word *Latino* rather than *Hispanic*, as do the editors of this book. However, *Hispanic* is the term used by the U.S. Census. Most Hispanics in the United States speak Spanish and are mestizos. A *mestizo* is a person of mixed biological heritage. Most Hispanics in the United States have an Indian as well as a Spanish heritage. Many of them also have an African biological and cultural heritage.

The largest groups of Hispanics in the United States are Mexican Americans (Chicanos), Puerto Ricans, and Cubans. According to the U.S. Census, 29,348,000 documented Hispanics lived in the United States in 1997, which was about 11 percent of the U.S. population. In 1997, there were 18.7 million Mexican Americans, 3.1 million Puerto Ricans in the mainland United States, 1.3 million Cubans, and 6.4 million Hispanics from other nations (Pollard & O'Hare, 1999).

Hispanics are one of the nation's fastest-growing ethnic groups of color. They increased 101 percent between 1980 and 1997, from 14.6 to 29.3 million. The nation's total population increased 19 percent during between 1980 and 1998 (Pollard & O'Hare, 1999). The U. S. Census projects that Hispanics will makeup 24 percent of the nation's population in 2050.

It is misleading to view Hispanics as one ethnic group. Some Hispanics believe that the word *Hispanics* can help to unify the various Latino groups and thus increase their political power. The primary identity of most Hispanics in the United States, however, is with their particular group, such as Mexican American, Puerto Rican, or Cuban.

Mainstream American A United States citizen who shares most of the characteristics of the dominant ethnic and cultural group in the nation. Such an individual is usually White Anglo-Saxon Protestant and belongs to the middle class or a higher social-class status.

Mainstream-centric curriculum A curriculum that presents events, concepts, issues, and problems primarily or exclusively from the points of view and perspectives of the mainstream society and the dominant ethnic and cultural group in the United States—White Anglo-Saxon Protestants. The mainstream-centric curriculum is also usually presented from the perspectives of Anglo males.

Mainstreaming The process that involves placing students with disabilities into the regular classroom for instruction. They might be integrated into the regular classroom for part or all of the school day. This practice was initiated in response to Public Law 94–142 (passed by Congress in 1975), which requires that students with disabilities be educated in the least restricted environment.

Multicultural education A reform movement designed to change the total educational environment so that students from diverse racial and ethnic groups, both gender groups, exceptional students, and students from each social-class group will experience equal educational opportunities in schools, colleges, and universities. A major assumption of multicultural education is that some students, because of their particular racial, ethnic, gender, and cultural characteristics, have a better chance to succeed in educational institutions as they are currently structured than do students who belong to other groups or who have different cultural and gender characteristics. See the *Handbook for Research on Multicultural Education* (Banks & Banks, 1995) for a further discussion of multicultural education.

Multiculturalism A philosophical position and movement that assumes that the gender, ethnic, racial, and cultural diversity of a pluralistic society should be reflected in all of the institutionalized structures of educational institutions, including the staff, the norms and values, the curriculum, and the student body.

Native Americans United States citizens who trace their biological and cultural heritage to the original inhabitants in the land that now makes up the United States. The term *Native American* is sometimes used synonymously with *American Indian*. There were about 2.4 million Native Americans (including American Indians, Eskimos, and Aleuts) in the United States in 1998. In 1990, only four tribes, the Cherokee, Navajo, Chippewa, and Sioux, had more than 100,000 persons. Most tribes had a population of less than 10,000. The two largest tribes were the Cherokee (308,000) and the Navajo (219,000).

People of color Groups in the United States and other nations who have experienced discrimination historically because of their unique biological characteristics that enabled potential discriminators to identify them easily. African Americans, Asian Americans, and Hispanics in the United States are among the groups referred to as *people of color*. Most members of these groups still experience forms of discrimination today.

Positionality An idea that emerged out of feminist scholarship stating that variables such as an individual's gender, class, and race are markers of her or his relational position within a social and economic context and influence the knowledge that she or he produces. Consequently, valid knowledge requires an acknowledgment of the knower's position within a specific context. (See Chapter 7 in this book.)

Prejudice A set of rigid and unfavorable attitudes toward a particular individual or group that is formed without consideration of facts. Prejudice is a set of attitudes that often leads to discrimination, the differential treatment of particular individuals and groups.

Race Refers to the attempt by physical anthropologists to divide human groups according to their physical traits and characteristics. This has proven to be very difficult because human groups in modern societies are highly mixed physically. Consequently, different and often conflicting race typologies exist. An excellent book on race is *Whiteness of a Different Color: European Immigrants and the Alchemy of Race* (Jacobson, 1999).

Racism A belief that human groups can be validly grouped according to their biological traits and that these identifiable groups inherit certain mental, personality, and cultural characteristics that determine their behavior. Racism, however, is not merely a set of beliefs but is practiced when a group has the power to enforce laws, institutions, and norms, based on its beliefs, that oppress and dehumanize another group. An informative reference on racism is *Man's Most Dangerous Myth: The Fallacy of Race* (Montagu,1997).

Religion A set of beliefs and values, especially about explanations that concern the cause and nature of the universe, to which an individual or group has a strong loyalty and attachment. A *religion* usually has a moral code, rituals, and institutions that reinforce and propagate its beliefs.

Sex The biological factors that distinguish males and females, such as chromosomal, hormonal, anatomical, and physiological characteristics.

Sexism Social, political, and economic structures that advantage one sex group over the other. Stereotypes and misconceptions about the biological characteristics of each sex group reinforce and support sex discrimination. In most societies, women have been the major victims of sexism. However, males are also victimized by sexist beliefs and practices.

Social class A collectivity of people who have a similar socioeconomic status based on such criteria as income, occupation, education, values, behaviors, and life chances. *Lower class, working class, middle class*, and *upper class* are common designations of social class in the United States.

References

Appiah, K. A. & Gates, H. L., Jr. (Eds.). (1999). *Africana: The Encyclopedia of the African and African American Experience*. New York: Perseus Books Group.

Asante, M. K. (1991). The Afrocentric Idea in Education. *The Journal of Negro Education*, *60*(2), 170–180.

Asante, M. K. (1998). *The Afrocentric Idea* rev. ed. Philadelphia: Temple University Press.

Banks, J. A. & Banks, C. A. M. (Eds.). (1995). *Handbook of Research on Multicultural Education*. New York: Macmillan.

Jacobson, M. F. (1999). *Whiteness of a Different Color: European Immigrants and the Alchemy of Race*. Cambridge, MA: Harvard University Press.

Montagu, A. (1997). *Man's Most Dangerous Myth: The Fallacy of Race* (6th ed.). Walnut Creek, CA: AltaMira Press.

Pollard, K. M. & O'Hare, W. P. (1999). America's Racial and Ethnic Minorities. *Population Bulletin*, *54*(3), pp. 1–48. Washington, DC: Population Reference Bureau.

U. S. Bureau of the Census. (1998). *Statistical Abstract of the United States: 1998* (118th ed.). Washington, DC: U.S. Government Printing Office.

Contributors

Jean Anyon is chairperson of the education department and director of the Institute for Outreach and Research in Urban Education, Rutgers University-Newark, NJ. She is author of *Ghetto Schooling: A Political Economy of Urban Educational Reform* (Teachers College Press). As a widely regarded expert on inner-city revitalization and school reform, she has been interviewed on numerous radio and television programs and has been an invited keynote speaker at gatherings and conferences in cities throughout the United States. Professor Anyon has published many scholarly articles on educational issues involving race, social class, and the urban context.

Cherry A. McGee Banks is associate professor of education at the University of Washington, Bothell. Professor Banks has contributed to such journals as *Phi Delta Kappan, Social Studies and the Young Learner, Educational Policy, Theory Into Practice*, and *Social Education*. She is also associate editor of the *Handbook of Research on Multicultural Education* and co-author of *Teaching Strategies for the Social Studies* (with James A. Banks). Professor Banks is on the editorial boards of *Educational Foundations, Multicultural Perspectives*, and *American Educational Research Journal*. In 1997, she received the Distinguished Teaching Award from the University of Washington, Bothell.

James A. Banks is professor and director of the Center for Multicultural Education at the University of Washington, Seattle. He has written or edited more than a dozen books in multicultural education and in social studies education. Professor Banks is a past president of the National Council for the Social Studies (NCSS) and the American Educational Research Association (AERA). His books include *Teaching Strategies for Ethnic Studies; Educating Citizens in a Multicultural Society; Teaching Strategies for the Social Studies;* and *Cultural Diversity and Education: Foundations, Curriculum, and Teaching*. He is the editor of the *Handbook of Research on Multicultural Education* and of the Multicultural Education Series of books published by Teachers College Press, Columbia University.

Professor Banks has received fellowships from the National Academy of Education, the Kellogg Foundation, and the Rockefeller Foundation. In 1986, he was named a Distinguished Scholar/Researcher on Minority Education by the American Educational Research Association. In 1994, he received the AERA Research Review Award. He has received honorary doctorates from the Bank Street College of Education and the University of Alaska, Fairbanks. Professor Banks is a member of the Board on Children, Youth, and Families of the National Research Council of the National Academy of Sciences.

Jill Bevan-Brown is a senior lecturer in special education at Massey University College of Education, New

Zealand. Being of Maori heritage (the indigenous people of New Zealand), she has a particular interest in the special education needs of Maori children and has concentrated her writing and research efforts in this area. At present, she has responsibility for the Maori section of a three-year, government-commissioned, national research project to evaluate special education policy and provisions throughout New Zealand.

Johnnella E. Butler is professor of American ethnic studies and adjunct professor of English and women studies at the University of Washington, Seattle. Professor Butler is a specialist in African American literature, American ethnic literature and criticism, and multicultural studies. She is particularly interested in the relationships among American ethnic literatures, their theory and pedagogy. She is editor and lead contributor of the forthcoming *Color Line to Borderlands: Ethnic Studies and the Matrix of Higher Education* (University of Washington Press). She is also co-editor of the *Encyclopedia of American Studies*.

Rodney A. Cavanaugh is an associate professor of special education at Plattsburgh, State University of New York. A former teacher of students with learning and behavior disorders in Michigan and Ohio, he currently teaches graduate and undergraduate courses in special education and research methods and supervises practice teaching. He is the president of the New York State Council for Exceptional Children Subdivision of Mental Retardation/Developmental Disabilities. His current interests focus on effective teaching strategies and teacher-as-researcher components in teacher education. Dr. Cavanaugh was named the 1995 New York State Professor of the Year by the Carnegie Foundation for the Advancement of Teaching.

Frederick Erickson is the George F. Kneller Professor of Anthropology of Education at the University of California, Los Angeles, where he teaches in the Graduate School of Education and Information Studies. His publications include *The Counselor as Gatekeeper: Social Interaction in Interviews; Sights and Sounds of Life in Schools;* a chapter on qualitative research methods in the *Handbook of Research on Teaching* (3rd ed.); and articles on ethnicity and on ethnographic description in *Sociolinguistics: An International Handbook of the Science of Language and Society*. He is a past president of the Council on

Anthropology and Education of the American Anthropological Association. He received the Council's George and Louise Spindler Award for outstanding scholarly contributions to educational anthropology in 1991. He is a past editor of the *Anthropology and Education Quarterly*. In 1998–99 he was a Spencer Fellow at the Center for Advanced Study in the Behavioral Sciences.

Geneva Gay is professor of education and associate of the Center for Multicultural Education at the University of Washington, Seattle. She is nationally and internationally known for her scholarship in multicultural education, particularly as it relates to curriculum design, staff development, classroom instruction, and culture and learning. Her writings include more than 115 book chapters, books, and journal articles. Among these are *At the Essence of Learning: Multicultural Education* (Kappa Delta Pi, 1994) and *Culturally Responsive Teaching: Research, Theory, and Practice* (Teachers College Press, 2000). International consultations on multicultural education have taken her to Canada, Brazil, Taiwan, Finland, Japan, England, and Scotland.

Carl A. Grant is a Hoefs-Bascom Professor at the University of Wisconsin, Madison. He has written or edited seventeen books in multicultural teacher education. These books include *Making Schooling Multicultural: Campus and Classroom* (with Mary L. Gomez); *Educating for Diversity; Making Choices for Multicultural Education* (with Christine E. Sleeter); *Research and Multicultural Education* (1993); and *After the School Bell Rings* (with Christine E. Sleeter). Professor Grant has written more than 100 articles and book chapters. His writings and the programs that he directed have received awards. He is a former teacher and administrator. He was a Fulbright Scholar in England and was chosen by the Association of Teacher Education as a leader in teacher education. He is a past president of the National Association for Multicultural Education (NAME).

Beth Harry entered the field of special education as a parent of a child with cerebral palsy. She is associate professor of special education at the University of Miami, Florida, and her particular interests are in families and cultural issues. Her research and teaching focus on the impact of culture and social status on the needs and perspectives of families of children with disabilities, and on professionals' interactions with such families. She uses ethnographic research methods to investigate these issues, with particular regard to African American and Latino parents. She is the author of *Cultural Diversity, Families and the Special Education System*, a study of Puerto Rican parents' perspectives, and of several articles published in leading educational journals.

William L. Heward is professor and coordinator of the Ph.D. program in special education at The Ohio State University. In 1985, he received OSU's highest honor for teaching excellence: the Alumni Association's Distinguished Teaching Award. He has had several opportunities to teach abroad, most recently in 1993, when he served as a visiting professor at Keio University in Tokyo, Japan. His books include *Exceptional Children: An Introduction to Special Education* (6th ed.), and *A Dozen Teaching Mistakes and What To Do Instead* (forthcoming). Professor Heward's current research interests focus on low-tech methods classroom teachers can use to increase the frequency with which each student actively responds and participates during group instruction and on methods for promoting the generalization and maintenance of newly learned skills.

Gess LeBlanc is assistant professor in the department of educational foundations and counseling programs at Hunter College, New York. Professor LeBlanc's research focuses on how children's learning develops through spontaneous and informal interactions with their peers and addresses the role of peer-based instruction in children's learning. Through research supported by the Spencer Foundation, he developed a model for designing after-school programs. The New York City public junior high schools are currently using his model. More recent interests include gifted education with respect to multicultural populations and developing techniques for enhancing achievement motivation in adolescents.

Luanna Meyer is pro vice-chancellor of the Massey University College of Education, New Zealand, where she administers programs in education at undergraduate and graduate levels on campuses in Auckland, Napier, Palmerston North and Wellington, Aotearoa, New Zealand. Prior to her current position, she was professor of education at Syracuse University, New York, where she directed the Inclusive Elementary and Special Education Program and the Consortium for Collaborative Research on Social Relationships of Children and Youth with Diverse Abilities. She has been an executive board member of TASH and AAMR and editor of JASH. She is internationally known for her work in special and inclusive education, having published more than 200 books, journal articles, and book chapters.

Sonia Nieto is professor of education, University of Massachusetts, Amherst. Her research centers on multicultural education, the education of Latinos, and Puerto Rican children's literature. She has written numerous book chapters and journal articles, and her books include *Affirming Diversity: The Sociopolitical Context of Multicultural Education; The Light in Their Eyes: Creating Multicultural Learning Communities;* and *Puerto Rican Students in U.S. Schools.* Dr. Nieto has received numerous awards for her activism and advocacy, including the 1995 Drylongso Award for Anti-Racism Activism from Community Change in Boston, the 1997 Educator of the Year Award from NAME (the National Association for Multicultural Education), and an Annenberg Institute Fellowship (1998–2000). In 1999, she was awarded an Honorary Doctorate in Humane Letters from Lesley College, Cambridge, MA.

Carlos J. Ovando is professor of education at Indiana University, Bloomington. He has taught at Oregon State University, University of Alaska, Anchorage, and University of Southern California. Professor Ovando specializes in bilingual and multicultural education and has contributed numerous publications in these fields. He guest-edited two special issues of the *Educational Research Quarterly* and contributed to the *Handbook of Research on Multicultural Education, Peabody Journal of Education, Bilingual Research Journal, Phi Delta Kappan, Teacher Educator, Educational Leadership, Kappa Delta Pi Record,* and *Harvard Educational Review.* He is senior author of *Bilingual and ESL Classrooms* and senior editor of *The Politics of Multiculturalism and Bilingual Education.* Professor Ovando has presented papers in Canada, Costa Rica, Egypt, England, Guam, Mexico, Nicaragua, the Netherlands, the Philippines, and Spain.

David Sadker is a professor at the American University in Washington, DC. His research and writing document gender bias from the classroom to the boardroom. His work has been reported in *Harvard Educational Review, Educational Leadership, Phi Delta Kappan, USA Today, Business Week, The Washington Post, The London Times, The New York Times, Time,* and *Newsweek.* Professor Sadker received the American Educational Research Association Research (AERA) Review Award in 1991, its professional service award in 1995, and The Eleanor Roosevelt award from the American Association of University Women in 1995. Dr. Sadker coauthored *Failing at Fairness: How Our Schools Cheat Girls* (Touchstone Press, 1995) and *Teachers, Schools and Society* (McGraw Hill, 2000).

Myra Sadker was a professor of education at the American University in Washington, DC, and director of the Master of Arts in Teaching program. She also served as dean of the School of Education and director of the Teacher Preparation Programs. Professor Sadker, who was a language arts teacher, contributed to numerous journals and books and offered workshops on sex equity in more than forty states. She and Professor David Sadker co-authored a number of books, including *Sex Equity Handbook for Schools* and *Failing at Fairness: How Our Schools Cheat Girls.*

Mara Sapon-Shevin is professor of education in the Teaching and Leadership Division of the School of Education at Syracuse University. She teaches in the university's Inclusive Elementary and Special Education Teacher Education Program, which prepares teachers for inclusive, heterogeneous classrooms. She is active in working with schools to promote the full inclusion of all students and the creation of cooperative school communities. Professor Sapon-Shevin is past co-president of the International Association for the Study of Cooperation in Education and the Convenor of the Invisible College on Social Justice Teaching. She gives presentations and writes on topics of cooperative learning, full inclusion, diversity education, and the politics of gifted education. She is also active in antiracism and social justice work within her community. Her most recent book is *Because We Can Change the World: A Practical Guide for Building Cooperative, Inclusive Classroom Communities.*

Janet Ward Schofield is professor of psychology and a senior scientist in the Learning Research and Development Center at the University of Pittsburgh. She has also served as a faculty member at Spelman College. She received her Ph.D. from Harvard University in 1972. Professor Schofield is a social psychologist whose major interest for more than twenty years has been social processes in desegregated schools. She has published more than two dozen papers in this area as well as two books. Her book *Black and White in School: Trust, Tension or Tolerance?* was awarded the Society for the Psychological Study of Social Issues Gordon Allport Intergroup Relations Prize. She is a contributing author of the *Handbook of Research on Multicultural Education.* Professor Schofield's work in her other major area of interest, the impact of computer technology on classroom processes, has resulted in numerous publications, including the book *Computers and Classroom Culture.*

Christine E. Sleeter is a professor at California State University, Monterey Bay. She coordinates the Master of Arts in Education program and directs the Institute for Advanced Studies in Education. She consults nationally and internationally in multicultural education and multicultural teacher education. She has published numerous books and articles in multicultural education. Her most recent books include *Multicultural Education as Social Activism; Developing Multicultural Teacher Education Curricula* (with Joseph Larkin); and *Multicultural Education, Critical Pedagogy and the Politics of Difference* (with Peter McLaren). She edits the series The Social Context of Education for SUNY Press. She served as program chair of the American Educational Research Association (AERA) annual meeting in 1998.

Rena F. Subotnik is a professor of education at Hunter College, New York. She has been awarded research and training grants with the National Science Foundation, the U.S. Department of Education, and the Spencer Foundation. She currently serves on the editorial boards of *Roeper Review, Gifted Child Quarterly, High Ability Studies,* and *Educational Horizons.* Professor Subotnik conducts featured interviews in the *Journal for the Education of the Gifted* under the title "Conversations with Masters in the Arts and Sciences." She is author of *Genius Revisited: High IQ Children Grown Up* (1993) and co-editor of *Beyond Terman: Contemporary Longitudinal Studies of Giftedness and Talent* (1994), *Remarkable Women: Perspectives on Female Talent Development* (1997), and *International Handbook of Research on Giftedness and Talent*

(2nd ed.) (2000). Professor Subotnik has served as an American Psychological Association Congressional Fellow in Child Policy. She is co-editor of the *Journal for Secondary Gifted Education.*

Mary Kay Thompson Tetreault is provost and vice president for Academic Affairs at Portland State University, Oregon. She also served as vice president for Academic Affairs at California State University, Fullerton, where she previously held the position of dean of the School of Human Development and Community Service. She also worked as a professor of secondary education, a department chair and an assistant dean at Lewis and Clark College, and taught social studies in high schools near Boston and Chicago. Tetreault received her B.A. in history from Benedictine College, a Master of Arts in Teaching from the University of Chicago, and her doctorate in Social Education and Womens Studies from Boston University. Professor Tetreault is the author (with Frances Maher) of *The Feminist Classroom* (Basic Books, 1994). She also edited *Women in America: Half of History*, a collection of primary-source materials for secondary school students.

James K. Uphoff is associate director for the Center for Teaching and Learning at Wright State University (Ohio), where he a professor emeritus in teacher education. He has been an educator for more than forty years and serves as the facilitator for the ASCD Religion and Public Education Network. Professor Uphoff is a Malone Faculty Fellow in Arab-Islamic Studies, was co-founder of the Public Education Religion Studies Center at WSU, and has been honored by his university for his teaching, scholarship, and service. He has also been a local school board member since 1989 and currently serves as president-elect of the Ohio School Boards Association.

Index